IVY CHEN
$25.00

ISBN 0-314-07210-1

TEXT IS PRINTED ON 10% POST
CONSUMER RECYCLED PAPER

CASES AND MATERIALS ON
POVERTY LAW:
THEORY AND PRACTICE

By

Julie A. Nice
Assistant Professor of Law
University of Denver College of Law

Louise G. Trubek
Clinical Professor of Law
University of Wisconsin Law School

WEST PUBLISHING CO.
ST. PAUL, MINN., 1997

To my mother,
who showed me the compatability of believing
in a strong work ethic and compassion

To my late father,
who taught me not to take myself
too seriously

To my partner, Martha,
who inspired me, a sprinter,
to complete this, a marathon

J.A.N.

To my parents,
who supported the struggle for a just society

L.G.T.

PREFACE

More than twenty years ago, the last legal textbook designed to teach poverty law was published. Since that time, law professors and students have continued to study how law regulates poverty and welfare. Professors created their own teaching materials reflecting the changes in law, practice, and societal understandings. This constant interest in poverty law during the last twenty years was enriched by two developments within law schools: clinical education and scholarship on lawyering. Clinical education is based on the commitment of law schools to provide services to disadvantaged clients while educating law students; practicing poverty law within law schools enables lawyers, professors, and students to reflect and practice on behalf of poor people. Scholarly writing on poverty law is crucial to the field; the recent explosion of writing with regard to poverty, race, and gender reinvigorates the intellectual debate.

Continued teaching of poverty law courses, initiation of clinical education, and explosion of scholarship enabled us to contemplate the writing and publishing of a new poverty law textbook. We were inspired by poverty law professors active in the Section on Poverty Law of the American Association of Law Schools who encouraged us to see that the time has come for a new poverty law textbook which incorporates the contemporary complexity of poverty theory and practice.

Our primary obstacle in creating an effective poverty law textbook was accounting for the many different approaches to teaching this subject. We collected a mountain of information from other professors. Because nearly every aspect of law affects poor people, some teachers preferred that poverty issues be integrated throughout the law school curriculum. Others taught courses devoted to poverty law, sometimes emphasizing social welfare policy, and sometimes teaching the subjects traditionally practiced by legal services lawyers (public benefits, housing law, family law, juvenile law, employment law, and consumer law). A third approach was a seminar focusing on just one of these issues. Most clinical professors also taught about poverty, some discussing the substantive legal issues emerging from client's cases, and others discussing the broader societal implications of the law's impact on low-income people. Reviewing these various approaches yielded one conclusion: there is no one way to teach about poverty. In light of this conclusion, our goal here is to provide a foundation for any of the approaches just enumerated.

To meet the variety of teaching needs in a poverty law class, we have structured this casebook in three major sections: (1) theory; (2) practice; and (3) an integrated application of theory and practice. Doctrine is central to all three sections; students acquire in-depth knowledge of the legal rules, an understanding of how these rules work, and their wider implications. We also include a Complaint and exercises that are particularly crafted to give the student concrete experience to prepare to litigate poverty law cases. A professor can focus on any third of the book, or selections of each third, according to the nature of her or his course.

Section I introduces students to theoretical issues which recur throughout the textbook. We first discuss the factual realities of poverty in American society today, including the data, the categories of assistance, the experiences of poor people, and the rhetoric that dominates discussions about poverty (Chapter 1). We next provide an historical overview which focuses on the legacies of racial and gender discrimination, and the specific anti-poverty benefits programs that emerged in the 1930s, 1960s, and 1990s (Chapter 2). We turn then to policy perspectives from the political right, middle, and left which fuel the never-ending debate about government's role in addressing poverty (Chapter 3).

Section II examines poverty law practice by exploring historical and contemporary challenges for poverty lawyers, including how to improve poverty lawyering and how to obtain judicial access for poor people (Chapter 4). The next three chapters focus on constitutional lawyering issues related to due process (Chapter 5), equal protection (Chapter 6), and the confounding unconstitutional conditions dilemma (Chapter 7).

Section III integrates theory and practice in the context of welfare reform (Chapter 8), with a particular focus on the family (Chapter 9) and the fight for work (Chapter 10).

All three sections incorporate a wide variety of materials, including cases, law review articles, statutes, and excerpts from interdisciplinary books. Our notes and questions are designed to be user friendly by listing topic headings, providing helpful summaries of authors' points, and leaving the questions for the tougher issues.

We tried to make the textbook format as easy to read as possible by editing out less relevant material and marking those omissions with asterisks. However, footnote and citation omissions are not noted in the text. When we retained a footnote, we used its original number.

One important note: we completed these materials on September 30, 1996, one day before many provisions of the 1996 Personal Responsibility and Work Opportunity Reconciliation Act (PRA) took effect. The PRA completely revolutionized 60 years of poverty law by abolishing the federal entitlement to welfare, limiting welfare benefits to five years, and allowing states to create their own programs with federal block grant funds. Many provisions of the 1996 legislation are in this text, with headings designed to bring them to your attention. Our source for these materials was the Conference Report on H.R. 3734 which set out the text of the legislation and the joint explanation of the conference committee, since United States Code citations were not available.

Our debts are numerous and immense. We thank Tom Geraghty of Northwestern University's Legal Clinic, who provided the inspiration, opportunity, and guidance for Julie Nice to create the initial draft of these materials to teach poverty law during her teaching fellowship at Northwestern. We thank the administration of the University of Denver College of Law who provided Julie with valuable research support from Dean Dennis Lynch and from the Hughes Research and Development Fund Committee, which included Dean Emeritus Robert B. Yegge, Victor Rosenblum, Millard Rudd, and Richard D. Schwartz. We thank the Interuniversity Consortium on Poverty Law, a group of law professors funded by the Ford Foundation, who provided community and funding for Louise Trubek's initial exploration of poverty law. We thank Professor Martha Fineman of Columbia University and Professor June Weisberger who provided Louise with the oppportunity and inspiration to teach poverty law at the University of Wisconsin Law School.

We are indebted to the many people at the University of Denver College of Law who brought this textbook to fruition. We thank Diane Burkhardt, Caryl Shipley, and Terry Gould for library support, David Dudra for copy center support, Vicki O'Brien for administrative support, and law students Molly Homan ('96), Kristen Nocella ('98), Karla Robertson ('98), Terri Texas ('98), and Christine Thurlow-Harrison ('97) for research assistance. We especially thank the three people who coordinated and literally created this textbook in succession, two brilliant Denver law graduates, Kim Montagriff ('94) and Sue Chrisman ('96), and one extraordinary paralegal and computer specialist, Leslie Pagett.

Most of all, we thank our partners, Martha Ertman and David Trubek, for their belief in and daily support of us and this project.

Finally, we gratefully acknowledge the copyright holders who generously granted permission to reprint the following excerpts from their materials:

Peter B. Edelman, Toward a Comprehensive Antipoverty Strategy: Getting Beyond the Silver Bullet, 81 Georgetown Law Journal 1697 (1993), reprinted with the permission of the publisher, copyright © 1993 The Georgetown Law Journal & Georgetown University.

Austin Sarat, ". . . The Law Is All Over": Power, Resistance, and the Legal Consciousness of the Welfare Poor, 2 Yale Journal of Law & the Humanities 343 (1990), reprinted with the permission of the author and the publisher, copyright © 1990 Yale Journal of Law & the Humanities.

Thomas Ross, The Rhetoric of Poverty: Their Immorality, Our Helplessness, 79 Georgetown Law Journal 1499 (1991), reprinted with the permission of the publisher, The Georgetown Law Journal, copyright © 1991 & Georgetown University.

Martha L. Fineman, Images of Mothers in Poverty Discourses, 1991 Duke Law Journal 274 (1991), reprinted with the permission of the publisher, copyright © 1991 Duke Law Journal.

Rennard Strickland, Genocide-at-Law: An Historic and Contemporary View of the Native American Experience, 34 Kansas Law Review 713 (1986), reprinted with the permission of the publisher, copyright © 1986 Kansas Law Review.

Mimi Abramovitz, Regulating the Lives of Women (1988), reprinted by permission of the publisher, copyright © 1988 South End Press.

Joel Handler, "Constructing the Political Spectacle": The Interpretation of Entitlements, Legalization, and Obligations in Social Welfare History, 56 Brooklyn Law Review 899 (1990), reprinted with the permission of the publisher, copyright © 1990 Brooklyn Law Review.

Charles Murray, Losing Ground: American Social Policy 1950-1980 (1984), reprinted by permission of BasicBooks, a division of HarperCollins Publishers, Inc., copyright © 1984 by Charles Murray.

Lawrence M. Mead, The New Politics of Poverty: The Nonworking Poor in America (1992), reprinted by permission of BasicBooks, a division of HarperCollins Publisher, Inc., © 1992 by Lawrence M. Mead.

William Julius Wilson, The Truly Disadvantaged: The Inner City, The Underclass and Public Policy (1987), reprinted by permission of the author and publisher, copyright © 1987 by The University of Chicago Press.

William H. Simon, The Invention and Reinvention of Welfare Rights, 44 Maryland Law Review 1 (1985), reprinted by permission of the author, copyright © 1985 William H. Simon.

Lucie E. White, No Exit: Rethinking "Welfare Dependency" from a Different Ground, 81 Georgetown Law Journal 1961 (1993), reprinted with the permission of the publisher, copyright © 1993 The Georgetown Law Journal & Georgetown University.

Martha Davis, Brutal Need (1993), reprinted by permission of the publisher, copyright © 1993 Yale University Press.

Allen Redlich, Who Will Litigate Constitutional Issues for the Poor?, 19 Hastings Constitutional Law Quarterly 745 (1992), reprinted with permission from the publisher, copyright © 1992 University of California, Hastings College of the Law.

Marc Feldman, Political Lessons: Legal Services for the Poor, 83 Georgetown Law Journal 1529 (1995), reprinted by permission of the author, copyright © 1995 Marc Feldman.

Alan W. Houseman, Political Lessons: Legal Services for the Poor--A Commentary, 83 Georgetown Law Journal 1669 (1995), reprinted by permission of the author, copyright © 1995 Alan W. Houseman.

Gary Bellow & Jeanne Charn, Paths Not Yet Taken: Some Comments on Feldman's Critique of Legal Services Practice, 83 Georgetown Law Journal 1633 (1995), reprinted by permission of the authors, copyright © 1995 Gary Bellow & Jeanne Charn.

john a. powell, Race and Poverty: A New Focus for Legal Services, Clearinghouse Review, Special Issue (1993), reprinted by permission of the publisher, copyright © 1993 National Clearinghouse for Legal Services, Inc.

Louise G. Trubek, Critical Lawyering: Toward a New Public Interest Practice, 1 Public Interest Law Journal 49 (1991), reprinted by permission of the author, copyright © 1991 Louise G. Trubek.

Theresa Glennon, Lawyers and Caring: Building an Ethic of Care into Professional Responsibility, 43 Hastings Law Journal 1175 (1992), reprinted by permission of the author and publisher, copyright © 1992 University of California, Hastings College of the Law.

Lucie E. White, Subordination, Rhetorical Survival Skills, and Sunday Shoes: Notes on the Hearing of Mrs. G., 38 Buffalo Law Review 1 (1990), reprinted by permission of the publisher, copyright © 1990 Buffalo Law Review.

Barbara Bezdek, Silence in the Court: Participation and Subordination of Poor Tenants' Voices in Legal Process, 20 Hofstra Law Review 533 (1992), reprinted by permission of the publisher, copyright © 1992 Hofstra Law Review.

William Clune: New Answers to Hard Questions Posed by Rodriguez: Ending the Separation of School Finance and Educational Policy by Bridging the Gap Between Wrong and Remedy, 24 Connecticut Law Review 721 (1992), reprinted by permission of the publisher, copyright © 1992 Connecticut Law Review.

Louise G. Trubek, Is Health Care a Right? Passage of This Proposal Will Make It So, Milwaukee Journal, April 3, 1994, reprinted by permission of the author, copyright © 1994 Louise G. Trubek.

Vernellia R. Randall, Does Clinton's Health Care Reform Proposal Ensure [E]Quality of Health Care for Ethnic Americans and the Poor? 60 Brooklyn Law Review 167 (1994), reprinted by permission of the publisher, copyright © 1994 Brooklyn Law Review.

Julie A. Nice, Making Conditions Constitutional by Attaching Them to Welfare: The Dangers of Selective Contextual Ignorance of the Unconstitutional Conditions Doctrine, 72 Denver University Law Review 971 (1995), reprinted by permission of the publisher, copyright © 1995 Denver University Law Review.

Marilyn A. Friedman, Women in Poverty and Welfare Equity, in Poverty, Justice and the Law, edited by George R. Lucas, Jr., (1986), reprinted by permission of the author, copyright © 1986 University Press of America.

David T. Ellwood, Poor Support: Poverty in the American Family (1988), reprinted by permission of BasicBooks, a division of HarperCollins Publishers, Inc., copyright © 1988 by Basic Books, Inc.

Lucy Williams, The Ideology of Division: Behavior Modification Welfare Reform Proposals, 102 Yale Law Journal 719 (1992), reprinted by permission of the author and the publisher, copyright © 1992 Yale Law Journal.

Susan Bennett & Kathleen Sullivan, Disentitling the Poor: Waivers and Welfare "Reform," 26 University of Michigan Journal of Law Reform 741 (1993), reprinted by permission of the publisher, copyright © 1993 University of Michigan Journal of Law Reform.

Yvette Marie Barksdale, And the Poor Have Children, 14 Law & Inequality 1 (1995), reprinted by permission of the publisher, copyright © 1995 Law & Inequality Law Journal.

Stephen D. Sugarman, Financial Support of Children and the End of Welfare As We Know It, 81 Virginia Law Review 2523 (1995), reprinted by permission of the publisher, copyright © 1995 Virginia Law Review.

Peter Pitegoff, Child Care Enterprise, Community Development, and Work, 81 Georgetown Law Journal 1897 (1993), reprinted with the permission of the publisher, copyright © 1993 The Georgetown Law Journal & Georgetown University.

Mary L. Heen, Welfare Reform, Child Care Costs, and Taxes, 13 Yale Law & Policy Review 173 (1995), reprinted by permission of the publisher, copyright © 1995 Yale Law & Policy Review.

Randi Mandelbaum, Trying to Fit Square Pegs into Round Holes: The Need for a New Funding Scheme for Kinship Caregivers, 22 Fordham Urban Law Journal 907 (1995), reprinted by permission of the publisher, copyright © 1995 Fordham Urban Law Journal.

Martha Minow, What Ever Happened to Children's Rights, 80 Minnesota Law Review 267, reprinted by permission of the publisher, copyright © (1995) Minnesota Law Review.

Larry L. Orr & Felicity Skidmore, The Evolution of the Work Issue in Welfare Reform, in Welfare Reform in America, edited by Paul M. Sommers (1982), reprinted by permission of the publisher, copyright © 1982 by Kluwer-Nijhoff Publishing.

Joanna K. Weinberg, The Dilemma of Welfare Reform: "Workfare" Programs and Poor Women, 26 New England Law Review 415 (1991), copyright © New England School of Law 1991. All rights reserved. Reprinted by permission.

Julie A. Nice, Welfare Servitude, 3 Georgetown Journal on Fighting Poverty 340 (1994), reprinted by permission of the publisher, copyright © 1994 Georgetown Journal on Fighting Poverty.

Teresa L. Amott & Julie A. Matthaei, Race, Gender, & Work: A Multicultural Economic History of Women in the United States (1991), reprinted with permission from the publisher, South End Press, 116 Saint Botolph Street, Boston MA 02115, copyright © 1991 South End Press.

Fran Ansley, Standing Rusty and Rolling Empty: Law, Poverty and America's Eroding Industrial Base, 81 Georgetown Law Journal 1757 (1993), reprinted with the permission of the publisher, copyright © 1993 The Georgetown Law Journal & Georgetown University.

Robert Reich, The Revolt of the Anxious Class, reprinted with permission from Daily Labor Report, No. 224, pp. E-1 - E-3 (Nov. 23, 1994). Published by the Bureau of National Affairs, Inc. (800-372-1033).

Deborah Maranville, Changing Economy, Changing Lives: Unemployment Insurance and the Contingent Workforce, 4 Boston University Public Interest Law Journal 291 (1995), reprinted by permission of the author, copyright © 1995 Deborah Maranville.

Stephen Bingham, Replace Welfare for Contingent Workers with Unemployment Compensation, 22 Fordham Urban Law Journal 937 (1995), reprinted by permission of the publisher, copyright © 1995 Fordham Urban Law Journal.

Deborah Maranville, Feminist Theory and Legal Practice: A Case Study on Unemployment Compensation Benefits and the Male Norm, 43 Hastings Law Journal 1081 (1992), reprinted by permission of the author and publisher, copyright © 1992 University of California, Hastings College of Law.

Anne L. Alstott, The Earned Income Tax Credit and the Limitations of Tax-based Welfare Reform, 108 Harvard Law Review 533 (1995), reprinted by permission of the publisher, copyright © 1995 by the Harvard Law Review Association.

Rebecca Arbogast, et al., Revitalizing Public Interest Lawyering in the 1990s: The Story of One Effort to Address the Problem of Homelessness, 34 Howard Law Journal 91 (1991), reprinted by permission of the publisher, copyright © 1991 Howard Law Journal.

JULIE A. NICE
LOUISE G. TRUBEK

September 30, 1996

SUMMARY OF CONTENTS

TABLE OF CONTENTS

TABLE OF CASES

The principal cases are in bold type. Cases cited or discussed in the text are roman type. References are to pages. Cases cited in principal cases and within other quoted materials are not included.

SECTION I: CONCEPTUALIZING POVERTY LAW THEORY

CHAPTER 1: REALITIES OF EXISTENCE

A. INTRODUCTION: SCRUTINIZING POVERTY

Defining our task

Our mission is to engage in a process of scrutinizing poverty. We will examine carefully how society uses law to impact the realities of existence[1] for poor people. We will explore an emerging orthodoxy--that government welfare programs harm more than they help. In this first section of the book, we focus on conceptualizing poverty law theory through exploring current poverty, the historical legacies influencing welfare policy, and competing public policy perspectives on welfare. In the second section, we examine poverty law practice, including challenges for poverty lawyers and the constitutional issues related to due process, equal protection, and the unconstitutional conditions dilemma. In the third section, we turn to welfare reform and its focus on family and work.

Scrutiny in Law

Consider what it means to scrutinize poverty. Law schools certainly teach about scrutiny. Decisions about the level of deference or scrutiny applied by judges to the decisions of other legal actors, such as juries, legislatures, or administrative agencies, pervade the traditional study of law. For example, civil procedure students learn that appellate judges defer to findings of fact made at trial, but scrutinize and substitute their own judgments on questions of law.

---

[1]The Chapter Title, Realities of Existence, refers to language from the famous case *Rosado v. Wyman*, 397 U.S. 397, 419 (1970) (holding that the Social Security Act prohibited states from eliminating items previously used to determine the standard of need for welfare benefits, "unless a State can demonstrate that the items formerly included no longer constituted part of the reality of existence for the majority of welfare recipients").

Presumably this difference between the deference afforded findings of fact and the scrutiny applied to questions of law reflects careful consideration. It seems based on the greater capabilities of triers of fact to observe and evaluate the credibility of witnesses, compared to the limited written record available for appellate judges to review. The overarching question is always why we choose to apply more deference and less scrutiny, or more scrutiny and less deference.

Scrutiny for Poor People: Too Little and Too Much

Issues of scrutiny also arise outside of procedural contexts. In constitutional law, for example, judges apply strict scrutiny for equal protection challenges to legislation or regulations impacting either a suspect class or a fundamental right. When judges apply strict scrutiny, typically government defendants must show that a challenged law is narrowly tailored to achieve a compelling interest. The law currently does not recognize poor people as a suspect class, nor subsistence as a fundamental right. Consequently, strict scrutiny rarely applies to challenges pursued by people who live in poverty. Although poor people do not receive the protection of heightened scrutiny from the judicial branch of government, people who live in poverty certainly know about scrutiny. Legislators and administrators scrutinize nearly every aspect of poor peoples' lives. Regulations typically require welfare recipients to report regularly to administrators about their income and assets, expenses, household composition, familial and intimate relationships, job search efforts, in-kind contributions to the family, and numerous other details. Although law generally tends to subject the actions and decisions of poor people to constant scrutiny, the actions and decisions of legislators and administrators who govern the lives of poor people receive great deference. Frequently, when confronted with questions relating to the law's impact on people living in poverty, courts recite a treasured mantra--decisions relating to social and economic welfare policy are best left to legislatures. If courts abdicate their function of providing some meaningful judicial review of legislative actions, what checks and balances operate to protect poor people, a relatively politically powerless minority, from oppression by the majority?

The Study of Poverty

When poverty was prevalent as a topic at the top of the domestic agenda during the 1960s, poverty was also popular as a topic for study in higher education. College and law professors added courses in social welfare policy and poverty to the curriculum. Some wrote textbooks and treatises exploring poverty law subjects. Then poverty lost its fashionable status both on the national policy agenda and in law schools. The process of scrutinizing the use of law to respond to poverty disappeared from visibility for much of the mid-1970s to the 1990s. Poverty law simply was not in style.

Increasing Poverty Today

While the study of poverty steadily fell, the incidence of poverty in society waxed and waned. As of 1995, 36.4 million people in the United States lived in poverty. The poverty rate as measured by the federal government was 13.8% of the total population. Nearly one in four children under 6 lived below the poverty line. The poverty rates for racial minorities exceeded even that of children, with the poverty rate for African-Americans exceeding 29% and for Hispanics exceeding 30%, compared to just over 10% for whites. In raw numbers, however, two-thirds of all poor people were white.

Current Rhetoric

In recent years, the intensity of rhetoric related to poverty rivals that of the 1930s and 1960s. But one major difference emerges. In the 1930s and 1960s, politicians and commentators called for a war on poverty. Today, the war seems to be waged against welfare, rather than poverty. And it seems to be focused on some of welfare's beneficiaries, especially single mothers, children, immigrants, and unemployed adults. According to dominant rhetoric, poor people cause their poverty by failing to act responsibly. The government welfare programs in turn encourage this irresponsibility by providing an income safety net. Poor people, competing against this rhetoric, call for more work opportunities, and fewer rules that constrain them from getting ahead.

Framing the Causes

While the details of anti-poverty programs differ from one

snapshot of time to another, the primary issues and themes consistently revolve around understanding the causes of, and solution to, poverty. Debate continues on the basic questions relating to the causes of poverty. *What* is poverty? What method do we use to measure it? *Who* counts as poor? Should we focus on individuals or families? Should we concentrate on the raw numbers or on the disproportionate trends? *When* do people fall into poverty? Are adults more likely to be poor if they lived in poverty as children? Do people fall into poverty following a loss of employment? Does employment loss follow recessionary trends? *Where* do people fall into poverty? Is poverty concentrated in inner cities and/or in rural areas? Do we find more poverty in some regions? *Why* do people fall into poverty? Is it caused more by personal problems or societal failures? *How* do people fall into poverty? Is it typically temporary, sporadic, or permanent?

Experimenting with Solutions

A similar debate continues on the basic questions relating to the solutions to the poverty problem. *What* should society do to respond to poverty? Should survival of the fittest be the rule? Or should we intervene to eliminate poverty? *Who* is best situated to respond to poverty--individuals, families, neighborhoods, private charities, government entities, or international institutions? If government remains involved in addressing poverty, should that happen through legislatures or agencies, or through local, state, or federal actors? *When* should society intervene--through early preventive programs or later remedial measures? *Where* should society intervene--in families, in schools, in neighborhoods, through private enterprise, in welfare offices? *How* should society eliminate or ameliorate the effects of poverty--through harsh incentives to increase self-sufficiency, through short-term treatment of symptoms, or through long-term treatment of the underlying causes? The preferred answers to these questions have changed over time, depending on the particular historical context.

Assessing Your Views at the Outset

Most of us are experts on welfare policy. Or at least we pretend to be. Discussions about welfare reform do not lack opinionated participants. Poverty law seems similar to family law in that respect--most of us have experience dealing with the need to earn income, so we think we understand the problem of poverty, and we espouse solutions that reflect our personal values and experiences. Consider your own views about poverty. What do you think counts as poverty? What do you think causes poverty? What remedies do you prefer? What experiences in your own life contributed to your beliefs? Are you open to considering whether your views match the reality experienced by poor people? We encourage you to identify at the outset your own perceptions and beliefs about poverty and wealth.

You may have elected to study poverty because you wanted knowledge to support your views. Or you may have selected this course for a true inquiry--for seeking information, developing knowledge, and challenging your views and those of others. Of course, some of you may be reading this because it is required. No matter your motivation, we invite your full participation in this course. No matter your perspective, you have something to offer our study. The study of poverty is a value-laden enterprise, as is all study of law. But with poverty law, the ideological nature of the enterprise seems more apparent. Our challenge to you is twofold, and somewhat dialectical--be both open and critical. You will identify strengths and weaknesses in every idea or argument presented, including your own.

B. THE NUMBERS

What are the realities of existence of poor people in the United States today? How many people live in poverty? Who are they? How do they experience poverty? What rhetoric characterizes or mischaracterizes their experiences? We begin with this reality check to balance the discourse about poverty and welfare by adding doses of reality to the excess of ideology, which we will study in Chapter 3.

Defining Poverty

We begin with a general definition of poverty: the state of lacking means to meet subsistence needs. Of course, what seems necessary for each of us to continue to exist entails both objective and relative aspects. We each need sufficient nourishment and protection from the elements to keep our physical selves alive. Most of us understand that we have material, emotional, social, intellectual, and other needs as well. Our senses of need reflect our expectations, which differ among individuals and among cultures of people. These observations, while very simple, offer a challenge for grounding our discussions about poverty throughout this course. As we explore various statistical trends and generalizations about poor people, consider whether these numbers and groupings tell the entire story.

How do we measure poverty? The federal Office of Management and Budget defines poverty by setting money income thresholds for various family sizes. The federal Census Bureau in turn surveys the population to estimate the number of families who live below these threshold income levels. It counts the family's pre-tax money income, including wages, salaries, and Social Security and cash welfare benefits. It does not include capital gains or noncash benefits such as food stamps, health insurance payments, or medical benefits. The poverty line is adjusted annually to account for changes in the Consumer Price Index. Table 1-1 provides figures for 1993 and 1995. For example, a family of two lived below the official poverty threshold in 1995 if it had an annual income less than $9,933. The figure for a family of four was $12,158.

Poverty Line Income Thresholds

Table 1-1

	1993	1995
Family of 1	$7,343	$7,763
Family of 2	$9,414	$9,933
Family of 3	$11,522	$12,158
Family of 4	$14,763	$15,569

Source: ELEANOR BAUGHER AND LEATHA LAMISON-WHITE, U.S. BUREAU OF THE CENSUS, CURRENT POPULATION REPORTS, SERIES P60-194, POVERTY IN THE UNITED STATES: 1995 (1996).

The Number of Poor Persons

As of 1993, more people lived in poverty than in over thirty years (see Table 1-2). In 1962, the total population included over 184 million people. The poverty rate was 21%, meaning over 38 million people lived below the poverty line. In 1993, the total population included nearly 260 million people. The poverty rate was 15.1%, meaning over 39 million people lived below the poverty line again. In 1994, poverty decreased slightly, so that over 38 million people lived below the poverty line. In 1995, the raw number of people living below the poverty line again fell to 36.4 million people.

Poverty in the United States Table 1-2

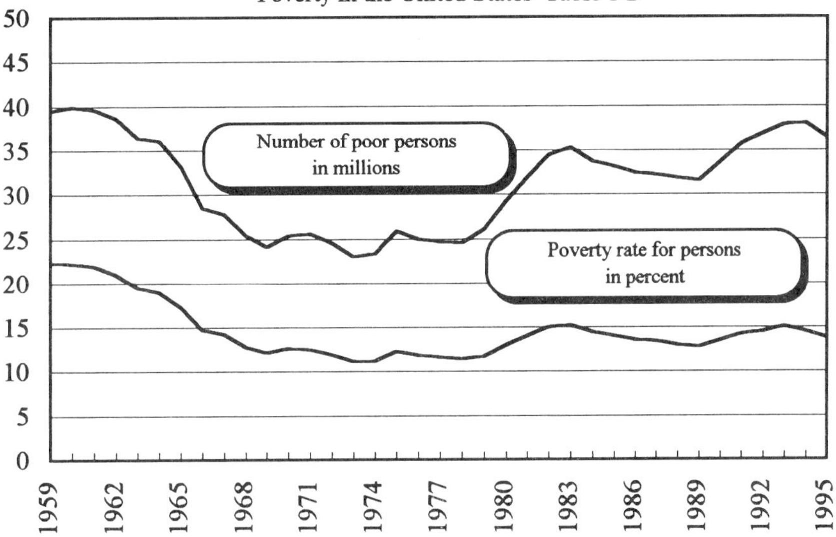

Source: ELEANOR BAUGHER AND LEATHA LAMISON-WHITE, U.S. BUREAU OF THE CENSUS, CURRENT POPULATION REPORTS, SERIES P60-194, POVERTY IN THE UNITED STATES: 1995, App. Table C-1, at C-2 (1996).

The Poverty Rate

After the Census Bureau counts the number of poor people who lived below the poverty line during the previous calendar year, it announces the poverty rate for that year. The poverty rate is the percentage of the total population who lived below the poverty line. As Table 1-2 details, the poverty rate prior to the 1960s' War on Poverty exceeded 20% of the population. The poverty rate dipped to a low of 11.1% in 1973. It sporadically increased to a high of 15.2% in 1983, then decreased again. The rate exceeded 15% again in 1993, when 15.1% of the population lived below the poverty line. As the economy strengthened in 1994 and 1995, the poverty rates for those years fell to 14.5% and 13.8%.

Poverty and Age

Since 1974, children under eighteen years of age have suffered from the highest poverty rate, compared to other age groups. For the fifteen years from 1966 through 1980, less than 20% of children lived in poverty. But as of 1993, the child poverty rate of 22.7% was higher than it had been for 30 years (see Table 1-3). The child poverty rates for 1994 and 1995 declined slightly to 21.8% and 20.8% respectively. Perhaps more disturbing, the rate for children under six was 25.6% in 1993 and 23.7% in 1995.

Many elderly people also live below or near the poverty line. While persons 65 and over made up 12% of the population in 1995, they constituted only 9% of the poor. But of the "near poor" population 18% were elderly.

Poverty Rates by Age Table 1-3

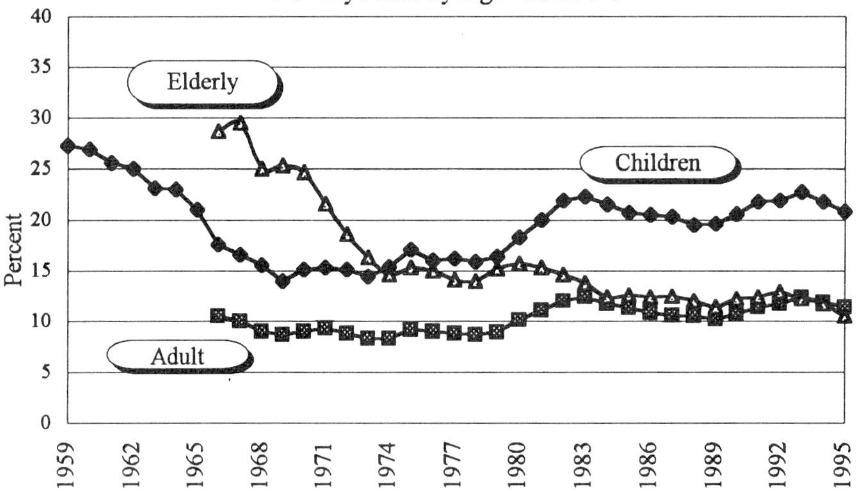

Note: Adults are between the ages of 18 and 64; elderly are 65 and over; and children are under 18.

Source: ELEANOR BAUGHER AND LEATHA LAMISON-WHITE, U.S. BUREAU OF THE CENSUS, CURRENT POPULATION REPORTS, SERIES P60-194, POVERTY IN THE UNITED STATES: 1995 App. Table C-1, at C-5 (1996).

Poverty and Race

According to Census Bureau categories, approximately two-thirds of poor people in 1995 were White. Racial minorities, however, were disproportionately affected by poverty. In 1995, only 11.2% of Whites, compared to 29.3% of Blacks, 30.3% of Hispanics (who may be of any race), and 14.6% of Asians and Pacific Islanders, lived below the poverty line (see Table 1-4). Over time, the poverty rate for Whites and Blacks has remained relatively steady, while the rate for Hispanics gradually has increased.

Poverty Status by Race Table 1-4

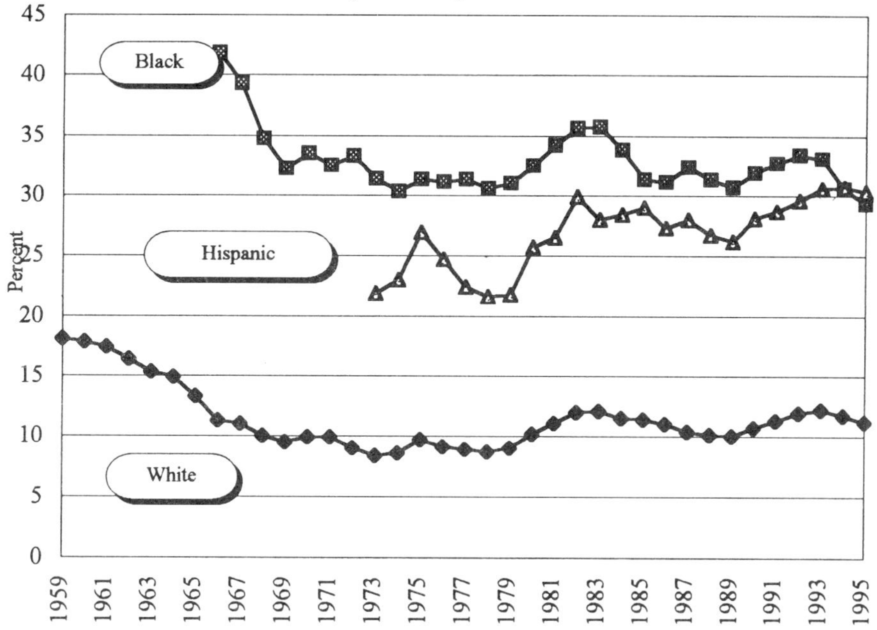

Source: ELEANOR BAUGHER AND LEATHA LAMISON-WHITE, U.S. BUREAU OF THE CENSUS, CURRENT POPULATION REPORTS, SERIES P60-194, POVERTY IN THE UNITED STATES: 1995 App. Table C-1, at C-4 (1996).

Poverty and Gender

Over 32% of families headed by women lived below the poverty line in 1995. Moreover, over half of all poor families were headed by women (54%), while only 18% of all families were headed by women.

Income Inequality

Recently, greater attention has been paid to the trend toward increasing income inequality between the poorest fifth of the population (lowest 20%) and the wealthiest fifth (top 20%). The income inequality between the poorest and wealthiest in our society is great, and it is growing larger. As of 1992, the wealthiest fifth of our population earned nearly 47% of total income, while the poorest fifth earned less than 4% of total income. Table 1-5 reveals that income of the poorest fifth has remained nearly unchanged for more than 20 years. Between 1972 and 1992, the mean income of the poorest fifth of our population barely increased from $7,124 to $7,328. In contrast, during those same twenty years, the mean income of the wealthiest fifth rose from $78,385 in 1972 to $91,494 in 1992. How much did the income of the top 5% of the population rise between 1972 and 1992?

Mean Income Table 1-5

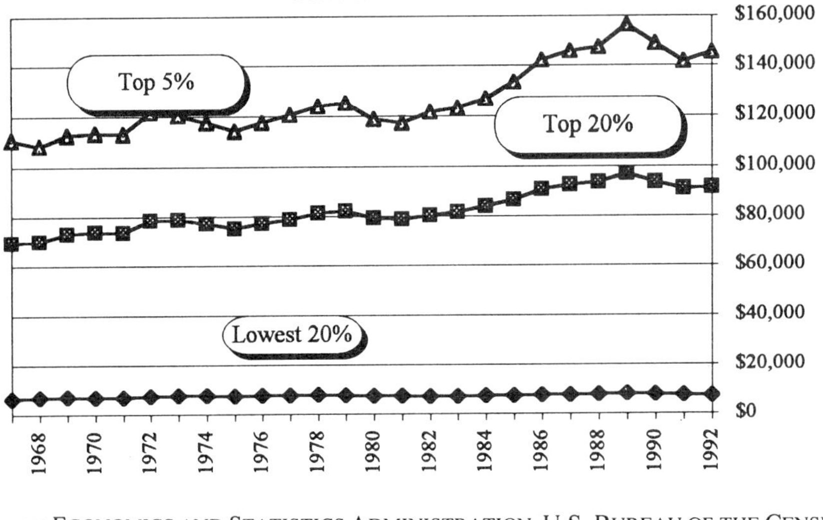

Source: ECONOMICS AND STATISTICS ADMINISTRATION, U.S. BUREAU OF THE CENSUS, MONEY INCOME OF HOUSEHOLDS, FAMILIES, AND PERSONS IN THE UNITED STATES: 1992 App. Table B-3, at B-6 (1993).

In percentage terms, the share of total income received by the wealthiest fifth of the population increased from 43.9% in 1972 to 46.9% in 1992. In contrast, the poorest fifth's share of income decreased from 4.1% in 1972 to 3.8% in 1992 (see Table 1-6). What happened to the share of income of the middle 60%? Of the top 5%?

In addition to the increasing income gap, an enormous wealth gap exists. According to 1989 Federal Reserve figures, the wealthiest 1% of the population owned 40% of property, and the wealthiest fifth owned 80%. In the spring of 1995, news articles reported that the United States surpassed Britain as the nation with the largest gap between the rich and the poor.

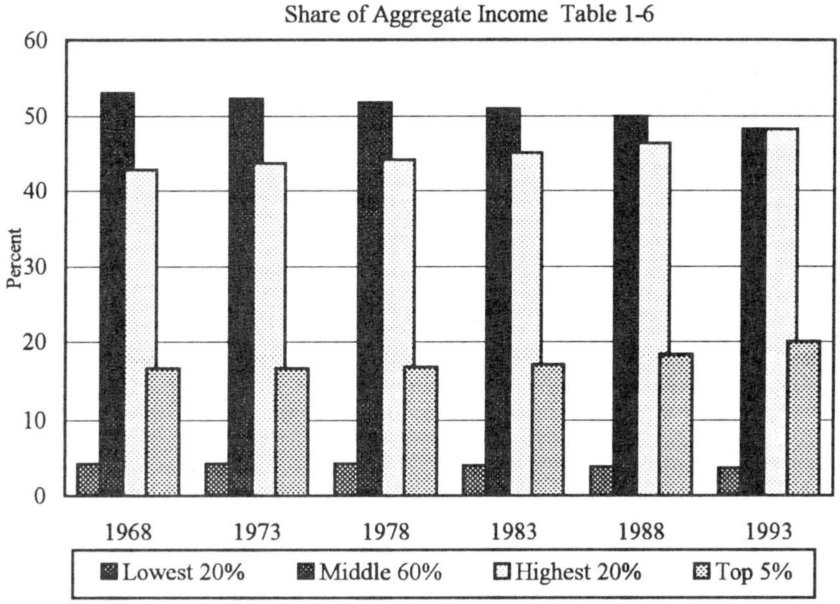

Source: ECONOMICS AND STATISTICS ADMINISTRATION, U.S. BUREAU OF THE CENSUS, INCOME, POVERTY, AND VALUATION OF NONCASH BENEFITS: 1993 xii (1995).

Poverty and Location

The South consistently experiences the highest poverty rate among the nation's four regions. In 1995, the poverty rates were 15.7% in the South, 14.9% in the West, 12.5% in the Northeast, and 11% in the Midwest. The poverty rate outside of metropolitan areas was 15.6% in 1995, higher than the metropolitan area poverty rate of 13.4%.

More telling perhaps is the distribution of the poor among the regions. Around 40% of the poor lived in the South over the twenty years between the early 1970s and the early 1990s. No other region hosted more than one-quarter of poor people during this period.

Poverty and Welfare

Not all poor people receive welfare. Less than half of the people living in poverty in the early 1990s received cash assistance such as Aid to Families with Dependent Children (AFDC). Over one-quarter of people who lived below the poverty line received neither cash nor noncash assistance. Moreover, most people who received cash assistance still lived below the poverty level even after their assistance was counted as income.

Welfare does not lift recipients above the poverty line because amounts paid out are modest. For example, the average monthly AFDC grant for 1993 was $373. This amount brought the average poor family's income up to about half of the poverty line. No state provided AFDC benefits at a level high enough to lift a family out of poverty.

Because welfare spending amounts are small, they account for a tiny segment of the government's budget. For example, AFDC spending in the early 1990s accounted for around 1% of the federal budget and about 3.5% of the average state budget. Nor are welfare spending amounts increasing to compensate for inflation. Between 1970 and 1993, AFDC benefits fell by 45% in real dollar terms.

Finally, major segments of the poor population do not receive basic health coverage. For example, while over 46% of poor people received some Medicaid coverage in 1995, 11 million poor people, or over 30%, had neither Medicaid nor any other health insurance during 1995.

Poverty and Work

Many poor people work. In 1995, 41% of poor persons 16 years and older worked, and 11% worked full time all year. How can working people remain poor?

In 1995, the federal minimum wage was $4.25. A parent working full-time all year at the federal minimum wage earned a gross income of $8,840, less than the amount required to support one child above the poverty line. A parent attempting to support two children from a steady minimum wage job earned an income more than 25% below the poverty line for a family of three. In their study, Christopher Jencks and Kathryn Edin estimated that AFDC recipients needed to earn $16,000 per year as of 1990 to pay for food, shelter, transportation, child care, and medical costs.[1]

Congress increased the federal minimum wage to $4.75 in mid-1996 and to $5.15 effective July, 1997. Will these increases lift minimum wage workers above the poverty line?

C. THE CATEGORIES

Even as we review data about the numbers of poor people and the rates of poverty, we see the prevalence of categorization. When the Census Bureau releases its statistics about poverty each fall, the spin placed on those numbers tells more about trends among demographic categories of poor people than about the poor as a group. News reports frequently focus on an increase in poverty among racial minorities or children or female-headed households. Within poverty law, policies differ greatly among categories that vary based on whether society excuses the adult from participating in the labor force. Peter Edelman explains.

Peter B. Edelman

TOWARD A COMPREHENSIVE ANTIPOVERTY STRATEGY: GETTING BEYOND THE SILVER BULLET

81 GEORGETOWN LAW JOURNAL 1697 (1993)

* * *

The poor are not a monolithic group. They have differing needs and their situations involve differing policies. America has always had a regard for the "deserving" among its poor, and the categories of deserving poor have broadened as time has passed, a salutary development that must be noted positively.

In the nineteenth century, the blind, the deaf, and the incurably insane were treated fairly consistently as deserving--objects of state assistance not subject to discretionary judgments about their individual morality or worth. Civil War veterans and orphans also were treated reasonably well. No other categories of the poor fared

---

[1]CHRISTOPHER JENCKS, RETHINKING SOCIAL POLICY: RACE, POVERTY, AND THE UNDERCLASS 225 (1992).

particularly well. . . . The use of the poorhouse eventually faded, but the tradition of allowing significant discretion to state and local authorities regarding the nonelderly, nondisabled poor remains strong to this day.

With the passage of the Social Security Act in 1935, the elderly became the first large category of the poor to be treated as deserving, although they remained disproportionately poor for nearly a half century after the enactment of the Social Security Act. The indexing of social security benefits to inflation and the enactment of Supplemental Security Income (SSI) in 1972 cemented the elderly's status as deserving, but it was not until 1982 that the elderly as a group finally became less poor than the rest of the population. Even so, there were still 3.8 million elderly poor in 1991 (out of a total of 35.7 million poor people that year).

* * *

The disabled joined the ranks of the deserving poor in 1956, with their addition to insured status under the Social Security Act, albeit with significant initial limitations as to the age of entitlement to benefits and the definition of disability. The subsequent broadening of coverage and growth in the disability rolls brought a backlash in the 1980s in the form of a serious effort by the Reagan Administration to cleanse the rolls. This, however, was followed by a counter-movement in Congress, the courts, and the states that ultimately defeated the Reagan rollback initiative. The surprisingly easy enactment of the Americans with Disabilities Act in 1990 proved the disabled had "arrived" as a category of the deserving poor. The Census tells us that 7.2 million of the poor were totally or severely disabled in 1991, demonstrating that although this group is "deserving," not all of their needs are being met.

* * *

Beginning with the enactment of the Earned Income Tax Credit (EITC) in 1975, the working poor have moved toward deserving status. The EITC has been increased a number of times, and the pace of its expansion accelerated in the late 1980s. Conservative members of Congress speak warmly of those who work hard but are still unable to escape poverty, and President Clinton has proposed a large expansion of the Earned Income Tax Credit. On the other hand, given that there are 2.1 million people with year-round, full-time work who do not earn enough to lift their families out of poverty, and 2.6 million more who work part-time or only part of the year because they cannot find full-time work, the working poor can hardly be said to have fully joined the ranks of the deserving.

Children are a huge and disproportionate group among the poor, totaling 14.3 million in 1991. They comprise over forty percent of the poor, and their poverty rate--21.8%--is far in excess of the poverty rate for the population as a whole. Their situations vary enormously, of course, because their poverty is derivative of the problems of their parents, but we know a lot about their poverty. If they are the children of a female-headed household with no spouse present, they are vastly more likely to be poor. If they were born to an unmarried mother there is a sixty-two percent chance that they will be poor for the first ten years of their life, whereas if they were born to a two-parent family, their chance of a ten year spell of poverty is just two percent. If they are African American or Latino, they are much more likely to be poor, and if they are the child of an unmarried African-American or Latino mother, they will likely be poor at a yet higher rate. The size of the family is a variable, as is the educational attainment of the mother, so that poverty rates rise among larger families and families headed by women who did not graduate from high school. Thus, the rate of poverty among families headed by an African-American mother who did not finish high school is 72.4%.

Could we characterize children as "deserving" poor? Based on the rhetoric of elected officials, editorial writers, community leaders, and others one might say yes, but a sober look at the rate of poverty among children suggests the opposite conclusion. In significant part this is because, whatever our rhetoric, what we actually do for particular children depends upon what we think of their parents. It also relates to the complexity and cost of the preventive and developmental policies that are necessary to maximize a child's chances of growing up to self-sufficient adulthood, to say nothing of the policies that would maximize the child's possibility of growing up in a healthy, stable, economically self-sufficient family setting.

* * *

Who is left? The remaining poor in this typology are the working age, nondisabled, and nonworking persistently poor. They are a widely diverse group. A major element of their diversity is their geographic location--a large number live in rural areas where there are no available jobs within scores, if not hundreds, of miles. A subgroup of considerable size lives in inner cities; the fact that they live among high concentrations of poor people complicates the quality of their lives and the possibility of change for their children.

Another significant element of diversity among the persistently poor is their varying ability to undertake employment, a question wholly apart from whether there is employment available to them. They have varying innate capacities, varying levels of skills and other employment readiness, and varying damage from the vicissitudes of life. They face varying barriers to employment, including lack of child care, loss of health insurance coverage if they go to work, and racial discrimination.

* * *

However one measures the so-called "underclass," and however successful one is in subdividing groups needing a job, education or job training, child care, health coverage, or some combination of these, a residual group will still remain that is unable to achieve self-sufficiency, in many cases because they have serious problems that make them unable to function successfully in the labor market. As implied earlier, conservatives in the policy debate in effect suggest abandoning this population. But this response ignores important long-term consequences. In leaving the hardcore poor to their own devices, we run a significant risk of condemning their children to a similar fate, which is neither efficient nor humane.

Notes and Questions

1. *Deserving versus Undeserving.* According to Professor Edelman, we currently categorize elderly and disabled people as deserving, the working poor as nearly deserving, and children and unemployed adults as undeserving. How do you expect this categorization to impact poverty policy? Do these categories make sense to you?

2. *Demographics.* Edelman explains that poor people are categorized according to other demographic criteria. For example, we create and study categories of poor people based on their family composition, such as two-parent or one-parent families, female-headed or male-headed families, and families of various sizes. We also study poverty among various racial groups. Edelman notes other

differences among poor people, such as the educational or employment skill levels of poor adults. How might these other categories help us to better understand poverty?

3. *Changes in Categories.* Categorization of people who are poor for various reasons has changed over time. What factors influenced these changes? Do you predict future changes in these categories? What strategies might you use to change the current categorization?

D. THE EXPERIENCE

Many discussions about poverty ignore the views of poor people themselves. But poor people are not entirely invisible in the public debate. Media representations frequently provide images of poor people, but these more often than not are the worst-case examples of lazy freeloaders or cheats. These images of poor people, which we will explore later, serve to create a rhetoric. But what about the reality of poor peoples' experiences?

During the welfare rights movement of the 1960s, poor people spoke, and many Americans listened. Perhaps the most prominent spokesperson was Johnnie Tillmon, who served as Executive Director of the National Welfare Rights Organization. *See* Robert McG. Thomas, Jr., *Johnnie Tillmon Blackston, Welfare Reformer, Dies at 69,* N.Y. TIMES, Nov. 27, 1995. Tillmon was an Arkansas sharecropper's daughter who had tried to support her six children working in a laundry before accepting welfare benefits. *Id.* She was oft-quoted for comparing the welfare bureaucracy to a bad husband:

> You trade in "a" man for "The" Man. But you can't divorce him if he treats you bad. He can divorce you, of course--cut you off--any time he wants. But in that case, "he" keeps the kids, not you.
>
> "The" Man runs everything. In ordinary marriage, sex is supposed to be for your husband. On A.F.D.C. you're not supposed to have sex at all. You give up control of your body. It's a condition of aid. "The" Man, the welfare system, controls your money. "He" tells you what to buy and what not to buy, where to buy it and what things cost.

Id. For a description of the early welfare rights movement, *see*

FRANCES FOX PIVEN AND RICHARD A. CLOWARD, POOR PEOPLE'S MOVEMENTS: WHY THEY SUCCEED, HOW THEY FAIL (1977).

Some grassroots movements of welfare recipients endure, but they receive relatively little media attention. A few former welfare recipients have written about their experiences. *See, e.g.*, THERESA FUNICIELLO, TYRANNY OF KINDNESS: DISMANTLING THE WELFARE SYSTEM TO END POVERTY IN AMERICA (1993). Several journalists have also written moving accounts of the lives of poor children. *See, e.g.*, JONATHAN KOZOL, RACHEL AND HER CHILDREN: HOMELESS FAMILIES IN AMERICA (1988); JONATHAN KOZOL, SAVAGE INEQUALITIES: CHILDREN IN AMERICA'S SCHOOLS (1991); ALEX KOTLOWITZ, THERE ARE NO CHILDREN HERE: THE STORY OF TWO BOYS GROWING UP IN THE OTHER AMERICA (1991). Some scholars who study poverty have also focused their work on examining the lives of poor people. *See, e.g.*, MARK ROBERT RANK, LIVING ON THE EDGE: THE REALITIES OF WELFARE IN AMERICA (1994).

Consider what you can learn from poor people directly by listening to them. Austin Sarat shares some of what he learned from Spencer and others who live in poverty.

Austin Sarat

". . . THE LAW IS ALL OVER": POWER, RESISTANCE AND THE LEGAL CONSCIOUSNESS OF THE WELFARE POOR

2 YALE JOURNAL OF LAW & THE HUMANITIES 343 (1990)

"For me the law is all over. I am caught, you know; there is always some rule that I'm supposed to follow, some rule I don't even know about that they say. It's just different and you can't really understand." These words were spoken by Spencer, a thirty-five-year-old man on public assistance (general relief), whom I first encountered in the waiting room of a legal services office. I introduced myself and told him that I was interested in talking to him about law and finding out why he was using legal services; I asked if he would be willing to talk with me and allow me to be present when he met with his lawyer. While he seemed, at first, both puzzled and amused that I had, as he put it, "nothing more important to do," he agreed to both of my requests.

As my research unfolded, what Spencer said in our first conversation, ". . . the law is all over," served as a reference point for understanding the meaning and significance of law in the lives of the welfare poor. His words helped me interpret how people on welfare think about law and use legal ideas as well as how they respond to problems with the welfare bureaucracy. In this paper I present that interpretation and describe what I call the legal consciousness of the welfare poor. I suggest that the legal consciousness of the welfare poor is a consciousness of power and domination, in which the keynote is enclosure and dependency, and a consciousness of resistance, in which welfare recipients assert themselves and demand recognition of their personal identities and their human needs.

The legal consciousness of the welfare poor is, I will argue, substantially different from other groups in society for whom law is a less immediate and visible presence. Law is, for people on welfare, repeatedly encountered in the most ordinary transactions and events of their lives. Legal rules and practices are implicated in determining whether and how welfare recipients will be able to meet some of their most pressing needs. Law is immediate and powerful because being on welfare means having a significant part of one's life organized by a regime of legal rules invoked by officials to claim jurisdiction over choices and decisions which those not on welfare would regard as personal and private. Thus, Spencer's sense that ". . . the law is all over" is an introduction to the pervasiveness and obtrusiveness of legal rules and practices in the lives of people on welfare.

For Spencer and other welfare recipients law is not a distant abstraction; it is a web-like enclosure in which they are "caught." It is a space which is not their own and which allows them only a "tactical" presence. It is both a metaphorical trap and a material force. Like the man from the country in Franz Kafka's parable "Before the Law," law is, for Spencer and others on welfare, an irresistible and inescapable presence. For them, however, it is an already entered space, an enclosure seen from the inside, an enclosure whose imperative power, whose "supposed to'(s)," is clothed in the categories and abstractions of rules.

The rules Spencer confronts are a series of "they say(s)." The rules speak, but what Spencer hears is the embodied voice of law's bureaucratic guardians. For him, as for Kafka's character, the power of legal rules and practices is derived, at least in part, from the incomplete, yet authoritative, representation of law's categories and abstractions by officials authorized to say what the law is. Legal rules and practices are all around, immediately and visibly present; yet the law itself remains a shadowy presence.

The law that the welfare poor confront is neither a law of reason and justification nor of sacred texts and shared normative commitments. Spencer and others like him are not invited to participate in the interpretation of those texts, and they are included in neither the official explication of welfare law nor in the construction of meaningful accounts of the legal practices they regularly encounter. They are "caught" inside law's rules, but are, at the same time, excluded from its interpretive community. In all of their dealings with welfare they act on "a terrain imposed . . . and organized by the law of a foreign power." Their law is a law of power and of compulsion, and their experience of being inside, but yet excluded, is one indication of the way that power is exercised over the welfare poor.

While the welfare poor are surrounded and entrapped by legal rules as well as by officials and institutions which claim authority to say what the law is and what the rules mean, they are not, like the man from the country, transfixed or paralyzed. In this paper I argue that the welfare poor subscribe to neither an allegedly hegemonic "myth of rights" nor to a picture of law as autonomous, apolitical, objective, neutral and disinterested. They are not the passive recipients of an ideology encoded in doctrine which is allegedly taken seriously among legal elites. Power and domination are thus only part of the story of the legal consciousness of the welfare poor. Because welfare recipients are trapped or "caught," because they are involved in an ongoing series of transactions with officials visibly engaged in the interpretation and use of rules, the welfare poor have access to inside knowledge not generally available to those whose contacts with law are more episodic or for whom law is less visible. This inside knowledge means, as we will see, that they have few illusions about what law is or what it can do. They are, as a result, able, when the need arises, to respond strategically, to maneuver and to resist the "they say(s)" and "supposed to(s)" of the welfare bureaucracy.

Resistance exists side-by-side with power and domination. Thus, when people like Spencer seek legal assistance or go to legal services they fight the welfare bureaucracy and its "legal order" even as they submit themselves to another of law's domains. They use legal ideas to interpret and make sense of their relationship to the welfare bureaucracy even as they refine those ideas by making claims the meaning and moral content of which are often at variance with dominant understandings. They resist those understandings by "vigilantly making use of the cracks that particular conjunctions open in . . . proprietary powers. . . ." Yet their use of legal services and legal ideas further inscribes them in the world of state law and helps to reproduce official understandings of law and justice. It is, however, always an incomplete inscription.

Spencer and others like him stand in a contradictory, paradoxical and ambivalent relationship to legal authority, mobilizing one set of legal officials against another, moving from one arena of rules to another, seeking recognition and help while being very dubious about the treatment they receive and seeking to establish spaces for, or moments of, resistance. While they seek *legal* redress for wrongs done in the name of law, they contest what are sometimes said to be key symbols of law and legal authority, in particular the association of law with neutrality, disinterestedness, rule determinacy and rights.

The dynamic of power and resistance that I observed is, of course, played out on the "foreign" terrain of the lawyer's office, and the welfare poor seem very conscious of the fact that neither here nor in their dealings with the welfare bureaucracy are they able to find a "*place* that can be delineated as . . . [their] own and serve as a base from which relations of *exteriority* . . . can be managed." The recognition that ". . . the law is all over" expresses, in spatial terms, the experience of power and domination; resistance involves efforts to avoid further "spatialization" or establish unreachable spaces of personal identity and integrity.

Power and domination are, however, represented in the legal consciousness of the welfare poor in temporal as well as spatial terms; thus, the people I studied often spoke of an interminable waiting that they said marks the welfare experience. In that waiting they are frozen in time as if time itself were frozen; power defines whose time is valued and whose time is valueless. For the welfare poor resistance involves a use of time against space, an insistence on the *immediacy* of their material needs, an attempt to substitute human for bureaucratic time. Thus metaphors of space and time become important signs of the way the welfare poor understand power and resistance as well as a currency for tactical maneuvers within a "world bewitched by the . . . powers of the Other."

To this point I have talked about the welfare poor as if they were a homogeneous group whose legal consciousness and relationship to power and resistance were uniform. There is, however, considerably more fragmentation and division among people on welfare than might be suggested by my repeated references to *the* welfare poor. As Spencer put it, "all welfare recipients aren't the same." He reminded me that the welfare poor are not a natural social group. They neither share a distinctive background nor common ties of sentiment; they vary greatly in their life situations, their ability to survive without public assistance and their disposition to do so.

Spencer insisted that many welfare recipients have lives not unlike my own only without the material comfort which a regular job would provide, that many have stable ties to their community and its major social institutions. They are often regular church-goers, who maintain close relationships with their extended families. They invest heavily in the effort to attain symbols of respectability even as they confront conditions of material deprivation. Others lack such stable social ties and aspirations. They are cut off from their families or do not know the identities of parents and relatives; some are involved in serious drug use and have criminal records.

* * *

These differences suggest that legal consciousness among people on welfare may be as internally divided and plural as it is different from the legal consciousness of other social groups.

Notes and Questions

1. *Invasion.* Professor Sarat recounts how some poor people experience being caught in a web of power and domination spun by the welfare bureaucracy. He explains that this involves an invasion of their time and space. Welfare recipients certainly spend a great deal of time waiting in welfare offices. Once their number is finally called, they must report to government employees about the details of their personal lives. They must answer all questions, or suffer the

penalty for "failure to cooperate." They must submit to home visits or inspections by their caseworkers.

Consider a former welfare recipient's description of applying for welfare: "I remember feeling inadequate in the sense that I had to justify and prove to a welfare worker that I was who I said I was, that my children in fact were my children, and that we actually had no source of income and no relatives around to help us. My life stopped being personal and private at that moment. As they kept dissecting me as a person, piece by piece, I felt that I was unable to speak up because I believed I would put in jeopardy my children's next meal or the roof over our heads, which we eventually lost anyway." Nitza I. Vera, *Remarks Of A Former Welfare Recipient On Selected State Legislative Developments In Welfare,* 3 JOURNAL OF GENDER & LAW 153, 154 (1995).

Is this invasion of personal privacy necessary? Is it reasonable? Do scholars perpetrate a similar invasion when they study poor people's lives?

2. *Strategies.* Poor people organized themselves into a national organization to advocate for policies that would serve their interests during the 1960s. Many organizations similar to the National Welfare Rights Organization now survive on a state or local level. In addition, Sarat describes how individual poor people resist the welfare system by acting strategically to minimize bureaucratic interference in their lives. Does this response seem reasonable to you? Is it reasonable for policy makers to expect poor people to be any less self-protective than any other group?

3. *Diversity.* Sarat reminds us of the vast diversity among poor people. How do you think poor people compare to other groups? Are poor people more or less internally diverse than members of any particular race or gender or other class?

E. THE RHETORIC

Poor people struggle, as part of the reality of their existence, with the rhetoric that controls the debate about poverty policy. In this context, we use "rhetoric" to mean an unsupported or inflated discourse. It refers especially to the language and images used to signify poor people. The poverty rhetoric tends to present the most despised stereotype as the norm. For example, politicians, pundits and reporters frequently refer to "welfare mothers" as a shorthand for poor people. Thomas Ross provides a historical overview that may help us to understand how this rhetoric functions.

Thomas Ross

THE RHETORIC OF POVERTY: THEIR IMMORALITY, OUR HELPLESSNESS

79 GEORGETOWN LAW JOURNAL 1499 (1991)

Poor people are different from us. Most of them are morally weak and undeserving.

* * *

The first rhetorical step, the creation of the abstraction the "poor," is an easily overlooked yet powerful part of the rhetoric of poverty. We are so used to speaking of the poor as a distinct class that we overlook the rhetorical significance of speaking this way. By focusing on the single variable of economic wealth and then drawing a line on the wealth continuum, we create a class of people who are them, not us. Creating this abstraction is, in one sense, merely a way of speaking. We do this because to speak of the world in sensible ways we must resort to categories and abstractions. There are meaningful differences between the circumstances of people below the poverty line and the circumstances of middle class people, and to ignore these real differences can lead to injustice. Thus, to speak of the "poor" is a sensible way to talk. In the rhetorical context, however, it is also much more.

The creation of the category of the "poor", also makes possible the assertion of their moral weakness. To assert their moral weakness, "they" must exist as a conceptually distinct group. There is a long history of speaking of the poor as morally weak, or even degenerate. Thus, when we hear legal rhetoric about the poor, we often hear an underlying message of deviance: we are normal, they are deviant. Our feelings about their deviance range from empathy to violent hatred. Still, even in the most benevolent view, they are not normal. Their deviance is a product of a single aspect of their lives, their relative wealth position. All other aspects of their lives are either distorted by the label of deviance or ignored. By creating this class of people, we are able at once to distinguish us from them and to appropriate normalcy to our lives and circumstances.

* * *

The Immorality of the Poor

The separation and stigmatization of people in poverty is not new. In various manifestations, it has been a constant feature of our culture. In fact, the cultural separation and stigmatization of the poor has been a feature of most Western cultures throughout modern history. In one fashion or another the poor have always been separated by class distinctions and labels. They have been labeled "paupers," "peasants," and "strangers." They have been cast as different, deviant, and morally weak. These assumptions make coherent the physical separation of the poor from the affluent.

Just as the separation and stigmatization of the poor is a recurring cultural assumption, the intensified suffering of those in poverty in times of natural or man-made disaster has been a recurring societal reality. During the great plagues of Europe, for example, the poor were left in what became ghettos of disease and death while the affluent left for enclaves outside the cities. As a result, the plagues took the lives of a much larger percentage of the poor. Famine, wars, and natural disasters have followed a similar pattern, with the burdens falling disproportionately on the poor. The cultural assumptions and the societal realities cannot be disconnected. The assumptions make the disproportionate suffering coherent.

The particular assumptions made about the poor have varied greatly across cultures and time.[14] Still, the recurrent expression of

---

[14]At certain places and times, separation and stigmatization have all but disappeared. Poverty, measured by the lack of basic necessities, has been virtually banished by Sweden.

> We have in post-World-War II Sweden a situation in which the war on poverty has been won; urban rehabilitation is a fact; housing is subsidized so that the working class pays no higher share of its income for a home than does the middle class; medical and dental care at nominal fees is available to all; education up through the doctorate is free; unestablished newlyweds receive loans to set up housekeeping guaranteed by the state; every expectant mother is given care, and families automatically receive child support; a parent can take leave from work with pay to care for a sick child; early retirement with nearly full pension is a realizable goal for everyone; no one suffers destitution because of loss of earning power, and so on.

their immorality in world history makes this assumption one that cannot be easily sloughed off by those who live today. We would like to think that our assumptions about poor people are not anything like the assumptions of our European ancestors who walled the poor into plague-ridden urban ghettos. Yet, throughout this country's history the poor have been distinguished from those not in poverty and have been, in one fashion or another, the subject of moral censure.

In eighteenth century America, laws typically imposed some responsibility on communities to assist poor members. Poor people found within the boundaries of the community who were not members of the community were forced to leave. Communities expended many resources shunting poor people out and resisting the claims of the outsiders.

Many American communities in the late eighteenth and early nineteenth centuries concluded that even the burden of providing assistance to members of the community had become too great. The problem, they concluded, was the able-bodied, and hence undeserving, recipient of public assistance. The solution was to purge undeserving poor from the system of public assistance. To do so required that the community make a distinction that to this day remains etched in our cultural and legal conceptions of poverty--the distinction between the deserving and the undeserving poor. The distinction created a line running through the poor, putting the aged, infant, and disabled on one side of the line, and the able-bodied on the other side.

In the nineteenth century the label for the able-bodied poor was "paupers." The Reverend Charles Burroughs, preaching at the opening of a chapel in a New Hampshire poorhouse in 1834, spoke of the distinction between "poverty" and "pauperism:"

> In speaking of poverty, let us never forget that there is a distinction between this and pauperism. The

---

> . . . [A person's] right to care and help is as solid as his right to vote or own property. . . . In the period since World War II, Sweden has organized humanitarianism from top to bottom, cradle to grave, like no other part of the world.

Zetterberg, *The Rational Humanitarians*, in NORDEN--THE PASSION FOR EQUALITY 94-95 (1986).

> former is an unavoidable evil. . . . It is the result, not of our faults, but of our misfortunes . . . . Pauperism is the consequence of wilful error, of shameful indolence, of vicious habits. It is a misery of human creation, the pernicious work of man, the lamentable consequence of bad principles and morals.

This moral censure of the able-bodied recipient of public assistance has never left us.

The Depression, as with all great social dislocations, changed somewhat the way we thought about things. The commonly held assumptions regarding the able-bodied man, unemployed and poor, were obviously affected by the experience of the Depression. Nonetheless, the social stigma attached to the receipt of public assistance remained. Even during times of catastrophic levels of unemployment, we could not shake the idea that there was something wrong about an able-bodied man receiving public assistance.

A special and enduring legacy of the Depression and the New Deal was yet another line drawn through the ranks of the poor--the distinction between those receiving "public assistance" and "social insurance." Social insurance, exemplified by the Social Security benefit programs for the aged and the disabled, was thought of as a form of insurance against the "natural" events that impose financial hardships on all of us. People who were merely poor, on the other hand, depended instead on "public assistance." This distinction ignored the fortuities that might have forced the poor person into her current status, and did not bother with the fact that the benefits paid out to the aged and the disabled under Social Security may exceed the value of the private contributions made. These new categories served to underscore the undeserved quality of the benefits extended to recipients of public assistance.

Societal line drawing and moral censure took a brief detour in the 1960s. The "War on Poverty" was the product of a period of unrelenting growth in the gross national product and unbounded optimism about society's ability to abolish poverty without any real sacrifice. During this time, people spoke of the cruel error of assuming a correlation between poverty and moral weakness. As more Americans focused on the eradication of poverty, there was less interest in separating and stigmatizing the poor. Yet, as the "War on Poverty" came unraveled in the wash of blood, here and in Southeast

Asia, and as people came to see the actual sacrifice entailed in eliminating poverty, the public discourse soon drifted back to the theme of moral weakness.

The rhetoric of poverty in the 1980s was exemplified by the myth of the welfare mother with a Cadillac and by the rise of yet another category of the poor, the "underclass." This new category of the poor included:

> (a) the passive poor, usually long-term welfare recipients; (b) the hostile street criminals who terrorize most cities, and who are often school dropouts and drug addicts; (c) the hustlers, who, like street criminals, may not be poor and who earn their livelihood in an underground economy, but rarely commit violent crimes; (d) the traumatized drunks, drifters, homeless shopping-bag ladies and released mental patients who frequently roam or collapse on city streets.

Membership in the underclass was determined by behavior which was either patently immoral or socially deviant. The concept of the underclass etched deeper the division between us and them. It also connected perfectly with the rhetorical theme of moral weakness. Except for some examples of the "traumatized" members of the underclass, the behavior that characterized the underclass was criminal, deviant, or that of a person without hope or dignity. The idea of the "passive" poor, people beyond hope and without any sense of initiative, expressed the pervasive notion that poor people were unwilling to pull themselves up by their bootstraps and were instead happy to feed at the public trough.

The "underclass" thus was a late twentieth century form of the historically persistent category, the undeserving poor. And like its historical antecedents, the idea of the "underclass" seemed to be driven more by ideology than by any attempt accurately to generalize about the circumstances and nature of poverty in America. Michael Katz contrasted the idea of the underclass and the reality:

> [A]s a metaphor, the underclass obscures more than it reveals. It glosses over differences in condition that require varied forms of help, and it passes lightly over two salient features of poverty and welfare in America: their widespread and transient character.

> . . . In truth, the forces that push individuals and families into poverty originate in the structure of America's political economy. Some of us are lucky, not different.

As a metaphor, the underclass is the perfect expression of the rhetorical themes of difference and deviance. Perhaps because it so perfectly expresses these persistent historical themes, it has remained as part of the public discourse on poverty notwithstanding its metaphoric and distorting quality.

The precise content of the commonly held assumptions about the poor has changed throughout American history. The idea of the nineteenth century "pauper" is different from the idea of the late twentieth century "underclass." Still, the basic premises of the rhetoric of poverty run through history, drawing lines between groups of people and labeling categories as deviant and undeserving. There has always been an "us/them" conception of people in poverty. We have always found ways to make their suffering intellectually coherent.

* * *

Notes and Questions

1. *Separation.* While Professor Ross notes some differences between specific rhetorical devices, poverty rhetoric across American and English history seems strikingly consistent. First, Ross describes the rhetorical separation of "them," the poor, from the rest of "us." This separation seems especially persistent because, unlike race or gender which most of us cannot change, our class status is not biologically determined. Regardless of whether children of poor parents are more or less likely to be poor, any one of us could be poor. What role does this possibility play in poverty rhetoric and policy? Certainly middle class Americans hit hard times and fall into poverty. As their plight gets more press, our perception of the danger of poverty increases. Perhaps separating "us" from "them" distances non-poor from their fear of becoming impoverished. Should such fear drive policy?

2. *Stigmatization.* Following separation of the poor from the rest of us, society then stigmatizes the poor for their plight. This stigmatization is the second step in the creation of poverty rhetoric as described by Ross. In particular, we construct moral weakness as the

primary characteristic of poor people. This moral judgment then sets the stage for constructing an ideological debate about poverty.

We use "ideology" to mean the beliefs and ideas that serve the needs and desires of particular groups. The prevalent ideology reflects the ideas that serve the needs and desires of the non-poor. These needs and desires are constructed by society. For example, the non-poor could want to eliminate or limit poverty, an oft-stated goal during the War on Poverty. More commonly, the non-poor want to eliminate or limit any shared social responsibility for the poor. The poor, for their part, could want to eliminate or limit any individual responsibility for their poverty, as some conservative commentators suggest. But more commonly, the non-poor want to eliminate or limit poverty. For a brief period, both the non-poor and poor seemed to share an ideology aimed toward eliminating poverty. But for most periods of time, the tension between social versus individual responsibility frames the debate about poverty policy. The current dominant ideology about poverty relies heavily on a societal judgment about the individual moral weakness of the poor. Rather than using a clear, judgment-free lens for viewing poverty, we apply a shaded, value-laden lens. Through this lens, poverty appears not as a social circumstance that society might rectify, but as an individual failure that we need to punish.

3. *Division.* The third step in the evolution of modern poverty rhetoric is the division among poor people. Ross describes the categories of deserving versus undeserving, poor versus paupers, and social insurance recipients versus public assistance recipients. The modern complexities in poverty rhetoric require understanding this division among poor people. Rather than stigmatizing and abandoning all people who live in poverty, rhetoric makes more selective moral judgments. Those who are not expected to work or are poor due to innocent misfortune are viewed as deserving of compassion. They typically receive benefits based on a quasi-insurance system of contributions paid by them, their provider, or colleagues. Those who are expected to work or are poor due to their individual failure are deemed undeserving paupers for whom we begrudgingly and barely provide some public assistance.

4. *Deviance.* A recent fourth step complicates modern poverty rhetoric. During the 1980s, the undeserving poor welfare recipients were lumped together with many other groups of people

who were similarly separated and stigmatized by society. Ross describes these categories as hostile street criminals, hustlers, and traumatized drifters. With welfare recipients added to their ranks, they became the "underclass" that torments society with deviant and expensive behavior. This regrouping of undeserving poor people with other immoral or deviant actors constituted the underclass. What ideological purposes does the creation of the concept of underclass serve?

5. *Ideology versus Reality.* Ross suggests that poverty rhetoric reflects ideology more than reality. Based on what you have learned about poverty and poor people thus far, do you agree?

Martha L. Fineman

IMAGES OF MOTHERS IN POVERTY DISCOURSES

1991 DUKE L.J. 274

I. Introduction

This Essay focuses on the construction of the concept of "Mother" in poverty discourses. It addresses the role of patriarchical ideology in the process whereby a characteristic typical of a group of welfare recipients has been selected and identified as constituting the cause as well as the effect of poverty. I am particularly interested in those political and professional discourses in which single Mother status is defined as one of the primary predictors of poverty. This association of characteristic with cause has fostered suggestions that an appropriate and fundamental goal of any proposed poverty program should be the eradication of the status and practice of single motherhood. This goal is to be accomplished through appropriate coupling of the single mother with the child's father--who would thereby assume his "rightful" place in the family and fulfill his financial obligations. By his so doing, the paramount welfare reform objective--letting the state off the economic hook--will have been achieved.

Although many commentators prefer sanctified mother/father relationships, the coupling of the single mother and the financially-endowed male anticipated by such reforms need not be accomplished through the formation of a formal marital bond. The objective of such proposals is the creation of a legal tie between the male who is presumed to be economically-viable, and the dependent single mother and child. Through this legal tie, child support obligations can be established and enforced. Neither the mother's nor the father's wishes regarding the establishment of a legal tie are considered relevant.

The paternity proceeding is the legal process through which this tie is accomplished. Increased reliance on this process has been a mainstay of recent welfare reforms. It is an essential step in assuring that the family, and not the state, takes the responsibility for children. Generally, recent welfare reforms assume as a normative matter that children should be firmly anchored (financially, morally, and legally) within the nuclear family. The socially and economically based deprivations that poor children and their mothers suffer are thereby transformed into deprivations attributable to and based upon their deviant family form. Economic and social salvation will therefore come about through the restructuring of these families to conform as closely as possible to the "natural" (nuclear) family, thereby perpetuating traditional roles.

* * *

The Family Support Act of 1988 was the first major piece of legislation addressing poverty to pass Congress in several decades. It reflects the belief that welfare dependency is a significant societal problem that requires a dramatic reorientation of welfare policy. The Act's primary objective is to link poverty with the lack of a work ethic, thereby attaching welfare recipients to a new workfare scheme. This is accomplished by mandating that the single mother work (or train for work) and/or by substituting state support with support from fathers, transforming a child's primary source of support from public to private hands.

* * *

Other provisions of the Family Support Act mandate stricter enforcement of child support orders, including wage-withholding. Beginning in 1992, states are required to meet federal standards to establish paternity of children born out of wedlock as a method of obtaining child support from absent fathers.

* * *

The significance of the paternity action and child support provisions of the Act in reinforcing traditional norms of the male-headed family and its responsibility for children is evident in the political rhetoric surrounding the reforms. In addressing the Family Support Act in the Senate, for example, Senator Moynihan began his address by commending President Bush for his remarks at the United Nations World Summit for Children. He stated:

> One sentence [of President Bush's remarks is] especially notable. "We want to see the day when every American child is part of a strong and stable family." The importance of this statement is elemental. Unlike the problems of children in much of the world; age-old problems of disease, new problems of ecological disaster, the problems of children in the United States are overwhelmingly associated with the strength and stability of their families. Our problems do not reside in nature, nor yet are they fundamentally economic. Our problems derive from behavior.

* * *

Moynihan's rhetoric attributes the problems of the poor to their own behavior--thereby furthering the simplistic tendency in poverty discourses to categorize negatively mothers according to their relationship with men. Single mothers are generally deemed to present potential social problems for which they alone are largely responsible. Women who have become single mothers due to the death of their spouses, however, are excused from such condemnation--considered worthy as sympathetic widows.

* * *

In some discourses, however, poor women who become single mothers because of divorce are increasingly included within the category of deserving mothers. This classification is permitted by the recent changes in the way we consider marital dissolution, epitomized by the advent of no-fault divorce, that was built upon the popular perception that the failure of a marriage is a joint responsibility.

* * *

The imagery of welfare discourse, however, remains laden with moral and normative judgments that are founded on stereotypical assumptions about single mothers in the poverty context. The decisions to become or remain a single mother, particularly when undertaken by a woman who has never been married, is the decisive issue for whether one is to be considered a "good" mother. If they are not single as a result of death (or, perhaps, divorce), poor, single mothers are deemed "bad" mothers. Their conduct is considered to have "earned" them this designation, and stereotypes about their motivations and behavior abound.

* * *

The characterization of some single mothers as "bad" corresponds to the larger popular and political currents that classify the poor as either "deserving" or "undeserving." This classification is often based on the public's perception of whether the impoverished individual is poor because of her personal choices and actions, or as a result of forces beyond her control. Furthermore, this distinction between deserving and undeserving has concrete and material implications attached to its ideological categories; the way that one becomes a single mother often dictates the source of public assistance to which one may turn. Widows are typically entitled to generous social security benefits; whereas mothers who are divorced or who never marry are left to the variability of the child support system or AFDC. Such distinctions, therefore, go beyond social stigma (which, in and of itself, is significant); they have a real impact on the material future of a large number of single mothers and their children.

Yet the stigma that society attaches to certain single mothers provides the conceptual basis for the disparate economic outcomes that such groups experience. The parsimonious treatment of poor women who chose to become mothers without marrying, or those whose choices are limited because of circumstances that grow out of poverty, is justified because they can be considered undeserving poor. Recently, in poverty discourses emanating from a broad spectrum of groups, these single mothers have been lumped together with drug addicts, criminals, and other socially-defined "degenerates" in the newly-coined category of "underclass." The undeserving status of single-mother families in this context is established partly by their lack of relationship to the work force (either through their own jobs or through their attachment to a male breadwinner) and partly by their asserted role as mothers in the perpetuation of poverty.

* * *

We speak of the "broken" family, the "disintegration" of the family, the "crisis" in the family, the "unstable" family, the "decline" of the family, and, perhaps inevitably from some perspectives, the "death" of the family. Underlying such labels is the specter of single motherhood--statistically on the upswing--pathological and disease-like, contaminating society, contributing to its destruction and degeneration. With this perspective so pervasive, it is little wonder that many reformers urge efforts to curb the practice of single motherhood.

* * *

A critical examination of poverty discourse discloses that patriarchy is the dominant family ideology that fixes the core concepts and images about motherhood. . . . Although this traditional image has undergone some revisions in light of the modern concerns with gender equity and equality, the nuclear family form, with a sexual affiliation between man and woman as the paradigmatic intimate associational bond, is still the focus in policy discourses. Patriarchical ideology may have adapted to twentieth-century shifts in expressions of sexuality and redefinitions of gender roles, but the fundamental composition and nature of the core images remain constant. Mother and child are defined by their relationship to the patriarch.

When one considers the relationship between motherhood and patriarchy, it seems that motherhood has always been, and continues to be, a colonized concept--an event physically practiced and experienced by women, but occupied and defined, given content and value, by the core concepts of patriarchical ideology. Single motherhood is viewed as a practice of resistance to patriarchal ideology, particularly because it represents a "deliberate choice" in a world with birth control and abortion. As such, the existence of single motherhood as an ever-expanding practice threatens the hold of the dominant ideology.

* * *

Dominant ideologies are subtly and conclusively expressed and repressed in the very creation and recreation of social norms and conventions. They define the contours of culture and of society and its institutions. A dominant ideology is transmitted through everyday language, symbols, and images, as well as through the operations of formal institutions and structures of power.

Patriarchy is such a dominant ideology. It has as one of its organizing premises the belief that the primary affiliation in society is the sexual bond. In our legal and political culture, consistent with the demands of the ideology, it is this affiliation that is privileged as the paradigmatic manifestation of connection. In popular culture, sexual expression (particularly heterosexual expression traditionally realized through marriage) is portrayed as the quintessential indication of maturity, completeness, success, and power. Historically, deviance from the heterosexual paradigm brought with it social and even legal sanctions, as well as condemnation in the discourses of psychology, social work, and medicine. In recent years, the legal and heterosexual aspects of the paradigm have been challenged by demands to consider other forms of sexual intimacy as equally privileged as formal marriage. Alternative family legislation has been enacted that recognizes sexual affiliations other than heterosexual formal marriage. I consider these reforms to be complicit with patriarchical ideology, however, because by duplicating the privileging based on heterosexual affiliation, these relationships merely affirm the centrality of sexuality to the fundamental ordering of society and nature of intimacy. The nexus or affiliating circumstances of these "alternatives," although not the traditional "conjugal family," is still the sexual connection.

Single motherhood, therefore, could be considered deviant and threatening simply because it is a rejection of the primacy of the sexual connection as the core organizing familial concept and the privacy basis for social organization. The very label "single mother" separates some practices of motherhood from the institution of "Mother" by reference to the mother's marital status. Mother, as constructed and defined in this discourse, is modified by her relationship (formal and legal) to the father. By contrast, the institution when practiced in its "normal" form is not so modified. No one speaks of a "married mother"; the primary connection of husband and wife is assumed in the unadorned designation of "mother." It is only the deviant form of motherhood that needs qualification and, by implication, justification. In this process of distinguishing the deviant variation of motherhood from the norm, a complementary cluster of stereotypical designated family roles are implied to form the contemporary images of the "ideal" family.

* * *

An examination of motherhood in terms of its changing manifestations reveals that patriarchy as an ideology has adapted to ostensibly challenging discourses and absorbed seemingly significant challenges while ensuring the relatively undisturbed continuation of power distributions within the family structure. This adaptation or modification of patriarchy was necessitated by the "crisis" of the rising divorce rate in the twentieth century. The traditional family formation was disrupted, but the acceptance of joint custody and the idea of shared parenting has ensured continued male control over children and, through them, over their mothers, even as divorce has become available virtually on demand.

Mandatory paternity laws were fashioned in response to the increasing number of women who chose to become single mothers (this has also been designated as a crisis). These laws were first enacted in the context of AFDC single mothers, but are now expanding into other areas of the law. In Wisconsin, for example, under a rhetorical bludgeon that dictates that every child has a "legal right" to a father (or at least to a father's name on a birth certificate), legislation has been passed that requires all single mothers to participate in paternity proceedings. These proceedings are mandated even if the state is not likely to ever be asked to provide economic support for the child. The core tenets of the ideology of patriarchy--that "natural" families have two parents and that the male position is one of financial primacy and family control--are thus ensured.

* * *

The [major architect of the legislation] . . . does not mention that the mother's cooperation in this paternity program will require her to reveal details of her sexual and personal life, or risk the potential sanction of incarceration through a court's contempt power. Nor does he note that the legal father's paternal involvement with the child will not be mandated by the court beyond (perhaps) payment of child support. Also absent is the fact that a legal father can exercise legal rights and become an unwanted or even abusive presence in the mother's and child's life merely because he fathered the child.

Changes in behavior precipitated by alterations in divorce laws and women's expanding economic security (which allow them to choose to become single mothers) have required the remodeling of patriarchy. The remodeling, however, has not substantially altered, let alone led to the rejection of, the core images of the ideology. The foundation remains stable. Society may now be grudgingly forced to accept single-mother households as an unfortunate byproduct of the social and economic dislocations that characterize the latter part of this century, but they are seldom treated as an acceptable, let alone a desirable, family form. In expressions of popular culture, as well as in public policy, single motherhood may be perceived at best as requiring an uneasy accommodation with the dominant ideology. The societal aspiration, however, remains to complete the "family" by the addition of a man.

In the context of the treatment of single mothers in poverty discourses, the focus on family form obscures the economic deprivations that make it difficult for single women to raise their children. Rather than addressing their needs as single mothers, reforms tend to try to push them into a model of family life that is increasingly discredited, even in the middle class from which it arose. The dominance of family imagery contained in the ideology of patriarchy has required the rejection of economic subsidies that would truly support single mother families. Instead, their deviation must be punished and deterred, and their practice of resistance curtailed.

Notes and Questions

1. *Effect As Cause.* Professor Fineman identifies one of the primary methods common in poverty rhetoric: a characteristic typical of some welfare recipients is identified as both the cause and effect of poverty. Fineman focuses on one characteristic typically used in this fashion: single motherhood. The resulting rhetorical arguments emphasize their theme: single motherhood causes poverty; poverty causes single motherhood; if poverty is bad, then single motherhood must also be bad. Are there any defects in this reasoning?

2. *Legal Families.* In order to solve the problem of single motherhood, Fineman argues that law makers have required the formation of a legal tie between an economically-viable male and the single mother and each child. In so doing, the law creates a legal family. Can law create families?

3. *Single Mothers.* Fineman traces the logic of anti-welfare rhetoricians who identify selected behavior as deviant, blame the actors for their behavior, and then label them as undeserving of societal assistance to lessen their plight. With regard to poor single mothers, what behavior is blameworthy? According to Fineman, society blames each poor single mother for having no man and no job, and for perpetuating another generation of poverty. How are these circumstances blameworthy? How does society distinguish between the circumstances of poor single mothers who have never married compared with those who have been divorced or widowed?

4. *Resistance.* Fineman argues that patriarchal ideology sets out the sexual affiliation between a man and a woman as the core organizing concept for family. Through this universal concept, society regulates both sexuality and economics. Is the practice of single motherhood a form of resistance to this norm, as Fineman suggests? How likely is it that law will be any more successful than these powerful ideological and rhetorical forces in pushing single mothers into the nuclear family model?

We can learn a great deal about a society's social values from its rhetoric about poverty. We also can learn a great deal about how rhetoric shapes legal policy. Perhaps Leonard Long summed it up best:

> If you want me to believe that we care for the poor, I will believe we care for the poor. If you want me to believe that we have made an honest, concerted effort to address the problems of poverty in American society, I will believe we have seriously tried. And, if you want me to believe that we truly hold sacred the liberal, egalitarian creed that all humans are created equal and ought to be treated on their individual merits, I will believe in this as well. Still, I know what I know. And I know that the truth is in the pudding, the social pudding of our laws, our customs, and, most importantly, our values and actions, both individual and collective.
>
> Do our laws, customs, values and actions tend to unite and warm us to the poor and others who are less fortunate than ourselves? Or do they instead tend to isolate and distance the nonpoor from the poor? Do our laws, customs, values and actions tend to facilitate the empowerment, self-sufficiency, and upward mobility of the underclass? Or do they tend to deepen their political impotency, dependency, and stagnation? Do our laws, customs, values and actions tend to allow for weighing each and every individual on his or her merits? Or do these tend to reinforce discrimination on the ignoble basis of economic class, ethnicity, race, gender and parentage, over which the individual has little or no control?
>
> Wishing that American society would live up to its professed values does not make it so. Believing that as a society, we are what we say we are does not ensure that we

> are what we believe ourselves to be. Perceptions and realities are seldom a perfect match. While belief is one necessary condition for knowledge, it is not the only condition for knowledge. I'll believe what you want me to believe about the compassion of American society. But, I know what I know.

Leonard J. Long, *Optimum Poverty, Character, and the Non-Relevance of Poverty Law,* 47 RUTGERS LAW REVIEW 693 (1995).

CHAPTER 2: THE HISTORICAL LEGACIES

Societies around the world have struggled throughout time with the task of relieving poverty. Law has been an integral social tool in this history. The United States learned about welfare policy from English law. With the benchmark Elizabethan poor laws of 1601, England established its policy as one of prohibiting private relief of poverty outside of established almshouses (institutions that housed poor people in exchange for their labor). To what extent do you think this policy has influenced American welfare law?

The particular histories of racial, gender, and economic struggles in the United States also have influenced a good deal of American welfare policy. This chapter explores the legacies of race and gender, and the specific anti-poverty programs they influenced.

A. POVERTY AND RACE

Most of the people who lived below the poverty line in the early 1990s, indeed two-thirds, were white. Yet the relationship between race and poverty continues to dominate much of the public debate about welfare. Perhaps we focus on race because we know that members of racial minority groups disproportionately tend to fall into poverty. In the early 1990s, historically disadvantaged racial minorities were approximately three times as likely as whites to live below the poverty line.[1] Why?

We turn first to history to explain these current poverty trends. In particular, consider whether higher poverty rates among racial minorities stem from historical oppression of groups, such as the systematic destruction of Native American cultures and the brutal enslavement of African-Americans. Consider also the extent to which welfare rules and practices over time reflect racism by directly excluding racial minorities, subjecting them to discretion of white bureaucrats, and requiring assimilation to white cultural norms as a prerequisite to eligibility.

---

[1]Recall that, in 1995, over 29% of African-Americans and over 30% of Hispanics lived below the poverty line, compared to only approximately 11% of Whites.

1. Native Americans and the Creation of Poverty

Rennard Strickland

GENOCIDE-AT-LAW: AN HISTORIC AND CONTEMPORARY VIEW OF THE NATIVE AMERICAN EXPERIENCE

34 KANSAS LAW REVIEW 713 (1986)

Genocide is a new word for an old tragedy. The term, coined only in the twentieth century, describes the decimation of a people, of a nation. Webster's Collegiate Dictionary defines genocide as "the deliberate and systematic destruction of a racial, political, or cultural group." We most commonly think of genocide as synonymous with the Nazi holocaust, the loss of six million or more lives, or in the context of the Chinese Communist extermination of eighteen to twenty million dissidents. The term also describes the Native American experience.

* * *

Legal Genocide

In the early nineteenth century, the picture for American Indians was not so bright. At this time, it appeared as if the Indian genocide would be total. Alexis de Tocqueville contrasts the styles of extermination of the Spanish and of the Americans of the United States. De Tocqueville, writing in the mid-1830's, concludes:

> The Spaniards pursued the Indians with bloodhounds, like wild beasts; they sacked the New World like a city taken by storm, with no discernment or compassion; but destruction must cease at last and frenzy has a limit. . . . The conduct of the Americans of the United States towards the aborigines is characterized, on the other hand, by a singular attachment to the formalities of law. . . .
>
> The Spaniards were unable to exterminate the Indian race by those unparalleled atrocities which brand them with indelible shame, nor did they succeed even in wholly depriving it of its rights; but the Americans of the United States have accomplished this twofold purpose with singular felicity, tranquilly; legally, philanthropically, without shedding blood and without violating a single great principle of morality in the

> eyes of the world. It is impossible to destroy men with more respect for the laws of humanity.

* * *

There were, of course, great and tragic Indian massacres and bitter exiles and exoduses, illegal even under the laws of war. We know these acts of genocide by place names--Sand Creek, the Battle of the Washita, Wounded Knee--and by their tragic poetic codes--the Trail of Tears, the Long Walk, the Cheyenne Autumn. . . . I am talking not about these cold-blooded atrocities but about law and the ways in which genocidal objectives have been carried out under color of law. . . . These were legally enacted policies whereby a way of life, a culture, was deliberately obliterated. As the great Indian orator Dragging Canoe concluded, "[W]hole Indian Nations have melted away like balls of snow in the sun leaving scarcely a name except as imperfectly recorded by the destroyers."

The legal genocide, cultural as well as physical, practiced against the American Indian could only have been the product of a society such as ours, a society with a strong sense of the "rule of law." Even while physically exterminating the Indian--shooting Native men, women, and children like deer or buffalo--the state legislature of Georgia passed a formal resolution legalizing their actions by declaring Indians to be outlaws, beyond the protection of the law. Before we move to the more subtle forms of cultural genocide, let me read to you from that 1789 statute legalizing what amounted to an Indian hunting season:

> Be it enacted by the Representatives of the Freemen of the State of Georgia, in General assembly met, and by the authority of the same, That from and immediately after the passing of this Act, the Creek Indians shall be considered as without the protection of this state, and *it shall be lawful for the Government and people of the same, to put to death or capture the said Indians* wheresoever they may be found within the limits of this state; except such tribes of the said Indians which have not or shall not hereafter commit hostilities against the people of this state, of which the commanding officer shall judge.

Another excellent example is the series of legal steps whereby the State of Georgia in the late 1820's and 1830's transferred all

Indian lands from tribal hands to white hands. The procedure looks and sounds and feels oh so legal. The legal process was simple. New counties are created out of Indian lands; land belonging to the Indians is declared surplus; individual Indians are given a right to renounce tribal membership and reclaim their own land; county courts and county judges administer the program with seals, leather-bound tomes and oaths sworn on Bibles. There is even a right to appeal their decisions--to a court system from which Indian testimony is barred. If the Indian refused to renounce tribal citizenship, the Indian lost all claims to his treaty lands. It was thusly under full color of law that the vast majority of Indian land in the southeast passed into white hands and with it the passage of the Indian way of life which it had sustained. This story was repeated again and again. Thus, the law and the courts became the principal institution for acquisition of Indian lands.

* * *

Assimilation and Genocide: Law, Education, and Allotment

* * *

The Indian was caught on the crest of one of those great cycles that recur throughout American history. Westward expansion was itself an old story. Many Indians, including the Shawnees, the Iroquois, the Cherokees, the Senecas, and the Creeks, had been caught in earlier stages of the cycle. But this post-Civil War expansion was different. It was driven, more determined, better organized, much faster, more efficient, and more difficult to resist. Powered not only by technological marvels such as the railroads, the steam engine, and the mechanical harvester, the new expansion was also propelled by the "go-getter" spirit that infused the nation after the war. The military energy of the Union victory survived on the frontier. A determination to thrust the nation westward ruled in Congress and, more importantly, in the boardrooms, taverns, and churches. Landless Americans from older sections of the nation and newer emigrants who had temporarily settled elsewhere demanded Indian lands. There was no place left to remove the Indian, and there was little sympathy for the preservation of a way of life that left farmlands unturned, coal unmined, and timber uncut.

The old Indian hunter way and the new white agricultural and industrial way could not coexist. One had to die. The Plains Indians' roaming hunter culture with the seasonal migration patterns following the herds was targeted for extinction on both economic and moral grounds. The goals and values of white and Indian civilization were incompatible. The legal and philosophical justification for cultural genocide was beginning to be developed.

* * *

Land that was exclusively Indian-owned had to be taken out of common tribal ownership. At the same time, a new economic focus had to be created. Thus, from the Indian side, we are dealing both with acculturation, or change of Indian culture, and with allotment, or distribution of Indian lands. These goals became the twin tasks of assorted nineteenth century Indian reform policies, including the Dawes Act of 1887 and the Curtis Act of 1898. Because white settlement, Indian land allotment, and the attempted cultural transformation all occurred at approximately the same time, it is difficult to deal with the genocidal aspects of each in isolation. Taken together, these tasks dominated the life of Indians into the twentieth century.

During this period, nearly 100 million acres of Indian land passed from Indian into white hands. In 1887, when the Dawes Act provided for dividing tribal lands among individual Indians, the already shrunken American Indian heritage in land totaled 138 million acres. Less than fifty years later, when the allotment policy was formally abandoned, only forty-eight million acres were left in Indian hands. Even more dramatic was the almost total collapse of the Indians' tribal holdings. For example, before allotment the entire Indian Territory of twenty million acres in eastern Oklahoma was the exclusive property of self-governing tribal entities, primarily the Cherokees, the Creeks, the Choctaws and Chickasaws, and the Seminoles. Today, virtually the entire acreage of this rich domain of prosperous agricultural and mineral lands has passed away from the Native American. At the turn of the century, "there was not a pauper Indian amongst them." Today, three-quarters of a century later, the heartlands of these once-powerful tribes are filled with unemployment and destitution. The Indian settlement areas are primary battlegrounds for any war on poverty.

How did this happen? How was the entire Indian Territory, a maturing political entity at one time destined to become the Indian state of Sequoyah, so quickly transferred from Indian to white hands? What transformed many of these Indian people from proud, prosperous, self-reliant citizens of their own small republics into poverty stricken, landless, manipulated outcasts in a white state? The conventional wisdom is that these Indians suffered at the hands of mighty enemies--land-hungry railroad barons and zealous land developers--who were able to translate evil designs into Indian policy with bribes and six-shooter diplomacy.

There is some truth in these old myths, but the most disastrous policies for the tribes of the old Indian Territory were not the exclusive product of frontier villains. They were duly enacted, legally endorsed creations which were supported and ultimately adopted by liberal, pro-Indian Christian reformers. The "good works" of the Indians' friends created conditions ripe for the "evil deeds" of the Indians' exploiters. Ironically, nineteenth century Indian genocide was as friendly as it was legal. Over the years, the Indians' friends have been particularly troublesome to native people.

* * *

The white advocates of reform policy, the Indians' friends, were determined to make little red Farmer Joneses and native Old MacDonalds out of the American Indians. The Indian was to become another lost race in the American melting pot. He was to abandon his tribal lands, own his own farm, and compete for material goods. Two stages of development were thus required. Plains Indians and other nomadic tribes had to be settled on fixed reservations, since only then could their tribal lands be assigned to individuals. Indian lands that were declared "surplus lands" would then become available for white settlement, with the allotted lands becoming available for later purchase from the Indian allottee by whites. To accomplish all this called for a government-supervised division of the commonly owned and held tribal lands among the individual members of the tribes. Implicit in this program was the assumption that this was the Christian God's plan and man's reward.

* * *

The long-range result of federal policy was that many Indians were handed land with a negotiable title. It was a fee simple absolute title in many cases, and in other cases subject only to a limitation or restriction by supervision for a term of years. A great many Indians were destined to become landless, because Indian tribes no longer held the land and title soon passed to whites. Thus was Indian land lost, allotted over the protests of the vast majority of Indians who wished to retain tribal ownership.

* * *

To assure that white values lived and Indian civilization died, the federal government used the full power of the law. They established "courts of Indian offenses," the goal of which was to eliminate "heathenish practices".

* * *

The thrust of this federal criminal law was to end Indian culture. That objective is reflected in the text of "Rules for Indian Court," which defined offenses as follows:

> Dance, etc--Any Indian who shall engage in the sun dance, scalp dance or war dance, or any other similar feast, so-called, shall be deemed guilty of an offense. . . .
>
> Practices of Medicine Men--Any Indian who shall engage in the practices of so-called medicine men, or who shall resort to any artifice or device to keep the Indians of the reservation from adopting and following civilized habits and pursuits, or shall adopt any means to prevent the attendance of children at school, or shall use any arts of a conjurer to prevent Indians from abandoning their barbarous rites and customs, shall be deemed to be guilty of an offense.
>
> * * *
>
> Misdemeanors--And provided further, that if an Indian refuses or neglects to adopt habits of industry or to engage in civilized pursuits or employments, but habitually spends his time in idleness and loafing, he shall be deemed a vagrant and guilty of a misdemeanor.

* * *

[Strickland next reviewed experiences of Indians in the educational reform programs aimed at assimilating children to white culture. Then he turned to the process of allotment, the division of tribal land to individuals. Next, he discussed the legal mechanisms used to take land from the Indians.] . . . A few of the more common devices were:

1. Fraudulent deeds, approved by courts of law, signed by other than the owner of the land;

2. Purchase prices far below market or actual appraised value of the land, again approved by courts of law;

3. Payments of bribes for court approval of fraudulent land sales;

4. Excessive administrative and guardianship fees;

5. Embezzlement of Indian money and personal expenditure of Indian trust funds for the benefit of the trustee;

6. False heirship claims or destruction of Indian wills; and

7. Gifts to charities or individual citizens of Indian assets without knowledge or approval of the Indian.

* * *

In the midst of this corruption, lawyers who ought to have been guarding the Indians, preserving the integrity of the judicial process, and policing the behavior of their colleagues, were often themselves guilty. Too many other lawyers, who were not participants, stood by while their brothers at the bar stole the small allotments of fullbloods and major fortunes, either by outright theft or through unwarranted or excessive charges for their services. "Few attempts," Angie Debo records, "were ever made to disbar attorneys for unprofessional conduct." This is not an ennobling chapter in the history of professional relations with Indian people. Knowing of this earlier chapter should help us understand, at least in part, Indian hostility toward lawyers and courts.

The friends of the Indian did not envision that their policies would produce pillage and murder. Nonetheless, the Indian condition, which made such wholesale crime possible, would have been apparent to them had they attempted to understand the Indian and his value system. The vast majority of these Indians did not speak English, had no conception of Anglo-American land ownership, and were used to living in a society with a strong sense of shared common values that emphasized cooperation rather than competition. They, as a people, were not selfish, not acquisitive, and certainly not sophisticated in terms of a money economy and a system of real estate sales and arm's-length contract negotiations. The reformers refused to listen to the Indian side. The Indian, with great regularity, attempted to draw these facts and conditions to the attention of both Congress and the Indian reformers. There are more than 150 Native

American memorials written by Indian tribes. In these testimonials, the Native American quite accurately predicted these abuses.

The allotment experience tells us a good bit about playing with law and manipulating culture. We learn, empirically, that it is difficult, if not impossible, to forcibly graft white institutions onto the Indian body politic. For law, as we all know, is organic. Law is the product of a specific time and an actual place. The Dawes and Curtis acts failed because the provisions of these laws were not suited to Indian values, to Indian attitudes regarding land, and to Indian use of resources.

* * *

Notes and Questions

1. *How History Matters.* Professor Strickland describes Native American cultures as once prosperous and self-reliant. He recounts the destruction of the Indian economy, as non-Native Americans displaced tribes of Indian people from their lands. He laments that "the heartlands of these once-powerful tribes are filled with unemployment and destitution." He then suggests that Indian reservations are "primary battlegrounds for any war on poverty." Should this history affect current welfare policy with respect to Indian people? If so, how? Some argue that today's society shares no responsibility for a history it cannot change. Do you agree?

2. *Lessons.* Certainly large numbers of Native Americans live in poverty today. Strickland's account of part of Indian history provides information that allows us to view Native American poverty in historical context. Can we also extrapolate Native American experiences to poor people generally? How well can we compare the situation of poor people today with that of Native Americans?

Not all Native-Americans shared the same cultural beliefs. Do poor people today share a common culture? Do they experience socially constructed behavior patterns and beliefs? Strickland concluded that laws regulating the Indians failed because they were not suited to many Indian values. Are welfare laws at similar risk?

3. *Good Intentions.* What particular lessons can be learned about law as a social tool from this chapter of American history? Strickland describes the most disastrous policies as "duly enacted, legally endorsed creations which were supported and ultimately adopted by liberal, pro-Indian Christian reformers" who destroyed

Indian culture through their attempts to assimilate Indians into "little red Farmer Joneses and native Old McDonalds." In her study of the early history of federal welfare, Winifred Bell echoed Strickland's observation, noting that "it was often difficult to distinguish between genuine concern and demagoguery." WINIFRED BELL, AID TO DEPENDENT CHILDREN 67 (1965). Does this sound a cautionary note for those today who believe they have the interests of poor people at heart? If so, how could anti-poverty policy planners prevent similar disasters? Did the pro-Indian reformers listen to the Indians' articulation of their needs? Are advocates for poor people today listening to what poor people say they need?

4. *Role of Law.* Law and lawyers played key roles in the decimation of Indian culture. Alexis de Tocqueville was struck by non-Native Americans' respect for law and morality, as they simultaneously and systematically destroyed Indian cultures. How do you imagine de Tocqueville would assess our current use of legal tools and moral rhetoric to address our poverty problem? What role do lawyers play in the lives of poor people? Are lawyers today enriching themselves at the direct, or indirect, expense of poor people?

2. African Americans and Welfare Policy

In 1965, Winifred Bell wrote the book, *Aid to Dependent Children.* This book remains one of the most informative and cogent analyses of how welfare restrictions both attempted to limit the "immoral" behavior of recipients and enforced racial inequality. She described how the states limited their Mother's Pensions benefits (antecedents to modern welfare benefits) to "fit and deserving" widows. A 1931 study of the Mother's Pensions caseload revealed that 96% of the recipients were white. North Carolina and Florida each had only one African-American family in the entire state which received benefits. No blacks received benefits in Houston, Texas, although blacks were 21% of the population, or in Indianapolis, Indiana, although blacks were 11% of the population. WINIFRED BELL, AID TO DEPENDENT CHILDREN 9-10 (1965). Bell concluded that the vagueness of the suitable home requirement guaranteed its adaptability to local and regional prejudices. *Id.* at 10, 18.

Perhaps the more things change, the more they stay the same.

Consider how Bell's description of the first federal Aid to Dependent Children program sounds remarkably like the current Temporary Assistance for Needy Families block grant program (part of the 1996 Personal Responsibility and Work Opportunity Act). Bell explained that "the Act required that programs be in operation throughout the state, that they be administered by a single state agency, and that states share in the cost." *Id.* at 21. But the federal government did not establish a national standard of need. "Nor were states obliged to provide sufficient assistance to meet minimum standards of health and decency. The level of public support to be provided, in other words, was entirely within the state's discretion. Also, all matters relating to the selection, qualifications, tenure, and compensation of personnel were initially reserved to states." *Id.* The Act did specify the maximum federal money grant to be provided. *Id.* at 22. Bell argued that, because Southern states were the most impoverished, and had the highest proportion of black children, these children suffered "particularly severe deprivation." *Id.* at 24.

After the creation of Aid to Dependent Children, states continued to impose "suitable home" requirements, and these continued to result in the disproportionate exclusion of racial minority children. For example, the state of Georgia imposed a quota system that fixed the ratio of black and white recipients. *Id.* at 34-35.

Some states also imposed seasonal employment requirements that disproportionately excluded racial minorities. For example, Louisiana required recipients to be refused assistance whenever workers were needed in cotton fields. Bell reported that, in one parish, this included children as young as 7 years old. Because cotton field work was relegated to African-Americans, Bell believed they were disproportionately excluded from benefits by this rule. *Id.* at 46. Consider the following exchange between a Louisiana parish grand jury investigating welfare costs, and the local welfare director, as reported by Bell:

> "I should like to know why you have so many Negro women on your payrolls," one juror asked the local welfare director. "Why can't they go back to the country and work instead of staying in the city and living on public welfare?"
>
> "We can't just strike them from the payrolls unless work is available to them," was her reply. "If,

> however, we do find a job for them in the country, we can offer them employment and if they refuse, then we can take them off the welfare lists."

Id. at 64.

After World War II, progress was made toward more coverage for needy minority children. But some states responded by increasing their restrictions against "undeserving" applicants. Bell explained, "It was possible for perceptive observers to view the signs of mounting public impatience with poor Negro and illegitimate children and their parents as a 'last stand' against the rising demand for income protection and equality of opportunity for all families regardless of their birth status, race, or geographical location." *Id.* at 58. As a result, welfare benefits became one of the "easily accessible whipping boys." *Id.* at 61. Bell reported that welfare's critics enjoyed the offensive, while its supporters "found it strangely difficult to defend the program." *Id.* Politicians began to investigate allegations of welfare fraud, although one statewide study found only approximately 1.5% fraud. *Id.* at 62. Ultimately, states began reducing financial support for welfare benefits. *Id.* at 66. Bell quoted Pulitzer-Prize winning journalist Edgar May, who said in 1961, "when tax bills and tempers rise correspondingly, a wave of social ills--ranging from illegitimacy to poverty itself--is blamed on welfare."

Winifred Bell's early study of Aid to Dependent Children serves as a rich source about the history of poverty and race. In recent years, the problem of how racial discrimination has influenced welfare policy has received important new attention. In her 1994 book, *The Color of Welfare: How Racism Undermined the War on Poverty*, Jill Quadagno provides a compelling analysis of how America's inability or unwillingness to confront racial inequality impeded the 1960s war on poverty. In Andrew Hacker's 1992 book, *Two Nations: Black and White, Separate, Hostile, Unequal*, he explores the racial division in American society. He tackles tough issues, including racial differences in marriage rates, in earned income, and in educational quality. He concludes that "[a] huge racial chasm remains, and there are few signs that the coming century will see it closed. A century and a quarter after slavery, white America continues to ask of its black citizens an extra patience and perseverance that whites have never required of themselves. So the question for white Americans is essentially moral: is it right to impose on members of an entire race a lesser start in life, and then to expect from them a degree of resolution that has never been demanded from your own race?" *Id.* at 219.

3. Immigrants and Welfare Policy

In 1996, Congress established new restrictions that prohibit both "unqualified" immigrants and legal immigrants from receiving federal welfare benefits. We explore these issues in Chapter 6 regarding Equal Protection for immigrants, and in Chapter 8 regarding Welfare Reform. For now, consider Congress' statement of national policy concerning welfare and immigration, adopted as part of the Personal Responsibility and Work Opportunity Reconciliation Act of 1996.

> The Congress makes the following statements concerning national policy with respect to welfare and immigration:
>
> (1) Self-sufficiency has been a basic principle of United States immigration law since this country's earliest immigration statutes.
>
> (2) It continues to be the immigration policy of the United States that--
>
> > (A) aliens within the Nation's borders not depend on public resources to meet their needs, but rather rely on their own capabilities and the resources of their families, their sponsors, and private organizations, and
> >
> > (B) the availability of public benefits not constitute an incentive for immigration to the United States.
>
> (3) Despite the principle of self-sufficiency, aliens have been applying for and receiving public benefits from Federal, State, and local governments at increasing rates.
>
> (4) Current eligibility rules for public assistance and unenforceable financial support agreements have proved wholly incapable of assuring that individual aliens not burden the public benefits system.
>
> (5) It is a compelling government interest to enact new rules for eligibility and sponsorship agreements in order to assure that aliens be self-reliant in accordance with national immigration policy.

> (6) It is a compelling government interest to remove the incentive for illegal immigration provided by the availability of public benefits.
> (7) With respect to the State authority to make determinations concerning the eligibility of qualified aliens for public benefits in this title, a State that chooses to follow the Federal classification in determining the eligibility of such aliens for public assistance shall be considered to have chosen the least restrictive means available for achieving the compelling governmental interest of assuring that aliens be self-reliant in accordance with national immigration policy.

What does this policy statement reveal about Congressional attitudes toward immigrants? What is Congress trying to achieve by specifying its compelling government interests and by describing its methods of achieving those interests as the least restrictive means?

B. POVERTY AND GENDER

The relationship between poverty and gender continues to baffle most, and disturb many. Commentators across the political spectrum worry about the apparently increasing poverty risk for women who head households. At the end of the 1950s, women headed less than one-quarter of the families living in poverty. That figure doubled by the end of the 1980s, when women headed more than half of the families living in poverty.

Scrutinizing poverty requires analyzing women's economic roles. Historical analysis provides a broader perspective for viewing both the idealized and actual roles of women in the American economy. In colonial times, economic productivity, including that of women, was centered in the home. As industrial capitalism transformed American society, economic productivity shifted to the market. Mimi Abramovitz explains that this shift divided labor on gender lines, with men moving to the market and women staying in the home. Many women, however, needed to work in the market to alleviate their poverty. These women faced conflicting demands both to have and raise children, to keep house, and to bring home a market wage. Consider the extent to which this tension in demands confronting poor women continues today.

Mimi Abramovitz
REGULATING THE LIVES OF WOMEN (1988)

The Rise of the Industrial Family Ethic

The rise of industrial capitalism in the early nineteenth century and the concurrent separation of household and market production restructured both the labor market and the family system. The requirements of the new market economy gradually undermined the ability of the colonial family ethic to regulate the work and family life of white women. Indeed, the changing economy created a new gender division of labor, which assigned men to the market and women to the home. Women's new "place" in the home evolved as the changing economy moved economic production from the household to the market, a trend which developed first and considerably more rapidly in major urban areas. As women's domestic labor shifted away from production (the transformation of raw or unfinished material into finished goods) to reproduction and maintenance (the bearing of children, caring for family members, and managing household affairs), it significantly increased the time women spent on household and caretaking activities. The symmetry of this exchange was imperfect, however, because both poverty and the needs of the new market economy required women's labor outside the home. Moreover, in rural areas, life remained virtually unchanged. Eventually, the changing role of white women and the conflicting demand for their reproductive and productive labor rendered the colonial family ethic obsolete. In the early nineteenth century, it was replaced by a new definition of women's roles--the industrial family ethic--more suited to the needs of the emerging economic order.

The Decline of the Colonial Family Ethic

The process of industrialization unsettled and transformed the organization of both work and family life. The growth of market production and its increased efficiency gradually weakened white women's role as an economically productive helpmeet. In 1790, for example, women produced all their own yarn and wove their own cloth. But the sharp fall in the price of manufactured brown shirting after 1815, from 42 cents to 7.5 cents a yard, made it less worthwhile for women to sit at the loom. The changing economy made cash income virtually indispensable to most families who increasingly purchased market goods, borrowed from banks, and needed more productive farm machinery. The need for cash led more and more men and some women to leave home-based agricultural work for paid market labor.

The growth of the market economy also restructured women's role in the family, particularly in urban areas. The pull of men into the market, the increased consumption of manufactured rather than handmade products, the reduced need for children's labor on the farm, and the growing importance of socialization to the success and productivity of the next generation all modified women's homemaking and caretaking activities. These changing conditions required someone to create a relaxing home for the market-weary breadwinner, to oversee the consumption of market-produced goods and services, and to spend more time rearing children. These expanded family-maintenance tasks were assigned exclusively to women, in part because declining household production freed them for other tasks. But the social assignment of family responsibilities to women also reflected prevailing ideas that a woman's nature made her suitable for the job.

Paradoxically, as the new economic order enlarged women's reproductive tasks in the home, it also increased the need for women's market labor. The conviction that an independent republic depended on land ownership, the resulting scarcity and high cost of male labor, concerns about the idleness of women displaced from the household economy, and the rising dependency of poor women on public aid all contributed to the demand for women workers outside the home. The emerging manufacturing class, desirous of cheap labor and seeking ways to counter the idea that the growth of manufacture threatened society's agrarian base, offered to employ women.

* * *

The demand for women's market labor clashed with the terms of the colonial family ethic which favored economic productivity by women only if it occurred within the confines of the home. It also conflicted with the new industrial family ethic and the expansion of women's reproductive responsibilities in the home. However, since the early manufacturing system relied heavily on pre-factory, home-based production, married women could remain in compliance with the colonial and industrial family ethic by earning an income while working at home. Because merchants contracted for this labor through the male household head, these early manufacturing systems also protected prevailing patriarchal relations. The growing mechanization of manufacture disturbed this delicate balance by making centralized factory production more efficient and profitable than home production. The invention of the water-driven cotton mill in Pawtucket, Rhode Island in 1789 and the introduction of the power loom in New England in 1813 made it possible to consolidate the processes of power-driven spinning and weaving under one roof. By 1815, textile mills located mostly in New England numbered in the hundreds and eventually eliminated the profitability of home-based production.

Because married women preferred to earn an income by working at home, the early factories had to rely heavily on young single women. Hoping to make factory work compatible with the colonial family ethic, the owners initially offered them "sheltered" living and working conditions. For example, mill-owners in Lowell, Massachusetts, the most-well known factory town in New England, created a system of strictly supervised boarding houses and jobs, and promised to protect a young woman's virtue, her availability for marriage, and the primacy of her place in the home. Mill work actually conferred some status on "the Lowell girls" as they came to be called. Eventually, however, market pressures caused the factory owners to eliminate supervised lodgings, de-skill the labor process, reduce wages, lengthen the work day, increase the pace of work, and essentially remove the respectability and appeal of factory work to the white, native-born, often middle-class farmer's daughter. Once factory conditions ceased to dignify womanhood, it became increasingly difficult to mediate the tension between the need for low-paid labor and the colonial family ethic's proscription of women's work outside the home. Both deteriorating work conditions and the availability of new jobs for women, such as teaching, sent many young women out of the New England mills. Their places were filled by male and female farm laborers wiped out by poor soil, depressions, and the high cost of farm machinery, as well as by free blacks in need of work and, beginning in the 1840s, by newly arrived Irish immigrants, half of whom were women. Owing to their poverty, the single and married mostly foreign-born women who replaced the "Lowell girls" became part of the permanent urban labor force whose survival depended on their labor and uncertain market conditions. Segregated by gender and ethnicity and paid less than the native-born workers, they could not return to the farm when factory work dropped off.

The efforts to protect native-born, white women who had to work against the stigma associated with departures from the colonial family ethic did not extend to black women. White society defined and treated black women as laborers rather than as homemakers and denied them the patriarchal "protections" accorded to white women. . . . In addition to working in the fields and in the "big house," a small number of owners rented both male and female slaves to outside employers. . . . In the early nineteenth century, slave women built levees, laid railroad track, and labored in mines, foundries, saltworks, sugar refineries, turpentine camps, and food and tobacco processing plants. . . . Racism and economic necessity forced free black women into the paid labor force. Attempting to abide by the family ethic, free black married women also took in wash and boarders so that they could be at home with their children.

The restructuring of home and family life meant that the colonial family ethic was less applicable to the reality of women's lives. The decline of women's economically productive role in the home, for example, violated the colonial family ethic's mandate against idleness. Yet economically productive work, now available only through the marketplace, brought women out of the home, thus contradicting the family ethic's mandate that women not leave the domestic sphere. The simultaneous expansion of women's caretaking activities in the home only compounded these conflicts, especially since this new "work" was not defined as economically productive. These developments, which created new tensions between the demand for women's home and market labor, marked the decline of the colonial family ethic and the rise of a new one more suited to the changing times.

The Industrial Family Ethic

The industrial family ethic first appeared in the 1790s, became institutionalized in the 1830s, and was further refined after the Civil War. By making reproduction rather than production the centerpiece of women's life and defining women's paid labor outside the home as deviant, the new family ethic helped to explain and institutionalize women's new role, popularly referred to as her "place in the home." More suited to the conditions of industrial capitalism, the industrial family ethic provided the rationale needed to exclude women from economic productivity, to expand their reproductive and maintenance tasks, and to define the home as "women's sphere".

* * *

Under these revised gender norms, women and men who previously shared, however unequally, responsibility for household production now legitimately occupied seemingly "separate spheres." Pious, inferior, subordinate, and confined to the home as before, the terms of women's role in the new industrial family ethic elevated marriage, motherhood, homemaking, and the overseeing of family life to new ideological heights. In addition to the loss of a recognized productive role, the industrial family ethic defined proper women as "moral mothers" and "asexual wives," and denied their previously acknowledged sexual needs.

* * *

The terms of the industrial family ethic were conveyed to women by ministers, educators, and by the popular advice books and sentimental novels that began to flood the market after the invention of inexpensive printing machinery in the 1830s. Reflecting the experience of white, middle-class women and targeted primarily at them, women from other classes and races had difficulty subscribing to the terms of the industrial family ethic. Nonetheless, it was eventually encoded in all societal institutions and, especially in urban areas, exercised considerable ideological power. Fulfilling the terms of the new family ethic, also known as the domestic code, "the cult of domesticity," and "the cult of true womanhood," established a woman's femininity, her womanhood, and her social respectability. Non-compliance brought penalties for stepping out of role.

* * *

The Industrial Family Ethic, White Working-Class Women, and Women of Color

The industrial family ethic described the ultimate nineteenth-century female, an imaginary woman whose traits increasingly defined the roles of white, middle-class women. But the wide discrepancy between ideology and reality meant that few women, even those in the middle class, could match its idealized terms. Nonetheless, the industrial family ethic became encoded in virtually all societal institutions and operated as a powerful social force influencing the norms of the white working class, the free black community, as well as those of the white middle and upper classes.

Nineteenth-century working-class families attempted to comply with the prevailing ideology of women's roles. Working-class men and their unions fought for the "family wage" that is, wages adequate for a man to support his dependents. . . . The ideal of "normal" manhood contained in the notion of a "family wage" was premised on the economic dependency of women on men and supported women's exclusion from the labor force. To promote the family wage, but also because working-class men worried that women's employment lowered male wage levels and took away male jobs, the working-class press regularly extolled the virtues of the home and women's place in it.

* * *

If compliance with the industrial family ethic was viewed as offering white middle-class women an opportunity to develop themselves as mothers and homemakers, such compliance intensified the domestic labor of working-class women and involved major sacrifices in the organization and comfort of their family life. Not being "allowed" to work outside the home, working-class women had to make up for the lost income by limiting family consumption and risking the health of their children by sending them to work. They also gave up the privacy of their home and increased their household tasks by taking in boarders, increasing the production of household goods, and taking in piece work. Like those women who did enter the labor force, those at home also faced a double work day.

The black community also accepted the industrial family ethic and strived to meet its terms. Black men, both slave and free, defined their manhood in terms of male supremacy in the family. As early as 1773, male slaves petitioned for freedom on the grounds, among other things, that male slaves had no family authority. A convention of free black males in 1855 declared, "As a people we have been denied the ownership of our bodies, *our wives*, homes, children and the products of our own labor" (emphasis added). . . . Black husbands also took pride in buying fashionable dresses, pretty hats, and delicate parasols for their women. A well-dressed wife legitimized their relationship and his role as a successful provider.

* * *

After the Civil War, black families strived to keep women closer to home where they performed domestic chores, took care of children, raised vegetables, and tended to farm animals. When he withdrew his family members from the fields after the Civil War, a Tennessee freedman explained to his employer: "When I married my wife, I married her to wait on me and she has got all she can do right here for me and the children." Boston cotton brokers attributed the disastrous cotton-crop losses in 1867-68 to the decision of "growing numbers of Negro women to devote their time to their homes and children".

* * *

Despite its widespread acceptance, the industrial family ethic failed to reflect the experience of many white working-class and immigrant women and women of color. The similarity even among white married women who shared an exclusion from the paid labor force quickly disappeared in the inequality of their husband's income. Women with means often substituted leisure for the rigors of domesticity prescribed by the family ethic. They became "ladies of leisure" who entrusted the care of their children and households to hired help. . . . The delicate clothes worn by upper-class women prohibited strenuous exercise, made walking difficult, and testified to the wearer's exemption from or incapacity for any "vulgarly" productive employment. To a British observer, the idleness of the American lady exceeded that of other countries. "There is in America," she wrote, "a large class of ladies who do absolutely nothing".

* * *

Women whose poverty, race, or lack of a male breadwinner forced them to work for wages outside the home could not conform to the family ethic. . . . By 1840, when about 10 percent of all women over age ten worked for wages outside the home, women filled nearly half of all manufacturing jobs and 90 percent of those in shoe factories, textile mills, and millinery shops.

* * *

The industrial family ethic hardly reflected the experience of many black women who, owing to a lack of marriage and work opportunities, had even less ability to fulfill its terms. A demographic shortage of black men and their exclusion from all but the most menial jobs limited the marriage possibilities of black women relative to whites. Although the majority of black families contained husbands and fathers, many free black women, particularly urban women, headed their own households.

* * *

Even when they married, poverty sent many free black women into the labor force, causing them to violate the family ethic. . . . Employed black women did not, however, receive what little protection employers offered to white women working outside the home. Virginia tobacco factories, for example, which employed white and black women in the 1850s, carefully placed white women in sex-segregated jobs suitable for "respectable ladies." Black women, by contrast, worked side-by-side with black men as they always had.

After the Civil War, whites continued to deny black women the rights of womanhood under the terms of the industrial family ethic. The white stereotypes of black women typically held her to be a laborer, dominant in the family (indomitable grandmother or unnatural matriarch), and sexually loose--characteristics which put her in direct contradiction of the family ethic. The black homemaker drew derision, while employers contemptuously and hypocritically referred to freed women who refused to work in the fields as "playing the lady," as "most lazy," and as demanding that their husbands "support them in idleness".

* * *

All Women Not Quieted by the Family Ethic

The power of the family ethic inhibited but did not totally forestall militant reactions. White, working-class women protested their wages and working conditions, and fought against their isolation and subordination; black women of both classes resisted the impact of racism on their lives. The first white women workers to strike on their own in America were the members of the United Tailoresses Society of New York who, in 1825, called their first meeting and demanded higher wages, and, despite chastisement for "clamorous and unfeminine declarations of personal rights," struck for more than 5 weeks in 1831.

* * *

The protests and organization of women workers, which continued after the Civil War, provoked considerable public disapproval and raised questions about women's proper role. Critics attacked the striking women for their lack of femininity, referred to them as "amazonian," and suggested a "gynocracy" would emerge if the militia were not called out. The response signaled an emerging public concern with the tension between women's work and their "place in the home."

Societal disapproval also greeted the white middle-class women who became involved in various religious and social reform organizations and started a movement to secure women's rights. Some historians suggest that the isolation and frustration of middle-class women helps explain why so many more women than men participated in the evangelical revivals that swept through New England and New York State in the early nineteenth century.

* * *

Denied access to the vote, to formal education, and to most professional jobs, many white, middle-class women also stepped out of their "place in the home" to join moral reform associations and benevolent societies which attacked prostitution, the double standard, drinking, and other symbols of male domination. Others focused on equity for women. . . . By 1848, the year of the first Women's Rights convention in Seneca, New York, middle-class women were actively involved in seeking property rights in the family and equal opportunity in the wider social order. Their extension of women's terrain from the private to the previously exclusively male, public sphere challenged patriarchal norms. Like their working-class sisters, they were denounced as "unnatural," as "semi-woman and mental hermaphrodites" and were scorned for tampering with society and undermining civilization.

Black women also fought poverty, white supremacy, slavery, poor wages, and dangerous working conditions. Black slaves who could not quit, organize, or strike, resisted their oppression by slowing down their work pace, laboring carelessly, and otherwise undermining the full use of their labor. . . . Slave women educated themselves, engaged in sabotage, operated the underground railroad, refused to breed slave children for their masters, and risked being burned at the stake for their participation in slave revolts.

* * *

During the nineteenth century and prior to similar efforts made on their behalf by whites, free, black women called for the abolition of slavery, started black grammar schools, and created formal organizations to fight for their rights and to deal with problems created by racism. Katy Ferguson, an ex-slave, established a school in New York City for poor black and white children in 1793--some forty years before the well-known school for young black girls opened in Connecticut by the white teacher Prudence Crandall.

* * *

The Industrial Family Ethic and the Political Economy

The industrial family ethic emerged at a time when the nation needed to adjust to the deep, disturbing, and often tumultuous changes that accompanied the development of capitalist production. The emerging economy required a new gender division of labor that assigned women to the private arena of home and community, and men to the more powerful public arena of work, politics, and society.

* * *

The industrial family ethic helped convince women as well as men to accept their place in the new social order. Its terms offered women a new status and the comforts of "patriarchal protection" while fostering women's oppression in ways that served the needs of capital and patriarchy. Unpaid caretaking and homemaking labor benefitted capital by cushioning the family from the effects of an increasingly ruthless and cut-throat market and assuring the reproduction of the labor force and the maintenance of the non-working members of society. The economy needed women to provide a tranquil retreat for market-weary men, socialize children to fulfill appropriate gender and class roles, and assure the consumption of market-produced goods and services.

* * *

The devaluation of women at home and in the market went a long way towards restoring patriarchal power in both spheres. The unequal treatment of women in the market placed them at the bottom of male-dominated job hierarchies. The poverty that resulted from women's economic marginalization caused them to turn to marriage for support, reinforced their economic, if not psychological, dependence on men, and locked them into devalued and subordinated family roles.

* * *

The family ethic also harnessed the male work ethic, which encouraged the development and disciplining of a male labor force. "The only way to make husbands sober and industrious," observed the *New York Post* in 1829, "was to keep women dependent on them."

. . . The good breadwinner worked hard, supported his family, and competed effectively with other men in the race for wealth. Only if he failed did his wife go out to work. Combined with the pressures of economic survival and upward mobility, the economic responsibility placed on men reinforced industry's ability to exploit and control the male labor force.

* * *

Finally, the family ethic rationalized the class stratification which became more pronounced in the nation's cities beginning in the late eighteenth century. The growing wealth of the industrial capitalists, regarded as vulgar, ambitious, and dangerously powerful by the agrarian gentry, contrasted sharply with the living standards of the urban laborers who worked for them. As if to deny this reality, the newly democratic social order rejected the idea of ascribed status and all classifications except "natural" ones which included gender, race, and achieved status such as "self-made" wealth. In this context, the idea of common domestic vocation for all women gained enormous appeal. The democratic possibility left those who failed to achieve this goal personally responsible for their departures.

In the long run, however, the many female workers and female paupers in America became visible. Indeed, their growing numbers, along with other changes, eventually created a crisis for the colonial poor law system, paving the way for its "reform." The results . . . were a set of punitive new ideas about the cause of poverty, an attack on outdoor relief, and the development of institutional care. In a period of intense social change, the emerging poor law system, which encoded and enforced the industrial family ethic, also helped to adjust workers to the rules of wage labor, to reinforce family discipline and to reconcile the competing demands for women's paid labor in the market and her unpaid labor in the home.

* * *

Notes and Questions

1. *Shift Toward An Industrial Economy.* Primarily during the nineteenth and early twentieth centuries, the American economy shifted from agriculture to industrialized manufacturing. Professor Abramovitz describes the competing demands various groups of women faced during this transformation. In broad strokes, she

connects gender, race, and class to the needs of the economic order. How should anti-poverty programs account for these connections?

2. *Shift Toward A Service Economy.* Current indicators suggest another economic transformation, away from an industrialized and nationalized economy toward a more service-oriented and global economy. Do the patterns described by Abramovitz predict gender, race, and class problems for this current economic transformation?

3. *Feminism and Poverty.* Many feminist scholars and activists include poverty in the lists of pressing problems facing women. Yet some criticize the organized feminist community for focusing on the goals of middle and upper class women and ignoring the problems of poor women. This criticism is not limited, however, to feminists. Because poverty strikes no identity group predominantly, many organizations devoted to eliminating racism, sexism, heterosexism, or other intolerant beliefs and practices fail to target eliminating poverty as part of their political agendas. Do the National Organization for Women, or the National Association for the Advancement of Colored People, or other civil rights organizations share responsibility for eliminating poverty? Should these types of organizations choose to spend their limited time, energy, money, and political capital on eliminating poverty? If they don't, who will represent poor people in the political process?

4. *Resistance.* Abramovitz recounts portions of the resistance waged against economic injustice by women during the transformation to industrialization. Do you see similar protests today?

5. *Moralism.* During this period of transformation to industrialization, a belief in democratic opportunity allowed those favored by capitalism to blame the remainder who were "personally responsible" for failing to achieve self-sufficiency. Abramovitz suggests this moral judgment set the stage for punitive reform of poverty law. How does this historical reform compare to modern reform efforts, including blaming individuals for causing poverty, attacking welfare benefits as contributing to dependency, and proposing institutional care (such as the 1994 Republican call for orphanages to house children displaced from homes when welfare is eliminated)? *See, e.g., Orphanages Are No Solution,* N.Y. TIMES, Dec. 12, 1994, at A14; David Van Biema, *The Storm Over Orphanages*, TIME, Dec. 12, 1994, at 58; *The Orphanages*,

NEWSWEEK, Dec. 12, 1994, at 28; Douglas J. Besharov, *Orphanages Aren't Welfare Reform*, N.Y. TIMES, Dec. 21, 1994, at A19.

C. THE ANTI-POVERTY PROGRAMS

Inequities of race and gender continue to be associated with welfare programs. Women and racial minorities constitute a disproportionate percentage of public assistance recipients. Indeed, understanding the structure of anti-poverty programs requires understanding the politics that frame the policy debate about these programs. We offer a framework which divides discussion about anti-poverty programs into three parts. Each part represents a set of defining moments for welfare programs which occurred in the 1930s, the 1960s, and the 1990s.

1. The 1930s: War on Unemployment

We begin with the 1930s. In the following article, Joel Handler describes a critical dilemma in anti-poverty policy--the balance between maintaining "labor discipline" and relieving poverty. The need to balance between these aims caused a now-familiar division of poor people into two camps, the deserving poor who were excused from labor and merited relief, and the undeserving poor who were not excused from labor and, therefore, did not merit relief.

Joel Handler

"CONSTRUCTING THE POLITICAL SPECTACLE": THE INTERPRETATION OF ENTITLEMENTS, LEGALIZATION, AND OBLIGATIONS IN SOCIAL WELFARE HISTORY

56 BROOKLYN LAW REVIEW 899 (1990)

* * *

A (Very) Brief History

The Normative Order[*]

Who the poor are and what to do about their poverty form the basis of welfare policy. The construction of the nature, causes, and remedies for poverty reflects fundamental values about how society should be organized, how people should act, and how to assign blame. Poverty policy is part of the normative order of the political economy. From at least the time of Henry VIII, the overarching tension has been to balance the need to maintain labor discipline with the need to relieve misery. Under liberal capitalism, the state offers protection, comfort, and support for those who participate in the productive system. For those who cannot because of conditions beyond their control, the state provides relief. Thus, the heart of poverty policy centers on the question of who is excused from work. Those who are excused are the "deserving poor"; those who must work are the "undeserving." Ultimately, this is a moral distinction. It involves deciding the nature and significance of the work ethic, the causes and extent of disability, the impact, both real and perceived, of incentives and disincentives on human behavior, and the consequences to the individual, the family, and the community of failing to abide by conventional norms.

The normative order of the political economy involves far more than work. The construction of the family--gender roles, child rearing, and socialization--are integral parts of this political economy, as are race and ethnicity. Thus, poverty policy is influenced by and, in turn, influences labor discipline, gender and family roles, socialization, and race and ethnicity. All are part of the ideological construction of welfare policy.

The Formative Years

Women in the Paid Labor Force

Central to an understanding of welfare is the role of poor women in the paid labor force. From the earliest days of the country, poor women were *never* morally excused from the paid labor force. During the colonial and early national periods, women from all social classes were encouraged to seek paid labor. Starting about the 1830s, the situation changed. With the rise of the "domestic code," the patriarchal family was defined by the husband in the paid labor force and the wife and mother in the home. The spheres were to be separate; the female role was morally defined in terms of the purer sex, the provider of sanctuary, and the moral educator of the children. Many reasons are given for the rise of the domestic code, including competition from male wage earners, employers who blamed working women for low wages, and social reformers who feared the destruction of the family.

The domestic code had serious, negative effects on poor

women and mothers. These women *had* to work; there were no alternatives. Yet, they were severely condemned for working. They were blamed for competition and for undermining working conditions, and they were attacked for bad mothering--neglecting their children, or if married--neglecting their husbands as well. The moral degradation of these women was compounded by additional factors. The poorer the woman, the worse the job--in laundries, in factories, as domestic servants, taking in boarders--jobs that were the least "feminine." African-Americans and immigrants were disproportionately represented at the bottom of the paid labor force. Finally, the number of poor women in the paid labor force was not small. Thus, they were perceived as a social menace. Poor mothers, especially single mothers, were in an inescapable dilemma. They had to work--there were no sources of aid--yet, by working they violated the domestic code and faced the loss of their children. In the latter part of the century, Progressive child protectors "discovered" child neglect. Neglect became an expansive concept, covering a wide range of "bad mothering." Child protection agencies claimed that they never removed a child for poverty alone, but poverty was never alone and a disproportionate number of cases that came to the attention of the authorities involved single poor mothers. One of the reforms of that period was the juvenile court, which asserted jurisdiction over delinquent, neglected, and dependent children. Neglected and dependent children were considered pre-delinquent, and therefore, in need of state control.

The Fight against Pauperism

Why were there no welfare programs for poor mothers? During this period, the country was preoccupied with the control of pauperism. Pauperism was equated with vice, criminality, prostitution, and delinquency. In the latter part of the century, as a result of the worsening recessions, bands of unemployed men roamed the countryside creating fear of disorder and crime. A prime cause of pauperism, it was firmly believed, was the indiscriminate giving of outdoor relief which would only encourage permanent dependency. It was difficult, in practice, to distinguish those who were morally at fault for their poverty from those who were blameless. Strenuous campaigns to abolish outdoor relief were led by the most prominent social reformers of the day. This was the period of "scientific charity"; its enemy was pauperism.

Poor mothers were caught in the campaigns in two senses. Because they were part of the paid labor force, giving them aid would undermine labor discipline. The giving of aid would also weaken the family, lessen the husband's obligations, or encourage desertion. The task of social policy, argued the reformers, was to force the husband to return to the family by affirming obligations, not encouraging dependency. Accordingly, throughout the century, there was no outdoor relief for single mothers. From time to time, local work programs were established for "worthy" widows, but these programs were largely unsuccessful. What is important about these programs is that they insisted on work for these poor women.

* * *

The Rise of the Categories

Yet, there was the need to relieve misery and to help the blameless poor. The nineteenth century witnessed the rise of categories--aid for particular categories of the poor who were considered blameless. This approach has remained a basic characteristic of American social welfare policy. Institutions were created for the blind, the deaf, and the insane, and later, for orphans. A separate pension system was created for Civil War veterans, which eventually grew into a massive welfare program.

The first of the twentieth century categorical programs--Aid to Dependent Children (ADC)--was enacted in 1911 and quickly spread throughout the country. This program, popularly called "Mothers' Pensions," was designed to provide income support for single mothers to maintain their homes. Thus, the programs were interpreted as a major change in social welfare policy towards poor single mothers: these women were removed from the paid labor force--the hallmark of the deserving poor.

In fact, nothing was further from the truth. At this time, single mothers and their children, as a category, were indistinguishable from the mass of the poor; that is, they were undeserving and required to work. Some Progressive social reformers, recognizing the economic and social trap of poor single mothers and the futility of child protection (and removal) began to argue for in-home support; a poor home was now considered by them to be better than no home. However, their proposals were bitterly contested, especially by some of the most prominent organizations and members of scientific charity. The grounds were familiar--aid would lessen the responsibility of the fathers and encourage single motherhood. As with outdoor relief, in general, pauperism would be encouraged because of the difficulty of distinguishing the worthy from the unworthy. The programs that were enacted reflected historical rather than reform values. Many were administered by the juvenile court; thus, worthy mothers functioned as a form of privatized probation. All the programs were very restrictive; only a small number of white widows were enrolled. In many jurisdictions, local governments refused to establish programs. In many others, administration was placed in the hands of the social organizations that had opposed the programs in the first place. The ADC programs were a gesture only; the vast bulk of poor single mothers and their children were untouched. They were still part of the paid labor force, the undeserving poor.

Aid to the Blind was enacted during this period but under very different circumstances. The programs sought to separate the blind from the general mass of paupers. Eligibility was clearly defined; there were very few conditions. The blind were not considered part of the labor force.

Relief for the dependent aged came a bit later, but was much contested. At this time, there was no agreed-upon retirement age; hence, capitalists opposed these programs on labor-supply grounds as well as differing local taxes. Relief for the aged, it was felt, compromised traditional family values of saving and intergenerational responsibility. Accordingly, these programs spread very slowly and were filled with conditions designed to weed out the morally unfit. As a category, the dependent aged were still part of the undeserving poor; they were still part of the labor market.

One other program that emerged during this period deserves mention--workmen's compensation. By the first decades of the century, capitalists were searching for solutions to combat the financial costs of industrial accidents. Common law defenses were being eroded, and cases were going to juries. In addition, as a result of reports and exposés, public indignation was rising. Employers, and their insurance companies, wanted to regularize and reduce costs and defuse the adverse publicity. They got what they wanted in the workmen's compensation reforms. Over the opposition of labor, claims were removed from the courts and handled by administrative agencies according to formula. Benefits were low. The Progressive reformers thought that they were getting an insurance scheme and that insurance would spread to other social problems. They were disappointed in both respects; workers still bore most of the loss, and insurance did not spread. For our purposes, workmen's compensation is important for two reasons. Despite its insurance rhetoric, it was designed to maintain industrial discipline. It was also a social control program that was rule-bound.

This brings us to the New Deal, the great watershed in the American welfare state. Before proceeding, it is well to review the landscape. A few categories of the poor were considered deserving--that is, morally excused from work: the institutionally disabled and the blind. The vast bulk of the poor, including single mothers and their children were considered undeserving and a part of the labor force. From time to time, certain members of these categories--some worthy white widows, some dependent aged, some others no doubt--would be let into public programs, but the important point is that *most* of the members of these categories were *excluded*; they had to work, get private help, or starve.

The New Deal

The New Deal consisted of four parts: (1) work relief; (2) unemployment insurance; (3) Social Security for the retired; and (4) the grant-in-aid programs for aid to dependent children, old-age assistance, and aid to the blind. Together, these parts show continuity with the past by the strengthening of the categories.

The first and most immediate crisis facing the new administration was massive unemployment. There was significant local disorder and serious concern about threats to social order at all levels of government. The initial New Deal reforms were constructed during this state of crisis and widespread poverty. The Roosevelt administration quickly put together an extensive system of public employment. While these programs turned out to be temporary, their brief history tells us much about the future course of the American welfare state.

Within a year, more than 4,500,000 families and single people were receiving some sort of relief. Even though administration was through grants-in-aid to the states, the federal government insisted on separate administrative agencies (to distinguish these programs from welfare), the prohibition of racial, religious, and political discrimination, and uniform benefits. Between 1.4 and 2.4 million people per month worked at wages higher than both direct relief and market wages. Nevertheless, despite the apparent success of the work programs, they were instantly and bitterly attacked, and ultimately seriously crippled by the business community on the grounds that the federal programs did not follow traditional welfare requirements and compromised industrial discipline. Under extreme pressure, Congress rescinded the minimum wage, imposed a means test, and shortly, despite their national popularity, scaled back the programs drastically.

The reasons for the demise of work relief are telling. Despite the fact that the vast number of recipients were the submerged middle class and in no sense the stereotypical malingerer, the perceived need to preserve industrial discipline was overwhelming. Capitalists insisted that employed workers had to be reminded that if they lost their jobs, there was no reliable cushion for them to fall back on.

Race politics also became more overtly important at this time. Prior to the New Deal, African-Americans were simply excluded from welfare. They were the most undeserving of the undeserving poor. The Roosevelt administration tried to open up the new programs, which incurred the wrath of the South. The South, at this time, was largely a plantation economy, with African-American tenant farming taking the place of slavery. The great majority of African-Americans lived in the South and on the land. As a one-party region, with a large part of its citizenry disenfranchised, the South exercised a virtual veto power in Congress. Southern politicians refused to tolerate any federal intervention in their labor and race relations. Southern race and labor politics would prove to be very important in the other New Deal programs as well.

President Roosevelt himself was opposed to the work relief programs. He feared the creation of a large, permanent, entrenched bureaucracy and worried about the effects of relief on work incentives. His Committee on Economic Security unsuccessfully floated a guaranteed public employment program. However, the position of business was that all relief programs should be returned to the states, work relief should be abolished, and direct relief payments should be reduced. The resulting program produced a small number of public jobs only for those not employable in the private sector.

This was the context in which the Social Security Act was debated. Despite the massive unemployment and the impressive accomplishments of the work programs, traditional attitudes towards relief and labor discipline prevailed. Even though the Depression poor were in no sense the stereotypical malingerer, regulating employment was more a matter of industrial discipline and preventing dependency than meeting need. Moreover, the federal government was not to be trusted. Social control was best left to the states and local governments, which were more sensitive to local labor markets. It was this dominant ideology towards work and relief that explains the outcome of the first major task of the Social Security reformers: unemployment insurance.

Here, an important influence was the experience of the Civil War pensions system. Initially tied to service-connected injuries or death, this program, under political pressure, expanded into a vast social welfare program blanketing all veterans and their families. In practice, ninety days of service and old age (sixty-two) became the test. Most northern white males or their widows were covered; excluded were African-Americans, southerners, and immigrants. By the turn of the century, the program was infected with political patronage and corruption, and this strongly affected the Progressive-era social reformers who were arguing for professionally administered social insurance systems in the European tradition. Their fears of corruption-prone, public-spending programs were fueled by the post-World War I experience in Europe, especially in Britain, where the unemployment insurance system yielded to an open-ended system of relief for the unemployed.

The experience of the Civil War pension system, the specter of Europe, and the work relief experience helped determine the fate of unemployment insurance. Roosevelt insisted that unemployment insurance be separate from relief, and be actuarily "sound"--that is, financed by contributions and taxes. There would be maximum state control. This was of central importance; in fact, the dispute over the administrative form of unemployment insurance was *the* dominant political issue in 1934. Why were state interests so important? It was in local labor markets that the interests of capitalists and labor were fought out. "Sensitivity" or "control over local labor markets" was the code for the social control of marginal workers; the capitalists insisted that the price and availability of local labor not be disturbed. The South was able to make sure that all the provisions of the Social Security Act, including unemployment insurance, left undisturbed its economy and race relations.

In the end, state unemployment insurance laws reflected these positions; programs were state and local and they failed to reach those most in need, the "less deserving" workers such as employees of small firms, agricultural workers, women, African-Americans, and migrants. State benefits varied widely, but the most common was sixteen weeks at half pay, with a maximum of fifteen dollars per week. Significantly, the maximum was about the average federal work relief (WPA) rate. Once benefits were exhausted, there was no other relief available except WPA, which was difficult to obtain. In sum, unemployment insurance was more in the nature of temporary emergency relief. Moreover, it was for the deserving workers--those who worked in steady, reliable, covered employment. Benefits were calibrated to length of employment and rates of pay. There were waiting periods. Workers were excluded if they quit voluntarily, were discharged for cause or a labor dispute, or failed to register at a public employment office and be available for suitable alternative work. All attempts to impose significant, substantive national standards on the states were defeated.

The centerpiece of the Social Security Act was the establishment of a contributory, national pension for the aged--old age insurance (OAI). As we have seen, prior to the New Deal, aid to the dependent aged was controversial, and the South considered such pensions as family grants which would weaken control over African-American farm tenants. By 1935, however, the political climate outside the South had changed. The elderly, along with the working population, were politically active and various radical redistribution plans were being proposed. Nevertheless, Roosevelt was strongly committed to an actuarily sound contributory insurance system and adamantly opposed to anything resembling the dole. He believed that the program would only attain solid legitimacy if it was "earned," if it was financed by contribution, if it had no means test, if it clearly defined the risks, and if it had a fixed retirement age. Benefits would reflect wages, thus strengthening incentives rather than redistribution. Only in this way would recipients avoid the stigma of welfare. The program was (and is) sold on its insurance features. This was a dignified program paying individually earned benefits as of right rather than relief for people who had to demonstrate need.

There was now a strong desire to get older workers out of the labor market. Families had changed, and young people did not want their parents moving back in. In contrast to unemployment insurance, there were strong arguments in favor of a uniform, national scheme. It was in the interests of big business to avoid different state taxes, and the fact that there was a general relationship between wages and benefits (and not much redistribution), meant that wage structures and regional variations would not be disturbed. The South was opposed, and insisted on the exclusion of agricultural and domestic workers, insuring that planter control over African-Americans would not be disturbed. The exclusion of these workers, plus the elimination of national standards from state old-age assistance, meant that the vast majority of elderly African-Americans were almost completely excluded.

Why was OAI national while Unemployment Insurance (UI) was not? The arguments in favor of a national OAI applied as well to UI--namely, the mobility of labor and uniform taxes. The reason lies in the differential effects on labor markets. OAI wanted its beneficiaries *out* of the labor market; UI wanted to make sure that its beneficiaries stayed in. And in the United States, the regulation of work tests are invariably at the local level. Local businesses want to keep close control over economic issues (and avoid taxes), and the local community wants to keep control over moral behavior. OAI, as originally conceived, touched on these issues in the South, but the exclusion of agricultural and domestic workers left race relations undisturbed. Once a consensus was reached on this "deserving" category, the program could be nationalized.

The last piece of the Social Security Act were the grants-in-aid to the states to rescue their old age, aid to the blind, and aid to dependent children programs. At this time, the separation of OAI and old age assistance was not a foregone conclusion. There was strong support for a universal, national, flat pension for the aged. By now, the aged were excused from work. Again, the influence of the South was crucial. As the price of southern support, important national standards, which would have allowed federal funds to go directly to African-Americans, were stripped from old age assistance. The states could set their own eligibility requirements and enjoy an independent administration. Southern intentions were carried out. They were the slowest to enact old age assistance programs; eligibility was more stringent; administration was at the local level under broad discretion; there were strict residency requirements and removal powers--characteristics of traditional poor law. In the South, the African-American aged agricultural tenant farmer was still considered part of the labor force since the South considered an old age grant to be a family subsidy. Benefits to African-Americans were substantially lower than to whites and carefully monitored. Elsewhere, old age assistance was popular, especially since substantial numbers of insurance retirees were not scheduled to receive OAI benefits until 1942. Programs spread rapidly; benefits and federal contributions were higher than they were with aid to dependent children (ADC).

Of course, the plight of poor single mothers worsened during the Depression. Divorce and desertion increased, as did joblessness and homelessness. Nevertheless, despite the lobbying efforts of the Federal Children's Bureau, there was little interest in ADC on the part of either the administration or Congress. The basic thinking was that as OAI took hold, more and more of the elderly and widows would be covered and that public assistance as well as ADC would wither. The old problems continued to dog this category of the poor--the stigma of poor single mothers, labor discipline, and race. "[N]o one in 1935 imagined throwing millions of dollars into broken homes." Some important federal requirements, however, were imposed--for example, programs had to be implemented statewide, eligibility standards were broadened, benefits had to be paid in cash, and there had to be fair hearings.

However, while access to ADC was increased formally, in practice the programs stayed the same. In contrast to Old Age Assistance (OAA), most states lagged in buying into grant-in-aid and did little to encourage enrollments. Congress did not encourage the states to either adopt grant-in-aid or enroll poor single mothers. Despite the different federal subsidies and benefits between OAA and ADC (the latter were lower than the former), which were noticed during the Social Security Act deliberations, there was little interest expressed by either Congress or the administration in harmonizing the programs. This pattern of treating the adult programs (OAA and Aid to the Blind) more generously than ADC was not a mere oversight.

In fact, higher appropriations, matching formulae and benefit levels for the former continue to the present.

At the local level, social control of the poor single mother continued. Through the use of "suitable home" and "employable mother" policies, states were able to exclude the unworthy, maintain labor markets, and reduce costs. Even under the Social Security Act, ADC remained small and primarily for white widows.

In the meantime, what was happening to the general mass of poor? During the 1920s, there had been a rapid growth of public relief programs at the local level. These were, of course, overwhelmed by the Depression, and there was little change during the New Deal period. Public relief for the undifferentiated poor (which included the great bulk of single mothers and their children who were excluded from ADC) was always miserly. In the Depression, there was simply no money left for the noncategorical poor.

Post-World War II

The distinctions drawn by the Social Security Act continued in the post-World War II period. Unemployment Insurance retained its basic character, a limited program for the deserving worker. The big change came with the elderly. There was strong pressure to expand Old Age Assistance, which prior to the war was far larger than OAI. States were pressing for a flat-grant old age "pension" without a means test. While the Social Security Administration, anxious to protect its program, insisted on need, several states streamlined the program and raised benefits. The ultimate goal of these "flat grant" advocates was a national, generous, non-means tested, uniform pension which would replace OAI. As late as the 1950s, more people were on OAA than the slowly maturing Social Security system. The Social Security Administration responded in two ways. It insisted on need for OAA, to preserve the distinction between relief and insurance, and it expanded OAI. Timetables for benefits were shortened, eligibility expanded (adding survivors in 1939 and OASI), and benefits were liberalized. Still, the South refused to allow the program to be extended to agricultural and domestic workers. Southern opposition lessened when agriculture became mechanized, African-Americans migrated, a poor aged population became an increasing welfare burden, southern congressional power declined, and civil rights took hold.

In 1969, President Nixon introduced the Family Assistance Act which proposed sweeping changes in all of the categorical programs. The proposal was defeated--primarily because of the proposed changes in ADC (by now Aid to Families with Dependent Children, AFDC)--but there was strong support for reforming the other programs. In 1974, Supplementary Security Income (SSI) was enacted, thus federalizing Old Age Assistance, Aid to the Blind, and Aid to the Totally and Permanently Disabled (which had been established in 1954). SSI is completely federally funded and administered (by the Social Security Administration) with national eligibility standards and a basic uniform grant (there is optional state supplementation). SSI was not controversial. The aged and the blind are not in the labor force; they are now full members of the deserving poor.

Social Security expanded only slowly; until the 1960s, it was a low-level income-maintenance program. The big changes came in 1968 and 1974 when benefits were raised substantially and indexed to the cost of living, moves which coincided with the liberalization of OAA and the enactment of SSI. Today, Social Security is a major source of income for the vast majority of the aged in America. It has not only become a retirement wage; it has also become a "citizen's wage," an entitlement that has significant redistribution effects. It has significantly reduced poverty among the elderly, and it is comparable to the most advanced systems in Western Europe.

Despite the Social Security Administration's effort to keep them separate, there was a convergence between the dependent aged and the retirees. For both groups of the elderly, there was pressure to *remove* them from the labor force. When this ideological transformation was finally completed in the South, all of the dependent aged were treated as the deserving poor.

The story is different for the unemployed. As distinguished from the aged, helping the unemployed affects the bargaining power of labor, lessens the pressure to take less desirable jobs, and lessens the pressure to limit strikes. Accordingly, the basic features of UI have remained in place. Various attempts to assert national standards have failed. There is great variation among the states, but in general, benefits remain low. It is estimated that a single worker could meet daily subsistence needs, but not an unemployed worker with a family --probably the most important segment of the work force.

UI is funded entirely through the payroll tax, and employers are experience-rated. These features, unique in the industrialized world, evidence the central relation of this program to the market. Meanwhile, the program remains seriously inadequate. The distinction between the deserving and undeserving worker remains in place. Coverage has declined sharply: since 1985, to less than a third of the unemployed. This means that in an average month, in 1988, 4.6 million jobless workers did not receive any unemployment insurance benefits. Coverage is even worse for African-Americans (21 percent) and Hispanics (14 percent). There are very few alternative income supports for the able-bodied unemployed who are no longer covered by UI. Both Aid to Families with Dependent Children with an Unemployed Parent (AFDC-UP) and General Relief are very restrictive; needless to say, poverty rates among the long-term unemployed are very high.

AFDC is also different. From the New Deal to post-World War II, the patterns set during the Mothers' Pension era continued. There was some expansion during the war and the 1950s. The big changes started in the late 1950s, and took two contradictory paths. There was a period of liberalization. For a variety of reasons--the civil rights movement, African-American migrations, urban riots, welfare rights, the widespread campaigns of the National Welfare Rights Organization (NWRO), the War on Poverty--benefits were raised and several of the social control features of eligibility were eliminated. The rolls exploded, and the composition of the program changed from widows to women who had been deserted or never married, and became increasingly African-American. However, costs rose and the programs became massive and appeared out of control, especially in terms of integrity. Popular attention, with thinly disguised racial overtones, began to focus on costs, the moral consequences of marital disruption, single parenthood, and generational dependency.

The federal government and the states responded in several ways. There was a clampdown on benefits. In 1967, the first federal work requirement--the Work Incentive Program (WIN)--was enacted. Quality control was introduced. Programs became computerized; clerical workers replaced social workers; there was close supervision and vigorous pursuit of overpayments. There was a dramatic tightening of administrative practices, and the program became much more bureaucratic and rule-bound.

In sum, AFDC changed, but hardly in the direction of the categorical adult programs. In part, it was federalized (the financial elements). But, in contrast with the other programs where federalization has meant liberalization, with AFDC it has been used to clamp down on recipients and control portions of benefits such as work expenses and income-deeming rules. But in the main, AFDC is still primarily a state and local program in basic benefit levels, administration, and work requirements.

The most fundamental test of the difference between the deserving and undeserving poor is work. Prior to the 1960s, the various states had work tests for their AFDC recipients. In addition, since most poor single mothers were excluded from the program, they had to work or starve as did the rest of the poor. Thus, whether in or out of AFDC, poor single mothers were undeserving. In the 1960s, the local gatekeepers lost control, and the previously excluded single mothers now streamed into the program. Congress responded, in 1967, by passing the WIN program. WIN had a two-pronged approach: incentives to seek market employment and a coercive administrative work test. The prevailing view in Congress was that welfare undermined family stability and work incentives, that the economy could absorb all who wanted to work and that the jobs that recipients would obtain would allow them to leave welfare. Congress also felt that welfare recipients had inappropriately high standards for what constituted acceptable work. At first WIN was mandatory for males and voluntary for women.

WIN was destined to fall short of congressional expectations. Local offices faced incredible obstacles: determinative, yet uncontrollable local labor markets, recipients with multiple barriers to employment, and seriously inadequate resources. Local offices responded predictably by allocating resources to those most likely to succeed (those most likely to be employed to begin with ("creaming")), and figuring out ways to deflect the rest. The vast bulk of the eligible AFDC population was put on administrative hold. It is not clear whether those who did find jobs would not have found them otherwise; it is also not clear that there would have been even greater welfare savings without WIN.

Reacting to continually rising welfare costs, Congress

toughened the work requirements in 1971 (WIN II, or the Talmadge Amendments). The focus shifted from education and institutional training to placement in entry-level jobs; the program was made mandatory for mothers with children over the age of six. Nevertheless, WIN II was just as unsuccessful as WIN I. When federal funding was at its peak, the average spent per recipient was only two hundred and fifty dollars. Under the best scenario, WIN was able to remove less than two percent of the AFDC recipients from the rolls, and of those attaining employment, a third were paid less than the minimum wage. The vast bulk of the population was not affected. With the apparent failure of WIN, the Reagan administration again toughened the work requirements. Work-related expenses were reduced, and while the Congress refused to go along with mandated work-relief jobs, it did allow the states the option of imposing such requirements in the form of Community Work Experience (CWEP). A number of states operated work-relief programs. Despite very modest results, under small, demonstration conditions, several major states adopted workfare programs. Although there is variation among the states, workfare generally requires client employability assessment, job search, education and training (if appropriate), and work-relief. The Family Support Act of 1988, in effect, codifies state workfare options. Although states are required to adopt many elements of workfare--for example, every state has to establish a Job Opportunities and Basic Skills Program (JOBS)--there are enough loopholes to allow the states to be tough or lenient. It is too early to tell how the state programs will fare. As with WIN, much depends on local labor markets and funding, but early signs are not promising. History is likely to repeat itself.

In the meantime, AFDC rolls and costs were stable for quite some time. Grants were frozen for years, and there has been a real decline in income for recipients. Birth rates have also been declining, and the average AFDC family is smaller than in the past. Does this mean that the welfare "crisis" is over? Not at all. The country is now fixated on the "underclass." While the underclass, however difficult to define, is broader than the AFDC population--it includes, for example, the homeless, male unemployed, school drop-outs, criminals, and gangs--two images dominate: the young African-American mother and the African-American youth. These two groups have come to be equated with joblessness, drugs, and crime. Thus, the stereotypical AFDC recipient is considered a prime contributor to this new scourge. And, as we learn from Lawrence Mead, many think that welfare (AFDC) is at least one of the faults.

This brief review demonstrates the variety and complexity of our response to poverty. What is the meaning of this history? What is social welfare policy doing?

* * *

Notes and Questions

1. *Categorization.* Poverty law centers around categorization. Professor Handler reviews the historical creation of categories, from the blind, deaf, insane, orphans and veterans of the nineteenth century to the addition of dependent children, the dependent aged, and the injured workers of the early twentieth century. The New Deal expanded the categories to include the unemployed and the retired, and strengthened existing categories. Does it make sense to organize anti-poverty policy around categories? What purposes does categorization serve?

2. *Work Ethic.* The need to maintain labor discipline permeates poverty law history. The could the American work ethic conceivably support a system of public employment as the welfare system of last resort?

As Handler describes, the work relief programs of the New Deal were short-lived because business leaders believed they compromised labor discipline. This same concern impacted non-work relief programs as well. Legislators historically excluded categories of people expected to work from receiving relief. For most of American history then, mothers, children, disabled people, and elderly people were expected to work and either excluded from relief or limited in the type or amount of relief. How should we decide who we expect to work? Do economic needs drive these political choices?

3. *Racism.* The politics of racial control seem closely related to the need to maintain labor discipline. Handler describes the close relation between labor and race relations revealed by southern politicians' exclusion of African-Americans from relief, typically by denying benefits to agricultural, domestic, and migrant laborers. Are the politics of race still affecting poverty policy today?

4. *Federalism.* Struggles over federalism also pervade poverty law history. As categories of people were excused from

labor, their benefits typically were nationalized. Benefits for elderly people serve as a prime example of this trend. Society initially expected the elderly to work, to have saved for their old age, or to have raised children to care for them. Gradually politicians provided aid to elderly people who were needy, and eventually to elderly people who were retired from work. The needy elderly received means-tested state-controlled benefits. The retired elderly received wage-tested nationally-controlled benefits. As social values shifted over time, society excused both groups of elderly from labor force participation. As a result, all benefits for elderly people were nationalized. Nationalization entailed setting uniform floors for benefit levels and indexing benefits to the cost of living.

5. *Repeating History.* Perhaps Handler's brief history to the current debate about poverty shows that the more things change, the more they stay the same. For example, do you see evidence of the "inescapable" gender dilemma described by Mimi Abramovitz and echoed by Handler? Are poor women still forced to work, but condemned for working? Similarly, do welfare critics today argue that providing relief encourages dependency and causes poverty? If similar themes and strategies recur throughout history, should anti-poverty advocates simply anticipate the pattern or attempt to alter it?

2. The 1960s: War on Poverty

The 1960s emerged as a truly exceptional period, where society focused more on helping the poor than on blaming them. Peter Edelman provides a close-up view of the innovative programs during the War on Poverty.

Peter B. Edelman

Toward a Comprehensive Antipoverty Strategy: Getting Beyond the Silver Bullet

81 Georgetown Law Journal 1697 (1993)

In a very real sense, the 1960s *are* the beginning of the modern American history of antipoverty policy. If there had been millions in poverty in the 1930s, it was because the economy had collapsed. If there were still millions in poverty in the 1960s, albeit fewer millions, it was now poverty in the midst of plenty, a new

American phenomenon. Initiatives to deal with that poverty were a new departure.

* * *

The Great Society

President Johnson, signing the Economic Opportunity Act (the War on Poverty) on August 20, 1964, said, "[T]he measure . . . offers the answer that its title implies--the answer of opportunity. For the purpose of the Economic [Opportunity] Act of 1964 is to offer opportunity, not an opiate." The strategy of the Great Society was, as an analysis of its programs will show, primarily a strategy of providing an equal start and an equal opportunity to all Americans, regardless of their race or economic background.

* * *

Reexamination of President Johnson's actual remarks in 1964, however, is revealing. In fact, poverty was not his sole, or even his major focus, and big government was most definitely not his solution. He said, . . . "[T]he Great Society . . . is not a safe harbor, a resting place, a final objective, a finished work. It is a challenge constantly renewed, beckoning us toward a destiny where the meaning of our lives matches the marvelous products of our labor." After stating a series of problems needing national attention, including poverty as one item in a lengthy list, Johnson specifically concluded, "The solution to these problems does not rest on a massive program in Washington, nor can it rely solely on the strained resources of local authority. They require us to create new concepts of cooperation, a creative federalism, between the National Capital and the leaders of local communities."

* * *

The Great Society as it related to poverty consisted of not only the war on poverty itself, as embodied in the Economic Opportunity Act of 1964, but also an array of other policies and programs. A long list of these initiatives is now widely accepted and regarded as excellent public policy. The Civil Rights Act of 1964 and the Voting Rights Act of 1965, which, respectively, challenged racially discriminatory barriers to opportunity and to participation in the political process, are appropriately viewed in part as antipoverty initiatives. Medicare and Medicaid, which have assured health care access to millions of the elderly and the poor, have had a positive impact on health indicators for the poor and therefore belong on everyone's list of positive antipoverty programs of the 1960s. The Elementary and Secondary Education Act of 1965, which provided help to poor children with their reading and other basic skills, has been favorably evaluated and has survived the Reagan onslaught of the 1980s, despite the Act's antipoverty emphasis.

The list of accepted antipoverty initiatives also includes numerous pieces of the original war on poverty itself: Head Start, Job Corps, neighborhood health centers, Volunteers in Service in America (VISTA), Foster Grandparents, Upward Bound, and neighborhood legal services (now the Legal Services Corporation, still a favorite right-wing target but also championed for years by the organized bar and a hardy survivor).

If all of these laws and programs are now more or less widely accepted, what is the source of the continuing mantra reciting that the Great Society failed? . . . The vast majority of Great Society initiatives are, as indicated above, quite widely supported. From a narrower programmatic perspective, there seem to be two items that might be the basis of the indictment: community action and Model Cities.

Community action was a key part of the Economic Opportunity Act. The drafters did not want the individual programs that they were creating either run or overseen by traditional social service agencies in city government, county government, or the private nonprofit sector. They believed, with considerable evidentiary support, that these agencies were unresponsive to the poor and were part of the problem rather than part of the solution. Therefore, Title II of the Act authorized the creation of local quasigovernmental entities called community action (CAP) agencies, which would have the responsibility for running or coordinating the various individual programs contemplated by the Act. These CAP agencies would be governed by a majority of people from the community, i.e., not under the thumb of the mayor or county executive. The catch phrase for governance was "maximum feasible participation of the poor."

Although Community Action was never massively funded, receiving only about $325 million at its zenith, Title II's CAP agencies quickly became a lightning rod for criticism. This was because, given their independence from local government, CAP agencies became organizing points for advocacy directed at local government. Mayors were infuriated to find buses, chartered with federal funds, filled with demonstrators coming to city hall with lists of nonnegotiable demands. Led by Mayor Richard Daley of Chicago, the mayors played their own, far more potent political cards. Just three years after the original enactment of the Economic Opportunity Act, the mayors got Congress to enact the Green Amendment, which transferred effective control of the CAP agencies to local government.

* * *

What about Model Cities? Policymakers whose entry point into urban antipoverty work was in housing and physical community development had from the beginning been skeptical of the War on Poverty and the CAP agencies; or at least they had felt the Office of Economic Opportunity (OEO) approach was not sufficient, even if constructive, to fight poverty. In the wake of the Watts riot in 1965, the Newark and Detroit riots in 1966, and dozens of serious disturbances in other cities, they felt a renewed urgency to propose a new initiative.

Officials at the newly minted Department of Housing and Urban Development and their allies believed instead that it was necessary to tie services, even innovative services, and job training to housing and community development activities. They proposed a Demonstration Cities Act (which became Model Cities when it was pointed out that the initial title had a most unfortunate connotation at a time of widespread urban unrest) that would in effect create a more sophisticated multidisciplinary antipoverty endeavor in a limited number of cities. At the subcity level, but tied to local government, an entity would be created with the jurisdiction to spearhead initiatives that would cut across and include low- and moderate-income housing, community facilities, health, education, and various social services. At the federal level, metropolitan "expediters" would pull together funds from all relevant federal agencies to pour into the multipronged neighborhood initiative contemplated by the proposal.

The idea was promising, but it never happened as envisioned. Model Cities was enacted, but it was underfunded and lacked the capacity to draw in additional funds from other agencies and programs. Members of Congress insisted on the inclusion of more cities than originally contemplated, thereby diluting the money available for each city. The war in Vietnam even more severely reduced the availability of funds. The metropolitan expediters were never created. By 1973, having spent most of its infancy under the less than benign tutelage of the Nixon Administration, Model Cities was pronounced a failure and mutated into the community development revenue sharing program, which effectively gave big-city mayors a small free grab bag for various "community development" initiatives that often fell far afield from low-income neighborhoods.

Community action and Model Cities are the only negative items that surface if one dissects the criticism of the Great Society. Of course, President Bush painted with a much broader brush in his 1991 speech, arguing that "programs intended to help people out of poverty invited dependency." It would appear that what he had in mind was welfare. AFDC, the federal welfare program, was, of course, not a Great Society initiative, but rather a part of the original Social Security Act--a creation of the New Deal. In fact, the massive expansion of cash and in-kind assistance programs (although not of AFDC itself) occurred during the Nixon Administration, not the Johnson Administration.

In fact, Lyndon Johnson proposed only one even modestly significant piece of legislation relating to welfare. The heart of it was to require states to pay recipients the full amount of the standard of need as the state itself had defined it--not a radical idea. Whatever the possibilities of enactment would have been with the massive Democratic majorities of the 89th Congress in 1965 and 1966, this idea was offered to the slimmed-down 90th Congress, which was trying to come up with funds to fight a war and was distinctly less friendly to the poor than its immediate predecessor. Johnson's initiative was transformed by an unfriendly Congress into a two year freeze on federal funding for AFDC and the first-ever compulsory work requirement for AFDC recipients. History reveals, therefore, that the Johnson Administration was not the administration, if ever there was one, that promoted dependency.

The Great Society did, in fact, reflect a strategy--an opportunity strategy with a little advocacy thrown in for spice (controversial spice, as it turned out). Head Start, federal aid for the education of poor children, Upward Bound, job training, and a number of other programs were all geared to prepare people to participate fully in the economy. The civil rights laws were enacted to break down barriers of discrimination, and legal services for the poor were designed to create access for the poor to protection by way of the courts. Access to health care for the poor was geared towards creating a healthy work force.

Because it was an opportunity strategy, the Great Society guaranteed no outcomes, whether in the form of a guaranteed job or a guaranteed income. When Senators Joseph Clark and Robert Kennedy took the Senate floor to propose an $850 million initiative to create jobs for young people who could not find them on their own, the Johnson Administration opposed them and they were defeated. The economic theory of the Great Society was that macroeconomic policy would create the jobs; the purposes of government programs and policies were to get people ready for the jobs and to break down barriers of discrimination.

The Great Society strategy was a reasonable approach in the context of a "hot" economy in which overall unemployment was low, and it was reasonably successful in what it set out to do, at least as reflected in the continuing political support for its programs. The Great Society created a structure of poverty prevention, human resource development, and antidiscrimination laws that has survived, albeit underfunded and underenforced. On the other hand, the Great Society lacked any initiative to create employment or credential-building work experience for people unable to find employment on their own, a gap that is even more noticeable in an economy featuring far higher unemployment across the board.

* * *

The Seventies and Eighties

The 1973 Arab oil shock was the first in a series of blows to the American economy that have kept it in a tailspin from which it has never recovered. Since that time unemployment has been consistently higher than it was throughout the 1960s, and an associated weakening in the labor market at the low-wage end of the spectrum has left many more people unable to earn enough to stay out of poverty even though they do have employment. High-paying manufacturing jobs disappeared offshore and were replaced, if at all, by lower-paying service jobs. A huge number of people entered the labor market during the 1970s: women, babyboomers, and wave after wave of new immigrants, both legal and illegal, sought work. It is a testament to the residual strength of the economy at the time that it performed as well as it did in absorbing new labor market entrants.

* * *

The 1970s did not lack for antipoverty policy. In the early Nixon years much was accomplished by a Democratic Congress responding to popular liberal impulses continuing from the 1960s and relating to a President who was more interested in foreign affairs. The Congress indexed Social Security, created Supplemental Security Income, vastly expanded food stamps, increased Medicare and Medicaid funding, passed the Basic Educational Opportunity Grant program (now Pell Grants), enacted the Comprehensive Employment and Training Act of 1973 (CETA), and created the Section 8 housing program. The Earned Income Tax Credit came onto the statute books during the Ford Administration, and low-income energy assistance was added during the Carter Administration.

Apart from Pell Grants, CETA, and a few smaller items, the initiatives of the 1970s did not pursue the opportunity strategy of the 1960s, but rather provided income support, whether in cash or in kind. These initiatives constituted extremely important public policy in setting stronger income floors for the elderly and the disabled and a basic nutritional guarantee for all of the poor, but they were not focused directly on either the people of the inner city or the nonelderly, nondisabled poor who are unable to find work, i.e., the welfare population. The latter, whose benefits were not indexed for inflation (except for food stamps) commenced suffering losses in real income that have continued for twenty years, and the former were left to rely disproportionately on welfare in the absence of jobs and were otherwise ignored. In an economy that has been weak for two decades, with concomitant results in the loss of "good" jobs and wages of young workers, the results for inner cities have been disastrous.

The situation of the poor has been aggravated in the 1980s by public policies that have widened the gap between rich and poor. Specific policies at both the rich end and the poor end of the spectrum have had negative effects, dividing even more unevenly a pie that was already shrinking for macroeconomic reasons.

For example, changes in tax policy in 1981 enabled the wealthy to keep a far larger portion of their income. The result was that the after-tax share of the top one percent of earners in the national income grew from seven to twelve percent between 1977 and 1989, the share of the top five percent grew from eighteen percent to twenty-four percent, the share of the top twenty percent grew from forty-four percent to forty-nine percent, and the share of the bottom fifth dropped from six percent to four percent. The middle three quintiles lost ground as well, so that only the top twenty percent of American earners had an increased share in the pie by the end of the decade.

* * *

For the first two and a half postwar decades, income inequality did not play as substantial a role in our political discourse as it does today. That period was marked by a decrease in poverty, across-the-board income growth, and a decrease in income inequality. The Reagan and Bush Administrations, however, succeeded in changing the distribution of income in the United States to favor the wealthy far more substantially.

Changes in welfare policy at the same time also hurt the poor. Only some of these changes affected the income shares just discussed, because only cash benefits are included in income for purposes of measuring poverty and income shares. Cuts in in-kind assistance, including food stamps, Medicaid, and housing assistance, injured the poor as well, but they are not included in the income figures.

The picture on the benefits end of the spectrum is even worse when examined through a twenty year lens. Aid to Families with Dependent Children, the major cash program for nonelderly families, is not indexed to inflation. Thus, inflation reduced the real dollar value of the average AFDC grant for a family of three by forty-one percent between 1972 and 1991. When food stamps, which are indexed, are taken into account, benefits eroded by twenty-seven percent.

Where Are We Now?

Thus, the poor have taken it on the chin since 1973. The job market has very substantially weakened, and income maintenance programs have deteriorated. Let us now turn to the present state of antipoverty policy.

Our current antipoverty policy is essentially maintenance-oriented. Yet we blame the recipients for continuing to depend on welfare when that is all we offer in an economy that is not producing enough jobs at decent wages, or, indeed, enough jobs at all. We speak the rhetoric of self-sufficiency, but we arrange things so it is fundamentally impossible for a large number of people to achieve such sufficiency.

We have policies and programs to prevent poverty, and especially to prevent it from being passed on from generation to generation, but these policies and programs are underfunded and inadequate in scope. Each year significant numbers of young people come to the age at which they should either go to college or enter the labor market, and they do neither. Many lack the skills to perform a job even if they could find one, although, symbiotically, many have not bothered to acquire the skills because they see no possibility of getting a job even if they could perform the work.

From prenatal care to early childhood development to elementary and secondary education to job training to a variety of family support services that might make a difference, we are suffering huge gaps in the quantity and quality of needed offerings. We are, consequently, not producing young adults who are ready and able to perform on the job (even as we fail to produce enough jobs to employ them if large numbers should suddenly be prepared for jobs). From housing to community economic development to law enforcement, we have similar gaps. We are, consequently, producing neither any increase in economic opportunity close to home nor community environments that can nurture people with an ethos of success that accords with the values of the larger society.

The consequence of all of this is that the major antipoverty program we have for adults is called welfare: cash and food stamp assistance that keeps people dependent, but at least enables them to survive--barely. It is no wonder, perhaps, that ordinary citizens and the people they elect to represent them see only the dependency and react by blaming the recipients. The fact, however, is that the enemy is not the poor. As Walt Kelly's comic strip character Pogo used to say, "We has met the enemy and it is us."

Notes and Questions

1. *Selective Survival.* Several of the 1960s innovations survived at least another two and a half decades. Head Start and Upward Bound achieved relative popularity. VISTA was phased out, but the Clinton administration attempted a partial resurrection of a national service program. The Legal Services Corporation survived persistent attacks throughout the 1980s, only to suffer an outright assault in the mid-1990s. Why do you think these initiatives of the 1960s have survived, while others disappeared?

2. *Maximum Feasible Participation.* Most current government anti-poverty programs eschew any focus on community action and development. What happened to the ideal of "maximum feasible participation of the poor" in solving their own community problems?

3. *Underfunding.* Many anti-poverty initiatives at various times have suffered from severe underfunding. As a result, many strategies for engaging problems related to poverty never get tried, even on an experimental basis. Does this persistent lack in funding limit our knowledge base about poverty?

3. The 1990s: War on Welfare

As we have seen, welfare has never been popular, and its recipients have been the persistent targets of legislative efforts attempting to control recipient behavior and to reduce costs. Welfare's unpopularity hit one of its high points during the 1990s. Its unpopularity in the 1990s grew out of the bipartisan consensus of the late 1980s that welfare had failed.

In 1988 Congress passed the Family Support Act with great fanfare about its balance between providing support and requiring responsibility. The Family Support Act marked the emergence of a bipartisan consensus among federal legislators who agreed that welfare programs failed to move recipients from welfare to work. So the Family Support Act created the Job Opportunities and Basic Skills (JOBS) program. JOBS required recipients to find work or be subject to sanctions, and it required states to move designated percentages of recipients off welfare into work. Congress provided support for recipients' work efforts by funding education and training, child care, transportation, and health care. But neither Congress nor the states allocated adequate funds to support the work requirements. In 1992, for example, only 6% of adult AFDC recipients nationwide participated in more than twenty hours of work activities per week, largely because states did not allocate the matching funds required to make them eligible for federal dollars.

As both the poverty rate and the numbers of people living below the poverty line climbed during the early 1990s, frustration with the welfare system increased. In his first presidential campaign, Bill Clinton promised to "end welfare as we know it." Once elected,

President Clinton first focused his major policy initiative on his proposal to reform health care, which dominated national debate until it died in September, 1994. During the 1994 elections, Republicans gained control over Congress. Congress then passed two versions of the Personal Responsibility Act, but President Clinton vetoed them in late 1995 and early 1996. Then, after months of a stalemate, President Clinton reached an agreement with Congress on welfare reform in the Summer of 1996, during his second presidential campaign. President Clinton signed the Personal Responsibility and Work Opportunity Reconciliation Act (PRA) in August, 1996.

In the Act, Congress abolished Aid to Families with Dependent Children and replaced it with the Temporary Assistance for Needy Families (TANF) block grant program. TANF eliminated the federal entitlement to welfare benefits. TANF does not require states to provide any cash assistance to families, but instead gives states broad discretion to use the federal block grant funds in any manner reasonably calculated to serve the purposes of the statute. TANF's purposes are to provide assistance to needy families, to end the dependence of needy families on welfare benefits by promoting work and marriage, to prevent and reduce the incidence of out-of-wedlock pregnancies, and to encourage the formation and maintenance of two-parent families. TANF also caps the amount of money the federal government will spend for welfare benefits.

Moreover, TANF imposes various restrictions on the states, including limiting benefits to families with children, prohibiting states from providing benefits to families for more than 60 months, prohibiting benefits to unmarried teenage parents unless they complete their high school education and live with a supervising adult, and prohibiting benefits to most immigrants. TANF also requires recipients to engage in "community service employment" after receiving benefits for 2 months (unless the state opts out), and to engage in work as soon as the state deems them ready but no later than after receiving 24 months of benefits. Finally, TANF requires states to maintain some effort toward welfare assistance; specifically states must contribute 80% of their 1994 spending level toward welfare benefits, except states which meet mandatory work participation rates must only contribute 75% of their 1994 spending level.

We will explore various TANF provisions throughout this text, and in greater detail in Chapter 8 on Welfare Reform. For now, consider how TANF compares to the federal welfare programs as initially adopted in the 1930s and expanded in the 1960s.

CHAPTER 3: COMPETING POLICY PERSPECTIVES

Discussions about welfare currently revolve around questions of public policy. In particular, what principles should guide welfare policy? And what procedures and programs will best serve those principles? As with most issues about policy, the discourse tends to feature debates between political commentators who favor particular values. Taken together, these perspectives reflect the ambiguity felt by most Americans who are torn between their belief in self-sufficiency and their tendency toward compassion.

A. FROM THE RIGHT

During the 1980s, voices speaking against welfare emerged. One of the most persistent commentators has been Charles Murray. When he initially called for dismantling welfare in the mid-1980s, his position was viewed as fairly radical. Most commentators were calling instead for merely reforming welfare to better encourage work. Within a decade, Murray's call to fully dismantle welfare had become mainstream, with other commentators and politicians in the mid-1990s agreeing that welfare caused more problems than it solved.

Charles Murray
LOSING GROUND: AMERICAN SOCIAL POLICY 1950-1980 (1984)

If social policy may be construed . . . as transfers from the haves to the have-nots, the proper first question is, "What is the justification for any transfers at all?" Why should one person give *anything* to a stranger whose only claim to his help is a common citizenship?

Suppose that I am not opposed to the notion of government transfers, but neither do I think that equality of outcome is always a good in itself. I attach considerable value to the principle that people get what they deserve. In other words, "I" am a fairly typical citizen with a middle-of-the-road, pragmatic political philosophy.

I am asked to consider the case of a man who has worked steadily for many years and, in his fifties, is thrown out of his job because the factory closes. Why should I transfer money to him--provide him with unemployment checks and, perhaps, permanent welfare support? The answer is not difficult. I may rationalize it any number of ways, but at bottom I consent to transfer money to him because I want to. The worker has plugged along as best he could, contributed his bit to the community, and now faces personal disaster. He is one of my fellows in a very meaningful way--"There but for the grace of God. . . ."--and I am happy to see a portion of my income used to help him out. (I would not be happy to see so much of my income transferred that I am unable to meet my obligations to myself and my family, however.)

A second man, healthy and in the prime of life, refuses to work. I offer him a job, and he still refuses to work. I am called upon to answer the question again: Why should I transfer money to him? Why should I not let him starve, considering it a form of suicide?

It is a question to ponder without escape hatches. I may not assume that the man can be made to change his ways with the right therapeutic intervention. I may not assume that he has some mental or environmental handicap that relieves him of responsibility. He is a man of ordinary capacities who wishes to live off my work rather than work for himself. Why should I consent?

Suppose that I decide not to let him starve in the streets, for reasons having to do with the sanctity of life (I would prevent a suicide as well). The decision does not take me very far in setting up an ideal policy. At once, I run into choices when I compare his situation (we will call him the drone) with that of the laid-off worker.

Suppose that I have only enough resources either (a) to keep both alive at a bare subsistence level or (b) to support the laid-off worker at a decent standard of living and the drone at a near-starvation level. What would be the just policy? Would it be right, would it be fair, to make the worker live more miserably so that I might be more generous to the drone?

We may put the question more provocatively: Suppose that scarce resources were not a problem--that we could afford to support both at a decent standard of living. Should we do so? Is it morally appropriate to give the same level of support to the two men? Would it be right to offer the same respect to the two men? The same discretionary choice in how to use the help that was provided?

These are not rhetorical questions nor are they questions about expedient policy. They ask about the justice and humanity of the alternatives. I submit that it is not humane to the laid-off worker to treat him the same as the drone. It is not just to accord the drone the respect that the laid-off worker has earned.

The point is that, in principle, most of us provide some kinds of assistance gladly, for intuitively obvious reasons. We provide other kinds of assistance for reasons that, when it comes down to it, are extremely hard to defend on either moral or practical grounds. An ethically ideal social policy--an *intuitively* satisfying one--would discriminate among recipients. It would attach a pat on the back to some transfers and give others begrudgingly.

We have yet to tackle the question of whether the point has anything to do with recipients in the workaday world. Who is to say that the drone has no justification for refusing to work (he was trained as a cook and we offer him a job sweeping floors)? Who is to say whether the laid-off worker is blameless for the loss of his job (his sloppy workmanship contributed to the factory's loss of business to the Japanese)? Who is to say that the income of the taxpaying donor is commensurate with his value to society--that he "deserves" his income any more than the drone deserves the gift of a part of it? But such questions define the operational barriers to establishing a social policy that discriminates among recipients according to their deserts. They do not touch on the legitimacy of the principle.

Robbing Peter to Pay Paul: Transfers from Poor to Poor

When we think of transfers, we usually think in terms of economic transfers from richer to poorer. In reality, social policy can obligate one citizen to turn over a variety of "goods" as a donation on behalf of some other person; access to parking spaces reserved for the handicapped is a simple example.

Sometimes these noneconomic transfers, like the economic ones, are arranged so that the better-off give up something to the worse-off, and the argument about whether the transfer is appropriate follows the lines of the issues I have just raised. But in a surprising number of instances the transfers are mandated by the better-off, while the price must be paid by donors who are just as poor as the recipient.

* * *

When job-training programs were set up to function at the level of the least competent, it was the most competent trainees who had to sacrifice their opportunities to reach their potentials. When social policy reinforced the ethic that certain jobs are too demeaning to ask people to do, it was those who preferred such jobs to welfare whose basis for self-respect was stripped from them.

More generally, social policy after the mid-1960s demanded an extraordinary range of transfers from the most capable poor to the least capable, from the most law-abiding to the least law-abiding, and from the most responsible to the least responsible. In return, we gave little to these most deserving persons except easier access to welfare for themselves--the one thing they found hardest to put to "good use."

* * *

The Net Happiness Challenge

If the first questions of social policy ask why we approve of transfers at all, the next questions ask how we know whether our expectations are being justified. How, in an ideal world, would we measure "success" in assessing a transfer?

The social scientists who measure the effects of transfers look for success at two levels and of necessity ignore a third. The first level is, "Did the transfer reach the people it was intended to reach in the intended form?" (Do Food Stamps reach people who need extra food money?) The second level is, "Did the transfer have the intended direct effect on the behavior or condition of the recipients?" (Do Food Stamps improve nutrition?) The third, unattainable level is, "Did the transfer, in the long run, add to net happiness in the world?"

We may presume that better housing, nutrition, and medical care contribute to less misery and more happiness; so also do good parents, a loving spouse, safe streets, personal freedom, and the respect of one's neighbors. We know how to measure some of these aspects of the quality of life; others we cannot measure at all; and, most certainly, we are unable to compare their relative worth or to add up a net total. We have no "misery" or "happiness" indexes worthy of the name. But the concept of reducing misery and increasing happiness is indispensable to deciding whether a social policy is working or failing.

With that in mind, let us consider yet another hypothetical example. In this case, I am deciding upon my stance in support or opposition of a policy that automatically provides an adequate living allowance for all single women with children. I am informed that one consequence of this policy is that large numbers of the children get better nutrition and medical care than they would otherwise obtain. Using this known fact and no others, I support the program.

Now, let us assume two more known facts, that the program induces births by women who otherwise would have had fewer children (or had them under different circumstances), and that child abuse and neglect among these children runs at twice the national average. Does this alter my judgment about whether the allowance is a net good--that it is better to have it than not have it? I must now balance the better health of some children against the pain suffered by others who would not have suffered the pain if the program had not existed. I decide--although I wish I could avoid the question altogether--that, all in all, I still support the program.

What if the incidence of abuse and neglect is three times as high? Five times? Ten times? A hundred times?

The crossover point will be different for different people. But a crossover will occur. At some point, I will say that the benefits of better nutrition and medical care are outweighed by the suffering of the abused and neglected children. What then is the humane policy? Once more I must avoid false escape hatches. I may continue to search for a strategy that does not have the overbalancing side-effects. But what is my position toward the existing program in the meantime?

* * *

The first conclusion is that transfers are inherently treacherous. They can be useful; they can be needed; they can be justified. But we should approach them as a good physician uses a dangerous drug--not at all if possible, and no more than absolutely necessary otherwise.

The second conclusion is that, as a general rule, compulsory transfers from one poor person to another are uncomfortably like robbery. When we require money transfers from the obviously rich to the obviously poor, we at least have some room for error. Mistaken policies may offend our sense of right and wrong, but no great harm has been done to the donor. The same is not true of the noneconomic transfers from poor to poor. We have no margin for error at all. If we are even a little bit wrong about the consequences of the transfer, we are likely to do great injustices to people who least deserve to bear the burden.

And that, finally, is what makes the question of social policy not one of polite philosophical dispute but one of urgent importance. . . . [These] examples . . . are not really hypothetical. . . . It is impossible to examine the statistics on a topic such as single teenaged mothers without admitting that we are witnessing a tragedy. *If* it had been inevitable, *if* there had been nothing we could have done to avoid it, then we could retain the same policies, trying to do more of the same and hoping for improvement. But once we must entertain the possibility that we are bringing it on ourselves, as I am arguing that both logic and evidence compel us to do, then it is time to reconsider a social policy that salves our consciences ("Look how compassionate I am") at the expense of those whom we wished to help.

* * *

Laws of Social Programs

> **#1. The Law of Imperfect Selection.** Any objective rule that defines eligibility for a social transfer program will irrationally exclude some persons.

It can always be demonstrated that some persons who are excluded from the Food Stamps program are in greater need than some persons who receive Food Stamps. It can always be demonstrated that someone who is technically ineligible for Medicaid really "ought" to be receiving it, given the intent of the legislation.

These inequities, which are observed everywhere, are not the fault of inept writers of eligibility rules, but an inescapable outcome of the task of rule-writing. Eligibility rules must convert the concept of "true need" into objectified elements. The rules constructed from these bits and pieces are necessarily subject to what Herbert Costner has called "epistemic error"--the inevitable gap between quantified measures and the concept they are intended to capture. We have no way of defining "truly needy" precisely--not those who truly need to stop smoking, nor those truly in need of college scholarships or subsidized loans or disability insurance. Any criterion we specify will inevitably include a range of people, some of whom are unequivocally the people we intended to help, others of whom are less so, and still others of whom meet the letter of the eligibility requirement but are much less needy than some persons who do not.

Social welfare policy in earlier times tended to deal with this problem by erring in the direction of exclusion--better to deny help to some truly needy persons than to let a few slackers slip through.

Such attitudes depended, however, on the assumption that the greater good was being served. Moral precepts had to be upheld. Whenever a person was inappropriately given help, it was bad for the recipient (undermining his character) and a bad example to the community at large.

When that assumption is weakened or dispensed with altogether, it follows naturally that the Law of Imperfect Selection leads to programs with constantly broadening target populations. If persons are not to blame for their plight, no real harm is done by giving them help they do not fully "need." No moral cost is incurred by permitting some undeserving into the program. A moral cost is incurred by excluding a deserving person. No one has a scalpel sharp enough to excise only the undeserving. Therefore it is not just a matter of political expedience to add a new layer to the eligible population rather than to subtract one (though that is often a factor in the actual decision-making process). It is also the morally correct thing to do, given the premises of the argument.

> **#2. The Law of Unintended Rewards.** Any social transfer increases the net value of being in the condition that prompted the transfer.

A deficiency is observed--too little money, too little food, too little academic achievement--and a social transfer program tries to fill the gap--with a welfare payment, Food Stamps, a compensatory education program. An unwanted behavior is observed--drug addiction, crime, unemployability--and the program tries to change that behavior to some other, better behavior--through a drug rehabilitation program, psychotherapy, vocational training. In each case, the program, however unintentionally, *must* be constructed in such a way that it increases the net value of being in the condition that it seeks to change--either by increasing the rewards or by reducing the penalties.

For some people in some circumstances, it is absurd to think in terms of "net value," because they so clearly have no choice at all about the fix they are in or because the net value is still less desirable than virtually any alternative. Paraplegics receiving Medicaid cannot easily be seen as "rewarded" for becoming paraplegics by the existence of free medical care. Poor children in Head Start cannot be seen as rewarded for being poor. Persons who are in the unwanted condition *completely involuntarily* are not affected by the existence of the reward.

But the number of such pure examples is very small. Let us return to the case of the middle-aged worker who loses his job, wants desperately to work, but can find nothing. He receives Unemployment Insurance, hating every penny of it. He would seem to be "completely involuntarily" in his situation and his search for a job unaffected by the existence of Unemployment Insurance. In fact, however, his behavior (unless he is peculiarly irrational) *is* affected by the existence of the Unemployment Insurance. For example, the cushion provided by Unemployment Insurance may lead him to refuse to take a job that requires him to move to another town, whereas he would take the job and uproot his home if he were more desperate. Most people (including me) are glad that his behavior is so affected, that he does not have to leave the home and friends of a lifetime, that he can wait for a job opening nearby. But he is not "completely involuntarily" unemployed in such a case, and the reason he is not is that the Unemployment Insurance has made the condition of unemployment more tolerable.

* * *

Let us consider the implications in terms of the archetypical social program for helping the chronic unemployed escape their condition, the job-training program.

Imagine that a program is begun that has the most basic and benign inducement of all, the chance to learn a marketable skill. It is open to everybody. By opening it to all, we have circumvented (for the time being) the Law of Unintended Rewards. All may obtain the training, no matter what their job history, so no unintended reward is being given for the condition of chronic unemployment.

On assessing the results, we observe that the ones who enter the program, stick with it, and learn a skill include very few of the hardcore unemployed whom we most wanted to help. The typical "success" stories from our training program are persons with a history of steady employment who wanted to upgrade their earning power. This is admirable. But what about the hardcore unemployed? A considerable number entered the program, but almost all of them dropped out or failed to get jobs once they left. Only a small proportion used the training opportunity as we had hoped. The problem of the hardcore unemployed remains essentially unchanged.

We may continue to circumvent the Law of Unintended Rewards. All we need do is continue the job-training program unchanged. It will still be there, still available to all who want to enroll, but we will do nothing to entice participation. Our theory (should we adopt this stance) is that, as time goes on, we will continue to help at least a few of the hardcore unemployed who are in effect skimmed from the top of the pool. We may even hope that the number skimmed from the top will be larger than the number who enter the pool, so that, given enough time, the population of hardcore unemployed will diminish. But this strategy is a gradualist one and relies on the assumption that other conditions in society are not creating more hardcore unemployed than the program is skimming off.

The alternative is to do something to get more of the hardcore unemployed into the program, and to improve the content so that more of them profit from the training. And once this alternative is taken, the program planner is caught in the trap of unintended rewards. Because we cannot "draft" people into the program or otherwise coerce their participation, our only alternative is to make it more attractive by changing the rules a bit.

Suppose, for example, we find that the reason many did not profit from the earlier program was that they got fired from (or quit) their new jobs within a few days of getting them, and that the reason they did so had to do with the job-readiness problem. The ex-trainee was late getting to work, the boss complained, the ex-trainee reacted angrily and was fired. We observe this to be a common pattern. We know the problem is not that the ex-trainee is lazy or unmotivated, but that he has never been socialized into the discipline of the workplace. He needs more time, more help, more patience than other workers until he develops the needed work habits. Suppose that we try to compensate--for example, by placing our trainees with employers who are being subsidized to hire such persons. The employer accepts lower productivity and other problems in return for a payment to do so (such plans have been tried frequently, with mixed results). Given identical work at identical pay, the ex-trainee is being rewarded for his "credential" of hardcore unemployment. He can get away with behavior that an ordinary worker cannot get away with.

May we still assume that the program is making progress in

preparing its trainees for the real-world marketplace? Will the hardcore unemployed modify their unreliable behavior? What will be the effect on morale and self-esteem among those trainees who were succeeding in the program before the change of rules? It is tempting to conclude that the program has already ceased to function effectively for anyone anymore, that the change in rules has done more harm than good. But my proposition is for the moment a more restricted one: The reward for unproductive behavior (both past and present) now exists.

What of the case of a drug addict who is chronically unemployed because (let us assume) of the addiction? It might seem that the unintended reward in such a case is innocuous; it consists of measures to relieve the addict of his addiction, measures for which the nonaddict will have no need or use. If we were dealing with an involuntary disability--our paraplegic again--the argument would be valid. But in the case of drug addiction (or any other behavior that has its rewards), a painless cure generally increases the attractiveness of the behavior.

* * *

The program that seeks to change behavior must offer an inducement that unavoidably either adds to the attraction of, or reduces the penalties of engaging in, the behavior in question. The best-known example in real life is the thirty-and-a-third rule for AFDC recipients. It becomes more advantageous financially to hold a job than not to hold a job (the intended inducement for AFDC recipients to work), but it also becomes more advantageous to be on AFDC (the unintended reward to nonrecipients).

We are now ready to tackle the question of when a social program can reasonably be expected to accomplish net good and when it can reasonably be expected to produce net harm. Again let us think in terms of a continuum. All social programs, I have argued, provide an unintended reward for being in the condition that the program is trying to change or make more tolerable. But some of these unintended rewards are so small that they are of little practical importance. Why then can we not simply bring a bit of care to the design of such programs, making sure that the unintended reward is *always* small? The reason we are not free to do so lies in the third law of social programs:

#3. The Law of Net Harm. The less likely it is that the unwanted behavior will change voluntarily, the more likely it is that a program to induce change will cause net harm.

A social program that seeks to change behavior must do two things. It must induce participation by the persons who are to benefit, as described under the Law of Unintended Rewards. Then it must actually produce the desired change in behavior. It must succeed, and success depends crucially on one factor above all others: the price that the participant is willing to pay.

The more that the individual is willing to accept whatever needs to be done in order to achieve the desired state of affairs, the broader the discretion of the program designers. Thus, expensive health resorts can withhold food from their guests, hospitals can demand that their interns work inhuman schedules, and elite volunteer units in the armed forces can ask their trainees to take risks in training exercises that seem (to the rest of us) suicidal. Such programs need offer no inducement at all except the "thing in itself" that is the *raison d'être* of the program--a shapelier body, a career as a physician, membership in the elite military unit. Similarly, the drug addict who is prepared to sign over to a program a great of deal of control over his own behavior may very well be successful--witness the sometimes impressive success rates of private treatment clinics.

The smaller the price that the participant is willing to pay, the greater the constraints on program design. It makes no difference to an official running a training program for the hardcore unemployed that (for example) the Marine Corps can instill exemplary work habits in recruits who come to the Corps no more "job-ready" than the recruits to the job-training program. If the training program tried for one day to use the techniques that the Marine Corps uses, it would lose its participants. Boot camp was not part of the bargain the job trainees struck with the government when they signed on. Instead, the training program must not only induce persons to join the program (which may be fairly easy). It must also induce them to stay in the program, induce them to cooperate with its curriculum, and induce them, finally, to adopt major changes in outlook, habits, and assumptions. The program content must be almost entirely carrot.

There is nothing morally reprehensible in approaches that are constrained to use only positive inducements. The objections are practical.

First, it is guaranteed that success rates will be very low. The technology of changing human behavior depends heavily on the use of negative reinforcement in conjunction with positive reinforcement. The more deeply engrained the behavior to be changed and the more attractions it holds for the person whose behavior is involved, the more important it is that the program have both a full tool kit available to it *and* the participant's willingness to go along with whatever is required. The Marine Corps has both these assets. Social programs to deal with the hardcore unemployed, teenaged mothers, delinquents, and addicts seldom do.

Second, as inducements become large--as they must, if the program is dealing with the most intractable problems--the more attractive they become to people who were not in need of help in the first place. We do not yet know how large they must finally become. We do know from experience, however, that quite generous experimental programs have provided extensive counseling, training, guaranteed jobs, and other supports--and failed. We can only guess at what would be enough--perhaps a matter of years of full-time residential training, followed by guaranteed jobs at double or triple the minimum wage; we do not know. Whatever they are, however, consider their effects on the people not in the program. At this point, it appears that any program that would succeed in helping large numbers of the hardcore unemployed will make hardcore unemployment a highly desirable state to be in.

The conditions that combine to produce net harm are somewhat different in the theoretical and the practical cases, but they come to the same thing. Theoretically, any program that mounts an intervention with sufficient rewards to sustain participation and an effective result will generate so much of the unwanted behavior (in order to become eligible for the program's rewards) that the net effect will be to increase the incidence of the unwanted behavior. In practice, the programs that deal with the most intractable behavior problems have included a package of rewards large enough to induce participation, but not large enough to produce the desired result.

My conclusion is that social programs in a democratic society tend to produce net harm in dealing with the most difficult problems.

They will inherently tend to have enough of an inducement to produce bad behavior and not enough of a solution to stimulate good behavior; and the more difficult the problem, the more likely it is that this relationship will prevail. The lesson is not that we can do no good at all, but that we must pick our shots.

* * *

Notes and Questions

1. *Murray's Drone.* Mr. Murray sets up a hypothetical comparison between a "drone" and a laid-off worker. Note that Murray assumes the drone has an offer of a job, but refuses to work. How important is this assumption of job availability to Murray's logic, and to his persuasiveness? Is this hypothetical drone typical among the poor; are jobs typically available to poor people? Does it matter whether the available job will provide income sufficient for the drone to meet his subsistence needs, or those of his family?

2. *Deserving versus Undeserving.* Murray pits the drone against the laid-off worker. Regardless whether society has scarce or full resources, Murray suggests that the laid-off worker deserves a higher level of support than the drone. What values are served by a welfare policy that "discriminates among recipients according to their deserts?" What values are neglected by such a policy?

3. *Welfare As Drug.* Murray characterizes welfare as "inherently treacherous." He posits that it should be used like a dangerous drug, preferably not at all or at least no more than absolutely necessary. Under what circumstances is welfare absolutely necessary?

How persuasive is Murray's use of the analogy between a dangerous drug and welfare? For example, if a person would die without a dangerous drug, he or she typically elects to take the drug. Perhaps if a person would die without welfare, he or she typically would elect to take the assistance. Are the supposed dangers of the drug and of welfare comparable? Who is harmed by the side effects?

4. *Murray's Laws.* Murray sets out 3 "laws" of social programs. He first suggests that selection will be imperfect, that welfare cannot be perfectly tailored to achieve *all* its desired results, and *only* its desired results. Second, he suggests that welfare rewards and encourages "deficiency" and "unwanted behavior." Third, he concludes that welfare will cause net harm. In short, Murray suggests

that doing nothing about poverty is better than doing something, because doing something causes so many other problems. Has he conducted a full cost-benefit analysis of doing nothing? What are the individual and societal costs of people who have absolutely nothing to lose?

Are the imperfections decried by Murray limited to welfare? Or are other social policies subject to similar complaints? For example, do family laws *always* select the best parent for custodian? Do they sometimes encourage unwanted behavior, like seeking custody in the hope of achieving a lower child support payment? Or, to explore another context, are environmental laws that regulate the competing interests between economic development and conservation subject to similar criticism? Can you think of laws that are not only narrowly tailored but perfectly tailored to achieve their underlying goals? Are Murray's arguments therefore under-inclusive themselves? In other words, taken to his logical extreme, isn't Murray arguing for dismantling all law because of its imperfections, rather than only welfare law?

Lawrence M. Mead
The New Politics of Poverty: The Nonworking Poor in America (1992)

The problem of entrenched poverty in the United States has caused a sea change in American politics. Since poverty first became a leading issue thirty years ago, the questions that most bitterly divide Americans have shifted from how to secure working Americans more of the good things of life to how to cope with the problems of seriously poor and dependent Americans, most of whom do not work. Once, the most divisive demands on government were inspired by the working class; they now arise from the nonworking underclass. The New Deal and union rights used to be fighting words. Today, controversies over the homeless, welfare, and "law and order" are more bitter.

Some say the nation has become more conservative. The poor do receive less attention from government today than they did fifteen or twenty years ago. The Reagan administration cut some social programs, and the "kinder, gentler" Bush administration has declined to initiate much of any new antipoverty policy. The idea of throwing money at social problems is decidedly passé. But the nation has not moved very far to the right in the traditional sense. For all Ronald Reagan's persuasion, big government is still popular with the voters, and overall social spending--for the poor and middle class alike--went right on growing in the Reagan years, albeit more slowly than before.

The very meanings of right and left have changed. The public wants government used to combat the disorders of the ghetto. Republicans have made that appeal their own, and ridden it to the White House, while many Democrats have resisted. That has altered what the parties stand for. Today conservatism still means smaller government, but it also means using government more vigorously against crime, welfarism, and the failure of ghetto children to learn in school. Liberalism still means bigger government, but it also connotes resistance to enforcement and a greater tolerance for disorder, dependency, and ethnic pluralism. The two sides now differ more sharply on questions of social authority than they do about the scale of government.

Up through the mid-1960s, an era that I call progressive, the leading question was how to help ordinary Americans obtain advancement. Liberals favored greater government intervention in the private economy, while conservatives favored less. The underlying dispute was over economic class--whether to accept the unequal rewards meted out by the marketplace or to try to equalize them by raising wages and giving public benefits to workers and their families. In the new era, which is characterized by what I call dependency politics, the leading issue is how to respond to the disorders of the inner city. Conservatives usually want to repress nonwork and crime, while liberals continue to seek solutions mainly through providing benefits. The focus of politics is now conduct rather than class.

The new agenda goes back to the later 1960s, when the welfare rolls doubled, crime soared, and riots erupted in the ghettos of major cities. These episodes raised issues of order and propriety much more sharply than had the earlier class politics. Ever since then, the closely linked problems of poverty, welfare, and the inner city have dominated the domestic agenda. The claims of broader groups, including minorities and women as well as workers, have not gone unnoticed, but they no longer command center stage. Classes and economic interests still jostle for advantage in Washington, yet the deepest concern is disadvantage. Issues of dependency and dysfunction, not equality among workers, now preoccupy our affairs.

This has happened not because concern for the poor is lapsing, but because efforts to help them in the old ways achieved little. The fact that policies to promote new opportunities, by both the right and the left, failed to integrate the urban poor inevitably shifted attention from social change to the personal capacities of the needy. It has become harder to find social barriers that explain why so few poor adults work regularly--the immediate reason most of them are needy. Whether one sees barriers at all increasingly hinges on judgments made about the personal capacity of the poor rather than social inequities. Liberals are the readiest to see further impediments and call for more programs, because they see the poor as victims without ability to proceed on their own; conservatives doubt that there are barriers because they think the poor can take care of themselves as well as other people.

I do not mean to say that dependency issues are entirely new. How to cope with the poor has been an issue for centuries. But in American politics the question was largely a local one. At the national level, poverty and the problems tied to it have a prominence today that they never had before. Progressive-style battles among classes and economic factions continue even during the dependency era, but they no longer set the tone of national politics at the highest levels. In domestic affairs, presidential and party programs mostly revolve around how to overcome urban decay or to regenerate the economy. Prosecuting the old battles of business versus workers is secondary.

It is true that Democrats and liberals still seek a redistribution of income, while Republicans and conservatives resist. Economic inequality has recently increased, and some think a new age of conflict between rich and poor is upon us. Short of an economic collapse, I find that difficult to imagine. Most Americans are a lot more afraid of rising crime, welfarism, and declining schools than they are of their employers. Government is perceived as having failed to solve today's social problem. Until it succeeds, it will receive no new mandate to tackle the older problem of unequal fortunes.

For the left, nonworking poverty has been a political disaster. Only people who try to help themselves, above all by working, are seen as deserving by most Americans; only they can be the objects of a reform crusade or the recipients of mainstream benefits such as Social Security or Medicare. Thus, when poverty became largely nonworking in the 1960s and 1970s, support fell for governmental social change. That is a major reason why conservatives have controlled the presidency and the national agenda for most of a generation.

Dependency politics is growing in importance not only in the United States, but in the West as a whole. In Europe, disputes over the social behavior of low-income groups, often immigrant minorities, have become more contentious than traditional conflicts between organized labor and capitalism. As in the United States, the claims of workers are being shoved back on the agenda by controversies over groups at the periphery of society.

The Welfare Issue

Progressive debates revolved around employment and its rewards. The question, in today's parlance, was how to generate the most "good jobs at good wages" as well as support workers when they were unable to work. Liberals looked to achieve these aims through government programs, conservatives by relying on the private sector. That battle has largely ceded to questions of providing for those outside the economy altogether. The most important welfare program is Aid to Families with Dependent Children (AFDC), which supports poor, mostly single-parent families with a combination of federal and local funding. Since the 1960s, the leading question in social politics has been how to reform AFDC so as to minimize dependency by people who many feel could support themselves.

Welfare dependency has displaced labor issues as a question presidents feel they must address. Ronald Reagan, for example, took office as a conservative of the old school, his main purpose being to cut government spending and taxation. But if voters wanted cheaper government, they also wanted something done about urban disorders. Fortunately for him, Reagan also took tough stands on crime, welfare, and education. He asserted that moralism about "values" which is the conservatives' key resource in the new politics. In the end, despite his preferences, Reagan may have had more impact on social than economic policy. His cuts in federal spending barely slowed the growth in government, and his tax cuts will probably be reversed over time due to the budget deficit. But if Reagan did not cut the size of the welfare state by much, he did begin to change its character. It became marginally less generous, but also more demanding. Reforms passed under Reagan for the first time seriously required that able-bodied welfare recipients work or prepare for work in return for support.

Like the public, the Washington governing class has come to worry more about urban social problems than the scale of government. Government experts and analysts endured the Reagan spending and tax cuts, which put some of them out of work. They responded much more avidly when, on 4 February 1986, in his State of the Union address, the president announced a new study of welfare to try to achieve "lasting emancipation" from the "spider's web of dependency." In the antipoverty community, pent-up concern broke out as if a dam had burst. Over the next eighteen months, a flood of new studies of poverty and welfare poured forth from groups of every political persuasion. Great attention was paid to the new and apparently successful state-level work programs authorized by Congress in 1981. On 13 October 1988, Reagan signed the Family Support Act (FSA), the most thoroughgoing reform of welfare ever, whose key provisions will expand work programs.

FSA was a triumph, but it also signaled the passing of Reagan's economic politics from center stage. Congressional debate turned not so much on questions of benefits or costs as on the expectations to be made of the dependent in return for support. Were the poor to be held morally responsible for helping themselves or not?

The Work Issue

The welfare debate already suggests the most fundamental difference between the old politics and the new: Progressive politics was about how to advance *working* people, while dependency politics is largely about how to cope with *nonworking* people. Nonwork--by which I mean a failure to work or look for work by the employable--is the immediate reason for destitution and dependency among most of today's working-aged poor, who are the most controversial of the needy. For mysterious reasons, poor adults no longer work as regularly as they once did, a fact too often neglected. Nonwork persisted even in the face of steady economic growth in the 1980s, and it has resisted all solutions, whether of the right or the left.

In *How the Other Half Lives*, a classic of social reportage, the journalist Jacob Riis described New York's Lower East Side at the turn of the century. Then, whole families of immigrants living in fetid tenements slaved long hours in sweatshops for the lowest wages merely to survive. It is still true today that new immigrants are among the hardest workers in the city, taking the lowest-paid jobs in an effort to get ahead. An atmosphere of hustle and hard work can still be felt in the new immigrant areas of New York or Los Angeles, but in the poorest sections, bustle is much less evident. A great many native-born New Yorkers do not work. At the height of the recent boom in 1988-89, unemployment fell to 3.9 percent in New York City, compared to a national rate of 5.6 percent. Yet only 56 percent of adults in the city were either working or looking for work, a figure 11 points below the national norm. Among youth--those aged sixteen to nineteen--only 23 percent were in the labor force, less than half the rate for the nation generally. The situation is similar in other large cities. Somehow many poor people do not connect with the jobs that are available.

* * *

Nonwork has devastated large sections of New York. Formerly working-class neighborhoods like Spanish Harlem lost their aspiring character during the 1970s and 1980s, when welfare and the drug trade replaced legitimate employment as the economic bases of the community. When older residents look back, what they remember is "People worked hard." There remain many hardworking, self-reliant people in East Harlem, but, with over a third of the residents on welfare, workers no longer set the tone. People barely survive, despite the wealth all around them. One woman laments, "All those generations on welfare. There is no respect any more because people haven't worked."

The poor in Riis's day lived mostly in two-parent families, and children worked alongside their parents. The answer to poverty was higher wages, which economic growth eventually provided. Today we see mostly female-headed families living on welfare and single men, among whom not even the adults work regularly. On the whole, the immigrant poor of old were poor *despite* work, while the current poor are needy for *lack* of it. Wages in low-skilled jobs may still seem too low to support families, but, as I will show, poverty is very uncommon among adults who work usual hours at any legal wage. The "working poor" are considerably outnumbered by the nonworking. The leading domestic issue has changed from how to raise wages and benefits for working people to how to turn more poor people into workers.

* * *

The Decline in Work Effort

Since the 1960s, when poverty became a major public concern, work effort among the poor has dropped sharply, a trend that has received too little attention. Falling work levels have operated as an undertow, defeating the government's best efforts to overcome poverty. Table 3.1 details the changes, with the poor defined as those families who fall under the federal poverty line. In 1989, less than half the heads of poor families had any earnings at all, a drop of nearly a fifth since 1959, when over two-thirds were employed. The proportion in full-time, full-year work has dropped by half, to only 16 percent in 1989. Correspondingly, the share of heads of poor households without work has risen from less than a third to over half.

Much of this reduction comes not from the same persons working less, but from shifts in population. The poor as a percentage of the U.S. population dropped substantially in these years, from 22 percent in 1959 to 13 percent in 1989, mostly as a result of economic growth, which raised what wages could buy and thus enabled working families to lift themselves above need. The working poor left poverty, and the poor became almost by definition nonworking. Rather than ask why so few poor people work, we might as well ask why we still have so many poor.

One can also categorize the poor as those who are needy relative to normal family income. Table 3.2 shows work levels among all families and among those in the top and bottom quintile, or fifth, of the distribution of family incomes. If we take the poor to be the bottom fifth, the poverty line is not fixed, but rises with earnings. This means the needy do not separate as cleanly from the rest of the population over time as in Table 3.1, but a difference in work effort remains apparent. In 1986, working hours, measured in units of full-time, full-year workers, were almost seven times as great among the top fifth of incomes as among the bottom. There is not much change in overall work levels in either the top or bottom quintile, but there is among families with children, which account disproportionately for the needy. Work effort among such families rises in the top fifth and falls in the bottom fifth, among both female-headed and two-parent families. These work differences go far to explain the radical income differences among families at the top and bottom of society.

* * *

Work Experience of Heads of Poor Families, 1959-89

Table 3-1

Percent of all heads who:	**1959**	**1975**	**1989**
Worked at any time in year	67.5	50.4	48.9
Worked full-year, full-time	31.5	15.9	16.2
Did not work	30.5	49.1	50.8
Percent of single female heads who:			
Worked at any time in year	42.9	36.5	41.6
Worked full-year, full-time	10.9	5.6	8.8
Did not work	57.1	63.5	58.4
Percent of all other heads who:			
Worked at any time during the year	74.9	61.5	56.8
Worked full-year, full-time	37.6	24.2	24.1
Did not work	22.5	37.5	42.6

NOTE: "Full-year" means at least fifty weeks a year, "full-time" at least thirty-five hours a week. "Other heads" are mostly men, with or without spouses, but include some married women. Proportions working and not working do not add to 100 because heads in the armed forces are omitted.

SOURCE: Calculated from U.S. Department of Commerce, Bureau of the Census, *Characteristics of the Population below the Poverty Level: 1984*, Series P-60, no. 152 (Washington, D.C.: U.S. Government Printing Office, June 1986), table 4; idem, *Money Income and Poverty Status in the United States: 1989*, Series P-60, no. 168 (Washington, D.C.: U.S. Government Printing Office, September 1990), table 23.

[I]t is not at all clear how to explain the decline. One might suppose that the poor are working less because fewer of them are working-aged. Traditionally, the poor were composed mostly of children and the elderly, since the working-aged could use earnings to escape need. The overall American population is, in fact, aging, but the working-aged proportion of the poor population is rising, not falling. Between 1959 and 1989, the share of the poor aged sixty-five or over fell from 14 to 11 percent, while the share under age eighteen fell from 44 to 40 percent, leaving 49 percent of the poor of working age. The main reasons for these changes are that most of the elderly and disabled have been lifted out of poverty by rising Social Security payments, and poor Americans, like the better-off, are having fewer children than they once did.

Today's poor are mainly found among female-headed families and single adults. In both groups, the great majority of adults are nonelderly, yet they work less often than the intact families that previously predominated among the poor. Between 1959 and 1989, the total number of poor Americans dropped from 39 to 32 million, but the number of poor living in female-headed families grew from 7 to 12 million and the number of poor single people grew from 5 to 7 million. Together, the two groups comprised 30 percent of the poor in 1959, but 58 percent by 1989. The fact that both groups grew absolutely, not only as a share of the poor, shows that the work decline is not just an artifact of the fall in poverty.

Some might blame the decline on the upsurge in female-headed poor households, on the argument that mothers abandoned by their husbands must inevitably work little because of their child care responsibilities. Much of the decline is indeed related to the fact that more poor families today are female-headed. Since such families typically work less than two-parent families, the shift lowers the overall work level among the poor. But as Table 3.1 shows, there has been a substantial work decline among heads of family other than single women, due apparently to male workers withdrawing from the labor force. Some of these are elderly men retiring earlier due to higher Social Security, but fewer working-aged, low-income men also work today to support families. The economists Sheldon Danziger and Peter Gottschalk estimate that the proportion of employable men heading poor families with children who worked at least forty-eight weeks a year dropped from 72 to 46 percent between 1967 and 1984, while the share not working at all jumped from 8 to 17 percent. Meanwhile, the proportion drawing government income benefits of some kind more than doubled, from 17 to 38 percent.

Equivalent Number of Full-Time Full-Year Workers by Income Quintile, 1970-86

Table 3-2

	1970	**1978**	**1986**
All families at all incomes	.76	.75	.76
Families with children	.91	.94	.97
Married couples	.98	1.05	1.12
Single mothers	.36	.40	.42
All families in top income quintile	1.23	1.25	1.25
Families with children	1.28	1.36	1.42
Married couples	1.31	1.37	1.45
Single mothers	.75	.91	.92
All families in bottom income quintile	.19	.15	.18
Families with children	.42	.33	.27
Married couples	.63	.62	.61
Single mothers	.05	.03	.03

SOURCE: Congressional Budget Office, *Trends in Family Income: 1970-1986* (Washington, D.C.: U.S. Government Printing Office, February 1988), table A-15. Entries are based on tabulations of Current Population Survey data, 1971-87.

The decline in employment has been especially great among black men, a principal reason why poverty today is much higher among blacks than whites. In 1960, 83 percent of both white and black men were working or looking for work. By 1988, the white rate had dropped to 77 percent, the black rate to 71 percent. Black unemployment rates, which typically run twice those for whites, reached 20 percent during the 1980s, and among black male teenagers an astounding 49 percent.

Although female-headed households have lower family incomes, it is too simple to say they must be poor or dependent. For the population as a whole, as Table 3.2 shows, work effort by mothers, married and unmarried, is increasing. About half of all female family heads are working, nearly three-quarters of them full-time. Among those not dependent, the work rate is about 85 percent. Somehow, welfare mothers differ. Their numbers have doubled since the 1960s, and only 6 percent of them work at a given time, even part-time. One might suppose that they suffer special impediments, such as large numbers of children or a lack of child care. But, as I will show, this does not seem to be the case.

Even if one exempts many of the adult poor as unable to work, a decline in work effort is clear. Setting aside the elderly, students, the disabled, and mothers with preschool-aged children, Danziger and Gottschalk found the share of poor households headed by adults who might reasonably be expected to work rose from 37 to 47 percent between 1967 and 1984, yet the share of these heads actually working at least forty-eight weeks a year dropped from 54 to 32 percent in this same period. Meanwhile, the share not working at all rose from 22 to 32 percent. By 1984, 91 percent of these employable heads of households lacked sufficient earnings to keep a family of four above poverty.

The Failure of Reform

The appearance of nonworking poverty is one great fact driving the emergence of dependency politics. A second is the failure of the progressive approach to social reform to raise work levels. Traditionally, government's response to any social problem was to try to expand opportunity for the downtrodden. For Democrats, this meant extending the protections of government; for Republicans, cutting them back and relying more on the free market. Both approaches have been tried. The Great Society sharply expanded antipoverty benefits and programs, and the Reagan administration somewhat reduced them. If either policy had integrated the poor into the larger society, American politics would probably still revolve around questions of class and economic equality, rather than personal conduct. But neither approach worked. The poverty rate, after falling sharply through the 1960s, bottomed out at 11 to 12 percent in the 1970s. It rose and then fell in the 1980s, ending in 1989 at 13 percent. Just as important, social conditions among the poor radically deteriorated, with family breakdown, crime, and drug addiction becoming epidemic in America's inner cities.

Many social causes for nonwork among the poor have been proposed--low wages, lack of jobs or child care, racial discrimination, disincentives to work generated by welfare. But while each has some influence, my judgment is that none of them, individually or together, can explain nonwork on the scale now found among the poor. Most experts, left and right, agree that the causes of poverty remain mysterious.

* * *

I do not mean to say that social barriers are unimportant. Differences in opportunity explain much of the inequality in American society. People with less privileged backgrounds, particularly less education, do have less of a chance to succeed in our competitive society. But such differences mainly explain *inequality among workers*, not *failure to work at all*, which is the greater problem among today's poor. It is the failure of most poor adults to work steadily in *any* job, not the inferiority of their positions, that largely explains their predicament.

Trends in the society should have resulted in higher work levels among the needy, not lower. Since the 1960s, opportunities have grown for the low-skilled. Their education levels as well as the number of jobs have risen. Racial discrimination has fallen, as have welfare disincentives, with the failure of AFDC benefits, since the early 1970s, to keep pace with inflation. Yet, mysteriously, work levels have declined and remained low. Whatever outward causes one cites, a mystery at the heart of nonwork remains--the *passivity* of the seriously poor in seizing the opportunities that apparently exist for them.

It is true that the economy has shown some negative trends, paralleling those among the poor. After 1970, the country suffered several economic shocks: the baby boom generation flooded the job market, productivity stagnated, and foreign competition destroyed many manufacturing jobs, especially in the Northern and Midwestern cities where many poor and dependent people live. The decline of factory jobs and the shift toward a "high-tech" economy, among other factors, have increased inequality among workers. Many liberals contend that a mismatch between the remaining jobs and low-skilled job seekers largely explains nonwork in the inner city.

But research has failed to confirm these theories. Economic trends may have reduced wages for those with the least skills; they cannot explain why so many of the poor fail to take the jobs still available. The decline of the factory has been offset by an explosion of employment in service trades. While the high-tech economy does reward advanced education, the vast majority of jobs do not require it. Most of the inner-city poor appear able to find jobs, albeit not of the quality they would like. The clamor of immigrants from all over the world to come to the United States strongly suggests that opportunities for the unskilled are still abundant here.

To explain nonwork, I see no avoiding some appeal to psychology or culture. Mostly, seriously poor adults appear to avoid work, not because of their economic situation, but because of what they believe. To a detached eye, opportunity may appear to be available to the low-skilled, but nonworkers typically do not believe this. A combination of resistance to low wages, pessimism about long-term prospects, the isolation of the ghetto, and group memories of a harsher past cause many to turn aside from the chances to work that exist. Thus, the poor remain economically passive in a society where other low-skilled people find abundant opportunity.

Cautions

In mentioning these disturbing facts, I do not seek to be partisan, in terms of either the old or the new politics. I will not argue that the answer to poverty is either more government, in the simple sense of more spending or programs, or less. Like other conservatives, I am cautious about assuming that government has the answer to social problems, but I also believe that the degree to which government should intervene in society is a political question that I have no special competence to decide. It is an issue to be fought out in the progressive arena among functioning citizens.

My point is to stress the crucial importance of the work problem in shaping today's politics. It may not be clear how large government should be, but it is absolutely clear that employment is essential to being a functioning citizen. Only adults with a work connection have moral standing to demand either more government or less. Thus, once the nonworking poor became a presence on the national stage, the proper role of government could no longer be the central issue in politics. Instead, moralistic disputes about personal conduct came to the fore.

I will also not take a hard-and-fast position on the newer issues of dependency politics, which have to do with the moral responsibility and competence of the poor. I do not believe society is responsible for poverty to the extent it once was. At the same time, I believe that the poor as they now are need help. The poor may not be responsible for themselves at present, but they must become so. Competence cannot be the assumption of social policy, but it must be the goal.

It is too simple to say that conservatives are concerned about the disorders of the inner city while liberals are not. Liberals, too, disapprove of crime, nonwork, and welfarism. But they seek to overcome these problems by assuaging what they see as the underlying causes, rather than through imposing standards. It is also too simple to say that liberals are concerned about the poor while conservatives are not. For liberals, in their hesitation to levy expectations on the needy, reflect a less sanguine view of their capacities than most conservatives assert.

Whether the often-alleged social barriers explain poverty remains a matter of judgment, especially if one is seeking to generalize from a large body of technical research, as I do here. There is no rigorous way to sum up the various influences on poverty: low wages, racial discrimination, lack of jobs and child care, and so on. Some might say that these factors in combination, if not individually, can account for nonwork. I can only say that I find that conclusion unreasonable. It assumes that the explanations are all independent, each one accounting for a separate piece of the puzzle. In fact, the theories are largely competitive, each claiming to explain the same central mystery--the passivity of the long-term poor.

* * *

The poor differ widely among themselves. Most are not on welfare. Some do work, and many who do not, including children, the elderly, and the ill, would not be expected to by any humane society. These groups may need and deserve more assistance than they get. I concentrate on the working-aged, employable poor simply because they are the most controversial and thus, politically, the most significant. They have also proved the hardest to help. When the public, as opposed to government, thinks of "the poor," it is usually thinking of them.

Poverty is often transient. Most Americans who become poor also escape poverty within two years, and there is little reason to view them as distinct from the population in general. I focus on the long-term poor--the 6 to 7 percent of Americans who are poor for more than two years, and especially the 4 to 5 percent who are employable, that is, not elderly or disabled. This is a narrower group than all the poor, but it is also broader than the homeless or the underclass, meaning the most dysfunctional poor. Within it, experts agree, there are two crucial subgroups--long-term welfare mothers and nonworking single men--and I will focus mainly on them. The initial reason for most working-aged poverty is simply that fathers in ghetto areas tend not to provide for their children, while the mothers usually go on welfare rather than work themselves. Whether the parents, both fathers and mothers, could work more than they do, and why they do not, are the leading questions in social policy today.

Nonwork, also, is only one of the many social problems afflicting poor Americans. Some argue that crime, drug addiction, failure in school, or unwed childbearing are more fundamental causes of poverty than nonwork. The needs of weak families and poor children, especially in inner-city ghettos, are certainly pressing. Disputes about how to solve these problems are as much a part of dependency politics as the work issue. They dramatize the embarrassing, *personal* nature of today's social dilemma, even more than nonwork. Tragic spectacles such as "crack babies" abandoned by drug-addicted mothers have even more power than panhandling men to drive the claims of working Americans off the front pages.

Politically, however, nonwork is much the most significant aspect of poverty. Except for crime, it is the behavior of the poor that most offends the nonpoor. It has prompted the most sustained policy-making at the federal level, more than either crime or family problems. It is the problem about which research has taught us the most, though mysteries remain. It is also the respect in which the condition of the poor is most clearly deteriorating. Levels of crime and unwed parenthood appear to have peaked in the ghetto, but nonwork continues to increase. Nonwork constitutes the core of the social problem, if not the whole of it.

Nonwork is the aspect of poverty that has the widest political implications. Crime and family problems arise initially mostly from private causes; employment problems have much more evident connections to social opportunities. Work is public behavior for which society has always accepted some responsibility. Employable workers who are idle for long periods become a political issue to which government must respond. The failure of traditional reforms to solve the work problem, therefore, has effects that reach beyond social policy. It suggests the bankruptcy of the entire progressive tradition--of our image of self-reliance as central to American politics. More than any other development, nonwork explains the appearance of a new politics focused on dependency rather than the claims of workers.

* * *

My main point is to define the essence of the new dependency politics and contrast it with the progressive past. Secondarily, I will argue that dependency issues are now more important than older, progressive disputes. By this I mean that they control the commanding heights of politics, that is, the national agenda and, to a great extent, presidential elections.

* * *

Progressive Politics

The baseline for the change I discuss is the progressive era. By this I mean the period up through the mid-1960s when politicians debated primarily how to advance the *progress* of ordinary, working Americans toward greater wealth and status. Next only to preserving basic law and order, promoting broad-based mobility has been the overriding purpose of American domestic government since the nation's founding. Most politicians have shared Lincoln's belief at the purpose of democracy is to "elevate the condition of men" or, as Richard Hofstadter phrases it, "to provide opportunities for social ascent to those born in its lower ranks."

The issues in progressive politics were structural, having to do with the basic organization of society. Politicians differed, above all, over whether the economy should be guided more by government or the marketplace. While American leaders, like the people, have always believed in capitalism, they have disputed how far government should interfere in the free economy to promote this or that economic or social interest. Especially they differed over whether more or less government was best for the hopes of working Americans to support their families and advance their position in the world. The meaning of social reform was impersonal: it meant to re-form society by adjusting the relationship of government and the economy.

The term progressive usually connotes governmental measures to protect workers (the minimum wage), redistribute income (the income tax), or provide support to those unable to work (Unemployment Insurance, Social Security). Progressivism as I use it also includes proposals by conservatives to attain the same ends with less government, through greater reliance on the free market. The American right has served the interests of business, but in the belief that unfettered capitalism also served the interests of ordinary people. Both sides claim to provide more "opportunity." For liberals that word suggests public benefits and protections from the marketplace, while for conservatives it means faster growth, and hence more and better jobs, in the private sector. The first choice provides more security and equality in an immediate sense, the latter stronger incentives to work and invest and hence, it is argued, greater wealth and opportunity in the long run. Each philosophy makes a genuine appeal to the interests of ordinary people, and each has enjoyed greater support at different times.

This debate dominated domestic affairs throughout the Western world for two centuries. The kind of economic interventions that Americans call liberalism have, taken to greater lengths, produced socialism in Europe and communism in the Soviet bloc. In Europe as in the United States, a period of ambitious governmental growth has lately been followed by retrenchment. Many nations are struggling to find the mix of public controls and market incentives that will best promote growth and affluence over the long haul.

The former Soviet Union represented one extreme of the progressive continuum. The statist Soviet economy guaranteed employment, and wages had little connection to effort. There was little incentive for workers to produce or managers to economize. Consumers, too, were protected from the market by subsidies for food and housing. . . . In the American economy, much closer to the market extreme, incentives to effort and efficiency are much stronger, but there is also more risk that workers will be unemployed and investments will fail. The chance of greater wealth and growth comes at the price of greater insecurity.

* * *

At home, the progressive meaning of social reform retains considerable appeal. Demands for greater opportunity, earlier made by distressed workers and farmers, were picked up by blacks and women in the 1960s and 1970s. The civil rights and feminist movements were the last expressions of progressive claim making to obtain salience in American politics. They succeeded as movements of working people seeking greater opportunity within the mainstream economy. The fact that both groups were seen as functional was one reason their leading demands were granted. The effect of reforms, as designed, was to expand the black middle class and advance women in business and professional life.

The limitation of progressivism is that it assumes employment. Both liberalism and conservatism in their traditional meanings were theories on behalf of *working* people. The big-government and the free-market visions of society disagree about how much government workers require, but each presumes that ordinary people can and do work. Only the employed and their dependents benefit from labor regulations such as the minimum wage or qualify for mainstream social benefits such as Social Security or Medicare, which are more generous than welfare. It is also the employed, and those seeking work, who benefit most from the free-market economy. Both left and right assume that most of the help ordinary people need to get through life can be provided by expanding the rewards of employment.

Progressivism can deal with nonwork only if the problem is traceable to some reformable impediment outside the jobless. Some feature of society--economic depression, low wages, an unfair labor market--must be keeping people out of work or depressing the quality of jobs they can get. Only then does the progressive remedy of altering the scope of government apply. This is so regardless of whether one thinks the answer lies in expanded or reduced controls on the economy.

For a long time, this limitation went unnoticed. Over the course of American history, government and the economy together have succeeded mightily in improving the material situation of ordinary Americans. The combination of growing wages and government benefits has raised the incomes of workers and their families to levels undreamt of a century ago. As recently as 1938, probably two-thirds of Americans were poor by today's definition. From World War II through the 1960s, poverty was driven down rapidly by growing wages and benefits earned by the still-numerous working poor. But after that, the decline first slowed sharply, then reversed. Due largely to nonwork, the remaining poverty no longer responded much to either government programs or a growing economy. Before these facts, the progressive tradition stood disarmed.

The Competence Assumption

The progressive approach took for granted a goal-oriented view of human nature. The traditional left and right shared the assumption that the individual is willing and able to advance his or her own economic interests. Not just the businessperson, but the ordinary citizen is a maximizer, seeking not just survival, but advancement, in material terms--supporting one's family and propelling oneself to a higher station in society.

* * *

This view of human nature, which I call the competence assumption, has permeated all conventional American political thinking. The Declaration of Independence reckoned the pursuit of happiness as an essential human right. This reflected the view of the Founders, according to Hofstadter, that the "rapacious" pursuit of self-interest was among the "necessary qualities of man." There was no need to spur people to seeking thcir own advantage.

Competence here means all the qualities that allow a person to get ahead in economic terms--not only intelligence, but foresight, energy, discipline, and the ability to sacrifice for the future. It did not mean that people were moral, that is, willing to serve others before themselves, only that they were effective in pursuing their own interest. To reconcile the individual interest with the general interest was society's problem. A harmony might be achieved either through the invisible hand of the marketplace or through the visible hand of government.

Both varieties of progressivism assert this view of human nature. They differ almost entirely over the organization of society. Liberals have a more favorable view of government, conservatives of the marketplace, but each conceives of ordinary citizens as self-reliant. Traditionally, conservatives may have had a more confident view of personality than liberals, who are quicker to assert that people need some insulation from the market, but the difference is small. Even liberal measures, for example to subsidize higher education or home mortgages, presume that the beneficiaries will earn the money they need to make good use of these opportunities.

The vigorous pursuit of economic advantage has widely been seen the keynote of American society. In the early 1830s, Alexis de

Tocqueville noted that Americans put much more energy into both work and politics than was usual in Europe. All was "activity and bustle," he wrote, "everybody works," and no store was set on "idleness," even among the elite. There was no other country where "all those who work are so keen on making themselves prosperous."

The United States has been known for a severe work ethic and, correspondingly, a suspicious attitude toward the poor. Intellectuals are typically critical, believing that a democracy should be especially tolerant of the needy. Tocqueville concluded, however, that democracy fostered a strong work norm. Economic effort was a way people earned the respect of one another in a society with few ascriptive distinctions. "Among democratic peoples where there is no hereditary wealth, every man works for his living, or has worked, or comes from parents who have worked. Everything, therefore, prompts the assumption that to work is the necessary, natural, and honest condition of all men."

Intellectuals also say that Americans insist on too hard a line between government and the economy. They worship the free market and resist government interfering even to help the vulnerable. But it would be more accurate to say that the hard division is between groups who are seen as deserving and those who are seen as undeserving. Typically, people who can claim economic interests based on employment get some assistance from government; those without economic functions do not. In America, this moral distinction is a lot clearer than the separation of the public and private sectors.

Historically, there never was a time when American government was not involved in the economy. Almost from the founding, the idea developed, wrote Vernon Parrington, that "a democratic state stands in *loco parentis* to the economic interests of its citizens." Throughout the nineteenth century, government at all levels showered subsidies on entrepreneurs and others seeking to develop the country. It helped finance turnpikes and canals, donated land for railroads, levied tariffs to protect growing industries, and provided infrastructure and services to farmers and industrialists. Most of the largesse went to well-connected businessmen, but homesteaders received land, Civil War veterans received pensions, and the retainers of politicians received government jobs.

The New Deal marked the high tide of this sort of

intervention. Government regimented the private economy as never before, and major benefit programs were enacted for the unemployed, aged, and destitute. Academics write of the United States establishing a welfare state on the European model, one that shielded the needy from the marketplace, but, in fact, the traditional tie between aid and economic function was preserved. The most generous of the new benefits--Unemployment Insurance and Social Security--limited eligibility to people who had earlier paid payroll taxes. True to the American tradition, claimants on government must first of all be workers.

If the progressive tradition neglects anyone, it is people outside the economy. The political problem for today's poor is precisely that they usually are not workers. They cannot make the same demands on a helpful government as people with a work history. They do not satisfy the competence assumption. Some argue that the destitute should get more from government to compensate for their failure to get much from the economy, but the moral logic of American political economy is just the opposite: Workers get more from the economy *and* from government than nonworkers do, because they are seen as more deserving. If today's poor worked more, they would be seen as more, not less, deserving of government aid, even though they would be less needy.

Dependency Politics

In essence, dependency politics arises when the competence assumption comes into question. How does one cope with people who seem unable to advance even their own interests, let alone society's? That is the essential problem in domestic policy today. We debate less and less how to reform society and more and more whether the poor can be responsible for their own conduct. Progressive politics, a battle of ideologies, has given ground to moralistic disputes over individual behavior.

During the last three decades, most antipoverty policies paid homage to the competence assumption by assuming that the poor would get ahead if they were given the chance. That was as true of liberal training and service programs for the disadvantaged as of conservative reliance on economic growth. But the progressive assumption that opportunity was enough to overcome destitution proved invalid. Work levels actually fell among the poor, and many social programs came to operate in practice, if not intention, as substitutes for employment.

In the old politics, it was never doubted that individuals, even the poor, were responsible for their personal probity, if not for their economic fortunes. In the new era, the question of moral responsibility has become intensely divisive. Liberals deny that the poor are responsible for nonwork, crime, or family problems, on grounds they face a hostile society; conservatives defend responsibility and seek to enforce it.

In the old era, the political extremes disagreed about the organization of society but agreed that ordinary people could take care of their own interests, if not other people's. In the new era, the situation reverses. The two sides disagree less sharply about the role of government but more sharply about the competence to be expected of the poor. Liberals assert that the needy want to work and obey other mainstream mores, but are unable to in practice. Conservatives tend to doubt, not the competence, but the morality of the poor.

The rhetoric of dependency politics often uses progressive categories to debate the new issues. Liberals still talk of social barriers keeping the poor from working, while conservatives doubt this. But because the impediments cited are usually much more limited than those of thirty or fifty years ago, the debate is less impersonal than it seems. It is one thing to say people cannot work because of a literal lack of jobs or rigid racial bars to all employment--impediments that are rarely found today. It is quite another to say that lack of skills, transportation, or child care prevent work, since these are difficulties that a great many low-skilled people overcome every day.

When liberals appeal to such problems, they implicitly assume a lesser competence in the poor than do conservatives, who think opportunity is available. *Every view of barriers rests on a view of competence, usually unspoken.* Although the debate may be couched in the most arcane statistics about whether jobs or child care is available, the real difference is about human nature. Are poor people able to organize their lives to assume the burdens of employment? Or are they helpless victims of whom nothing can be expected? The very exhaustion of the more obvious barriers to employment brings these issues to the fore.

The drift of antipoverty policy during the 1970s and 1980s was away from social reformism of either the left or the right and toward efforts to reorder the personal lives of the poor. Work programs in welfare are the leading instance, but the same idea underlies recent reforms in law enforcement and education. The chief aim is no longer to enlarge opportunity by changing social structure, but rather to help make the poor more able to take advantage of existing opportunities. The new measures are more paternalist than liberal or conservative in the traditional sense. They do not reorder society, but neither do they dismantle protections and throw the vulnerable into the marketplace. Rather, they seek to build a structure around the dependent that will conduce to more functional behavior.

The practical question in social policy is the proper character of this new regime. Should it be indulgent or demanding? Liberals still want to help people in the style of the Great Society, with voluntary programs such as special training and education. The tendency of policy, though, has been toward the conservative preference, which is to enforce social standards. I see no speedy end to these differences as long as social conditions among the poor continue to deteriorate. To restore progressive politics will take a long struggle to raise work levels. Only then could personal responsibility and competence once again be taken for granted.

* * *

Notes and Questions

1. *Nonwork.* Professor Mead frames the current welfare problem as one of nonwork. Murray seems likely to agree with that formulation. Do you detect any differences between the conservative perspectives of Murray and Mead?

Do their methods of analysis differ? How does Murray's use of logic and hypotheticals compare to Mead's series of topical essays relating to contemporary politics? Do you imagine they were designed for, or appeal to, different audiences?

How do you compare the substance of their critiques? Do you think Murray blames individuals more? For example, he seems to assume that the primary problem is one of individual laziness. In comparison, Mead targets government policies as more to blame for creating and encouraging welfare dependency.

2. *Conservative Activism.* Mead focuses heavily on what he characterizes as a recent shift in politics. He acknowledges that

conservatives still want a smaller government, but one that is more activist in enforcing social norms to fight "welfarism." He asserts that liberals continue to desire bigger government, but one that is more passive in tolerating dependency. He argues that progressive politics (apparently referring to policies designed to redistribute income and wealth) cannot solve the general, intangible problem of nonwork. On what does he base this conclusion? What does he suggest as an alternative?

3. *Assumptions.* Mead also suggests that conservatives are more likely to assume that poor people are competent actors, whereas liberals are more likely to view poor people as incompetent victims. Do you agree? What purposes does this argument serve for conservative advocates?

4. *Language.* Consider the language Mead uses in his analysis. He argues that the focus has shifted from class, poverty, and social barriers to a concern with what Mead characterizes as conduct, crime, dependency, disorder, dysfunction, family breakdown, nonwork, and passivity. How do these characterizations influence his analysis?

5. *Begging the Question.* Mead targets nonwork as the current cause of poverty. Does that advance your understanding of the problem? Does it suggest any particular solution? If Mead is right that nonwork actually causes poverty, then work must solve it. Will conservatives and liberals respond differently to the goal of creating more work? Won't their policies depend on what they think causes nonwork? So, for example, liberals might continue their fight to dismantle social barriers to women and racial minorities. Conservatives might continue to assume competence and encourage individual self-sufficiency. So how are these politics really new, as Mead suggests?

* * *

B. FROM THE MIDDLE

As demonstrated by the perspectives of Murray and Mead, conservative commentators tend to blame both *individual* poor people for engaging in irresponsible behavior and lacking initiative, and *government* for providing welfare and creating dependency. As we will study after this section, liberal commentators tend to identify *societal* forces, especially the inadvertent or intentional unequal economic distribution resulting from capitalism, and blame *government* for failing to redistribute income and wealth more equitably.

More moderate scholars reject the simplicity of either the conservative or liberal analysis, in favor of what they might characterize as a more balanced approach. As the following excerpt from the work of William Julius Wilson demonstrates, middle of the road scholars tend to identify numerous individual and societal factors that contribute to poverty. They similarly view the solution to poverty as much more complex, requiring intricate policy packages to address the various causes.

William Julius Wilson
THE TRULY DISADVANTAGED: THE INNER CITY, THE UNDERCLASS AND PUBLIC POLICY (1987)

The Ghetto Underclass and Social Dislocations

Why have the social conditions of the ghetto underclass deteriorated so rapidly in recent years? Racial discrimination is the most frequently invoked explanation, and it is undeniable that discrimination continues to aggravate the social and economic problems of poor blacks. But is discrimination really greater today than it was in 1948, when black unemployment was less than half of what it is now, and when the gap between black and white jobless rates was narrower?

* * *

Those who cite discrimination as the root cause of poverty often fail to make a distinction between the effects of *historic* discrimination (i.e., discrimination prior to the mid-twentieth century) and the effects of *contemporary* discrimination. Thus they find it hard to explain why the economic position of the black underclass started to worsen soon after Congress enacted, and the White House began to enforce, the most sweeping civil rights legislation since Reconstruction.

The point to be emphasized is that historic discrimination is more important than contemporary discrimination in understanding the plight of the ghetto underclass--that in any event there is more to the story than discrimination (of whichever kind). Historic discrimination certainly helped create an impoverished urban black community in the first place. . . . [B]lack newcomers from the rural South were far more severely discriminated against in northern cities than were the new white immigrants from southern, central, and eastern Europe. Skin color was part of the problem but it was not all of it.

The disadvantage of skin color--the fact that the dominant whites preferred whites over nonwhites--is one that blacks shared with the Japanese, Chinese, and others. Yet the experience of the Asians, who also experienced harsh discriminatory treatment in the communities where they were concentrated, but who went on to prosper in their adopted land, suggests that skin color per se was not an insuperable obstacle. . . . Because changes in immigration policy cut off Asian migration to America in the late nineteenth century, the Japanese and Chinese population did not reach large numbers and therefore did not pose as great a threat as did blacks.

Furthermore, the discontinuation of large-scale immigration from Japan and China enabled those Chinese and Japanese already in the United States to solidify networks of ethnic contacts and to occupy particular occupational niches in small, relatively stable communities. For blacks, the situation was different. The 1970 census recorded 22,580,000 blacks in the United States but only 435,000 Chinese and 591,000 Japanese.

If different population sizes accounted for a good deal of the difference in the economic success of blacks and Asians, they also helped determine the dissimilar rates of progress of urban blacks and the new European arrivals. European immigration was curtailed during the 1920s, but black migration to the urban North continued through the 1960s. With each passing decade there were many more blacks who were recent migrants to the North, whereas the immigrant component of the new Europeans dropped off over time. Eventually, other whites muffled their dislike of the Poles and Italians and Jews and directed their antagonism against blacks.

In addition to the problem of historic discrimination, the black migration to New York, Philadelphia, Chicago, and other northern cities--the continued replenishment of black populations there by poor newcomers--predictably skewed the age profile of the urban black community and kept it relatively young. The number of central-city black youths aged sixteen to nineteen increased by almost 75 percent from 1960 to 1969. Young black adults (aged twenty to twenty-four) increased in number by two-thirds during the same period, three times the increase for young white adults. In the nation's inner cities in 1977, the median age for whites was 30.3, for blacks 23.9. The importance of this jump in the number of young minorities in the ghetto, many of them lacking one or more parents, cannot be overemphasized.

Age correlates with many things. For example, the higher the median age of a group, the higher its income; the lower the median age, the higher the unemployment rate and the higher the crime rate (more than half of those arrested in 1980 for violent and property crimes in American cities were under twenty-one). The younger a woman is, the more likely she is to bear a child out of wedlock, head up a new household, and depend on welfare. In short, part of what had gone awry in the ghetto was due to the sheer increase in the number of black youth.

The population explosion among minority youth occurred at a time when changes in the economy were beginning to pose serious problems for unskilled workers. Urban minorities have been particularly vulnerable to the structural economic changes of the past two decades: the shift from goods-producing to service-producing industries, the increasing polarization of the labor market into low-wage and high-wage sectors, innovations in technology, and the relocation of manufacturing industries out of the central cities.

Most unemployed blacks in the United States reside within the central cities. Their situation, already more difficult than that of any other major ethnic group in the country, continues to worsen. Not only are there more blacks without jobs every year; men, especially young males, are dropping out of the labor force in record proportions. Also, more and more black youth, including many who are no longer in school, are obtaining no job experience at all.

However, the growing problem of joblessness in the inner city exacerbates and is in turn partly created by the changing social composition of inner-city neighborhoods. These areas have undergone a profound social transformation in the last several years, as reflected not only in their increasing rates of social dislocation but also in the changing class structure of ghetto neighborhoods. In the 1940s, 1950s, and even the 1960s, lower-class, working-class, and middle-class black urban families all resided more or less in the same ghetto areas, albeit on different streets. Although black middle-class professionals today tend to be employed in mainstream occupations outside the black community and neither live nor frequently interact with ghetto residents, the black middle-class professionals of the 1940s and 1950s (doctors, lawyers, teachers, social workers, etc.) resided in the higher-income areas of the inner city and serviced the ghetto community. The exodus of black middle-class professionals from the inner city has been increasingly accompanied by a movement of stable working-class blacks to higher-income neighborhoods in other parts of the city and to the suburbs. Confined by restrictive covenants to communities also inhabited by the urban black lower classes, the black working and middle classes in earlier years provided stability to inner-city neighborhoods and perpetuated and reinforced societal norms and values. In short, their very presence enhanced the social organization of ghetto communities. If strong norms and sanctions against aberrant behavior, a sense of community, and positive neighborhood identification are the essential features of social organization in urban areas, inner-city neighborhoods today suffer from a severe lack of social organization.

Unlike in previous years, today's ghetto residents represent almost exclusively the most disadvantaged segments of the urban black community--including those families that have experienced long-term spells of poverty and/or welfare dependency, individuals who lack training and skills and have either experienced periods of persistent unemployment or have dropped out of the labor force altogether, and individuals who are frequently involved in street criminal activity. The term *ghetto underclass* refers to this heterogeneous group of families and individuals who inhabit the cores of the nation's central cities. The term suggests that a fundamental social transformation has taken place in ghetto neighborhoods, and the groups represented by this term are collectively different from and much more socially isolated than those that lived in these communities in earlier years.

The significance of changes embodied in the social transformation of the inner city is perhaps best captured by the concepts *concentration effects* and *social buffer*. The former refers to the constraints and opportunities associated with living in a neighborhood in which the population is overwhelmingly socially disadvantaged--constraints and opportunities that include the kinds of ecological niches that the residents of these communities occupy in terms of access to jobs, availability of marriageable partners, and exposure to conventional role models. The latter refers to the presence of a sufficient number of working- and middle-class professional families to absorb the shock or cushion the effect of uneven economic growth and periodic recessions on inner-city neighborhoods. The basic thesis is not that ghetto culture went unchecked following the removal of higher-income families in the inner city, but that the removal of these families made it more difficult to sustain the basic institutions in the inner city (including churches, stores, schools, recreational facilities, etc.) in the face of prolonged joblessness. And as the basic institutions declined, the social organization of inner-city neighborhoods (defined here to include a sense of community, positive neighborhood identification, and explicit norms and sanctions against aberrant behavior) likewise declined.

* * *

In underlining joblessness as an important aspect of inner-city social transformations, we are reminded that in the 1960s scholars readily attributed poor black family deterioration to problems of employment. Nonetheless, in the last several years, in the face of the overwhelming attention given to welfare as the major source of black family breakup, concerns about the importance of joblessness have diminished, despite the existence of evidence strongly suggesting the need for renewed scholarly and public policy attention to the relationship between the disintegration of poor black families and black male labor-market experiences.

* * *

Research has demonstrated, for example, a connection between an encouraging economic situation and the early marriage of young people. In this connection, black women are more likely to delay marriage and less likely to remarry. Although black and white teenagers expect to become parents at about the same ages, black teenagers expect to marry at later ages. The black delay in marriage and the lower rate of remarriage, each associated with high percentages of out-of-wedlock births and female-headed households, can be directly tied to the employment status of black males. Indeed, black women, especially young black women, are confronting a shrinking pool of "marriageable" (that is economically stable) men.

* * *

The Limits of Race-specific Public Policy

In the early 1960s there was no comprehensive civil rights bill and Jim Crow segregation was still widespread in parts of the nation, particularly in the Deep South. With the passage of the 1964 Civil Rights Bill there was considerable optimism that racial progress would ensue and that the principle of equality of individual rights (namely, that candidates for positions stratified in terms of prestige, power, or other social criteria ought to be judged solely on individual merit and therefore should not be discriminated against on the basis of racial origin) would be upheld.

Programs based solely on this principle are inadequate, however, to deal with the complex problems of race in America because they are not designed to address the substantive inequality that exists at the time discrimination is eliminated. In other words, long periods of racial oppression can result in a system of inequality that may persist for indefinite periods of time even after racial barriers are removed. This is because the most disadvantaged members of racial minority groups, who suffer the cumulative effects of both race and class subjugation (including those effects passed on from generation to generation), are disproportionately represented among the segment of the general population that has been denied the resources to compete effectively in a free and open market.

On the other hand, the competitive resources developed by the *advantaged minority members*--resources that flow directly from the family stability, schooling, income, and peer groups that their parents have been able to provide--result in their benefiting disproportionately from policies that promote the rights of minority individuals by removing artificial barriers to valued positions.

Nevertheless, since 1970, government policy has tended to focus on formal programs designed and created both to prevent discrimination and to ensure that minorities are sufficiently represented in certain positions. This has resulted in a shift from the simple formal investigation and adjudication of complaints of racial discrimination to government-mandated affirmative action programs to increase minority representation in public programs, employment, and education.

However, if minority members from the most advantaged families profit disproportionately from policies based on the principle of equality of individual opportunity, they also reap disproportionate benefits from policies of affirmative action based solely on their group membership. This is because advantaged minority members are likely to be disproportionately represented among those of their racial group most qualified for valued positions, such as college admissions, higher paying jobs, and promotions. Thus, if policies of preferential treatment for such positions are developed in terms of racial group membership rather than the real disadvantages suffered by individuals, then these policies will further improve the opportunities of the advantaged without necessarily addressing the problems of the truly disadvantaged such as the ghetto underclass. The problems of the truly disadvantaged may require *nonracial* solutions such as full employment, balanced economic growth, and manpower training and education (tied to--not isolated from--these two economic conditions).

* * *

The Hidden Agenda: From Group-specific to Universal Programs of Reform

Comprehensive economic policies aimed at the general population but that would also enhance employment opportunities among the truly disadvantaged--both men and women--are needed. . . . Moreover, underclass absent fathers with more stable employment are in a better position to contribute financial support for their families. Furthermore, since the majority of female householders are in the labor force, improved job prospects would very likely draw in others.

I have in mind the creation of a macroeconomic policy designed to promote both economic growth and a tight labor market. The latter affects the supply-and-demand ratio and wages tend to rise. It would be necessary, however, to combine this policy with fiscal and monetary policies to stimulate noninflationary growth and thereby move away from the policy of controlling inflation by allowing unemployment to rise. Furthermore, it would be important to develop policy to increase the competitiveness of American goods on the international market by, among other things, reducing the budget deficit to adjust the value of the American dollar.

In addition, measures such as on-the-job training and apprenticeships to elevate the skill levels of the truly disadvantaged are needed. . . . In this connection, instead of focusing on remedial programs in the public sector for the poor and the unemployed, emphasis would be placed on relating these programs more closely to opportunities in the private sector to facilitate the movement of recipients (including relocation assistance) into more secure jobs. Of course there would be a need to create public transitional programs for those who have difficulty finding immediate employment in the private sector, but such programs would aim toward eventually getting individuals into the private sector economy. Although public employment programs continue to draw popular support, . . . "they must be designed and administered in close conjunction with a nationally oriented labor market strategy" to avoid both becoming "enmeshed in congressionally reinforced local political patronage" and being attacked as costly, inefficient, or "corrupt."

Since national opinion polls consistently reveal strong public support for efforts to enhance work in America, political support for a program of economic reform (macroeconomic employment policies and labor-market strategies including training efforts) could be considerably stronger than many people presently assume. However, in order to draw sustained public support for such a program, it is necessary that training or retraining, transitional employment benefits, and relocation assistance be available to all members of society who choose to use them, not just to poor minorities.

It would be ideal if problems of the ghetto underclass could be adequately addressed by the combination of macroeconomic policy, labor-market strategies, and manpower training programs. However, in the foreseeable future employment alone will not necessarily lift a family out of poverty. Many families would still require income support and/or social services such as child care. A program of welfare reform is needed, therefore, to address the current problems of public assistance, including lack of provisions for poor two-parent families, inadequate levels of support, inequities between different states, and work disincentives. A national AFDC benefit standard adjusted yearly for inflation is the most minimal required change. We might also give serious consideration to programs such as the Child Support Assurance Program developed by Irwin Garfinkel and colleagues at the Institute for Research on Poverty at the University of Wisconsin, Madison. This program, currently in operation as a demonstration project in the state of Wisconsin, provides a guaranteed minimum benefit per child to single-parent families regardless of the income of the custodial parent. The state collects from the absent parent through wage withholding a sum of money at a fixed rate and then makes regular payments to the custodial parent. If the absent parent is jobless or if his or her payment from withholdings is less than the minimum, the state makes up the difference. Since all absent parents regardless of income are required to participate in this program, it is far less stigmatizing than, say, public assistance. Moreover, preliminary evidence from Wisconsin suggests that this program carries little or no additional cost to the state.

Many western European countries have programs of family or child allowances to support families. These programs provide families with an annual benefit per child regardless of the family's income, and regardless of whether the parents are living together or whether either or both are employed. Unlike public assistance, therefore, a family allowance program carries no social stigma and has no built-in work disincentives.

* * *

Finally, the question of child care has to be addressed in any program designed to improve the employment prospects of women and men. Because of the growing participation of women in the labor market, adequate child care has been a topic receiving increasing attention in public policy discussions. For the overwhelmingly female-headed ghetto underclass families, access to quality child care becomes a critical issue if steps are taken to move single mothers into education and training programs and/or full- or part-time employment. However, I am not recommending government-operated child care centers. Rather it would be better to avoid additional federal bureaucracy by seeking alternative and decentralized forms of child care such as expanding the child care tax credit, including three- and four-year-olds in preschool enrollment, and providing child care subsidies to the working-poor parents.

If the truly disadvantaged reaped disproportionate benefits from a child support enforcement program, child allowance program, and child care strategy, they would also benefit disproportionately from a program of balanced economic growth and tight-labor-market policies because of their greater vulnerability to swings in the business cycle and changes in economic organization, including the relocation of plants and the use of labor-saving technology. It would be shortsighted to conclude, therefore, that universal programs (i.e., programs not targeted at any particular group) are not designed to help address in a fundamental way some of the problems of the truly disadvantaged, such as the ghetto underclass.

By emphasizing universal programs as an effective way to address problems in the inner city created by historic racial subjugation, I am recommending a fundamental shift from the traditional race-specific approach of addressing such problems. It is true that problems of joblessness and related woes such as poverty, teenage pregnancies, out-of-wedlock births, female-headed families, and welfare dependency are, for reasons of historic racial oppression, disproportionately concentrated in the black community. And it is important to recognize the racial differences in rates of social dislocation so as not to obscure problems currently gripping the ghetto underclass. However, as discussed above, race-specific policies are often not designed to address fundamental problems of the truly disadvantaged. Moreover, as also discussed above, both race-specific and targeted programs based on the principle of equality of life chances (often identified with a minority constituency) have difficulty sustaining widespread public support.

Does this mean that targeted programs of any kind would necessarily be excluded from a package highlighting universal programs of reform? On the contrary, as long as a racial division of labor exists and racial minorities are disproportionately concentrated in low-paying positions, antidiscrimination and affirmative action programs will be needed even though they tend to benefit the more advantaged minority members. Moreover, as long as certain groups lack the training, skills, and education to compete effectively on the job market or move into newly created jobs, manpower training and education programs targeted at these groups will also be needed, even under a tight-labor-market situation. For example, a program of adult education and training may be necessary for some ghetto underclass males before they can either become oriented to or move into an expanded labor market. Finally, as long as some poor families are unable to work because of physical or other disabilities, public assistance would be needed even if the government adopted a program of welfare reform that included child support enforcement and family allowance provisions.

For all these reasons, a comprehensive program of economic

and social reform (highlighting macroeconomic policies to promote balanced economic growth and create a tight-labor-market situation, a nationally oriented labor-market strategy, a child support assurance program, a child care strategy, and a family allowances program) would have to include targeted programs, both means tested and race-specific. However, the latter would be considered an offshoot of and indeed secondary to the universal programs. The important goal is to construct an economic-social reform program in such a way that the universal programs are seen as the dominant and most visible aspects by the general public. As the universal programs draw support from a wider population, the targeted programs included in the comprehensive reform package would be indirectly supported and protected. Accordingly *the hidden agenda for liberal policymakers is to improve the life chances of truly disadvantaged groups such as the ghetto underclass by emphasizing programs to which the more advantaged groups of all races and class backgrounds can positively relate.*

* * *

[I]t is imperative that the political message underline the need for economic and social reforms that benefit all groups in the United States, not just poor minorities. Politicians and civil rights organizations, as two important examples, ought to shift or expand their definition of America's racial problems and broaden the scope of suggested policy programs to address them. They should, of course, continue to fight for an end to racial discrimination. But they must also recognize that poor minorities are profoundly affected by problems in America that go beyond racial considerations. Furthermore, civil rights groups should also recognize that the problems of societal organization in America often create situations that enhance racial antagonisms between the different racial groups in central cities that are struggling to maintain their quality of life, and that these groups, although they appear to be fundamental adversaries, are potential allies in a reform coalition because of their problematic economic situations.

The difficulties that a progressive reform coalition would confront should not be underestimated. It is much easier to produce major economic and social reform in countries such as Sweden, Norway, Austria, the Netherlands, and West Germany than in the United States. What characterizes this group of countries . . . is the interaction of solidly organized, generally centralized, interest groups--particularly professional, labor, and employer associations with a centralized or quasi-centralized government either compelled by law or obliged by informal agreement to take the recommendations of the interest groups into account or to rely on their counsel. This arrangement produces a consensus-making organization working generally within a public framework to bargain and produce policies on present-day political economy issues such as full employment, economic growth, unemployment, wages, prices, taxes, balance of payments, and social policy (including various forms of welfare, education, health, and housing policies).

In all of these countries . . . social policy is integrated with economic policy. This produces a situation whereby, in periods of rising aspirations and slow economic growth, labor--concerned with wages, working conditions, and social security--is compelled to be attentive to the rate of productivity, the level of inflation, and the requirements of investments, and employers--concerned with profits, productivity, and investments--are compelled to be attentive to issues of social policy.

* * *

[C]ountries that rely the least on public assistance, such as Sweden, West Germany, and France, provide alternative income transfers (family allowances, housing allowances, child support, unemployment assistance), stress the use of transfers to augment both earnings and transfer income, provide both child care services and day-care programs, and emphasize labor-market policies to enhance high employment. . . . By contrast, the United States relies more heavily than all the other countries (Sweden, West Germany, France, Canada, Austria, the United Kingdom, and Israel) on public assistance to aid poorer families. "The result is that these families are much worse off than they are in any of the countries."

* * *

Notes and Questions

1. *Defining Moderate.* How is Professor Wilson more conservative or liberal? Wilson frames the problems underlying poverty quite differently than either Murray or Mead. He does not seem to blame either individuals for causing their own poverty or government for causing welfare dependency. But neither does he

view public provision of welfare as the primary solution to welfare. He refers to partnerships between public and private initiatives to facilitate rehabilitation of the poor.

On the one hand, Wilson seems closer to the liberal camp insofar as he views the problems and solutions as centering on social and economic organization. But is he really letting individuals off the hook? To what extent does his analysis depend on enforcement of social norms relating to proper individual work ethic?

On the other hand, his concern about the breakdown of the family and his assumptions about the desirability of replacing these broken families with the ideal family seem to place him closer to the conservative camp. The ideal family implicit in his analysis seems to be made of heterosexual, married, steadily employed spouses with children who live in what can probably best be described as middle class neighborhoods. Many who absorbed a middle class socialization may share this implicit notion of the ideal family. Is the restoration of the traditional nuclear family necessary to eliminate poverty? Is it sufficient? How important is it? Why do you suppose that notions of family and poverty are so closely linked today?

2. *Considering Race.* Wilson views historic understanding of racial oppression as central to understanding poverty. He argues specifically that this history of racial subjugation is more important than contemporary discrimination in understanding poverty. Wilson emphasizes how the cumulative effects of both race and class subjugation deny "the resources to compete effectively in a free and open market" to the most disadvantaged members of racial minority groups. In contrast, he argues that general civil rights laws tend to benefit the most economically advantaged racial minorities. As a result, race-based policies cannot fully address the problem of poverty, even for poor members of racial minority groups.

Although Wilson proposes shifting antipoverty policies away from a race-based focus, he does not propose the elimination of race-based programs. He favors the continuation of policies designed to help specific racial groups as long as these groups continue to suffer disproportionate disadvantage.

What do you think of Wilson's proposed shift of focus away from race and toward disadvantage? While his proposal to design programs for the truly disadvantaged has not gained much ground, his corollary suggestion to shift away from race-specific programs has become quite popular. Race-based affirmative action programs are under attack by officials from each branch of government, executives, legislators and judges. Do you think Wilson's proposal foreshadowed, or contributed to, the current attack on race-based programs? Do you think his proposal of a universal program to rehabilitate anyone who suffers disadvantage will fare better than current affirmative action or welfare programs?

3. *Central Cities.* Wilson provides insights about the social structure of central city neighborhoods. In particular, he suggests that neighborhoods populated predominantly by socially disadvantaged people suffer *concentration effects* or constraints on opportunity. He also links the lack of *social buffer* (or cushion formerly provided by middle class families) with the decline of social institutions in central city neighborhoods. In particular, he suggests that the absence of the black middle class in poor neighborhoods causes limitations in "access to jobs, availability of marriageable partners, and exposure to conventional role models," which he in turn links to the breakdown of black families.

To what extent is Wilson correct in describing central city neighborhoods as lacking social organization? Certainly other views of these neighborhoods resonate from recent times. The police officers' beating of Rodney King, and the 1992 rioting in South Central Los Angeles that followed their acquittal, left powerful images of angry and violent black youth reminiscent of the race riots of the late 1960s. From a considerably different perspective, Carol Stack described the strength of extended black family networks in central city neighborhoods in her widely acclaimed 1974 book, *All Our Kin.* Can Stack's words compete with repetitive television images of self-destruction? When do we see central city neighborhoods depicted? Do we see their everyday workings? Or do we see them only when they are newsworthy, usually meaning when riots or crime occur? At the very least, it might behoove us to be cognizant of the danger of generalizing about neighborhoods which have suffered from media portrayal which reinforces existing stereotypes.

4. *Solutions.* Wilson does not limit himself to a critique, but constructs a package of policies designed to fight poverty. He identifies as pieces of this package: *macroeconomic policies* that support a tight, full employment labor market and stimulate balanced,

noninflationary economic growth; *employment development* including training, retraining, transitional employment benefits, and relocation assistance; *welfare* or income support improved by providing benefits to two-parent families, increasing the levels of income support and adjusting them yearly for inflation, eliminating inequities between different states, and eliminating work disincentives; and *child care* support through expansion of the child care tax credit, earlier preschool enrollment, and subsidies to working poor parents. What do you think of Wilson's proposed package solution to poverty?

C. FROM THE LEFT

Liberal or Radical?

Any attempt to describe policy perspectives from the left immediately confronts the difficulty of combining liberal and radical critiques in one category. Indeed, one of the persistent themes of left scholarship about welfare is the continuing dialogue about whether welfare helps or harms. Some scholars, more frequently described by themselves or others as liberal, maintain their focus on the goal of compassionate relief. Other scholars, typically characterized as radical, argue that welfare creates and pacifies a dependent underclass. The tension within this dialogue among left scholars leaves the position of the left category about the desirability of welfare appearing somewhat ambiguous. In fairness, many similar tensions exist among scholars on the right and in the middle as well. For whatever reasons, however, the position of scholars on the right seems to reflect a greater consensus toward increasing individual responsibility and reducing government involvement. The left, in comparison, seems more conflicted about whether increasing or reducing government involvement will provide greater empowerment of poor people, with liberals maintaining greater faith in the capability of government to redistribute wealth and radicals envisioning a grassroots movement by poor people to force economic equality.

The Emergence of Legal Doctrine

Modern left scholarship about welfare was transformed by Charles Reich's contribution of *The New Property* in 1964.[1] In this law review article, Professor Reich encompassed welfare benefits into a broader category of government largesse, including franchises, licenses, tax credits and other forms of government subsidies. Because recipients rely on this largesse, Reich reasoned that these benefits constitute property, with the accompanying ramification that the benefits could not be discontinued without due process of law. In the landmark 1970 case, *Goldberg v. Kelly*, the United States Supreme Court cited and adopted Reich's analysis in holding that due process required a hearing prior to termination of welfare benefits.

The announcement of a due process hearing right for welfare recipients coincided with the culmination of a decade of expansion of the welfare rolls. According to welfare historian Linda Gordon, the numbers of recipients receiving Aid to Families with Dependent Children rose by only 17% during the 1950s, but by 107% during the 1960s. Scholars typically attribute this dramatic increase in the welfare rolls to the politicization of poor, urban African-Americans.

In *The Promised Land*,[2] Nicholas Lehman provides a riveting account of the mass migration of African-Americans from southern, agricultural regions to the northern industrial cities. The influx of this predominantly young population proved to be more than the northern urban economies could support. As the civil rights movement facilitated political education, African-Americans learned of their eligibility for welfare benefits. In addition to this politicization, the structure of welfare provided greater leniency in approving applications for benefits, primarily because the new northerners were no longer limited by the discretion exercised by southern welfare bureaucrats which had resulted in the mass exclusion of African-Americans from southern welfare rolls.

Some scholars believe that these two factors, the political education of potential welfare recipients and changes in the welfare structure, fail to tell the whole story. The left critique grew more

---

[1]Charles A. Reich, *The New Property*, 73 YALE L.J. 733 (1964).

[2]NICHOLAS LEHMAN, THE PROMISED LAND (1991).

radical in 1971, when a political scientist and a sociologist teamed up to present an account more incriminating of government actors.

The Shift to a Social Science Analysis

In 1971, Frances Fox Piven and Richard Cloward published their groundbreaking work, *Regulating the Poor: The Functions of Public Welfare*.[3] They examined the impact and reaction of government to the unrest that grew, in part, out of the northern migration. In particular, they described widespread unemployment in the northern cities, resulting in political unrest, both in the streets and at the polls. According to Piven and Cloward, national politicians responded to this unrest by extending welfare benefits.

Rich in detail and broadsweeping in concept, this book articulated the left's critique of poor relief in the United States. Linda Gordon provides an apt summary:

> Following a distinguished tradition of critique of poor relief/social welfare, Piven and Cloward interpreted welfare programs as a form of social control, but gave to that position a new specificity and argumentation. First, they argued that public welfare served to regulate the labor force: pushing workers in and out of the labor force to create a better balance between supply and demand, thus reducing unemployment and attendant unrest; and enforcing the work ethic. They made an historical as well as a theoretical case for this. Second, they traced the roots of the 1960s welfare crisis to the specific conditions of black Americans: to the historical processes that destroyed their already marginal sharecropping existence, and to social disorder and civil-rights militance. Third, they showed that welfare programs were by no means an automatic, functional response to need, but were stimulated by civil protest and disruption.[4]

The goal of labor regulation, the intertwined history of welfare with

---

[3]A second edition of Regulating the Poor was published in 1993, containing two additional chapters about developments from the 1970s to the 1990s.

[4]Linda Gordon, *What Does Welfare Regulate?*, 55 SOCIAL RESEARCH 609 (1988).

racial and gender discrimination, and the prevention of civil unrest were not entirely new themes in the study of welfare history. Piven and Cloward combined them, however, to form a theoretical framework for understanding the role of welfare as a means of social control.

Although Piven and Cloward's groundbreaking work articulated a critique for the radical left, it did not, by itself, resolve the underlying tension about the desirability of welfare among left scholars. Consider how these tensions played out in the following debate between Professors William Simon and Joel Handler about the legitimacy of an entitlements-based approach to welfare.

William H. Simon
THE INVENTION AND REINVENTION OF WELFARE RIGHTS
44 MARYLAND LAW REVIEW 1 (1985)

Reich styled The New Property as an attack on Progressive jurisprudence, which he thought had become "a doctrine monstrous and oppressive." As he saw it, the essence of this doctrine, in the form that had come to dominate the postwar public interest state, was that "a man or woman . . . has no rights which may not be taken away to serve some public policy." For him, one of the ugliest manifestations of the doctrine was the philosophy of welfare administration of the public interest state.

Reich and his followers did not describe comprehensively the welfare doctrine they were reacting against, and they are perhaps not entirely responsible for the historical account of welfare rights that became conventional among liberal lawyers in the years following The New Property, but they contributed to it. According to this account, welfare benefits were not regarded as rights prior to the 1960s. They were regarded as gratuities to be dispensed in accordance with administrative whim. The welfare system was dominated by social workers committed to an ideology of condescending moralism. These social workers considered poverty a symptom of personal failing and considered poor people, like children and lunatics, to be incapable of rational and responsible choice. They sought to condition material assistance on recipients' submission to supervision of their housekeeping, child rearing, and sexual practices.

Such supervision was designed to get the recipient to act like, and ultimately to transform her into, the middle class person's ideal of a working class person- industrious, economizing, sexually ascetic, politically complacent, and socially unambitious. The "man-in-the-house" rules that disqualified families on the basis of the mother's sexual conduct, and the "midnight raids" designed to enforce such rules, typified this regime. The regime went unchallenged-so the story goes-until lawyers and the federal judiciary intervened in the 1960s. The lawyers and judges established the principle that welfare was a legal right and, under the banner of this principle, purged the system of condescending moralism and arbitrary administration. The critical milestones in this account are Reich's 1964 article, the 1968 case of *King v. Smith*, in which the Supreme Court struck down the "man-in-the-house" rules, and the 1970 case of *Goldberg v. Kelly*, in which the Court held that due process required a hearing prior to the termination of a welfare benefit.

***

[T]he principle of welfare as a legal right had been fully accepted and elaborated within an important sector of the welfare system long before the lawyers took an interest in the system. Yet although social work jurisprudence anticipated and overlapped the New Property in many ways -- in its repudiation of condescending moralism, its insistence on the dignity of the recipient, and its attack on arbitrary administration -- there were important differences between the social workers' and the lawyers' conceptions of welfare rights.

***

Social work jurisprudence grew out of the Progressive critique of classical legalism early in this century. By classical legalism I mean the conservative legal thought of the substantive due process era, the era of *Lochner v. New York.* There were three principal elements to the classical conception of a legal right. The first element was the view that the basic value underlying the legal system is individual independence. Independence connoted a Utopian image of autarchy or self-sufficiency. It meant security against the pleas or demands of others. It meant immunity from having to rely on the sympathy or goodwill of others. The greatest threat to independence was the state, which represented the concentrated collective power of the others. A basic purpose of rights was to protect independence from the collective power of the state. The type of rights suitable for this purpose were absolute or categorical. Absolute rights were designed to create zones of nonaccountability; they prescribed certain and unbreachable boundaries of autonomy. Such rights merited recognition regardless of the consequences to others. Rhetorically, they were understood as trumps. They closed dialogue by precluding rebuttal.

The second element of the classical scheme was a set of premises about just distribution. The classicists thought they had deduced from the basic value of independence distributive principles that might be summarized as, first, entitlement to the fruits of one's efforts, and second, the legitimacy of voluntary exchange. For the classicists only wealth acquired through effort or exchange could appropriately be considered a matter of right.

The third element of the classical scheme was a set of legal rules specifying particular rights. These were basically the turn-of-the-century private law rules of contract, tort, and property. The classicists purported to deduce most of these rules from the distributive principles of effort and exchange and in turn from the basic value of independence.

The basic notion of right was thus associated with private law. In contrast, public law consisted of two types of subsidiary norms. One type was designed to further the basic collective goal of rights enforcement. These norms provided for the state to protect the individual's rights against trespasses by other individuals and to prevent the state itself from interfering with rights. The other set of public law norms regulated the residual power of the state to provide for a variety of collective goals other than rights enforcement, goals often grouped under the rubrics of health, welfare, safety, and morals.

Thus, in the classical view, individuals were free to exercise their wills within the spheres defined by rights. So long as they stayed within these spheres, they were not accountable to others. At the same time, the state was empowered to pursue a variety of residual public goals subject to the basic constraint that it not violate rights.

Within this framework, the interests of welfare beneficiaries were not considered rights. While the notion of right was founded on the morally fundamental value of independence, welfare benefits were held to be inextricably associated with the phenomenon of dependence. To some, welfare beneficiaries were incapable of exercising the autonomy that the system of rights was designed to protect. To them, dependence connoted an impairment of the will. Eligibility for or receipt of welfare was either a cause or a consequence of such an impairment; in either case, welfare status was at least presumptive evidence of incapacity. It resembled in this respect the statuses of infancy and insanity. Classical legalism considered such statuses exceptions to the basic norm of independence calling for regulation based on principles other than the general private rights scheme.

Moreover, even classicists who conceded the competence of welfare beneficiaries could not see welfare as a matter of right because welfare was not consistent with the intermediate distributive premises of effort and exchange. The distributive premise of welfare was need, a concededly important value but one which the classical legalists could not square with their notion of right. From this perspective, dependence connoted the morally inferior status of living on income not acquired through effort or exchange. Finally, the classicists could not fit welfare benefits into their rights scheme because such benefits were not among the interests protected by the private law rules with which classicism associated the idea of right.

The Progressives attacked classical legalism from a variety of angles. Perhaps their broadest and most powerful approach was to argue that the specific regime of private law rights that the classical legalists defended did not follow from any plausible understanding of the basic value of individual independence. In one line of attack, they showed that the classical private right regime did not operate uniformly to provide security, but that it enhanced security for some only at the expense of reducing it for others. They showed how the rules of contract and property could be seen as enforcing the servitude of those who lacked assets and bargaining power to those who had them. These rules had in fact operated to leave the working class in a state of great insecurity and vulnerability to, for example, economic downturn, sickness, and injury. At the same time, another line of attack showed that a variety of public programs not recognized in the classical rights regime (for example, social insurance) could be seen as entailed by the fundamental notion of independence. These programs increased the security of their beneficiaries by providing them relatively certain benefits in the event of misfortune.

These attacks had two consequences of particular interest here.

First, they undermined the classical distinction between public and private law. Not only did the Progressives show that a panoply of public regulatory and welfare benefits could be rationalized in terms of the basic classical norm of independence (and even in terms of the intermediate distributive premises of effort and exchange), they also showed that a variety of interests associated with classical private rights could be justified, if at all, only in terms of the type of public policy considerations classicism had associated with the police power. For example, the enforcement of a form contract by a business against a consumer represented not the effectuation of a voluntary exchange, but the ratification of a power of regulation in the business, which would be proper only to the extent compatible with public norms of efficiency and fairness.

Second, the Progressive attacks undermined the basic classical distinction between individual right and collective or state power. They portrayed many of the forms of power threatening individual independence as arising from citizens engaged in activities classicism characterized as the exercise of rights. The most prominent example was the large corporation, which the Progressives described as a concentration of power rather than as a rightholder. Conversely, the Progressives showed that many of the welfare and regulatory activities of the state could be described-even if one started with the basic moral premises of the classicists-as rights enforcement.

Now the Progressive critique might have led to a posture of apolitical skepticism or analytical detachment. But most of the Progressives saw their jurisprudence as linked to the liberal politics of the expansion of the welfare-regulatory state. They thus had to face the question of how legal thought could be reconstructed from the rubble of classicism in a manner compatible with their program. Although they and their successors responded to this challenge in many quite complex ways, two strategies are of particular importance to the question of welfare rights. One strategy was to appeal to the notions of entitlement that classicism associated with private law to legitimate the liberal program of regulation and welfare. This strategy would embrace the classical premise of individual independence and the premises of effort and exchange, but insist that these premises supported, not the classical private right regime, but the programs of the New Deal and subsequent liberal administrations.

The second strategy was less compromising. It was inspired

not only by the jurisprudential critique of the classical effort to deduce its private rights regime from the ideal of independence, but by a cultural objection that some Progressives pressed against this ideal and its implicit Utopian image of autarchy. The cultural objection was that the classical norms seemed to foster a social order of self-seeking materialism that stultified personal growth, generated alienation, and ironically, promoted conformity. It subverted the kinds of collaboration and conflict essential to both individual development and a vital culture. This second strategy sought to replace or at least revise the ideal of independence in a way that emphasized the social or communal dimension of the self and of legal entitlement. While it did not repudiate the principles of effort and exchange outright, it denied their exclusive status; it portrayed them as two among several legitimate principles of distribution, and it considered need as another such principle of at least equal legitimacy and dignity.

* * *

Although Reich was thus correct in characterizing the Progressive approach to thinking about rights as balancing, he was wrong in attributing to Progressivism the "fallacy" of "treating the 'individual interest' as affecting only the party to the case" and thus allowing it to be outweighed routinely by the interests of the collectivity. As Roscoe Pound had shown in response to similar criticisms of the classicists, this characterization presupposed the very distinction between individual and collective that the Progressives disputed. For the Progressives, the commitment to individual freedom and autonomy was a social commitment, and claims of right based on this commitment implicated collective concerns just as much as claims based on, say, economic productivity. The enforcement of one person's rights is of concern to the others because it defines the society in which they all live.

The New Property jurisprudes were also wrong to suggest that the Progressives denied the validity of any form of interest in individual nonaccountability or immunity that might limit the kind of inquiry and dialogue implicit in the dialectical notion of right. The Progressives dealt with such interests under the rubric of privacy. (The most influential Progressive legal thinker--Brandeis--is, of course, the father of the modern constitutional and common law doctrines of privacy.) Their approach differed from that of the classicists in three respects. First, the Progressives denied that privacy rights were paradigmatic of rights generally. The point of developing doctrines of privacy is to distinguish interests in immunity and nonaccountability from other forms of entitlement. Second, unlike the classicists, the Progressives found such interests relatively more important in the sphere of "personal" than of "material" interests. Third, the Progressives denied that the boundaries of even these interests could ever be defined deductively or with certainty.

* * *

While the classicists saw rights enforcement as a matter of the state leaving people alone (or forcing others to leave them alone), the social workers saw it as a matter of helping people define and effectuate their goals. A claim of right was not only a claim against others and the state but a claim for their assistance. Rights did not exist to effectuate previously willed ends; they were part of the process by which people came to understand their ends. They did not constitute a fortress for the individual against the state, but rather an encounter between the individual and the state in which the identity of each was partly up for grabs.

* * *

Reich thought that, since the New Deal, the welfare state had become infected pervasively by the pathologies of invasion of privacy, punitive moralism, disrespect for civil liberties, and "capture" by powerful private interests. He didn't exactly blame Progressive jurisprudence for these pathologies, but he thought it powerless to oppose them. His basic proposal was a notion of entitlement alien to Progressivism.

Reich insisted that his proposal did not represent a return to classicism, and in some respects this claim was correct, but the notion of entitlement advanced in The New Property was a watered down version of the classical notion. Like the classicists, Reich saw the basic problem as protecting the independent individual from the power of the state. "The institution called property guards the troubled boundary between man and the state," reads the famous opening sentence. He used the term property to connote the zone of immunity or nonaccountability of the classical notion of right.

Property draws a circle around the activities of each private individual or organization. Within that circle, the owner has a greater degree of freedom than without. Outside, he must justify or explain his actions, and show his authority. Within, he is master, and the state must explain and justify any interference. Sometimes Reich spoke as if rights simply "shifted the burden of proof;" at other points he spoke more ambitiously of "zones within which the majority has to yield to the owner" or "sanctuaries or enclaves where no majority can reach." At some points he seemed to concede the need for balancing and to argue simply for more weight for individual interests; at others he seemed to repudiate balancing. Although he shied away from the absolutistic rhetoric of classicism, he invoked the same goal-individual independence; portrayed the same danger-the power of the state; and proposed the same solution-rights as immunities.

However, when one turns from the basic notion of entitlement to the level of specific rights and powers, Reich departed strikingly from classicism. He revised the contents of the categories of right and power. One revision was to take large corporations out of the right category and put them in the power category; they were portrayed as part of the problem rather than as part of the solution. Corporations were not seen as right-bearing individuals (or as institutions facilitating the exercise of rights by individuals), but rather as agglomerations of state-created power. Reich rejected the classical public/private, power/right categorization in this area because here government and the private sector "are often partners rather than opposing interests" and government power "aids rather than limits the objectives of those private sectors." As a result, "[t]oday it is the combined power of government and the corporations that presses against the individual." Because of this partnership, interests of large corporations are "not individual property but arbitrary power over other human beings."

Of course, Reich's most famous revision was the recategorization of right. The interests of large corporations were taken out. While a variety of forms of tangible "individual" property remained, they held little interest for Reich. The most prominent occupants of the redefined rights domain were interests in economic "status," notably interests "intimately bound up with the individual's freedom to earn a living" and welfare benefits.

By far the most frequently expressed concern in the article was for occupational interests, and, indeed, with a particular type of occupational interest. Reich showed little concern for the interests of capitalists and managers in earning a living (most of their interests were banished to the realm of power); nor did he say much of relevance to unskilled workers. Most of his heroes and martyrs were small businessmen, professionals, and skilled workers: "[d]octors, lawyers, real estate brokers, . . . taxi drivers" and "the businessman, the teacher, the professional man," all threatened by state licensing and regulatory schemes.

* * *

Thus the substantive reform implications of the New Property differ significantly from those of social work jurisprudence in that Reich's approach does not assert the primacy of need-based distribution; it is concerned with the protection of interests in economic status generally. Reich sought to convert his redefined category of property interests into zones of immunity or nonaccountability. At its most ambitious, the program contemplated prohibition of the impairment of interests in economic status without compensation. More modestly, it proposed that such interests not be "conditioned" in ways that impaired the claimant's autonomy, and especially on the waiver of constitutionally protected liberties. And still more modestly, it proposed an attitude of deference and respect for property, an attitude that gave substantial weight in any balancing that had to be done to the interests of independence secured by property as a zone of immunity.

Reich's discussion of the interaction of officials and right-holders makes clear that for the New Property, as for classicism, autonomy is a stipulated premise of the system. In contrast to social work jurisprudence, he showed no interest in the process by which citizens become aware of and communicate their goals and no concern with ambivalence and false consciousness. For example, the only illustration The New Property gave in the area of public assistance was a 1941 New York case upholding a welfare department's denial of cash benefits to an old man because he insisted on living in unsanitary conditions. The man slept on a pile of dirty rags in a barn. Now on the narrow question of whether assistance should be denied on such grounds, social work jurisprudence would have agreed entirely with Reich. But there are important differences between the two approaches. Reich summarily assumed that the old man's choice was a matter of "freedom of action," and he implied that the old man's rights would have been fully vindicated by a decision awarding him the cash assistance. Things are more complicated in social work jurisprudence. The social work conception cannot be applied without more information about the old man's practical opportunities and about the process by which he made his decision. Did the state enable the old man to secure decent shelter? If not, then its failure to do so is as important an infringement of his autonomy as the withdrawal of cash benefits. If so, one needs the kind of understanding of his choice that can only emerge through dialogue with him before one can decide whether his choice is really autonomous.

The vision of public administration in The New Property was also quite different from that of social work jurisprudence. Its most fundamental theme was the repudiation of administrative discretion. The principal reforms Reich proposed were administrative adjudication and judicial review. Others derived from Reich's analysis a more ambitious program diametrically opposed to that of the social workers. Its principal themes were the formalization of entitlement, the bureaucratization of administration, and the proletarianization of the lower tier workforce. They derived this program from the basic Reichian notion of entitlement as the opposite of state power and the Reichian equation of the problem of freedom with the control of state power. Formality was supposed to limit state power by limiting the number of factors the state could consider in decisionmaking; bureaucratization was supposed to do so by subjecting initial decisionmakers to the control of higher level decisionmakers; and proletarianization was supposed to do so by recruiting and socializing people who would divorce their personal goals from their work.

Reich's general notion of welfare rights as immunities from state power and the reform program derived from that notion have dominated liberal legal thinking about the welfare system for the past two decades. After Reich wrote, a substantial literature emerged seeking to ground welfare entitlement in natural rights philosophy--an approach Reich specifically declined to take. This literature resembled Reich's article in its individualistic premises, but it resembled social work jurisprudence in its emphasis on need- based distribution. Its implications for public administration were more ambiguous than those of Reich's and the social workers' analyses. But it was Reich's rhetoric rather than that of the natural rights lawyers that became the banner of liberal legal reform in the 1960s and 1970s. The New Property is quite justly regarded as one of the most influential pieces of legal scholarship ever written, and it can fairly be treated as both source and summary of liberal legal thinking about welfare in the 1960s and 1970s.

* * *

The most basic defect of classicism, which Reich repeated, was the reification of individual rights and state power as distinct and opposed entities. The most telling criticism that the Progressives made about the classical notion of (old) property was that it portrayed as a relation between a person and a thing what was really a relation among people. The important legal aspect of old property was not intrinsic to the material objects; it lay in the ability of the right-holder to call upon the power of the state to exclude others or in the ability that this state-backed power of exclusion gave the right-holder to exact concessions from others (again enforceable through state power) in exchange for access to the property.

To put it more generally: Under the interdependent conditions of modern society, very little activity can be seen as affecting only the actor. Moreover, to the extent that activity does affect only the actor, the concept of right is superfluous. Appeals to right occur only when activities and goals conflict; their function is to determine whose side the state will take. A successful claim of right gives the right-holder the opportunity to pursue her activities and goals with the help of the state and without regard to the interests of the other.

In these circumstances, all rights involve the state-private partnership that Reich and the small town Progressives associated only with the large corporation. You cannot use rights to limit "arbitrary power over the lives of other human beings" because rights (understood as zones of immunity) are arbitrary power over the lives of other human beings. Any redefinition or recategorization of rights could enhance a person's independence only at the expense of diminishing the independence of others. Nor does rights expansion diminish the power of the state; it increases those aspects of state power that derive from its role as rights enforcer.

Now the Progressives did not apply their critique to public law rights because classicism had no scheme of public law rights. But if, as Reich proposes, the idea of rights-as-immunities is to be extended to the material interests of the welfare-regulatory state, then so should the Progressive critique. The Progressives' point may be harder to grasp in public than in private law because of a further misleading practice that the classicists and Reich share: the reification of the state. While in private law rights are in form "against" other individuals, in public law they are in form "against the state." But this usage simply invites us to ignore that the "state" and its agencies exist only through and for people. The enforcement of rights "against the state" really involves the redistribution of wealth and power among the people advantaged and disadvantaged by the welfare and regulatory activities of state officials.

* * *

And by portraying welfare benefits as things that protect the independence of beneficiaries, Reich's analysis obscures the fact that such benefits represent a coercive transfer of wealth from one group of right-holders to another. In Reich's vivid and extensive description of the myriad activities of the expanding welfare state, one kind of state activity receives almost no mention at all: taxation. For the classicists, explicit redistribution from one recognizable group to another-"taking from A to give to B"-was mortal constitutional sin. They could reconcile their rights scheme to welfare activities only by asserting that taxation meeting certain formal requirements was not confiscation and that welfare spending was not a matter of distributive entitlement but a matter of public policy. The Progressives refuted these views. They showed both that taxation, like many other forms of government intervention, was indistinguishable from many types of confiscation and that this fact was not incompatible with regarding tax-funded benefits as rights, since all rights were fundamentally a matter of coercive transfer. Reich adopted the point that welfare could be seen as a right (without giving the Progressives credit for it), but he ignored its premise: That right is a form of power, not a safeguard against power.

Reich's failure to heed lessons that the social workers learned from Progressive legal thought accounts for two striking paradoxes of the New Property. The first paradox is that, while Reich's argument is clearly designed to legitimate the redistributive activities of the welfare state, it has curiously conservative and anti-redistributive implications. Reich's most ambitious substantive proposal was to treat interests in government largesse as "vested" and to require "payment of just compensation" for their impairment. But if, as the article suggests, both old and New Property are to be so regarded-if all the material incidents of economic status are to be constitutionalized--then it is hard to see how there could ever be any legitimate impairment, or given such an impairment, how there could be compensation. Compensation for the impairment of one person's property could only be achieved by impairing someone else's. If all wealth is to be regarded as "vested," then there can be no coercive redistribution.

Reich's more modest substantive proposal was that government largesse not be conditioned on waiver of independently protected constitutional rights. He gave as an example the case of *Sherbert v. Verner* in which the Supreme Court held that a state could not disqualify a woman for unemployment insurance benefits because religious activities protected by the first amendment made her unavailable for work on Saturdays. After two decades of development of the doctrine of unconstitutional conditions, it is apparent that, not only does the New Property idea offer nothing that cannot be more easily explained through elaboration of the independently protected rights, but it seems to compound the central difficulty that has arisen with respect to unconstitutional conditions. This difficulty concerns the relationship between constitutional liberties and the distribution of wealth. The problem is to distinguish plausibly a set of particular impermissible conditions, burdens, deprivations, penalties, etc., from the general background regime of state-defined economic rights that determines the distribution of wealth, and in turn, the extent to which people can make use of their constitutional liberties. Since Sherbert these distinctions have repeatedly broken down, so that people are constantly arguing that the recognition of a constitutional right entails an obligation to redistribute wealth in a way that makes it possible to exercise the right. Thus, people argue that the right to a criminal appeal requires the state to transfer funds to poor defendants so that they can afford to appeal, or that freedom of expression requires the state to force media owners to afford access for nonowners to their media, or that the right to education requires the state to transfer revenues from wealthy school districts to poor ones. Reich's more modest proposal thus leads to the same paradox as the compensation requirement: It requires a kind of redistribution that can only be accomplished through the infringement of some of the rights it is designed to protect.

The problems with the substantive program are in part a

consequence of the fact that Reich's argument bypasses the distributive issues. The paradox of the proposal simply to legalize "economic status" can only be resolved by some criteria for assigning priorities to different types of status to indicate which would warrant enforcement at the expense of others. Similarly, the paradox of the proposal to limit power through rights creation can only be resolved through criteria for distinguishing legitimate from illegitimate power, and this distinction in turn requires judgments about the relative justice of the ends for which different types of power might be used.

Why didn't Reich discuss such criteria? Perhaps part of the answer is that it would have been difficult for him to address the distributive issue directly without making his article more controversial. To do so might have made the piece more controversial jurisprudentially because it would have placed it somewhat at odds with the individualist, anti-state rhetorical tradition on which it relied. To defend explicitly the distributive premises of welfare, Reich would have had to take on the claim that welfare cannot be a right because it requires coercive redistribution that infringes the independence of the non-needy. He would have had to take on the further claim that, because the principle of need is hard to limit or because it is sensitive to unexpected contingency, it is incompatible with the kind of absolute or categorical rights required by the value of independence. Moreover, confronting the distributive issue directly might have made the article more controversial by identifying it with a recognizably political program. By sublimating his distributive concerns, Reich created the impression of a distinctively legal program that stood above political conflict.

The second paradox of the New Property is that, while it was clearly designed to legitimate the expansion of the welfare state, it proceeded by portraying the state as a menace. This paradox was partially obscured by the practice of the New Property jurisprudes of characterizing their administrative program of formalization, bureaucratization, and proletarianization as reducing the power or discretion of the state. Yet even if this characterization were accurate, progressive jurisprudence suggests that one cannot say, as a matter of abstract jurisprudence, whether reducing the power or discretion of the state will serve the independence of the individuals with whom it deals. If by discretion we mean, not arbitrariness, but flexible, complex judgment, then discretion may be necessary to help people find their way through the legal system or to respond to unexpected contingencies in their lives. Reducing state power can limit the capacity of officials to harm citizens, but it can also limit their capacity to help them. Here again the individual right/state power framework obscures the real stakes. It makes it hard to understand the ways in which individuals are necessarily dependent on the state; it makes it impossible to consider that the state might empower individuals.

Moreover, the paradox of the state leads to a more fundamental problem. The thrust of the administrative program is not to limit state power or discretion at all; it is simply to shift it around. In particular, the program tends to shift power from lower tier officials toward upper tier officials and judges. Unless one arbitrarily assumes that upper tier officials and judges are not part of the state, these reforms in no way affect the magnitude of state power.

Reich appears to have misunderstood the Progressive critique of the classical portrayal of the state. He associated the Progressive repudiation of rights-as- immunities and of bureaucratized administration with a naive faith in the expertise or altruism of public officials. It is not unfair to charge the Progressives with naivete in these respects, but the charge is not an adequate response to their arguments that rights are not a plausible solution to the problem of official misconduct (since their enforcement depends on official conduct) and that formality and bureaucracy are as likely to injure as they are to vindicate the interests of the beneficiaries of the welfare-regulatory state. Indeed, Reich's own program is every bit as dependent on official expertise and altruism as the one he criticizes. The only difference is in the identity of the officials on whom he relies.

Just as Reich's substantive program lacks needed criteria to distinguish material interests entitled to protection from competing interests that might be sacrificed, so his procedural program lacks needed criteria for distinguishing types of people or of organization that can be trusted to exercise power from those that cannot be trusted. Although Reich's preferences are clear, they do not follow from the premise of independence and the right/power framework. Here, too, one reason Reich did not address such criteria may be that the effort would have threatened the notion of right-as-immunities by bringing the discussion explicitly into the realm of group conflict and controversial political judgments.

* * *

The New Property view of welfare rights is incoherent as jurisprudence and exhausted as politics. It is irrelevant to what ought to be the two principal concerns of liberal welfare jurisprudence. The first is to develop doctrines that acknowledge the importance of need as a distributive principle and design programs that adequately respond to need. The second is to develop an ideal and a program of public administration that recognizes the value of a responsible state as well as the dangers of an irresponsible one and that fosters conditions in which the street level public workforce can work responsibly and effectively. These were precisely the central concerns of the New Deal social workers, and contemporary lawyers still have a lot to learn from their efforts.

Joel F. Handler

"Constructing the Political Spectacle": The Interpretation of Entitlements, Legalization, and Obligations in Social Welfare History

56 Brooklyn Law Review 899 (1990)

From Entitlements to Legalization and Obligations

In *The New Property*, Charles Reich called for a re-construction of the relationship between citizens and government. After pointing out the increased dependency of citizens on their relationships to government, he argued that these relationships should be considered legal entitlements. This conceptualization, which he called the New Property, would protect the holders of these entitlements from discretionary government acts either by clear rules or procedural due process. Legal entitlements to government relationships would perform the same work as traditional property. Reich talked about a wide range of relationships--licenses, franchises, employment contracts, and also welfare. The United States Supreme Court, in *Goldberg v. Kelly*, encoded this legal theory into public law: statutory welfare grants were legal entitlements; as such, they could only be withheld or terminated according to due process of law. The Court explicitly rejected the prior construction that welfare was a mere privilege. An AFDC recipient was entitled to a fair hearing before benefits could be terminated.

The New Property and *Goldberg v. Kelly* seized the historical moment. There was a vast change in legislation and administrative codes recognizing the new legal status of welfare and granting procedural due process. To a large extent, this change in both the ideology and practice of welfare reflected broader currents in American public life--civil rights, rights of other vulnerable groups (the handicapped, the mentally ill, women, and children), and consumer and environmental protection. There was heady talk among the poverty law community of a constitutional "right to life" that would finally move America toward the fulfillment of the social rights of citizenship.

The hopes for a vanguard Supreme Court were short-lived. Within a few years, the Court squashed all thought of substantive interference with state control over welfare benefits and restricted *Goldberg v. Kelly*. In the meantime, the ideology of entitlements has taken a curious turn. It has been attacked from the left by Professor William Simon for further dividing the poor, for failing to protect welfare recipients from substantive cutbacks in benefits and for contributing to the "legalization of welfare." By legalization, Simon is referring to the increased use of rules in welfare to deny or reduce benefits. At the same time, conservatives, such as Lawrence Mead, have used entitlements to justify the new efforts at social control in welfare, namely, "workfare."

For a long time now, welfare has taken a bad turn. Benefits have declined substantially. Payments have been extensively restricted by detailed rules designed to reduce administrative errors. As a result, massive numbers of applicants are denied aid or have their benefits terminated through "paper" errors. For almost twenty-five years, the federal government has been trying to impose work requirements. The latest welfare reform consensus, the Family Support Act of 1988, has "workfare" as its centerpiece. Has the concept of entitlements helped chart this path? Has the reconstruction of the welfare relationship provided the ideological grounding for these developments? Simon and Mead say, "yes." While Mead, of course, applauds this development, Simon harshly condemns *The New Property*.

The result, if true, is startling. It has long been argued that social rights--the entitlement to the minimum, decent provisions of life, however difficult to define--were essential to full citizenship rights, that civic and political rights were hollow without social rights. Does the American welfare experience mean that the conceptual move toward entitlements refutes this argument? What is the argument against welfare entitlements? Does that argument explain the course of welfare policy in the United States?

Entitlements

Simon's argument against the New Property rights-based jurisprudence of welfare is twofold. In contrast to traditional property rights, welfare rights, by themselves, provide no basis for redistribution (taking property from some and giving it to others). The distributive principles of property rights are based on the entitlement to one's own efforts and the legitimacy of voluntary exchange, neither of which can ground welfare rights. Simon argues that welfare distribution (and rights) can only be grounded on needs, which Reich refused to do. As long as there was an expanding social pie, welfare rights could claim a share for recipients. But when new property came into conflict with old property, with the decline in growth in the late 1970s, property rights were better grounded in distributive principles. New property had no theoretical justification for redistribution; welfare as property rights failed.

Reich argued that rights are incompatible with discretion. He was referring to the moralistic, paternalistic intrusion of social work. The emphasis on rights paved the way for the elimination of discretion and the replacement of social workers with eligibility clerks. The new system was designed to protect recipients by clearly defining rights, and by exercising management control over field-level discretion. Simon argues that this approach made sense only on the assumption that liberals would be in control. When the conservatives took over, these rules were turned against the poor. The reduction of discretion through the imposition of tightly drawn rules administered by bureaucratic clerks allowed managers to institute quality control. Ostensibly combating "waste, fraud, and abuse," managers focused primarily on overpayment errors. Many errors were "paper" errors--that is, failure to comply with rules that did not involve substantive eligibility--for example, the failure to have a Social Security number for a child. Vast numbers of cases were closed, how many permanently is unknown. Michael Lipsky coined the phrase "bureaucratic disentitlement" to describe the practice. While the ideology of entitlements cannot be completely blamed for these developments, according to Simon, by focusing on rights and excluding consideration of needs and by attacking both discretion and social workers, legal rights advocates became the handmaiden of subsequent control by the conservatives.

Obligations

According to Mead, a major reason for "entrenched" poverty is nonwork on the part of the poor--both the inability to find work and the failure to even look for work. Whatever the reasons for nonwork, he argues, both liberals and conservatives have come to the conclusion that neither macroexpansionary economic programs nor civil rights enforcement will affect nonwork. Rather, the government must now engage in specific programs aimed at raising the work levels of the poor. This means requiring employable welfare recipients to work or to prepare for work. Mead's moral argument is that citizenship entitlements necessarily entail obligations.

Mead concedes that the poor *want* to work. He does not believe that the structural barriers to employment explain the high levels of nonwork. What, then, is the problem? As a result of civil rights, our society has become permissive. Conventional work norms have lost their moral authority. Facilitating work for the poor will no longer do; rather, work must be enforced. Prior work programs failed because they either relied on incentives, and if the welfare poor were responsive to incentives, they would not be poor in the first place, or on public jobs[18] which were better than what the poor could command in the private economy, and thus disguised welfare. Instead of relying on incentives, work relief programs tied to welfare should be expanded. The principal benefit is to increase the motivation of welfare recipients to work. Because workfare is mandatory, welfare agencies have the authority to "demand effort and cooperation from the clients *in return* for the benefits they are receiving." Thus, welfare entitlements are matched by obligations.

For Mead, equal citizenship means the same rights and obligations as enjoyed by those not on welfare. Nonwork is an antisocial act that justifies making employment a publicly enforced duty. Citizens have the moral obligation to become "competent"; by this he means, the successful discharge of their obligations; for him, moral worth is found in the market.

The Consensus on Welfare Reform

---

[18]The Comprehensive Employment Training Act (CETA) funded as many as 750,000 jobs per year during the 1970s.

In a curious way, some liberals have adopted Mead's argument. This is reflected in the contemporary consensus on welfare reform. The centerpiece of the reform consensus is workfare. Workfare used to mean "work relief"--the age-old system whereby welfare recipients were required to work for the welfare grant. Today, "workfare" is much broader. It includes both the requirement that a welfare recipient engage in a number of work-related activities--such as job search and work preparation (e.g., education, training)--and "work relief," whereby the recipient works in return for the welfare grant. Child-care and other benefits are provided for participants. Workfare is required; failure to participate is sanctioned.

The justification that liberals give for supporting workfare is that because the majority of non-poor mothers, even of small children, are now in the paid labor force, societal norms have changed. Therefore, it is reasonable to expect a similar obligation on the part of welfare mothers. It is the language of obligation that attaches to citizenship. The poor and the non-poor are to be treated alike; they are to have similar obligations.

Thus, we see the importance of ideological reconstruction. Reconstructing the welfare relationship in terms of entitlements has either undermined citizenship social rights (Simon) or affirmed the obligations of citizenship (Mead). Reconstructing gender roles, combined with entitlements, has brought liberals on board a conservative welfare reform.

Entitlements thus carry a heavy burden--not only the dashed hopes of a more complete citizenship, but also responsibility for a significant change in our attitudes towards poor mothers. Is this a correct analysis of the role of the ideology of welfare policy? Do these stories explain the changes that have taken place in welfare policy?

In my view, all three positions--Simon, Mead, and the liberals who have joined the reform consensus--are telling the wrong story about welfare. They have misconstrued the ideologies of welfare policy. Their error is focusing on the rhetoric of entitlement to interpret welfare policy and to justify positions. . . . What I argue is that language, including legal language, is malleable, and that a deeper analysis of the multiple *meanings* of welfare history reveals a far more complex story than presented by the three positions.

* * *

The meaning of welfare history has been constructed around

the master ideologies of class--I prefer the term industrial discipline--gender (patriarchy and child rearing), race, and ethnicity. Welfare history both reflects and constructs these ideologies. I view that history as the institutionalized production of deviant symbols designed to shore up dominant ideology. The history and development of the Aid to Families with Dependent Children (AFDC) program not only illustrates patriarchy and race, but also the importance of the deviant status of poor mothers in the paid labor force. Worker's compensation shows the relation between ideological consensus and administrative structure in a repressive program. The rise and fall of the New Deal work relief programs explains the social control features and jurisdictional characteristics of unemployment insurance. The conflict between programs for the dependent aged and Social Security insurance shows that formal distinctions between needs and entitlements are malleable: *needs* become social *rights*, indistinguishable, for the most part, from entitlements. It is the moral conception of the particular category of the poor that is decisive.

Notes and Questions

1. *Tensions Among the Left.* Does the debate between Professors Simon and Handler reflect tensions among left scholars? If so, how?

2. *Entitlement Status.* Will deeming welfare to be a legal entitlement help or harm poor people?

3. *Confronting the Right.* The entitlement debate among left scholars neither attempted nor accomplished the construction of arguments designed to engage and respond to the growing conservative voices. Many poverty law scholars in the 1990s have attempted to fill this void. Lucie White, in the article excerpted below, undertook the task of examining the reality experienced by a welfare recipient who could probably serve well as a conservative example of the worst case scenario resulting from liberal welfare policies. White did not rely solely on explanations typically provided by liberal commentators to explain poor people's plight, such as systematic racial and gender discrimination in employment. Instead, she carefully considered how Elaine Preston might fare with proffered conservative solutions to her predicament.

Lucie E. White

NO EXIT: RETHINKING "WELFARE DEPENDENCY" FROM A DIFFERENT GROUND

81 GEORGETOWN LAW JOURNAL 1961 (1993)

* * *

I turn now to the words of one woman--I will call her Elaine Preston[38]--who readily describes herself as trapped on welfare because she is lazy. Ms. Preston is a parent in a Head Start program in a rural county in North Carolina.

* * *

Elaine Preston was born on May 19, 1955. She was the oldest of eight children, four boys and four girls. Her father left the family when she was a young child. To support her children, Elaine's mother, who had been trained as a cosmetologist, styled hair in the daytime and washed dishes at night. As early in her childhood as Elaine can remember, she was expected to take care of younger brothers and sisters. She has never liked taking care of children. She recalls that it was hard to be called on to do this kind of work while still a child herself.

Elaine's memories of school are all negative: "It was boring. . . . I had the most snobby teachers, and hateful teachers. . . . They didn't care . . . [s]o I didn't care." The one teacher Elaine distinctly remembers, Ms. Diggs, stands out because, "she took her time with me. And if I ever had a problem I could also go to her." Ms. Diggs was the exception, however. Elaine became a "loncr" in school. She recalls looking forward to the end of the school day, so she could go back home--deal with thc younger children--and then watch TV.

Elaine recalls that as a child, she had wanted to be a nurse's aid. At fifteen, however, she got pregnant and then "just stopped" going to school. She remembers that "a few people" tried to talk to her about going back, but "it didn't do no good." Of the eight children in the Preston household, Elaine was the only one who did not graduate from high school.

After leaving school and having a baby, Ms. Preston found occasional work as a maid in a local motel. This felt better to her than school, because it allowed her to spend more time watching TV. "I love television," she explains. Early on, she had learned to escape

---

[38]Elaine Preston is a pseudonym.

from her own maternal responsibilities, her boredom, her mother's cares, and the things that she did not feel comfortable talking to me about, by watching TV. "I just like watching television. I just love it. I don't know why. . . . I can just sit there and turn it on and look at it all day."

Ms. Preston now lives in a public housing project that has a growing crack cocaine problem. In addition to an adult daughter who was raised by Ms. Preston's mother, she has two young boys. Over the years, she has made a living by working intermittently in restaurants, motels, and spinning mills . . . getting laid off or quitting . . . and then signing up for AFDC. All her jobs have paid minimum wage. Welfare, when she gets it, pays her family $272.00 a month. She hates being on AFDC: "I know they be wanting to *know* everything. They are so nosy. They control your life. I don't like it." But when she gets laid off, or gets so fed up with work that she quits, she feels that she has no other choice except to go back on AFDC.

When I met Elaine Preston she was on AFDC. Under the terms of the 1988 Family Support Act as it was administered by her state, she was required to attend a literacy class as a condition for receiving AFDC payments. Nearly all of the students in this class, like Ms. Preston, had children in Head Start. Two mornings a week the literacy class would meet at the Head Start center, so the mothers could work on prereading activities with their children.

Ms. Preston's son loves Head Start. It offers him "a lot more stuff . . . a lot more games . . . fun things" than when she was in school. In contrast to what Ms. Preston remembers from her own schooling, at Head Start "they *make* you like it." Especially important to Ms. Preston is the involvement of the mothers: "I believe if my mom had come [to my school] . . . would've had time . . . she had several kids outside . . . I would've graduated. . . . There is a lot of stuff that used to be so hard. . . . [W]hen I go in there and see the little smile on their face, how I make 'em feel good on the inside, it makes you feel good too!" Elaine sums up her reaction to Head Start by noting that the program feels "like a little family."

About two weeks after my first taped interview with Elaine Preston in January of 1992, she disappeared from the literacy class for almost two months. In an interview in early April, she explained her extended absence: her kids got sick, there was a death in her family, she "just got lazy," and she wanted to see if her AFDC worker would notice that she was gone or take the time to track her down. As Elaine Preston would have predicted, however, in spite of the requirement that she attend the literacy class, it took her social worker two months to respond to her absence by telephoning her with a warning to return. Just before she received this phone call, however, she had already returned to the class on her own. She went back because she had gotten bored with watching TV, and because her son missed his mother's absence from his Head Start classroom.

"Exploding the Boulder. . ."[70]

The story of Elaine Preston poses something of a dilemma within liberal welfare discourse. Traditionally, such discourse seeks to avoid blaming either poor people themselves, or welfare, for entrenched poverty. Yet at the same time, this tradition values the work incentive and views prolonged "welfare dependency" as a bad thing. Within this normative framework, it is difficult to respond to Elaine Preston's self-proclaimed laziness, her apparently capricious regard for her own self-interest, her confessed addiction to TV, and her seemingly random drift from one dead-end job to another, with periodic detours through AFDC. Rather than seeking to make sense of this life experience, liberal welfare discourse has simply ignored--erased--women like Elaine Preston. Meanwhile, conservative writers have focused upon women like Elaine Preston, extracting details that will promote negative stereotypes about their moral worthiness, and about the welfare programs that are crucial to their families' survival.

What if we diverge from this rhetoric of denial and move Ms. Preston's life story from the margins to the center of our attention?

---

[70]The reference is to an insight of Alice Walker's main character, Tashi, in POSSESSING THE SECRET OF JOY (1992). Tashi struggles to give words to an unbearably painful recollection from her own childhood. Through this struggle, she begins to comprehend how speaking about such experiences is a crucial step in the process of surviving them. When Tashi finally manages to give words to her own pain, she describes the moment as follows:

> There was a boulder lodged in my throat. . . . I knew what the boulder was; that it was a word; and that behind that word I would find my earliest emotions. . . . I took a deep breath and exhaled it against the boulder blocking my throat: [I spoke] . . . exploding the boulder. . . . No longer would my weeping be separate from what I *knew*. . . .

Id. at 73-74.

What if we listen carefully to what she has said? Will such a project yield any insight about welfare and poverty, insight that might help us contest the hegemonic conservative gospel that welfare and its victims are bad?

According to this gospel, Elaine Preston is a woman of intrinsically weak character, who has been enticed by the guarantee of a welfare check to lose all incentive to seek a genuinely self-sufficient future. This reading of Ms. Preston's life, however, may not account very fully for her experience. For her life has not been stagnant over the last thirty years. Rather, Ms. Preston has made repeated attempts to exit welfare and enter into the world of self-supporting social citizenship. But every time she has made such an effort, she has found the widely advertised exit corridors of education, work, and marriage to be blocked by threats of violence. When she is "laying low"--by drawing welfare to support her children and watching a lot of TV--Ms. Preston's life is fairly quiet. But when she starts on the routes out of poverty--like education, employment, or marriage--she opens herself up to a heightened risk of physical, sexual, and psychic injury.

Therefore, the image of Ms. Preston as a woman who has been rendered passive by welfare may not really do justice to the facts of her life. Ms. Preston may not be a woman whose incentive has been sapped by welfare, so much as a woman in continual, determined, but also often futile motion. Elaine Preston might best be understood as a woman who has resolved to survive--one way or another--in the face of a plethora of double binds. The recurring pattern of welfare, attempted exit, violence, and retreat that marks Ms. Preston's life becomes more clear when her experiences are placed beside accounts of other women whose lives intersect with her own.

"Get An Education"

From the time that they are children, poor women are exhorted to "get an education" if they want to escape poverty. After the desegregation cases of the 1970s purported to implement *Brown v. Board of Education,* children of color have been expected to believe that the courts have finally dismantled Jim Crow in the public schools. Therefore, when these children fail to complete high school, they are made to feel that it is their own lack of initiative, determination, or smarts that is to blame.

This message ignores the social facts about public education for poor children that have been amassed by journalists, sociologists, lawyers, and educators in their efforts to reform the schools. This work paints a familiar composite picture: unequal and inadequate funding; overcrowded classrooms; overworked teachers; and entrenched, unresponsive, and sometimes corrupt bureaucracies. What these accounts often leave unnamed, however, is the emotional reality of the school experience, particularly for the generation of young adults of color who, like Ms. Preston, went to school during the first years of court-ordered integration.

Elaine Preston spoke to me from a distance about school. She noted that her teachers were "snobby" and concurred with me that for her, school was a "bust." She could recall only a single teacher who had cared for her; she longed for the kind of school experience, the "little family," that she felt in her son's Head Start. She dropped out of school at fifteen, before finishing the tenth grade. Twenty years later, when she was required to attend a literacy class to receive AFDC, she felt, once again, a compulsion to withdraw from school. But within these broad outlines, Ms. Preston gave little detail about her day to day life in school. "All that she remembered" had become a vague dark cloud.

The stories of other women, Ms. Preston's contemporaries, suggest what some of those repressed memories might have been. Other women in Ms. Preston's Head Start program have recalled scenes of being called "nigger" or being spat upon by white classmates, and then getting blamed for the ensuing fight. They have recalled white teachers casually lamenting to one another that "those coloreds just can't learn like us," or white students chiding each other for "playing with blacks." Some women still recall the feeling of not getting chosen for the softball team or the cheerleading squad, or of not getting invited to parties at white students' houses.

* * *

"Get A Job"

The next exit route that is presented to Elaine Preston is employment. She is repeatedly counseled that she can exit poverty by finding and keeping a job. She is led to believe that this strategy has worked for other dispossessed groups, especially the groups of immigrants that have been considered members of the "white" race. Therefore, if employment fails to work for Elaine Preston and her peers, it must be because all those years on welfare have sapped their work incentive. Elaine Preston hears this message at the welfare office, on television, at church, and at her son's Head Start. She even hears it from the other welfare women in her literacy class. The message is reinforced by a culture within the AFDC program--of sub-poverty level benefits, continual surveillance, and "hateful" bureaucrats--that seems calculated to force her to leave. It should come as no surprise, therefore, that Elaine Preston repeatedly heeds the message, leaves her children in the care of others, and seeks work.

When Ms. Preston takes this route, what does she discover? What jobs are available for a thirty-seven year-old African-American woman, with two young children and a ninth grade education, in the rudderless economy of her home county? There are basically three kinds of work that she has any chance of finding. She can work in food service. She can work in one of the region's many chicken processing plants. Or she can work, like many of her African-American foremothers, as a maid. Because of the dollar for dollar deduction of wages from AFDC benefits, full-time jobs in any of these industries would probably "succeed" in getting Ms. Preston off of welfare. But would they also succeed in improving her financial situation, or according her the social dignity to which tax-paying citizens are supposedly entitled?

First, let us consider the food service jobs that Ms. Preston might hope to find. In "sit down" restaurants where patrons give tips, the jobs for black women are just about all behind the scenes--washing pots, cleaning toilets, or mopping floors. In spite of the Civil Rights Act of 1964, which long ago made job segregation by race or gender against the law, it is still unusual in Ms. Preston's community for a "girl" who isn't white to get a job waiting tables or working as a cashier. Additionally, like most jobs for women, restaurant work carries a constant risk of sexual violation. At fast food establishments, on the other hand, Ms. Preston can get jobs with public contact, but no tips. Not only do these jobs pay less than the full service restaurants; they also tend to have impossible hours for single mothers with kids. A woman might have to report to work at four a.m. to make the breakfast biscuits, or stay until midnight to close up. Finally, the food service jobs in the region seldom provide health coverage or sick leave, and leave workers at risk of being fired for cause for missing work to care for a sick child.

In the chicken processing plants, pay and benefits may be slightly better, but working conditions are often much worse. For in spite of state and federal regulations to the contrary, these jobs often mean being locked inside cold rooms with icy water on the floors and fire exits that are barred from the outside. The workers must chop and wrap meat for hours at a time on production lines where speed is more important than safety. The workers are regimented so closely that often they are not allowed to go to the toilet or sit down, except on designated breaks.

These conditions were tragically brought to public attention on September 3, 1991, when a fire at the Imperial Food Processing plant in Hamlet, North Carolina killed twenty-five workers. A subsequent investigation revealed numerous violations of federal and state safety and health regulations, including locked fire exits, no sprinkler system, and no fire exit plan. Yet the state's worker safety agency had never inspected the plant. Indeed, at the time of the fire the state's agency was so understaffed that it would have needed a hundred years to inspect every workplace that was subject to regulation. As a result of the investigation, three plant officials were charged with criminal manslaughter. The state added seventy-cight additional inspectors to its workplace inspection program, and Congress convened hearings to consider mandating tighter federal supervision of state-managed workplace safety programs. It remains unclear whether these initiatives will result in long-term reforms in the chicken processing industry.

Unlike most industries that were recruited to the mid-South in the 1950s and 1960s by promises of "cheap labor," chicken processing plants cannot run away from the region if southern workers--or new federal laws--begin to demand better working conditions or higher pay. These plants must be located near the farms where the chickens are raised. Therefore, in the chicken plants, in contrast to the textile mills, individualized retaliation, more than the threat of plant closure, has become the routine method to keep labor costs down. With a large pool of potential workers and no advocacy assistance for enforcing their legal protections, the employees in this industry take for granted that if they choose to complain about working conditions, they are also choosing to quit.

If Ms. Preston finds a job as a maid, particularly in private homes, she must face the multiple hazards of work that is outside the de jure as well as the de facto boundaries of government regulation.

. . . In the county where Ms. Preston lives, elderly white people recall how a few decades ago African-American servants were still taken outside and whipped if they displeased their masters. In addition to the routinized humiliation that Ms. Preston still faces in these jobs because of her race, she also faces a particularly high risk of sexual violence. Women can expect sexual harassment in any job, but in household service, the isolation of work sites and the historical assumption of the servant's sexual availability to the master makes the risk of unwanted sexual advances unusually high.

Occasionally, the few spinning mills that remain in the region will hire African-American women. In these coveted jobs, there is less risk of sexual molestation, or of slicing one's own fingers with a cold knife. But for the lucky ones who do not get laid off after a few months, there are the risks of carpal tunnel syndrome, lower back pain, chronic depression, and brown lung disease.

Together these employment options show that, as stated by the African-American folk and gospel group Sweet Honey in the Rock, Ms. Preston can indeed expect to collect "More Than a Paycheck"[115] when she leaves welfare to seek paid work. But her perks are more likely to be physical and psychic violence than dignity and independence.

Progressive poverty advocates have repeatedly demonstrated that AFDC is irrational if its underlying policy goal is to give recipients the incentive to enter the labor market. For, all things considered, welfare typically offers poor women a better deal than

---

[115]*See* SWEET HONEY IN THE ROCK, MORE THAN A PAYCHECK (Flying Fish Records 1981):

> We bring more than a paycheck
> to our loved ones and family
> . . .
> We bring asbestosis, silicosis,
> brown lung, black lung disease
> radiation hits the children
> before they really been conceived
> . . .
> If not disease then injury,
> may befall your lot
> If not injury then stress, is going to tie you up in knots . . . .

Id.

work. When Ms. Preston subtracts the real costs of working--in the form of subsidy reductions as well as out of pocket expenses--from her minimum wage paychecks, she is left with little more than her meager monthly AFDC stipend. This contradiction within a program whose major purpose, according to the current bipartisan consensus, is to push poor people into the labor market surely needs to be addressed.

But the progressive advocates' dollar per dollar comparison neglects the much deeper systemic problems that sap women's motivation to enter the labor market and, once there, drive them back into the demeaning "haven" of AFDC. These deeper disincentives cannot be corrected by tinkering with a few of the figures in the current AFDC benefit schedule, nor even by increasing the number of low wage slots in the current labor market. For these deterrents to finding and keeping paid employment arise from the violent or demeaning work culture of the jobs that are open to welfare recipients, even more than from the lack of job security and the lousy pay.

"Find A Man"

The third exit from poverty that is pushed on poor women is marriage. The notion that marriage provides economic security is grounded in an often noted demographic trend: the chance that an American family will be poor is many times greater if that family is headed by a woman, particularly a woman of color, than if it is headed by a man. Furthermore, over the last decade, the correlation between female-headed families and poverty has become dramatically more pronounced. But the statistics neither reveal the historical and social causes behind the trend, nor specify the appropriate policy responses. Yet in a kind of voodoo logic that has often been invoked over the last decade, the numbers have been cited by male welfare pundits to convince women that their best route off of welfare is a trip to the altar.

* * *

But the numbers do not necessarily lead to the conclusion that marriage is a successful route off of poverty. As feminist scholars have repeatedly pointed out, we might conclude from the same numbers that poverty in America is linked to the dismal work options of single mothers, and to the striking absence in our country of the kind of universal family policy that shields most children from poverty in other industrial countries.[122] We might seek social policies that bring wages above subsistence in traditionally female jobs, and that require quality on-site childcare, health coverage, and family leave as conditions of every job. We might also design enforcement mechanisms that ensure that every workplace is free from the physical, psychic, and sexual hazards that drive poor women to quit their jobs. We might use the numbers about poverty among single mothers to show that the need for such policies is beyond debate, and then put our heads and our purses together to cover their substantial costs. But instead of facing this hard fiscal question, it has seemed easier for armchair moralists to point a finger at poor women and accost them to escape poverty by catching a man.

When women seek to heed this advice, they are likely to confront violence. Elaine Preston did not talk to me much about her own father, the fathers of her children, or other men that might have passed through her life. But other women in her community have shared their experiences in some detail. Barbara Sutton, another mother in Ms. Preston's Head Start program, for instance, gave the following account.[123]

After having a child on her own, Ms. Sutton tried for two years to make ends meet as a single mother. Finally, she met a man who seemed both eligible and responsible, and she dutifully fell in love. Her story, in her own assessment, then began to sound like a worn-out cliche. First, there was a whirlwind romance, with lots of roses and a church wedding that made her parents proud. After a few weeks, with no warning, there was an occasional slap, a few vile

---

[122] *See* TIMOTHY CASEY, CENTER FOR SOC. WELFARE POL'Y & L., PUB. NO. 803, CHILDHOOD POVERTY AND PUBLIC TRANSFERS IN INTERNATIONAL PERSPECTIVE 2-3 (1991) (comparing childhood poverty rates around 1980 in the United States and seven other countries with advanced market economies to show that the U.S. post-transfer childhood poverty rate is the highest among these eight countries, largely because our government's income transfer programs did "exceptionally little" to reduce pretransfer poverty). The two striking features of our public income transfer programs that set them apart from the more successful programs in these other nations are AFDC's exceptionally low--indeed, sub-poverty level--benefit ceiling, and our country's lack of a universal family allowance program. *Id.* at 3-4.

[123] Barbara Sutton is a pseudonym.

words. Then the cursing got fierce and the slaps became blows. There were outbursts of jealousy that led him to search through her things, hide her birth control pills so she could not cheat on him, and take her car keys so she would not leave the house.

She tried hard to calm his anger--by talking less or cooking better or avoiding "those looks" that he didn't trust. But it didn't always work. Once he put his intent bluntly. "I'm going to break you, break your spirit," she recalls him telling her, "even if I have to kill you first." Still she tried to hold the marriage together--because she loved him, and in order to give a future to her child. She explained how "you're taught, as a woman that it is your job to keep the family together, and that if it breaks up--no matter what he did to you--it's your fault."

Finally, after the beatings got so bad that her mother started asking questions about her swollen face, Barbara Sutton went to the courthouse for a restraining order. At the time, she was pregnant with his child. In court, she had to answer to a magistrate who called her "honey" and asked her what she had done to get on his nerves. Then the magistrate told her to "go on home and tell him you're sorry," but she would not follow his advice. Instead, she got a restraining order and a judicial separation. The sheriff moved her husband out of their mobile home. Though she grieved for the end of her marriage, she thought she had gotten away.

Three months later he came back with a box cutter to slit her throat. She crouched in a corner of her trailer, shielding her face with her hands. When he fled, vowing to come back to finish the job, her three year-old daughter sought refuge in her mother's lap. When the ambulance came, the medics had to pull the child away. With her tendons slashed, Barbara Sutton's hand is now permanently disabled; her face is disfigured in ways that plastic surgery can only partially repair. Her daughter is in counseling for emotional trauma. Her husband was convicted of assault, rather than attempted murder, and given a twelve year sentence with an option of early parole.

Stories like Ms. Sutton's--a rape, routine verbal and physical beating, a week in the hospital for a broken jaw--have repeatedly surfaced in interviews that began with innocent open questions about Head Start. Welfare scholars and advocates have not generally considered domestic violence "their" problem, for it is not unique to women who are poor. Yet when their silence about this problem is coupled with direct or implicit advice that poor women should get married, those women are left with a grim choice. They can get treated "like dirt" on welfare, or they can try to beat the odds of injury from a spouse.

Whenever I listen intently to poor women talk about their lives, I hear stories of violence: the violence of racism and class bias that they remember--and expect--from school; the violence of industrial hazards, brain-deadening routines, repressive discipline, and sexual harassment that they face in the few available jobs; and the violence inherent in the bargain when they seek to secure their children's futures through a man. Poor women are thus trapped in a no-win predicament. They face shame if they stay on welfare. Yet the "exits" they are offered are really traps, for rather than providing opportunities, these exits repeatedly expose them to violence.

Mainstream welfare discourse has been silent about this dilemma. Even progressive welfare scholars have too often failed to attend to women's accounts of the violence that they face when they try to leave. Even feminists have too often failed to look for patterns in the multiple stories of violence that poor women tell.

* * *

To break out of this silence, we must first relocate our scholarly and policy discourses on welfare precisely at the center of the double binds that poor women face--"On the edge of hell." Once there, we must refuse to turn back to the old, comfortable, consensus conversations about welfare. We must refuse to turn back to those old conversations, even when our own talk about "welfare" moves us away from topics like work requirements and child support enforcement in AFDC, and toward topics like grassroots democracy in schools, factories, and social programs, and androgynous, fuzzy-bordered families whose homes bridge the "public" and the "private" spheres. If we can be more bold about staking out such a counterhegemonic academic and political discourse about welfare, then women like Ms. Preston might not feel quite so alone, as they continue the interpretive--and physical--battles they cannot escape in their own lives. They might then find it possible, on occasion, to defy the normative and institutional presumptions on which their poisoned choices are premised, rather than merely absorbing the blame for the tragic costs that either making--or evading--those choices entails.

A Primer on Evading Double Binds

One need not read too deeply in psychology to learn that human beings can and do learn to cope when they feel trapped within double binds. We can and do manage to live in such fixes, to flee from our own awareness that we are locked inside a universe of options that are all unsafe. As the psychological literature suggests, however, those strategies of survival are ultimately self-defeating. This is because those strategies too often work by undermining the person who deploys them, rather than by deconstructing the bind. This section examines three strategies that Elaine Preston devised to evade the choice between shame and violence that her life in poverty repeatedly compelled. It may be presumptuous for me, a well-off white woman, to interpret Elaine Preston's actions. Elaine Preston, after all, is quite capable of speaking for herself. Yet right-wing welfare moralists have been bold about interpreting women's lives in order to buttress the myth of welfare dependency. Perhaps my presumption can help open up a conversation about welfare dependency in which those conservative voices are not the only ones that dare to speak.

Preemption

Perhaps the most striking feature of my interviews with Elaine Preston was her readiness to describe herself as "just lazy." When explaining her actions she states, "It [was] just, just *laziness,* that's all it was." When Ms. Preston used this familiar stereotype to describe herself, she did not explain what she sought to accomplish. Some might say that Elaine Preston had internalized the stigma of being on welfare; she had accepted the stereotypes of the dominant culture as the truth about herself. Yet when Elaine Preston pronounced herself "lazy," her meaning was hardly clear. Rather, like the haunting gospel harmonies I heard at her church, her voice seemed to strain to blend discordant emotions--irony, defiance, and exhaustion--into coherent sound.

As scholars of subordination have persuasively demonstrated, theories of internalized domination, or "false consciousness," describe the subjectivity of systematically subordinated people from the outside. Those who have lived race or class subordination are more likely to use themes like double consciousness, or multiple strategies of self-presentation, to describe their own work of claiming "identity" in the face of pervasive hate. Rather than simply *believing* that she was "lazy," it is more likely that Elaine Preston was *deploying* that insult for multiple strategic ends.

Elaine Preston might have called herself lazy in self-defense: to deflect "nosy" questions from one more outsider whom she had no reason to trust. Indeed, she volunteered this self-description so quickly that it sounded like something she had rehearsed before. She might also have called herself "lazy" to preempt my chance to impose the insult upon her, thereby dulling its psychic sting.

* * *

This strategy of preemption worked to shield Elaine Preston from the shame of welfare. It worked to dull the intensity of the double bind. But it also inflamed her anger--toward herself, perhaps, but also toward a "community" that would ask one of its members to pay such a price for her own peace of mind. For no matter how much irony she managed to call up when she said it, calling herself "lazy" hurt Elaine Preston's pride.

Escape

Self-blame helps Elaine Preston cope with the double bind of shame and violence by giving her some psychic distance from the stigma of welfare, thereby making it easier for her to stay on the welfare rolls. A second set of strategies focuses more on the violence than the shame. These strategies send her into mercurial, evasive motion whenever she is forced into an institutional sphere in which she fears violence. Throughout her life, Ms. Preston has perfected what might be called a performance artistry--a range of well-rehearsed movements that permit her to evade the psychic, economic, and physical harm that she fears from the institutional authorities with which she must engage.

I saw her use this artistry in the literacy class. In that class, each student's assignments were tailored to her own needs. Thus, while Ms. Preston attended the class, she was able to control--and minimize--her work-load by "playing dumb" to the teacher. This strategy, however, reinforced in her teacher a stereotyped misperception about Ms. Preston's intellectual potential. Thus the strategy carried a self-defeating cost, for even as Ms. Preston repeatedly sought to out-wit her teacher, she also seemed, at times, to want the teacher's approval.

I saw a further display of this artistry whenever Ms. Preston's teacher tried to engage her student. At these moments, Ms. Preston would evade, and indeed parody, the teacher's attempts at connection. Ms. Preston might begin such a session by feigning intense interest in the material, thereby encouraging her teacher's enthusiasm. When the teacher was thoroughly engaged, Ms. Preston might feign sudden boredom, and then sit back while her teacher scrambled to respond to the abrupt change. Ms. Preston made her boldest gesture of evasion when she disappeared from the class for two months and then suddenly returned.

In short, Elaine Preston is sinking a lot of creative energy into subverting the "opportunity" that the literacy class is intended to offer. But Elaine Preston does not experience the class as an "opportunity." Rather, to her it feels more like a psychic land mine. For one thing, she distrusts the teacher's power to cut off students' AFDC benefits if they fail to show up for class. She also distrusts the teacher's efforts to engage her. For though this teacher is clearly trying to be sincere, Elaine Preston expects that sooner or later a careless comment will betray the teacher's inevitable prejudices about her intellectual capacity. Even if this teacher turns out to be a rare exception, it won't make any difference in the long run, because eventually, just like Ms. Diggs before her, she will go away.

When viewed from her perspective, then, Elaine Preston's strategies of subversion make complete sense. By playing dumb, she limits her psychic investment in the enterprise, as well as her workload. By playing games with the teacher's emotions, Ms. Preston acts out some of her rage at all the white people who have appeared to be well intentioned and then have let her down. Her games also put her in charge of the scene with the teacher, defining its plot line and setting its pace. Indeed, Ms. Preston's sudden departure confirms what she takes to be her teacher's indifference, in spite of prior gestures of care. It also makes Ms. Preston feel in control of the welfare system, exposing its hollow threat to sanction her for missing the literacy class.

Thus Elaine Preston's evasive strategies are very effective. Through her maneuvers, she has staked out a sphere of protected psychic space within a threatening arena; she has subverted an institution's power to do her harm. But Elaine Preston's strategies of self-protection have also subverted her own needs. We got a glimpse of those needs when she spoke of her son's Head Start experience; we got a glimpse of Elaine Preston's hope for what her own education might have been. She remembers that her own past schooling thwarted that hope, and anticipates that the literacy class will be more of the same. As a determined and very strategically sophisticated adult, Elaine Preston might have negotiated this new experience in a way that did not repeat the old hurt, affirming rather than denying her hopes for the future. But her ingenious strategies of self-protection--of guarding her own emotions, acting out her anger, and seizing petty beachheads of control--systematically blocked that possibility. It is this contradictory logic--this convergence of self-protection and self-defeat--that marks the strategies that people are driven to design when they must cope with double binds.

Drugs

Elaine Preston's third set of coping strategies are at once the most blunt in their mechanism and the most extreme in their self-defeating side-effects. These are the familiar strategies of self-medication, of defeating the double bind by psychically or chemically escaping the world. Even the most resilient of temperaments will eventually be driven to such strategies when repeatedly confronted by double binds.

One way that people in impoverished rural communities like Ms. Preston's sought psychic relief during the harsh decade of the 1980s was through a new, commercialized version of evangelical Christianity. This movement had roots in African and Christian religious traditions. Unscrupulous people, however, drew upon these traditions to devise a new, high tech evangelism, and then to market it in communities like Elaine Preston's for huge profits. This phenomenon seems to have peaked with the fall of Jim and Tammy Bakker. Yet many of the local congregations that were a part of the Bakkers' PTL network are still going strong. This kind of religion is all-consuming; it transports its adherents from the everyday frustrations of their lives. But according to Elaine Preston, it works best for people who are both highly disciplined and highly gullible. For to feel its full effects, one must follow an arduous daily regime, and one must not ask too many questions. Elaine Preston is too much a skeptic for this kind of religion to work for her in a sustained way.

For her, a more reliable route to psychic relief has been TV. Elaine Preston discovered the drug-like effects of television as a young child. When she feels particularly vulnerable, she can close out the world by watching television for hours at a stretch. Nothing gets in the way of the calm that Elaine Preston feels when her attention is fixed on the TV--not her own anger, not the kids, not even the program that happens to be on the screen. Sleep is also effective to give Elaine Preston interludes of psychic escape. With small children at home in the afternoons and neighbors who tend to get rowdy at night, however, it is harder for her to secure. Indeed, one of the things that Ms. Preston and other women appreciate about Head Start is that it takes their kids for a few hours in the mornings, so they can sleep.

Beyond religion, television, and sleep are the real drugs, the ones that Elaine Preston only resorts to when her anger and frustration get impossible to bear. There has always been hard liquor and heroin, but now there is crack cocaine as well. In the last four or five years, crack has been pushed on women like Elaine Preston, even in rural communities, right at their front doors. Ms. Preston has seen what crack does to women and children, and she knows about AIDS. But still, crack is hard to resist. Its salesmen are so persistent, and compared to the alternatives it works--at least for those first few minutes--so incomparably well. Philosopher and social critic Cornel West has described crack as "the highest form of addiction known to humankind, [in] that it provides a feeling ten times more pleasurable than orgasm." He goes on to mourn how this drug and the AIDS epidemic that has followed it into despairing African-American communities have mangled lives in ways that defy description. These lives are not being lost through ignorance, or carelessness, or a will to die. Rather, from Elaine Preston's perspective, people in her position must sometimes risk their lives in order to seek relief from their pain.

The range of coping strategies that are available to Elaine Preston and similarly situated women are at once dazzling in their scope and self-defeating in their ultimate effects. Ms. Preston can preempt welfare's stigma by inflicting it on herself; she can subvert the treacherous "opportunities" that come her way; or she can numb herself with a spirit-killing drug. She can also try to summon up the "strength of character" to wrestle free of the double binds on her own. Remarkably, the majority of women on welfare succeed in this feat. They do make it off the welfare rolls--at least temporarily--within a few years. They do get through the gates of "opportunity" without getting maimed or killed. For many of these women, however, as well as for the large minority like Elaine Preston, life on the edge of welfare has been described . . .: "If I think about my life I feel like I'm going insane . . . . I just need to scream."

* * *

Notes and Questions

1. *Listening and Analyzing.* In this article, Lucie White shares her careful listening to and thinking about some of the life experiences of one intermittent welfare recipient. Admittedly, she does not conduct any scientific survey to discern demographic statistics. Is her approach helpful to your understanding about the experiences of welfare recipients? How does her approach compare to Charles Murray's use of hypothetical welfare recipients?

2. *Victimization.* White describes Elaine Preston as confronting violence at every turn, in the psychic destruction of her school years and the potential physical and sexual hazards of available jobs and possible relationships. Conservatives frequently accuse liberals of treating welfare recipients as mere victims. Does Lucie White view Elaine Preston as a victim?

SECTION II: EXAMINING POVERTY LAW PRACTICE

CHAPTER 4: CHALLENGES FOR POVERTY LAWYERS

Poor people experience legal problems of every variety. Those needing assistance undoubtedly have received the occasional aid of a lawyer who offered services for a reduced fee or none at all. Most legal needs of poor people, however, never receive a lawyer's attention. This chapter examines the provision of legal services to the poor by setting the historical stage, raising challenges for poverty lawyering, and examining ongoing issues of access to justice.

A. A BRIEF HISTORY

1. Early Legal Aid

Martha Davis
BRUTAL NEED (1994)

Poor Law and Poverty Lawyers

Until the 1960s practicing poverty law meant little more than giving routine legal advice to poor people. A handful of lawyers--most notably the 400 or so employed by Legal Aid societies across the country--had specialized in representing the poor since the late nineteenth century, but no cohesive body of poverty law had been developed by the litigants or the courts. Except in a few academic circles, labor law, family law, administrative law, and constitutional law were not recognized as having unique impacts on poor people. Instead, legal theorists held to the laissez-faire notion that the law was class-blind.

Poverty law changed dramatically in the 1960s. Between 1963, when federal grants were first made available to experimental offices in New Haven, Connecticut, and New York City, and 1971, when the federally funded legal services program was in full swing, the number of lawyers for poor people rose by 650 percent to more than 2,500. In 1959 Legal Aid Society lawyers took only 6 percent of their cases to court while the rest of their clients made do with advice or assistance with out-of-court negotiations; by 1971 federally funded legal services lawyers took 17 percent of their client's cases to court. Until 1965 no course on poverty law had ever been taught at a law school; by 1967 poverty law courses were offered at thirty-six law schools. Despite eighty-nine years of representing the poor, Legal Aid lawyers had never appealed a case to the U.S. Supreme Court; but from 1965 to 1974 the new poverty lawyers appealed 164 cases to the Court on behalf of their clients. Seven percent of all Supreme Court opinions written during those years were decisions in poverty law cases.

From the nineteenth century through the 1960s a succession of organizations--the Legal Aid Society, settlement houses, Mobilization for Youth, and the Center on Social Welfare Policy and Law--used New York City as a base for efforts to address the problems of poverty through litigation and law reform.

The Legal Aid Society exercised a virtual monopoly over the representation of poor people in New York from its creation in 1876 until 1964, when the Mobilization for Youth (MFY) Legal Unit was chartered. Originally called Der Deutsche-Rechtsschutz-Verein, the society was founded by Edward Salomon, former governor of Wisconsin, to "render legal aid and assistance, gratuitously, to those of German birth, who may appear worthy thereof, but who from poverty are unable to procure it." Only after Salomon's retirement in 1889 was the society's charter amended to allow it to render free legal assistance to all.

By that time the wave of German immigration had subsided; the newest influx of immigrants to New York was made up of Russian and Eastern European Jews. According to Arthur Von Briesen, president of the New York Legal Aid Society from 1890 to 1915, the society had a mission to introduce these immigrants to democracy. "Once a poor jobless fellow-being learns that in this country he will have his rights ensured and enforced," Von Briesen asserted, "be he ever so poor, he will promptly join the ranks of those who are the most ardent supporters of our institutions."

Von Briesen's tenure at the society was marked by dogged fund-raising and steady expansion as he worked to achieve this goal. The society had been funded almost exclusively through the contributions of German immigrants and staffed primarily by volunteers when Von Briesen assumed control. Its annual budget was about $3,000. Von Briesen moved to establish a stable and sizable budget through membership drives and law firm contributions, refusing financial support from New York City itself. In addition, Legal Aid Society clients were required to pay a retaining fee of up to twenty-five cents, if possible, and attorneys were authorized to collect a 10 percent commission on all sums recovered in excess of five dollars. In 1904 alone the society collected $5,483, about one-quarter of its budget, in this way. By 1906 the New York Legal Aid Society's budget had risen to $28,553, by far the largest of any Legal Aid society in the country.

Von Briesen's tenacity translated into expanded services for New York's poor. In 1900, for example, the Legal Aid Society expeditiously handled 14,365 cases--almost triple the caseload in 1898 --recovering $96,704.45 for its clients at an average overhead of less than a dollar a case. This rise in activity was attributable, in part, to Von Briesen's innovative decision to dilute the resources of Legal Aid's main office in the heart of downtown Manhattan to establish branch offices in New York's most impoverished neighborhoods.

One satellite office was the East Side Branch, established in 1899 at the University Settlement House at 185 Eldridge on the Lower East Side. At the time the Lower East Side was the most densely populated neighborhood in the world, housing more than 1,000 people per acre. Most of the neighborhood's inhabitants lived in dumbbell tenements, five- or six-story structures built around dark, narrow air shafts with few windows. Because of the overcrowding, filth, and crime bred by the tenements, the death rate on the Lower East Side was double that of any other part of the city.

The national origin of Legal Aid's clients at the East Side Branch during the first two and a half months of 1899 reflected the neighborhood's character: sixty-six clients were Russian; thirty-seven, German; twenty-eight, Austrian; fourteen, Polish; eight, American; six, Rumanian; two, Irish; one, Scottish; one, Italian; one, Turkish; and one, Hungarian. Less than a third were U.S. citizens; 115 of the clients were men, and 50 were women.

As recent arrivals learning the mores of the United States, many of these clients required only basic advice regarding contracts, real estate transactions, or family troubles. According to the attorney in charge of the office, "Common sense is a greater requisite than the law." A few additional cases sought "redress for misfortunes common to us all, and with which the law has little to do."

The great majority of the cases handled by the East Side Branch, however, involved unpaid wages, a common denominator of the sweatshop employment that prevailed on the Lower East Side. A typical wage case, according to a Legal Aid attorney, arose when

> the 'greener' just over from Poland, Russia, or Roumania [sic] looks about for a chance to earn a living. He sees in one of the Yiddish papers an attractive advertisement to teach beginners machine operating or cigarette and cigar making. He applies at the shop and is told that he must learn for four weeks and then he will be employed steadily, with pay. To this end he gives the fee of from $5 to $15, which generally takes the last cent he owns . . . . At the end of that time the apprentice is very apt to be discharged at once, or else told that he is not fit to earn money and must keep working for nothing if he wishes to stay. Whether the man leaves in disgust or is discharged, the result is the same: the master has the money and the apprentice is in a desperate situation . . . . We have complaints of this sort every week, and there is little that can be done in the majority of them.

The Legal Aid Society's policy was to settle most of these wage cases; only six were brought to trial in 1899. Of the six, four were initially settled to the lawyer's satisfaction, but the client, "through obstinacy or ill-temper," insisted on taking the case to trial. According to Legal Aid staff attorney Samuel Goldberg, "It is undoubtedly true that our clients are naturally litigious." Staff attorney Arthur G. H. Lester agreed that "the spirit of compromise does not exist with them."

Despite their clients' obstinacy, the Legal Aid Society enforced a "general policy of reasonable compromise," whatever the client's wishes. Placards distributed to each of the Legal Aid Society's offices in 1907 admonished lawyers to settle cases if at all possible. Legal Aid lawyers reasoned that an early settlement was preferable to waiting for a trial: "The clients lived from hand to mouth and needed their money without delay. The local courts were frightfully congested." Both to maximize their own time and to speedily obtain at least some recompense for their clients, Legal Aid lawyers focused on settling cases.

The dire conditions on the Lower East Side also attracted more than a dozen fledgling settlement houses that were, like the Legal Aid Society, devoted to reforming the poor by exposing them to middle-class values--a sort of American chivalry for recent immigrants.

Influenced by the philosophy of Felix Adler, founder of the Ethical Culture Society, and moved by Jacob Riis's 1890 book *How The Other Half Lives*, an account of ghetto life on the Lower East Side, settlement house residents believed that they could reform the conditions that created New York's ghettos by living and working among the poor. These aspirations were inextricably linked to the development and institutionalization of social work. Not only did the social work profession emerge from the settlement house movement, but the profession's early focus on social justice and reform was a direct result of settlement house goals and ideology.

The University Settlement on the Lower East Side--home of the Legal Aid Society's East Side Branch--was the first settlement house in the United States, founded in 1886. Its purpose was to bring "men of education into closer relations with the laboring classes of the city, for mutual instruction and benefit," by establishing "'settlements' in the tenement-house districts, where college men interested in the workers may live, and mingle with their poor neighbors, on terms of perfect equality."

The settlement house idea caught on quickly, particularly among young women in cities like Philadelphia, Chicago, and New York, which were inundated with tens of thousands of impoverished immigrants. Settlement houses offered this first generation of college-educated women independence from their families and a respectable, challenging career other than teaching or nursing. At least one of New York's settlement houses, College Settlement (affiliated with Smith College), was operated exclusively by women. Several others, such as the famous Hull House in Chicago headed by Jane Addams and the Henry Street Settlement House in New York directed by Lillian Wald, were founded by women.

The University Settlement was the only settlement house in New York that provided *direct* legal services to its clients (through the Legal Aid Society), but as settlement house residents moved into the arena of Progressive politics, law reform became a significant part of their work. Reflecting Progressives' emphasis on scientific management as an alternative to the cronyism prevalent in city and state governments, settlement houses published reams of sociological data gathered from their clients, then used this data to promote Progressive policies. New York's Lower East Side was their laboratory. Between 1897 and 1909 the Henry Street Settlement investigated dispossessed tenants, the licensing of midwives, child labor, and working conditions for women. In 1900 the University Settlement conducted an early survey of the criminal courts. The College Settlement mounted a comprehensive survey of unemployment. Settlement residents lobbied to get nurses in the public schools and helped organize the Women's Trade Union League and the National Association for the Advancement of Colored People. Beginning in 1902 a coalition of settlement leaders led the fight to enact national child labor laws, an effort that culminated in 1912 when Congress passed a bill establishing the Children's Bureau in the Department of Labor.

Ironically, Legal Aid lawyers--serving the same poor constituency as settlement houses--contributed little to the settlements' law reform work, which was handled by settlement house leaders in consultation with elite private attorneys. Lillian Wald of the Henry Street Settlement House, for example, relied on the prominent corporate lawyer Louis Marshall of Guggenheim, Untermeyer & Marshall for advice concerning her efforts in support of laws regulating night work for women. Florence Kelley, a fixture at the Henry Street Settlement House, enlisted the able representation of Louis D. Brandeis in 1908 when the issue of regulating women's work was presented to the U.S. Supreme Court in *Muller v. Oregon*.

In part, Legal Aid chose to stay on the sidelines in order to maintain an image of professional objectivity. But Legal Aid's absence from the great law reform debates of the day also reflected the meager political clout wielded by the society. Von Briesen had envisioned Legal Aid as a "stepping stone to success" for young lawyers, much like a physician's internship, but in reality Legal Aid attracted women and Jews, who were excluded from most law firms. As a result, these lawyers were marginalized even in the area with which they were most familiar--poverty law.

Legal Aid's apolitical stance did, however, help save it from the financial insecurity of the settlement house movement. Funding for settlement houses came almost exclusively from individuals, and as the movement came of age, many patrons withdrew support because of the residents' participation in Progressive politics, advocacy of women's suffrage, support of labor unions, and outspoken pacifism. By the 1920s the type of activist social work pioneered by settlement houses was no longer fundable. Social workers increasingly stressed individual casework and psychology rather than the social context and community of their clients. Settlement houses were forced to change their focus or disband.

In contrast, Legal Aid societies had a pool of well-heeled potential supporters in the legal profession. Bar associations were initially uneasy about Legal Aid societies, as many attorneys viewed Legal Aid as a potential competitor for scarce clients. But the societies tailored their programs to allay this fear. New York's Legal Aid Society turned away personal injury cases that, because of potential damage awards, might seem attractive to the private bar. As Von Briesen reassured his colleagues, "The attorneys of The Aid Society never take charge of cases which lawyers in actual practice would be ready to undertake."

It was, however, the great influx of immigrants from southern and eastern Europe between 1905 and 1914 that finally convinced bar leaders that supporting Legal Aid was in their own best interests. As immigration increased, so did the "lawlessness and disorder" of the ghettos and the potential for social unrest unless clients were shown that "their rights could and would be enforced by the mechanisms of the existing capitalistic order." With increased financial support of elite lawyers, the number of Legal Aid societies nationwide jumped from five to forty-one between 1905 and 1920. In 1921, after decades on the sidelines of the poverty debate, the legal profession's most powerful organization, the American Bar Association, appointed a standing committee on legal aid. Two years later, the National Association of Legal Aid Organizations was formed.

The architect of the alliance between Legal Aid societies and the organized bar was Reginald Heber Smith, a young partner at the Boston law firm Hale & Dorr and general counsel to Boston's two-person Legal Aid Society. In 1917 the Carnegie Foundation hired Smith to undertake a nationwide survey of the delivery of legal services to the poor. In *Justice and the Poor*, his 1919 report to the foundation, Smith candidly concluded that "the administration of American justice is not impartial, the rich and the poor do not stand on an equality before the law, [and] the traditional method of providing justice has operated to close the doors of the courts to the poor, and has caused a gross denial of justice in all parts of the country to millions of persons." According to Smith, merely providing Legal Aid lawyers to advise the poor would not solve the problem. He advocated that Legal Aid societies use their expertise to lobby for broad legal reforms.

Published at a time when the country was struggling to absorb millions of recent arrivals, Smith's report might easily have led to a broad reexamination of the legal system--the restrictive educational requirements for practicing law and the bar's monopoly over judicial appointments and courtroom representation, as well as other privileges that attend the profession. Instead, Smith's conclusion that America's institutions were fraught with class injustice was diluted--apparently with Smith's acquiescence--by bar leaders interested in using the survey to strengthen the bar's exclusive access to legal institutions.

In his foreword to *Justice and the Poor*, for example, Elihu Root, Sr.--former Secretary of State, Secretary of War, and U.S. senator from New York--wrote that Smith's report was addressed to "the multitude of Americans who are interested in the Americanization of the millions of foreigners who have immigrated to this country, and who fail to understand or who misunderstand American institutions." Through the efforts of Root and other bar leaders, Americanization rather than class injustice became the central focus when the American Bar Association considered Smith's report. The organized bar endorsed this goal by providing financial and administrative support to Legal Aid societies. Instead of tying up the courts with the myriad problems of poor people or putting private attorneys in the uncomfortable position of turning away clients who could not afford assistance, Legal Aid societies would both socialize the poor and efficiently dispose of their cases, extending rough justice to people who otherwise had no hope for justice at all.

The support of the organized bar, though nominal in some areas of the country, continued to stimulate the growth of the Legal Aid movement: thirty new Legal Aid organizations were started in the 1920s, and the number of cases handled by Legal Aid societies nearly doubled, rising from 96,034 in 1920 to 171,961 in 1929. But with the onset of the Depression, the interests of many in the legal profession shifted again. Established clients of small firms cut back on the luxury of legal advice. Individuals who might have once hired attorneys instead joined the lines at Legal Aid societies. From 1929 to 1932 the nationwide Legal Aid caseload almost doubled again, from 171,000 to more than 307,000 cases. At the same time, financial support for Legal Aid declined. For example, only 229 of 17,000 lawyers practicing in New York City made contributions to the Legal Aid Society in 1934.

Small law firms and sole practitioners specializing in representing individuals languished during the Depression. But law firms handling corporate work--the province of lawyers from the most prestigious schools and elite backgrounds--kept busy with bankruptcies and corporate reorganizations and, as one attorney stated, were "very little affected" by the economy. The widening gap between individuals of low or moderate income who needed legal assistance and those corporations and wealthy individuals who could actually afford assistance again exposed lawyers and legal institutions to charges of class bias.

This time, no less a personage than Supreme Court Justice Harlan F. Stone led the attack on his profession. In a widely publicized address at the University of Michigan Law School in 1934 Stone asserted that lawyers' primary allegiance now went to corporations rather than to communities. This development had transformed "the learned profession of an earlier day [into] the obsequious servant of business, and tainted it with the morals and manners of the market place in its most anti-social manifestations."

Law professors rallied around Stone. Fueled by the public antagonism against big business during the Depression years, they published a series of devastating critiques of large law firms and their powerful place in the legal profession. The most influential of these critical theories, "legal realism," argued that law, far from being a collection of formal, objective rules, was a product of politics and morality. Legal realists argued that the orthodoxy that judges decided cases on objective rules was a "wishful" rationalization; they maintained that because a judge's decision was, in essence, a political response to the facts presented, lawyers could use law as an instrument of social change through their presentation of the facts and selection of litigation tactics. According to Karl Llewellyn of Columbia Law School, legal realism represented "a new and timely voicing of the function of law: to serve society. Society as a whole, not merely the

White-collars and the Haves . . . . Let this be written large, for senior partners in law-factories to ponder on: Law does not exist for corporation executives alone."

Legal realism and its attendant cynicism about the supposed classless nature of the law was particularly popular among liberal lawyers who moved between university law schools and New Deal agencies during the Roosevelt administration. The president's willingness to initiate bold new federal programs coincided with lawyers' own ideas that federal intervention was justified, as a legal matter, by the social policy needs of the country. The realists' readiness to use law for social change, combined with the extreme exigencies of the Depression, contributed to the significant reworking and partial federalization of welfare laws in the Social Security Act of 1935.

Incredibly, the dramatic changes in welfare law and policy did not, by and large, pierce the consciousness of Legal Aid lawyers representing the poor in the 1930s and 1940s. For instance, soon after World War I Legal Aid organizations adopted a standard classification scheme for civil cases to facilitate statistical studies. Yet as late as 1951 these classifications did not include public assistance among the types of cases routinely handled by Legal Aid societies.

Though legal realists continued to harangue the legal profession for its failure to serve the poor, only those at the political fringes of the profession took the occasion to reassess the existing model for delivery of legal aid. In response to realists' criticism, the leftist National Lawyers Guild in 1938 initiated a small-scale experiment to provide legal services to the poor and to members of the middle class. With the blessings of Llewellyn and Reginald Heber Smith, guilds in Chicago and Philadelphia set up neighborhood offices to provide low-cost legal services. The experiments were a modest success; by 1949 the Philadelphia office was serving 4,200 clients annually and operating at a profit. Yet similar offices were not opened elsewhere, perhaps because of the organized bar's resistance to competition.

Lawyers for the NAACP Legal Defense and Educational Fund also incorporated the realists' philosophy into their legal strategy for the desegregation of public schools. Realism not only influenced their view of litigation's potential to effect change, it also expanded the scope of their factual arguments against segregation. As envisioned by the Legal Defense Fund lawyers, the constitutional argument for desegregation under the equal protection clause was inseparable from the sociological evidence that separate schools were inevitably unequal--a direct reflection of the realists' argument that all law, even constitutional law, was at bottom social policy.

These innovations at the margins of the profession had little effect on either the bar associations or the Legal Aid societies. The organized bar's support for poverty law continued to stagnate until 1950, when Great Britain instituted its Legal Aid and Advice Scheme, which mandated that every member of the legal profession be available to provide legal aid to the poor, to be reimbursed by the government. A vocal minority of the profession, led by members of the National Lawyers Guild, took up the call for a similar program in the United States. According to the guild's estimates, two-thirds of the American population was unable to afford legal services. It was time for a radical reworking of Legal Aid.

Terrified lest a plan modeled on the British scheme be adopted in the United States--setting a precedent for restricting the bar's self--regulation--state and local bar associations stepped into the breach to demonstrate the continued viability of American Legal Aid societies. By the end of the 1950s Legal Aid lawyers reported "a breakthrough. Whereas in 1949 . . . 43% of the large cities were without offices, the percentage . . . was reduced to 21% by the end of 1959."

While shoring up support for privately funded legal aid, the American Bar Association launched a counteroffensive against the guild and others who might support the "socialization" of law. The association's Special Committee to Study Communist Tactics, Strategy, and Objectives concluded that the time had come to "drive such lawyers from the profession" and to exclude those found guilty of "embracing and practicing" communism or Marxism-Leninism. Many state bar associations adopted loyalty oaths as a prerequisite to practice. Even Reginald Heber Smith warned in 1951 that "it is a fundamental tenet of Marxian Communism that law is a class weapon used by the rich to oppress the poor through the simple device of making justice too expensive." Comprehensive legal services to the poor, the organized bar asserted, was un-American.

Throughout the 1950s the organized bar was largely successful in forestalling federally sponsored legal services for the poor. At the same time, however, a West Coast academician was laboring to develop a legal theory that would redefine the rights of poor people and lead to dramatic changes in the practice of poverty law, whether by traditional legal aid organizations or by government lawyers.

Jacobus TenBroek, blinded in a bow and arrow accident at age seven, earned two law degrees from Berkeley's Boalt Hall and one from Harvard before his appointment to the speech and political science faculties at University of California at Berkeley. A founder of the National Federation for the Blind, TenBroek was dedicated to integrating the blind into sighted society. To demonstrate his commitment, he insisted on moving about the Berkeley campus without a guide.

TenBroek's academic interest--poverty--was also a personal crusade. He began to lay the intellectual foundations of welfare law in the late 1940s, more than a decade before it was recognized as a field of legal practice and scholarship.

At that time the meaning of the equal protection clause of the Constitution was in flux. In 1944, in *Korematsu v. United States* --which challenged the restrictions on the movement of Japanese Americans in the United States during World War II--the Supreme Court suggested that the equal protection clause might allow federal courts to scrutinize and strike down state laws that used racial classifications. According to Justice Hugo L. Black's opinion, "All legal restrictions which curtail the civil rights of a single racial group are immediately suspect." This proposition was confirmed and explained in 1954 in the Supreme Court's decision in *Brown v. Board of Education*. But TenBroek argued in 1949 that poor people, as well as racial groups, should be considered a class requiring special judicial attention and that state laws resulting in unequal treatment of the poor should be struck down by the courts. He believed that "the mere state of being without funds [should be] a neutral fact" under the law.

In 1955 TenBroek detailed a compelling example of the unequal treatment of the poor. Many states had enacted onerous residency requirements that denied welfare benefits to individuals who had not resided in the state for a specified length of time, in some cases several years. As a result, welfare recipients could not move to another state to be with family and friends or to search for a job without forgoing their meager benefits. These laws, TenBroek argued, "operate as an impairment of the [constitutional] right to free movement" of U.S. citizens. TenBroek's logic was beyond question, but no court had yet agreed with his interpretation of the law.

TenBroek's magnum opus, a three-part article published in 1965 in the *Stanford Law Review*, reformulated his arguments around the idea that welfare laws create dual systems of family law in the United States, one for the indigent and one for everyone else. Under the welfare regime, for example, residency laws restricted recipients' movements, and regulations required that women receiving AFDC keep men out of their homes, even if the men were simply boyfriends who had no obligation to support children of a prior relationship. Relying on the *Brown* opinion and the intimations in *Gideon v. Wainwright*--which ruled that states must provide trial counsel for indigents in criminal proceedings--TenBroek argued that poverty commanded the special solicitude of the courts. He called again for the application of the equal protection clause to strike down laws that used public assistance to impose special standards of behavior on poor people.

By the close of the 1950s these emerging legal theories were beginning to challenge the fundamental assumptions of the welfare system. Legal Aid societies, however, by and large failed to respond to these changes. Despite the bar's concerted resistance to federal involvement in the provision of legal services, Legal Aid and the private bar seemed unable to meet the legal needs of the poor.

* * *

Notes and Questions

1. *Funding of Private Legal Aid.* Martha Davis describes the formation of legal aid societies funded not by government but by private charitable donations in the late nineteenth and early twentieth centuries. She notes that New York's Legal Aid Society required clients to pay a small retaining fee and a commission on recovered funds. Today the funding controversy revolves around whether legal services lawyers should be publicly or privately funded. What are the pros and cons of each type of funding?

2. *Immigrants as Clients.* Martha Davis reports one survey of New York's early Legal Aid Society showing that two thirds of its clients were not United States citizens. Current rules prohibit legal services lawyers from representing most undocumented immigrants. Should the history of immigrant representation influence the contemporary debate over whether legal services lawyers should represent undocumented residents? If a return to private funding of

legal services lawyers would free them to represent immigrants, would this be desirable?

3. *Role of Legal Services Lawyers.* What should be the proper role of a legal services lawyer? Martha Davis describes early legal aid lawyers' distance from the settlement social change movement. Should legal services attorneys represent clients according to the client's individual interests and desires, or should they consider the broader impact of their activities on the general population of poor people? Should legal services lawyers be responsive to contemporary social movements?

4. *Quality of Representation.* Davis also describes the historical caseload pressures on legal services lawyers to settle disputes. Long before the legal services funding cutbacks of the mid 1990s, the American Bar Association estimated that lawyers generally met only 20% of the legal needs of poor people. (The American Bar Foundation estimated that government funded legal services meet about 12% of the legal needs of poor persons.) Does the pressure to meet the needs of other clients encourage legal services lawyers to settle cases of existing clients? If so, what effect is such pressure likely to have on the quality of representation?

5. *Competition.* Davis notes legal services lawyers' uneasy relations with the private bar. Do legal services lawyers compete with the private bar for clients, or do they fill an otherwise unmet need? Are legal services lawyers unfairly free from the economic pressures of private practice (as some of their opponents claim), or do their caseload pressures suffice to at least even the playing field (as Davis suggests)? The private bar, primarily through the American Bar Association, has fought consistently against the 1980s and 1990s cutbacks in funding for legal services. What does the ABA's advocacy for legal services reveal about the contemporary relations between legal services and the private bar?

2. Federally Funded Legal Services

During the 1960s, the federal government began to fund legal services programs. As Allen Redlich explains below, legal services lawyers brought welfare issues to the attention of the United States Supreme Court, resulting in a host of decisions that will be explored in the remaining chapters of this section.

Allen Redlich

WHO WILL LITIGATE CONSTITUTIONAL ISSUES FOR THE POOR?

19 HASTINGS CONSTITUTIONAL LAW QUARTERLY 745 (1992)

* * *

The Origins and Development of the Legal Services Program

When the "war against poverty" began, the poor saw the law as a part of the criminal justice system, as a hostile organ of government, or as a tool used by the landlord or creditor. Lewis Powell, then President of the American Bar Association, said: "Of . . . long-range importance is the attitude of the poor towards the law. Many of them have come to regard the law as an enemy." What little organized civil legal representation the poor received came from legal aid societies that failed to provide meaningful services because of sparse resources and a charity-oriented perspective that accepted and never challenged the systemic practices that adversely affected the poor. A 1964 survey spoke of legal aid attorneys with annual caseloads of 1678 cases. The heavy caseload meant there was no time to do research, to investigate the facts, or to litigate. At best, the legal aid lawyer could rush to the courthouse to delay an eviction. Even this tiny bit of defensive litigation would disappoint a waiting room filled with others in need.

In 1964, Charles Reich published *The New Property*, noting the growth of government grants of "largesse," such as licenses, subsidies, contracts and income maintenance expenditures, and government conditioning of these grants, sometimes on a waiver of the grantee's constitutional rights. Reich suggested that government "largesse" had become so important to the social order that it deserved the procedural and substantive protection afforded to the holders of property rights. This perspective, namely that one has a right to largesse, became the bedrock of the litigations that would be brought in the late 1960s and early 1970s on behalf of the poor. Shortly before Reich's article was published, demonstration projects had begun in New York City, New Haven, and Washington, where lawyers were assigned to social agencies to assist the agencies' clients. The New York City program was operated by a social agency called Mobilization for Youth, located in the mostly Puerto Rican slums of New York City. This program was the most publicized of these projects due to the talents of its director, Edward V. Sparer, who would soon become the "war's" most respected spokesman and strategist. At this time, Edgar and Jean Cahn published another seminal article, *The War on Poverty: A Civilian Perspective*, which advocated establishment of neighborhood law firms to represent poor communities "with an eye toward making public officials, private service agencies, and local business interests more responsive to the need and grievances of the neighborhood." The congruence of Reich's theory of entitlement, Sparer's success, the Cahns' call for "neighborhood law offices," and President Johnson's "war against poverty" resulted in a call for federally funded legal services for the poor. A memorable Law Day speech by Attorney General Robert Kennedy at the University of Chicago Law School, a series of conferences on the subject, and the support of the prestigious American Bar Association, led to a decision by the newly created Office of Economic Opportunity to establish and fund a Legal Services Program.

By September of 1966, the handful of pre-existing legal aid offices had been augmented by hundreds of federally funded offices staffed by more than a thousand lawyers, with more to come. The national staff of the Legal Service Program (LSP) and its advisory committee quickly adopted "law reform" as its principal goal. Legal services programs were, in the course of serving clients, to use the law to achieve social change. They did so with a passion. Hundreds of major litigations began and flourished. One student of the subject, Susan E. Lawrence, concluded, "During its nine-year tenure, 1965 through 1974, the LSP sponsored 164 cases before the Supreme Court, 119 of which were accepted for review. The eighty LSP cases that received plenary consideration represent 7 percent of all written opinions handed down during this era."

The Constitutional Litigations

The literature discussing the major constitutional litigations instituted by legal services lawyers generally discusses only the leading cases, *Shapiro v. Thompson*, *Goldberg v. Kelly*, *Lindsey v. Normet*, *Dandridge v. Williams*, *San Antonio Independent School District v. Rodriguez*, and *Wyman v. James*. This approach tends to overlook other related constitutional issues raised by legal services lawyers. For example, in addition to deciding *Shapiro v. Thompson* on equal protection grounds, the Court utilized equal protection on other occasions. In *United States Department of Agriculture v. Moreno*, the Court invalidated a provision of the Food Stamp Act that denied "unrelated" members of households access to the program. In *Graham v. Richardson*, aliens were protected against state welfare statutes that subjected them to durational residency tests. *James v. Strange* precluded states from attempts to recover the costs of legal defenses provided indigents. *Jimenez v. Weinberger* invalidated a statutory provision that denied Social Security disability benefits to certain categories of illegitimate children. In *Pease v. Hansen*, recipients of non- categorical assistance, or "poor relief," were afforded the same constitutional protections as recipients of federally funded welfare. In *Williams v. Illinois*, the Court used equal protection to limit the length of imprisonment for involuntary nonpayment of fines.

In the area of due process, Justice Brennan held in *Goldberg v. Kelly* that welfare benefits could not be terminated unless the recipient first was offered a hearing satisfactory to the essential elements of due process. He reasoned that without a continuation of benefits, the recipient would not survive, survival was necessary for a meaningful hearing, and due process thus mandated that the hearing precede the termination. The Court also invoked due process on other occasions. *Fuentes v. Shevin* invalidated a state prejudgment replevin statute. *Goss v. Lopez* gave a modicum of process to public school students threatened with suspension. *O'Connor v. Donaldson* upheld the due process rights of persons improperly committed to state mental institutions. *Stanley v. Illinois* upheld the due process rights of natural fathers threatened with loss of custody of their children. The Court also invalidated a number of state statutes that conflicted with federal law, asserting that the state laws were preempted, sometimes relying on the Supremacy Clause.

The Court also acted in the area of access to justice. In *Boddie v. Connecticut*, the Court held a destitute woman need not pay publication costs as a prerequisite to divorcing her missing spouse. But the Court refused to go farther, holding in *United States v. Kras* that bankruptcy filing fees must be paid, even by the indigent; and in *Ortwein v. Schwab*, the Court held an appeal from a welfare department decision could be conditioned on payment of the court's filing fee.

The Court refused to use equal protection in many instances. More precisely, the Court applied the rational or reasonable basis test to state actions or inactions. In *Dandridge v. Williams*, the Court held states could "cap" welfare grants, which in effect meant each child in a large family would receive less than a child in a smaller family. The Court accepted the state's argument that the cap provided a work incentive, because welfare allotments higher than one could earn working at the minimum wage were a disincentive to work. The Court announced, in the best tradition of Pontius Pilate, that allocation of state resources in the area of public assistance was not a matter of judicial concern. The Court also threw up its hands at the thought of involvement in school financing, stating there was no constitutional right to a public school education. In *Lindsey v. Normet*, the Court declined future involvement with housing.

Dandridge shattered the hopes of those who thought social change could quickly be achieved in the courts. The decision came at a moment when everything seemed to be going particularly well. In the spring of 1969, the State of New York had enacted a statute that sharply reduced welfare benefits. *Rosado v. Wyman*, a major, complex challenge to the state plan, was quickly commenced. Months later, *Rothstein v. Wyman* was instituted, as an afterthought, when *Rosado* floundered. While *Rosado*, the carefully planned litigation, sat on a Supreme Court docket, a three-judge district court in *Rothstein* held that the state's disparate treatment of residents of New York's suburbs violated the Equal Protection Clause of the Fourteenth Amendment. Rejecting the state's assertion that the "higher social cost of living" in New York City justified the differential, the Court stated:

> Receipt of welfare benefits may not at the present time constitute the exercise of a constitutional right. But among our Constitution's expressed purposes was the desire to "insure domestic tranquility" and "promote the general Welfare." Implicit in those phrases are certain basic concepts of humanity and decency. One of these, voiced as a goal in recent years by most responsible governmental leaders, both federal and state, is the desire to insure that indigent, unemployable citizens will at least have the bare minimums required for existence, without which our expressed fundamental constitutional rights and liberties frequently cannot be exercised and therefore become meaningless. . . . It can hardly be doubted that the subsistence level of our indigent and unemployable aged, blind and disabled involves a more crucial aspect of life and liberty than

> the right to operate a business on Sunday or to extract gas from subsoil. We believe that with the stakes so high in terms of human misery the equal protection standard to be applied should be stricter than that used upon review of commercial legislation and more nearly approximate that applied to laws affecting fundamental constitutional rights.

Sparer's strategy had envisioned attacks on substantive and procedural flaws in state welfare programs, followed by challenges to the adequacy of state-wide benefit levels, implicitly based on a constitutional right to subsistence. Finally having achieved those goals, the poor would demand a national welfare system or, at the very least, a national standard of benefits. State welfare systems had already been battered by thousands of cases. The constitutional challenge to the level of benefits provided by particular states had arrived swiftly, but just as swiftly was resolved by the Court in *Dandridge*; the battle, but not the war, was over.

The Demise of the Legal Services Program
The Nixon and Reagan Years

President Nixon, on taking office, began a lengthy multi-faceted war of attrition aimed at legal services. Nixon's appointed Director of the Office of Economic Opportunity frequently attacked the program and its personnel in concert with numerous other administration officials and supporters led by his Vice-President. Attacks by state officials directed at various local programs, such as the attack on California Rural Legal Assistance (CRLA) by then-Governor Reagan and other California officials, were only grudgingly rebuffed, as internal attacks on the program continued. After a few years, the administration and the program's supporters, recognizing neither side could win the battle, agreed to "depoliticize" legal services by setting up a public corporation to be funded by the federal government. After a three-year political battle over the details, the Legal Services Corporation Act was passed. The ravages of inflation during the dispute over the terms of the Act, when the level of program funding had been frozen, led to large decreases in the number of program offices and lawyers, massive attorney turnover, and a decline in the availability and quality of necessary support services.

There was also a change in program goals. The Corporation now spoke of "equal access to justice," rather than of "achieving social change." The Corporation distributed its largesse based primarily on the number of potential clients in a program's geographic area. One observer, noting the new corporate language ("[l]ocal programs became 'recipients'. . . clients became 'applicants'. . . attorneys became employees"), commented that "the terminology changes reflected a subtle bureaucratization or management orientation of the programme." The voluminous and incredibly detailed statistical reports compiled and issued by the Corporation tell the reader nothing about the program's accomplishments other than the number of cases handled and clients served, evidencing its lack of concern about quality.

The Nixon experience was heavenly compared to co-existing with President Reagan, who remembered his prior defeats in California. His bare-knuckled attacks on CRLA while governor of California were a predictor of his performance as President. The budgets he submitted to Congress never requested any funds for the Legal Services Corporation, forcing its Congressional supporters to fight, year after year, to secure enough funds for LSC's survival. One year the program's funds were reduced by 25 percent. Salaries for legal services attorneys, already low, suffered in comparison with salaries earned by other attorneys in both the public and private sectors. The decision by the Corporation to create programs in the South and Southwest increased the number of potential clients at the same time the disintegrating salary structure led to massive staff turnover.

As early as 1977, Gary Bellow commented that "despite their commitment to avoid the kind of cautious, detached, client controlling services that so many public bureaucracies--public housing authorities, welfare departments--seem to provide . . . this is precisely the kind of service our clients are receiving." Bellow listed typical traits of legal service programs such as routine processing of cases, low client autonomy, narrow definitions of client concerns, and "inadequate" outcomes. Bellow, seemingly echoing descriptions of mid-century legal aid, noted:

> When one learns, from the limited empirical work available on legal aid practice, that legal services attorneys are regularly handling caseloads of one

> hundred and fifty ongoing cases, generally seeing their clients only once in the course of an entire representation, and spending an average of twenty minutes per interview on the client's substantive legal problems, it seems a certainty that the cases are being superficially and minimally handled.

A law firm that staffed its litigation department with law school graduates, paid them less than competing firms, trained them in a cursory manner, did not expose them to the work habits and ethics of experienced litigators, and saw them leave after one or two years to be replaced with a new group of graduates would have a short existence. Unhappily, this is the manner in which most legal services programs have operated during the past years.

Litigation and Its Relationship to Good Lawyering

Lack of involvement in litigation by legal services programs evidences a failure to provide quality services to their clients. Most of the cases that confront poverty lawyers require advice, referral, or other non-litigative approaches. This is not to denigrate legal services lawyers engaging in these activities or representing clients before administrative tribunals or local courts. Many of the problems of the poor, however, can be resolved only through litigation. Others cannot be resolved in an appropriate manner without a credible threat of litigation. When litigation is the appropriate option and it is not undertaken, the client is effectively abandoned by the attorney. Even where there is complete disclosure of the litigation option and the client is told that it will not be exercised, there is a betrayal because unlike a corporate client, the poor cannot seek out other counsel. The need to litigate occurs when the adversary is a government agency bound by statutes, rules, regulations, interpretations, and policies that preclude an agency official from making a reasonable attempt to settle a dispute, even when the official is not disinclined to do so. Litigation is necessary when proceedings before administrative agencies fail to resolve the client's problem in a just and lawful manner. The need to litigate also exists when the statute or policy is itself unlawful. Many problems of poor clients are either-or situations where the client either loses or wins. Welfare eligibility is a good example: It cannot be parsed. Litigation is also necessary when the negotiation process fails to achieve a fair and just outcome. The poor rarely have bargaining power matching that of the government and other perennial adversaries of the poor. Since bargaining power dictates the outcome of negotiations, the poor generally do not do well.

Despite these myriad situations that require litigation and despite Legal Services Corporation's claim of 1,421,805 closed cases in 1987, 1,430,053 cases in 1988, and about 1,400,000 cases in 1990, there was little reported litigation during those years. The Westlaw data banks reveal that in 1987 there were 389 state court and 151 federal district court appearances, for a total of 540 court appearances. The year 1988 saw a decline to 361 state court and 103 federal district court appearances, for a total of 464. In 1990, while the total number of closed cases remained constant, there were only 95 appearances in federal district court and 273 in state court, for a total of 368 or about one reported litigated case in every 3,800. The decrease from 1987 to 1990 was 172 or 31.9 percent. The decrease from 1981, when there were 564 state court and 174 federal district court appearances for a 1981 total of 738 reported appearances, was 370, or just over a 50 percent decrease.

When representing people whose financial position is precarious, litigation is necessary to achieve even modest fiscal gains or to avoid modest financial loss. For example, a welfare department's decision to "recoup" a small prior overpayment by deducting a small amount from a family's monthly grant causes hardship. If the decision to recoup is erroneous as a matter of law, as is often the case, and negotiation and administrative procedures fail, litigation would seem to be the only option consistent with the "zealous" representation called for by the ethical standards of the profession.

One sometimes hears that a program does not litigate because of success in negotiation. A legal services program may argue that a good relationship with a particular agency's personnel makes litigation counterproductive and that to preserve a "relationship" with an agency, a poverty lawyer should consider the "sacrifice" of a "client" for the sake of future clients. Negotiation is a serious business, however, and the likelihood of litigation, its cost and its risks, not personal charm and relationships, are the factors which determine the benefit of a settlement.

Melvin Belli, a well-known litigator, once said, "I have to maintain my advocacy in court on trial in order to keep up my settlement value." Knowledge of the strengths and weaknesses of the other party's position, including its ability and willingness to litigate if dissatisfied with proposed settlements, is essential to a competent negotiator. When one party to a negotiation concludes litigation will not occur if that party makes no concessions, then any concessions made are gratuitous, and what one calls a "negotiation" is really a supplication. It follows that the paucity of litigation by legal service programs, despite the many cases where litigation is called for, makes negotiation a sham and evidences the absence of quality lawyering. The price paid includes not only a poor result for the particular client, but less than satisfactory results in negotiations for other clients.

Notes and Questions

1. *Change in Goals.* During the 1960s and early 1970s, legal services lawyers and programs reflected the activism and idealism of the times, unapologetically devoting their energies to reforming law and society. Reacting to the attack on their efforts launched by conservative leaders including former presidents Richard Nixon and Ronald Reagan, legal services attorneys shifted their goal to simply providing poor people with equal access to justice. Compare the goal of reforming society with the goal of providing equal access to justice. If you were a legal services lawyer, how would you have modified your practice in response to this change in goals?

2. *Bureaucratization.* Imagine what a poor client might experience when she contacts a legal services office. Because these offices receive more requests for assistance than they can handle, most clients' cases are screened in an intake process and then rejected. As a result, poor clients may feel that they have been processed in a manner not unlike what they experience at welfare or other government offices. Even supporters of legal services have decried its bureaucratization. Can it be avoided?

3. *Restrictions on Representation.* Over the years, congressional statutes and Legal Services Corporation regulations have added a variety of restrictions on the services that federally-funded lawyers for poor people may provide. First, they may not represent certain types of clients, generally prisoners or undocumented immigrants. (Do the restrictions on who legal services attorneys may represent present any constitutional problems?) Second, they may not handle cases involving abortion, legislative redistricting, eviction from public housing related to alleged drug activity, or welfare reform. (Are these restrictions on the subject matter of legal services lawyering

valid?) Third, they may not solve their clients' problems through lobbying legislators or administrative regulators to change the law or through filing class actions. (Do the restrictions on permissible methods of representation limit their ability to adequately, zealously, or otherwise ethically represent their clients?) Finally, although Congress reduced legal services funding by 30% in 1996, it prohibited legal services lawyers from seeking attorney fees in successful litigation.

Are legal services programs required to take the bitter (restrictions) with the sweet (federal funding)? Or might the Constitution limit the ability of Congress to impose restrictions? Consider these questions in connection with the materials presented in Chapter 7 relating to the unconstitutional conditions doctrine.

4. *Decline in Litigation.* Allen Redlich stresses the importance of litigation to poor clients. He argues that successful resolution of cases often depends on full litigation, or at least the credible threat of litigation. Bringing a court challenge may be the only method available, for example, to challenge welfare officials who are bound by legal rules that they are powerless to change. As counted by court appearances in the Westlaw data base, reported litigation by legal services lawyers decreased by just over 50% from 1980 to 1990. If accurate, how do you expect this decrease in litigation has impacted poor people? If the impact is likely harmful, how should it be remedied?

B. THE CONTEMPORARY DEBATE AND CHALLENGES

1. Attacks on Legal Services

During the first major wave of attacks against legal services in the early 1980s, conservative politicians accused legal services programs of furthering a liberal social reform agenda to redistribute wealth from society's haves to its have-nots. Legal services attorneys responded that the vast majority of their cases involved defending families against problems such as domestic violence, illegal eviction, or a parent's failure to pay child support. Although President Reagan "zero-funded" legal services in his budgets, members of Congress seemed to believe that legal services should be funded, but disagreed about the appropriate level of funding.

During the second major wave of attacks against legal services in the mid 1990s, conservatives expanded their accusations, this time charging that legal services were anti-family (for example, by representing one spouse against another in actions seeking divorces, orders of protection against domestic violence, or child support awards) and anti-community (for example, by representing drug dealers in evictions). This mid 1990s battle in Congress was not limited to a debate about the appropriate level of funding, but focused on whether legal services should be funded at all. Legal services won the latter battle, but suffered the loss of 30% of their funding in 1996, which could result in closing 30% of legal services offices, and turning away 30% of cases previously handled. Assuming the American Bar Foundation's previous estimate was still accurate, government funded legal services offices were handling only 12% of poor people's legal problems before the 30% cut. Assuming a reduction in representation proportional to the reduction in funding, legal services programs would be handling only 8.4% of poor people's legal problems after the 1996 cut.

What arguments support and oppose funding for legal services programs? Do legal services lawyers serve a political agenda? Should they? Should society care whether a poor person suffers a lack of legal representation? Is there a right to access to the judicial system? Or is access to the judicial system an important government interest? Should private attorneys engage in more pro bono publico representation to fill the gap left by the reduction of legal services? What incentive would private attorneys have to represent poor persons? Does it matter whether the economic demands of private practice enable such representation? Does it matter whether private attorneys have the expertise necessary to represent poor persons? Should law schools, bar associations, or governments require law students and attorneys to engage in a minimum amount of mandatory pro bono service?

2. Debates About Improving Legal Services

Although legal services advocates rallied to fight both the first and second waves of attacks, they often disagreed among themselves about how to best deliver legal services to poor clients. Consider the following debate about the proper role of legal services between Marc Feldman, Alan Houseman, Gary Bellow, and Jeanne Charn.

Marc Feldman

POLITICAL LESSONS: LEGAL SERVICES FOR THE POOR

83 GEORGETOWN LAW JOURNAL 1529 (1995)

Introduction

There are profound shortcomings in the legal work on behalf of the poor. Randomness pervades Legal Services lawyers' conception of role and legal work. The Legal Services lawyer is uncertain about whether she is a social worker, community organizer, or litigator. Staff autonomy in choice of work, in generalization or specialization, and in determining how to prosecute and when to conclude legal work is the norm. Case loads reflect insufficient concentration on any particular topic or issue.

The legal work fails to identify meaningfully the legal problems experienced by the poor. Legal Services lawyers identify the priorities for their work using a process that generates long lists of highly general problems. The lawyers rarely possess expertise about the local or larger political economy in which they work and their clients live. Nevertheless, they regularly fail to involve other disciplines that may offer such expertise. They think about and work on problems in ways that are defined by the very parties and bureaucracies that will be their adversaries in trying to alleviate client difficulties.

Legal Services lawyers subscribe to a dogma that divides legal activity into impact work and service work. Service work constitutes the bulk of their effort and, by definition, there is no ambition to reach beyond the details of a particular client's case to influence broader, more systematic problems. Randomly chosen individual clients and the pursuit of limited strategies on behalf of those individual clients intensifies the unfortunate consequences of this flawed conception.

Although programs may have identified priorities for the

selection of their legal work, these priorities are so general that they do not really help when it comes to actually deciding which cases to accept and which cases to refuse. Intentionality in the legal work is further diluted by the distraction and preoccupation of program staff by a host of "internal" nonclient activities.

Frequently, legal efforts result in inadequate solutions to client problems. Legal Services lawyers rarely engage in sustained litigation; instead, settlement and withdrawal typify the conclusion of client involvement. There is little or no accountability to clients; Legal Services lawyers rarely employ devices such as practice protocols, peer evaluation, and management oversight that would serve as substitutes. Even in those rare instances when the lawyers gain favorable judgments, they often lose this advantage by failing to follow-up or enforce the initial favorable results.

* * *

Legal education is an early and formative experience in constructing lawyers' views about law and legal process. Law school serves up in powerful fashion an account which is in important respects formalist. . . . I do not intend to offer a fully developed account of legal formalism or its notable limitations as an explanatory account upon which poverty lawyers should rely. Instead, I wish to signal some of those features central to formalism's telling about law. While all lawyers-to-be are exposed to this inculcation, there is special meaning for those who would represent the poor.

* * *

Formalism teaches that there are meaningful structures and patterns of law. Law is intellectually orderly. It has a clear subject matter organization, out of which problems arise and solutions are fashioned. Formalism describes the integrated hierarchy of the judiciary with similar notions of regularity. Judges' exercise of authority is extreme, even complete. Missing is complexity and a discussion of other social processes. With one "stroke of the pen" a decision is reached and implemented. The view from inside law classrooms is that when courts make decisions there is no limit to, or question of, judicial authority, for there is little or no consideration of implementation or enforcement of judicial orders. Regularity is thus coupled with extraordinary judicial autonomy in formalism's telling.

* * *

Many lessons about the structures, patterns, and consequences of law are taught indirectly. Inattention teaches and reinforces by leaving undisturbed larger cultural lessons with which students arrive at law school. The belief that our society is essentially meritocratic and the companion liberal article of faith that there is universal opportunity are two such examples. In recent years, study of gender and the law has been introduced in some law classrooms, but it is my suspicion that such efforts remain largely marginal in formative student experiences. Teaching and learning about race and sexuality is even more provisional; attention to class and economic status is virtually nonexistent. For future poverty lawyers, these are grievous omissions in their education about the workings of law.

* * *

Just as the first year of law school is formative in shaping Legal Services lawyers' views of law, the early years of practice are similarly powerful. Many poverty lawyers experience their first years of legal practice as harsh and betraying. The developmental patterns and underlying experiences of Legal Services lawyers reflect real variety; nevertheless, I suspect that for many the early years of practice are integral in fashioning the understandings and behavior they will exhibit for the remainder of their poverty practice careers. Insinuated alongside their partially formalist views of law are new views that might aptly be described as cynical, even nihilistic--formalism and cynicism, believed simultaneously, producing intellectual and emotional static and dissonance. Both are part of Legal Services lawyers' collective consciousness.

Many Legal Services lawyers suffer an intellectual and experiential crash shortly after beginning practice, as their formalist views encounter the real world. At the heart of the formalist regime, internalized and subscribed to by Legal Services lawyers, is a belief in meritocracy, which promises deserving outcomes not only for clients, but for lawyers as well. When representing the poor, one begins to accumulate experience (and disillusionment) at odds with any substantive claims legal formalism or meritocratic liberalism might make about achieving justice. The rhetorical promise of justice is as close as one will come.

* * *

It is hardly surprising, then, that in reaction Legal Services lawyers radically readjust their sights downward from their former ambitions. Betrayed by formalism's exaggerated intellectual claims and buffeted by the anxiety of early practice experiences, they become intellectually and emotionally defensive. Their perspectives narrow, and the moment of concern increasingly becomes the immediate. . . It is impossible to describe or strategize about the dynamics of social change. Alternative ideas, practices, and visions are rarely developed with enough operational detail to be considered possible, persuasive, or meaningful. Instead, discussion of alternatives remains crude and distant. Unprepared for and unsupported during their introduction to the harshness of poverty practice, Legal Services lawyers come to view law with a formalist residue in tension with a reactive skepticism.

* * *

In the following section, I develop three intertwined ideas as part of a discussion of the political environment that surrounds Legal Services. I argue that, in part, because of this environment, Legal Services fails to pursue aggressively the larger interests of poor clients and to engage in meaningful and constructive conflict.

The first idea is that the way the state arranges and exercises authority has changed. There has been a transfer of power from government to nominally private entities. Spurred by a range of forces, including market considerations, these entities have grown larger and more remote. Although less centralized, this privatized state power has nevertheless become more concentrated and less publicly accountable.

My second claim is that there have been important changes in social meaning. As there has been a privatization of state power, so too there has been a privatization of social life, although with very different meaning as to the accumulation and exercise of power. We have constructed and pursued individual lives that are increasingly psychomorphic. We seek psychic absorption, not social participation; we find social meaning in individual human feelings, not in collective civil activity.

Our psychic absorption is pervasive, and we are ill-served by such a commitment. Intimate society is ruled by personality; social meaning is accorded by reference to feeling. Romanticized models of human relationships narrow and dominate our ideas about human interaction. Whatever the setting--whether it be work, play, or avocation--the worth of a relationship is demonstrated by increasing personal revelation (as if each disclosure strengthens the bond between the persons) and its success or failure by affective satisfaction. Leadership is not evaluated by accomplishment nor so much by action. Instead, intention and "credibility" are the emotional measures through which we express our approval or disapproval. Even explanations about one's place in the world have yielded to understanding via personality and feeling. We have abandoned class as a meaningful construct, despite systematic inequalities of wealth and power. Rather, with Enlightenment sensibilities, we proclaim that each of us has equal potential and equal opportunity. In this way, what we accomplish (or fail to accomplish) and the inequalities some of us experience are the result of personal effort and ambition. Not class nor race nor gender, but individual character. Dignity for those who succeed, guilt for those who do not, and social isolation for all.

My third claim is that the state is waging an aggressive campaign against the poor using a full range of devices--from the manipulation of welfare programs to physical force. Historically, the poor have been targeted for social discipline by government and the market, but emboldened by the lessened public accountability of the new forms of state authority and a diminished public participation resulting from psychic absorption, current initiatives display a special vengeance towards the poor. This coercive activity excludes the poor from the economic and social functioning of the larger society.

In this setting the failure of Legal Services work is glaring. Legal Services does not help the poor fight back; it does not contest in meaningful fashion the new forms of authority employed against the poor. The question is why not? Part of the answer lies in the conception and execution of the actual legal work. Another part of the answer comes from the organization and structure of the workplace. Yet another part of the answer is attributable to the professional education and socialization of the lawyers. These partial answers, rooted in the formative decisions made at the beginning of Legal Services, together with the three claims I make with respect to contemporary society, help explain a collective personality characteristic of Legal Services lawyers. This collective personality, in turn, plays an important role in the shortcomings of Legal Services practice. A larger political climate of diffused state authority, generalized psychic absorption, and aggression against the poor has helped to produce Legal Services lawyers whose collective personality is intolerant of conflict. This desire to avoid conflict fuels the political perversion of their work.

* * *

In the new Legal Services, before undertaking legal work, lawyers should engage in a short period of deliberate and intense study. This is the time to build upon critique and insight, and to seek stimulation that can become imaginative material. For the first round or two, the study periods should be relatively general and unstructured. With experience, they should become more focused. Freed of case responsibilities, lawyers could walk the streets, wait in line, knock on doors, attend meetings, contact instigators, supporters, and opponents. They should remember and consult their everbetter documented program history. They should research, read, talk, and exchange drafts. The goal of this study should be the identification of widespread practices that disadvantage the poor and are susceptible to legal attack and change through targeted, disciplined effort. Although this may result in the continuation of some program priorities and work, I imagine that study plus the screen of "systematic practices" and "result orientation" will lead to largely new formulations.

Fresh from study, program lawyers would then concretize their formulations. There must be meaningful guides in deciding whether to accept a case, in knowing the ingredients of high-quality lawyering in pursuing such a case, and in safeguarding against self-interest in case resolution. This is a mandate for operational priorities, practice protocols, and outcome accountability.

* * *

For funding decisionmakers, I would encourage two initial policy initiatives. The first relates to the persons eligible to receive legal services. On an experimental basis, they should raise the financial ceilings governing eligibility to include the working- and near-poor. It has been suggested that there are important connections between those who have little and those who are the very poorest. Problems would be understood and approached differently, and it would enlarge and strengthen the political constituency of Legal Services clients. While this is an attractive claim, it is one fraught with the danger of further dilution of limited resources. The commonalities may prove superficial or afford little added political leverage. Yet, the need and demand for assistance would have grown dramatically without even proportional increase in funding. This strategic decision, about which we know far too little, should become the subject of study projects. These studies should be highly participatory, with aggressive efforts to reach beyond Washington, state capitals, and academic enclaves. These projects should be activist by funding actual demonstration sites where the focus of the legal work would be to explore the political utility of working in the intersections of the poor and near-poor.

The goal of my second "funder's" initiative is to support the establishment of an ethic of effectiveness. This would mean invigorating the anomie that so pervades Legal Services by disrupting present arrangements and encouraging innovation. To the greatest extent possible, I would, in the parlance, "reprogram" funds. I would award a significant portion of existing funds and all new funds that might become available via a process of competitive grants. For the near-term, I would respect current funding formulas for the purpose of insuring at least gross geographic distribution.

* * *

The task is to begin constructing a workplace where people think and feel very differently about what Legal Services lawyers do and how they do it. In practice, these lawyers must behave very differently: with forethought, discipline, aggression, and a tenacious commitment to the results they actually obtain. For these changes to occur, lawyers will have to confront shared attitudes about the attractions of self-absorption and intimacy. We will have to build a social architecture that supports a growing appreciation of difference and conflict, as well as engagement and gratification in the impersonal.

* * *

My final suggestion is for the creation of Legal Services institutes. Field programs and law schools should band together for the purpose of creating Legal Services training programs. Whether new funding is forthcoming for such an effort should not be dispositive. These institutes are sufficiently important that both schools and programs ought to redirect existing funds and reassign faculty and lawyers to undertake the project. Of all my suggestions, I imagine that these institutes would provide the counter-cultural setting most likely to succeed both in challenging prevailing conceptions and practices, and in nurturing alternatives.

Alan W. Houseman

POLITICAL LESSONS: LEGAL SERVICES FOR THE POOR--A COMMENTARY

83 GEORGETOWN LAW JOURNAL 1669 (1995)

Five Critical Elements of Legal Services

By 1970, the basic structure of the legal services program was in place. This structure has continued to this day with only slight modification. Also by 1970, five elements that differentiated "legal services" from "legal aid" had evolved. The architects of the national program and the leaders in field programs saw these elements as critical to effective legal services.

The first element was the notion of responsibility to all poor people as a "client community." Most legal services programs had developed to serve as a whole the poor people who resided in their geographic service area, not just individual clients who happened to be indigent. Additionally, some programs served specific segments of the poor, such as migrant farmworkers and Native Americans.

Second, legal services emphasized the right of clients to control decisions about the solutions to their problems and, through participation on the board of the local legal services program, to control in part what problems to address. Legal services was an advocate whose use was to be determined by poor people rather than an agency established to give services to poor people.

The third element was a commitment to redress historic inadequacies in the enforcement of legal rights of poor people caused by lack of access to the institutions that created those rights. Thus, legal services programs pursued the reform of law and practice to make them more responsive to poor people; legal services attorneys became the chief law enforcers for federal agencies that were not effectively policing local agencies and facilities subject to federal law and policies.

Fourth, legal services were responsive to legal need rather than to demand. Probably the greatest deficiency of the legal aid societies was that they responded only to uninformed demand--to those who walked into the office--so that large parts of the legal needs of the poor were not addressed, while resources were committed to the generally narrow range of legal problems that poor people recognized. Through community education, outreach efforts, and physical presence in the community, legal services programs were able to assist clients in identifying critical needs and fashioning legal responses.

The fifth and final element was a full range of service and advocacy tools--a range as full as that offered by private attorneys for the affluent. This included not only litigation and appeals in federal and state courts and administrative representation before agencies, but also legislative advocacy, rule drafting, and comprehensive strategies to implement policies advantageous to poor people.

The Problems Within

It is necessary to note the substantial dangers in critiquing, generalizing, and drawing conclusions about the problems of a large national program such as legal services. Many different types of programs coexist. There is no uniform structure or service area. Local programs range in size from a few hundred thousand dollars in resources and one or two professional staff members, to those with millions of dollars in resources and hundreds of professional staff members. Some are solely dependent on Legal Services Corporation (LSC) funds; others have substantial amounts of non-LSC funds. As a result, there are widely varying capacities, orientations to the work, and degrees of effectiveness.

Set out below is a discussion of ten of the problems within legal services, which counter many of Feldman's assumptions and suggestions. The analysis presented here is based on periodic interactions with virtually all of the 323 legal services programs, a review of the peer review evaluations conducted by LSC over the last two years, the insights of management consultants who have worked with many programs over the last ten years, and numerous conferences and workshops that have explored the problems within, including a national conference the author conducted last year on the future of legal services.

The Problem of Vision and Mission

In many legal services programs, directors, board, and staff do not have a shared long-term vision of what their program should be and where it should be heading. The reasons for a lack of a shared vision are complex. The national emphasis on access and local control need not have prevented individual programs from developing their own shared vision. Yet only a few have actually developed such a vision.

* * *

Developing a shared vision within particular programs with any real substantive content will be difficult today, not only because of fears about going public with a genuine vision, but also because of the varying perspectives within legal services about what the program is and should be. Many legal staff members view legal services as a social services program that provides necessary help but has no real political content; it is a job to be done as best as one can within the "helping" framework. Others view legal services as an advocate to enhance and protect the interests of the poor: to some it means using lawyers in courts and before legislative and administrative bodies to achieve social and economic justice for poor persons; still others view legal services as a means to empower the poor to act on their own behalf and help change their lives and the conditions under which they live and work.

Even among those who see legal services in terms of empowerment and social change, there are widely divergent views about how best to achieve meaningful impact on the lives of the poor. Some favor policy advocacy; others favor affirmative litigation; still others see work on individual cases focused on clear targets as equally important and having significant and lasting impact.

Nonetheless, having a clear mission and a shared vision among local program staff and management would help individual programs focus their scarce resources effectively, develop appropriate advocacy strategies and delivery approaches, and attract advocates with energy, commitment, and competence.

The Problem of Bureaucracy

The lack of a shared vision is compounded by legal services having become, in many ways, a social services bureaucracy that shares many characteristics with other social services bureaucracies. Some legal services programs may have become bureaucratized to such an extent that they cannot effectively respond to the problems of the poor in their service areas. Within many local programs, substantial time and resources are spent on internal struggles, not on the external problems faced by the poor. To add to the complexity, a majority of legal services staff members are in unions and thereby involved in the additional issues of collective bargaining and union management.

* * *

Quality and Productivity

Related to the concerns about bureaucracy are concerns about the quality of lawyering that exists in some programs and the productivity of some program staff. Gary Bellow first wrote about quality when he criticized the casework done by legal services advocates in the programs he observed, finding that much was of low quality and lacked an effective relationship to solving community problems. A review of the peer review reports done as part of the Comparative Demonstration Project, as well as other performance evaluations conducted in legal services, indicates that the quality of legal services advocacy in some programs is not at its highest and that productivity is low. Doug Besharov examined some data on legal services productivity and concluded somewhat tentatively that productivity had declined by as much as 20% since the program began.

All of these analyses, as well as the discussion by Feldman about the quality of legal work, are based on an examination of a very few programs. The fact is that we do not know what quality of lawyering exists in most programs, nor do we know the productivity of legal services staff, either in comparison with the past or in comparison with private lawyers and other legal providers. Only now is LSC beginning a systematic evaluation of all programs based on performance criteria that address the quality of legal work, and only now is LSC using a peer review process. Thus, generalizations about low quality and productivity are, at best, guesses based on limited data--data that itself is suspect.

On the other hand, there is no question that many programs are engaged in very effective legal work, whether it be routine or complex litigation at all levels of the judicial system, both federal and state, or whether it be before administrative agencies or legislative bodies. Much of this legal work is not captured in official case statistics reported to LSC because the LSC data format does not provide for reporting on legislative or administrative policy advocacy and does not distinguish among types of cases with regard to their time and complexity.

* * *

Support and Research

There are deficiencies in national and state advocacy and research capacities. The legal services system does not have sufficient capacity to identify and address new and emerging needs that do not fall within the expertise or work of existing organizations, or to think effectively about new substantive developments and strategies. In addition, there is no central coordination for training and technical assistance, and there are substantial problems of communication and information sharing among all levels of the support structure. Similarly, many states lack the capacity to undertake representation, coordination, and support at the state level.

A much deeper problem is the failure of some advocates to focus on substantive poverty law strategies and activities that can have a significant and realistic impact upon the long-term conditions in which the poor live and work. Legal services has focused largely on defending current programs rather than considering new programs or ideas that might address clients' needs more effectively. Moreover, there is a real question whether some legal services advocates are ready to shed the perspectives of the past and work on strategies that might actually succeed in today's environment.

* * *

Client Engagement and Involvement

Many legal services programs and staff members are distressingly isolated from the communities they are supposed to assist. Many program offices are centered outside of low-income neighborhoods; staff members and directors go to and from their offices with little real involvement in community institutions or participation in community activities. Few legal services staff members actually live in the communities they serve. Many do not relate to community efforts that are directed toward addressing systemic community problems. Others have not established effective relationships with a wide variety of community groups working on issues that affect the poor. Still others never venture beyond their offices to visit housing projects, welfare offices, nursing homes, homeless shelters, innercity schools, churches, or similar institutions. Few legal services programs intake at institutions serving community members, such as hospitals, welfare offices, and churches. Rarely do programs utilize community activists in their work or hire them on their staffs. Additionally, some programs do little to promote effective community education; only a few attempt to conduct self-help initiatives outside of their offices.

* * *

Insularity, Law Students, and the Private Bar

Legal services programs' isolation from the community is exacerbated by their insularity from the work of other advocacy organizations. In some communities, legal services staff have not sought out other organizations such as civil rights groups, children's advocacy organizations, and new community efforts of neighborhood and community revitalization.

In addition, although many communities have active law school clinical programs, legal services has not sought to effectively utilize them or law students who are interested in poverty legal work. By not developing effective relationships with such clinics, programs have failed to leverage the additional human resources that could increase the number of advocates available to provide representation. Nor has the legal services community as a whole considered how to incorporate the work of law school clinics into the work of the program, seeing clinics instead as unrelated, separate entities. Recently, this has begun to change. The new law school clinical grant program emphasizes interaction with, and integration of, law school clinical work and legal services programs. Far greater effort is needed in order to take advantage of the large and valuable resource of law students interested in poverty work.

A similar resource issue involves the failure of several legal services programs to effectively utilize private attorney involvement (PAI) for the range of legal problems they could handle.

New Approaches to Problem Solving

Legal services has been slow to respond to new approaches to problem solving, whether it is the use of private dispute resolution forums, community justice centers, self-help and nonlawyer advocacy, or cooperation with service delivery by other nonlegal sectors. These possibilities have not been adequately explored or their feasibility considered. Alternative dispute resolution (ADR) has been rejected both because use of ADR was politicized by critics of legal services who proposed replacing the staff attorney system with free-standing ADR programs and because advocates and managers remain unfamiliar with how ADR could be effective for the poor.

* * *

Priority Setting

In many respects the problems outlined above are compounded by the difficulties many programs have in undertaking effective planning and priority setting. Section 1007(a)(2)(c) of [The LSC Act and regulations] and Part 1620 of the LSC regulations require programs to set periodically (and annually update) priorities in order to allocate resources and determine which clients to serve. Every program does this in one form or another. Many procedures are used, including client-staff-board retreats, legal-needs surveys, focus groups, and community meetings. In fact, the idea that local programs should set local priorities and not be tightly controlled by the greater legal services community is central to the operation of the legal services program as a whole and vital for its continuing survival.

There are problems, however, in both the procedures used and the results obtained. Most significantly, program managers fail to conceive of priority setting as a dynamic management process that must be based on a sound management theory of organizational change. To be successful, priority setting requires strategic thinking by the staff and clients about the purposes of their work and the basic strategies to be pursued. In turn, strategic thinking requires those involved to confront and answer fundamental questions about the purposes of their work. After such thinking, program leaders must engage in strategic programming to reduce the products of this strategic thinking to goals and activities that are sufficiently specific to guide the day-to-day work of the program.

* * *

The Delivery System

The problems discussed above, and the many suggestions for change made by Feldman and others, suggest that it may be time to reconsider whether we should continue to maintain a delivery structure that is premised upon one primary provider for each geographic area and that excludes other providers from participating. Certainly there should be room for funding innovative or experimental efforts, even if this results in more than one provider in each geographic area. On the other hand, it does not make sense to dismantle a delivery system that has worked well in many states--a system that has developed skilled staff with expertise in the problems of the poor and promoted effective relationships with the bar, the low-income community, and the community generally. Thus, there is a real tension between preserving what works and ensuring that the delivery system also promotes innovation and change.

* * *

The Vision of Practice

The critique of legal services outlined above suggests a vision for legal services practice that differs sharply from that suggested by Feldman. His is a vision of the lawyer as an agent for social change and the legal services program as the key catalyst for changing the economic and social fabric that perpetuates poverty in this country. Feldman proposes a set of recommendations that he hopes will create a lawyer-dominated, tightly disciplined organization that is an "anti-state catalyst for change."

The core of this vision--the lawyer as an agent for social change and the program as leading the charge to alter the political economy--rests on a fundamentally flawed view of what is possible to achieve in the courts, agencies, and legislatures. The increasing poverty of many Americans and the widening income gap between rich and poor will not be solved by the activities of legal services lawyers acting through impact or "focused case" representation. Legal services cannot end poverty; nor are the courts going to redistribute wealth. As Edgar Cahn put it: "Any efforts undertaken by legal services attorneys to redistribute wealth, whether by legislation or litigation, are bound to meet with continued and increasing political and judicial resistance."

Moreover, this view of legal services as a catalyst for change will deter funding from the government, as well as from most private foundations and local charities. Government today refuses to fund far less threatening activities, such as welfare reform litigation, and foundation support for legal advocacy, which has never been substantial, is not increasing. Government and private entities will only fund access to, and delivery of, effective services.

Even if it were possible to obtain funding for some of the activities proposed by Feldman, the notion that legal services lawyers should lead the charge reinforces lawyer domination and does little or nothing to empower the poor to assert their own rights and interests.

Gary Bellow & Jeanne Charn

PATHS NOT YET TAKEN: SOME COMMENTS ON FELDMAN'S CRITIQUE OF LEGAL SERVICES PRACTICE

83 GEORGETOWN LAW JOURNAL 1633 (1995)

We have chosen to focus here on two [of Professor Feldman's] characterizations that seem particularly relevant to an appraisal of the program: 1) that the legal work of the legal services program, in large measure, neither produces results nor reflects judgments and actions that meet standards of "good practice" (hereafter the proficiency issue); and 2) that legal services programs resist or ignore significant possibilities for mobilizing clients or achieving institutional change in the ways they provide day-to-day service in individual cases (hereafter the politics issue).

* * *

[First, in order to address the problem of proficiency, Bellow & Charn recommend "a process that would permit a more grounded and informed discussion among and between legal services staff on this subject."]

* * *

To this end, we would urge upon legal services readers a simple, local experiment, requiring no special authorization or funding, which we believe will add to a more knowledgeable discussion of the problem, if indeed, there is one. Although many variations are possible, this essentially involves the following steps:

1. Assemble a group of program staff involved in day-to-day service (appropriate to the size of program and office) who will devote time and thought to assessing the quality of the program's work. This group should include people who have first-hand experience with casework in the program's primary practice areas (i.e., family, housing, Social Security, AFDC) and who are able to participate consistently in the case reviews and meetings devoted to the project.

2. Review with the group five or ten recently closed case files in two different areas of practice, in which the representation provided involved more than brief advice or referral. Focus both normatively and descriptively on (a) the problem or problems presented by the client or developed by the advocate; (b) the decisions made and actions taken in the handling of the case; (c) the obstacles and difficulties the case presented and how or whether they were

confronted; (d) the outcome of the case and the client's situation at its conclusion; (e) the forms, entries, letters and memos in the file; and, most important, (f) questions to ask the advocate (or client) that any of the above inquiries may suggest. The purpose of this exercise is to develop a preliminary consensus on what constitutes good practice in each area of the program's work. . . . If no member of the group seems knowledgeable enough to guide this process, the group should reach outside the program to other legal services programs or private practitioners doing analogous work in the jurisdiction. Additionally, at a later stage, the more experienced advocates in the program might undertake to do five to ten cases of a particular type to further test the realism of the emerging consensus.

3. Next, turn the group's attention to a more extensive review (of twenty-five to fifty cases) of selected advocates in the areas of practice previously chosen. This will involve not only a survey of the case files of the advocate, but also, whenever possible, a self-assessment by each advocate of his or her own performance on the cases, including the advocate's thinking, judgments, assumptions, and any important unwritten dimensions of the cases. The process should not be understood as the group's "judgment" of one of its coworkers, but as a form of participation in an effort to articulate grounded aspirations and criteria for assessing the program's casework. The extent to which this becomes a fair description of the process depends on how widely the participation extends, how much change the process generates, and the degree of respect, seriousness, and honest assessment it actually produces.

4. Extend the above process to more advocates, to intake, and finally to observations of performance and interactions by the staff in their day-to-day work. This final aspect regarding observations of performance should include assessment of achievements in improving the recordkeeping, strategic judgments, and outcomes identified in the first round of reviews. At the same time, continually alter the review team so that the roles of reviewer and reviewee become blurred. If done systematically, the entire office can, over time, be involved in an ongoing process of casework assessment.

[Second, in order to address the problem of politics, Bellow & Charn recommend further experimentation by legal services programs.]

* * *

1. Building on prior case reviews, initiate a discussion among

the staff engaged in this project about whether there are any typical responses that were made by adversaries, officials, or institutions in the cases reviewed that they would like to see changed. This discussion should include a realistic exploration of (a) the importance of the desired change to the program's clients; (b) the number of clients who are already coming to the office faced with the same problem; (c) the results that could be obtained and their potential duration should such a change be achieved; and (d) the strategies available to challenge the problem while continuing to provide service on the type of cases in which the problem arises. Note that this is an explicitly staff-driven effort working at the margins of the current handling of such cases. Accomplishment of staff goals depends on the program having already achieved a fairly high level of proficiency in the casework they are doing in this area.

2. From this array of problems and possible changes, select one or two areas of focus and develop ways to increase both caseload (sufficiently large to have some chance of achieving the desired result) and the aggregate impact of the way the cases are handled in these areas. This involves adding further requirements to the "proficiency-oriented" routines and standards of the office designed to encourage actions and interactions in cases which, consistent with the needs and desires of clients, tilt the cumulative effects of the casework in a desired direction. For example, hearings at a particular welfare office might routinely be followed by conversations with the worker involved concerning the practice that has been challenged, or regularly circulating appellate or hearing decisions touching on the agency's practice to the office's staff. Such low key challenges can sometimes affect future behavior on the issue involved, strengthening the influence of people in the office more sympathetic to the legal services position.

* * *

3. Finally, proceed and monitor the results from these strategies for some specified length of time. Focused casework produces surprisingly predictable reactions, many of which can and must be anticipated. And initial strategies inevitably run out as circumstances change or as efforts fail, succeed, or hit roadblocks that cannot easily be dislodged. Moreover, discussions about results inevitably implicate policy choices by the program that too often are not adequately addressed among day-to-day practitioners. Types of issues to be

discussed could include, for instance, whether protecting "problem tenants" in public housing from eviction should be pursued by the program; whether work requirements in welfare programs should be attacked; whether parents or spouses found to have engaged in violent conduct against their children or partners should be assisted by the office. These questions present difficult and complex problems of choice in which representation, particularly focused representation, will have consequences. These consequences are as surely goals of the program as those that are consciously embraced.

The most important thing to remember about these preliminary strategies is that they are opportunistic, partial, and unstable, offering possibilities rather than promises of impact. However, the experience and knowledge obtained from them, as well as their cumulative effects in both material outcome and learning for the clients, are a platform on which to build similar efforts in the future.

Notes and Questions

1. *Defining the Problem.* How does Marc Feldman's definition of the problems facing legal services compare to Alan Houseman's list? Do their differing perspectives of what ails legal services reflect competing views of the goals of legal services?

2. *Comparing Means and Ends.* Feldman posits the inertia of the status quo as a potential danger facing legal services. He suggests "disrupting" the status quo and "encouraging innovation." He also suggests that lawyers should play an active role in effectively fighting poverty. Houseman seems more concerned with maintaining those parts of the current legal services delivery system which work well. He also views the idea that lawyers can be agents for social change as "fundamentally flawed." To what extent do their disagreements reflect different goals? To what extent do their disagreements reflect different means toward those goals?

3. *Seeking Solutions.* How should legal services attorneys improve their effectiveness? What roles do Feldman, Houseman, and Bellow & Charn each envision for poverty lawyers? Should they be agents for social change? Could it be, as Bellow and Charn suggest,

that legal services programs simply need more study of their problems and concerted efforts aimed at solving them. They prescribe a series of steps that legal services programs could take to identify their own problems and solutions. Are these steps likely to be helpful?

3. Revisions of Poverty Lawyering

john a. powell

Race and Poverty: A New Focus for Legal Services

Clearinghouse Review, Special Issue 1993

* * *

The legal services community comprises the largest poverty organization that serves the needs of minority communities. In a number of urban areas, blacks and Latinos may comprise the majority of the legal services' clients. Despite this fact . . . legal services does not focus on the needs of the urban minority poor. I would like to explain further why this is the case.

An individual problem, particularly in the minority community, cannot be addressed adequately or understood without situating that problem in a larger context. The programs and priorities of legal services' agenda for minorities, however, tend to be the same as those used for poor whites, a group that, although also poor, has very different problems. Many of the strategies used by legal services are more appropriate for the poor not living in a concentrated poor urban community, isolated from goods and services, and locked in by discrimination. These strategies were not explicitly adopted to address the needs of the white poor and certainly not *only* the white poor. Instead, there was an assumption that these programs were universal and that poverty is color blind. However, while in theory this might be true, in practice it is certainly false. As in most apparently universal plans, there were and are hidden biases that are more sensitive to one group's needs and less sensitive to others'. While both the laws and the strategies for legal services attempted to be sensitive to the standard poor client, there is seldom recognition that there is no standard client and therefore no standard model, including the individual model, that is sufficiently sensitive to the needs of poor people.

* * *

Some have argued that the best way to help the poor is through a universal program that does not consider race, but merely economic status, in determining whom to assist. Legal services has traditionally followed this route. They have argued, for example, that race-based programs will be ineffective in helping blacks at poverty levels because such programs tend to help the black middle class, and not the poor. They argue that we should adopt universal programs to help anyone who is poor and that, in the process, the minority poor will benefit as well (possibly more, since the poor are disproportionately minority). Furthermore, general improvements in the economy will also improve the lot of the poor by providing more opportunities for economic gain. Along these lines, it is argued that programs for minorities only are not politically palatable and that, besides, poor whites also need help.

What the supporters of such a "universalist" approach do not acknowledge are that there are unique circumstances of being poor and minority and that, due to discrimination, such strategies are implemented in a way that impacts negatively on minorities. Indeed, a part of the apparent attraction to universal strategies is that one can avoid the hostility that many whites have toward people of color. [For example, w]hen it is recognized that housing is tied to access to community services, the need for integrated housing becomes clear. But it is difficult to conceive of an effective integrated housing strategy that does not take race into account. In addition, there is also the reality that the minority poor have a different cluster of problems from others. People who live in the inner city face more obstacles to the use of services provided by various poverty assistance programs; poor black inner-city residents are particularly difficult to reach and to help. The only way, in fact, to help them is to create a program explicitly designed for that purpose. Hiding inside another program for political reasons will not achieve that result--and, worse, we pretend that it does and hence take no further action. What the "universal" poverty programs actually do is help poor whites; they have not proven to be effective in addressing the needs of poor minorities.

Changing Racial Demographics

Sometime early in the next century, Latinos will replace blacks as the largest nonwhite racial/ethnic group in the United States. Also,

Asian Americans are by far the fastest growing racial group in the country. In California, for example, African Americans are actually outnumbered by both Latinos and Asians, and it is expected that in the first half of the next century, whites will make up less than 50% of the population, thus making no racial group the majority in that state. Of course, these groups are not monolithic, and the various subgroups will have different interests and levels of poverty among them. This only makes consideration of race in the provision of services that much more important.

* * *

The histories and experiences of Latinos and Asians in this country are quite different from those of either blacks or whites. A recent Vietnamese immigrant requires poverty-related services different from those needed by a Mexican American migrant worker, each of whom is different from the inner-city black, or a suburban or rural white. In order for a legal services organization to provide assistance effectively to these various groups, it must be sensitive to their various needs. For example, having a program that tries to aid Latinos, Filipinos, or other language minorities does not mean simply having a bilingual program that otherwise provides the same services. The program staff would also need to be aware of language discrimination issues, such as subjection to biases due to one's accent, as well as cultural issues, in which the relative importance of various concerns could be quite different from the way they are viewed by "white" society. Similarly, the term "Asian American" is clearly too broad to define the issues that such communities confront. The Japanese American community is likely to have very different problems from a Vietnamese or Laotian community.

There are also likely to be tensions and issues among the various minority communities. Consider the tension that caught the public eye in the Los Angeles riots between blacks and Latinos on the one hand and Koreans on the other. . . . There is some indication that many of the secondary jobs are being closed off to African Americans in favor of minority immigrants due to status. There are a number of important and difficult issues to address if strategies are to be developed to meet the needs of the various complex minority communities.

A service organization that treats all its poor clients in the same manner, as if they have the same needs, will in fact end up meeting fewer and fewer of the clients' needs as a larger percentage of the population find the services irrelevant. As the multicultural aspect of our society increases, there will be more and more issues to which one must be sensitive in order to serve the clientele appropriately. Of course, it will be harder, because of the number of complex subgroups, and the solutions to the problems may also be more complex. Having no awareness, however, of the differences among various groups simply means no help for most of them.

Developing Strategies to Address the Needs of Poor Urban Minorities

In order to address the specific needs of communities, programs should develop strategies that are sensitive to their needs. . . . The structure of most programs' priority setting is not sensitive to the issues of concentration and discrimination . . . . One goal then is to assist programs in developing a process that would be more likely to identify special minority needs. We must have national strategy conferences to see how the problem is occurring in other areas and to share what works. Perhaps the most important function of such a conference would be for us to think collectively about these issues.

The way in which legal services approached the homelessness issue might be instructive. Advocates recognized that homelessness is a problem that is occurring across the country and that the scope of the problem exceeds the scope and resources of any one program. It would not be appropriate to wait for individual clients to walk in the door to define the scope of the homelessness problem. The legal services community appropriately took a much more affirmative stance in trying to develop strategies. I believe that a similar approach is required in order to develop effective strategies to deal with the intersection of race and poverty.

* * *

Critical Lawyering

Louise G. Trubek

CRITICAL LAWYERING: TOWARD A NEW PUBLIC INTEREST PRACTICE

1 PUBLIC INTEREST LAW JOURNAL 49 (1991)

The practice of public interest law is ready for a change. While the public interest idea has its roots in older traditions of lawyer professionalism, the movement was inspired by the work of organizations like the ACLU and the NAACP. Current public interest practice, which I define as the practice of law for social change, was born in the 1960s and took institutional shape in the 1970s. As we look ahead to the 1990s, it is clear that public interest lawyers need a new vision to orient and sustain them. This commentary outlines such a vision, which I call "critical lawyering." Critical lawyering acknowledges the contradictions and difficulties of working for social change within the conventional framework of the legal system.

My vision comes from my experience as public interest practitioner for over a 20 year period. I have worked in a variety of public interest practice settings, including a small public interest women's rights group; a private minority rights agency; a mixed private and pro bono law firm; and a state-based, multi-issue public interest law firm associated with a law school clinic. For some time now, I have also directed the clinic. I have also worked on minority, health, elderly and consumer issues and women's rights, concentrating on the state level.

My work has shown me first hand the strengths and weaknesses of traditional public interest practice. My consciousness about the use of law for social change has changed over the years. My initial views were formed when I attended law school in the late 1950s: these ideas framed my approach in the early years of my practice in the late 1960s and early 1970s. These attitudes reflected ideals of professionalism and pluralism; my practice focused on government reforms and interest group politics. As the 1970s progressed, I became dissatisfied with these ideas. In order to continue working in the public interest sector and to increase my effectiveness, I rethought my practice and my goals. This rethinking was spurred by my work as a teacher, influenced by my concentration on state level questions, and inspired by generations of law students who have brought new questions and visions to our practice. My experience has given me the courage to propose a reconceptualization of the role of the public interest practitioner and, in this essay, I will describe how public interest law can be a practice of critical lawyering.

This new concept of public interest practice is grounded in a more critical vision of law and society. It recognizes that lawyering for social change and on behalf of subordinated groups presents challenges far greater and more complex than the public interest lawyers of the 1960s imagined. Critical legal practice, as I define it, involves two elements: seeking to empower oppressed groups and individuals, *and* initiating a trajectory of change towards a more just society. Attorneys can empower people in two ways: first, individually, within a supportive attorney-client relationship; second, through the process of organizing groups and encouraging them to speak out in the public sphere. My view of a just society, however, goes beyond formal equality and redistribution. Lawyers alone can't create a just society, but they can take actions to put society on a trajectory toward fundamental change. Both empowerment and transformative strategies are crucial, and critical practice should involve both. But it is also important to see them as distinct and independent objectives for social change lawyering.

In my practice, I have found that critical lawyering has six dimensions. Lawyers should encourage participation, personalize the issues, be skeptical of bureaucracy, be flexible in selecting advocacy arenas, organize with other lawyers, and apply feminist and anti-racist analyses. Each is useful in analyzing what cases or issues to emphasize, planning strategy, and choosing work partners. Thinking about these dimensions when a new issue arises has helped me to ensure that my work involves both aspects of critical practice--*empowerment* and *transformation*.

Encourage Participation

Critical lawyers should involve their clients in practice decisions. Traditional public interest lawyers tended to orient their advocacy toward court victories; they considered advocacy a professional task. While they often discussed strategies with clients, their view of client participation was limited. Critical practice recognizes that a broader view of participation is essential. Critical lawyers should seek client participation to raise client consciousness of the law's impact and to develop proposals that will continue to work and ensure empowerment. Participation includes client involvement in actual advocacy and in devising the goals that the lawyers will pursue.

An example from my practice illustrates this principle. A major issue confronting the elderly is provision of adequate long-term care. In a recent controversy in Wisconsin, insurance companies offered nursing home insurance as the solution. At first glance, many considered this an attractive option. Consultations with the constituency groups and individuals my organization represents, however, revealed the pitfalls of this plan because the insurance would favor nursing homes over other long-term care options. With our constituents, we devised a counter-proposal more suited to the needs and desires of the elderly. Wisconsin has, for several years, had a very successful community-based, individualized, tax-funded case-management system for long-term care. This was developed for younger disabled people but has been widely used for the elderly in the state. This "Community Options Program," which operates at the county level, has been extremely popular with elderly clients, as well as elderly advocacy groups. After many meetings with elderly groups, we decided to push for an expanded Community Options Program (COP), in which individuals decide for themselves what community-based services they need to remain in their own homes, e.g., chore service, home health aides, etc. We issued a position paper which opposed nursing home insurance and proposed funding for the community-based, individualized alternative.

The COP example illustrates both aspects of participation: elderly advocates developed the plan with the clients and the proposal requires client involvement in the creation of individual support packages. While this kind of participation seems necessary, traditional public interest lawyers often lost sight of the central importance of client-generated strategies.

Personalize the Issue

Critical lawyers should frame issues in human terms. Lawyers, including public interest practitioners, tend to think in terms of "causes of action" and technical solutions. But this approach keeps the issue and the advocacy within a narrow, professional arena. To be effective, public interest lawyers have to break out of this arena into a broader public space and make moral and emotional connections. For example, critical lawyers should view the media as a major resource. Lawyers can use the media to more effectively demonstrate the human implications of policies and laws, especially if the media tells the story from the client's perspective.

***

Especially in discussions with lawyers and government officials, public interest lawyers should emphasize the effects policies have on people. Decision-makers will conceptualize the problem and the solutions differently when faced with real people and multi-dimensional needs. For example, the Center for Public Representation worked on the implementation of the Wisconsin Family and Medical Leave Act to help parents balance family and work responsibilities. We urged government officials and business attorneys to look beyond procedural requirements and understand the stress felt by parents with work and childcare responsibilities. At conferences on the Family and Medical Leave Act, our lawyers analyzed each complaint filed under the Act. They described the human dilemmas behind the complaints rather than the technical statutory analysis. This allowed the audience of lawyers and business people to see the issue as a human problem, not merely an interpretation of an abstract set of rules. By showcasing people who use the Act and presenting the tensions and difficulties they face, we captured the sympathy of the endorsing agency and helped regulated businesses understand people's real concerns.

These efforts with the family and medical leave policies are transformative in that they seek to expand the Act to encourage businesses and unions to make more "family-sensitive" decisions. These efforts have also fostered client empowerment because our advocacy techniques involved clients telling their stories and presenting a multidimensional view of their concerns.

Don't Trust Bureaucracy

Public interest lawyers of my generation often thought the way to deal with a social problem was to create another agency or get new staff for an existing agency. Traditional public interest lawyers believed that a new director or new agency with a new mission--for example, providing health care for all--would create and carry out the solution that the advocates wanted. These lawyers thought that if they could frame a statute that gave agencies a mandate to bring about desired change and get it passed, their work ended. This was a very seductive image and many public interest lawyers were seduced. Too often, the bureaucratic structures abandoned the lawyers that created them. For example, I supported the creation of a state agency to regulate hospital rates, with the goal of controlling hospital costs to insure services for patients who lacked resources. No sooner was the agency created than hospital interests co-opted it. As a result, the agency clearly favored hospital interests and ignored the interests of needy clients. Moreover, the regulators actually discouraged the participation of the clients and advocates who had been instrumental in the creation of the agency.

Until recently, many of my proposals on health involved creation of oversight agencies designed to develop health care provisions. However, I have rethought that approach. I am thinking much more in terms of creating community programs that will provide health care directly, using both public and private dollars, plus whatever citizen energies we can mobilize. We can use the programs created in local communities to see what actually works. Then we will be better able to describe what we want for the state as a whole.

***

Don't Privilege Any Advocacy Arena

Law reformers often debate the effectiveness of litigation versus legislation and individual case representation versus class actions. Traditional public interest lawyers have preferred using the test case or statute that will set a new principle and have often disdained direct service to clients. Taking this position, traditional public interest lawyers assumed that direct service was tainted by the "system" and could never bring social change. In contrast, they assumed test cases were a purer approach to law reform, and that this constituted public interest lawyering beyond the system. They based these assumptions on a belief that the legal process itself did not replicate inequities in access. Law reformers see the professional arena as self-contained, their victories as self-enforcing,and, as we have seen, the bureaucracies as trustworthy. Critical lawyering recognizes that every arena contains opportunities for, and obstacles to, change. Rather than privileging any one arena, critical lawyering involves expanding professional boundaries. The critical lawyer looks for any opportunity to empower clients and transform society.

I have found that successful critical legal practice can start anywhere. Public interest lawyers should seize an issue, case or client that has resonance in the community and move from there. My public interest law center represents many thousands of individual senior citizens. From our experience in individual cases, we developed enough credibility and knowledge to enable us to advocate systematic changes like the Community Options Program for long-term care. Had we proposed that solution without having gained the ideas through providing individual representation, our proposals would have received scant attention. Also, the simple fact that we actually talked to many potential recipients gave us great credibility. Industry rarely comes to the legislature with first hand evidence.

On the other hand, sometimes we start at the legislative level and move to individual cases. For example, our work in the Family and Medical Leave Act, which provides unpaid leave for families, started with legislative work. After dramatizing the issue for the public, we provided direct information to employees and representation of cases before administrative agencies.

Organize

Public interest lawyers generally understand that they will be more successful in representing their clients' interests when their clients are well organized. Due to lack of resources, difficulty in perceiving inchoate client strengths, and professional distance, however, advocates rarely follow through on this understanding. This presents perhaps the most challenging tasks for social change lawyers because our professional education does not promote organizing skills and the value of community work. Also, resources for advocates to do organizing work are especially limited. Critical lawyers should join with and encourage client organizations whenever they arise.

Nevertheless, critical lawyers themselves *can* take leadership in organizing. Public interest lawyers must do more to create an advocacy community so that we can learn from each other and more effectively promote transformative strategies. Frequently, advocacy success stories involve lawyers getting together to plan, strategize jointly and support each other.

***

Apply Feminist and Anti-Racist Analyses

Traditional public interest lawyers working in areas other than civil rights and women's rights did not address the systemic nature of the subordination of women and minorities in America. Critical lawyers have come to understand the structural persistence of racism and sexism and to recognize it in our advocacy. We have seen that our failure to look specifically at the effect of advocacy solutions on women and minorities may have unwittingly contributed to their continued subordination.

For example, in our work on behalf of the elderly on long-term care issues we initially failed to see how certain policy solutions might harm women as a group. If legislation emphasizes keeping older people at home, women will likely end up as caretakers. This will affect working women and increase the pressure for women to return to unpaid work in the home. When my public interest law center realized this, we redesigned some proposals. Now we emphasize creating resources to assist women caretakers and avoid forcing a choice between care and career. For a family choosing home-based care, we seek to make home health aides paid for by the state or private insurance available so family members can continue their work outside the home. We are demanding paid caretaking leave so that caretakers can miss work for caretaking without facing an employer's penalties. Our work with unions seeks to secure adequate pay and working conditions for home health workers; and we are seeking state or insurance based compensation plans at market rates for family caretakers who choose to work full-time providing long-term care. Without an analysis of the policies' effects on women, we would short-circuit the ability of women to empower themselves in the workplace and at home.

Closer attention to racism and the persistence of racial inequality has had a similar impact on our thinking and our practice. Two examples illustrate the impact of critical race thinking on my center's activities. We have long advocated a right to health care for all in Wisconsin. Initially, we advocated for a universal health care program based on state financing and private insurance. But, once we began to look closely at the different impacts of programs on subordinated groups, we began to see that a universal plan would not necessarily deal effectively with the problem of minorities in the inner city.

For example, in the Milwaukee inner city, very few clinics exist and almost no minority physicians work in them. A universal plan for health care might have little impact in this area, because no delivery system exists. Thus we shifted our emphasis to highlight the need for neighborhood clinics and specialized services *as well as* universal financing plans. We proposed legislation to create such clinics, believing them necessary components of providing adequate health care for all. Once again, critical analysis moved us away from universal and bureaucratic plans to more decentralized and participatory approaches.

A similar set of issues arose when we examined drug treatment plans. Here, both race analysis and feminist analysis applied. In the last year, the state has embarked on a general effort to develop more drug treatment centers in Wisconsin. When we looked at the program's impact in Milwaukee, however, we found that because the programs had few minority counselors, they had little sensitivity to the needs of minorities. In addition, lack of child care availability excluded many minority women with children from participation. Along with a local coalition of black health advocates, we have sought to dramatize this issue and to press for the creation of more culturally sensitive programs, participation of more minority counselors, and increased day care availability for these groups.

Living in the Contradiction

Critical lawyering requires careful attention to each of the six dimensions outlined. Public interest lawyers should constantly remember the need for participation, personalization, organization and anti-racist and feminist analyses. Critical lawyers must avoid the lure of professional discourse, privileged arenas and bureaucratic "quick-fixes." But it is not enough to foster participation, personalize issues, reject bureaucratic solutions, explore all arenas, encourage organization and pay special attention to the impact of policies on women and minorities within client groups. We as critical lawyers must also learn how to live in the contradiction. We have to learn to deal with the central paradox of our peculiar vocation: helping bring about basic change and social mobilization while working within a legal system rooted in the status quo and oriented towards professional decision-making.

What does it mean to "live in the contradiction?" Three points help answer this question. First, as public interest lawyers, we should never assume we have the answers or that we can solve social problems. Critical lawyering demands constant criticism of our work, our interaction with others and our workplaces. Second, we must understand that no definite solutions or final victories exist. Agencies we helped create one day became enemies the next day as they interpreted statutory gains away and ignored or overruled successful cases. Nevertheless, if we do our work, some empowerment will take place in each case and some movement along a transformative trajectory will occur. Admittedly, we must look hard to recognize these positive moments, and we cannot despair when the inevitable setbacks occur. Finally, we have to care about our own workplaces and not let the pursuit of ideal goals in legislation or litigation blind us to the need to constantly make our everyday work life exemplary for the world we want to create. Public interest law practice should reflect the same goals we seek for our clients. For example, increased attention should be paid to race and gender issues.

These three elements of living in the contradiction are related. Self-criticism is necessary to maintain an exemplary workplace, and to help lawyers avoid false hopes and premature despair. A supportive workplace helps create an environment conducive to self-criticism and enables us to act on the insights that criticism generates. To sustain their hope and energy, critical lawyers must seek an understanding of the complex and contradictory nature of public interest practice.

Critical lawyering presents a sober and realistic outlook at the possibilities of lawyering for social change. It requires recognition that advocates for subordinated groups will win few easy victories. It forces us to insist that all actions foster empowerment. It demands a view of how our advocacy will lead to fundamental change. Critical lawyering requires public interest lawyers to move beyond the professional arena into a wider public space and beyond bureaucracy towards decentralized, participatory approaches to social problems.

Caring Lawyering

If you came to law school because you wanted to assist disadvantaged people, consider how your law school experience has influenced your goal. Theresa Glennon, in the excerpt that follows, describes how she structured a law school course to reinforce an ethic of care. As you read about her approach, consider how each individual law student and lawyer could build a similar ethic of care into their daily activities.

Theresa Glennon

LAWYERS AND CARING: BUILDING AN ETHIC OF CARE INTO PROFESSIONAL RESPONSIBILITY

43 HASTINGS LAW JOURNAL 1175 (1992)

* * *

The public debate concerning the responsibility of the private bar to provide legal services to people living in poverty has focused largely on whether this should be a mandatory obligation. This focus on enforceable rules reflects the usual treatment given to questions of professional responsibility in legal education. . . . This constrained view of professional responsibility excludes deeper questions of lawyers' moral conduct and their role in creating or perpetuating injustice.

* * *

The dominant approach rests upon a political and moral theory that values individual rights, the duty not to interfere with the rights of others, and the fair resolution of the conflict of rights among separate individuals. In this vision the role of morality is to keep that competition fair by limiting interference with the rights of others.

* * *

A more compelling account of professional responsibility is available, but it rests on a different vision of social reality and on political and moral theories that place responsibility to others at the heart of human freedom and fulfillment. This account draws on a vision of the social world in which the responsibility of individuals to each other and their community, rather than the possession of individual rights, creates and maintains the conditions that guard human freedom. Civic responsibility is not antithetical to individual fulfillment. Rather, the human spirit finds fulfillment by assuming this responsibility to others.

* * *

[In my course on Legal Theory and Practice and Civil Procedure], I made an effort to replace a vision of professional responsibility based solely on individual rights with one that includes an "ethic of care." The effort to incorporate an ethic of care focused on two ideas: first, that students' professional work is deeply connected to those who are disadvantaged by the legal system; and second, that practicing law with others can be based on care and connection. In implementing these ideas, I employed teaching methodologies that emphasized regard for and connection to others.

* * *

The course provided students with opportunities to build connections with individuals living in poverty and emphasized the role of care in their professional lives. For example, the usual discussion in a civil procedure class concerning complaints focuses primarily on the minimum requirements to prevent dismissal of a complaint. In [my course], however, this discussion centered on the elements of a good complaint. In particular, we focused on responding to the client's goals and helping the client tell his or her story in a clear and compelling way. I hoped that students who listened carefully to their client's story would begin to see the world through their clients' eyes. This effort was encouraged in classes on basic lawyering skills, such as interviewing, counseling, and fact gathering. In each case, incorporating regard for clients and trying to understand their perspectives and their humanity was depicted as essential to responsible lawyering.

* * *

Working with individual clients enabled students to see how difficult it was for their clients to obtain services to which they were entitled. Education rights that appeared generous in statutes were often inaccessible to their clients. Students saw how difficult it was for their clients to speak up when confronted by "professionals" at meetings. They learned that for their clients, a hearing might not be the "opportunity" it is always described as in their casebook, but a threat by school officials.

* * *

Students were also encouraged to make connections between their legal work and the broader context in which they operated, and to bring their care for others to this broader context. They encountered some of the structural barriers to education faced by children who are homeless, and advocated for the removal of those barriers. Students saw that school officials, confronted by scarce resources, would pit the needs of one group against another, and also saw the role that racial and gender stereotypes play in the allocation of those scarce resources.

* * *

People living in poverty need lawyers who work together. Lawyers who work for those people need relationships with other lawyers as well. Relationships among lawyers that include care and the sharing of ideas and problems help lawyers to be motivated and effective. Thus, students were encouraged to form these relationships with each other and to recognize their benefits.

I encouraged students to provide emotional support to each other and to think through problems together. Collegial structures were established throughout all aspects of the course.

* * *

These cooperative and supportive relationships were brought into classroom discussion as well. Instead of relying solely on the

Socratic method, in many classes students were treated as members of a practice group who had a problem to solve. Thus, students used class time to plan their arguments together and marshal their evidence for a motion for class certification. In addition, students were asked to present their ideas to each other, in order to signal that their views and their attempts to give meaning to what they read and experienced were valued.

Providing legal services to people living in poverty is hard and often painful work. Instead of trying to submerge this aspect of lawyering, students were encouraged to share their responses. For some students, poverty is a shock. Other students come to the course with their own experiences of poverty, racism, and bureaucratic indifference. Many students experience for the first time the uncertainties involved in lawyering--that it is hard to know what choices to make, who should make those choices, what information is needed, and how to get it. Students were encouraged both to support each other and to investigate their responses to see what they could learn about the legal structures in which they practiced.

Students' work with other attorneys illustrated the importance of caring work relationships to motivation and effectiveness. The students who worked with private pro bono attorneys saw that, in general, these attorneys did their public service in isolation, and often at the end of a busy work day. These attorneys thus were unable to share in the benefits of a collegial practice for their pro bono work. . . . Some students vividly witnessed the isolation that many of the attorneys felt about their pro bono cases, and ways in which that work was marginalized by their firm. They saw and heard from some of the attorneys how difficult it can be to provide effective representation without others' ideas and support. . . . While the students were impressed by the tenacity of some of the pro bono attorneys, they saw the limits of this manner of providing legal services, because the pro bono attorneys were not part of a concerted, coordinated effort to improve education services for poor children.

Students who worked with attorneys in public interest organizations observed that these attorneys had opportunities unavailable to many of the pro bono attorneys to work together and to plan and implement projects that might improve the education of many children. These organizations also offered the possibility of caring relationships among the lawyers and between lawyers and clients, as well as with the lawyer community. Through discussions with students, these issues were brought to light, and students were encouraged to think about how to organize legal work on behalf of people living in poverty to make that work both meaningful and effective.

Notes and Questions

1. *Race-Conscious or Not?* According to john powell, legal services programs must affirmatively take race into account and develop strategies to reach the needs of poor members of various racial minority groups. What reasons support powell's argument for race-conscious strategies by legal services lawyers?

Recall the analysis of William Julius Wilson in Chapter 3. Wilson argued that race-based programs help economically advantaged minorities, rather than the truly disadvantaged. Do powell and Wilson disagree, or is it possible to reconcile their ideas?

2. *Diversity Among Minorities.* Even powell acknowledges that minority groups are not monolithic, but instead are quite diverse. The limitless nature of diversity boggles the mind. How are legal services lawyers to accomplish what society has not, namely to understand the needs of each group as well as each individual? If you were directing a legal services program, how would you approach the task of educating your lawyers to understand our multicultural society? Do poor people share common characteristics that might simplify your task?

3. *Critical Lawyering.* Professor Trubek offers six concrete strategies for new critical public interest lawyering. She recommends that public interest lawyers: (1) encourage client participation in decision-making; (2) frame issues in human terms; (3) focus on community development, rather than creation of bureaucracy; (4) be open to new issues, and flexible in addressing them; (5) organize client communities; and (6) address the systemic subordination of women and racial minorities. Who is Professor Trubek addressing--legal services lawyers, and/or pro bono lawyers? Can legal services lawyers lawfully engage in these strategies today? Do these strategies seem feasible? How could they be accomplished by individual lawyers? Are there tensions between any of these strategies? Are there tensions between these strategies and lawyers' ethical responsibilities?

4. *Ethic of Care.* Does morality play a role in determining lawyers' ethical responsibilities? Should morality play such a role?

Professor Glennon argues that professional ethics should focus less on individual rights and more on "the responsibility of individuals to each other and their community" which "creates and maintains the conditions that guard human freedom." What do you think she means? How would an ethic of care change the study and practice of law? Should such an ethic be part of the formal ethical rules which govern lawyers?

5. *Rejecting Litigation?* Professors powell, Trubek, and Glennon urge lawyers to be more engaged in communities and to try new approaches to solving client problems. Advocates of alternative dispute resolution have urged lawyers to attempt more creative and/or more mutually beneficial methods to solve client problems. *See* Linda Singer, et al., *Alternative Dispute Resolution and the Poor,* 26 CLEARINGHOUSE REVIEW 142 (May/June 1992). To what extent should lawyers reject litigation as a viable strategy for achieving lawyering goals? For example, consider the views of Professor Kimberly O'Leary:

> Most challenges to subsidized housing anti-crime measures have been based upon constitutional analyses. Constitutional analysis has traditionally failed to address issues that must be resolved in fashioning anti-crime measures that will work. Methodologies based on dialogue between affected parties are more likely to result in practices that are workable to housing authority staff, law enforcement, residents, and members of the community. A policy which comes out of this process will take into account the needs of a variety of affected parties, protecting minority as well as majority interests in most instances. Public interest attorneys must take affirmative steps to increase the opportunities for meaningful dialogue to take place. Attorneys should consider whether the time and money spent on litigation will ultimately result in policies and practices that will benefit their clients. If litigation is needed, lawyers should consult different perspectives and present the information to the court. Attorneys can craft settlement plans that will pay community leaders

> to organize meaningful dialogue concerning the underlying issues that prevent anti-crime measures from working effectively. They can also encourage their clients to begin discussions about these underlying issues. If resident and community needs are to shape the policies and practices of the future, public interest attorneys must find ways to create and sustain dialogue between those parties who would be defined as opponents in traditional litigation.

Kimberly E. O'Leary, *Dialogue, Perspective and Point of View As Lawyering Method: A New Approach to Evaluating Anti-Crime Measures in Subsidized Housing,* 49 JOURNAL OF URBAN AND CONTEMPORARY LAW 133 (1996).

Theoretics of Practice

Unsatisfied with the constraints that litigation and causes of action impose, some critical legal scholars have explored the use of narratives to convey and explore the meaning of people's experiences. *See, e.g.*, DERRICK BELL, AND WE ARE NOT SAVED (1987) and PATRICIA J. WILLIAMS, THE ALCHEMY OF RACE AND RIGHTS (1991). A related "theoretics of practice" movement has emerged among some clinical and poverty law scholars calling for a reconstruction of poverty law practice. *See, e.g.*, Symposium, *Theoretics of Practice: The Integration of Progressive Thought and Action*, 43 HASTINGS LAW JOURNAL 717 (1992). Many theoretics of practice scholars criticize traditional law practice of fitting, or forcing, client experiences into cause-of-action pigeonholes. They propose instead that lawyers tell their clients' own narratives. According to Anthony Alfieri, poverty lawyers subject clients to what he calls "interpretive violence," which consists of lawyer practices of "marginalization, subordination, and discipline. Marginalization establishes client inferiority. Subordination entrenches inferiority in a lawyer-client hierarchy of subject-object relations. Discipline enforces hierarchy by excluding the expression of the voices of client narratives." *See* Anthony V. Alfieri, *Reconstructive Poverty Law Practice: Learning Lessons of Client Narrative*, 100 YALE LAW JOURNAL 2107, 2125 (1991). Alfieri proposes that poverty lawyers reconstruct their practice through four methods: suspicion, metaphor, collaboration, and redescription. *Id.* at 2134. He explains:

> Suspicion is the practice of investigating the primary contradiction of the poverty lawyer's interpretive tradition: the image of client dependency. This image and its attendant meaning are contradicted by the client's public and private assertions of power.
>
> * * *
>
> Through the practice of metaphor, the lawyer imagines that events composing the client story may signify a double meaning or constitute a double referent. The first meaning is prosaic, referring to the concreteness of specific events. This is the meaning inscribed by traditional lawyer practice. . . . A more complete account requires the lawyer to search for a deeper, normative meaning within client events. [For example, one client tells of her struggle through the metaphors of dignity, caring, community, and rights.]
>
> * * *
>
> The practice of collaboration commands lawyer-client co-equal participation in the telling of client story. As a means of guiding all aspects of lawyer-client advocacy, collaboration overrides lawyer claims of neutral and universal narratives.
>
> * * *
>
> Redescription is the revisionist practice of retelling client story consonant with the voices of client narratives. In this retelling, the poverty lawyer discredits traditional images of client dependency by crediting client narratives of daily struggle. The practice of redescription honors client integrity by sifting out the narrative richness of client story omitted by traditional practices of interpretation.

Id. at 2134, 2138, 2140-41. *See* Clark D. Cunningham, *The Lawyer As Translator, Representation As Text: Towards an Ethnography of Legal Discourse,* 77 CORNELL LAW REVIEW 1298 (1992).

Some theoretics of practice scholars have criticized the movement's tendency to rely too heavily on theory. For example, Lucie White criticizes Alfieri's work "as the bringing of static, prepackaged insights to poverty lawyers from a perspective that is curiously freed from the concrete engagement, the partiality, and hence the ambiguity of its own vantage-point." Lucie White, *Paradox, Piece-Work, and Patience,* 43 HASTINGS LAW JOURNAL 853, 855 (1992). White explains, "If we lose patience with the slow, dialogic exploration of the collective practices in which we are embedded, and leap toward an imperial, imperative style of doing theory, we risk repeating within our own theories the very 'interpretive violence' that our theories seek to move us beyond." *Id.* at 856.

Other scholars have criticized the theoretics of practice movement for devaluing the skills that lawyers offer clients. For example, Binny Miller criticizes narrative scholars for having "virtually ignored the critical role that case theory can play in linking client stories to the narratives that lawyers tell on behalf of their clients." Binny Miller, *Give Them Back Their Lives: Recognizing Client Narrative in Case Theory*, 93 MICHIGAN LAW REVIEW 485, 487 (1994). Miller argues that case theory links the legal case to the client's experience "with an eye toward the ultimate audience--the trier of fact." *Id.* As another scholar concluded:

> Poverty law clients seek out poverty attorneys because they have legal problems, and because poverty attorneys are trained as lawyers. Poverty law clients need poverty lawyers to obtain for them the legal results to which they are entitled. To assume that poverty clients also need poverty attorneys for normative validation and conveyance, or to assume that if poverty attorneys take control in the legal setting poverty clients are disempowered and marginalized in all other settings, conceives for poverty attorneys a paternalistically greater role than poverty attorneys have in their clients' lives. Most dangerously, these assumptions lead to practice suggestions which ignore the very reason the clients seek the help of poverty attorneys--because they are attorneys.

Cathy Lesser Mansfield, *Deconstructing Reconstructive Poverty Law: Practice-Based Critique of the Storytelling Aspects of the Theoretics of Practice Movement*, 61 BROOKLYN LAW REVIEW 889 (1995).

Much of the debate about the theoretics of practice gets bogged down in the question whether the lawyer or the client should control the story the lawyer tells on the client's behalf. Why should either one "control"? Why shouldn't lawyers and clients collaborate in making these decisions? Gerald Lopez calls for such collaboration in his book, REBELLIOUS LAWYERING: ONE CHICANO'S VISION OF PROGRESSIVE LAW PRACTICE (1992). Lopez described traditional law practice as "regnant," in which lawyers pose as experts and rescuers of poor victims. As an alternative to regnant lawyering, he proposed a "rebellious" approach, in which lawyers work in collaboration with community members. Does Lopez' call for collaboration merely beg the question whether lawyer or client should control the storytelling, or does it offer a meaningful way to resolve the question?

C. ACCESS AND BARRIERS

Even if a poor person obtains the services of a lawyer to help her with a legal problem, and even if that lawyer wants to tell the client's story, she may face additional barriers to gaining access to the judicial system. For example, poor clients may not be able to afford the fees required for filing pleadings with a court. Or the court may not recognize any formal cause of action which would entitle the poor person to raise a claim or defense in a judicial proceeding. We turn now to these issues, including the enforceability of the 1996 Temporary Assistance for Needy Families block grant legislation.

1. Court Fees

BODDIE v. CONNECTICUT

401 U.S. 371

Justice HARLAN delivered the opinion of the Court.

Appellants, welfare recipients residing in the State of Connecticut, brought this action in the Federal District Court for the District of Connecticut on behalf of themselves and others similarly situated, challenging, as applied to them, certain state procedures for the commencement of litigation, including requirements for payment of court fees and costs for service of process, that restrict their access to the courts in their effort to bring an action for divorce.

It appears from the briefs and oral argument that the average cost to a litigant for bringing an action for divorce is $60. Section 52--259 of the Connecticut General Statutes provides: "There shall be paid to the clerks of the supreme court or the superior court, for entering each civil cause, forty-five dollars . . . ." An additional $15 is usually required for the service of process by the sheriff, although as much as $40 or $50 may be necessary where notice must be accomplished by publication.

There is no dispute as to the inability of the named appellants in the present case to pay either the court fees required by statute or the cost incurred for the service of process. The affidavits in the record establish that appellants' welfare income in each instance barely suffices to meet the costs of the daily essentials of life and includes no allotment that could be budgeted for the expense to gain access to the courts in order to obtain a divorce. Also undisputed is appellants' "good faith" in seeking a divorce.

Assuming, as we must on this motion to dismiss the complaint, the truth of the undisputed allegations made by the appellants, it appears that they were unsuccessful in their attempt to bring their divorce actions in the Connecticut courts, simply by reason of their indigency. The clerk of the Superior Court returned their papers "on the ground that he could not accept them until an entry fee had been paid." Subsequent efforts to obtain a judicial waiver of the fee requirement and to have the court effect service of process were to no avail.

* * *

Our conclusion is that, given the basic position of the marriage relationship in this society's hierarchy of values and the concomitant state monopolization of the means for legally dissolving this relationship, due process does prohibit a State from denying, solely because of inability to pay, access to its courts to individuals who seek judicial dissolution of their marriages.

I

At its core, the right to due process reflects a fundamental value in our American constitutional system. Our understanding of the value is the basis upon which we have resolved this case.

Perhaps no characteristic of an organized and cohesive society is more fundamental than its erection and enforcement of a system of rules defining the various rights and duties of its members, enabling them to govern their affairs and definitively settle their differences in an orderly, predictable manner. Without such a "legal system," social organization and cohesion are virtually impossible; with the ability to seek regularized resolution of conflicts individuals are capable of interdependent action that enables them to strive for achievements without the anxieties that would beset them in a disorganized society. Put more succinctly, it is this injection of the rule of law that allows society to reap the benefits of rejecting what political theorists call the "state of nature."

* * *

As this Court on more than one occasion has recognized, marriage involves interests of basic importance in our society. It is not surprising, then, that the States have seen fit to oversee many aspects of that institution. Without a prior judicial imprimatur, individuals may freely enter into and rescind commercial contracts, for example, but we are unaware of any jurisdiction where private citizens may covenant for or dissolve marriages without state approval. Even where all substantive requirements are concededly met, we know of no instance where two consenting adults may divorce and mutually liberate themselves from the constraints of legal obligations that go with marriage, and more fundamentally the prohibition against remarriage, without invoking the State's judicial machinery.

Thus, although they assert here due process rights as would-be plaintiffs, we think appellants' plight, because resort to the state courts is the only avenue to dissolution of their marriages, is akin to that of defendants faced with exclusion from the only forum effectively empowered to settle their disputes. Resort to the judicial process by these plaintiffs is no more voluntary in a realistic sense than that of the defendant called upon to defend his interests in court. For both groups this process is not only the paramount dispute-settlement technique, but, in fact, the only available one. In this posture we think that this appeal is properly to be resolved in light of the principles enunciated in our due process decisions that delimit rights of defendants compelled to litigate their differences in the judicial forum.

II

These due process decisions, representing over a hundred years of effort by this Court to give concrete embodiment to this concept, provide, we think, complete vindication for appellants' contentions. In particular, precedent has firmly embedded in our due process jurisprudence two important principles upon whose application we rest our decision in the case before us.

A

Prior cases establish, first, that due process requires, at a minimum, that absent a countervailing state interest of overriding significance, persons forced to settle their claims of right and duty through the judicial process must be given a meaningful opportunity to be heard. . . . Although "[m]any controversies have raged about the cryptic and abstract words of the Due Process Clause," as Justice Jackson wrote for the Court, . . . "there can be no doubt that at a minimum they require that deprivation of life, liberty or property by adjudication be precedent by notice and opportunity for hearing appropriate to the nature of the case."

Due process does not, of course, require that the defendant in every civil case actually have a hearing on the merits. A State, can, for example, enter a default judgment against a defendant who, after adequate notice, fails to make a timely appearance, or who, without justifiable excuse, violates a procedural rule requiring the production of evidence necessary for orderly adjudication. What the Constitution does require is "an opportunity . . . granted at a meaningful time and in a meaningful manner, . . . for [a] hearing appropriate to the nature of the case." The formality and procedural requisites for the hearing can vary, depending upon the importance of the interests involved and the nature of the subsequent proceedings. That the hearing required by due process is subject to waiver, and is not fixed in form does not affect its root requirement that an individual be given an opportunity for a hearing before he is deprived of any significant property interest, except for extraordinary situations where some valid governmental interest is at stake that justifies postponing the hearing until after the event. In short, "within the limits of practicability," a State must afford to all individuals a meaningful opportunity to be heard if it is to fulfill the promise of the Due Process Clause.

B

Our cases further establish that a statute or a rule may be held constitutionally invalid as applied when it operates to deprive an individual of a protected right although its general validity as a measure enacted in the legitimate exercise of state power is beyond question. Thus, in cases involving religious freedom, free speech or assembly, this Court has often held that a valid statute was unconstitutionally applied in particular circumstances because it interfered with an individual's exercise of those rights.

No less than these rights, the right to a meaningful opportunity to be heard within the limits of practicality, must be protected against denial by particular laws that operate to jeopardize it for particular individuals.

In *Mullane* [*v. Central Hanover Bank & Trust Co.*], this Court held that the statutory provision for notice by publication in a local newspaper, although sufficient as to beneficiaries of a trust whose interests or addresses were unknown to the trustee, was not sufficient notice under the Due Process Clause for known beneficiaries. Similarly, *Covey* [*v. Town of Somers*] held that notice by publication in a foreclosure action, even though sufficient to provide a normal person with an opportunity for a hearing, was not sufficient where the defendant was a known incompetent. The Court expressly rejected an argument that "the Fourteenth Amendment does not require the State to take measures in giving notice to an incompetent beyond those deemed sufficient in the case of the ordinary taxpayer."

Just as a generally valid notice procedure may fail to satisfy due process because of the circumstances of the defendant, so too a cost requirement, valid on its face, may offend due process because it operates to foreclose a particular party's opportunity to be heard. The State's obligations under the Fourteenth Amendment are not simply generalized ones; rather, the State owes to each individual that process which, in light of the values of a free society, can be characterized as due.

III

Drawing upon the principles established by the cases just canvassed, we conclude that the State's refusal to admit these appellants to its courts, the sole means in Connecticut for obtaining a divorce, must be regarded as the equivalent of denying them an opportunity to be heard upon their claimed right to a dissolution of their marriages, and, in the absence of a sufficient countervailing justification for the State's action, a denial of due process.

The arguments for this kind of fee and cost requirement are that the State's interest in the prevention of frivolous litigation is substantial, its use of court fees and process costs to allocate scarce resources is rational, and its balance between the defendant's right to notice and the plaintiff's right to access is reasonable.

In our opinion, none of these considerations is sufficient to override the interest of these plaintiff-appellants in having access to the only avenue open for dissolving their allegedly untenable marriages. Not only is there no necessary connection between a litigant's assets and the seriousness of his motives in bringing suit, but it is here beyond present dispute that appellants bring these actions in good faith. Moreover, other alternatives exist to fees and cost requirements as a means for conserving the time of courts and protecting parties from frivolous litigation, such as penalties for false pleadings or affidavits, and actions for malicious prosecution or abuse of process, to mention only a few. In the same vein we think that reliable alternatives exist to service of process by a state-paid sheriff if the State is unwilling to assume the cost of official service. This is perforce true of service by publication which is the method of notice least calculated to bring to a potential defendant's attention the pendency of judicial proceedings. We think in this case service at defendant's last known address by mail and posted notice is equally effective as publication in a newspaper.

We are thus left to evaluate the State's asserted interest in its fee and cost requirements as a mechanism of resource allocation or cost recoupment. Such a justification was offered and rejected in *Griffin v. Illinois*. In *Griffin* it was the requirement of a transcript beyond the means of the indigent that blocked access to the judicial process. While in *Griffin* the transcript could be waived as a convenient but not necessary predicate to court access, here the State invariably imposes the costs as a measure of allocating its judicial resources. Surely, then, the rationale of *Griffin* covers this case.

IV

In concluding that the Due Process Clause of the Fourteenth Amendment requires that these appellants be afforded an opportunity to go into court to obtain a divorce, we wish to re-emphasize that we go no further than necessary to dispose of the case before us, a case where the bona fides of both appellants' indigency and desire for divorce are here beyond dispute. We do not decide that access for all individuals to the courts is a right that is, in all circumstances, guaranteed by the Due Process Clause of the Fourteenth Amendment so that its exercise may not be placed beyond the reach of any individual, for, as we have already noted, in the case before us this right is the exclusive precondition to the adjustment of a fundamental human relationship. The requirement that these appellants resort to the judicial process is entirely a state-created matter. Thus we hold only that a State may not, consistent with the obligations imposed on it by the Due Process Clause of the Fourteenth Amendment, pre-empt the right to dissolve this legal relationship without affording all citizens access to the means it has prescribed for doing so.

Reversed.

Justice BRENNAN, concurring in part.

I join the Court's opinion to the extent that it holds that Connecticut denies procedural due process in denying the indigent appellants access to its courts for the sole reason that they cannot pay a required fee. "[C]onsideration of what procedures due process may require under any given set of circumstances must begin with a determination of the precise nature of the government function involved as well as of the private interest that has been affected by governmental action." When a State's interest in imposing a fee requirement on an indigent is compared to the indigent's interest in being heard, it is clear that the latter is the weightier. It is an unjustifiable denial of a hearing, and therefore a denial of due process, to close the courts to an indigent on the ground of nonpayment of a fee.

But I cannot join the Court's opinion insofar as today's holding is made to depend upon the factor that only the State can grant a divorce and that an indigent would be locked into a marriage if unable to pay the fees required to obtain a divorce. A State has an ultimate monopoly of all judicial process and attendant enforcement machinery. . . . In this case, the Court holds that Connecticut's unyielding fee requirement violates the Due Process Clause by denying appellants "an opportunity to be heard upon their claimed right to a dissolution of their marriages." . . . I see no constitutional distinction between appellants' attempt to enforce this state statutory right and attempt to vindicate any other right arising under federal or state law. . . . If fee requirements close the courts to an indigent he can no more invoke the aid of the courts for other forms of relief than he can escape the legal incidents of a marriage.

* * *

In addition, this case presents a classic problem of equal protection of the laws. The question that the Court treats exclusively as one of due process inevitably implicates considerations of both due process and equal protection. Certainly, there is at issue the denial of a hearing, a matter for analysis under the Due Process Clause. But Connecticut does not deny a hearing to everyone in these circumstances; it denies it only to people who fail to pay certain fees.

* * *

The rationale of *Griffin* covers the present case. Courts are the central dispute-settling institutions in our society. They are bound to do equal justice under law, to rich and poor alike. They fail to perform their function in accordance with the Equal Protection Clause if they shut their doors to indigent plaintiffs altogether. Where money determines not merely "the kind of trial a man gets," but whether he gets into court at all, the great principle of equal protection becomes a mockery.

* * *

Justice BLACK, dissenting.

This is a strange case and a strange holding. Absent some specific federal constitutional or statutory provision, marriage in this country is completely under state control, and so is divorce. . . .

The Court here holds, however, that the State of Connecticut has so little control over marriages and divorces of its own citizens that it is without power to charge them practically nominal initial court costs when they are without ready money to put up those costs.

* * 8

It is true, as the majority points out, that the Court did hold in *Griffin v. Illinois* . . . that indigent defendants in criminal cases must be afforded the same right to appeal their convictions as is afforded to a defendant who has ample funds to pay his own costs. But in *Griffin* the Court studiously and carefully refrained from saying one word or one sentence suggesting that the rule there announced to control rights of criminal defendants would control in the quite different field of civil cases. And there are strong reasons for distinguishing between the two types of cases.

Criminal defendants are brought into court by the State or Federal Government to defend themselves against charges of crime. They go into court knowing that they may be convicted, and condemned to lose their lives, their liberty, or their property, as a penalty for their crimes. Because of this great governmental power the United States Constitution has provided special protections for people charged with crime. They cannot be convicted under bills of attainder or ex post facto laws. And numerous provisions of the Bill of Rights--the right to counsel, the right to be free from coerced confessions, and other rights--shield defendants in state courts as well as federal courts.

* * *

Civil lawsuits, however, are not like government prosecutions for crime. Civil courts are set up by government to give people who have quarrels with their neighbors the chance to use a neutral governmental agency to adjust their differences. In such cases the government is not usually involved as a party, and there is no deprivation of life, liberty, or property as punishment for crime. Our Federal Constitution, therefore, does not place such private disputes on the same high level as it places criminal trials and punishment. There is consequently no necessity, no reason, why government should in civil trials be hampered or handicapped by the strict and rigid due process rules the Constitution has provided to protect people charged with crime.

* * *

Notes and Questions

1. *State-created Marriage.* The majority in *Boddie* reasoned that due process prohibits states from denying access to courts based on inability to pay fees for dissolution of marriage actions because of the importance of marriage and the state's monopoly over its dissolution. In his separate concurrence, Justice Brennan argued that states have a monopoly over all judicial proceedings, not only marriage, and that due process prohibits states from denying access to courts for any action. Should *Boddie*'s holding be interpreted narrowly to apply only to marriage, or should it apply to any denial of judicial access?

2. *Due Process for Plaintiffs.* The Supreme Court consistently has held that the due process clauses in the Fifth and Fourteenth Amendments require the federal and state governments to provide notice and an opportunity to be heard at a meaningful time and in a meaningful manner. Most due process decisions, however, involved the rights of defendants being summoned to court. How does due process protect the right of access to courts for plaintiffs?

3. *State's Interests.* The state of Connecticut argued that its fee requirements served three purposes: (1) preventing frivolous litigation; (2) rationally allocating scarce resources; and (3) reasonably balancing between defendants' rights to notice and plaintiffs' rights to access. Each of these purposes seems to be a legitimate government interest. Examine the Court's reasons for rejecting each asserted state purpose.

a. *Preventing Frivolous Litigation.* The Court first notes no general connection between whether an individual is poor and whether that individual is likely to bring frivolous court actions. The Court then reiterates that constitutional rights are guaranteed to individuals, and that the individuals involved brought their actions for dissolution in good faith.

Compare this analysis to the federal statute and rules governing Civil Procedure. Federal Rule of Civil Procedure 12(b)(6) allows courts to dismiss an action for failure to state a claim upon which relief may be granted. This rule applies to all litigants, regardless of wealth. A separate federal statute, 28 U.S.C. § 1915, allows courts to grant *in forma pauperis* petitions, thereby waiving court fees for indigent parties. This statute allows courts to dismiss any such action that was brought for frivolous purposes. What function does this statute serve? Does it accomplish anything more than Rule 12(b)(6), perhaps by allowing judges greater leeway to dismiss actions brought by poor people? If so, is this statute unconstitutional under the reasoning of *Boddie v. Connecticut*?

b. *Balancing Plaintiffs' and Defendants' Rights.* The Court suggests that defendants could be adequately notified by mail to their last known address if service by government officials proves too costly for plaintiffs or for the state. Would service by mail withstand a due process challenge? For starters, see *Mullane v. Central Hanover Bank & Trust Co.*, 339 U.S. 306 (1950) (upholding service by mail to trust beneficiaries whose addresses were unknown, but invalidating such service for beneficiaries with known addresses).

c. *Allocating Scarce Resources.* Many government regulations directed toward poor people arguably allocate government resources. Do we simply presume government resources to be scarce at all times, or should scarcity be proved in each case?

The Court in *Boddie* invokes a landmark decision that rejected the scarcity argument in the criminal content. In *Griffin v. Illinois*, the Court prohibited states from requiring defendants to pay for transcripts as a prerequisite to filing an appeal. Justice Black argued in his *Boddie* dissent that *Griffin* was inapplicable because criminal defendants have greater constitutional rights than civil parties. Should indigent parties be treated in a similar or different manner as between civil and criminal judicial proceedings?

4. *Equal Protection.* Justice Brennan argued in his concurrence that the state's different treatment of the rich and the poor constitutes a form of discrimination that should be analyzed under the Equal Protection doctrine. Do you agree?

2. Private Rights of Action

In addition to frequently needing waiver of applicable court access fees, indigent clients need a sufficient cause of action or legal claim. If they have experienced some breach of a defendant's common law duty, they simply assert such a claim. Poor plaintiffs often complain of actions by various government officials, whose conduct is governed by federal and state constitutions, statutes, and regulations. Plaintiffs, regardless of their wealth, may sue directly for constitutional violations, but generally must exhaust administrative remedies before seeking judicial review of agency actions.

When plaintiffs complain that government officials have violated the requirements of a statute designed to benefit them, they must allege that the statute either expressly or by implication gives them a right to enforce its terms, or that 42 U.S.C. § 1983 gives them a right to sue. If the statute does not expressly confer the right to enforce its terms, how can plaintiffs show that Congress intended them to enforce it? The following case demonstrates the worst-case-scenario for poor plaintiffs, litigating all the way to the United States Supreme Court only to be told they have no right to be in any court.

SUTER v. ARTIST M.

503 U.S. 347 (1992)

The CHIEF JUSTICE delivered the opinion of the Court.

This case raises the question whether private individuals have the right to enforce by suit a provision of the Adoption Assistance and Child Welfare Act of 1980 (Adoption Act or Act), either under the Act itself or through an action under 42 U.S.C. § 1983.[1] The Court of Appeals for the Seventh Circuit held that 42 U.S.C. § 671(a)(15)

---

[1]Section 1983 provides, in relevant part: "Every person who, under color of any statute, ordinance, regulation, custom, or usage, of any State or Territory or the District of Columbia, subjects or causes to be subjected, any citizen of the United States or other person within the jurisdiction thereof to the deprivation of any rights, privileges, or immunities, secured by the Constitution and laws shall be liable to the party injured in an action at law, suit in equity, or other proper proceeding for redress."

contained an implied right of action, and that respondents could enforce this section of the Act through an action brought under § 1983 as well. We hold that the Act does not create an enforceable right on behalf of the respondents.

The Adoption Act establishes a federal reimbursement program for certain expenses incurred by the States in administering foster care and adoption services. The Act provides that States will be reimbursed for a percentage of foster care and adoption assistance payments when the State satisfies the requirements of the Act.

To participate in the program, States must submit a plan to the Secretary of Health and Human Services for approval by the Secretary. Section 671 lists 16 qualifications which state plans must contain in order to gain the Secretary's approval. As relevant here, the Act provides:

> (a) Requisite features of State plan
> In order for a State to be eligible for payments under this part, it shall have a plan approved by the Secretary which--
>
> * * *
>
> (3) provides that the plan shall be in effect in all political subdivisions of the State, and, if administered by them, be mandatory upon them;
>
> * * *
>
> (15) effective October 1, 1983, provides that, in each case, reasonable efforts will be made (A) prior to the placement of a child in foster care, to prevent or eliminate the need for removal of the child from his home, and (B) to make it possible for the child to return to his home. . . .

Petitioners in this action are Sue Suter and Gary T. Morgan, the Director and the Guardianship Administrator, respectively, of the Illinois Department of Children and Family Services (DCFS). DCFS is the state agency responsible for, among other things, investigating charges of child abuse and neglect and providing services to abused and neglected children and their families. DCFS is authorized under Illinois law, to gain temporary custody of an abused or neglected child after a hearing and order by the Juvenile Court. Alternatively, the court may order that a child remain in his home under a protective supervisory order entered against his parents. Once DCFS has jurisdiction over a child either in its temporary custody, or in the child's home under a protective order, all services are provided to the child and his family by means of an individual caseworker at DCFS to whom the child's case is assigned.

Respondents filed this class-action suit seeking declaratory and injunctive relief under the Adoption Act. They alleged that petitioners, in contravention of 42 U.S.C. § 671(a)(15) failed to make reasonable efforts to prevent removal of children from their homes and to facilitate reunification of families where removal had occurred. This failure occurred, as alleged by respondents, because DCFS failed promptly to assign caseworkers to children placed in DCFS custody and promptly to reassign cases when caseworkers were on leave from DCFS. The District Court, without objection from petitioners, certified two separate classes seeking relief, including all children who are or will be wards of DCFS and are placed in foster care or remain in their homes under a judicial protective order.[4] The District Court denied a motion to dismiss filed by petitioners, holding, as relevant here, that the Adoption Act contained an implied cause of action and that suit could also be brought to enforce the Act under 42 U.S.C. § 1983.

The District Court then entered an injunction requiring petitioners to assign a caseworker to each child placed in DCFS custody within three working days of the time the case is first heard in Juvenile Court, and to reassign a caseworker within three working days of the date any caseworker relinquishes responsibility for a particular case. The three working day deadline was found by the District Court to "realistically reflec[t] the institutional capabilities of DCFS," based in part on petitioners' assertion that assigning caseworkers within that time frame "would not be overly burdensome." The District Court, on partial remand from the Court of Appeals, made additional factual findings regarding the nature of

---

[4]Specifically, the following classes were certified by the District Court: "Class A: Children who are or will be the subjects of neglect, dependency or abuse petitions filed in the Circuit Court of Cook County, Juvenile Division ('Juvenile Court'), who are or will be in the custody of [DCFS] or in a home under DCFS supervision by an order of Juvenile Court and who are now or will be without a DCFS caseworker for a significant period of time. Class B: Children who are or will be the subjects of neglect, dependency or abuse petitions filed in Juvenile Court who are or will be placed in DCFS' custody and who are or will be without a DCFS caseworker for a significant period of time." The "Class B" plaintiffs only raised a constitutional due process claim, which was dismissed by the District Court.

the delays in assigning caseworkers and the progress of DCFS reforms at the time the preliminary injunction was entered.

The Court of Appeals affirmed. Relying heavily on this Court's decision in *Wilder v. Virginia Hospital Assn.*, 496 U.S. 498 (1990), the Court of Appeals held that the "reasonable efforts" clause of the Adoption Act could be enforced through an action under § 1983. That court, applying the standard established in *Cort v. Ash*, 422 U.S. 66 (1975), also found that the Adoption Act created an implied right of action such that private individuals could bring suit directly under the Act to enforce the provisions relied upon by respondents. We granted certiorari, and now reverse.

In *Maine v. Thiboutot*, 448 U.S. 1 (1980), we first established that § 1983 is available as a remedy for violations of federal statutes as well as for constitutional violations. We have subsequently recognized that § 1983 is not available to enforce a violation of a federal statute "where Congress has foreclosed such enforcement of the statute in the enactment itself and where the statute did not create enforceable rights, privileges, or immunities within the meaning of § 1983." *Wright v. Roanoke Redevelopment and Housing Authority*, 479 U.S. 418, 423 (1987).

In *Pennhurst State School and Hospital v. Halderman*, 451 U.S. 1 (1981), we held that § 111 of the Developmentally Disabled Assistance and Bill of Rights Act of 1975 did not confer an implied cause of action. That statute, as well as the statute before us today, was enacted by Congress pursuant to its spending power.[7] In *Pennhurst*, we noted that it was well established that Congress has the power to fix the terms under which it disburses federal money to the States. As stated in *Pennhurst*:

> The legitimacy of Congress' power to legislate under the spending power thus rests on whether the State voluntarily and knowingly accepts the terms of the "contract." There can, of course, be no knowing acceptance if a State is unaware of the conditions or is unable to ascertain what is expected of it. Accordingly, if Congress intends to impose a condition on the grant of federal moneys, it must do so unambiguously.

[7]Article I, § 8, cl. 1, of the Constitution contains the spending power, which provides, "Congress shall have Power to . . . provide for the . . . general Welfare of the United States."

We concluded that the statutory section sought to be enforced by the Pennhurst respondents did not provide such unambiguous notice to the States because it spoke in terms "intended to be hortatory, not mandatory."

In *Wright*, the Brooke Amendment to existing housing legislation imposed a ceiling on the rent which might be charged low-income tenants living in public housing projects. The regulations issued by the Department of Housing and Urban Development in turn defined rent to include "'a reasonable amount for [use of] utilities,'" and further defined how that term would be measured. We held that tenants had an enforceable right to sue the Housing Authority for utility charges claimed to be in violation of these provisions. In *Wilder*, the Boren Amendment to the Medicaid Act required that Medicaid providers be reimbursed according to rates that the "'State finds, and makes assurances satisfactory to the Secretary,'" are "'reasonable and adequate'" to meet the costs of "'efficiently and economically operated facilities.'" Again, we held that this language created an enforceable right, on the part of providers seeking reimbursement, to challenge the rates set by the State as failing to meet the standards specified in the Boren Amendment.

In both *Wright* and *Wilder* the word "reasonable" occupied a prominent place in the critical language of the statute or regulation, and the word "reasonable" is similarly involved here. But this, obviously, is not the end of the matter. The opinions in both *Wright* and *Wilder* took pains to analyze the statutory provisions in detail, in light of the entire legislative enactment, to determine whether the language in question created "enforceable rights, privileges, or immunities within the meaning of § 1983." And in *Wilder*, we caution that "'[s]ection 1983 speaks in terms of "rights, privileges, or immunities," not violations of federal law.'"

Did Congress, in enacting the Adoption Act, unambiguously confer upon the child beneficiaries of the Act a right to enforce the requirement that the State make "reasonable efforts" to prevent a child from being removed from his home, and once removed to reunify the child with his family? We turn now to that inquiry.

As quoted above, 42 U.S.C. § 671(a)(15) requires that to obtain federal reimbursement, a State have a plan which "provides that, in each case, reasonable efforts will be made . . . to prevent or eliminate the need for removal of the child from his home, and . . . to make it possible for the child to return to his home. . . ." As recognized by petitioners, respondents, and the courts below, the Act is mandatory in its terms. However, in the light shed by *Pennhurst*, we must examine exactly what is required of States by the Act. Here, the terms of § 671(a) are clear: "In order for a State to be eligible for payments under this part, it shall have a plan approved by the Secretary." Therefore the Act does place a requirement on the States, but that requirement only goes so far as to ensure that the State have a plan approved by the Secretary which contains the 16 listed features.

Respondents do not dispute that Illinois in fact has a plan approved by the Secretary which provides that reasonable efforts at prevention and reunification will be made. Respondents argue, however, that § 1983 allows them to sue in federal court to obtain enforcement of this particular provision of the state plan. This argument is based, at least in part, on the assertion that 42 U.S.C. § 671(a)(3) requires that the State has a plan which is "in effect." This section states that the state plan shall "provid[e] that the plan shall be in effect in all political subdivisions of the State, and, if administered by them, be mandatory upon them." But we think that "in effect" is directed to the requirement that the plan apply to all political subdivisions of the State, and is not intended to otherwise modify the word "plan."

In *Wilder*, the underlying Medicaid legislation similarly required participating States to submit to the Secretary of Health and Human Services a plan for medical assistance describing the State's Medicaid program. But in that case we held that the Boren Amendment actually required the States to adopt reasonable and adequate rates, and that this obligation was enforceable by the providers. We relied in part on the fact that the statute and regulations set forth in some detail the factors to be considered in determining the methods for calculating rates.

In the present case, however, the term "reasonable efforts" to maintain an abused or neglected child in his home, or return the child to his home from foster care, appears in quite a different context. No further statutory guidance is found as to how "reasonable efforts" are to be measured. This directive is not the only one which Congress has given to the States, and it is a directive whose meaning will obviously vary with the circumstances of each individual case. How the State was to comply with this directive, and with the other provisions of the Act, was, within broad limits, left up to the State.

Other sections of the Act provide enforcement mechanisms for the reasonable efforts clause of 42 U.S.C. § 671(a)(15). The Secretary has the authority to reduce or eliminate payments to a State on finding that the State's plan no longer complies with § 671(a) or that "there is a substantial failure" in the administration of a plan such that the State is not complying with its own plan. The Act also requires that in order to secure federal reimbursement for foster care payments made with respect to a child involuntarily removed from his home the removal must be "the result of a judicial determination to the effect that continuation [in the child's home] would be contrary to the welfare of such child and (effective October 1, 1983) that reasonable efforts of the type described in section 671(a)(15) of this title have been made." While these statutory provisions may not provide a comprehensive enforcement mechanism so as to manifest Congress' intent to foreclose remedies under § 1983, they do show that the absence of a remedy to private plaintiffs under § 1983 does not make the reasonable efforts clause a dead letter.

The regulations promulgated by the Secretary to enforce the Adoption Act do not evidence a view that § 671(a) places any requirement for state receipt of federal funds other than the requirement that the State submit a plan to be approved by the Secretary. The regulations provide that to meet the requirements of § 671(a)(15) the case plan for each child must "include a description of the services offered and the services provided to prevent removal of the child from the home and to reunify the family." Another regulation, entitled "requirements and submittal," provides that a state plan must specify "which preplacement preventive and reunification services are available to children and families in need."[14] What is

[14]The regulation, 45 CFR § 1357.15(e)(2) (1990), goes on to provide a list of which services may be included in the State's proposal: "Twenty-four hour emergency caretaker, and homemaker services; day care; crisis counseling; individual and family counseling; emergency shelters; procedures and arrangements for access to available emergency financial assistance; arrangements for the provision of temporary child care to provide respite to the family for a brief period, as part of a plan for preventing children's removal from home; other services which the agency identifies as necessary and appropriate such as home-based family services, self-help groups, services to unmarried parents, provision of, or arrangements for, mental health, drug and alcohol abuse counseling, vocational counseling or vocational rehabilitation; and post adoption services."

significant is that the regulations are not specific, and do not provide notice to the States that failure to do anything other than submit a plan with the requisite features, to be approved by the Secretary, is a further condition on the receipt of funds from the Federal Government. Respondents contend that "[n]either [petitioners] nor amici supporting them present any legislative history to refute the evidence that Congress intended 42 U.S.C. § 671(a)(15) to be enforceable." To the extent such history may be relevant, our examination of it leads us to conclude that Congress was concerned that the required reasonable efforts be made by the States, but also indicated that the Act left a great deal of discretion to them.

Careful examination of the language relied upon by respondents, in the context of the entire Act, leads us to conclude that the "reasonable efforts" language does not unambiguously confer an enforceable right upon the Act's beneficiaries. The term "reasonable efforts" in this context is at least as plausibly read to impose only a rather generalized duty on the State, to be enforced not by private individuals, but by the Secretary in the manner previously discussed.

Having concluded that § 671(a)(15) does not create a federally enforceable right to "reasonable efforts" under § 1983, the conclusion of the Court of Appeals that the Adoption Act contains an implied right of action for private enforcement may be disposed of quickly. Under the familiar test of *Cort v. Ash*, 422 U.S. 66 (1975), the burden is on respondents to demonstrate that Congress intended to make a private remedy available to enforce the reasonable efforts clause of the Adoption Act.[16] The most important inquiry here as well is whether Congress intended to create the private remedy sought by the plaintiffs. As discussed above, we think that Congress did not intend to create a private remedy for enforcement of the "reasonable efforts" clause.

---

[16]As established in Cort v. Ash, 422 U.S. 66, 95 S.Ct. 2080, 45 L.Ed.2d 26 (1975), these factors are: "First, is the plaintiff one of the class for whose especial benefit the statute was enacted, that is, does the statute create a federal right in favor of the plaintiff? Second, is there any indication of legislative intent, explicit or implicit, either to create such a remedy or to deny one? Third, is it consistent with the underlying purposes of the legislative scheme to imply such a remedy for the plaintiff? And finally, is the cause of action one traditionally relegated to state law, in an area basically the concern of the States, so that it would be inappropriate to infer a cause of action based solely on federal law?" Id. at 78.

We conclude that 42 U.S.C. § 671(a)(15) neither confers an enforceable private right on its beneficiaries nor creates an implied cause of action on their behalf.

The judgment of the Court of Appeals is therefore

Reversed.

Justice BLACKMUN, with whom Justice STEVENS joins, dissenting.

The Adoption Assistance and Child Welfare Act of 1980 (Adoption Act) conditions federal funding for state child welfare, foster care, and adoption programs upon, inter alia, the State's express commitment to make, "in each case, reasonable efforts" to prevent the need for removing children from their homes and "reasonable efforts," where removal has occurred, to reunify the family. The Court holds today that the plaintiff children in this case may not enforce the State's commitment in federal court either under 42 U.S.C. § 1983 or under the Act itself.

In my view, the Court's conclusion is plainly inconsistent with this Court's decision just two Terms ago in *Wilder v. Virginia Hospital Assn.*, 496 U.S. 498 (1990), in which we found enforceable under § 1983 a functionally identical provision of the Medicaid Act requiring "reasonable" reimbursements to health care providers. More troubling still, the Court reaches its conclusion without even stating, much less applying, the principles our precedents have used to determine whether a statute has created a right enforceable under § 1983. I cannot acquiesce in this unexplained disregard for established law. Accordingly, I dissent.

I

A

Section 1983 provides a cause of action for the "deprivation of any rights, privileges, or immunities, secured by the Constitution and laws" of the United States. We recognized in *Maine v. Thiboutot*, 448 U.S. 1 (1980), that § 1983 provides a cause of action for violations of federal statutes, not just the Constitution. Since *Thiboutot*, we have recognized two general exceptions to this rule. First, no cause of action will lie where the statute in question does not "'create enforceable rights, privileges, or immunities within the meaning of § 1983.'" Second, § 1983 is unavailable where "Congress has foreclosed enforcement of the statute in the enactment itself."

In determining the scope of the first exception--whether a

federal statute creates an "enforceable right"--the Court has developed and repeatedly applied a three-part test. We have asked (1) whether the statutory provision at issue "'was intend[ed] to benefit the putative plaintiff.'" If so, then the provision creates an enforceable right unless (2) the provision "reflects merely a 'congressional preference' for a certain kind of conduct rather than a binding obligation on the governmental unit," or unless (3) the plaintiff's interest is so "'vague and amorphous'" as to be "'beyond the competence of the judiciary to enforce.'" The Court today has little difficulty concluding that the plaintiff children in this case have no enforceable rights, because it does not mention--much less apply--this firmly established analytic framework.

* * *

Each of the three elements of our three-part test is satisfied. First, and most obvious, the plaintiff children in this case are clearly the intended beneficiaries of the requirement that the State make "reasonable efforts" to prevent unnecessary removal and to reunify temporarily removed children with their families.

Second, the "reasonable efforts" clause imposes a binding obligation on the State because it is "cast in mandatory rather than precatory terms," providing that a participating State "shall have a plan approved by the Secretary which . . . shall be in effect in all political subdivisions of the State, and, if administered by them, mandatory upon them." Further, the statute requires the plan to "provid[e] that, in each case, reasonable efforts will be made." Moreover, as in *Wilder*, the statutory text expressly conditions federal funding on state compliance with the plan requirement and requires the Secretary to reduce payments to a State, if "in the administration of [the State's] plan there is a substantial failure to comply with the provisions of the plan." Under our holding in *Wilder*, these provisions of the Adoption Act impose a binding obligation on the State. Indeed, neither the petitioner state officials nor amicus United States dispute this point.

What petitioners and amicus United States do dispute is whether the third element of the *Golden State-Wilder-Dennis* test has been satisfied: They argue that the "reasonable efforts" clause of the Adoption Act is too "vague and amorphous" to be judicially enforced. Aware that *Wilder* enforced an apparently similar "reasonableness" clause, they argue that this clause is categorically different.

According to petitioners, the Court would not have found the Boren Amendment's reasonableness clause enforceable had the statute not provided an "objective benchmark" against which "reasonable and adequate" reimbursement rates could be measured. Reasonable and adequate rates, the Boren Amendment provides, are those that meet the costs that would be incurred by "an 'efficiently and economically operated facilit[y]' providing care in compliance with federal and state standards while at the same time ensuring 'reasonable access' to eligible participants." Petitioners claim that, given this benchmark, "reasonable and adequate" rates can be ascertained by "monetary calculations easily determined based on prevailing rates in the market." By contrast, they observe, there is "no market for 'reasonable efforts' to keep or return a child home, and such 'reasonable efforts' cannot be calculated or quantified."

* * *

There may be a "range" of "efforts" to prevent unnecessary removals or secure beneficial reunifications that are "reasonable." It may also be that a court, in reviewing a State's strategies of compliance with the "reasonable efforts" clause, would owe substantial deference to the State's choice of strategies. That does not mean, however, that no State's efforts could ever be deemed "unreasonable." As in *Wilder*, the asserted right in this case is simply not inherently "beyond the competence of the judiciary to enforce."

* * *

Federal courts, in innumerable cases, have routinely enforced reasonableness clauses in federal statutes. Petitioners have not shown that the Adoption Act's reasonableness clause is exceptional in this respect.

II

The Court does not explain why the settled three-part test for determining the enforceability of an asserted right is not applied in this case. Moreover, the reasons the Court does offer to support its conclusion--that the Adoption Act's "reasonable efforts" clause creates no enforceable right--were raised and rejected in *Wilder*.

The Court acknowledges that the Adoption Act is "mandatory in its terms." It adopts, however, a narrow understanding of what is "mandatory." It reasons that the language of § 671(a), which provides that "[i]n order for a State to be eligible for payments under this part, it shall have a plan approved by the Secretary," requires participating States only to submit and receive approval for a plan that contains the features listed in §§ 671(a)(1) to (16). According to the Court, the beneficiaries of the Act enjoy at most a procedural right under § 671(a)--the right to require a participating State to prepare and file a plan--not a substantive right to require the State to live up to the commitments stated in that plan, such as the commitment to make "reasonable efforts" to prevent unnecessary removals and secure beneficial reunifications of families. Since the State of Illinois has filed a plan that the Secretary has approved, the Court reasons, the State has violated no right enforceable in federal court.

The Court's reasoning should sound familiar: The state officials in *Wilder* made exactly the same argument, and this Court rejected it. In *Wilder*, we noted that the Medicaid Act expressly conditions federal funding on state compliance with the provisions of an approved plan, and that the Secretary is required to withhold payments from noncomplying States. In substantially identical language, the Adoption Act, too, requires States to live up to the commitments stated in their plans. To be sure, the Court's reasoning is consistent with the dissent in *Wilder*. But it flatly contradicts what the Court held in that case.

* * *

III

In sum, the Court has failed, without explanation, to apply the framework our precedents have consistently deemed applicable; it has sought to support its conclusion by resurrecting arguments decisively rejected less than two years ago in *Wilder*; and it has contravened 22 years of precedent by suggesting that the existence of other "enforcement mechanisms" precludes § 1983 enforcement. At least for this case, it has changed the rules of the game without offering even minimal justification, and it has failed even to acknowledge that it is doing anything more extraordinary than "interpret[ing]" the Adoption Act "by its own terms." Readers of the Court's opinion will not be misled by this hollow assurance. And, after all, we are dealing here with children. I would affirm the judgment of the Court of Appeals. I dissent.

Notes and Questions

1. *Enforcement of Federal Law.* One of the first questions that confronts plaintiffs who wish to challenge the constitutionality or application of a federal benefits statute is whether they have a federal cause of action. Article III of the United States Constitution gives the federal courts power to hear cases "arising under" the Constitution, federal laws, and treaties. Because this grant of power is not self-

executing, Congress exercises considerable control over the creation of federal causes of action.

Congress could authorize a suit based on a federal benefits statute in a variety of ways. First, the statute could provide explicit authorization for persons to enforce its provisions. Congress rarely creates such express rights of action in benefits legislation. Even when Congress creates an express right of action, plaintiffs, as always, must be sure they can demonstrate standing (generally, an injury in fact, causation fairly traceable to the defendant, judicial ability to redress the injury, and an interest within the zone of interests protected by the federal law). *See Lujan v. Defenders of Wildlife*, 112 S. Ct. 2130 (1992) (denying environmentalists standing to challenge the Secretary of the Interior's refusal to apply the Endangered Species Act to government activity occurring outside of United States boundaries, even though the statute contained a "citizen-suit" provision authorizing suits by any person for any violation).

Second, the statute could create an implied private right of action for persons to enforce it. Courts determine whether a statute created an implied private action by considering:

> (1) whether plaintiffs are part of the class for whose special benefit the statute was passed;
> (2) whether the indicia of legislative intent reveal a congressional purpose to provide a private cause of action;
> (3) whether a federal cause of action would further the underlying purposes of the legislative scheme; and
> (4) whether the cause of action is a subject traditionally relegated to state law.

See Cort v. Ash, 422 U.S. 66 (1975).

Third, the statute may be enforceable through 42 U.S.C. § 1983,[1] which provides:

> Every person who, under color of any statute, ordinance, regulation, custom, or usage, of any State or Territory, subjects, or causes to be subjected, any citizen of the United

[1] Other civil rights statutes also create important causes of action. 42 U.S.C. § 1981 creates a cause of action for racial discrimination related to property. 42 U.S.C. § 1982 creates a cause of action for racial discrimination related to contract disputes. 42 U.S.C. § 1985 creates a cause of action for conspiracies to deny civil rights.

> States or other person within the jurisdiction thereof to the deprivation of any rights, privileges, or immunities secured by the Constitution and laws, shall be liable to the party injured in an action at law, suit in equity, or other proper proceeding for redress.

The Supreme Court held in *Maine v. Thiboutot*, 448 U.S. 1 (1980) that plaintiffs may use § 1983 to enforce federal statutes.

Fourth, federal lawsuits may be possible against state officials who fail to comply with federal law. Although the Supreme Court has interpreted the Eleventh Amendment to bar federal court suits by private plaintiffs directly against states,[2] the Court held in *Ex Parte Young*, 209 U.S. 123 (1908) that private plaintiffs may bring federal court suits against state officials to compel compliance with federal laws. The Supreme Court limited plaintiffs to prospective relief, however, in *Edelman v. Jordan*, 415 U.S. 651 (1974) (upholding order requiring state official to pay prospective welfare benefits in compliance with federal law, but invalidating order requiring payment of retrospective benefits). Moreover, plaintiffs should be prepared to argue that Congress intended to make state officials subject to suit for failure to comply with federal law. *See Seminole Tribe v. Florida*, 116 S. Ct. 1114 (1996) (invalidating Indian Gaming Act provision which authorized suit against states for failure to negotiate with tribes in good faith because the Eleventh Amendment prevented Congress from authorizing suits directly against states, and finding no congressional intent to subject state officials to federal suit).[3] In *Seminole Tribe*, the Court noted that federal civil rights actions against states are not barred by the Eleventh Amendment because they are authorized by the later-enacted Fourteenth Amendment.

What are the advantages and disadvantages of pursuing each of the four approaches to enforcing a federal statute?

---

[2]Although the text of the Eleventh Amendment bars suits against states by citizens of another state or by citizens of foreign states, the Supreme Court interpreted it to also bar suits against a state brought by citizens of the defendant state. *See Hans v. Louisiana*, 134 U.S. 1 (1890).

[3]As of this writing, the Supreme Court had granted certiorari but had not yet decided a case that raises the question whether Congress may authorize federal suits against state officials, *Idaho v. Coeur D'Alene Tribe*, No. 94-1474.

2. *Common Sense.* If the federal statute required states to make reasonable efforts to maintain children in their homes, why couldn't these children enforce a state's failure to satisfy this requirement? Does it seem plausible to interpret the statute to require only that a state prepare a plan promising to make reasonable efforts? In other words, would Congress have been more interested in the plan than the promise?

3. *Legislative Trump.* When courts interpret statutes, they do not enjoy the last word. The legislature may simply speak again to trump judicial interpretation of its statute. Congress did precisely that following the *Suter v. Artist M.* decision.

After the Supreme Court's decision in *Suter v. Artist M.*, Congress enacted the Social Security Act Amendments of 1994. In these amendments, Congress overturned part of the reasoning but not the result of *Suter*. The relevant section reads:

> (a) IN GENERAL.--Part A of title XI of the Social Security Act (42 U.S.C. 1301-1320b-13) is amended by inserting after section 1122 the following:
>
> SEC. 1123. EFFECT OF FAILURE TO CARRY OUT STATE PLAN.
>
> In an action brought to enforce a provision of the Social Security Act, such provision is not to be deemed unenforceable because of its inclusion in a section of the Act requiring a State plan or specifying the required contents of a State plan. This section is not intended to limit or expand the grounds for determining the availability of private actions to enforce State plan requirements other than by overturning any such grounds applied in *Suter v. Artist M.*,(1992), but not applied in prior Supreme Court decisions respecting such enforceability; provided, however, that this section is not intended to alter the holding in *Suter v. Artist M.* that section 671(a)(15) of the Act is not enforceable in a private right of action.
>
> (b) APPLICABILITY.--The amendment made by subsection (a) shall apply to actions pending on the date of the enactment of this Act and to actions brought on or after such date of enactment.

What is the effect of this amendment? What grounds applied

in *Suter* were not applied in prior Supreme Court decisions regarding enforceability? The Court in *Suter* applied the same general test for enforceability as it had in *Wright*, namely whether Congress unambiguously conferred an enforceable right upon the statute's beneficiaries. Perhaps what seemed different in *Suter* was the Court's basis for its determination that the statute did not unambiguously confer an enforceable right: (1) the fact that the statute merely required a state plan; and (2) the fact that the statute provided alternative enforcement mechanisms by the Secretary of Health and Human Services. Did Congress mean then that in the future these factors should not be dispositive of whether Congress meant to confer enforceable rights? Or, perhaps because in the first sentence of the amendment Congress referred only to the plan requirement, they meant only to preclude judicial reliance on that requirement?

Lower courts have not settled the question. Some lower courts have ignored the congressional amendment entirely. For example, in *"Tony" L. v. Childers*, 71 F.3d 1182 (6th Cir. 1995), the Sixth Circuit ignored the effect of the congressional amendment, and held that, because the federal laws at issue used only the word "may," they were "more like those in *Suter* (no guidelines) than those in *Wilder* (mandatory guidelines)." *Id.* at 1189. Other courts have attempted to construe the effect of the congressional amendment, with no greater clarity than Congress achieved in the amendment itself. For example, the Tenth Circuit reasoned that "[w]hether or not *Suter* added to prior Court analysis, which addition is no longer to be followed, is irrelevant" when the federal law at issue "does not approach the specificity" required by prior case law for creating an enforceable right. *See, e.g., Stanberry v. Sherman*, 75 F.3d 581 (10th Cir. 1996).

4. *The Role of Precedent.* In determining whether Congress created an enforceable right, the Supreme Court requires that the statute impose a binding obligation on the states with clear guidelines for implementation. Regarding various statutes, the Supreme Court has concluded either that Congress did, or did not, create a right enforceable pursuant to § 1983. For example, it held that Congress did create enforceable rights in the Boren Amendment to the Medicaid Act which required states to pay reasonable rates of reimbursement to hospitals, *Wilder v. Virginia Hospital Association*, 496 U.S. 498 (1990), and in the Brooke Amendment to the Housing Act of 1937 which limited public housing utility rent charges to reasonable amounts, *Wright v. City of Roanoke Redevelopment & Housing*

Authority, 479 U.S. 418 (1987). The Court held, however, that Congress did not create an enforceable right in the Developmentally Disabled Assistance and Bill of Rights Act of 1975 which restricted federal funds to institutions that ensure appropriate treatment in the least restrictive environment, *Pennhurst State School & Hospital v. Halderman*, 451 U.S. 1 (1981).

Can you distinguish between the holdings in *Suter v. Artist M.* and *Wilder v. Virginia Hospital Association* or *Wright v. Roanoke Redevelopment and Housing Authority*? The statute requiring reasonable utility rates in public housing was enforceable by tenants in *Wright*, just as the statute requiring reasonable Medicaid reimbursement rates was enforceable by hospitals in *Wilder*. Can you identify a principled basis on which to justify the denial of enforcement in *Suter*? Is it any more difficult for judges to define the words "reasonable" in these various contexts? If not, then why did the Supreme Court depart from the prior precedents?

5. *The Established Test.* Why did the majority fail to apply what Justice Blackmun in dissent describes as the "settled three-part test"? That test allowed enforcement if the statute was intended to benefit plaintiffs, unless the statute did not reflect a binding obligation or the plaintiffs' interests were so vague and amorphous as to be beyond judicial competency. Justice Blackmun asserts that the majority must have relied on the final factor. Is a child's interest to remain in his or her home a vague and amorphous interest? Is it beyond judicial competence to determine whether Illinois' efforts, which included failure to promptly assign caseworkers, were reasonable?

6. *Lawyering Strategy.* What steps do you expect lawyers for poor plaintiffs might take to avoid the result suffered by the plaintiffs in *Suter v. Artist M.*?

Private Rights of Action and Temporary Assistance For Needy Families Block Grant Programs

In 1996, Congress abolished Aid to Families with Dependent Children and replaced it with Temporary Assistance for Needy Families (TANF) block grants to the states. Of what effect is the portion of the TANF statute which requires the state's Family Assistance Program plan to "set forth objective criteria for the delivery of benefits and the determination of eligibility and for fair and equitable treatment, including an explanation of how the State will provide opportunities for recipients who have been adversely affected to be heard in a State administrative or appeal process"? After *Suter* and the legislative amendment overturning some part of *Suter*, what meaning should courts give to the fact that Congress merely required states to explain in their plans how they will allow recipients to be heard?

Under the block grant TANF program, Congress explicitly stated in the section describing the purpose of the statute that it "shall not be interpreted to entitle any individual or family to assistance under any State program funded under this part." In the section prohibiting a state from using the block grant to provide assistance to a family for more than 60 months, Congress explicitly stated that such section "shall not be interpreted to require any State to provide assistance to any individual for any period of time under the State program funded under this part." What effect will these provisions have on the question whether Congress intended individual recipients of block grant funds to enforce the provisions of the statute? Does Congress' denial of an individual entitlement necessarily or practically imply the denial of a private right of action to enforce the statute?

Does Congress have the exclusive power to declare that its statute does not create any entitlement? If courts find, for example, that recipients have some property interest in receipt of block grant benefits, does Congress have the power to limit the amount of due process which recipients arc entitled to receive? Who should determine whether recipients have a property interest in a form of benefits, and what process must be afforded them prior to infringement of such benefits? Is this a question for Congress or the courts? Who typically interprets the Constitution? *See* Chapter 5 which explores due process issues, especially the discussion about *Cleveland Board of Education v. Loudermill*, 470 U.S. 532 (1985).

If Congress meant to prohibit individuals from enforcing the provisions of the statute, did it authorize the Secretary of Health and Human Services to have exclusive but full authority to enforce its provisions? Apparently not. Congress stated that "[n]o officer or employee of the Federal Government may regulate the conduct of States under this part or enforce any provision of this part, except to the extent expressly provided in this part."

Congress specified that states could be penalized for failure to comply with the TANF statute for the following violations:

(1) general and intentional violations, including:
(2) failure to submit required report;
(3) failure to satisfy minimum work participation rates;
(4) failure to participate in the income and eligibility verification system;
(5) failure to comply with paternity establishment and child support enforcement requirements;
(6) failure to timely repay a federal loan fund for state welfare programs;
(7) failure of any state to maintain a specified level of its historic welfare spending effort;
(8) substantial noncompliance of state child support enforcement program with federal requirements;
(9) failure to comply with 5-year limit on assistance;
(10) failure of state receiving amounts from contingency fund to maintain 100% of its historic welfare spending effort;
(11) failure to maintain assistance to adult single custodial parent who cannot obtain child care for child under age six; and
(12) failure to expend additional state funds to replace grant reduction.

Congress capped the total penalties against a state at 25%. It further prohibited the Secretary from imposing a penalty against a state if the Secretary determines that the state has reasonable cause for failing to comply with the requirement. Congress then granted various procedural rights to the states, including the rights to (1) notice and an opportunity to enter into a corrective compliance plan; (2) administrative review by the Department of Health and Human Services Appeals Board; and (3) federal court judicial review.

Does Congress have the power to prevent the executive branch of government from enforcing federal laws? If individual beneficiaries cannot enforce the statute's provisions, and if the Secretary of Health and Human Services can enforce only designated provisions, are the states free to disregard the remaining provisions of the statute?

Consider how the structure of the TANF block grant statute governs the power relations between the state governments and the federal government. First, the statute limits the federal government's power to enforce its provisions, and guarantees various procedural rights to the states. Does it, in effect, designate the states as the primary beneficiaries of the statute, and give them broad discretion, not only about how, but perhaps about whether, to comply with the federal statute's requirements? Does the provision denying general enforcement power to the Secretary, in effect, transform the seemingly mandatory provisions of the statute to merely hortatory or fully discretionary provisions? Who will serve as a check on the states for the provisions Congress designated as non-enforceable? Compare the power of the states as beneficiaries of the TANF statute, to the power of individual recipients as the beneficiaries of the former AFDC statute.

Consider how the structure of the TANF block grant statute governs the power relations between the state and federal governments and individual recipients of benefits.

CHAPTER 5: THE VALUE OF DUE PROCESS

A. THE RIGHT TO BE HEARD (IN SOME CONTEXTS)

The Fifth Amendment's due process clause prohibits the federal government from depriving any person of life, liberty, or property without due process of law. A similar due process clause in the Fourteenth Amendment applies to state governments. Courts traditionally have analyzed recipients' claims to benefits under the property prong of due process protection, and have not limited the meaning of property to so-called private property. The following cases show that if a recipient of a government benefit meets all eligibility requirements for continued receipt of that benefit, courts have considered that benefit to be a form of property belonging to the recipient. Once a court decides whether a sufficient deprivation is at issue, it then must decide what process is due. Traditionally, due process requires that the affected persons be provided an opportunity to be heard, at a meaningful time, and in a meaningful manner.

This part explores the extent of entitlement to due process hearings and the nature of those hearings in two contexts, first, administrative hearings regarding public assistance, and second, judicial hearings regarding eviction. In addition to the cases which determine the extent and nature of the due process right, we have included critiques provided by Professors Lucie White and Barbara Bezdek. They explore the value of contemporary forms of due process. Specifically, White explores whether a welfare hearing served the interests of Mrs. G., her client. Bezdek documents the processes of a typical urban eviction court. Both authors raise important questions about whether formal hearings serve the interests of poor clients in a meaningful way. Consider whether poor people are likely to favor alternatives to these hearings.

1. Administrative Public Assistance Hearings

GOLDBERG v. KELLY

397 U.S. 254 (1970)

Justice BRENNAN delivered the opinion of the Court.

The question for decision is whether a State that terminates public assistance payments to a particular recipient without affording him the opportunity for an evidentiary hearing prior to termination denies the recipient procedural due process in violation of the Due Process Clause of the Fourteenth Amendment.

This action was brought in the District Court for the Southern District of New York by residents of New York City receiving financial aid under the federally assisted program of Aid to Families with Dependent Children (AFDC) or under New York State's general Home Relief program.[1] Their complaint alleged that the New York State and New York City officials administering these programs terminated, or were about to terminate, such aid without prior notice and hearing, thereby denying them due process of law.[2] At the time

---

[1]AFDC was established by the Social Security Act of 1935. It is a categorical assistance program supported by federal grants-in-aid but administered by the States according to regulations of the Secretary of Health, Education, and Welfare. . . . Home Relief is a general assistance program financed and administered solely by New York state and local governments. It assists any person unable to support himself or to secure support from other sources.

[2]Two suits were brought and consolidated in the District Court. The named plaintiffs were 20 in number, including intervenors. Fourteen had been or were about to be cut off from AFDC, and six from Home Relief. During the course of this litigation most, though not all, of the plaintiffs either received a "fair hearing" or were restored to the rolls without a hearing. However, even in many of the cases where payments have been resumed, the underlying questions of eligibility that resulted in the bringing of this suit have not been resolved. For example, Mrs. Altagracia Guzman alleged that she was in danger of losing AFDC payments for failure to cooperate with the City Department of Social Services in suing her estranged husband. She contended that the departmental policy requiring such cooperation was inapplicable to the facts of her case. The record shows that payments to Mrs. Guzman have not been terminated, but there is no indication that the basic dispute over her duty to cooperate has been resolved, or that the alleged danger of termination has been removed. Home Relief payments to Juan DeJesus

the suits were filed there was no requirement of prior notice or hearing of any kind before termination of financial aid. However, the State and city adopted procedures for notice and hearing after the suits were brought, and the plaintiffs, appellees here, then challenged the constitutional adequacy of those procedures.

The State Commissioner of Social Services amended the State Department of Social Services' Official Regulations to require that local social services officials proposing to discontinue or suspend a recipient's financial aid do so according to a procedure that conforms to either subdivision (a) or subdivision (b) of § 351.26 of the regulations as amended.[3] The City of New York elected to promulgate a local procedure according to subdivision (b). That subdivision, so far as here pertinent, provides that the local procedure must include the giving of notice to the recipient of the reasons for a proposed discontinuance or suspension at least seven days prior to its

---

were terminated because he refused to accept counseling and rehabilitation for drug addiction. Mr. DeJesus maintains that he does not use drugs. His payments were restored the day after his complaint was filed. But there is nothing in the record to indicate that the underlying factual dispute in his case has been settled.

[3]The adoption in February 1968 and the amendment in April of Regulation § 351.26 coincided with or followed several revisions by the Department of Health, Education, and Welfare of its regulations implementing 42 U.S.C. § 602(a)(4), which is the provision of the Social Security Act that requires a State to afford a "fair hearing" to any recipient of aid under a federally assisted program before termination of his aid becomes final. This requirement is satisfied by a post-termination "fair hearing" under regulations presently in effect. A new HEW regulation now scheduled to take effect in July 1970, would require continuation of AFDC payments until the final decision after a "fair hearing" and would give recipients a right to appointed counsel at "fair hearings." Another recent regulation now in effect requires a local agency administering AFDC to give "advance notice of questions it has about an individual's eligibility so that a recipient has an opportunity to discuss his situation before receiving formal written notice of reduction in payment or termination of assistance." This case presents no issue of the validity or construction of the federal regulations. It is only subdivision (b) of § 351.26 of the New York State regulations and implementing procedure 68-18 of New York City that pose the constitutional question before us. Even assuming that the constitutional question might be avoided in the context of AFDC by construction of the Social Security Act or of the present federal regulations thereunder, or by waiting for the new regulations to become effective, the question must be faced and decided in the context of New York's Home Relief program, to which the procedures also apply.

effective date, with notice also that upon request the recipient may have the proposal reviewed by a local welfare official holding a position superior to that of the supervisor who approved the proposed discontinuance or suspension, and, further, that the recipient may submit, for purposes of the review, a written statement to demonstrate why his grant should not be discontinued or suspended. The decision by the reviewing official whether to discontinue or suspend aid must be made expeditiously, with written notice of the decision to the recipient. The section further expressly provides that "[a]ssistance shall not be discontinued or suspended prior to the date such notice of decision is sent to the recipient and his representative, if any, or prior to the proposed effective date of discontinuance or suspension, whichever occurs later."

Pursuant to subdivision (b), the New York City Department of Social Services promulgated Procedure No. 68-18. A caseworker who has doubts about the recipient's continued eligibility must first discuss them with the recipient. If the caseworker concludes that the recipient is no longer eligible, he recommends termination of aid to a unit supervisor. If the latter concurs, he sends the recipient a letter stating the reasons for proposing to terminate aid and notifying him that within seven days he may request that a higher official review the record, and may support the request with a written statement prepared personally or with the aid of an attorney or other person. If the reviewing official affirms the determination of ineligibility, aid is stopped immediately and the recipient is informed by letter of the reasons for the action. Appellees' challenge to this procedure emphasizes the absence of any provisions for the personal appearance of the recipient before the reviewing official, for oral presentation of evidence, and for confrontation and cross-examination of adverse witnesses. However, the letter does inform the recipient that he may request a post-termination "fair hearing." This is a proceeding before an independent state hearing officer at which the recipient may appear personally, offer oral evidence, confront and cross-examine the witnesses against him, and have a record made of the hearing. If the recipient prevails at the "fair hearing" he is paid all funds erroneously withheld. A recipient whose aid is not restored by a "fair hearing" decision may have judicial review. The recipient is so notified.

I

The constitutional issue to be decided, therefore, is the narrow one whether the Due Process Clause requires that the recipient be afforded an evidentiary hearing *before* the termination of benefits.[7] The District Court held that only a pre-termination evidentiary hearing would satisfy the constitutional command, and rejected the argument of the state and city officials that the combination of the post-termination "fair hearing" with the informal pre-termination review disposed of all due process claims. The court said:

> While post-termination review is relevant, there is one overpowering fact which controls here. By hypothesis, a welfare recipient is destitute, without funds or assets. . . . Suffice it to say that to cut off a welfare recipient in the face of . . . "brutal need" without a prior hearing of some sort is unconscionable, unless overwhelming considerations justify it.

The court rejected the argument that the need to protect the public's tax revenues supplied the requisite "overwhelming consideration."

> Against the justified desire to protect public funds must be weighed the individual's overpowering need in this unique situation not to be wrongfully deprived of assistance. . . . While the problem of additional expense must be kept in mind, it does not justify denying a hearing meeting the ordinary standards of due process. Under all the circumstances, we hold that due process requires an adequate hearing before termination of welfare benefits, and the fact that there is a later constitutionally fair proceeding does not alter the result.

Although state officials were party defendants in the action, only the Commissioner of Social Services of the City of New York appealed.

* * *

Appellant does not contend that procedural due process is not applicable to the termination of welfare benefits. Such benefits are a

---

[7]Appellant does not question the recipient's due process right to evidentiary review *after* termination.

matter of statutory entitlement for persons qualified to receive them.[8] Their termination involves state action that adjudicates important rights. The constitutional challenge cannot be answered by an argument that public assistance benefits are "a 'privilege' and not a 'right.'" Relevant constitutional restraints apply as much to the withdrawal of public assistance benefits as to disqualification for unemployment compensation. . . . The extent to which procedural due process must be afforded the recipient is influenced by the extent to which he may be "condemned to suffer grievous loss," and depends upon whether the recipient's interest in avoiding that loss outweighs the governmental interest in summary adjudication. Accordingly . . . "consideration of what procedures due process may require under any given set of circumstances must begin with a determination of the precise nature of the government function involved as well as of the private interest that has been affected by governmental action."

It is true, of course, that some governmental benefits may be administratively terminated without affording the recipient a pre-termination evidentiary hearing. But we agree with the District Court that when welfare is discontinued, only a pre-termination

---

[8]It may be realistic today to regard welfare entitlements as more like "property" than a "gratuity." Much of the existing wealth in this country takes the form of rights that do not fall within traditional common-law concepts of property. It has been aptly noted that

> [s]ociety today is built around entitlement. The automobile dealer has his franchise, the doctor and lawyer their professional licenses, the worker his union membership, contract, and pension rights, the executive his contract and stock options; all are devices to aid security and independence. Many of the most important of these entitlements now flow from government: subsidies to farmers and businessmen, routes for airlines and channels for television stations; long term contracts for defense, space, and education; social security pensions for individuals. Such sources of security, whether private or public, are no longer regarded as luxuries or gratuities; to the recipients they are essentials, fully deserved, and in no sense a form of charity. It is only the poor whose entitlements, although recognized by public policy, have not been effectively enforced.

Reich, *Individual Rights and Social Welfare: The Emerging Legal Issues*, 74 YALE L.J. 1245, 1255 (1965). *See also* Reich, *The New Property*, 73 YALE L.J. 733 (1964).

evidentiary hearing provides the recipient with procedural due process. For qualified recipients, welfare provides the means to obtain essential food, clothing, housing, and medical care. Thus the crucial factor in this context--a factor not present in the case of the blacklisted government contractor, the discharged government employee, the taxpayer denied a tax exemption, or virtually anyone else whose governmental entitlements are ended--is that termination of aid pending resolution of a controversy over eligibility may deprive an *eligible* recipient of the very means by which to live while he waits. Since he lacks independent resources, his situation becomes immediately desperate. His need to concentrate upon finding the means for daily subsistence, in turn, adversely affects his ability to seek redress from the welfare bureaucracy.

Moreover, important governmental interests are promoted by affording recipients a pre-termination evidentiary hearing. From its founding the Nation's basic commitment has been to foster the dignity and well-being of all persons within its borders. We have come to recognize that forces not within the control of the poor contribute to their poverty. This perception, against the background of our traditions, has significantly influenced the development of the contemporary public assistance system. Welfare, by meeting the basic demands of subsistence, can help bring within the reach of the poor the same opportunities that are available to others to participate meaningfully in the life of the community. At the same time, welfare guards against the societal malaise that may flow from a widespread sense of unjustified frustration and insecurity. Public assistance, then, is not mere charity, but a means to "promote the general Welfare, and secure the Blessings of Liberty to ourselves and our Posterity." The same governmental interests that counsel the provision of welfare, counsel as well its uninterrupted provision to those eligible to receive it; pre-termination evidentiary hearings are indispensable to that end.

Appellant does not challenge the force of these considerations but argues that they are outweighed by countervailing governmental interests in conserving fiscal and administrative resources. These interests, the argument goes, justify the delay of any evidentiary hearing until after discontinuance of the grants. Summary adjudication protects the public fisc by stopping payments promptly upon discovery of reason to believe that a recipient is no longer eligible. Since most terminations are accepted without challenge, summary adjudication also conserves both the fisc and administrative time and energy by reducing the number of evidentiary hearings actually held.

We agree with the District Court, however, that these governmental interests are not overriding in the welfare context. The requirement of a prior hearing doubtless involves some greater expense, and the benefits paid to ineligible recipients pending decision at the hearing probably cannot be recouped, since these recipients are likely to be judgment-proof. But the State is not without weapons to minimize these increased costs. Much of the drain on fiscal and administrative resources can be reduced by developing procedures for prompt pre-termination hearings and by skillful use of personnel and facilities. Indeed, the very provision for a post-termination evidentiary hearing in New York's Home Relief program is itself cogent evidence that the State recognizes the primacy of the public interest in correct eligibility determinations and therefore in the provision of procedural safeguards. Thus, the interest of the eligible recipient in uninterrupted receipt of public assistance, coupled with the State's interest that his payments not be erroneously terminated, clearly outweighs the State's competing concern to prevent any increase in its fiscal and administrative burdens. As the District Court correctly concluded, "[t]he stakes are simply too high for the welfare recipient, and the possibility for honest error or irritable misjudgment too great, to allow termination of aid without giving the recipient a chance, if he so desires, to be fully informed of the case against him so that he may contest its basis and produce evidence in rebuttal."

II

We also agree with the District Court, however, that the pre-termination hearing need not take the form of a judicial or quasi-judicial trial. We bear in mind that the statutory "fair hearing" will provide the recipient with a full administrative review.[14] Accordingly, the pre-termination hearing has one function only: to produce an initial determination of the validity of the welfare department's grounds for discontinuance of payments in order to protect a recipient against an erroneous termination of his benefits. Thus, a complete record and a comprehensive opinion, which would

[14]Due process does not, of course, require two hearings. If, for example, a State simply wishes to continue benefits until after a "fair" hearing there will be no need for a preliminary hearing.

serve primarily to facilitate judicial review and to guide future decisions, need not be provided at the pre-termination stage. We recognize, too, that both welfare authorities and recipients have an interest in relatively speedy resolution of questions of eligibility, that they are used to dealing with one another informally, and that some welfare departments have very burdensome caseloads. These considerations justify the limitation of the pre-termination hearing to minimum procedural safeguards, adapted to the particular characteristics of welfare recipients, and to the limited nature of the controversies to be resolved. We wish to add that we, no less than the dissenters, recognize the importance of not imposing upon the States or the Federal Government in this developing field of law any procedural requirements beyond those demanded by rudimentary due process.

"The fundamental requisite of due process of law is the opportunity to be heard." The hearing must be "at a meaningful time and in a meaningful manner." In the present context these principles require that a recipient have timely and adequate notice detailing the reasons for a proposed termination, and an effective opportunity to defend by confronting any adverse witnesses and by presenting his own arguments and evidence orally. These rights are important in cases such as those before us, where recipients have challenged proposed terminations as resting on incorrect or misleading factual premises or on misapplication of rules or policies to the facts of particular cases.

We are not prepared to say that the seven-day notice currently provided by New York City is constitutionally insufficient *per se*, although there may be cases where fairness would require that a longer time be given. Nor do we see any constitutional deficiency in the content or form of the notice. New York employs both a letter and a personal conference with a caseworker to inform a recipient of the precise questions raised about his continued eligibility. Evidently the recipient is told the legal and factual bases for the Department's doubts. This combination is probably the most effective method of communicating with recipients.

The city's procedures presently do not permit recipients to appear personally with or without counsel before the official who finally determines continued eligibility. Thus a recipient is not permitted to present evidence to that official orally, or to confront or cross-examine adverse witnesses. These omissions are fatal to the constitutional adequacy of the procedures.

The opportunity to be heard must be tailored to the capacities and circumstances of those who are to be heard. It is not enough that a welfare recipient may present his position to the decision maker in writing or secondhand through his caseworker. Written submissions are an unrealistic option for most recipients, who lack the educational attainment necessary to write effectively and who cannot obtain professional assistance. Moreover, written submissions do not afford the flexibility of oral presentations; they do not permit the recipient to mold his argument to the issues the decision maker appears to regard as important. Particularly where credibility and veracity are at issue, as they must be in many termination proceedings, written submissions are a wholly unsatisfactory basis for decision. The second-hand presentation to the decisionmaker by the caseworker has its own deficiencies; since the caseworker usually gathers the facts upon which the charge of ineligibility rests, the presentation of the recipient's side of the controversy cannot safely be left to him. Therefore a recipient must be allowed to state his position orally. Informal procedures will suffice; in this context due process does not require a particular order of proof or mode of offering evidence.

In almost every setting where important decisions turn on questions of fact, due process requires an opportunity to confront and cross-examine adverse witnesses. What we said in *Greene v. McElroy* is particularly pertinent here:

> Certain principles have remained relatively immutable in our jurisprudence. One of these is that where governmental action seriously injures an individual, and the reasonableness of the action depends on fact findings, the evidence used to prove the Government's case must be disclosed to the individual so that he has an opportunity to show that it is untrue. While this is important in the case of documentary evidence, it is even more important where the evidence consists of the testimony of individuals whose memory might be faulty or who, in fact, might be perjurers or persons motivated by malice, vindictiveness, intolerance, prejudice, or jealousy. We have formalized these protections in the requirements of confrontation and

> cross-examination. They have ancient roots. They find expression in the Sixth Amendment. . . . This Court has been zealous to protect these rights from erosion. It has spoken out not only in criminal cases, . . . but also in all types of cases where administrative . . . actions were under scrutiny.

Welfare recipients must therefore be given an opportunity to confront and cross-examine the witnesses relied on by the department.

"The right to be heard would be, in many cases, of little avail if it did not comprehend the right to be heard by counsel." We do not say that counsel must be provided at the pre-termination hearing, but only that the recipient must be allowed to retain an attorney if he so desires. Counsel can help delineate the issues, present the factual contentions in an orderly manner, conduct cross-examination, and generally safeguard the interests of the recipient. We do not anticipate that this assistance will unduly prolong or otherwise encumber the hearing.

* * *

Finally, the decisionmaker's conclusion as to a recipient's eligibility must rest solely on the legal rules and evidence adduced at the hearing. To demonstrate compliance with this elementary requirement, the decision maker should state the reasons for his determination and indicate the evidence he relied on, though his statement need not amount to a full opinion or even formal findings of fact and conclusions of law. And, of course, an impartial decision maker is essential. We agree with the District Court that prior involvement in some aspects of a case will not necessarily bar a welfare official from acting as a decision maker. He should not, however, have participated in making the determination under review.

Affirmed.

Justice BLACK, dissenting.

In the last half century the United States, along with many, perhaps most, other nations of the world, has moved far toward becoming a welfare state, that is, a nation that for one reason or another taxes its most affluent people to help support, feed, clothe, and shelter its less fortunate citizens. The result is that today more than nine million men, women, and children in the United States receive some kind of state or federally financed public assistance in the form of allowances or gratuities, generally paid them periodically, usually by the week, month, or quarter. Since these gratuities are paid on the basis of need, the list of recipients is not static, and some people go off the lists and others are added from time to time. These ever-changing lists put a constant administrative burden on government and it certainly could not have reasonably anticipated that this burden would include the additional procedural expense imposed by the Court today.

The dilemma of the ever-increasing poor in the midst of constantly growing affluence presses upon us and must inevitably be met within the framework of our democratic constitutional government, if our system is to survive as such. It was largely to escape just such pressing economic problems and attendant government repression that people from Europe, Asia, and other areas settled this country and formed our Nation. Many of those settlers had personally suffered from persecutions of various kinds and wanted to get away from governments that had unrestrained powers to make life miserable for their citizens. It was for this reason, or so I believe, that on reaching these new lands the early settlers undertook to curb their governments by confining their powers within written boundaries, which eventually became written constitutions. They wrote their basic charters as nearly as men's collective wisdom could do so as to proclaim to their people and their officials an emphatic command that: "Thus far and no farther shall you go; and where we neither delegate powers to you, nor prohibit your exercise of them, we the people are left free."

Representatives of the people of the Thirteen Original Colonies spent long, hot months in the summer of 1787 in Philadelphia, Pennsylvania, creating a government of limited powers. They divided it into three departments--Legislative, Judicial, and Executive. The Judicial Department was to have no part whatever in making any laws. In fact proposals looking to vesting some power in the Judiciary to take part in the legislative process and veto laws were offered, considered, and rejected by the Constitutional Convention. In my judgment there is not one word, phrase, or sentence from the beginning to the end of the Constitution from which it can be inferred that judges were granted any such legislative power. True, *Marbury v. Madison*, held, and properly, I think, that courts must be the final interpreters of the Constitution, and I recognize that the holding can provide an opportunity to slide imperceptibly into constitutional amendment and law making. But when federal judges use this judicial power for legislative purposes, I think they wander out of their field of vested powers and transgress into the area constitutionally assigned to the Congress and the people. That is precisely what I believe the Court is doing in this case. Hence my dissent.

The more than a million names on the relief rolls in New York, and the more than nine million names on the rolls of all the 50 States were not put there at random. The names are there because state welfare officials believed that those people were eligible for assistance. Probably in the officials' haste to make out the lists many names were put there erroneously in order to alleviate immediate suffering, and undoubtedly some people are drawing relief who are not entitled under the law to do so. Doubtless some draw relief checks from time to time who know they are not eligible, either because they are not actually in need or for some other reason. Many of those who thus draw undeserved gratuities are without sufficient property to enable the government to collect back from them any money they wrongfully receive. But the Court today holds that it would violate the Due Process Clause of the Fourteenth Amendment to stop paying those people weekly or monthly allowances unless the government first affords them a full "evidentiary hearing" even though welfare officials are persuaded that the recipients are not rightfully entitled to receive a penny under the law. In other words, although some recipients might be on the lists for payment wholly because of deliberate fraud on their part, the Court holds that the government is helpless and must continue, until after an evidentiary hearing, to pay money that it does not owe, never has owed, and never could owe. I do not believe there is any provision in our Constitution that should thus paralyze the government's efforts to protect itself against making payments to people who are not entitled to them.

Particularly do I not think that the Fourteenth Amendment should be given such an unnecessarily broad construction. That Amendment came into being primarily to protect Negroes from discrimination, and while some of its language can and does protect others, all know that the chief purpose behind it was to protect ex-slaves. The Court, however, relies upon the Fourteenth Amendment and in effect says that failure of the government to pay a promised charitable instalment to an individual deprives that individual of *his own property*, in violation of the Due Process Clause of the Fourteenth Amendment. It somewhat strains credulity to say that the government's promise of charity to an individual is property belonging to that individual when the government denies that the individual is honestly entitled to receive such a payment.

I would have little, if any, objection to the majority's decision in this case if it were written as the report of the House Committee on Education and Labor, but as an opinion ostensibly resting on the language of the Constitution I find it woefully deficient. Once the verbiage is pared away it is obvious that this Court today adopts the views of the District Court "that to cut off a welfare recipient in the face of . . . 'brutal need' without a prior hearing of some sort is unconscionable," and therefore, says the Court, unconstitutional. The majority reaches this result by a process of weighing "the recipient's interest in avoiding" the termination of welfare benefits against "the governmental interest in summary adjudication." Today's balancing act requires a "pre-termination evidentiary hearing," yet there is nothing that indicates what tomorrow's balance will be. Although the majority attempts to bolster its decision with limited quotations from prior cases, it is obvious that today's result doesn't depend on the language of the Constitution itself or the principles of other decisions, but solely on the collective judgment of the majority as to what would be a fair and humane procedure in this case.

* * *

The procedure required today as a matter of constitutional law finds no precedent in our legal system. Reduced to its simplest terms, the problem in this case is similar to that frequently encountered when two parties have an ongoing legal relationship that requires one party to make periodic payments to the other. Often the situation arises where the party "owing" the money stops paying it and justifies his conduct by arguing that the recipient is not legally entitled to payment. The recipient can, of course, disagree and go to court to compel payment. But I know of no situation in our legal system in which the person alleged to owe money to another is required by law to continue making payments to a judgment-proof claimant without the benefit of any security or bond to insure that these payments can be recovered if he wins his legal argument. Yet today's decision in no way obligates the welfare recipient to pay back any benefits wrongfully received during the pre-termination evidentiary hearings or post any bond, and in all "fairness" it could not do so. These recipients are by definition too poor to post a bond or to repay the benefits that, as the majority assumes, must be spent as received to insure survival.

The Court apparently feels that this decision will benefit the poor and needy. In my judgment the eventual result will be just the opposite. While today's decision requires only an administrative, evidentiary hearing, the inevitable logic of the approach taken will lead to constitutionally imposed, time-consuming delays of a full adversary process of administrative and judicial review. In the next case the welfare recipients are bound to argue that cutting off benefits before judicial review of the agency's decision is also a denial of due process. Since, by hypothesis, termination of aid at that point may still "deprive an *eligible* recipient of the very means by which to live while he waits," I would be surprised if the weighing process did not compel the conclusion that termination without full judicial review would be unconscionable. After all, at each step, as the majority seems to feel, the issue is only one of weighing the government's pocketbook against the actual survival of the recipient, and surely that balance must always tip in favor of the individual. Similarly today's decision requires only the opportunity to have the benefit of counsel at the administrative hearing, but it is difficult to believe that the same reasoning process would not require the appointment of counsel, for otherwise the right to counsel is a meaningless one since these people are too poor to hire their own advocates. Thus the end result of today's decision may well be that the government, once it decides to give welfare benefits, cannot reverse that decision until the recipient has had the benefits of full administrative and judicial review, including, of course, the opportunity to present his case to this Court. Since this process will usually entail a delay of several years, the inevitable result of such a constitutionally imposed burden will be that the government will not put a claimant on the rolls initially until it has made an exhaustive investigation to determine his eligibility. While this Court will perhaps have insured that no needy person will be taken off the rolls without a full "due process" proceeding, it will also have insured that many will never get on the rolls, or at least that they will remain destitute during the lengthy proceedings followed to determine initial eligibility.

For the foregoing reasons I dissent from the Court's holding. The operation of a welfare state is a new experiment for our Nation. For this reason, among others, I feel that new experiments in carrying out a welfare program should not be frozen into our constitutional structure. They should be left, as are other legislative determinations, to the Congress and the legislatures that the people elect to make our laws.

Notes and Questions

1. *Whether Due Process Applies.* The first question for the Court was whether welfare was a type of property protected by the due process guarantee. The Court answered in the affirmative, relying explicitly in footnote eight on the theory of Professor Charles Reich that welfare, like other forms of government benefits, should be treated as property, rather than as gratuities. Yet the Court has not maintained this view consistently. In other cases, the Court emphasizes instead the gratuitous nature of welfare. *See Bowen v. Gilliard*, discussed in Chapter 7. What makes any government benefit an entitlement? Are Reich and the *Goldberg* Court correct in concluding that welfare should be treated as an entitlement or protectable property interest? What are the strengths and weaknesses of this conclusion? Is the Court's recognition of the property interest in welfare benefits statutorily-based, or constitutionally-based, or both? In other words, to what extent did the Court rely on the statutory basis of entitlement for federal welfare benefits, and to what extent did the Court rely on its reasoning that eligible recipients should not be denied "the very means by which to live" while awaiting their decisions?

2. *What Test Governs What Process is Due.* The second question presented, once the Court decided that welfare was a protected form of property, asked what process was due. The Court employed the basic elements of the now-well-established balancing test, further developed in *Mathews v. Eldridge,* discussed in this chapter. The Court in *Goldberg* balanced two sets of interests: (1) the recipient's interest in continued receipt of welfare; and (2) the government's interests both in providing benefits and in containing its fiscal and administrative costs.

First, regarding the recipient's interest, the Court emphasized that the welfare recipient's interest is in "the very means by which to live while he waits" for a hearing, apparently giving this great weight. Second, regarding the government's interest, the key may have been the Court's willingness to consider the government's interest in providing benefits. In later decisions, such as *Mathews*, the Court limits the government's interest to saving costs. How should courts balance the competing government interests in providing the benefits but limiting their costs? Also, how important is the Court's willingness and ability to identify less restrictive means for the government to save costs. Finally, what influence, if any, did the risk of error have on the Court's conclusions?

3. *What Process is Due.* Although the Court concluded that the government must provide a hearing prior to termination of benefits, it required only "minimal procedural safeguards." The Court required: (1) an opportunity to orally present arguments and evidence and to confront adverse witnesses, (2) the right to retain an attorney, (3) a decision based solely on the law and the hearing record, and (4) an impartial decisionmaker. Are these safeguards sufficient?

Who benefits from not requiring formal rules of evidence, recipients or the government? What is the value of the right to retain an attorney to a poor person who cannot afford one? Why must the government supply counsel in some criminal cases, but not for welfare benefits cases? *See* the discussion of access to criminal justice in Chapter 6. Why are formal findings of fact and conclusions of law unnecessary? Is understanding the decisionmaker's reasoning less important for welfare decisions? In what respect would officials employed by a welfare department be "impartial" decisionmakers?

4. *Due Process in a Block-Grant Welfare System.* The state conceded in *Goldberg* that welfare constituted a form of property protected by the due process guarantee. The Court agreed, explaining that "[s]uch benefits are a matter of statutory entitlement for persons qualified to receive them." In a federal welfare system that provides block grants of funds for states to spend as they choose, are welfare benefits still a statutory entitlement? If welfare benefits are not a federal statutory entitlement, are they a state statutory entitlement? Would a federal or state's explicit provision specifying that welfare benefits are not a statutory entitlement be dispositive? Or does the *Goldberg* decision's reasoning in footnote eight that welfare benefits are one of the "sources of security" regarded as "essentials" by recipients require courts to consider welfare to be a form of property? In other words, are block-grant welfare benefits still more like property than a gratuity? Consider what Congress did in its Personal Responsibility and Work Opportunity Reconciliation Act of 1996

which abolished Aid to Families with Dependent Children and created the Temporary Assistance for Needy Families block grant program.

Due Process and Temporary Assistance For Needy Families Block Grant Programs

In the Personal Responsibility and Work Opportunity Reconciliation Act of 1996, Congress abolished Aid to Families with Dependent Children (AFDC). In so doing, Congress eliminated the federal statutory entitlement requiring states to provide AFDC benefits to all eligible individuals, and the procedural entitlement requiring states to grant disgruntled beneficiaries an opportunity for a fair hearing before the state agency. In place of AFDC, Congress created the Temporary Assistance for Needy Families (TANF) block grant program. The TANF block grant program allows states to create their own welfare programs and determine eligibility for requirements. Congress explicitly stated that the TANF statute "shall not be interpreted to entitle any individual or family to assistance under any State program funded under this part." Congress repeated this prohibition of entitlement status in the section restricting TANF benefits to five years, stating that the time limit "shall not be interpreted to require any State to provide assistance to any individual for any period of time under the State program funded under this part." *Id.* Congress required, however, that states set forth in their TANF Family Assistance Plan "objective criteria for the delivery of benefits and the determination of eligibility and for fair and equitable treatment, including an explanation of how the State will provide opportunities for recipients who have been adversely affected to be heard in a State administrative or appeal process." *Id.*

Of what effect is Congress' denial of entitlement status to TANF beneficiaries? Is entitlement status the same as a property interest? Is Congress' denial of entitlement status dispositive of whether beneficiaries have a property interest protected by the due process clauses? Of what effect are Congress' requirements that states establish objective criteria for fair and equitable treatment and explain how they will allow recipients to be heard?

Consider the Supreme Court's reasoning in *Board of Regents v. Roth,* 408 U.S. 564, 577 (1972), where the Court explained that an individual must have more than an abstract need for, or unilateral expectation of, a benefit, but instead must have a "legitimate claim of entitlement" to the benefit. The Court also stated that a property interest in a benefit depends on the statute defining eligibility for the benefit. *Id.* Compare these statements in *Roth* to the Court's later reasoning in *Cleveland Board of Education v. Loudermill,* 470 U.S. 532 (1985). In *Loudermill,* the Court made clear that a state legislature cannot limit the existence of a property interest by limiting the procedures available to enforce the interest. The Court explained that "the Due Process Clause provides that certain substantive rights--life, liberty, and property--cannot be deprived except pursuant to constitutionally adequate procedures. The categories of substance and procedure are distinct. Were the rule otherwise, the Clause would be reduced to a mere tautology. 'Property' cannot be defined by the procedures provided for its deprivation any more than can life or liberty." *Id.* at 541. As the Court explained in *Logan v. Zimmerman Brush Co.*, 455 U.S. 422 (1982), "once a state has created a property interest, the adequacy of the procedures employed to deprive an individual of that interest must be judged in constitutional terms."

How would *Goldberg, Roth*, and *Loudermill* apply to Congress' statements in TANF that denied entitlement status to TANF beneficiaries? How will they apply to each state's program created pursuant to the TANF block grant, none of which had been created as of this writing? Will it depend on whether each state explicitly disclaims the creation of any entitlement? What if a state conditioned eligibility for benefits on availability of funds? What if a state legislature explicitly delegated decision-making authority to the discretion of state officials? What if a state explicitly denied or limited appeal procedures? What if a state constitution created a fundamental right to subsistence? For analyses attempting to anticipate these issues, *see* John Bouman, *Due Process for Welfare Recipients Subject to Changing Program Rules: An Illinois Case Study,* 30 CLEARINGHOUSE REVIEW 109 (June 1996); Nancy Morawetz, *A Due Process Primer: Litigating Government Benefit Cases in the Block Grant Era,* 30 CLEARINGHOUSE REVIEW 97 (June 1996); Rebecca E. Zietlow, *Two Wrongs Don't Add Up to Rights: The Importance of Preserving Due Process in Light of Recent Welfare Reform Measures,* 45 AMERICAN UNIVERSITY LAW REVIEW 1111 (1996).

Even if courts determine that recipients have a property interest in TANF benefits, the question remains what process is due such recipients.

MATHEWS v. ELDRIDGE

424 U.S. 319 (1976)

Justice POWELL delivered the opinion of the Court.

The issue in this case is whether the Due Process Clause of the Fifth Amendment requires that prior to the termination of Social Security disability benefit payments the recipient be afforded an opportunity for an evidentiary hearing.

I

Cash benefits are provided to workers during periods in which they are completely disabled under the disability insurance benefits program created by the 1956 amendments to Title II of the Social Security Act.[1] Respondent Eldridge was first awarded benefits in June 1968. In March 1972, he received a questionnaire from the state agency charged with monitoring his medical condition. Eldridge completed the questionnaire, indicating that his condition had not improved and identifying the medical sources, including physicians, from whom he had received treatment recently. The state agency then obtained reports from his physician and a psychiatric consultant. After considering these reports and other information in his file the agency informed Eldridge by letter that it had made a tentative determination that his disability had ceased in May 1972. The letter included a statement of reasons for the proposed termination of benefits, and advised Eldridge that he might request reasonable time in which to obtain and submit additional information pertaining to his condition.

---

[1]The program is financed by revenues derived from employee and employer payroll taxes. It provides monthly benefits to disabled persons who have worked sufficiently long to have an insured status, and who have had substantial work experience in a specified interval directly preceding the onset of disability. Benefits also are provided to the worker's dependents under specified circumstances. When the recipient reaches age 65 his disability benefits are automatically converted to retirement benefits. . . .

In his written response, Eldridge disputed one characterization of his medical condition and indicated that the agency already had enough evidence to establish his disability.[2] The state agency then made its final determination that he had ceased to be disabled in May 1972. This determination was accepted by the Social Security Administration (SSA), which notified Eldridge in July that his benefits would terminate after that month. The notification also advised him of his right to seek reconsideration by the state agency of this initial determination within six months.

Instead of requesting reconsideration Eldridge commenced this action challenging the constitutional validity of the administrative procedures established by the Secretary of Health, Education, and Welfare for assessing whether there exists a continuing disability. He sought an immediate reinstatement of benefits pending a hearing on the issue of his disability.[3] The Secretary moved to dismiss on the grounds that Eldridge's benefits had been terminated in accordance with valid administrative regulations and procedures and that he had failed to exhaust available remedies. In support of his contention that due process requires a pretermination hearing, Eldridge relied exclusively upon this Court's decision in *Goldberg v. Kelly*, which established a right to an "evidentiary hearing" prior to termination of welfare benefits. The Secretary contended that *Goldberg* was not controlling since eligibility for disability benefits, unlike eligibility for welfare benefits, is not based on financial need and since issues of credibility and veracity do not play a significant role in the disability entitlement decision, which turns primarily on medical evidence.

The District Court concluded that the administrative procedures pursuant to which the Secretary had terminated Eldridge's benefits

---

[2]Eldridge originally was disabled due to chronic anxiety and back strain. He subsequently was found to have diabetes. The tentative determination letter indicated that aid would be terminated because available medical evidence indicated that his diabetes was under control, that there existed no limitations on his back movements which would impose severe functional restrictions, and that he no longer suffered emotional problems that would preclude him from all work for which he was qualified. In his reply letter he claimed to have arthritis of the spine rather than a strained back.

[3]The District Court ordered reinstatement of Eldridge's benefits pending its final disposition on the merits.

abridged his right to procedural due process. The court viewed the interest of the disability recipient in uninterrupted benefits as indistinguishable from that of the welfare recipient in *Goldberg*. It further noted that decisions subsequent to *Goldberg* demonstrated that the due process requirement of pretermination hearings is not limited to situations involving the deprivation of vital necessities. Reasoning that disability determinations may involve subjective judgments based on conflicting medical and nonmedical evidence, the District Court held that prior to termination of benefits Eldridge had to be afforded an evidentiary hearing of the type required for welfare beneficiaries under Title IV of the Social Security Act. Relying entirely upon the District Court's opinion, the Court of Appeals for the Fourth Circuit affirmed the injunction barring termination of Eldridge's benefits prior to an evidentiary hearing. We reverse.

* * *

III

A

Procedural due process imposes constraints on governmental decisions which deprive individuals of "liberty" or "property" interests within the meaning of the Due Process Clause of the Fifth or Fourteenth Amendment. The Secretary does not contend that procedural due process is inapplicable to terminations of Social Security disability benefits. He recognizes, as has been implicit in our prior decisions, that the interest of an individual in continued receipt of these benefits is a statutorily created "property" interest protected by the Fifth Amendment. Rather, the Secretary contends that the existing administrative procedures, detailed below, provide all the process that is constitutionally due before a recipient can be deprived of that interest.

This Court consistently has held that some form of hearing is required before an individual is finally deprived of a property interest. The "right to be heard before being condemned to suffer grievous loss of any kind, even though it may not involve the stigma and hardships of a criminal conviction, is a principle basic to our society." The fundamental requirement of due process is the opportunity to be heard "at a meaningful time and in a meaningful manner." Eldridge agrees that the review procedures available to a claimant before the initial determination of ineligibility becomes final would be adequate if disability benefits were not terminated until after the evidentiary hearing stage of the administrative process. The dispute centers upon what process is due prior to the initial termination of benefits, pending review.

* * *

More precisely, our prior decisions indicate that identification of the specific dictates of due process generally requires consideration of three distinct factors: First, the private interest that will be affected by the official action; second, the risk of an erroneous deprivation of such interest through the procedures used, and the probable value, if any, of additional or substitute procedural safeguards; and finally, the Government's interest, including the function involved and the fiscal and administrative burdens that the additional or substitute procedural requirement would entail.

We turn first to a description of the procedures for the termination of Social Security disability benefits, and thereafter consider the factors bearing upon the constitutional adequacy of these procedures.

B

The disability insurance program is administered jointly by state and federal agencies. State agencies make the initial determination whether a disability exists, when it began, and when it ceased. The standards applied and the procedures followed are prescribed by the Secretary, who has delegated his responsibilities and powers under the Act to the SSA.

In order to establish initial and continued entitlement to disability benefits a worker must demonstrate that he is unable "to engage in any substantial gainful activity by reason of any medically determinable physical or mental impairment which can be expected to result in death or which has lasted or can be expected to last for a continuous period of not less than 12 months. . . ." To satisfy this test the worker bears a continuing burden of showing, by means of

> "medically acceptable clinical and laboratory diagnostic techniques," that he has a physical or mental impairment of such severity that he is not only unable to do his previous work but cannot, considering his age, education, and work experience, engage in any other kind of substantial gainful work which exists in the national economy, regardless of whether such work exists in the immediate area in which he lives, or

> whether a specific job vacancy exists for him, or whether he would be hired if he applied for work.[14]

The principal reasons for benefits terminations are that the worker is no longer disabled or has returned to work. As Eldridge's benefits were terminated because he was determined to be no longer disabled, we consider only the sufficiency of the procedures involved in such cases.

The continuing-eligibility investigation is made by a state agency acting through a "team" consisting of a physician and a nonmedical person trained in disability evaluation. The agency periodically communicates with the disabled worker, usually by mail--in which case he is sent a detailed questionnaire--or by telephone, and requests information concerning his present condition, including current medical restrictions and sources of treatment, and any additional information that he considers relevant to his continued entitlement to benefits.

Information regarding the recipient's current condition is also obtained from his sources of medical treatment. If there is a conflict between the information provided by the beneficiary and that obtained from medical sources such as his physician, or between two sources of treatment, the agency may arrange for an examination by an independent consulting physician. Whenever the agency's tentative assessment of the beneficiary's condition differs from his own assessment, the beneficiary is informed that benefits may be terminated, provided a summary of the evidence upon which the proposed determination to terminate is based, and afforded an opportunity to review the medical reports and other evidence in his case file. He also may respond in writing and submit additional evidence.

The state agency then makes its final determination, which is reviewed by an examiner in the SSA Bureau of Disability Insurance. If, as is usually the case, the SSA accepts the agency determination, it notifies the recipient in writing, informing him of the reasons for the decision, and of his right to seek *de novo* reconsideration by the state agency. Upon acceptance by the SSA, benefits are terminated

---

[14]Work which "exists in the national economy" is in turn defined as "work which exists in significant numbers either in the region where such individual lives or in several regions of the country."

effective two months after the month in which medical recovery is found to have occurred.

If the recipient seeks reconsideration by the state agency and the determination is adverse, the SSA reviews the reconsideration determination and notifies the recipient of the decision. He then has a right to an evidentiary hearing before an SSA administrative law judge. The hearing is nonadversary, and the SSA is not represented by counsel. As at all prior and subsequent stages of the administrative process, however, the claimant may be represented by counsel or other spokesmen. If this hearing results in an adverse decision, the claimant is entitled to request discretionary review by the SSA Appeals Council, and finally may obtain judicial review.[21]

Should it be determined at any point after termination of benefits, that the claimant's disability extended beyond the date of cessation initially established, the worker is entitled to retroactive payments. If, on the other hand, a beneficiary receives any payments to which he is later determined not to be entitled, the statute authorizes the Secretary to attempt to recoup these funds in specified circumstances.

C

Despite the elaborate character of the administrative procedures provided by the Secretary, the courts below held them to be constitutionally inadequate, concluding that due process requires an evidentiary hearing prior to termination. In light of the private and governmental interests at stake here and the nature of the existing procedures, we think this was error.

Since a recipient whose benefits are terminated is awarded full retroactive relief if he ultimately prevails, his sole interest is in the uninterrupted receipt of this source of income pending final administrative decision on his claim. His potential injury is thus similar in nature to that of the welfare recipient in *Goldberg*.

* * *

Only in *Goldberg* has the Court held that due process requires an evidentiary hearing prior to a temporary deprivation. It was

---

[21]Unlike all prior levels of review, which are *de novo*, the district court is required to treat findings of fact as conclusive if supported by substantial evidence.

Goldberg contrasted

emphasized there that welfare assistance is given to persons on the very margin of subsistence:

> The crucial factor in this context--a factor not present in the case of . . . virtually anyone else whose governmental entitlements are ended--is that termination of aid pending resolution of a controversy over eligibility may deprive an *eligible* recipient of the very means by which to live while he waits.

Eligibility for disability benefits, in contrast, is not based upon financial need.[24] Indeed, it is wholly unrelated to the worker's income or support from many other sources, such as earnings of other family members, workmen's compensation awards, tort claims awards, savings, private insurance, public or private pensions, veterans' benefits, food stamps, public assistance, or the "many other important programs, both public and private, which contain provisions for disability payments affecting a substantial portion of the work force. . . ."

As *Goldberg* illustrates, the degree of potential deprivation that may be created by a particular decision is a factor to be considered in assessing the validity of any administrative decisionmaking process. The potential deprivation here is generally likely to be less than in *Goldberg*, although the degree of difference can be overstated. As the District Court emphasized, to remain eligible for benefits a recipient must be "unable to engage in substantial gainful activity." . . .[T]here is little possibility that the terminated recipient will be able to find even temporary employment to ameliorate the interim loss.

INJURY

As we recognized last Term in *Fusari v. Steinberg*, "the possible length of wrongful deprivation of . . . benefits [also] is an important factor in assessing the impact of official action on the private interests." The Secretary concedes that the delay between a request for a hearing before an administrative law judge and a decision on the claim is currently between 10 and 11 months. Since a terminated recipient must first obtain a reconsideration decision as a prerequisite to invoking his right to an evidentiary hearing, the delay

---

[24]The level of benefits is determined by the worker's average monthly earnings during the period prior to disability, his age, and other factors not directly related to financial need.

between the actual cutoff of benefits and final decision after a hearing exceeds one year.

In view of the torpidity of this administrative review process, and the typically modest resources of the family unit of the physically disabled worker, the hardship imposed upon the erroneously terminated disability recipient may be significant. Still, the disabled worker's need is likely to be less than that of a welfare recipient. In addition to the possibility of access to private resources, other forms of government assistance will become available where the termination of disability benefits places a worker or his family below the subsistence level. In view of these potential sources of temporary income, there is less reason here than in *Goldberg* to depart from the ordinary principle, established by our decisions, that something less than an evidentiary hearing is sufficient prior to adverse administrative action.

D

An additional factor to be considered here is the fairness and reliability of the existing pretermination procedures, and the probable value, if any, of additional procedural safeguards. Central to the evaluation of any administrative process is the nature of the relevant inquiry. In order to remain eligible for benefits the disabled worker must demonstrate by means of "medically acceptable clinical and laboratory diagnostic techniques," that he is unable "to engage in any substantial gainful activity by reason of any *medically determinable* physical or mental impairment. . . ." In short, a medical assessment of the worker's physical or mental condition is required. This is a more sharply focused and easily documented decision than the typical determination of welfare entitlement. In the latter case, a wide variety of information may be deemed relevant, and issues of witness credibility and veracity often are critical to the decisionmaking process. *Goldberg* noted that in such circumstances "written submissions are a wholly unsatisfactory basis for decision."

By contrast, the decision whether to discontinue disability benefits will turn, in most cases, upon "routine, standard, and unbiased medical reports by physician specialists," concerning a subject whom they have personally examined. In *Richardson* [*v. Perales*] the Court recognized the "reliability and probative worth of written medical reports," emphasizing that while there may be "professional disagreement with the medical conclusions" the "specter of questionable credibility and veracity is not present." To be sure, credibility and veracity may be a factor in the ultimate disability assessment in some cases. But procedural due process rules are shaped by the risk of error inherent in the truthfinding process as applied to the generality of cases, not the rare exceptions. The potential value of an evidentiary hearing, or even oral presentation to the decisionmaker, is substantially less in this context than in *Goldberg*.

The decision in *Goldberg* also was based on the Court's conclusion that written submissions were an inadequate substitute for oral presentation because they did not provide an effective means for the recipient to communicate his case to the decisionmaker. Written submissions were viewed as an unrealistic option, for most recipients lacked the "educational attainment necessary to write effectively" and could not afford professional assistance. In addition, such submissions would not provide the "flexibility of oral presentations" or "permit the recipient to mold his argument to the issues the decision maker appears to regard as important." In the context of the disability-benefits-entitlement assessment the administrative procedures under review here fully answer these objections.

The detailed questionnaire which the state agency periodically sends the recipient identifies with particularity the information relevant to the entitlement decision, and the recipient is invited to obtain assistance from the local SSA office in completing the questionnaire. More important, the information critical to the entitlement decision usually is derived from medical sources, such as the treating physician. Such sources are likely to be able to communicate more effectively through written documents than are welfare recipients or the lay witnesses supporting their cause. The conclusions of physicians often are supported by X-rays and the results of clinical or laboratory tests, information typically more amenable to written than to oral presentation.

A further safeguard against mistake is the policy of allowing the disability recipient's representative full access to all information relied upon by the state agency. In addition, prior to the cutoff of benefits the agency informs the recipient of its tentative assessment, the reasons therefor, and provides a summary of the evidence that it considers most relevant. Opportunity is then afforded the recipient to submit additional evidence or arguments, enabling him to challenge directly the accuracy of information in his file as well as the correctness of the agency's tentative conclusions. These procedures, again as contrasted with those before the Court in *Goldberg*, enable the recipient to "mold" his argument to respond to the precise issues which the decisionmaker regards as crucial.

Despite these carefully structured procedures, *amici* point to the significant reversal rate for appealed cases as clear evidence that the current process is inadequate. Depending upon the base selected and the line of analysis followed, the relevant reversal rates urged by the contending parties vary from a high of 58.6% for appealed reconsideration decisions to an overall reversal rate of only 3.3%. Bare statistics rarely provide a satisfactory measure of the fairness of a decisionmaking process. Their adequacy is especially suspect here since the administrative review system is operated on an open-file basis. A recipient may always submit new evidence, and such submissions may result in additional medical examinations. Such fresh examinations were held in approximately 30% to 40% of the appealed cases, in fiscal 1973, either at the reconsideration or evidentiary hearing stage of the administrative process. In this context, the value of reversal rate statistics as one means of evaluating the adequacy of the pretermination process is diminished. Thus, although we view such information as relevant, it is certainly not controlling in this case.

E

In striking the appropriate due process balance the final factor to be assessed is the public interest. This includes the administrative burden and other societal costs that would be associated with requiring, as a matter of constitutional right, an evidentiary hearing upon demand in all cases prior to the termination of disability benefits. The most visible burden would be the incremental cost resulting from the increased number of hearings and the expense of providing benefits to ineligible recipients pending decision. No one can predict the extent of the increase, but the fact that full benefits would continue until after such hearings would assure the exhaustion in most cases of this attractive option. Nor would the theoretical right of the Secretary to recover undeserved benefits result, as a practical matter, in any substantial offset to the added outlay of public funds. The parties submit widely varying estimates of the probable additional financial cost. We only need say that experience with the constitutionalizing of government procedures suggests that the ultimate additional cost in terms of money and administrative burden would not be insubstantial.

Financial cost alone is not a controlling weight in determining whether due process requires a particular procedural safeguard prior to some administrative decision. But the Government's interest, and hence that of the public, in conserving scarce fiscal and administrative resources is a factor that must be weighed. At some point the benefit of an additional safeguard to the individual affected by the administrative action and to society in terms of increased assurance that the action is just, may be outweighed by the cost. Significantly, the cost of protecting those whom the preliminary administrative process has identified as likely to be found undeserving may in the end come out of the pockets of the deserving since resources available for any particular program of social welfare are not unlimited.

But more is implicated in cases of this type than ad hoc weighing of fiscal and administrative burdens against the interests of a particular category of claimants. The ultimate balance involves a determination as to when, under our constitutional system, judicial-type procedures must be imposed upon administrative action to assure fairness. We reiterate the wise admonishment of Mr. Justice Frankfurter that differences in the origin and function of administrative agencies "preclude wholesale transplantation of the rules of procedure, trial, and review which have evolved from the history and experience of courts." The judicial model of an evidentiary hearing is neither a required, nor even the most effective, method of decisionmaking in all circumstances. The essence of due process is the requirement that "a person in jeopardy of serious loss [be given] notice of the case against him and opportunity to meet it." All that is necessary is that the procedures be tailored, in light of the decision to be made, to "the capacities and circumstances of those who are to be heard," to insure that they are given a meaningful opportunity to present their case. In assessing what process is due in this case, substantial weight must be given to the good-faith judgments of the individuals charged by Congress with the administration of social welfare programs that the procedures they have provided assure fair consideration of the entitlement claims of individuals. This is especially so where, as here, the prescribed procedures not only provide the claimant with an effective process for asserting his claim prior to any administrative action, but also assure a right to an evidentiary hearing, as well as to subsequent judicial review, before the denial of his claim becomes final.

We conclude that an evidentiary hearing is not required prior to the termination of disability benefits and that the present administrative procedures fully comport with due process.

The judgment of the Court of Appeals is

Reversed.

Justice BRENNAN, with whom Justice MARSHALL concurs, dissenting.

For the reasons stated in my dissenting opinion in *Richardson v. Wright*, I agree with the District Court and the Court of Appeals that, prior to termination of benefits, Eldridge must be afforded an evidentiary hearing of the type required for welfare beneficiaries under Title IV of the Social Security Act. I would add that the Court's consideration that a discontinuance of disability benefits may cause the recipient to suffer only a limited deprivation is no argument. It is speculative. Moreover, the very legislative determination to provide disability benefits, without any prerequisite determination of need in fact, presumes a need by the recipient which is not this Court's function to denigrate. Indeed, in the present case, it is indicated that because disability benefits were terminated there was a foreclosure upon the Eldridge home and the family's furniture was repossessed, forcing Eldridge, his wife, and their children to sleep in one bed. Finally, it is also no argument that a worker, who has been placed in the untenable position of having been denied disability benefits, may still seek other forms of public assistance.

Notes and Questions

1. *The Balancing Test.* The Court clarifies a three-part balancing test to evaluate the government's procedure, weighing: (1) the private interest affected, (2) the risk of an erroneous deprivation of such interest and the probable value of additional safeguards, and (3) the government's interests. Does the nature of this three-part inquiry for termination of disability benefits differ from the inquiry conducted in *Goldberg* for termination of welfare benefits?

2. *Private Interests.* The Court characterizes plaintiff Eldridge's interest as the "uninterrupted receipt" of disability benefits. This seems similar to plaintiff Kelly's interest in the uninterrupted receipt of welfare benefits. How does the Court distinguish their

interests? How do Justices Brennan and Marshall criticize the Court's reliance on these differences in their dissent?

3. *Risk of Error Under Existing Procedure and Probable Value of Additional Safeguards.* Do you agree that medical assessments are more reliable than welfare-need assessments, thus comparatively reducing the likelihood of error? Is the Court's attempt to discount the high reversal rates for appealed disability decisions convincing?

4. *Government and Public Interests.* The Court focuses on the administrative and fiscal burdens associated with requiring pre-termination hearings to disability benefit recipients. Are these the only government and public interests? Do the government and public have interests in continuous provisions of disability benefits to eligible recipients? Why doesn't the Court give weight to this part of the public interest?

5. Goldberg *as Baseline.* The *Mathews* Court uses the welfare recipients of *Goldberg* as its baseline for comparing the deprivation experienced by disability recipients. Is that comparison helpful and fair? Are any government benefits more essential than welfare?

6. *The Component Parts of the Balancing Test.* In *Brock v. Roadway Express, Inc.*, 481 U.S. 252 (1987), the Court discussed the due process balancing test with greater detail. Regarding the private interests at stake, the Court identified both the nature and the strength of the interest. Regarding the risk of erroneous deprivation, the Court identified the error that might occur, the likelihood of such error, the current procedures that protect against such error, the likelihood that current procedures would prevent error, the possible additional procedural safeguards, and the probable value of such safeguards. Finally, regarding the government's interests, the Court identified both the nature and strength of those interests. Future litigants might consider the need to clearly identify both the nature and degree of the recipient's and government's interests and the nature and likely effectiveness of both current and possible forms of procedure.

7. *Administrative Rights.* Consider whether the federal Administrative Procedure Act or a state's administrative procedure act creates procedural rights in beneficiaries of welfare programs. For example, would the relevant administrative procedure acts govern the processes states must afford to Temporary Assistance for Needy Families block grant beneficiaries?

Lucie E. White

SUBORDINATION, RHETORICAL SURVIVAL SKILLS, AND SUNDAY SHOES: NOTES ON THE HEARING OF MRS. G.

38 BUFFALO LAW REVIEW 1 (1990)

* * *

The Story[78]

Mrs. G. is thirty-five years old, Black, and on her own. She has five girls, ranging in age from four to fourteen. She has never told me anything about their fathers; all I know is that she isn't getting formal child support payments from anyone. She lives on an AFDC grant of just over three hundred dollars a month and a small monthly allotment of Food Stamps. She probably gets a little extra money from occasional jobs as a field hand or a maid, but she doesn't share this information with me and I don't ask. She has a very coveted unit of public housing, so she doesn't have to pay rent. She is taking an adult basic education class at the local community action center, which is in the same building as my own office. I often notice her in the classroom as I pass by.

The first thing that struck me about Mrs. G., when she finally came to my office for help one day, was the way she talked. She brought her two oldest daughters with her. She would get very excited when she spoke, breathing hard and waving her hands and straining, like she was searching for the right words to say what was on her mind. Her daughters would circle her, like two young mothers themselves, keeping the air calm as her hands swept through it. I haven't talked with them much, but they strike me as quite self-possessed for their years.

* * *

Mrs. G. and two daughters first appeared at our office one Friday morning at about ten, without an appointment. . . . She showed me a letter from the welfare office that said she had received an "overpayment" of AFDC benefits.

* * *

She told me that a few months before she had received a cash settlement for injuries she and her oldest daughter had suffered in a

[78]This story is based upon my work as a legal aid lawyer in North Carolina from 1982 to 1986. Certain details have been changed to avoid compromising client confidentiality.

minor car accident. After medical bills had been paid and her lawyer had taken his fees, her award came to $592. Before Mrs. G. cashed the insurance check, she took it to her AFDC worker to report it and ask if it was all right for her to spend it. . . . With a few exceptions, any "income" she reported would be subtracted, dollar for dollar, from her AFDC stipend. . . .

The worker . . . told Mrs. G. that the check would not affect her AFDC budget and she could spend it however she wanted.

Mrs. G. cashed her check that same afternoon and took her five girls on what she described to me as a "shopping trip." They bought Kotex, which they were always running short on at the end of the month. They also bought shoes, dresses for school, and some frozen food. Then she made two payments on her furniture bill. After a couple of wonderful days, the money was gone.

Two months passed. Mrs. G. received and spent two AFDC checks. Then she got the overpayment notice, asking her to repay to the county an amount equal to her insurance award.

* * *

I asked Mrs. G. if she could put together a list of all the things she had bought with the insurance money. If she still had any of the receipts, she should bring them to me. I would look at her case file at the welfare office and see her again in a couple of days.

The file had a note from the caseworker confirming that Mrs. G. had reported the insurance payment when she received it. The note also showed that the worker did not include the amount in calculating her stipend. The "overpayment" got flagged two months later when a supervisor, doing a random "quality control" check on her file, discovered the worker's note. Under AFDC law, the insurance award was considered a "lump sum payment."

* * *

[T]he insurance award did count as income for AFDC purposes under the state's regulations; indeed, the county should have cut Mrs. G. off of welfare entirely for almost two months on the theory that her family could live for that time off of the insurance award. . . . If the county didn't try to collect the sum from Mrs. G., it would be sanctioned for an administrative error.

I met again with Mrs. G. the following Friday. When I told her what I had pieced together from her file, she insisted that she had asked her worker's permission before spending the insurance money.

Then she seemed to get flustered and repeated what had become a familiar refrain. She didn't want to make any trouble. She hadn't meant to do anything wrong. I told her that it looked to me like it was the welfare office--and not her--who had done something wrong. I said I would try to get the county to drop the matter, but I thought we might have to go to a hearing, finally, to win.

Mrs. G. had been in court a few times to get child support and to defend against evictions, but she had never been to a welfare hearing. She knew that it was not a good idea to get involved in hearings, however, and she understood why. Fair hearings were a hassle and an embarrassment to the county. A hearing meant pulling an eligibility worker and several managers out of work for a few hours, which--given the chronic under-staffing of the welfare office--was more than a minor inconvenience. It also meant exposing the county's administrative problems to state-level scrutiny.

* * *

I could tell that Mrs. G. felt pressure from me to ask for a hearing, but she also seemed angry at the welfare office for asking her to pay for their mistake. . . . When she nervously agreed to file the request, I didn't second-guess her decision.

* * *

Mrs. G. brought all five of her girls to my office to prepare for the hearing. . . . I told her that I saw two stories we could tell. The first was the story she had told me. It was the "estoppel" story, the story of the wrong advice she got from her worker about spending the insurance check. The second story was one that I had come up with from reading the law. The state had laid the groundwork for this story when it opted for the "life necessities" waiver permitted by federal regulations. If a client could show that she had spent the sum to avert a crisis situation, then it would be considered "unavailable" as income, and her AFDC benefits would not be suspended. I didn't like this second story very much, and I wasn't sure that Mrs. G. would want to go along with it. How could I ask her to distinguish "life necessities" from mere luxuries, when she was keeping five children alive on three hundred dollars a month, and when she was given no voice in the calculus that had determined her "needs."

Yet I felt that the necessities story might work at the hearing, while "estoppel" would unite the county and state against us. According to legal aid's welfare specialist in the state capital, state officials didn't like the lump sum rule. It made more paper work for the counties. And, by knocking families off the federally financed AFDC program, the rule increased the pressure on state and county-funded relief programs. But the only way the state could get around the rule without being subject to federal sanctions was through the necessities exception. Behind the scenes, state officials were saying to our welfare specialist that they intended to interpret the exception broadly. In addition to this inside information that state officials would prefer the necessities tale, I knew from experience that they would feel comfortable with the role that story gave to Mrs. G. It would place her on her knees, asking for pity as she described how hard she was struggling to make ends meet.

The estoppel story would be entirely different. In it, Mrs. G. would be pointing a finger, turning the county itself into the object of scrutiny. She would accuse welfare officials of wrong, and claim that they had caused her injury. She would demand that the county bend its own rules, absorb the overpayment out of its own funds, and run the risk of sanction from the state for its error.

* * *

What story should we tell at the hearing, I wondered out loud.

* * *

Mrs. G. said she still felt like she'd been treated unfairly but--in the next breath--"I didn't mean to do anything wrong." Why couldn't we tell both stories?

* * *

I asked for the list she had promised to make of all the things she bought with the insurance money. Kotex, I thought, would speak for itself, but why, I asked, had she needed to get the girls new shoes? She explained that the girls' old shoes were pretty much torn up, so bad that the other kids would make fun of them at school. Could she bring in the old shoes? She said she could.

We rehearsed her testimony, first about her conversation with her worker regarding the insurance award and then about the Kotex and the shoes. Maybe the hearing wouldn't be too bad for Mrs. G., especially if I could help her see it all as strategy, rather than the kind of talking she could do with people she could trust.

* * *

The hearing itself was in a small conference room at the welfare office. Mrs. G. arrived with her two oldest daughters and five boxes of shoes.

* * *

We took our seats across the table from the AFDC director. The hearing officer set up a portable tape recorder and got out his bible. Mrs. G.'s AFDC worker, an African American woman about her age, entered through a side door and took a seat next to her boss. The hearing officer turned on the tape recorder, read his obligatory opening remarks, and asked all the witnesses to rise and repeat before god that they intended to tell the truth. Mrs. G. and her worker complied.

The officer then turned the matter over to me. I gave a brief account of the background events, and then began to question Mrs. G. First I asked her about the insurance proceeds. She explained how she had received an insurance check of about six hundred dollars following a car accident in which she and her oldest daughter had been slightly injured. She said that the insurance company had already paid the medical bills and the lawyer; the last six hundred dollars was for her and her daughter to spend however she wanted. I asked her if she had shown the check to her AFDC worker before she cashed it. She stammered. I repeated the question. She said she may have taken the check to the welfare office before she cashed it, but she couldn't remember for sure. She didn't know if she had gotten a chance to talk to anyone about it. Her worker was always real busy.

Armed with the worker's own sketchy notation of the conversation in the case file, I began to cross-examine my client, coaxing her memory about the event we had discussed so many times before. I asked if she remembered her worker telling her anything about how she could spend the money. Mrs. G. seemed to be getting more uncomfortable. It was quite a predicament for her, after all. If she "remembered" what her worker had told her, would her story expose mismanagement in the welfare office, or merely scapegoat another Black woman, who was not too much better off than herself?

When she repeated that she couldn't remember, I decided to leave the estoppel story for the moment. Maybe I could think of a way to return to it later. I moved on to the life necessities issue. I asked Mrs. G. to recount, as best she could, exactly how she had spent the insurance money. She showed me the receipts she had kept for the furniture payments and I put them into evidence. She explained that she was buying a couple of big mattresses for the kids and a new kitchen table. She said she had also bought some food--some frozen meat and several boxes of Kotex for all the girls. The others in the room shifted uneasily in their chairs. Then she said she had also bought her daughters some clothes and some shoes. She had the cash register receipt for the purchase.

Choosing my words carefully, I asked why she had needed to buy the new shoes. She looked at me for a moment with an expression that I couldn't read. Then she stated, quite emphatically, that they were Sunday shoes that she had bought with the money. The girls already had everyday shoes to wear to school, but she had wanted them to have nice shoes for church too. She said no more than two or three sentences, but her voice sounded different--stronger, more composed--than I had known from her before. When she finished speaking the room was silent, except for the incessant hum of the tape machine on the table and the fluorescent lights overhead. In that moment, I felt the boundaries of our "conspiracy" shift. Suddenly I was on the outside, with the folks on the other side of the table, the welfare director and the hearing officer. The only person I could not locate in this new alignment was Mrs. G.'s welfare worker.

I didn't ask Mrs. G. to pull out the children's old shoes, as we'd rehearsed. Nor did I make my "life necessities" argument. My lawyer's language couldn't add anything to what she had said. They would have to figure out for themselves why buying Sunday shoes for her children--and saying it--was indeed a "life necessity" for this woman. After the hearing, Mrs. G. seemed elated. She asked me how she had done at the hearing and I told her that I thought she was great. I warned her, though, that we could never be sure, in this game, who was winning, or even what side anyone was on.

We lost the hearing and immediately petitioned for review by the chief hearing officer. I wasn't sure of the theory we'd argue, but I wanted to keep the case open until I figured out what we could do.

Three days after the appeal was filed, the county welfare director called me unexpectedly, to tell me that the county had decided to withdraw its overpayment claim against Mrs. G. He explained that on a careful review of its own records, the county had decided that it wouldn't be "fair" to make Mrs. G. pay the money back. I said I was relieved to hear that they had decided, finally, to come to a sensible result in the case. I was sorry they hadn't done so earlier. I then said something about how confusing the lump sum rule was, and how Mrs. G.'s worker had checked with her supervisor before telling Mrs. G. it was all right to spend the insurance money. I said I was sure that the screw up was not anyone's fault. He mumbled a bureaucratic pleasantry and we hung up.

When I told Mrs. G. that she had won, she said she had just wanted to "do the right thing," and that she hoped they understood that she'd never meant to do anything wrong. I repeated that they were the ones who had made the mistake. Though I wasn't sure exactly what was going on inside the welfare office, at least this crisis was over.

* * *

Mrs. G. had a hearing in which all of the rituals of due process were scrupulously observed. Yet she did not find her voice welcomed at that hearing. A complex pattern of social, economic, and cultural forces underwrote the procedural formalities, repressing and devaluing her voice.

* * *

Intimidation: The Violence of Caste

Perhaps Mrs. G.'s strongest feelings, as she approached the hearing, were fear and intimidation. The people she had to face at the hearing were the same ones who would decide if she would get welfare and Food Stamps in the future. From her standpoint, they were also the ones who could take her children away, if they wanted to, or make it hard for her to stay in her apartment or find the occasional jobs she needed to make ends meet.

The ground of her fear was very deep. It reflected the long history of violence toward her people in that county and the daily reminders that the history was not over. But her fear also responded to her present-day relationship to the welfare office. First of all, a convergence of factors--a lack of child care, vocational training, and, most importantly safe, stable, decent-paying jobs--made her dependent on the county, the welfare office, and the housing authority, to survive. And she knew that the rules of welfare would give the county plenty of ways to make her life hard if she became known as a troublemaker.

Thus, her fear reflected the racial caste system that still structured social relations in the community, and the more particular welfare doctrines that gave the dominant caste, the white power structure--she called it simply "the Man"--a potent modern-day weapon for keeping her quiet. . . . Mrs. G.'s story suggests that, in spite of the sweeping changes that the Civil Rights era brought in social norms and legal structures, this system has not changed much for people like her in the half-century between the 1930s and the 1980s.

Her fear also reflected her sense that her welfare "entitlements" offered her no real security. . . . Initially, welfare advocates supported the formalization of eligibility rules as a way to extend benefits to Blacks and other groups who were excluded in the earlier regime of unfettered local discretion. But by the early 1980s, the formalization of eligibility rules was serving a very different political agenda. In the 1980s legalistic eligibility requirements were imposed to reduce welfare expenditures. In addition to providing new reasons for denying welfare to otherwise eligible clients, new procedural requirements made welfare programs too complex and burdensome for many poor people to negotiate.

In Mrs. G.'s experience, these highly formalized rules have a more important function than the wholesale exclusion of people from the rolls. They also keep people in fear. First of all, "churning," the occasional, arbitrary termination of large numbers of people for technical reasons, has the effect of keeping all recipients uncertain about whether their next check will come. And the technical rules, although they appear very rigid, actually conceal countless enclaves of discretion, hidden places for harassing clients who get out of line, and obscuring the human agency behind that harassment. Mrs. G. believed that "going to legal aid" or "asking for a hearing" were the best ways to make sure that this discretion would be used against her.

Thus, Mrs. G.'s fear of confronting the welfare office was engendered by concrete legal and social arrangements. These structures subverted the formal protections of the hearing process and posed a barrier to her speech. Had Mrs. G. not found her way to a lawyer, that barrier might have excluded her from the hearing process altogether: it would certainly have been safer for her simply to stay away. But even *with* a lawyer to protect her, Mrs. G.'s deep fear of retaliation was not completely put to rest. She did not need to be a legal scholar to understand that the law was largely impotent--or indifferent--to the subtle texture of retaliation in the welfare office. Her only real protection lay in the self-negating verbal strategies that she had learned so well--speaking female, crafting her words like a mirror to reflect what she sensed that the Other--"the Man"--wanted her to say.

Humiliation: The Stigma of Welfare Fraud

A second local force, the imagery of welfare fraud, posed a further barrier to Mrs. G.'s speaking frankly and with dignity at the hearing. While her social and economic marginality made her reluctant to speak at all, the mythology of welfare fraud worked to undermine her confidence and credibility when she did speak. This imagery predisposed the hearing officer to distrust Mrs. G. and led her to second-guess the integrity of her own actions. Furthermore, overbroad measures to control fraud deterred her from voicing any challenge to welfare officials.

"Welfare fraud" has long been one of the dominant themes expressing the ambivalence, indeed aversion, within modern political culture, to welfare. "Fraud" connotes an idea--a negative image of the "typical welfare recipient." At the same time, it justifies an elaborate regime for monitoring eligibility determinations and restricting the welfare rolls. In periods of constriction of welfare benefits, as in the last decade, the media has been flooded with stories about the extent of the fraud problem. At the same time the government has enacted overextensive programs of fraud control.

Given the inadequacy of AFDC benefit levels and the dollar for dollar reduction of benefits when a recipient reports work, many welfare recipients must add other income to their welfare stipends when they can. Furthermore, program rules are so complex and terminations so frequent and so arbitrary, that few recipients know how much they should be receiving, or why. In these circumstances, recipients typically feel themselves vulnerable to fraud charges. A finding of fraud means suspension from some benefit programs and a very real threat of jail. Thus "fraud" is a concrete image that focuses Mrs. G.'s diffuse fear of the welfare office. . . .

Furthermore, the obsession with fraud in the media and in the eligibility process itself, places a stigma on all welfare recipients. It leads some to forego welfare altogether. And the popular mythology about welfare recipients--embodied in the Black, jewel-bedecked, Cadillac-driving welfare queen--conveys this negative stereotype to the broader public. This image--superficially moralistic, but fundamentally racist and sexist--encourages others to disassociate themselves from the political interests of welfare recipients.

For a woman like Mrs. G., who does not have the option to forego welfare, fraud control becomes a constant message that she is not a person worthy of trust. Rather, fraud imagery suggests that she will try at every moment to cheat the system, to lie. This image resonates with the ancient stereotype of Woman as liar, as well as other negative images of poor women of color. With these deeply negative images evoked, she begins to doubt her own decisions and her own words. Thus, the fraud policy--so defensible on its face--is one of the structures that exacts silence, or self-defeating speech, from Mrs. G.--in the welfare office and at the hearing. When she is told so clearly, so incessantly, that she is expected to lie, her way of affirming her own dignity is to assume her own guilt, explaining that "I didn't *mean* to do anything wrong."

Objectification: The Logic of the Client State

A third local force that obstructed Mrs. G.'s full participation in the hearing is the bureaucratic structure of social welfare policy, and indeed, of the legal and political institutions that create it. This force entered the hearing through the questions that the advocate put to Mrs. G. The lawyer taught Mrs. G. to conform her words to the elements of the "lump sum" rule, the "life necessities" exception, and estoppel. Unlike the other two forces--which sought to silence Mrs. G. entirely or to undermine the value of her speech--this third force dictated the shape that Mrs. G. had to give to her story--its basic plot and its motivating themes--if she was to be heard.

Mrs. G.'s persistent feeling about being on welfare was, in her words, that she was "boxed in." None of the formal rules of welfare set up boundaries to protect her against churning or retaliation. Yet those rules confined her: they reduced her need to a mathematical formula for assistance. In all of her dealings with the welfare system --whether she was filling out forms at the welfare office, answering questions at a hearing, or casting her vote for those with the power to write the rules--Mrs. G. felt boxed in.

This bureaucratization of welfare was the third force that silenced Mrs. G. As public regulation of social life has expanded in complex societies, more and more activities have been made compatible with bureaucratic logic. That is, modes of acting--

intuitions and customs--have been "legalized," or reformulated as systems of explicit rules, and values have been translated into a uniform currency--or "monetized." Bureaucracy has been a means for centralized resource allocation and uniform policy implementation across large, diverse populations. But these apparent "efficiencies" of bureaucracy carry a significant hidden cost: many social critics argue that the process of bureaucratization has gotten "out of control" in the regulatory state. Although they use different language, these critics share the sense that the expanding bureaucratization of modern life threatens to destroy the face to face networks and practices that we rely on, as human actors, to make sense of our social experience. Some of these critics make the stronger argument that in capitalist or patriarchal societies bureaucracy becomes a specific vehicle of gender and class subordination.

Mrs. G. and her children are among the most vulnerable to this "pathology" of over-bureaucratization. Because they are stranded by the economy, they must depend directly on the state for their subsistence. To manage the task of maintaining them, the welfare bureaucracy constitutes the terms of their lives in a form, a currency, that it can process. It equates Mrs. G.'s need with the sum of the stipends the state is willing to pay her. It then contains her anger and her pain by locating those feelings as symptoms within a de-politicized "self" that psychiatric technologies are developed to manage.

Mrs. G. has no role in negotiating the meaning of either her psychiatrically-defined pathologies or her bureaucratically-constructed "needs." She is excluded on principle from the therapeutic discourse: it is the experts who had the prerogative to say how her psyche and culture are defective. Her status in the conversation about welfare policy is more problematic, however. According to the theory of representative democracy, she *should* feel herself a participant in the process that creates welfare policy. When she confronts the "lump sum rule" at her hearing, she should know that her vote gave her at least a *virtual* hand in creating that rule. Yet that "knowledge" is not part of her experience.

First of all, racism has kept her community from voting for much of its history. But Mrs. G.'s exclusion from the formulation of welfare policy has a deeper source as well. The public discussion of welfare--even among those who *have* access to the debate--has itself been framed by a bureaucratic logic. Its broad outlines reinforce deeply rooted moral judgments about the poor, but its details are left to experts--economists and managers--to design. The discourse has become one of costs and incentives, of crisis containment and systems management, rather than a search among citizens for the social meanings of their interdependent needs. In this discourse, welfare is defined, at once, as a moral stigma and a technical problem, rather than an ethical and political challenge to the entire community. In this discussion, Mrs. G.--the primary *target* of welfare policy--is not regarded as a speaking being. The talk she might do--plain, angry, personal, . . . uncertain--is not accepted as sensible speech. Rather, she occupies the familiar female position. She is the Object who is shaped by those with the authority to speak, to reflect the internal logic of their own systems of power.

Feminist scholars are beginning to expose the concrete ways that a welfare policy that is generated in this bureaucratized discussion has reflected and sustained women's subordination. Mothers' pensions, and their federalization in the Social Security Act, gave some poor women--generally from elite social groups--a small measure of economic power to escape patriarchal households if they so chose. Yet at the same time the Social Security Act systematically reinforced the male-headed nuclear family. All of the New Deal welfare programs were infused with incentives to encourage this family pattern at the expense of egalitarian or woman-centered alternatives. Furthermore, the AFDC program was unique among New Deal welfare programs in requiring claimants to open up their sexual lives to the scrutiny and control of welfare workers. In order to participate in AFDC, Mrs. G. had no choice but to conform her life to the conditions the program imposed.

At the fair hearing, it was Mrs. G.'s *voice*, rather than her behavior, which was compelled to assent to the bureaucratized--and arguably also gendered--logic of welfare. The law of evidence--doctrines of relevancy and materiality--commanded her to keep her speech within the categories that the legislative/administrative process had generated. Even though the technicalities of evidence law did not apply to her case, the hearing officer would only attend to the narrow issues that the AFDC regulations charged him to decide. Was Mrs. G.'s insurance award covered under the "lump sum" rule? Did Mrs. G.'s expenditures meet the administrative criteria of "life necessities"? Were the features of estoppel present in the case, and should the doctrine apply? Discrete responses to those questions--that was the measure of "participation" that this hearing gave to Mrs. G. She best not "fight the questions" if she wanted her voice to be heard at all. Rather, she had to speak her need as an accounting of how she had spent a few hundred dollars. Within these constraints, her speech might be worth that sum if she won; it would have no other consequence.

The Route Taken: Evasive Maneuvers or a Woman's Voice?

If we measure Mrs. G.'s hearing against the norms of procedural formality, it appears to conform. The hearing appears to invite Mrs. G. to speak on equal terms with all other persons. Yet within the local landscape of her hearing, Mrs. G.'s voice is constrained by forces that procedural doctrine will neither acknowledge nor oppose. Each of these forces attaches a specific social cost to her gender and race identity. The caste system implements race and gender ideology in social arrangements. The "fraud issue" revives misogynist and racist stereotypes that had been forced, at least partly, underground by the social movements of the 1960s and 1970s. And the welfare system responds to gender and race-based injustice in the economy by constructing the poor as Woman--as an object of social control. Given the power amassed behind these forces, we might predict that they should win the contest with Mrs. G. for her voice.

Yet to detect these forces, we have read the story through a structuralist lens, which shows only the stark dichotomy of subordination and social control. It is ironic that this lens, which works so well to expose the contours of Mrs. G.'s silence, also leaves her--as a woman actively negotiating the terrain in which she found herself--entirely out of focus. If we re-center our reading on Mrs. G., as a woman shaping events, unpredictably, to realize her own meanings, we can no longer say with certainty what the outcome will be. We cannot tell who prevailed at the hearing, or where the power momentarily came to rest. Rather, what we see is a sequence of surprising moves, a series of questions . . . . Why did she depart from the script she had rehearsed for the hearing, to remain silent before her own worker, and to speak about Sunday shoes? And why did the county finally abandon its claim to cut her stipend?

* * *

Why Did Mrs. G. Depart from her Script?

The lawyer had scripted Mrs. G. as a victim. That was the only strategy for the hearing that the lawyer, within the constraints of her own social position, could imagine for Mrs. G. She had warned her client to play the victim if she wanted to win. Mrs. G. learned her lines. She came to the hearing well-rehearsed in the lawyer's strategy. But in the hearing, she did not play. When she was cued to perform, without any signal to her lawyer, she abandoned their script.

* * *

For a moment she stepped out of the role of the supplicant. She ignored the doctrinal pigeonholes that would fragment her voice. She put aside all that the lawyer told her the audience wanted to hear. . . . When asked about "life necessities," she explained that she had used her money to meet *her own* needs. She had bought her children Sunday shoes.

* * *

When Mrs. G. talked about Sunday shoes, she was talking about a life necessity. For subordinated communities, physical necessities do not meet the minimum requirements for a human life. Rather, subordinated groups must create cultural practices through which they can elaborate an autonomous, oppositional consciousness. Without shared rituals for sustaining their survival and motivating their resistance, subordinated groups run the risk of total domination--of losing the *will* to use their human powers to subvert their oppressor's control over them. Religion, spirituality, the social institution of the Black Church, has been one such self-affirming cultural practice for the communities of African-American slaves, and remains central to the expression of Black identity and group consciousness today. By naming Sunday shoes as a life necessity, Mrs. G. was speaking to the importance of this cultural practice in her life, a truth that the system's categories did not comprehend.

At the same time that Mrs. G.'s statement affirmed the church, it condemned the welfare system. By rejecting the welfare's definition of life necessities, she asserted her need to have a say about *the criteria* for identifying her needs. Her statement was a demand for meaningful participation in the political conversations in which her needs are contested and defined. In the present welfare system, poor women--the objects of welfare--are structurally excluded from those conversations. When Mrs. G. insisted on her need to say for herself what her "life necessities" might be, she expanded, for a moment, the accepted boundaries of those conversations.

Mrs. G.'s statement also spoke to a third dimension of her "life necessity." When Mrs. G. talked about buying Sunday shoes, she defied the rules of legal rhetoric--the rule of relevancy, the rule against "rambling," the unwritten rule that told her to speak like a victim if she wanted to win. Had Mrs. G. spoken the language that was proper for her in the setting, her relevant, logical, submissive, hyper-correct responses to their questions might have been comprehended. But, by dutifully speaking the language of an institution from which subordinated groups have historically been excluded and in which Mrs. G. felt herself to have no stake, her voice would have repeated, and legitimated, the very social and cultural patterns and priorities that kept her down. Had she been a *respectful* participant in the legal ritual, Mrs. G. would have articulated someone else's need, or pleasure, rather than her own.

Mrs. G. did not boycott the hearing altogether. Rather, in her moment of misbehavior, she may have been standing her ground within it. Although she appeared, at first, to be deferring to the system's categories and rules, when she finally spoke, she animated those categories with her own experience. She stretched the category of "life necessity" to express her own values, and turned it around to critique the welfare's systemic disregard of her own point of view. By talking about Sunday shoes, Mrs. G. claimed, for one fragile moment, what was perhaps her most basic "life necessity." She claimed a position of equality in the speech community--an equal power to take part in the *making* of language, the making of shared categories, norms, and institutions--as she spoke through that language about her needs.

When Mrs. G. claimed this power, she affirmed the feminist insight that the dominant languages do *not* construct a closed system, from which there can be no escape. Although dominant groups may control the *social institutions* that regulate these languages, those groups cannot control the *capacity* of subordinated peoples to speak. Thus, women have evaded complete domination through their *practice* of speaking, like Mrs. G. spoke at her hearing, from their own intuitions and their own experience. Feminist writers have drawn three figures--play, archaeology, and poetry--to describe this emancipatory language practice.

When Mrs. G. construed "life necessities" to include Sunday shoes, she turned the hearing into a place where she could talk, on a par with the experts, about her "needs." For a moment she defied the rigid official meaning of necessity, and refused to leave nameless the values and passions that gave sense to her life. Adrienne Rich describes the process:

> For many women, the commonest words are having to be sifted through, rejected, laid aside for a long time, or turned to the light for new colors and flashes of meaning: power, love, control, violence, political, personal, private, friendship, community, sexual, work, pain, pleasure, self, integrity. . . . When we become acutely, disturbingly aware of the language we are using and that is using us, we begin to grasp a material resource that women have never before collectively attempted to repossess. . . .[161]

Mrs. G. might want to add "participation" and "need" to the poet's list.

* * *

The story tells us that the hearing officer ruled against Mrs. G., and then the county welfare department decided to drop the case, restoring her full stipend. But the text does not say how the men across the table experienced the hearing, or why the county eventually gave in. Did Mrs. G.'s paradoxical "strategy" disarm her audience? Did she draw a response from her audience that was different--more compelling--than the pity that her lawyer had wanted to play upon? Did her presentation of herself as an independent, church-going woman, who would exercise her own judgment, and was willing to say what she needed--did these qualities make the men fear her, respect her, regard her for a moment as a person, rather than a case? Did they feel a moment of anger--about the ultimately powerless roles that they were assigned to play in the bureaucracy that regulated all of their lives? Were these men moved, by the hearing, to snatch her case from the computer and subject it to their own human judgment?

* * *

[161]Adrienne Rich, *Power and Danger: Works of a Common Woman*, in ON LIES, SECRETS, SILENCE 247 (1977).

We do not know why the county decided to drop Mrs. G.'s case. What we do know, however, is that after the hearing Mrs. G. remained a Black, single mother on welfare--poor, dependent, despised. Mrs. G.'s unruly participation at her hearing was itself political action. Yet it was an act that did little to change the harsh landscape which constricts Mrs. G. from more sustained and more effective political participation. Substantial change in that landscape will come only as such fragile moments of dignity are supported and validated by the law.

* * *

Notes and Questions

1. *The Hearing.* Do you think Mrs. G.'s hearing furthered the *Goldberg* Court's goal of fostering her dignity and well-being? Did Mrs. G. sabotage both her estoppel and life necessities stories? Did the formalities of the hearing silence or empower Mrs. G.?

2. *The Explanations.* Professor White suggests that the hierarchy of courts, the ideology of welfare fraud, and the logic of bureaucracy each played a role in silencing Mrs. G. Do you agree?

3. *The Alternatives.* What would have improved Mrs. G.'s empowerment? Would less formality, such as an informal discussion between Mrs. G. and her caseworker, correct the silencing? What procedural mechanisms would have served Mrs. G.'s interests? Are some substantive problems beyond the reach of procedure?

4. *Theoretics of Practice.* Recall the discussion in Chapter 4 about theoretics of practice. Should Mrs. G.'s lawyer have handled her representation differently?

2. Eviction

LINDSEY v. NORMET

405 U.S. 56 (1972)

Justice WHITE delivered the opinion of the Court.

This case presents the question of whether Oregon's judicial procedure for eviction of tenants after nonpayment of rent violates either the Equal Protection Clause or the Due Process Clause of the Fourteenth Amendment.

The material facts were stipulated. Appellants were the month-to-month tenants of appellee Normet and paid $100 a month for the use of a single-family residence in Portland, Oregon. On November 10, 1969, the City Bureau of Buildings declared the dwelling unfit for habitation due to substandard conditions on the premises. Appellants requested appellee to make certain repairs which, with one minor exception, appellee refused to do. Appellants, who had paid the November rent, refused to pay the December rent until the requested improvements had been made. Appellee's attorney wrote a letter on December 15 threatening to "get a Court Order out on this matter" unless the accrued rent was immediately paid.

On January 7, 1970, however, before statutory eviction procedures were begun in the Oregon courts, appellants filed suit in federal district court under 42 U.S.C. § 1983 seeking a declaratory judgment that the Oregon Forcible Entry and Wrongful Detainer (hereinafter sometimes FED) Statute was unconstitutional on its face, and an injunction against its continued enforcement. A three-judge court was convened, a temporary restraining order was issued against the enforcement of the FED Statute, and appellants were ordered to make their rent payments into an escrow account during the pendency of the District Court proceeding. A lengthy stipulation of facts was agreed upon, a number of exhibits and depositions were submitted, and the District Court then granted appellee's motion to dismiss the complaint, after concluding that the statute was not unconstitutional under either the Due Process Clause or the Equal Protection Clause of the Fourteenth Amendment.

* * *

I

The Oregon Forcible Entry and Wrongful Detainer Statute establishes a procedure intended to insure that any entry upon real property "shall be made in a peaceable manner and without force." A landlord may bring an action for possession whenever the tenant has failed to pay rent within 10 days of its due date, when the tenant is holding contrary to some other covenant in a lease, and whenever the landlord has terminated the rental arrangement by proper notice and the tenant remains in possession after the expiration date specified in the notice. Service of the complaint on the tenant must be not less than two nor more than four days before the trial date; a tenant may obtain a two-day continuance, but grant of a longer continuance is conditioned on a tenant's posting security for the payment of any rent that may accrue, if the plaintiff ultimately prevails, during the period of the continuance. The suit may be tried to either a judge or a jury, and the only issue is whether the allegations of the complaint are true. The only award that a plaintiff may recover is restitution of possession. A defendant who loses such a suit may appeal only if he obtains two sureties who will provide security for the payment to the plaintiff, if the defendant ultimately loses on appeal, of twice the rental value of the property from the time of commencement of the action to final judgment.

Appellants' principal attacks are leveled at three characteristics of the Oregon FED Statute: the requirement of a trial no later than six days after service of the complaint unless security for accruing rent is provided; the provisions . . . which, either on their face or as construed, are said to limit the triable issues in an FED suit to the tenant's default and to preclude consideration of defenses based on the landlord's breach of a duty to maintain the premises; and the requirement of posting bond on appeal from an adverse decision in twice the amount of the rent expected to accrue pending appellate decision. These provisions are asserted to violate both the Equal Protection and Due Process Clauses of the Fourteenth Amendment. Except for the appeal bond requirement, we reject these claims.

II

We are unable to conclude that either the early-trial provision or the limitation on litigable issues is invalid on its face under the Due Process Clause of the Fourteenth Amendment. In those recurring cases where the tenant fails to pay rent or holds over after expiration of his tenancy and the issue in the ensuing litigation is simply whether he has paid or held over, we cannot declare that the Oregon statute allows an unduly short time for trial preparation. Tenants would appear to have as much access to relevant facts as their landlord, and they can be expected to know the terms of their lease, whether they have paid their rent, whether they are in possession of the premises, and whether they have received a proper notice to quit, if one is necessary. Particularly where, as here, rent has admittedly been deliberately withheld and demand for payment made, claims of prejudice from an early trial date are unpersuasive. The provision for continuance of the action if the tenant posts security for accruing rent means that in cases where tenant defendants, unlike appellants, deny nonpayment of rent and may require more time to prepare for litigation, they will not be forced to trial if they provide for rent payments in the interim. A requirement that the tenant pay or provide for the payment of rent during the continuance of the action is hardly irrational or oppressive. It is customary to pay rent in advance, and the simplicity of the issues in the typical FED action will usually not require extended trial preparation and litigation, thus making the posting of a large security deposit unnecessary. Of course, it is possible for this provision to be applied so as to deprive a tenant of a proper hearing in specific situations, but there is no such showing made here, and possible infirmity in other situations does not render it invalid on its face.

Nor does Oregon deny due process of law by restricting the issues in FED actions to whether the tenant has paid rent and honored the covenants he has assumed, issues that may be fairly and fully litigated under the Oregon procedure. The tenant is barred from raising claims in the FED action that the landlord has failed to maintain the premises, but the landlord is also barred from claiming back rent or asserting other claims against the tenant. The tenant is not foreclosed from instituting his own action against the landlord and litigating his right to damages or other relief in that action.

* * *

Underlying appellants' claim is the assumption that they are denied due process of law unless Oregon recognizes the failure of the landlord to maintain the premises as an operative defense to the possessory FED action and as an adequate excuse for nonpayment of rent. The Constitution has not federalized the substantive law of landlord-tenant relations, however, and we see nothing to forbid Oregon from treating the undertakings of the tenant and those of the landlord as independent rather than dependent covenants.

* * *

Justice DOUGLAS, dissenting in part.

* * *

Modern man's place of retreat for quiet and solace is the home. Whether rented or owned, it is his sanctuary. Being uprooted and put into the street is a traumatic experience. Legislatures can, of course, protect property interests of landlords. But when they weight the scales as heavily as does Oregon for the landlord and against the fundamental interest of the tenant they must be backed by some "compelling . . . interest." No such "compelling . . . interest" underlies this statutory scheme.

* * *

Oregon gives the tenant "not less than two or more than four days" after service of summons to go to trial. If service is on a Friday, trial could be on the following Monday. There can be no continuance for more than two days "unless the defendant . . . gives an undertaking . . . with good and sufficient security" covering the rent which may accrue during the trial.

For slum tenants--not to mention the middle class--this kind of summary procedure usually will mean in actuality no opportunity to be heard. Finding a lawyer in two days, acquainting him with the facts, and getting necessary witnesses make the theoretical opportunity to be heard and interpose a defense a promise of empty words. . . .

* * *

But where the right is so fundamental as the tenant's claim to his home, the requirements of due process should be more embracing. In the setting of modern urban life, the home, even though it be in the slums, is where man's roots are. To put him into the street when the slum landlord, not the slum tenant, is the real culprit deprives the tenant of a fundamental right without any real opportunity to defend. Then he loses the essence of the controversy, being given only empty promises that somehow, somewhere, someone may allow him to litigate the basic question in the case.

Notes and Questions

1. *Notice.* Due process requires notice and an opportunity to be heard at a meaningful time. The Oregon eviction statute provided two to four days notice of the lawsuit before the trial date, with the possibility of only a two-day continuance unless the tenant posts security for the accruing rent. Is this length of time sufficient for a tenant to seek counsel and/or prepare her case?

2. *Opportunity to be Heard.* Due process also requires an opportunity to be heard in a meaningful manner. The Oregon eviction statutes precluded tenants from raising defenses based on the property owner's breaches of obligations to maintain the premises. The Court allowed Oregon to treat the tenants' and landlords obligations as

independent. How do you think this compares to other contracts? For example, would due process allow government to limit the issues in a suit by a seller to whether a buyer paid the agreed price, requiring the buyer to pay first and then sue separately for defects in the goods purchased? Would such procedures provide a hearing at a meaningful time and in a meaningful manner?

On what factors did the Court rely to identify eviction procedures as unique? Does the greater economic power of a landlord justify judicial deference to those interests? Do the courts have a duty to check the government's involvement in relationships characterized by a power imbalance?

Barbara Bezdek

SILENCE IN THE COURT: PARTICIPATION AND SUBORDINATION OF POOR TENANTS' VOICES IN LEGAL PROCESS

20 HOFSTRA LAW REVIEW 533 (1992)

[In her empirical study of Baltimore's rent court, Professor Barbara Bezdek revealed some remarkable statistics. She found that, of the tenants appearing in court, 71% were women and 87% were African-American. As the following excerpt describes, few of the tenants were successful in advancing claims about the deplorable condition of their housing.]

Powerlessness is not possessed by the individual;
it is a collective phenomenon.[1]

Spend a morning on the hard benches of Baltimore's rent court and one readily concludes that the forum fails to provide redress for the claims of tenants with anything like the regard it accords the formal rights of landlords, which are delivered with smooth and speedy dispatch. Despite the enactment of tenant-protective legislation in the mid-1970s, the rent court operates in virtually the same manner as it did nearly twenty years ago. Today few tenants raise the available defenses; even fewer find it worth the candle.

---

[1] RICHARD E. FLATHMAN, THE PRACTICE OF POLITICAL AUTHORITY: AUTHORITY AND THE AUTHORITATIVE 149 (1980).

Beneath the veneer of due process and the ordered resolution of disputes, Baltimore's rent court systematically excludes from the law's prescriptions litigants who are members of socially subordinated groups. The exclusion is enacted over and over each day in rent court, where a single judge deals with as many as 2500 cases on a daily docket. The great proportion of tenants who appear are poor black women. The great proportion of housing leased to tenants summoned to rent court is in such a condition as to provide meritorious legal defense to the landlord's claim for nonpayment. Virtually every tenant is unrepresented and unassisted before, during or after her court appearance. Few tenants inform the court of the landlord's lapses. The handful who do attempt to press their own substantive rights are effectively not heard.[7]

It is this aspect of the court's operation, the functional voicelessness of virtually all tenants in this forum, to which this Article gives center stage.

Courts assigned to hear small claims were designed with the expectation that citizens would speak directly to courts without the aid or obstacle of formal rules of evidence, professionally trained representatives, or elaborate rules of entitlement or presentation. Yet, tenants are silenced by dynamics occurring in and around the court room. This is due both to differences in speech and to dissonant interpretations between speakers and listeners, since they do not share a culture of claiming. I explore these theses by using data gathered in one city's rent court. I expect the analysis to be applicable to the legal process found in the courts of the poor in many other cities.

* * *

One possible explanatory hypothesis, perhaps the standard one offered for the evident ineffectiveness of the formal provision of

---

[7]The tenants' words are not quite right: assertions are made indirectly, which neither express nor convey entitlement. The tenant's testimony is evidently accorded less value relative to the landlord or rental agent, in the course of which the tenant herself is devalued. She may be treated by the other players as uncomprehending the legally pertinent parameters, or as self-serving in her testimony, with greater frequency than are landlords or their agents. With very rare exception, the tenant has not anticipated the court's expectation of a paper trail or a written motion, or the devastation this lack will wreak in her hearing. Some tenants are thoroughly mystified in light of the judge's open-court statements that one goes to that court to "tell the judge" about the case.

tenants' rights to change the landlord-tenant relationship, proceeds from a view of law as a kind of cranky but adequate machinery that is capably protective when set in motion with a bit of special skill to assure that it operates properly.[19] Such a standard "access to justice" analysis of the defects of this particular legal institution is flawed and incomplete, because it proceeds from a view of law and society in which law is distinct from the social and political realms, and because of its correlative image of law as imparting "legal protection." This conception promotes the illusory notion that law is a source of power and authority disconnected from other power structures in society.

Without doubt, each of the enumerable constraints impeding poor tenants' court access is a substantial barrier to the assertion of claims by an appreciable numbers of tenants. Yet taken together, they are inadequate explanations for the magnitude of the silence of so many tenants. In this paper I suggest two more:

First, the operational premise of the rent court as an institution is to enforce the entitlement of the landlord to payment and possession, while it obscures the entitlements of tenants under the same governing law. In other words, in the absence of evidence produced by either party, the court uniformly awards judgment to the landlord. More than the formal statutory material is needed to explain this phenomenon. In important part, this is an expression of centuries of culture regarding landowning and its centrality to "worth," as well as an expression of judges' class-related assignments of parties' credibility and their conceptions of the social world. In order for tenants to articulate the claims available to them, they must challenge these powerful underlying premises held by the power-wielding figures in the room--the judge and the landlord.

Second, the great majority of defendants in these actions are members of groups that are, relatively speaking, socially powerless.

---

[19]The law students felt affinity for what are perhaps the predictable, first-round explanations for tenants' nonparticipation: lack of information about legal rights or of more specialized knowledge such as the kind they enrolled in law school to learn; the possible intimidation of the setting or of one's landlord; or, a final attribution, the tenant bargained for substandard housing in exchange for a preferred level of rent.

They are mostly women,[21] mostly black,[22] almost all poor, and tenants. The standard view of access-dysfunction largely ignores the dimensions of social power allocations in the ways our legal institutions, including the legal profession, fail poor people. At its root is the acculturated belief that the individual is the proper unit to scrutinize when analyzing disputes about performance under a lease agreement. This is a belief afforded only to socially mobile people and not to the "poor" people who lack the experience of individual power to affect one's status and circumstance. In matters where rights are asserted, including but not limited to civil litigation, this is manifested as an ideology of participatory election, i.e., that individuals autonomously decide whether to take steps when they believe they have been wronged. This premise operates throughout the civil law paradigm and thus, through the formal structure of tenants' rights. But it operates in our lowest courts, on our poorest citizens, in ways that are contrary both to the expressed intent and the evident spirit that accompanied the enactment of significant tenants' rights statutes in the mid 1970s. It also demeans and disables them from claiming, believing, and participating in the civic community which the courts ostensibly serve. This is violence in the form of spirit-murder.

* * *

Legal Rights: Formalism and Normalism

Each year in Baltimore, some 195,000 cases for summary ejectment are filed by landlords against tenants in district court. Over 736,000 people live in the city of Baltimore; of these, 49.7%, or approximately 355,300 people, are renters. The volume of ejectment cases is even more palpable after realizing that nearly 180,000 residents are under eighteen years of age, thus these numbers suggest that more than one-third of the city's householders, and nearly two-thirds of all adult tenants, are summoned to this court each year.

---

[21]Seventy-one percent of tenants appearing in court were women. A great many were accompanied by small children, although this observation in the courtroom was not recorded in our study. Census data for Baltimore indicates that 53.9% of all households include children, and that of all such households, 49.4% are headed by women.

[22]In our observation, 87% of tenants appearing were black and 13% were white.

The city has one of the highest concentrations of poor families in the United States: 20% of its families have incomes below the federal poverty level. The tenants who are sued for nonpayment are almost always poor, and the monthly rent claimed in these proceedings is typically under prevailing market rates. More than half of the tenant families paid more than half of their income for rent. The condition of the rented residences is poor also. Most of the rental housing stock consists of rowhouses which are two or three stories in height, half of it built before the 1940s, and most of it privately owned. Baltimore's public housing is home to about 38,000 people, with approximately 28,000 more on the waiting list. Families with children may wait for as long as ten years. At the last count, 63,442 occupied housing units in the city were deemed substandard including 35% of all rental units. Yet tenants' opportunities to find better housing are constrained by the scarcity of affordable housing and exacerbated by the city's or private owners' insufficient rehabilitation of existing units. The City does concede that at least 5,000 housing units remain vacant, however, the 1990 Census counted 27,222 vacant units.

The Legal Construction of Tenants' Rights in Possession, Rent and Habitability of Housing

As a formal matter, prior to the reforms of the early 1970s, thc laws of Baltimore City and Maryland which governed the obligations of landlords and tenants provided nothing more than a summary process for the eviction of nonpaying tenants. During the early 1970s, the winds of change sweeping the nation reached into landlord-tenant law in numerous jurisdictions, including Maryland. In 1969, the laws governing Baltimore were amended to authorize court-directed escrow of rent for leased premises having hazardous conditions and to proscribe retaliatory evictions for tenants' complaints about property condition. In 1971, Baltimore's law was amended to allow rescission where the premises were discovered to be unfit for habitation within the first 30 days of occupancy, and in 1975, the warranty of fitness for human habitation was extended to the entire tenancy. Each of these provisions permits tenants to raise the issue of defects in the property's condition and obtain specified remedies in either the landlord's summary proceeding for repossession or affirmatively by the tenant's own complaint.

These new tenant remedies appear significant. The court "shall make any order that the justice of the case may require," which may include but is not limited to an order of inspection, repair, and abatement of rent to reflect defective conditions, as well as limited receivership remedies under the escrow law. It may also award damages and rescission for breach of the statutory warranty of habitability. Although the state of the housing stock makes it probable that meritorious conditions defenses exist in the majority of nonpayment cases in Baltimore, such defenses are in fact rarely raised by tenants. Legal scholars have been consistent in attending to the rights and remedies of tenants in housing availability, cost, condition, and tenure. However, virtually none have ventured to study the operation of landlord-tenant courts on which the poorest citizens depend for the legal regulation of low-income housing. This study is meant to fill that gap.

Description of the Court in Operation

Our study includes data gathered from in-court observation, from court files, and from exit interviews with tenants. In the straightforward way of empirical efforts, it may be said that the study was intended to elicit whether tenants knew about the formal legal protections available to them, whether they were using the law's provisions, and with what frequency and result. However, these are all predicates to an exploration of the question, "Why are the tenants so silent?"

Court Characteristics

The entity called "rent court" is in fact a courtroom of the District Court for Baltimore City. A single judge and courtroom are assigned to the hearing of landlord-tenant disputes. Until recently, it was housed in the district court building of Baltimore's downtown, the only locus reasonably well served by the public transit system. In January 1989, the operation moved to a converted Sears department store, in one of the city's bedraggled and poverty-scarred neighborhoods far to the northeast of downtown. It shares the building with the "housing court," a half-time courtroom assigned to hear the State Attorney's prosecutions of housing code violations. This centralized processing is a great convenience for landlords, landlord's agents, and the judges of the district court. However, it is mightily inconvenient for the thousands of tenants who rent in the many poor parts of town miles away.

Inside, the six courtrooms on the main level are used primarily for criminal cases, which explains the number of police officers throughout the first floor. Rent court is in the basement past the offices of the Public Defender and the Constables who execute evictions. If one arrives before the morning session begins at 9 a.m., one sees the blankness of the wide, bright linoleum corridor, leading past closed doors that read, "Rent Court Clerk," "Eviction Prevention Office," and "Legal Aid." Around the corner, two sets of double doors are marked simply, "Silence--Court in Session."

Come an hour or so later, particularly in the busy middle of the month, and one sees an ever-replenished line of people who are mostly women, mostly black, and mostly with little kids. These tenants are waiting in turn to be called into the Eviction Prevention Office, where they will be quizzed about whether they are facing a "housing emergency" sufficient to entitle them to emergency assistance from the Department of Social Services ("DSS"). The tenants in line have already waited in the courtroom for their cases to be called. Each has received a "DSS slip" in exchange for which a judgment was entered against her for possession on the ground of nonpayment. Now they wait to be screened, and the lucky ones will be directed to their local DSS office to apply for an emergency assistance ("EA") grant. If the tenant has no other funds with which to satisfy the judgment and retain her housing, and if the tenant has not had two prior grants in the year, then she will likely receive an EA grant. But in no event will this grant ever exceed $250, and if there are no children in the household, or a prior grant has been made, it will in fact be less. Yet in 75% of the cases, the monthly rent sued for in rent court exceeds $250. Plainly, even the EA grant does not "prevent" the tenant's eviction.

As one heads for the double-doors to enter Courtroom 7, one may notice off to the right a tilted counter--the docket board. Stapled to it are the cases on the docket for the day, listed by address and case number alone--neither landlord's nor tenant's name appears. No explanation is posted. One might assume, as some tenants do, that the list indicates the order in which cases will be called. This is not so, since cases are called by the courtroom clerk so as to facilitate rapid disposition. Thus, periodically throughout the morning session, the clerk will call from the bench, "All those tenants paying rent to or renting from AB Management Company, come forward and bring your rent notice." Landlord agents (non-attorneys appearing on behalf of client landlords) prefer to have all of their cases heard in sequence, so that they can either come later in the docket or leave before its end. This wish is accommodated by court personnel as a matter of course.

Tenants, on the other hand, are extended no similar control over their schedule or expectation. They are given no idea when their case will be called, and throughout the long session they are at their peril should they leave the room to find the lavatory or to quiet the baby. In a few instances where the landlord appears on his or her own behalf rather than through an agent (no more than about 15% of the cases) the landlord and tenant may in fact know or recognize each other and realize that the momentarily missing party is in the court house. In the rare instances when this happens and it is brought to the judge's attention, the court may recall the case a few minutes later. Our court observation however, documented this only when the missing party was the landlord, never the tenant. But if a tenant's case is called and she does not move *directly* to the bench, the court will observe, "Landlord claims $330 rent due, tenant has failed to appear, judgment is entered for landlord for possession." It all takes less than a minute.

* * *

Aggregate Data About the "Cases" Heard in Court

The three sources of data, in-court observation, court record study, and exit interviews, together provide a detailed picture of the court's effectiveness in serving the rent-collection ends of the landlords. Tenants appeared almost always as defendants, and generally lost. While the study's structure did not permit follow-up of particular cases, the aggregate figures for tenant relief are shocking. Not a single order to the landlord to repair was observed in the sample. Abatement of rent to reflect housing violations was ordered in just 1.75% of all cases in the Observation Study.

Landlords prevailed outright in 67% of the cases observed. Tenants obtained judgment and were excused of claims for rent and possession in just 3.5% of all cases. Rent was ordered into escrow for a later determination of the parties' claims in 4.3% of all cases. In 5.5% of the cases, an initial claim by the tenant of unlawful housing conditions was credited sufficiently that the judge ordered a housing inspection and continued the case for a week in order to await the inspector's evidence. The balance of the cases were either dismissed, voluntarily or because the plaintiff failed to appear, or were continued.

In short, landlords avoided the imposition of rent abatement or damages for impaired habitability in 98.25% of all cases. The Court Record Survey also confirms that 84.7% of the judgments were entered on the defendant's default.

* * *

In the great majority of cases, the monetary stakes are small. Tenants are usually sued when there is but a single month's rent due. Economic considerations prevent attorneys from waiting around for two-minute, "two-bit" cases, thus appearances through non-attorney agents solves this problem cheaply. Landlord agents' specialization, experience, and familiarity with procedure and personnel, more than the limited law ever invoked, render them effective representatives for property owners.

Another advantage accruing to these repeat players is perhaps evidenced in the differential treatment accorded landlords and tenants when one party fails, or is slow to appear. Tenants were only half as likely to be awarded judgment when the opposing party failed to appear, whereas landlords secured a default judgment nearly every time. Not even in one case was any willingness to wait a few minutes for the tenant's arrival exhibited, although such a courtesy was extended in half the cases in which the tenant appeared and the landlord did not.

* * *

The study did document a few instances of "mom-and-pop" landlords bringing legitimate claims after informal efforts to collect rent had been unsuccessful. These actions were few and far between. The primary operators in the rent court are a class of business agents whose repeated participation in the forum is a kind of legal education in the scope and form of legal claiming which is adequate to preclude even a minimal contest by most tenants and sufficient to defeat the few tenants who muster more. The representatives' repetitious experience provides a confidence in conducting business before the court, borne of a certain amount of familiarity with the setting and its rhythms, as well as the presiding officials. Rent court, more than most other courts, is a theater of class conflict in which businesses and their hirelings constitute a class of professional claimants exercising significant advantages over the individual defendants whom they bring before the court, who are poor and poorly situated with respect to the attributes that garner respectful hearing in court rooms.

Reading the Local Scene: Legal Culture and Class Boundaries

Cases in which both landlord and tenant appear typically take no more than two minutes. The dullingly standard script proceeds as follows:

Judge:	"Landlord claims rent due of $297. Is that amount due?"
Tenant:	"Yes."
Judge:	"Is there anything else? Judgment for landlord for possession showing $297 due and unpaid."

In a frequent minor variation on this script, the judge may add to the tenant, "Would you like a slip for DSS? See the bailiff." Ordinarily the tenant's response is a nod, no other response seeming necessary. Whether this is the tenant's self-identified need or purpose, or just acquiescence to the judge's evident expectation is not possible to observe.

This typical transcript illustrates twin barriers to tenants' voicing of claims and the court granting a hearing to tenants. These are the dysfunctional premises embedded in legal culture, and the failure of the legal process to mediate the subtle, and not so subtle, intrusions of the larger culture's calculus of social and material status.

A tenant asserting her claim of rent-impairing defects must satisfy the judge on two levels of communication not likely to be familiar to her. These are the formal requirements for claiming within the official legal culture and the information gleaned from the tenant's presentation of herself and her claim, which the judge uscs to interpret the tenant before him. This interpretation encompasses attributions as to race and social class. In the elusive moment in which the tenant must state her claim or not, the tenant faces hurdles both of official legal culture and of the larger culture for which a lower court is scarcely a successful filter. As we shall see, both of these hurdles silence most tenants.

* * *

In a surprising number of cases, the landlord says nothing. He hardly needs to since the merits of a nonpayment case are extraordinarily simple and the judge conducts the landlord's case anyway. Has the tenant paid the rent? If not, the tenant has ceased to pay for the right to possess, thus the landlord is entitled to have this tenant removed. Formally, the dispute is one of possession and the landlord's remedy is regaining possession. In reality, however, the scene is one of debt collection.

Formal legal rights do not modify this essential transaction because of the barriers to tenants' assertions of such rights. The way the rent court operates, the familiar formal allocation among the parties of the burdens of presentation and proof, are in fact turned on their heads. This is explained only in part by the summary nature of the proceeding for repossession. It is strongly reinforced by the phenomenon, all too ordinary in rent court, of the judge trying the landlord's case.

* * *

The interplay of legal culture and class may be illustrated by the procedural hurdle of notice requirements most often employed to bar tenants from successfully claiming redress for defective conditions in the rented residences. Typically the judge requires that the tenant give written notice to the landlord more than thirty days before the tenant makes her claim to the court. Clearly "notice" to the landlord of the tenant's claim of defect and nonrepair is an essential element of the tenant's case. By law, the tenant is entitled to make her claim as an answer and defense to the landlord's suit for repossession which, as a summary proceeding, is scheduled for hearing within a week of the landlord's filing. Baltimore local law recognizes "actual notice" and notices issued by government inspectors as valid forms of notice. But it has been the practice of several rent court judges to prefer the statute's most stringent version of "notice" of defects--a tenant's certified letter to the landlord, of which the tenant has kept a copy and the returned receipt.

The cultural barrier is the judges' evident belief that it is "no big deal" for tenants to write letters or otherwise create paper trails for what they know. This may be both an unconscious projection of official legal culture or of a world view that one pilots one's own life, grounded in the social and economic status accompanying judges' professional station. Nevertheless, three points suggest that for many tenants, the letter requirement is clearly a significant hurdle to the hearing of real disputes by this court.

The first is Baltimore's legendary illiteracy rate--it has the least literate population of the nation's fifteen largest cities. One-third of the city's people above the age of sixteen are functionally illiterate, that is, unable to read bus and street signs or medicine bottles, much less the compound, complex "instructions" on the back of a tattered summons.

Second, the judges themselves have tended to raise the hurdle unreasonably high through their interpretation of simple letters which are submitted by some tenants. In one case the tenant's letter read:

> To whom it may concern, I am written you this letter
> to as you to fix these thing in the house i rent from.
>
> 1. Bathroom, toilet
> 2. all window needs to be fix
> 3. seil [ceiling] going up to the third floor

* * *

At trial, the judge rejected the letter as adequate notice, expressing concern that the letter did not sufficiently apprise the landlord that there was a defect in the toilet for which the landlord would be responsible. The landlord took the judge's cue that she did not "know" there was anything about the enumerated items to repair.

Third, although the court makes some scant effort to inform tenants of its formal expectations for notice, every instructional effort the court makes backfires. Intentional instructions are compromised by the concerns of docket management, and the unconscious instructions that are exuded in the court's operations teach tenants a bitter lesson. Instead of enabling poorer citizens to participate in the vindication of their rights, the obverse message is reiterated with a veneer of civility, dozens of times a day.

* * *

The dialogue concerning notice often proceeds as follows:

Judge:	"Did you tell your landlord?"
Tenant:	"Yes sir, I told him every time he came to get the rent" [or, "I told his workmen"].
Judge:	"When was that? . . . Mr. Landlord?"
Landlord:	"I didn't get the message."
Judge:	"Did you send your landlord a letter?"
Tenant:	"No, but I . . ."
Judge:	"I understand ma'am, but the landlord is entitled to 30 days notice. Now, he has to fix it if it is defective. If he hasn't fixed it in a reasonable time, then come back her next month and tell me you were here today.

Judgment for the landlord for the amount of rent claimed due, $xyz. Thank you."

The judge's preference for the most onerous of the three forms of notice permitted by statute thus becomes an operational imperative.

Tenant education in the rent court consists of a set of direct and powerful instructions. Informed by the judge's formal instructions at the start of docket, tenants are told that they cannot raise conditions issues if they did not have the foresight to write a letter, mail it certified, and keep a copy. Tenants see the judge try the landlords' cases. Tenants observe that few tenants participate or have much to say. The few tenants who do attempt to gain the judge's ear are not assisted in making their claims in ways parallel to the assistance afforded landlords. Tenants are placed under a different burden of production, presentation, and persuasion. The court makes no reference to tenants' rights and no admonishment to landlords at the start of docket in order to honor tenants' entitlements.

The very setting of the court conveys the differential experience and regard among the players. Tenants are confronted by the familiarity between court personnel and the landlord agents. The landlord agents know things that the tenant does not, such as who the people are, who has certain authority, what to expect, the language used, and the procedure utilized. In its fundamentals, coming to rent court is not an experience of a leveled playing field in neutral territory. Instead, it is a hoax of a court, an extension of one's social situations and relations unmitigated by "rights." It is the "same ole, same ole."

Silence and Speech

* * *

The puzzling question concerns the group of tenants who do appear in court, yet do not effectively "answer" in a manner attributed legal meaning. Of the tenants appearing, 87% do not speak so as to gain a hearing. One of two response types is common to the routine judicial inquiry, "Is there anything else you wish to tell me?" Many tenants say no, mumble something inaudible which is taken for no, or keep quiet. For others, the question prompts a human story which is not given legal credence, and thus with a short detour, the case concludes with judgment for the landlord.

The tenants who appear on the appointed day but who say nothing do not "default" in a technical sense, although they do fail to raise a cognizable claim. Why come to court then? Because they were summoned? Why take the time from work and risk losing the job, or ferry the kids across town, to get an adverse judgment, if one is not even going to contest the facts? The behavior might be explained by a judgment to submit to official power, or an intention to make a claim, or a sense of civic duty. What transpires in the time between arranging to come to court and the moment or two in front of the judge?

* * *

The tenant's decision to say little or nothing may be the summative effect of the court's instructions, not the least of which are those explicit and implicit interpretations of priority and credibility as between the landlords and the tenants, which are broadcast consistently throughout the long procession of short cases. These are scarcely interrupted by the refrain of "Judgment for the landlord for possession," which is the marginal tenant's worst fear.

* * *

Powerless Speech, Strategies of Subordinated Speakers

Among tenants who do give voice to claims, a subtler, recurring problem of access is evident: the presentational threshold required to have one's claim heard by the sitting judge.

* * *

A short stay in Baltimore's rent court shows that the "powerless" speech style predominates in tenants' usage when speaking with the judge. It coincides in aggregate with tenants' low success rate in Maryland's most-used court. The researchers' reports concerning hearers' assessments of the speech signals of those who feel powerlessness mirror phenomena observed repeatedly in this local setting. Virtually all tenants who attempt to claim the protection of the law find, in those moments before the judge, that tenants are neither credited with accurate or trustworthy reporting, nor are they helped in scaling the hurdles of filing claims--which the State's apparatus makes so undemanding for property owners.

The lesson ringing out from this research, and its manifestations in Baltimore, is that the language patterns that correlate with social subordination infect our nation's courtrooms, making them not tolerably "neutral." We are confronted with the socially and politically significant fact that important skills for meaningful participation are distributed by gender, race, and class. The burdens of stylistic powerlessness fall most heavily on women, minorities, the poor, and undereducated, with a disproportionate number of women and blacks in America being poor, undereducated, and relegated to the margins of economic and political power.

Judicial Domination in Courtroom Discourse

Tenants' socially distributed tendencies toward "powerless" speech in court are compounded by the expectations and directions of the presiding judge for the structure of the speech sequences constituting the "hearing."

The cases in which both tenant and landlord appear consist entirely of two discordant conversations. The first is conducted by the judge on the landlord's behalf, within the framework of the ordinary civil legal dispute, and casts the landlord's interests in rent, prompt payment, and repossession in a legally pertinent telling:

Judge: "Landlord claims $[265] due and unpaid. Is that correct?"

The second conversation is a (usually brief) colloquy in which the judge says to the tenant some version of:

Judge: "Is there anything you would like to tell me?"

In our observations, when invited in this way at this juncture, many tenants offer the court an explanation for their nonpayment. The judge either waits through the story or interrupts it, but at either point, tells the tenant that her remarks are irrelevant, and orders judgment for the landlord. This is the clash between the conventions for talking about troubles in noninstitutional settings and the law's conventions for speech within legal institutions, which the judge learned through formal education in law school and observation of other legal professionals' courtroom behavior.

* * *

In a court like Baltimore's that hears only a single kind of case, each aurally indistinguishable from the next, the discourse structured by the court is all there is of legal process. Invariably, the judge starts the hearing with the landlord's claim for rent. So the tenant starts her comments with rent. Most often, only rent has been spoken of when the judge dismisses the tenant's speech and rules for the landlord. As structured, it excludes virtually all tenants from meaningful participation in the conversation. This makes the legal process a charade.

* * *

"Powered" and "Empowered" Speech

To speak of power in the context of Baltimore's rent court, we must attend to the social situations importantly described by race and class, as well as the disturbingly persistent fact that people of color are disproportionately poor. What part may race play in the silencing enacted by this court and courts like it?

* * *

The public space of a courtroom, filled largely with black tenants and presided over by a succession of white judges, is a likely place for such mutual misinterpretations, particularly between people from "the neighborhood" and the typical judicial appointee.

* * *

Studies suggest that blacks and whites differ in their styles of public discussion, particularly in the calculus of what is appropriate as a matter of stance and level of spiritual intensity. Where the white mode is purposely "dispassionate and non-challenging," the black mode is "high-key, interpersonal, animated, [and] confrontational." This follows from the recognition of two kinds of argument in black community culture: argument for persuasion, and argument for the ventilation of anger and hostility. The distinction is in the degree of effect and intensity and not, as in formal white discourse, in their presence or absence.

Serious misinterpretation may occur when this style and its cultural meanings are transplanted to a white culture that fails to make these distinctions. This white culture sees vociferous argument as appropriate only to ventilate anger and hostility, not as a process of persuasion.

* * *

The paradigms enacted and reenacted by societal institutions, and thus by the people who play roles in them, teach each of us our parts, and at times even hand us our scripts. Therefore, the meaning of one's encounters with these institutions will depend in part on one's role. It will depend on one's perspective of the larger scene derived from one's locus and assigned role in it. But meaning also will depend on attributions made by others. The cultural, gender, racial, and ethnic identities of a person are not simply intrinsic to that person. Everyone's identity is relational and not simply personal, and depends both on one's self-understanding and on communal understandings.

This perspective offers an additional dimension of explanation for the mystery of why people bother to come to court and concede the rent is due, while making no claim, but stand there seeming to expect something else to occur. A fuller understanding of what transpires in the court acknowledges that virtually no tenant stands before the rent court judge as an autonomous individual. Instead, she is shadowed by the thousands who have preceded her, by the judge's culturally rooted premises and behaviors signalling she is out of place, and by her own experience. Her experience is not solely her own, but is constituted in significant part by the meaning she draws, and others have attributed about her identity, from her membership in culturally significant groups described by race, gender, and class.

If we turn the legalist lens on an institution like Baltimore's rent court, we should expect to see the adjudication of societally prescribed legal rights, carried out with presumably variable degrees of competence, efficacy, and equity. Yet the court I have described is riven by deep conflict. The rights of both parties are not being adjudicated. In its disfunction, the court fails one class of people and privileges another. While the pains and benefits it allocates are felt in the lives of individuals, it is at least as true to observe that they are distributed among socially identifiable groups of people. One's group memberships provide the best predictors of outcomes.

* * *

Notes and Questions

1. *Silence.* Why didn't the tenants pursue their legal claims more forcefully?

2. *Comparing Tenants to Mrs. G.* How did the tenants' hearings compare to the hearing of Mrs. G.? Certainly Mrs. G. had more time to develop her evidence in an administrative hearing than the Baltimore tenants had in their court hearings. And she had legal representation.

Both Mrs. G. and many of the tenants had meritorious claims. Yet the authors believe that both Mrs. G. and the tenants were silenced. Was Mrs. G.'s silence similar to the silence of the tenants?

3. *Role of Difference.* How could one's gender, race, or class affect one's ability or willingness to follow the formal rules of legal engagement?

4. *Alternatives.* What alternatives to the Baltimore rent court's assembly line processing of tenants would improve the plight of the tenants?

B. THE TIMING OF THE HEARING

MEMPHIS LIGHT, GAS AND WATER DIVISION v. CRAFT

436 U.S. 619 (1978)

Justice POWELL delivered the opinion of the Court.

This is an action brought under 42 U.S.C. § 1983 by homeowners in Memphis, Tenn., seeking declaratory and injunctive relief and damages against a municipal utility and several of its officers and employees for termination of utility service allegedly without due process of law. The District Court determined that respondents' claim of entitlement to continued utility service did not implicate a "property" interest protected by the Fourteenth Amendment, and that, in any event, the utility's termination procedures comported with due process. The Court of Appeals reversed in part. We granted certiorari to consider this constitutional question of importance in the operation of municipal utilities throughout the Nation.

Memphis Light, Gas and Water Division (MLG&W)[1] is a division of the city of Memphis which provides utility service. It is directed by a Board of Commissioners appointed by the City Council, and is subject to the ultimate control of the municipal government. As a municipal utility, MLG&W enjoys a statutory exemption from regulation by the state public service commission.

---

[1] Although MLG&W is listed as one of the petitioners, the District Court dismissed the action as to the utility itself because a "municipality or governmental unit standing in that capacity is not a 'person' within the meaning" of § 1983. The Court of Appeals did not disturb that determination, and respondents have not sought review of the point in this Court. The individual petitioners, who are sued in both their official and personal capacities, are the utility's president and general manager, vice president, members of the Board of Commissioners, and two employees who have had responsibility for terminating utility services. They will be referred to throughout as either "MLG&W" or petitioners.

Willie S. and Mary Craft, respondents here, reside at 1019 Alaska Street in Memphis. When the Crafts moved into their residence in October 1972, they noticed that there were two separate gas and electric meters and only one water meter serving the premises. The residence had been used previously as a duplex. The Crafts assumed, on the basis of information from the seller, that the second set of meters was inoperative.

In 1973, the Crafts began receiving two bills: their regular bill, and a second bill with an account number in the name of Willie C. Craft, as opposed to Willie S. Craft. Separate monthly bills were received for each set of meters, with a city service fee appearing on each bill. In October 1973, after learning from a MLG&W meter reader that both sets of meters were running in their home, the Crafts hired a private plumber and electrical contractor to combine the meters into one gas and one electric meter. Because the contractor did not consolidate the meters properly, a condition of which the Crafts were not aware, they continued to receive two bills until January 1974. During this period, the Crafts' utility service was terminated five times for nonpayment.

On several occasions, Mrs. Craft missed work and went to the MLG&W offices in order to resolve the "double billing" problem. As found by the District Court, Mrs. Craft sought in good faith to determine the cause of the "double billing," but was unable to obtain a satisfactory explanation or any suggestion for further recourse from MLG&W employees.

* * *

State law does not permit a public utility to terminate service "at will." MLG&W and other public utilities in Tennessee are obligated to provide service "to all of the inhabitants of the city of its location alike, without discrimination, and without denial, except for good and sufficient cause," and may not terminate service except "for nonpayment of a just service bill." An aggrieved customer may be able to enjoin a wrongful threat to terminate, or to bring a subsequent action for damages or a refund. The availability of such local-law remedies is evidence of the State's recognition of a protected interest. Although the customer's right to continued service is conditioned upon payment of the charges properly due, "[t]he Fourteenth Amendment's protection of 'property'. . . has never been interpreted to safeguard only the rights of undisputed ownership." Because petitioners may terminate service only "for cause," respondents assert a "legitimate claim of entitlement" within the protection of the Due Process Clause.

In determining what process is "due" in this case, the extent of our inquiry is shaped by the ruling of the Court of Appeals. We need go no further in deciding this case than to ascertain whether the Court of Appeals properly read the Due Process Clause to require (i) notice informing the customer not only of the possibility of termination but also of a procedure for challenging a disputed bill, and (ii) "'[an] established [procedure] for resolution of disputes'" or some specified avenue of relief for customers who "dispute the existence of the liability."

"An elementary and fundamental requirement of due process in any proceeding which is to be accorded finality is notice reasonably calculated, under all the circumstances, to apprise interested parties of the pendency of the action and afford them an opportunity to present their objections." The issue here is whether due process requires that a municipal utility notify the customer of the availability of an avenue of redress within the organization should he wish to contest a particular charge.

The "final notice" contained in MLG&W's bills simply stated that payment was overdue and that service would be discontinued if payment was not made by a certain date. As the Court of Appeals determined, "the MLG&W notice only warn[ed] the customer to pay or face termination." MLG&W also enclosed a "flyer" with the "final notice." One "flyer" was distributed to about 40% of the utility's customers, who resided in areas serviced by "credit counseling stations." It stated in part: "If you are having difficulty paying your utility bill, bring your bill to our neighborhood credit counselors for assistance. Your utility bills may be paid here also." No mention was made of a procedure for the disposition of a disputed claim.

* * *

Petitioners' notification procedure, while adequate to apprise the Crafts of the threat of termination of service, was not "reasonably calculated" to inform them of the availability of "an opportunity to present their objections" to their bills. The purpose of notice under the Due Process Clause is to apprise the affected individual of, and permit adequate preparation for, an impending "hearing." Notice in a case of this kind does not comport with constitutional requirements when it does not advise the customer of the availability of a procedure for protesting a proposed termination of utility service as unjustified. As no such notice was given respondents--despite "good faith efforts" on their part--they were deprived of the notice which was their due.

This Court consistently has held that "some kind of hearing is required at some time before a person is finally deprived of his property interests." We agree with the Court of Appeals that due process requires the provision of an opportunity for the presentation to a designated employee of a customer's complaint that he is being overcharged or charged for services not rendered.

* * *

Our decision in *Mathews v. Eldridge*, 424 U.S. 319 (1976), provides a framework of analysis for determining the "specific dictates of due process" in this case.

> [O]ur prior decisions indicate that identification of the specific dictates of due process generally requires consideration of three distinct factors: First, the private interest that will be affected by the official action; second, the risk of an erroneous deprivation of such interest through the procedures used, and the probable value, if any, of additional or substitute procedural safeguards; and finally, the Government's interest, including the function involved and the fiscal and the administrative burdens that the additional or substitute procedural requirement would entail.

Under the balancing approach outlined in *Mathews*, some administrative procedure for entertaining customer complaints prior to termination is required to afford reasonable assurance against erroneous or arbitrary withholding of essential services. The customer's interest is self-evident. Utility service is a necessity of modern life; indeed, the discontinuance of water or heating for even short periods of time may threaten health and safety. And the risk of an erroneous deprivation, given the necessary reliance on computers, is not insubstantial.

The utility's interests are not incompatible with affording the notice and procedure described above. Quite apart from its duty as a public service company, a utility--in its own business interests--may be expected to make all reasonable efforts to minimize billing errors and the resulting customer dissatisfaction and possible injury. Nor should "some kind of hearing" prove burdensome. The opportunity for a meeting with a responsible employee empowered to resolve the dispute could be afforded well in advance of the scheduled date of termination. And petitioners would retain the option to terminate service after affording this opportunity and concluding that the amount billed was justly due.

Petitioners contend that the available common-law remedies of a pretermination injunction, a post-termination suit for damages, and post-payment action for a refund are sufficient to cure any perceived inadequacy in MLG&W's procedures.

Ordinarily, due process of law requires an opportunity for "some kind of hearing" prior to the deprivation of a significant property interest. On occasion, this Court has recognized that where the potential length or severity of the deprivation does not indicate a likelihood of serious loss and where the procedures underlying the decision to act are sufficiently reliable to minimize the risk of erroneous determination, government may act without providing additional "advance procedural safeguards."

The factors that have justified exceptions to the requirement of some prior process are not present here. Although utility service may be restored ultimately, the cessation of essential services for any appreciable time works a uniquely final deprivation. Moreover, the probability of error in utility cutoff decisions is not so insubstantial as to warrant dispensing with all process prior to termination.

The injunction remedy referred to by petitioners would not be an adequate substitute for a pretermination review of the disputed bill with a designated employee. Many of the Court's decisions in this area have required additional procedures to further due process, notwithstanding the apparent availability of injunctive relief or recovery provisions. It was thought that such remedies were likely to be too bounded by procedural constraints and too susceptible of delay to provide an effective safeguard against an erroneous deprivation. These considerations are applicable in the utility termination context.

Equitable remedies are particularly unsuited to the resolution of factual disputes typically involving sums of money too small to justify engaging counsel or bringing a lawsuit. An action in equity to halt an improper termination, because it is less likely to be pursued and less likely to be effective, even if pursued, will not provide the same assurance of accurate decisionmaking as would an adequate administrative procedure. In these circumstances, an informal administrative remedy, along the lines suggested above, constitutes the process that is "due."

Because of the failure to provide notice reasonably calculated to apprise respondents of the availability of an administrative procedure to consider their complaint of erroneous billing, and the failure to afford them an opportunity to present their complaint to a designated employee empowered to review disputed bills and rectify error, petitioners deprived respondents of an interest in property without due process of law.

The judgment of the Court of Appeals is

Affirmed.

Justice STEVENS, with whom THE CHIEF JUSTICE and Justice REHNQUIST join, dissenting.

In my judgment, the Court's holding confuses and trivializes the principle that the State may not deprive any person of life, liberty, or property without due process of law. I have no quarrel with the Court's conclusion that as a matter of Tennessee law a customer has a legitimate claim of entitlement to continued utility services as long as the undisputed portions of his utility bills are paid. For that reason, a municipality may not terminate utility service without giving the customer a fair opportunity to avoid termination either by paying the bill or questioning its accuracy. I do not agree, however, that this record discloses any constitutional defect in the termination procedures employed by the Light, Gas and Water Division of the city of Memphis (Division).

The Court focuses on two aspects of the Division's collection procedures. First, according to the Court, the Division's standard form of termination notice did not adequately inform the customer of the availability of a procedure for protesting a proposed termination of service as unjustified. Second, the Division did not afford its customers an adequate opportunity to meet with an employee who had the authority to settle billing disputes. Whether we consider the evidence describing the unusual dispute between the Crafts and the Division, or the evidence concerning the general operation of the Division's collection procedures, I find no basis for concluding that either of the Court's criticisms is justified; its conclusion that a constitutional violation has been proved is truly extraordinary.

* * *

The Court's constitutional objection to the Division's notice rests entirely on the classic statement from *Mullane v. Central Hanover Trust Co.*, 339 U.S. 306 (1950),

> An elementary and fundamental requirement of due process in any proceeding which is to be accorded finality is notice reasonably calculated, under all the circumstances, to apprise interested parties of the pendency of the action and afford them an opportunity to present their objections.

That statement identifies the two essential characteristics of adequate notice: It must inform the recipient of the impending loss; and it must be given in time to afford the recipient an opportunity to defend. These essentials must, of course, be expressed in terms which the layman can understand. The Division's notice unquestionably satisfied these two basic requirements.[8]

* * *

Distinctions of this small magnitude are the appropriate concern of administrative rulemaking; they are too trivial to identify constitutional error.

The Court's pronouncement "that due process requires the provision of an opportunity for the presentation to a designated employee of a customer's complaint that he is being overcharged or charged for services not rendered," is equally divorced from the facts of this case. The Division processes more than 30,000 complaints of excess charges each year, and it has designated scores of employees to hear and investigate those complaints. Except for the Crafts' troubles, there is nothing in the record to suggest that the Division's customers are denied access to these employees, or that the employees lack the power to deal appropriately with meritorious complaints. Indeed, as already noted, there is no finding by either of the courts below that the Crafts themselves did not meet with responsible officials empowered to resolve their dispute.

* * *

Although the Division's terminations number about 2,000 each month, the record does not reveal any actual case of harm to health or

---

[8] It tells the customer that a cutoff is imminent and it allows the customer enough time to avoid a cutoff by paying under protest, by contacting the information center, or by beginning a legal action.

safety. The District Court found that the Division does not discontinue service when there is illness in a home. Since a customer can always avoid termination by the simple expedient of paying the disputed bill and claiming a refund, it is not surprising that the real emergency case is rare, if indeed it exists at all. When a true emergency does present a serious threat to health or safety, the customer will have ample motivation to take the important step of consulting counsel or filing suit even if the amount of his disputed bill is small. A potential loss of utility service sufficiently grievous to qualify as a constitutional deprivation can hardly be too petty to justify invoking the aid of counsel or the judiciary. Conversely, routine billing disputes too petty for the bench or the bar can hardly merit extraordinary constitutional protection.

Even if the customer does not consult counsel in a specific case, the potential damages remedy nevertheless provides far more significant protection against an unjustified termination than does the vague requirement of "some kind of hearing." Without the threat of damages liability for mistakes, the informal procedures required today would neither qualify the utility's ultimate power to enforce collection by terminating service nor deter the exercise of that power. On the other hand, even without specific informal procedures, the danger of substantial liability will by itself ensure careful attention to genuine customer disputes. The utility's potential liability therefore provides customers with real pretermination protection even though damages may not be recovered until later.

* * *

It is an unfortunate fact that when the State assesses taxes or operates a utility, it occasionally overcharges the citizen. It is also unfortunate that effective collection procedures sometimes require the citizen to pay an unjust charge in order to forestall a serious deprivation of property. But if the State has given the citizen fair notice and afforded him procedural redress which is entirely adequate when invoked by his lawyer, the demands of the Due Process Clause are satisfied. I do not believe the Constitution requires the State to employ procedures that are so simple that every lay person can always act effectively without the assistance of counsel.

I respectfully dissent.

Notes and Questions

1. *Property.* The Court held that continued utility service is a form of property because state law prohibited termination of service except "for cause." What if the reason for the Crafts' failure to pay their utility bills had been lack of sufficient income? Would they have had any claim that continued service was a "legitimate claim of entitlement"?

2. *Notice.* The Court cited classic language from *Mullane v. Central Hanover Trust Co.* that due process requires a "notice reasonably calculated, under all the circumstances, to apprise interested parties of the pendency of the action and afford them an opportunity to present their objections." The Court required, not only notice that service would be disconnected if the Crafts failed to pay their bill, but also notice of a procedure for resolving their billing dispute.

3. *Administrative Remedy.* The Court required some administrative process by which the Crafts could have attempted to reduce their billing dispute. Why weren't the available legal remedies sufficient?

C. THE ROLE OF REPRESENTATION

LASSITER v. DEPARTMENT OF SOCIAL SERVICES

452 U.S. 16 (1981)

Justice STEWART delivered the opinion of the Court.

[A North Carolina trial court terminated Abby Gail Lassiter's parental rights to her son William who had been adjudicated a neglected child. The trial court concluded that Ms. Lassiter had ample opportunity to seek counsel but had failed without just cause to do so. On appeal, Ms. Lassiter argued that Due Process entitled her to appointment of counsel because she was indigent.]

* * *

The pre-eminent generalization that emerges from this Court's precedents on an indigent's right to appointed counsel is that such a right has been recognized to exist only where the litigant may lose his physical liberty if he loses the litigation.

* * *

The case of *Mathews v. Eldridge* propounds three elements to be evaluated in deciding what due process requires, *viz.*, the private interests at stake, the government's interest, and the risk that the procedures used will lead to erroneous decisions. We must balance these elements against each other, and then set their net weight in the scales against the presumption that there is a right to appointed counsel only where the indigent, if he is unsuccessful, may lose his personal freedom.

This Court's decisions have by now made plain . . . that a parent's desire for and right to "the companionship, care, custody and management of his or her children" is an important interest that "undeniably warrants deference and, absent a powerful countervailing interest, protection." Here the State has sought not simply to infringe upon that interest but to end it. If the State prevails, it will have worked a unique kind of deprivation. A parent's interest in the accuracy and injustice of the decision to terminate his or her parental status is, therefore a commanding one.

Since the State has an urgent interest in the welfare of the child, it shares the parent's interest in an accurate and just decision. For this reason, the State may share the indigent parent's interest in the availability of appointed counsel. If, as our adversary system presupposes, accurate and just results are most likely to be obtained through the equal contest of opposed interests, the State's interest in the child's welfare may perhaps best be served by a hearing in which both the parent and the State acting for the child are represented by counsel, without whom the contest of interests may become unwholesomely unequal. North Carolina itself acknowledges as much by providing that where a parent files a written answer to a termination petition, the State must supply a lawyer to represent the child.

The State's interests, however, clearly diverge from the parent's insofar as the State wishes the termination decision to be made as economically as possible and thus wants to avoid both the expense of appointed counsel and the cost of the lengthened proceedings his presence may cause. But though the State's pecuniary interest is legitimate, it is hardly significant enough to overcome private interests as important as those here, particularly in light of the concession in the respondent's brief that the "potential costs of appointed counsel in termination proceedings . . . is [sic] admittedly

de minimis compared to the costs in all criminal actions."
Finally, consideration must be given to the risk that a parent will be erroneously deprived of his or her child because the parent is not represented by counsel. North Carolina law now seeks to assure accurate decisions by establishing the following procedures: A petition to terminate parental rights may be filed only by a parent seeking the termination of the other parent's rights, by a county department of social services or licensed child-placing agency with custody of the child, or by a person with whom the child has lived continuously for the two years preceding the petition. A petition must describe facts sufficient to warrant a finding that one of the grounds for termination exists, and the parent must be notified of the petition and given 30 days in which to file a written answer to it. If that answer denies a material allegation, the court must, as has been noted, appoint a lawyer as the child's guardian ad litem and must conduct a special hearing to resolve the issues raised by the petition and the answer. If the parent files no answer, "the court shall issue an order terminating all parental and custodial rights . . .; provided the court shall order a hearing on the petition and may examine the petitioner or others on the facts alleged in the petition." Findings of fact are made by a court sitting without a jury and must "be based on clear, cogent, and convincing evidence." Any party may appeal who gives notice of appeal within 10 days after the hearing.[4]

* * *

Yet the ultimate issues with which a termination hearing deals are not always simple, however commonplace they may be. Expert medical and psychiatric testimony, which few parents are equipped to understand and fewer still to confute, is sometimes presented. The parents are likely to be people with little education, who have had uncommon difficulty in dealing with life, and who are, at the hearing, thrust into a distressing and disorienting situation. That these factors may combine to overwhelm an uncounseled parent is evident from the findings some courts have made. Thus, courts have generally held that the State must appoint counsel for indigent parents at termination

---

[4]The respondent also points out that parental termination hearings commonly occur only after a custody proceeding in which the child has judicially been found to be abused, neglected or dependent, and that an indigent parent has a right to be represented by appointed counsel at the custody hearing. . . .

proceedings. The respondent is able to point to no presently authoritative case, except for the North Carolina judgment now before us, holding that an indigent parent has no due process right to appointed counsel in termination proceedings.

The dispositive question, which must now be addressed, is whether the three *Eldridge* factors, when weighed against the presumption that there is no right to appointed counsel in the absence of at least a potential deprivation of physical liberty, suffice to rebut that presumption and thus to lead to the conclusion that the Due Process Clause requires the appointment of counsel when a State seeks to terminate an indigent's parental status. To summarize the above discussion of the *Eldridge* factors: the parent's interest is an extremely important one (and may be supplemented by the dangers of criminal liability inherent in some termination proceedings); the State shares with the parent an interest in a correct decision, has a relatively weak pecuniary interest, and, in some but not all cases, has a possibly stronger interest in informal procedures; and the complexity of the proceeding and the incapacity of the uncounseled parent could be, but would not always be, great enough to make the risk of an erroneous deprivation of the parent's rights insupportably high.

If, in a given case, the parent's interests were at their strongest, the State's interests were at their weakest, and the risks of error were at their peak, it could not be said that the *Eldridge* factors did not overcome the presumption against the right to appointed counsel, and that due process did not therefore require the appointment of counsel. But since the *Eldridge* factors will not always be so distributed, and since "due process is not so rigid as to require that the significant interests in informality, flexibility and economy must always be sacrificed," neither can we say that the Constitution requires the appointment of counsel in every parental termination proceeding. We . . . leave the decision whether due process calls for the appointment of counsel for indigent parents in termination proceedings to be answered in the first instance by the trial court, subject, of course, to appellate review.

Here . . . "[i]t is neither possible nor prudent to attempt to formulate a precise and detailed set of guidelines to be followed in determining when the providing of counsel is necessary to meet the applicable due process requirements," since here, as in that case, "[t]he facts and circumstances . . . are susceptible of almost infinite variation.

. . ." Nevertheless, because child-custody litigation must be concluded as rapidly as is consistent with fairness, we decide today whether the trial judge denied Ms. Lassiter due process of law when he did not appoint counsel for her.

The respondent represents that the petition to terminate Ms. Lassiter's parental rights contained no allegations of neglect or abuse upon which criminal charges could be based, and hence Ms. Lassiter could not well have argued that she required counsel for that reason. The Department of Social Services was represented at the hearing by counsel, but no expert witnesses testified and the case presented no specially troublesome points of law, either procedural or substantive. While hearsay evidence was no doubt admitted, and while Ms. Lassiter no doubt left incomplete her defense that the Department had not adequately assisted her in rekindling her interest in her son, the weight of the evidence that she had few sparks of such interest was sufficiently great that the presence of counsel for Ms. Lassiter could not have made a determinative difference. True, a lawyer might have done more with the argument that William should live with Ms. Lassiter's mother--but that argument was quite explicitly made by both Lassiters, and the evidence that the elder Ms. Lassiter had said she could not handle another child, that the social worker's investigation had led to a similar conclusion, and that the grandmother had displayed scant interest in the child once he had been removed from her daughter's custody was, though controverted, sufficiently substantial that the absence of counsel's guidance on this point did not render the proceedings fundamentally unfair. Finally, a court deciding whether due proccss requires the appointment of counsel need not ignore a parent's plain demonstration that she is not interested in attending a hearing. Here, the trial court had previously found that Ms. Lassiter had expressly declined to appear at the 1975 child custody hearing, Ms. Lassiter had not even bothered to speak to her retained lawyer after being notified of the termination hearing, and the court specifically found that Ms. Lassiter's failure to make an effort to contest the termination proceeding was without cause. In view of all these circumstances, we hold that the trial court did not err in failing to appoint counsel for Ms. Lassiter.

In its Fourteenth Amendment, our Constitution imposes on the States the standards necessary to ensure that judicial proceedings are fundamentally fair. A wise public policy, however, may require that higher standards be adopted than those minimally tolerable under the Constitution. Informed opinion has clearly come to hold that an indigent parent is entitled to the assistance of appointed counsel not only in parental termination proceedings, but also in dependency and neglect proceedings as well. Most significantly, 33 States and the District of Columbia provide statutorily for the appointment of counsel in termination cases. The Court's opinion today in no way implies that the standards increasingly urged by informed public opinion and now widely followed by the States are other than enlightened and wise.

For the reasons stated in this opinion, the judgment is *affirmed.*

Justice BLACKMUN, with whom Justice BRENNAN and Justice MARSHALL join, dissenting.

The Court today denies an indigent mother the representation of counsel in a judicial proceeding initiated by the State of North Carolina to terminate her parental rights with respect to her youngest child. The Court most appropriately recognizes that the mother's interest is a "commanding one," and it finds no countervailing state interest of even remotely comparable significance. Nonetheless, the Court avoids what seems to me the obvious conclusion that due process requires the presence of counsel for a parent threatened with judicial termination of parental rights, and, instead, revives an ad hoc approach thoroughly discredited nearly 20 years ago . . . . Because I believe that the unique importance of a parent's interest in the care and custody of his or her child cannot constitutionally be extinguished through formal judicial proceedings without the benefit of counsel, I dissent.

This Court is not unfamiliar with the problem of determining under what circumstances legal representation is mandated by the Constitution. In *Betts v. Brady*, it reviewed at length both the tradition behind the Sixth Amendment right to counsel in criminal trials and the historical practices of the States in that area. The decision in Betts--that the Sixth Amendment right to counsel did not apply to the States and that the due process guarantee of the Fourteenth Amendment permitted a flexible, case-by-case determination of the defendant's need for counsel in state criminal trials--was overruled in *Gideon v. Wainwright*, 372 U.S. 335 (1963). The Court in *Gideon* rejected the *Betts* reasoning to the effect that counsel for indigent criminal defendants was "'not a fundamental right, essential to a fair trial.'" Finding the right well founded in its precedents, the Court further concluded that "reason and reflection require us to recognize that in our adversary system of criminal justice, any person haled into court, who is too poor to hire a lawyer, cannot be assured a fair trial unless counsel is provided for him."

* * *

Outside the criminal context, however, the Court has relied on the flexible nature of the due process guarantee whenever it has decided that counsel is not constitutionally required.

* * *

[T]he Court has recognized that what process is due varies in relation to the interests at stake and the nature of the governmental proceedings. Where the individual's liberty interest is of diminished or less than fundamental stature, or where the prescribed procedure involves informal decisionmaking without the trappings of an adversarial trial-type proceeding, counsel has not been a requisite of due process. Implicit in this analysis is the fact that the contrary conclusion sometimes may be warranted. Where an individual's liberty interest assumes sufficiently weighty constitutional significance, and the State by a formal and adversarial proceeding seeks to curtail that interest, the right to counsel may be necessary to ensure fundamental fairness. To say this is simply to acknowledge that due process allows for the adoption of different rules to address different situations or contexts.

It is not disputed that state intervention to terminate the relationship between petitioner and her child must be accomplished by procedures meeting the requisites of the Due Process Clause. Nor is there any doubt here about the kind of procedure North Carolina has prescribed. North Carolina law requires notice and a trial-type hearing before the State on its own initiative may sever the bonds of parenthood. The decisionmaker is a judge, the rules of evidence are in force, and the State is represented by counsel. The question, then, is whether proceedings in this mold, that relate to a subject so vital, can comport with fundamental fairness when the defendant parent remains unrepresented by counsel. As the Court today properly acknowledges, our consideration of the process due in this context, as in others, must rely on a balancing of the competing private and public interests, an approach succinctly described in *Mathews v.*

Eldridge. As does the majority, I evaluate the "three distinct factors" specified in *Eldridge*: the private interest affected; the risk of error under the procedure employed by the State; and the countervailing governmental interest in support of the challenged procedure.

At stake here is "the interest of a parent in the companionship, care, custody, and management of his or her children." This interest occupies a unique place in our legal culture, given the centrality of family life as the focus for personal meaning and responsibility. "[F]ar more precious . . . than property rights," parental rights have been deemed to be among those "essential to the orderly pursuit of happiness by free men," and to be more significant and priceless than "'liberties which derive merely from shifting economic arrangements.'" Accordingly, although the Constitution is verbally silent on the specific subject of families, freedom of personal choice in matters of family life long has been viewed as a fundamental liberty interest worthy of protection under the Fourteenth Amendment. Within the general ambit of family integrity, the Court has accorded a high degree of constitutional respect to a natural parent's interest both in controlling the details of the child's upbringing.

In this case, the State's aim is not simply to influence the parent-child relationship but to extinguish it. A termination of parental rights is both total and irrevocable. Unlike other custody proceedings, it leaves the parent with no right to visit or communicate with the child, to participate in, or even to know about, any important decision affecting the child's religious, educational, emotional, or physical development. It is hardly surprising that this forced dissolution of the parent-child relationship has been recognized as a punitive sanction by courts, Congress, and commentators. The Court candidly notes, as it must, that termination of parental rights by the State is a "unique kind of deprivation."

The magnitude of this deprivation is of critical significance in the due process calculus, for the process to which an individual is entitled is in part determined "by the extent to which he may be 'condemned to suffer grievous loss.'" Surely there can be few losses more grievous than the abrogation of parental rights. Yet the Court today asserts that this deprivation somehow is less serious than threatened losses deemed to require appointed counsel, because in this instance the parent's own "personal liberty" is not at stake.

I do not believe that our cases support the "presumption" asserted, that physical confinement is the only loss of liberty grievous enough to trigger a right to appointed counsel under the Due Process Clause. Indeed, incarceration has been found to be neither a necessary nor a sufficient condition for requiring counsel on behalf of an indigent defendant.

* * *

Rather than opting for the insensitive presumption that incarceration is the only loss of liberty sufficiently onerous to justify a right to appointed counsel, I would abide by the Court's enduring commitment to examine the relationships among the interests on both sides, and the appropriateness of counsel in the specific type of proceeding. The fundamental significance of the liberty interest at stake in a parental termination proceeding is undeniable, and I would find this first portion of the due process balance weighing heavily in favor of refined procedural protections. The second *Eldridge* factor, namely, the risk of error in the procedure provided by the State, must then be reviewed with some care.

The method chosen by North Carolina to extinguish parental rights resembles in many respects a criminal prosecution. . . . [T]he termination procedure is distinctly formal and adversarial. The State initiates the proceeding by filing a petition in district court, and serving a summons on the parent. A state judge presides over the adjudicatory hearing that follows, and the hearing is conducted pursuant to the formal rules of evidence and procedure. In general, hearsay is inadmissible and records must be authenticated.

In addition, the proceeding has an obvious accusatory and punitive focus. In moving to terminate a parent's rights, the State has concluded that it no longer will try to preserve the family unit, but instead will marshal an array of public resources to establish that the parent-child separation must be made permanent. The State has legal representation through the county attorney. This lawyer has access to public records concerning the family and to professional social workers who are empowered to investigate the family situation and to testify against the parent. The State's legal representative may also call upon experts in family relations, psychology, and medicine to bolster the State's case. And, of course, the State's counsel himself is an expert in the legal standards and techniques employed at the termination proceeding, including the methods of cross-examination.

* * *

The legal issues posed by the State's petition are neither simple nor easily defined. The standard is imprecise and open to the subjective values of the judge. A parent seeking to prevail against the State must be prepared to adduce evidence about his or her personal abilities and lack of fault, as well as proof of progress and foresight as a parent that the State would deem adequate and improved over the situation underlying a previous adverse judgment of child neglect. The parent cannot possibly succeed without being able to identify material issues, develop defenses, gather and present sufficient supporting nonhearsay evidence, and conduct cross-examination of adverse witnesses.

* * *

The risk of error thus is severalfold. The parent who actually has achieved the improvement or quality of parenting the State would require may be unable to establish this fact. The parent who has failed in these regards may be unable to demonstrate cause, absence of willfulness, or lack of agency diligence as justification. And errors of fact or law in the State's case may go unchallenged and uncorrected. Given the weight of the interests at stake, this risk of error assumes extraordinary proportions. By intimidation, inarticulateness, or confusion, a parent can lose forever all contact and involvement with his or her offspring.

The final factor to be considered, the interests claimed for the State, do not tip the scale against providing appointed counsel in this context. The State hardly is in a position to assert here that it seeks the informality of a rehabilitative or educative proceeding into which counsel for the parent would inject an unwelcome adversarial edge. As the Assistant Attorney General of North Carolina declared before this Court, once the State moves for termination, it "has made a decision that the child cannot go home and should not go home. It no longer has an obligation to try and restore that family."

The State may, and does, properly assert a legitimate interest in promoting the physical and emotional well-being of its minor children. But this interest is not served by terminating the rights of any concerned, responsible parent. Indeed, because North Carolina is committed to "protect[ing] all children from the unnecessary severance of a relationship with biological or legal parents," "the State spites its own articulated goals when it needlessly separates" the parent from the child.

The State also has an interest in avoiding the cost and administrative inconvenience that might accompany a right to appointed counsel. But, as the Court acknowledges, the State's fiscal interest "is hardly significant enough to overcome private interests as important as those here." The State's financial concern indeed is a limited one, for the right to appointed counsel may well be restricted to those termination proceedings that are instituted by the State. Moreover, no difficult line-drawing problem would arise with respect to other types of civil proceedings. The instant due process analysis takes full account of the fundamental nature of the parental interest, the permanency of the threatened deprivation, the gross imbalance between the resources employed by the prosecuting State and those available to the indigent parent, and the relatively insubstantial cost of furnishing counsel. An absence of any one of these factors might yield a different result. But where, as here, the threatened loss of liberty is severe and absolute, the State's role is so clearly adversarial and punitive, and the cost involved is relatively slight, there is no sound basis for refusing to recognize the right to counsel as a requisite of due process in a proceeding initiated by the State to terminate parental rights.

The Court's analysis is markedly similar to mine; it, too, analyzes the three factors listed in *Mathews v. Eldridge*, and it, too, finds the private interest weighty, the procedure devised by the State fraught with risks of error, and the countervailing governmental interest insubstantial. Yet, rather than follow this balancing process to its logical conclusion, the Court abruptly pulls back and announces that a defendant parent must await a case-by-case determination of his or her need for counsel. Because the three factors "will not always be so distributed," reasons the Court, the Constitution should not be read to "requir[e] the appointment of counsel in every parental termination proceeding." This conclusion is not only illogical, but it also marks a sharp departure from the due process analysis consistently applied heretofore. The flexibility of due process, the Court has held, requires case-by-case consideration of different decisionmaking contexts, not of different litigants within a given context. In analyzing the nature of the private and governmental interests at stake, along with the risk of error, the Court in the past has not limited itself to the particular case at hand. Instead, after addressing the three factors as generic elements in the context raised by the particular case, the Court then has formulated a rule that has general application to similarly situated cases.

Procedural norms are devised to ensure that justice may be done in every case, and to protect litigants against unpredictable and unchecked adverse governmental action. Through experience with decisions in varied situations over time, lessons emerge that reflect a general understanding as to what is minimally necessary to assure fair play. Such lessons are best expressed to have general application which guarantees the predictability and uniformity that underlie our society's commitment to the rule of law. By endorsing, instead, a retrospective review of the trial record of each particular defendant parent, the Court today undermines the very rationale on which this concept of general fairness is based.

* * *

Petitioner plainly has not led the life of the exemplary citizen or model parent. It may well be that if she were accorded competent legal representation, the ultimate result in this particular case would be the same. But the issue before the Court is not petitioner's character; it is whether she was given a meaningful opportunity to be heard when the State moved to terminate absolutely her parental rights. In light of the unpursued avenues of defense, and of the experience petitioner underwent at the hearing, I find virtually incredible the Court's conclusion today that her termination proceeding was fundamentally fair. To reach that conclusion, the Court simply ignores the defendant's obvious inability to speak effectively for herself, a factor the Court has found to be highly significant in past cases. I am unable to ignore that factor; instead, I believe that the record, and the norms of fairness acknowledged by the majority, compel a holding according counsel to petitioner and persons similarly situated.

* * *

Notes and Questions

1. *The Strength of the Parental Interests.* Did the majority and dissent differ in their views about the strength of the parental interests involved in *Lassiter*? The majority conceded that a parent's interest in the care of her children is an important interest and that the

termination of parental rights worked a unique kind of deprivation. The dissent regarded the parental interests as part of the fundamental liberty protected by the Fourteenth Amendment. The dissent also emphasized there could be "few losses more grievous than the abrogation of parental rights."

2. *The Risk of Erroneous Deprivation.* Did the majority and dissent differ in their views about the risk of erroneous deprivation? The majority noted that the factors involved in termination hearings "may combine to overwhelm an uncounseled parent" and that all courts other than the North Carolina court had held that indigent parents had a due process right to appointed counsel in termination proceedings. The dissent emphasized the "extraordinary" possibilities for error involved in such hearings.

3. *The Strength of the Government's Interests.* Did the majority and dissent differ in their views about the government's interests? Both the majority and dissent acknowledged the government's interests, first, in an accurate and just decision, and second, in the containment of costs.

4. *The Meaning of Liberty.* One of the major disagreements between the majority and dissent was whether due process protects more than physical liberty. Both opinions argued that precedents supported their views. If *Lassiter* were reconsidered today, would or should the outcome change?

5. *Ad Hoc Determinations.* On what basis did the majority conclude that presiding trial judges and reviewing appellate judges should decide whether due process requires appointment of counsel for a parent in each case? On what should this depend? Will courts decide that some parent's have less of a liberty interest in participating in the care of their children than others? Will the government's interests in protecting the best interests of the child vary among cases? Should the relative merits affect the courts' views of the process required? Identify the factors deemed relevant to the Court in its determination that due process did not require appointment of counsel for Ms. Lassiter.

6. *The Role of Counsel.* What could counsel have done for Ms. Lassiter in her termination proceeding?

CHAPTER 6: THE QUEST FOR EQUAL PROTECTION

A Brief Overview of Equal Protection Doctrine

The Fourteenth Amendment of the United States Constitution expressly prohibits government from denying to any person the equal protection of the laws, and it applies only to state governments. The U.S. Supreme Court held that the Fifth Amendment's Due Process Clause implies that the federal government also may not deny equal protection of the laws. In this decision, *Bolling v. Sharpe*, 347 U.S. 497 (1954), the Court invalidated racial segregation of public schools in the District of Columbia. As a result, both the states and federal governments are bound by the guarantee to all individuals that they will receive the equal protection of the laws.

To bring an equal protection challenge, a claimant must show that some government action impacted the claimant differently than others who were otherwise similarly situated. Most laws discriminate in the sense that they distinguish between various sorts of characteristics or behaviors. For example, persons over a certain age, typically sixteen, may be licensed to drive a car, while persons under that age are categorically excluded from eligibility for a driver's license. Such a distinction serves a state's interest in licensing only people with the requisite maturity to handle the responsibilities of driving an automobile. The law substitutes a classification, people over a certain age, for individual determinations of ability to drive. Most classifications are not perfectly tailored, however, but are overinclusive or underinclusive. For example, a minimum driving age law may be overinclusive in that it allows licensing of drivers who lack the requisite maturity of judgment. The law also may be underinclusive in that it prohibits licensing of drivers who are sufficiently capable of responsible driving.

Courts do not see every form of discrimination between classes of people as problematic. Courts subject most laws to mere *rationality review*, and will uphold those laws against equal protection challenges so long as the law's classification *rationally furthers a legitimate interest of the government*. Rationality review involves minimal judicial scrutiny and maximum deference to the legislature or administrative body that created the law at issue. Courts tend to accept the government's argument that the law rationally furthers some legitimate government interest.

Courts review laws with greater care, and with correspondingly less deference to the government, in one of two instances. Laws that disadvantage a *suspect class* or interfere with a *fundamental right* receive some form of *heightened scrutiny.*

Traditionally, suspect classes were groups who were "discrete and insular minorities." This language originated in the famous footnote four of *United States v. Carolene Products Co.*, 304 U.S. 144, 152 n.4 (1938), in which Justice Stone opined that "prejudice against discrete and insular minorities may be a special condition, which tends seriously to curtail the operation of those political processes ordinarily to be relied upon to protect minorities, and which may call for a correspondingly more searching judicial inquiry. . . ." Generally speaking, a group is discrete if it is identifiable and it is insular if it is isolated or segregated from the rest of society. Over time courts interpreted this phrase to require consideration of three factors: (1) whether the group experienced historical discrimination; (2) whether the group was politically less powerful or underrepresented compared to others; and (3) whether the trait identifying the group was an immutable characteristic that was not readily subject to change. Not all courts, however, have considered all three factors. Indeed, some uncertainty about the continued viability of these three factors persists.

Certain groups convinced courts that their group was a suspect class. Courts generally reversed laws that treated them differently. For example, African-Americans obtained the form of heightened scrutiny known as *strict scrutiny*, meaning the government must prove that its classification *was necessary to serve a compelling government interest.* Women, by comparison, achieved only *intermediate scrutiny*, meaning the government must prove that its classification *substantially furthered an important government interest.* Ironically, after African-Americans and women convinced the courts that their classes of people suffered greater discrimination and therefore deserved greater judicial scrutiny of laws affecting them, courts then generalized this protection to the broader relevant classifications, race and gender. Under current doctrine, not only do laws adversely affecting African-Americans and women receive heightened judicial scrutiny, but laws adversely affecting any race or gender of people receive similar heightened scrutiny.

Courts are much less settled about the appropriate level of scrutiny for other classes or groups of people. Nevertheless, some generalizations emerge. In addition to racial classifications, laws that classify based on alienage or ethnicity tend to be subjected to strict scrutiny. In addition to gender classifications, laws that classify based on the marital status of a child's parents tend to be subjected to intermediate scrutiny. Finally, laws that classify based on age and citizenship status receive mere rationality review, presumably because groups of certain ages or citizenship statuses do not constitute suspect classes. Most courts historically have granted only mere rationality review to classifications based on sexual orientation.

In addition to subjecting classifications that disadvantage suspect classes to strict scrutiny review, courts also utilize strict scrutiny where legal classifications burden fundamental rights. When government benefit programs are at issue, two levels of inquiry emerge. The first inquiry asks whether recipients have a direct fundamental right to the benefit at issue. For example, do poor people enjoy a fundamental right to subsistence? If so, does the government have a duty to provide welfare benefits? The second level of inquiry addresses whether limitations placed on receipt of welfare may burden other fundamental rights, albeit indirectly. For example, does a state's length of residency requirement burden a welfare applicant's fundamental right to interstate travel?

This chapter will explore these levels of scrutiny as they relate to poor people.

A. RATIONALITY REVIEW

1. Minimum Rationality

When a court decides that a group is not a suspect class and that the burdened interest is not a fundamental right, it rejects heightened scrutiny and employs mere rationality review. Courts sometimes apply mere rationality review without explaining why they rejected heightened scrutiny. Consider the extent to which the case below, *Dandridge v. Williams*, addresses whether either poor people or welfare recipients are a suspect class and whether subsistence is a fundamental right. The case involves a challenge to a state's maximum grant, referring to the rule that a family may receive a maximum amount of benefits regardless of the family's actual size or need.

DANDRIDGE v. WILLIAMS

397 U.S. 471 (1970)

Justice STEWART delivered the opinion of the Court.

This case involves the validity of a method used by Maryland, in the administration of an aspect of its public welfare program, to reconcile the demands of its needy citizens with the finite resources available to meet those demands. Like every other State in the Union, Maryland participates in the Federal Aid to Families With Dependent Children (AFDC) program, which originated with the Social Security Act of 1935. Under this jointly financed program, a State computes the so-called "standard of need" of each eligible family unit within its borders. Some States provide that every family shall receive grants sufficient to meet fully the determined standard of need. Other States provide that each family unit shall receive a percentage of the determined need. Still others provide grants to most families in full accord with the ascertained standard of need, but impose an upper limit on the total amount of money any one family unit may receive. Maryland, through administrative adoption of a "maximum grant regulation," has followed this last course. This suit was brought by several AFDC recipients to enjoin the application of the Maryland maximum grant regulation on the ground that it is in conflict with the Social Security Act of 1935 and with the Equal Protection Clause of the Fourteenth Amendment. A three-judge District Court, convened pursuant to 28 U.S.C. § 2281, held that the Maryland regulation violates the Equal Protection Clause. . . .

The operation of the Maryland welfare system is not complex. By statute the State participates in the AFDC program. It computes the standard of need for each eligible family based on the number of children in the family and the circumstances under which the family lives. In general, the standard of need increases with each additional person in the household, but the increments become proportionately smaller. The regulation here in issue imposes upon the grant that any single family may receive an upper limit of $250 per month in certain counties and Baltimore City, and of $240 per month elsewhere in the

State. The appellees all have large families, so that their standards of need as computed by the State substantially exceed the maximum grants that they actually receive under the regulation. The appellees urged in the District Court that the maximum grant limitation operates to discriminate against them merely because of the size of their families, in violation of the Equal Protection Clause of the Fourteenth Amendment. They claimed further that the regulation is incompatible with the purpose of the Social Security Act of 1935, as well as in conflict with its explicit provisions.

* * *

The appellees contend that the maximum grant system is contrary to § 402(a)(10) of the Social Security Act, as amended, which requires that a state plan shall "provide . . . that all individuals wishing to make application for aid to families with dependent children shall have opportunity to do so, and that aid to families with dependent children shall be furnished with reasonable promptness to all eligible individuals." The argument is that the state regulation denies benefits to the younger children in a large family. Thus, the appellees say, the regulation is in patent violation of the Act, since those younger children are just as "dependent" as their older siblings under the definition of "dependent child" fixed by federal law. Moreover, it is argued that the regulation, in limiting the amount of money any single household may receive, contravenes a basic purpose of the federal law by encouraging the parents of large families to "farm out" their children to relatives whose grants are not yet subject to the maximum limitation.

It cannot be gainsaid that the effect of the Maryland maximum grant provision is to reduce the per capita benefits to the children in the largest families. Although the appellees argue that the younger and more recently arrived children in such families are totally deprived of aid, a more realistic view is that the lot of the entire family is diminished because of the presence of additional children without any increase in payments. It is no more accurate to say that the last child's grant is wholly taken away than to say that the grant of the first child is totally rescinded. In fact, it is the *family* grant that is affected. Whether this per capita diminution is compatible with the statute is the question here. For the reasons that follow, we have concluded that the Maryland regulation is permissible under the federal law.

* * *

The States must respond to this federal statutory concern for preserving children in a family environment. Given Maryland's finite resources, its choice is either to support some families adequately and others less adequately, or not to give sufficient support to any family. We see nothing in the federal statute that forbids a State to balance the stresses that uniform insufficiency of payments would impose on all families against the greater ability of large families--because of the inherent economies of scale--to accommodate their needs to diminished per capita payments. The strong policy of the statute in favor of preserving family units does not prevent a State from sustaining as many families as it can, and providing the largest families somewhat less than their ascertained per capita standard of need. Nor does the maximum grant system necessitate the dissolution of family bonds. For even if a parent should be inclined to increase his per capita family income by sending a child away, the federal law requires that the child, to be eligible for AFDC payments, must live with one of several enumerated relatives. The kinship tie may be attenuated but it cannot be destroyed.

The appellees rely most heavily upon the statutory requirement that aid "shall be furnished with reasonable promptness to all eligible individuals." But since the statute leaves the level of benefits within the judgment of the State, this language cannot mean that the "aid" furnished must equal the total of each individual's standard of need in every family group. Indeed the appellees do not deny that a scheme of proportional reductions for all families could be used that would result in no individual's receiving aid equal to his standard of need. As we have noted, the practical effect of the Maryland regulation is that all children, even in very large families, do receive some aid. . . . So long as some aid is provided to all eligible families and all eligible children, the statute itself is not violated.

* * *

Although a State may adopt a maximum grant system in allocating its funds available for AFDC payments without violating the Act, it may not, of course, impose a regime of invidious discrimination in violation of the Equal Protection Clause of the Fourteenth Amendment. Maryland says that its maximum grant regulation is wholly free of any invidiously discriminatory purpose or effect, and that the regulation is rationally supportable on at least four entirely valid grounds. The regulation can be clearly justified, Maryland argues, in terms of legitimate state interests in encouraging gainful employment, in maintaining an equitable balance in economic status as between welfare families and those supported by a wage-earner, in providing incentives for family planning, and in allocating available public funds in such a way as fully to meet the needs of the largest possible number of families.

* * *

In the area of economics and social welfare, a State does not violate the Equal Protection Clause merely because the classifications made by its laws are imperfect. If the classification has some "reasonable basis," it does not offend the Constitution simply because the classification "is not made with mathematical nicety or because in practice it results in some inequality."

* * *

Under this long-established meaning of the Equal Protection Clause, it is clear that the Maryland Maximum grant regulation is constitutionally valid. We need not explore all the reasons that the State advances in justification of the regulation. It is enough that a solid foundation for the regulation can be found in the State's legitimate interest in encouraging employment and in avoiding discrimination between welfare families and the families of the working poor. By combining a limit on the recipient's grant with permission to retain money earned, without reduction in the amount of the grant, Maryland provides an incentive to seek gainful employment. And by keying the maximum family AFDC grants to the minimum wage a steadily employed head of a household receives, the State maintains some semblance of an equitable balance between families on welfare and those supported by an employed breadwinner.

It is true that in some AFDC families there may be no person who is employable. It is also true that with respect to AFDC families whose determined standard of need is below the regulatory maximum, and who therefore receive grants equal to the determined standard, the employment incentive is absent. But the Equal Protection Clause does not require that a State must choose between attacking every aspect of a problem or not attacking the problem at all. It is enough that the State's action be rationally based and free from invidious discrimination. The regulation before us meets that test.

We do not decide today that the Maryland regulation is wise, that it best fulfills the relevant social and economic objectives that Maryland might ideally espouse, or that a more just and humane system could not be devised. Conflicting claims of morality and intelligence are raised by opponents and proponents of almost every measure, certainly including the one before us. But the intractable economic, social, and even philosophical problems presented by public welfare assistance programs are not the business of this Court. The Constitution may impose certain procedural safeguards upon systems of welfare administration. But the Constitution does not empower this Court to second-guess state officials charged with the difficult responsibility of allocating limited public welfare funds among the myriad of potential recipients.

The judgment is reversed.

Justice MARSHALL, whom Justice BRENNAN joins, dissenting.

* * *

At the outset, it should be emphasized exactly what is involved in determining whether this maximum grant regulation is consistent with and valid under the federal law. In administering its AFDC program, Maryland has established its own standards of need, and they are not under challenge in this litigation. Indeed, the District Court specifically refused to require additional appropriations on the part of the State or to permit appellees to recover a monetary judgment against the State. At the same time, however, there is no contention, nor could there be any, that the maximum grant regulation is in any manner related to calculation of need.[1] Rather, it arbitrarily cuts across state-defined standards of need to deny any additional assistance with respect to the fifth or any succeeding child in a family. In short, the regulation represents no less than the refusal of the State to give any aid whatsoever for the support of

[1]The Court is thus wrong in speaking of "the greater ability of large families--because of the inherent economies of scale--to accommodate their needs to diminished per capita payments." Those economies have already been taken into account once in calculating the standard of need. Indeed, it borders on the ludicrous to suggest that a large family is more capable of living on perhaps 50% of its standard of need than a small family is on 95%.

certain dependent children who meet the standards of need that the State itself has established.

Since its inception in the Social Security Act of 1935, the focus of the federal AFDC program has been to provide benefits for the support of dependent children of needy families with a view toward maintaining and strengthening family life within the family unit. . . . In meeting these objectives, moreover, Congress has provided the outlines that the AFDC plan is to follow if a State should choose to participate in the federal program. The maximum grant regulation, however, does not fall within these outlines or accord with the purposes of the Act. And the Court by approving it allows for a complete departure from the congressional intent.

* * *

[Justice MARSHALL asserts that the Maryland regulation violates the federal AFDC provisions by: (1) creating "in effect a class of otherwise eligible dependent children with respect to whom no assistance is granted"; (2) providing for the State's continued receipt of "a federal subsidy for each and every dependent child even though the State passes none of this subsidy on to the large families for the use of the additional dependent children"; and (3) providing "a strong economic incentive to the disintegration of large families."]

* * *

The Maryland AFDC program in its basic structure operates uniformly with regard to all needy children by taking into account the basic subsistence needs of all eligible individuals in the formulation of the standards of need for families of various sizes. However, superimposed upon this uniform system is the maximum grant regulation, the operative effect of which is to create two classes of needy children and two classes of eligible families: those small families and their members who receive payments to cover their subsistence needs and those large families who do not.

This classification process effected by the maximum grant regulation produces a basic denial of equal treatment. Persons who are concededly similarly situated (dependent children and their families), are not afforded equal, or even approximately equal, treatment under the maximum grant regulation. Subsistence benefits are paid with respect to some needy dependent children; nothing is paid with respect to others. Some needy families receive full subsistence assistance as calculated by the State; the assistance paid to other families is grossly below their similarly calculated needs.

Yet, as a general principle, individuals should not be afforded different treatment by the State unless there is a relevant distinction between them and "a statutory discrimination must be based on differences that are reasonably related to the purposes of the Act in which it is found."

* * *

In the instant case, the only distinction between those children with respect to whom assistance is granted and those children who are denied such assistance is the size of the family into which the child permits himself to be born. The class of individuals with respect to whom payments are actually made (the first four or five eligible dependent children in a family), is grossly underinclusive in terms of the class that the AFDC program was designed to assist, namely, *all* needy dependent children. Such underinclusiveness manifests "a prima facie violation of the equal protection requirement of reasonable classification," compelling the State to come forward with a persuasive justification for the classification.

The Court never undertakes to inquire for such a justification; rather it avoids the task by focusing upon the abstract dichotomy between two different approaches to equal protection problems that have been utilized by this Court.

Under the so-called "traditional test," a classification is said to be permissible under the Equal Protection Clause unless it is "without any reasonable basis." On the other hand, if the classification affects a "fundamental right," then the state interest in perpetuating the classification must be "compelling" in order to be sustained.

* * *

In my view, equal protection analysis of this case is not appreciably advanced by the *a priori* definition of a "right," fundamental or otherwise. Rather, concentration must be placed upon the character of the classification in question, the relative importance to individuals in the class discriminated against of the governmental benefits that they do not receive, and the asserted state interests in support of the classification. As we said only recently, "In determining whether or not a state law violates the Equal Protection Clause, we must consider the facts and circumstances behind the law, the interests which the State claims to be protecting, and the interests of those who are disadvantaged by the classification."

It is the individual interests here at stake that, as the Court concedes, most clearly distinguish this case from the "business regulation" equal protection cases. AFDC support to needy dependent children provides the stuff that sustains those children's lives: food, clothing, shelter. And this Court has already recognized several times that when a benefit, even a "gratuitous" benefit, is necessary to sustain life, stricter constitutional standards, both procedural and substantive, are applied to the deprivation of that benefit.

Nor is the distinction upon which the deprivation is here based--the distinction between large and small families--one that readily commends itself as a basis for determining which children are to have support approximating subsistence and which are not. Indeed, governmental discrimination between children on the basis of a factor over which they have no control--the number of their brothers and sisters--bears some resemblance to the classification between legitimate and illegitimate children which we condemned as a violation of the Equal Protection Clause in *Levy v. Louisiana*.

The asserted state interests in the maintenance of the maximum grant regulation, on the other hand, are hardly clear. In the early stages of this litigation, the State attempted to rationalize the maximum grant regulation on the theory that it was merely a device to conserve state funds, in the language of the motion to dismiss, "a legitimate way of allocating the State's limited resources available for AFDC assistance.". . . The District Court quite properly rejected this asserted justification, for "[t]he saving of welfare costs cannot justify an otherwise invidious classification."

In post-trial proceedings in the District Court, and in briefs to this court, the State apparently abandoned reliance on the fiscal justification. In its place, there have now appeared several different rationales for the maximum grant regulation, prominent among them being those relied upon by the majority--the notions that imposition of the maximum serves as an incentive to welfare recipients to find and maintain employment and provides a semblance of equality with persons earning a minimum wage.

With regard to the latter, Maryland has urged that the maximum grant regulation serves to maintain a rough equality between wage earning families and AFDC families, thereby increasing the political support for--or perhaps reducing the opposition to--the AFDC program. It is questionable whether the Court really relies on this ground, especially when in many States the prescribed family maximum bears no such relation to the minimum wage. But the Court does not indicate that a different result might obtain in other cases. Indeed, whether elimination of the maximum would produce welfare incomes out of line with other incomes in Maryland is itself open to question on this record. It is true that government in the United States, unlike certain other countries, has not chosen to make public aid available to assist families generally in raising their children. Rather, in this case Maryland, with the encouragement and assistance of the Federal Government, has elected to provide assistance at a subsistence level for those in particular need--the aged, the blind, the infirm, and the unemployed and unemployable, and their children. The only question presented here is whether, having once undertaken such a program, the State may arbitrarily select from among the concededly eligible those to whom it will provide benefits. And it is too late to argue that political expediency will sustain discrimination not otherwise supportable.

Vital to the employment-incentive basis found by the Court to sustain the regulation is, of course, the supposition that an appreciable number of AFDC recipients are in fact employable. For it is perfectly obvious that limitations upon assistance cannot reasonably operate as a work incentive with regard to those who cannot work or who cannot be expected to work. In this connection, Maryland candidly notes that "only a very small percentage of the total universe of welfare recipients are employable." The State, however, urges us to ignore the "total universe" and to concentrate attention instead upon the heads of AFDC families. Yet the very purpose of the AFDC program since its inception has been to provide assistance for dependent *children*. The State's position is thus that the State may deprive certain needy children of assistance to which they would otherwise be entitled in order to provide an arguable work incentive for their parents. But the State may not wield its economic whip in this fashion when the effect is to cause a deprivation to needy dependent children in order to correct an arguable fault of their parents.

Even if the invitation of the State to focus upon the heads of AFDC families is accepted, the minimum rationality of the maximum grant regulation is hard to discern. The District Court found that of Maryland's more than 32,000 AFDC families, only about 116 could be classified as having employable members, and, of these, the number to which the maximum grant regulation was applicable is not disclosed by the record. The State objects that this figure includes only families in which the father is unemployed and fails to take account of families in which an employable mother is the head of the household. At the same time, however, the State itself has recognized that the vast proportion of these mothers are in fact unemployable because they are mentally or physically incapacitated, because they have no marketable skills, or, most prominently, because the best interests of the children dictate that the mother remain in the home. Thus, it is clear, although the record does not disclose precise figures, that the total number of "employable" mothers is but a fraction of the total number of AFDC mothers. Furthermore, the record is silent as to what proportion of large families subject to the maximum have "employable" mothers. Indeed, one must assume that the presence of the mother in the home can be less easily dispensed with in the case of large families, particularly where small children are involved and alternative provisions for their care are accordingly more difficult to arrange. In short, not only has the State failed to establish that there is a substantial or even a significant proportion of AFDC heads of households as to whom the maximum grant regulation arguably serves as a viable and logical work incentive, but it is also indisputable that the regulation at best is drastically *overinclusive* since it applies with equal vigor to a very substantial number of persons who like appellees are completely disabled from working.

Finally, it should be noted that, to the extent there is a legitimate state interest in encouraging heads of AFDC households to find employment, application of the maximum grant regulation is also grossly *underinclusive* because it singles out and affects only large families. No reason is suggested why this particular group should be carved out for the purpose of having unusually harsh "work incentives" imposed upon them. Not only has the State selected for special treatment a small group from among similarly situated families, but it has done so on a basis--family size--that bears no relation to the evil that the State claims the regulation was designed to correct. There is simply no indication whatever that heads of large families, as opposed to heads of small families, are particularly prone to refuse to seek or to maintain employment.

* * *

In the final analysis, Maryland has set up an AFDC program structured to calculate and pay the minimum standard of need to dependent children. Having set up that program, however, the State denies some of those needy children the minimum subsistence standard of living, and it does so on the wholly arbitrary basis that they happen to be members of large families.

* * *

The basis of that discrimination--the classification of individuals into large and small families--is too arbitrary and too unconnected to the asserted rationale, the impact on those discriminated against--the denial of even a subsistence existence--too great, and the supposed interests served too contrived and attenuated to meet the requirements of the Constitution. In my view Maryland's maximum grant regulation is invalid under the Equal Protection Clause of the Fourteenth Amendment.

I would affirm the judgment of the District Court.

Notes and Questions

1. *Assumptions Underlying the Statutory Interpretation.* The Court first considered whether Maryland's family cap violated the federal AFDC statute's requirement that "all eligible individuals" receive benefits. In rejecting the plaintiffs' argument that the fifth and later children of a family receive no benefits, the Court assumed that large families spread their benefits among all family members and that they benefit from "the inherent economies of scale." How did the majority of the Court justify these assumptions? Are these assumptions matters of logic? Are they empirical questions better determined based on credible evidence?

2. *Equal Protection Claim.* What is the equal protection challenge in *Dandridge*? What similarly situated classes are treated differently? If, as Justice Marshall suggested, the classes are needy children in large families compared to needy children in small families, does this case squarely raise the issue of whether either poor people or welfare recipients are a suspect class? If not, should

Dandridge affect the determination of whether poor people are a suspect class?

Notice that the Court never discussed the criteria for suspect class analysis, including: (1) historical disadvantage; (2) political powerlessness or underrepresentation; and (3) immutability or difficulty of changing the relevant characteristic. Have poor people been subjected to discrimination historically? Are poor people disadvantaged in effecting political change? How difficult is it to move out of poverty?

3. *Reverse Scrutiny.* The Court seemed to declare that all laws affecting welfare, whether they may disadvantage a suspect class or interfere with a fundamental right, shall only receive mere rationality review. In these passages, the Court established a sort of reverse-scrutiny. It suggested that the "intractable" difficulties of welfare programs justifies complete deference to legislators and welfare administrators. Is this complete deference appropriate?

4. *The Fit Between the Maximum Grant and Encouraging Employment.* The court identified encouraging employment as one of the state's legitimate interests. Yet the state also wanted to encourage employment of small welfare families. So the family cap was underinclusive in encouraging employment. And some welfare families do not have an employable member. So the family cap was overinclusive in encouraging employment. Why did the Court decide that such an overinclusive and underinclusive law was nevertheless "rationally based"?

5. *The Fit Between the Maximum Grant and Not Discriminating Against the Working Poor.* The Court supported the State's interest in not discriminating between needy welfare families and needy families of the working poor. Are these two groups distinct? While some may have thought so then, studies now show that 40% of welfare families are working poor families. Does this undercut the Court's analysis? Does it mean that large working poor welfare families suffer the greatest combined disadvantages (low wages and capped welfare benefits), which the legislature may have failed to recognize?

6. *Marshall's Balancing Test.* Justice Marshall proposed that the Court balance the relevant factors, including the character of the classification, the relative importance of the benefits, and the states interests. Would this balancing test better serve the interests of the

welfare recipient? How did Justice Marshall counter the majority's arguments in his dissent? For a defense of Justice Marshall's approach, *see* Gay Gellhorn, *Justice Thurgood Marshall's Jurisprudence of Equal Protection of the Laws and the Poor,* 26 ARIZONA STATE LAW JOURNAL 429 (1994).

7. *Family Cap.* To what extent is the *Dandridge* maximum grant similar to the contemporary family cap experiments which typically deny additional benefits for children born while the family receives welfare? Does *Dandridge* determine the constitutionality of contemporary family cap rules?

2. Heightened Rationality

Courts occasionally subject a law to mere rationality review, but nevertheless invalidate the classification. Consider whether any differences between *Dandridge* and the cases that follow justify the different outcomes.

UNITED STATES DEPARTMENT OF AGRICULTURE
v.
MORENO

413 U.S. 528 (1973)

Justice BRENNAN delivered the opinion of the Court.

This case requires us to consider the constitutionality of § 3(e) of the Food Stamp Act of 1964, which, with certain exceptions, excludes from participation in the food stamp program any household containing an individual who is unrelated to any other member of the household. In practical effect, § 3(e) creates two classes of persons for food stamp purposes: one class is composed of those individuals who live in households all of whose members are related to one another, and the other class consists of those individuals who live in households containing one or more members who are unrelated to the rest. The latter class of persons is denied federal food assistance. A three-judge District Court for the District of Columbia held this classification invalid as violative of the Due Process Clause of the Fifth Amendment. We noted probable jurisdiction. We affirm.

The federal food stamp program was established in 1964 in an effort to alleviate hunger and malnutrition among the more needy segments of our society. Eligibility for participation in the program is determined on a household rather than an individual basis. An eligible household purchases sufficient food stamps to provide that household with a nutritionally adequate diet. The household pays for the stamps at a reduced rate based upon its size and cumulative income. The food stamps are then used to purchase food at retail stores, and the Government redeems the stamps at face value, thereby paying the difference between the actual cost of the food and the amount paid by the household for the stamps.

As initially enacted, § 3(e) defined a "household" as "a group of related or non-related individuals, who are not residents of an institution or boarding house, but are living as one economic unit sharing common cooking facilities and for whom food is customarily purchased in common." In January 1971, however Congress redefined the term "household" so as to include only groups of related individuals. Pursuant to this amendment, the Secretary of Agriculture promulgated regulations rendering ineligible for participation in the program any "household" whose members are not "all related to each other."

Appellees in this case consist of several groups of individuals who allege that, although they satisfy the income eligibility requirements for federal food assistance, they have nevertheless been excluded from the program solely because the persons in each group are not "all related to each other." Appellee Jacinta Moreno, for example is a 56-year-old diabetic who lives with Ermina Sanchez and the latter's three children. They share common living expenses, and Mrs. Sanchez helps to care for appellee. Appellee's monthly income, derived from public assistance, is $75; Mrs. Sanchez receives $133 per month from public assistance. The household pays $135 per month for rent, gas and electricity, of which appellee pays $50. Appellee spends $10 per month for transportation to a hospital for regular visits, and $5 per month for laundry. That leaves her $10 per month for food and other necessities. Despite her poverty, appellee has been denied federal food assistance solely because she is unrelated to the other members of her household. Moreover, although Ms. Sanchez and her three children were permitted to purchase $108 worth of food stamps per month for $18, their participation in the program will be terminated if appellee Moreno continues to live with them.

Appellee Sheilah Hejny is married and has three children. Although the Hejnys are indigent, they took in a 20-year-old girl, who is unrelated to them because "we felt she had emotional problems." The Hejnys receive $144 worth of food stamps each month for $14. If they allow the 20-year-old girl to continue to live with them, they will be denied food stamps by reason of § 3(e).

Appellee Victoria Keppler has a daughter with an acute hearing deficiency. The daughter requires special instruction in a school for the deaf. The school is located in an area in which appellee could not ordinarily afford to live. Thus, in order to make the most of her limited resources, appellee agreed to share an apartment near the school with a woman who, like appellee, is on public assistance. Since appellee is not related to the woman, appellee's food stamps have been, and will continue to be, cut off if they continue to live together.

These and two other groups of appellees instituted a class action against the Department of Agriculture, its Secretary, and two other departmental officials, seeking declaratory and injunctive relief against the enforcement of the 1971 amendment of § 3(e) and its implementing regulations. In essence, appellees contend, and the District Court held, that the "unrelated person" provision of § 3(e) creates an irrational classification in violation of the equal protection component of the Due Process Clause of the Fifth Amendment.[5] We agree.

Under traditional equal protection analysis, a legislative classification must be sustained, if the classification itself is rationally related to a legitimate governmental interest. The purposes of the Food Stamp Act were expressly set forth in the congressional "declaration of policy":

> It is hereby declared to be the policy of Congress . . . to safeguard the health and well-being of the Nation's population and raise levels of nutrition

---

[5]"[W]hile the Fifth Amendment contains no equal protection clause, it does forbid discrimination and is so unjustifiable as to be violative of due process."

> among low-income households. The Congress hereby finds that the limited food purchasing power of low-income households contributes to hunger and malnutrition among members of such households. The Congress further finds that increased utilization of food in establishing and maintaining adequate national levels of nutrition will promote the distribution in a beneficial manner of our agricultural abundances and will strengthen our agricultural economy, as well as result in more orderly marketing and distribution of food. To alleviate such hunger and malnutrition, a food stamp program is herein authorized which will permit low-income households to purchase a nutritionally adequate diet through normal channels of trade.

The challenged statutory classification (households of related persons versus households containing one or more unrelated persons) is clearly irrelevant to the stated purposes of the Act. As the District Court recognized, "[t]he relationships among persons constituting one economic unit and sharing cooking facilities have nothing to do with their abilities to stimulate the agricultural economy by purchasing farm surpluses, or with their personal nutritional requirements."

Thus, if it is to be sustained, the challenged classification must rationally further some legitimate governmental interest other than those specifically stated in the congressional "declaration of policy." Regrettably, there is little legislative history to illuminate the purposes of the 1971 amendment of § 3(e). The legislative history that does exist, however, indicates that that amendment was intended to prevent so-called "hippies" and "hippie communes" from participating in the food stamp program. The challenged classification clearly cannot be sustained by reference to this congressional purpose. For if the constitutional conception of "equal protection of the laws" means anything, it must at the very least mean that a bare congressional desire to harm a politically unpopular group cannot constitute a legitimate governmental interest. As a result, "[a] purpose to discriminate against hippies cannot, in and of itself and without reference to [some independent] considerations in the public interest, justify the 1971 amendment."

Although apparently conceding this point, the Government maintains that the challenged classification should nevertheless be upheld as rationally related to the clearly legitimate governmental interest in minimizing fraud in the administration of the food stamp program.[7] In essence, the Government contends that, in adopting the 1971 amendment, Congress might rationally have thought (1) that households with one or more unrelated members are more likely than "fully related" households to contain individuals who abuse the program by fraudulently failing to report sources of income or by voluntarily remaining poor; and (2) that such households are "relatively unstable," thereby increasing the difficulty of detecting such abuses. But even if we were to accept as rational the Government's wholly unsubstantiated assumptions concerning the differences between "related" and "unrelated" households we still could not agree with the Government's conclusion that the denial of essential federal food assistance to all otherwise eligible households containing unrelated members constitutes a rational effort to deal with these concerns.

At the outset, it is important to note that the Food Stamp Act itself contains provisions, wholly independent of § 3(e), aimed specifically at the problems of fraud and of the voluntarily poor. . . . The existence of these provisions necessarily casts considerable doubt upon the proposition that the 1971 amendment could rationally have been intended to prevent those very same abuses.

* * *

Traditional equal protection analysis does not require that every classification be drawn with precise "mathematical nicety." But the classification here in issue is not only "imprecise," it is wholly without any rational basis. The judgment of the District Court

[7]The Government initially argued to the District Court that the challenged classification might be justified as a means to foster "morality." In rejecting that contention, the District Court noted that "interpreting the amendment as an attempt to regulate morality would raise serious constitutional questions.". . . [T]he District Court observed that it was doubtful at best, whether Congress, "in the name of morality," could "infringe the rights to privacy and freedom of association in the home.". . . The Government itself has now abandoned the "morality" argument.

holding the "unrelated person" provision invalid under the Due Process Clause of the Fifth Amendment is therefore affirmed.

Affirmed.

Justice DOUGLAS, concurring.

* * *

This case involves desperately poor people with acute problems who, though unrelated, come together for mutual help and assistance. The choice of one's associates for social, political, race, or religious purposes is basic in our constitutional scheme.

I suppose no one would doubt that an association of people working in the poverty field would be entitled to the same constitutional protection as those working in the racial, banking, or agricultural field. I suppose poor people holding a meeting or convention would be under the same constitutional umbrella as others. The dimensions of the "unrelated" person problem under the Food Stamp Act are in that category. As the facts of this case show, the poor are congregating in households where they can better meet the adversities of poverty. This banding together is an expression of the right of freedom of association that is very deep in our traditions.

* * *

Congress might choose to deal only with members of a family of one or two or three generations, treating it all as a unit. Congress, however, has not done that here. Concededly an individual living alone is not disqualified from the receipt of food stamp aid, even though there are other members of the family with whom he might theoretically live. Nor are common-law couples disqualified: they, like individuals living alone, may qualify under the Act if they are poor--whether they have abandoned their wives and children and however antifamily their attitudes may be. In other words, the "unrelated" person provision was not aimed at the maintenance of normal family ties. It penalizes persons or families who have brought under their roof an "unrelated" needy person. It penalizes the poorest of the poor for doubling up against the adversities of poverty.

* * *

The "unrelated" person provision of the present Act has an impact on the rights of people to associate for lawful purposes with whom they choose. When state action "may have the effect of curtailing the freedom to associate" it "is subject to the closest scrutiny." The "right of the people peaceably to assemble" guaranteed by the First Amendment covers a wide spectrum of human interests--including "political, economic, religious, or cultural matters." Banding together to combat the common foe of hunger is in that category.

* * *

Justice REHNQUIST, with whom THE CHIEF JUSTICE concurs, dissenting.

* * *

I am unable to agree with the Court's disposition of this case. Here appellees challenged a provision in the Federal Food Stamp Act, which limited food stamps to related people living in one "household." The result of this provision is that unrelated persons who live under the same roof and pool their resources may not obtain food stamps even though otherwise eligible.

The Court's opinion would make a very persuasive congressional committee report arguing against the adoption of the limitation in question. Undoubtedly, Congress attacked the problem with a rather blunt instrument and, just as undoubtedly, persuasive arguments may be made that what we conceive to be its purpose will not be significantly advanced by the enactment of the limitation. But questions such as this are for Congress, rather than for this Court; our role is limited to the determination of whether there is any rational basis on which Congress could decide that public funds made available under the food stamp program should not go to a household containing an individual who is unrelated to any other member of the household.

I do not believe that asserted congressional concern with the fraudulent use of food stamps is, when interpreted in the light most favorable to sustaining the limitation, quite as irrational as the Court seems to believe. A basic unit which Congress has chosen for determination of availability for food stamps is the "household," a determination which is not criticized by the Court. By the limitation here challenged, it has singled out households which contain unrelated persons and made such households ineligible. I do not think it is unreasonable for Congress to conclude that the basic unit which it was willing to support with federal funding through food stamps is some variation on the family as we know it--a household consisting of related individuals. This unit provides a guarantee which is not provided by households containing unrelated individuals that the household exists for some purpose other than to collect federal food stamps.

Admittedly, as the Court points out, the limitation will make ineligible many households which have not been formed for the purpose of collecting federal food stamps, and will at the same time not wholly deny food stamps to those households which may have been formed in large part to take advantage of the program. But, as the Court concedes, "[t]raditional equal protection analysis does not require that every classification be drawn with precise mathematical nicety." * * *

The limitation which Congress enacted could, in the judgment of reasonable men, conceivably deny food stamps to members of households which have been formed solely for the purpose of taking advantage of the food stamp program. Since the food stamp program is not intended to be a subsidy for every individual who desires low-cost food, this was a permissible congressional decision quite consistent with the underlying policy of the Act. The fact that the limitation will have unfortunate and perhaps unintended consequences beyond this does not make it unconstitutional.

Notes and Questions

1. *Purposes of the Benefit Program.* The Court emphasized that the rule limiting Food Stamps to households consisting of related family members does not serve either of the stated purposes of the Food Stamp Act, improving nutrition or strengthening the agricultural economy. Could a similar argument be applied in *Dandridge*? Does any maximum grant or family cap serve the purpose of providing benefits to needy children?

2. *Purposes of the Benefit Restrictions.* The federal government argued that the related household restriction served to prevent fraud in the Food Stamp program, arguing that households of unrelated members were more likely to abuse the program and were more difficult to detect because they were relatively unstable. The federal government contended that Congress "might reasonably have thought" these assumptions were true. The Court characterized them as "wholly unsubstantiated assumptions" and rejected them. When

would these assumptions be proved or challenged? During a Congressional hearing? During litigation? Does rationality review compel courts to determine as a factual matter what purposes the lawmakers sought to serve with their law? Does rationality review compel courts to determine whether the assumptions made by the lawmakers are accurate? How accurate? By a preponderance of the evidence?

3. *"Fit" between Means and Ends.* The Court did not determine whether the government's assumptions were accurate, but held that the denial of Food Stamps to all unrelated households did not rationally serve to prevent fraud. In other words, the "fit" between the ends sought and the means utilized was insufficient. Can you ascertain how close the fit between ends and means must be? How does the fit between ends and means in *Moreno* compare to the fit between the end of encouraging employment and the means of capping family benefits in *Dandridge*? Does the ends-means fit change when you consider the other end in *Dandridge*, not discriminating between needy welfare families and needy working poor families?

How did Justice Rehnquist and Chief Justice Burger address the fit between ends and means in their *Moreno* dissent?

4. *First Amendment Right of Association.* Justice Douglas in his concurrence suggested that the government's restriction of food stamps to households of related family members violates the First Amendment right to free association of persons who choose to live in households with others who are unrelated. Because alleged infringements of freedom to associate are subject to "the closest scrutiny," Justice Douglas believed that the government regulation should have been invalidated. Is it possible that a challenge based on a constitutional provision other than the equal protection guarantees could heighten judicial scrutiny of welfare laws? How does this square with the majority's language in *Dandridge* that "the intractable economic, social, and even philosophical problems presented by public welfare assistance programs are not the Business of this Court"? For further exploration of these ideas, read the materials on the unconstitutional conditions doctrine in Chapter 7.

5. *Animosity.* The Supreme Court cited the *Moreno* decision with approval in *Romer v. Evans*, 116 S. Ct. 1620 (1996), in which

the Court invalidated an anti-gay initiative amendment to Colorado's constitution which prohibited any part of Colorado's government from adopting or enforcing any policy that prohibited discrimination based on sexual orientation. The Court reasoned that mere animosity against a group could not serve as a rational basis for a law, even if that animosity were grounded in moral tradition. The Court concluded that "[a] state cannot so deem a class of persons a stranger to its laws." The Court applied rationality review but struck down the law at issue in *Romer v. Evans*. Could this be useful as a precedent for litigation on behalf of poor people? Do anti-welfare laws demonstrate animosity toward poor people? Do they create a caste system in which poor people are treated as second class citizens?

B. HEIGHTENED SCRUTINY

1. Suspect Classes or Classifications

a. (Not Yet) Wealth

HARPER v. VIRGINIA STATE BOARD OF ELECTIONS

383 U.S. 663 (1966)

Justice DOUGLAS delivered the opinion of the Court.

These are suits by Virginia residents to have declared unconstitutional Virginia's poll tax.

* * *

While the right to vote in federal elections is conferred by Art. I, § 2, of the Constitution . . . , the right to vote in state elections is nowhere expressly mentioned. It is argued that the right to vote in state elections is implicit, particularly by reason of the First Amendment and that it may not constitutionally be conditioned upon the payment of a tax or fee. . . . For it is enough to say that once the franchise is granted to the electorate, lines may not be drawn which are inconsistent with the Equal Protection Clause of the Fourteenth Amendment. That is to say, the right of suffrage "is subject to the imposition of state standards which are not discriminatory and which do not contravene any restriction that Congress, acting pursuant to its constitutional powers, has imposed."

* * *

We conclude that a State violates the Equal Protection Clause of the Fourteenth Amendment whenever it makes the affluence of the voter or payment of any fee an electoral standard. Voter qualifications have no relation to wealth nor to paying or not paying this or any other tax. Our cases demonstrate that the Equal Protection Clause of the Fourteenth Amendment restrains the States from fixing voter qualifications which invidiously discriminate.

* * *

We say the same whether the citizen, otherwise qualified to vote, has $1.50 in his pocket or nothing at all, pays the fee or fails to pay it. The principle that denies the State the right to dilute a citizen's vote on account of his economic status or other such factors by analogy bars a system which excludes those unable to pay a fee to vote or who fail to pay.

It is argued that a State may exact fees from citizens for many different kinds of licenses; that if it can demand from all an equal fee for a driver's license, it can demand from all an equal poll tax for voting. But we must remember that the interest of the State, when it comes to voting, is limited to the power to fix qualifications. Wealth, like race, creed, or color, is not germane to one's ability to participate intelligently in the electoral process. Lines drawn on the basis of wealth or property, like those of race are traditionally disfavored. To introduce wealth or payment of a fee as a measure of a voter's qualifications is to introduce a capricious or irrelevant factor. The degree of the discrimination is irrelevant. In this context--that is, as a condition of obtaining a ballot--the requirement of fee paying causes an "invidious" discrimination that runs afoul of the Equal Protection Clause.

* * *

[T]he Equal Protection Clause is not shackled to the political theory of a particular era. In determining what lines are unconstitutionally discriminatory, we have never been confined to historic notions of equality, any more than we have restricted due process to a fixed catalogue of what was at a given time deemed to be the limits of fundamental rights. Notions of what constitutes equal treatment for purposes of the Equal Protection Clause do change. This Court in 1896 held that laws providing for separate public facilities for white and Negro citizens did not deprive the latter of the equal protection and treatment that the Fourteenth Amendment commands. . . . When, in 1954--more than a half-century later--we repudiated the "separate-but-equal"doctrine of *Plessy* [*v. Ferguson*] as respects public education we stated: "In approaching this problem, we cannot turn the clock back to 1868 when the Amendment was adopted, or even to 1896 when *Plessy v. Ferguson* was written." [citing *Brown v. Board of Education*, 347 U.S. 483, 492 (1954)].

* * *

We have long been mindful that where fundamental rights and liberties are asserted under the Equal Protection Clause, classifications which might invade or restrain them must be closely scrutinized and carefully confined. Those principles apply here. For to repeat, wealth or fee paying has, in our view, no relation to voting qualifications; the right to vote is too precious, too fundamental to be so burdened or conditioned.

Reversed.

* * *

Justice HARLAN, whom Justice STEWART joins, dissenting.

The final demise of state poll taxes, already totally proscribed by the Twenty-Fourth Amendment with respect to federal elections and abolished by the States themselves in all but four States with respect to state elections, is perhaps in itself not of great moment. But that fact that the *coup de grace* has been administered by this Court instead of being left to the affected States or to the federal political process should be a matter of continuing concern to all interested in maintaining the proper role of this tribunal under our scheme of government.

* * *

Property qualifications and poll taxes have been a traditional part of our political structure. In the Colonies the franchise was generally a restricted one. Over the years these and other restrictions were gradually lifted, primarily because popular theories of political representation had changed. Often restrictions were lifted only after wide public debate. The issue of woman suffrage, for example, raised question of family relationships, of participation in public affairs, of the very nature of the type of society in which Americans wished to live; eventually a consensus was reached, which culminated in the Nineteenth Amendment no more than 45 years ago.

* * *

Property and poll-tax qualifications, very simply, are not in accord with current egalitarian notions of how a modern democracy should be organized. It is of course entirely fitting that legislatures should modify the law to reflect such changes in popular attitudes. However, it is all wrong, in my view, for the Court to adopt the political doctrines popularly accepted at a particular moment of our history and to declare all others to be irrational and invidious, barring them from the range of choice by reasonably minded people acting through the political process. It was not too long ago that Mr. Justice Holmes felt impelled to remind the Court that the Due Process Clause of the Fourteenth Amendment does not enact the laissez-faire theory of society. . . . The times have changed, and perhaps it is appropriate to observe that neither does the Equal Protection Clause of that Amendment rigidly impose upon America an ideology of unrestrained egalitarianism.

I would affirm the decision of the District Court.

Notes and Questions

1. *Suspect Classification or Fundamental Right?* Consider the Court's specific language in holding that Virginia's poll tax violated the Equal Protection Clause of the Fourteenth Amendment:

> Wealth, like race, creed, or color, is not germane to one's ability to participate intelligently in the electoral process. Lines drawn on the basis of wealth or property, like those of race, are traditionally disfavored.

By their plain meaning, these words seem to identify wealth as a suspect class. This wealth classification occurred, however, in the context of voting rights. As the court explained, "the right to vote is too precious, too fundamental to be so burdened or conditioned." As a result, *Harper* has been interpreted to require heightened scrutiny because it involved a wealth classification that burdened a fundamental right, the Court's language referring to wealth classifications as "traditionally disfavored" notwithstanding.

2. *The Evolution of Equal Protection.* The Court admitted in *Harper* that its Equal Protection doctrine has changed. The Court previously had upheld poll taxes. And the dissent accurately explained that poll taxes played a longstanding role in our

government system. The Court did not duck the dissent's accusations, but faced them squarely, explaining that notions of what constitutes equal treatment changes over time. The dissent responded that changes in the meaning of equality should be effectuated by the voters, not by the Supreme Court. The voters through their federal and state representatives had amended the Constitution to prohibit poll taxes in federal elections; certainly voters could have amended the Constitution to prohibit poll taxes in state elections.

Should the existence of the opportunity for voters to amend the Constitution cause the judiciary to defer to the voters? If so, what issues would be left for the judiciary to decide?

Should the judiciary defer to voters only on issues that have been the subject of a societal change of mind? Given the Supreme Court's tendency to decide cases involving relatively novel issues, how would the justices determine whether their views and votes reflect a traditional understanding or a societal change of mind?

Should the "notions of what constitutes equal treatment" change over time? If not, should the Supreme Court overrule its decisions that reflect such changes, such as decisions relating to race and gender relations?

JAMES v. VALTIERRA

402 U.S. 137 (1971)

Justice BLACK delivered the opinion of the Court.

These cases raise but a single issue. It grows out of the United States Housing Act of 1937, which established a federal housing agency authorized to make loans and grants to state agencies for slum clearance and low-rent housing projects. In response, the California Legislature created in each county and city a public housing authority to take advantage of the financing made available by the federal Housing Act. At the time the federal legislation was passed the California Constitution had for many years reserved to the State's people the power to initiate legislation and to reject or approve by referendum any Act passed by the state legislature. The same section reserved to the electors of counties and cities the power of initiative and referendum over acts of local government bodies. In 1950, however, the State Supreme Court held that local authorities' decisions on seeking federal aid for public housing projects were "executive" and "administrative," not "legislative," and therefore the state constitution's referendum provisions did not apply to these actions. Within six months of that decision the California voters adopted Article XXXIV of the state constitution to bring public housing decisions under the State's referendum policy. The Article provided that no low-rent housing project should be developed, constructed, or acquired in any manner by a state public body until the project was approved by a majority of those voting at a community election.

The present suits were brought by citizens of San Jose, California, and San Mateo County, localities where housing authorities could not apply for federal funds because low-cost housing proposals had been defeated in referendums. The plaintiffs, who are eligible for low-cost public housing, sought a declaration that Article XXXIV was unconstitutional because its referendum requirement violated: (1) the Supremacy Clause of the United States Constitution; (2) the Privileges and Immunities Clause; and (3) the Equal Protection Clause. A three-judge court held that Article XXXIV denied the plaintiffs equal protection of the laws and it enjoined its enforcement. . . . For the reasons that follow, we reverse.

* * *

While the District Court cited several cases of this Court, its chief reliance plainly rested on *Hunter v. Erickson*, 393 U.S. 385 (1969). . . . The court below erred in relying on *Hunter* to invalidate Article XXXIV. Unlike the case before us, *Hunter* rested on the conclusion that Akron's referendum law denied equal protection by placing "special burdens on racial minorities within the governmental process." In *Hunter* the citizens of Akron had amended the city charter to require that any ordinance regulating real estate on the basis of race, color, religion, or national origin could not take effect without approval by a majority of those voting in a city election. The Court held that the amendment created a classification based upon race because it required that laws dealing with racial housing matters could take effect only if they survived a mandatory referendum while other housing ordinances took effect without any such special election. The opinion noted: "Because the core of the Fourteenth Amendment is the prevention of meaningful and unjustified official distinctions based on race, . . . racial classifications are 'constitutionally suspect'. . . and subject to the 'most rigid scrutiny.'. . . They 'bear a far heavier burden of justification' than other classifications." The Court concluded that Akron had advanced no sufficient reasons to justify this racial classification and hence that it was unconstitutional under the Fourteenth Amendment.

Unlike the Akron referendum provision, it cannot be said that California's Article XXXIV rests on "distinctions based on race." The Article requires referendum approval for any low-rent public housing project, not only for projects which will be occupied by a racial minority. And the record here would not support any claim that a law seemingly neutral on its face is in fact aimed at a racial minority. The present case could be affirmed only by extending *Hunter*, and this we decline to do.

California's entire history demonstrates the repeated use of referendums to give citizens a voice on questions of public policy. A referendum provision was included in the first state constitution, and referendums have been a commonplace occurrence in the State's active political life. Provisions for referendums demonstrate devotion to democracy, not to bias, discrimination, or prejudice. Nonetheless, appellees contend that Article XXXIV denies them equal protection because it demands a mandatory referendum while many other referendums only take place upon citizen initiative. They suggest that the mandatory nature of the Article XXXIV referendum constitutes unconstitutional discrimination because it hampers persons desiring public housing from achieving their objective when no such roadblock faces other groups seeking to influence other public decisions to their advantage. But of course a lawmaking procedure that "disadvantages" a particular group does not always deny equal protection. Under any such holding, presumably a State would not be able to require referendums on any subject unless referendums were required on all, because they would always disadvantage some group. And this Court would be required to analyze governmental structures to determine whether a gubernatorial veto provision or a filibuster rule is likely to "disadvantage" any of the diverse and shifting groups that make up the American people.

Furthermore, an examination of California law reveals that persons advocating low-income housing have not been singled out for mandatory referendums while no other group must face that obstacle. Mandatory referendums are required for approval of state constitutional amendments, for the issuance of general obligation long-term bonds by local governments, and for certain municipal territorial annexations. California statute books contain much legislation first enacted by voter initiative, and no such law can be repealed or amended except by referendum. Some California cities

have wisely provided that their public parks may not be alienated without mandatory referendums.

The people of California have also decided by their own vote to require referendum approval of low-rent public housing projects. This procedure ensures that all the people of a community will have a voice in a decision which may lead to large expenditures of local governmental funds for increased public services and to lower tax revenues.[4] It gives them a voice in decisions that will affect the future development of their own community. This procedure for democratic decisionmaking does not violate the constitutional command that no State shall deny to any person "the equal protection of the laws."

The judgment of the three-judge court is reversed and the cases are remanded for dismissal of the complaint.

Reversed and remanded.

Justice MARSHALL, whom Justice BRENNAN and Justice BLACKMUN join, dissenting.

By its very terms, the mandatory prior referendum provision of Art. XXXIV applies solely to

> any development composed of urban or rural dwellings, apartments or other living accommodations for persons of low income, financed in whole or in part by the Federal Government or a state public body

---

[4]Public low-rent housing projects are financed through bonds issued by the local housing authority. To be sure, the Federal Government contracts to make contributions sufficient to cover interest and principal, but the local government body must agree to provide all municipal services for the units and to waive all taxes on the property. The local services to be provided include schools, police, and fire protection, sewers, streets, drains, and lighting. Some of the cost is defrayed by the local governing body's receipt of 10% of the housing project rentals, but of course the rentals are set artificially low. Both appellants and appellees agree that the building of federally financed low-cost housing entails costs to the local community.

> or to which the Federal Government or a state public body extends assistance by supplying all or part of the labor, by guaranteeing the payment of liens, or otherwise.

Persons of low income are defined as "persons or families who lack the amount of income which is necessary . . . to enable them, without financial assistance, to live in decent, safe and sanitary dwellings, without overcrowding." The article explicitly singles out low-income persons to bear its burden. Publicly assisted housing developments designed to accommodate the aged, veterans, state employees, persons of moderate income, or any class of citizens other than the poor, need not be approved by prior referenda.

In my view, Art. XXXIV on its face constitutes invidious discrimination which the Equal Protection Clause of the Fourteenth Amendment plainly prohibits. . . . Article XXXIV is neither "a law of general applicability that may affect the poor more harshly than it does the rich," nor an "effort to redress economic imbalances." It is rather an explicit classification on the basis of poverty--a suspect classification which demands exacting judicial scrutiny.

The Court, however, chooses to subject the article to no scrutiny whatsoever and treats the provision as if it contained a totally benign, technical economic classification. Both the appellees and the Solicitor General of the United States as amicus curiae have strenuously argued, and the court below found, that Art. XXXIV, by imposing a substantial burden solely on the poor, violates the Fourteenth Amendment. Yet after observing that the article does not discriminate on the basis of race, the Court's only response to the real question in these cases is the unresponsive assertion that "referendums demonstrate devotion to democracy, not to bias, discrimination, or prejudice." It is far too late in the day to contend that the Fourteenth Amendment prohibits only racial discrimination; and to me, singling out the poor to bear a burden not placed on any other class of citizens tramples the values that the Fourteenth Amendment was designed to protect.

Notes and Questions

1. *Definition of the Class.* The Court noted that the plaintiff class was comprised of persons who were eligible for low income housing, but identified "persons advocating low-income housing" as the class affected by requirement of voter approval of new low-

income housing. Justice Marshall's dissenting opinion argued that the voter approval requirement burdened low income people through its explicit poverty classification in plain violation of the equal protection guarantee. Did the definition of the class affect the court's analysis? Given that the majority did not define the affected class as poor people, is this decision dispositive on the question whether poor people are a suspect class?

2. *Political Powerlessness.* One of the suspect class criteria suggests that the judiciary should more carefully scrutinize laws that burden any group which has difficulty protecting its interests in the political process. The voter approval requirement subjects poor people to an extraordinary political hurdle, namely convincing not elected representatives but a majority of the populace to support their interests. How likely is it that poor people or low income housing will receive popular political approval? Does voter passage of a law limiting a group's political remedies to majority voter approval exacerbate the disadvantage suffered by poor people? What check or balance will temper the likely negative effect on poor people if the judiciary refuses to scrutinize such legislation? For an argument that courts should apply heightened scrutiny to claims of poor people due in part to their lack of political power, *see* Stephen Loffredo, *Poverty, Democracy and Constitutional Law,* 141 UNIVERSITY OF PENNSYLVANIA LAW REVIEW 1277 (1993).

Although the Supreme Court has not yet held that either poor people or welfare recipients constitute a suspect class, or that classifications based on wealth are suspect, it has considered classifications based on race, gender, and the marital status of a child's parents as suspect. The Court, accordingly, applies heightened scrutiny, either strict or intermediate scrutiny, to such classifications. This raises two questions. First, if welfare classifications disadvantage recipients based on their race, gender, or parental marital status, should such classifications be reviewed with heightened scrutiny? Second, if the class of welfare recipients disproportionately includes women or racial minorities or non-marital children, should regulations that generally burden welfare recipients be reviewed with heightened scrutiny? Consider the extent to which these questions are answered in the following cases.

b. Race

JEFFERSON v. HACKNEY

406 U.S. 535 (1972)

Justice REHNQUIST delivered the opinion of the Court.

Appellants in this case challenge certain computation procedures that the State of Texas uses in its federally assisted welfare program. Believing that neither the Constitution nor the federal welfare statute prohibits the State from adopting these policies, we affirm the judgment of the three-judge court below upholding the state procedures.

Appellants are Texas recipients of Aid to Families With Dependent Children (AFDC). They brought two class actions, which were consolidated in the United States District Court for the Northern District of Texas, seeking injunctive and declaratory relief against state welfare officials. A three-judge court was convened pursuant to 28 U.S.C. § 2281.

The Texas State Constitution provides a ceiling on the amount the State can spend on welfare assistance grants. In order to allocate this fixed pool of welfare money among the numerous individuals with acknowledged need, the State has adopted a system of percentage grants. Under this system, the State first computes the monetary needs of individuals eligible for relief under each of the federally aided categorical assistance programs. Then, since the constitutional ceiling on welfare is insufficient to bring each recipient up to this full standard of need, the State applies a percentage reduction factor in order to arrive at a reduced standard of need in each category that the State can guarantee.

Appellants challenge the constitutionality of applying a lower percentage reduction factor to AFDC than to the other categorical assistance programs. They claim a violation of equal protection because the proportion of AFDC recipients who are black or Mexican-American is higher than the proportion of the aged, blind, or disabled welfare recipients who fall within these minority groups. Appellants claim that the distinction between the programs is not rationally related to the purposes of the Social Security Act, and violates the Fourteenth Amendment for that reason as well.

* * *

We turn, then, to appellants' claim that the Texas system of percentage reductions violates the Fourteenth Amendment. Appellants believe that once the State has computed a standard of need for each recipient, it is arbitrary and discriminatory to provide only 75% of that standard to AFDC recipients, while paying 100% of recognized need to the aged, and 95% to the disabled and the blind. They argue that if the State adopts a percentage-reduction system, it must apply the same percentage to each of its welfare programs.

This claim was properly rejected by the court below. It is clear from the statutory framework that, although the four categories of public assistance found in the Social Security Act have certain common elements, the States were intended by Congress to keep their AFDC plans separate from plans under the other titles of the Act. A State is free to participate in one, several, or all of the categorical assistance programs, as it chooses. It is true that each of the programs is intended to assist the needy, but it does not follow that there is only one constitutionally permissible way for the State to approach this important goal.

This Court emphasized only recently, in *Dandridge v. Williams*, 397 U.S. 471, 485 (1970), that in "the area of economics and social welfare, a State does not violate the Equal Protection Clause merely because the classifications made by its laws are imperfect." A legislature may address a problem "one step at a time," or even "select one phase of one field and apply a remedy there, neglecting the others." So long as its judgments are rational, and not invidious, the legislature's efforts to tackle the problems of the poor and the needy are not subject to a constitutional straitjacket. The very complexity of the problems suggests that there will be more than one constitutionally permissible method of solving them.

The standard of judicial review is not altered because of appellants' unproved allegations of racial discrimination. The three-judge court found that the "payment by Texas of a lesser percentage of unmet needs to the recipients of the AFDC than to the recipients of other welfare programs is not the result of racial or ethnic prejudice and is not violative of the federal Civil Rights Act or the Equal Protection Clause of the 14th Amendment." The District Court obviously gave careful consideration to this issue, and we are cited by its opinion to a number of subsidiary facts to support its principal finding quoted above. There has never been a reduction in the amount of money appropriated by the legislature to the AFDC program, and between 1943 and the date of the opinion below there had been five increases in the amount of money appropriated by the legislature for the program, two of them having occurred since 1959. The overall percentage increase in appropriation for the programs between 1943 and the time of the District Court's hearing in this case was 410% for AFDC, as opposed to 211% for OAA and 200% for AB. The court further concluded: "The depositions of Welfare officials conclusively establish that the defendants did not know the racial make-up of the various welfare assistance categories prior to or at the time when the orders here under attack were issued." Appellants in their brief in effect abandon any effort to show that these findings of fact were clearly erroneous, and we hold they were not.

Program	Year	Percentage of Negroes and Mexican-Americans	Percentage of White-Anglos	Number of Recipients
OAA	1969 1968 1967	39.8 38.7 37.0	60.2 61.3 63.0	230,000
APTD	1969 1968 1967	46.9 45.6 46.2	53.1 54.4 53.8	4,213
AB	1969 1968	55.7 54.9	44.3 45.1	14,043
AFDS	1969 1968 1967	87.0 84.9 86.0	13.0 15.1 14.0	136,000

Appellants are thus left with their naked statistical argument: that there is a larger percentage of Negroes and Mexican-Americans in AFDC than in the other programs, and that the AFDC is funded at 75% whereas the other programs are funded at 95% and 100% of recognized need. As the statistics cited in the footnote demonstrate, the number of minority members in all categories is substantial. The basic outlines of eligibility for the various categorical grants are established by Congress, not by the States; given the heterogeneity of the Nation's population, it would be only an infrequent coincidence that the racial composition of each grant class was identical to that of the others. The acceptance of appellants' constitutional theory would render suspect each difference in treatment among the grant classes, however lacking in racial motivation and however otherwise rational the treatment might be. Few legislative efforts to deal with the difficult problems posed by current welfare programs could survive such scrutiny, and we do not find it required by the Fourteenth Amendment.

Applying the traditional standard of review under that amendment, we cannot say that Texas' decision to provide somewhat lower welfare benefits for AFDC recipients is invidious or irrational. Since budgetary constraints do not allow the payment of the full standard of need for all welfare recipients, the State may have concluded that the aged and infirm are the least able of the categorical grant recipients to bear the hardships of an inadequate standard of living. While different policy judgments are of course possible, it is not irrational for the State to believe that the young are more adaptable than the sick and elderly, especially because the latter have less hope of improving their situation in the years remaining to them. Whether or not one agrees with this state determination, there is nothing in the Constitution that forbids it.[19]

* * *

[19]Just as the State's actions here do not violate the Fourteenth Amendment, we conclude that they do not violate Title VI of the Civil Rights Act of 1964. The Civil Rights Act prohibits discrimination in federally financed programs. We have, however, upheld the findings of nondiscriminatory purpose in the percentage reductions used by Texas, and have concluded that the variation in percentages is rationally related to the purposes of the separate welfare programs. The Court's decision in *Griggs v. Duke Power Co.*, 401 U.S. 424 (1971), is therefore inapposite. In *Griggs*, the employment test having racially discriminatory effects were found not to be job-related, and for that reason were impermissible under the specific language of Title VII of the Civil Rights Act. Since the Texas procedure challenged here is related to the purposes of the welfare programs, it is not proscribed by Title VI simply because of variances in the racial composition of the different categorical programs.

In conclusion, we re-emphasize what the Court said in *Dandridge v. Williams*, 397 U.S. at 487:

> We do not decide today that the [state law] is wise, that it best fulfills the relevant social and economic objectives that [the State] might ideally espouse, or that a more just and humane system could not be devised. Conflicting claims of morality and intelligence are raised by opponents and proponents of almost every measure, certainly including the one before us. But the intractable economic, social, and even philosophical problems presented by public welfare assistance programs are not the business of this Court. . . . [T]he Constitution does not empower this Court to second-guess state officials charged with the difficult responsibility of allocating limited public welfare funds among the myriad of potential recipients.

Affirmed.

Justice MARSHALL, with whom Justice BRENNAN joins, and with whom Justice STEWART joins as to Part I only, dissenting.

* * *

The record contains numerous statements by state officials to the effect that AFDC is funded at a lower level than the other programs because it is not a politically popular program. There is also evidence of a stigma that seemingly attaches to AFDC recipients and no others. This Court noted that AFDC recipients were often frowned upon by the community. The evidence also shows that 87% of the AFDC recipients in Texas are either Negro or Mexican-American. Yet, both the District Court and this Court have little difficulty in concluding that the fact that AFDC is politically unpopular and the fact that AFDC recipients are disfavored by the State and its citizens, have nothing whatsoever to do with the racial makeup of the program. This conclusion is neither so apparent, nor so correct in my view.

Moreover, because I find that each one of the State's reasons for treating AFDC differently from the other programs dissolves under close scrutiny, as is demonstrated, I am not at all certain who should bear the burden of proof on the question of racial discrimination. Nor am I sure that the "traditional" standard of review would govern the case as the Court holds. In *Dandridge v. Williams*, *supra*, on which the Court relies for the proposition that strict scrutiny of the State's action is not required, the Court never faced a question of possible racial discrimination. Percentages themselves are certainly not conclusive, but at some point a showing that state action has a devastating impact on the lives of minority racial groups must be relevant.

The Court reasons backwards to conclude that because appellants have not proved racial discrimination, a less strict standard of review is necessarily tolerated. In my view, the first question that must be asked is what is the standard of review and the second question is whether racial discrimination has been proved under the standard. It seems almost too plain for argument that the standard of review determines in large measure whether or not something has been proved.

These are all complex problems, and I do not propose to resolve any of them here. It is sufficient for me to note that I believe that the constitutional issue raised by appellants need not be reached, and that in choosing to reach it, the Court has so greatly oversimplified the issue as to distort it.

Appellants also challenge the distinction between programs under Title VI of the 1964 Civil Rights Act: "No person in the United States shall, on the ground of race, color, or national origin, . . . be subjected to discrimination under any program or activity receiving Federal financial assistance." Only last Term in *Griggs v. Duke Power Co.*, 401 U.S. 424 (1971), we had occasion to strike down under Title VII of the 1964 Act, 42 U.S.C. § 2000e, employment practices that had a particularly harsh impact on one minority racial group and that could not be justified by business necessity. We indicated in that case that "good intent or absence of discriminatory intent does not redeem employment procedures or testing mechanisms that operate as 'built-in headwinds' for minority groups." We said, in fact, that "Congress directed the thrust of the Act to the consequences of employment practices, not simply the motivation." That decision even placed the burden on the employer "of showing that any given requirement must have a manifest relationship to the employment in question."

There has been a paucity of litigation under Title VI, and I am not prepared at this point to say whether or not a similar analysis to that used in *Griggs* should be used in Title VI cases. This is a question of first impression in this Court, and I do not think we have to reach it in this case. I include this section only to make plain that I do not necessarily reject the argument made by appellants; I simply do not reach it.

This brings me to what I believe disposes of the question presented: the disparity between the various social welfare programs is not permissible under the federal statutory framework.

The four social welfare programs offered by Texas are funded in part by the Federal Government. Each program is governed by a separate statute: OAA, 42 U.S.C. § 301 et seq.; AFDC, 42 U.S.C. § 601 et seq.; AB, 42 U.S.C. § 1201 et seq.; APTD, 42 U.S.C. § 1351 et seq. No State is compelled to participate in any program, and any State that wants to participate can choose to do so in one, several, or all of the programs.

There is no doubt that States are free to choose whether or not to participate in these programs, and it is also clear that each State has considerable freedom to allocate what it wants to one or more programs by establishing different standards of need to compute eligibility for aid. It is also true, however, that the basic aims of the four programs are identical. Indeed, when Congress first enacted the programs in 1935, it viewed them all as necessary to provide aid to families unable to obtain income from private employment. The beneficiaries of the various programs shared the basic characteristics of need and dependence. While the programs as they now exist go well beyond merely furnishing financial assistance as they did originally they still maintain similar goals.

Moreover, all four programs were simultaneously amended in 1956 to provide for social and rehabilitative services to enable all needy individuals to attain the maximum economic and personal independence of which they were capable. Each program now requires a State to describe, in its plan for each social welfare program it administers, the services it offers to accomplish this objective.

Congress has given the States authority to set different standards of need for different programs. But where, as here, the State concludes that the standard of need is the same for recipients of aid under the four distinct statutes, it is my opinion that Congress required that the State treat all recipients equally with respect to actual aid. In other words, as I read the federal statutes, they are designed to accomplish the same objectives, albeit for persons disadvantaged by different circumstances.

States clearly have the freedom to make a bona fide determination that blind persons have a greater need than dependent children, that adults have a higher standard of need than children, that the aged have more need than the blind, and so forth.

But, in this case, Texas made an independent determination of need, and it determined that the need of all recipients was equal. In this circumstance, I find nothing in the federal statute to enable a State to favor one group of recipients by satisfying more of its need, while at the same time denying an equally great need of another group. The purposes and objectives of the statutes are the same, those eligible for aid are suffering equally, and Congress intended that once a State chose to participate in the programs similarly situated persons would be treated similarly.

Everything in this record indicates that the recipients of the various forms of aid are identically situated. Although the District Court accepted the State's contentions that there are differences between AFDC children and other recipients which warranted different treatment under the federal statutes, I find each of the reasons offered totally unpersuasive.

First, Texas argues that AFDC children can be employed, whereas recipients of other benefits cannot be. Assuming arguendo that this is true, it is an argument that falls of its own weight. Whatever income the children earn is subtracted from need, or it is excluded from consideration under § 402(a)(8) to encourage self-help. Thus, income is already reflected in the computation of payments, or it is excluded in order that a specific legislative goal may be furthered. Thus, income is irrelevant in any explanation of the differences between the percentage reductions applied to the various programs. It should also be noted that a recipient's income is also taken into consideration in programs other than AFDC.

Second, the State maintains that AFDC families can secure help from legally responsible relatives more easily than recipients under other programs. Assuming again for purposes of discussion that this is true, it should be plain that any support from any relatives is subtracted from the State's grant. Moreover, appellants properly point out that recipients of aid in non-AFDC programs often have a source of aid unavailable to AFDC recipients--the federal old age insurance. Thus, there is no substance to this argument.

Third, Texas points to the likelihood of future employment for AFDC recipients, a likelihood that it says is non-existent for older persons and others who receive aid. Federal law provides that a State may only consider income that is currently available in allocating funds. This contention is therefore irrelevant.

The State makes only two other arguments. One has already been rejected. Texas urges that the purposes of the federal programs differ, but the history belies this contention. The other is that the numbers of AFDC recipients is rising and this program should therefore bear the burden of monetary limitations. The obvious problem with this argument is that one fundamental purpose of AFDC aid is to enable people to escape the welfare rolls. But, under the Texas system, the aid is presently insufficient, people are unable to escape from dependency, and the rolls become larger. Had Texas not funded AFDC at a lower level than other programs, it is possible that the number of recipients would not have grown so large. The State's argument is a self-fulfilling prophecy on which it cannot rely to penalize AFDC recipients. Furthermore, there is nothing in the federal legislation to indicate that aid is to be reduced in a program merely because the number of beneficiaries of that program increases at a more rapid rate than in other programs. On the contrary, Congress has indicated that increased eligibility for AFDC is desirable, see 42 U.S.C. § 602(a)(23); *Rosado v. Wyman*, *supra*. It would be extreme irony if AFDC recipients were penalized by a State because their numbers grew in accordance with congressional intent.

The conclusion that I draw from the statutes is that Congress intended equal treatment for all persons similarly situated. Congress left to the States the determination of who was similarly situated by permitting States to determine levels of need. Since Texas has decided that AFDC recipients have precisely the same need as recipients of other social welfare benefits, it is my opinion that the federal legislation requires equal treatment for all.

This conclusion finds support in the legislative history of the 1950 amendments to the social welfare legislation. In those amendments Congress made clear its intent to put AFDC recipients on a par with recipients of other welfare aid.

> Today more than 1.1 million children under 18 years of age are receiving aid to dependent children through the State-Federal program because one or both of their

> parents are dead, absent from the home, or incapacitated. These children, regardless of the State in which they now live, will someday find their place in the productive activities of the Nation and, should the necessity arise, will take part in defending our Nation. Many of these children will be seriously handicapped as adults because in childhood they are not receiving proper and sufficient food, clothing, medical attention, and the other bare necessities of life. The national interest requires that the Federal Government provide for dependent children at least on a par with its contributions toward the support of the needy aged and blind.

Congress recognized that "families with dependent children need as much in assistance payments as do aged and blind persons." It concluded that sound national policy was "for the States to provide payments for aid to dependent children comparable to those for the needy aged and blind." It is evident that Congress rejected the notion that where AFDC recipients had the same need as other welfare beneficiaries, they should get less money. As Senator Benton said on the floor of the Senate:

> There seems no reasonable basis for such inequitable treatment of mothers and of children by the Federal Government. All of us with children know that it costs as much if not more to rear children in health, decency, and self-respect than to maintain an adult. It is surely no less important to make this investment in our future citizens than it is to provide decently for those who have retired.

In the 1950 amendments, Congress increased the federal funding of AFDC so that its beneficiaries would receive treatment equivalent to that received by beneficiaries of the other federal-state social welfare legislation. Where the needs of the people receiving aid under the various programs differed, Congress recognized that the amount of aid forth-coming should also differ. But where need was determined by the State to be equal for all recipients, Congress intended that all should receive an equal amount of aid. There is absolutely no indication in any subsequent congressional action that the intent of Congress has changed.

Accordingly, I would reverse the judgment of the District Court and remand the case . . . .

Notes and Questions

1. *Proof.* Texas provided less of their need to AFDC recipients than to aged, blind, and disabled recipients. The plaintiffs claimed that part of the reason for lower AFDC amounts was that AFDC recipients were disproportionately African-American and Mexican-American. Their statistical data showed that African-Americans and Mexican-Americans constituted between 37% and 55.7% of aged, blind, and disabled recipients, whereas they constituted between 84.9% and 87% of AFDC recipients. AFDC recipients received 75% of need, whereas the other groups received 95-100% of need. The Supreme Court majority referred to the plaintiff's claims as "unproved allegations of racial discrimination." Why?

The Court also noted that the Texas legislature had increased AFDC amounts several times, and state welfare officials had denied knowing the racial make-up of the various programs. Do these findings rebut the claim of racial discrimination?

2. *Cart Before the Horse.* Justice Marshall in dissent accused the majority of failing to first determine the proper level of scrutiny and then apply it to the proof. The majority indeed noted that plaintiffs' theory "would render suspect each difference in treatment" which few laws could survive. Did the majority decide that the classifications should be upheld, and therefore refused to apply the level of scrutiny that would invalidate them? In other words, did the Court put the cart before the horse?

3. *Actuality of Purpose.* The Court suggested that the State of Texas "may have concluded" that young AFDC recipients were more "adaptable" than disabled and elderly recipients were. Should the Court have required the State to prove what its actual purposes were, and what evidence supported the assumptions or finding underlying its purposes?

4. Dandridge *revisited.* The Court concluded its decision by quoting the famous language from *Dandridge v. Williams* that "the intractable economic, social, and even philosophical problems

presented by public welfare assistance programs are not the business of this Court." Did the Court mean that welfare decisions are presumptively rational and that courts should not review them? Does the *Dandridge* language foreclose the possibility of judicial review? Does it make welfare decisions irrebuttably rational?

5. *The Mere Rationality Blues.* Justice Marshall in dissent lamented the majority's facile conclusion that the state's disfavor toward AFDC recipients had nothing to do with the racial makeup of the program. He asserted instead that "a showing that state action has a devastating impact on the lives of minority racial groups must be relevant." What level of scrutiny was appropriate? Does the Court normally require proof of the merits of a racial discrimination claim prior to applying heightened scrutiny? Why did it do so here?

6. *Strength of Texas' Interests.* Justice Marshall identified several state interests: (1) assuming employability of AFDC children; (2) encouraging AFDC recipients to seek assistance from non-welfare sources; (3) encouraging employment of AFDC recipients; and (4) placing a greater monetary burden on AFDC recipients due to the program's growth. Are these interests legitimate, substantial, or compelling? Does providing less aid to AFDC recipients rationally, substantially, or indispensably further any of these interests?

c. Gender

We know that women disproportionately experience poverty. The figures for 1993 showed that over half of all poor families were headed by women, while only 18% of all families were headed by women. Could welfare regulations that burden welfare recipients generally be challenged as discrimination based on gender? What about welfare regulations that treat mothers differently than fathers? What about regulations that provide benefits or conditions that restrict reproductive choices?

CALIFANO v. WESTCOTT

443 U.S. 76 (1979)

Justice BLACKMUN delivered the opinion of the Court.

Section 407 of the Social Security Act, part of the Aid to Families with Dependent Children program, provides benefits to families whose dependent children have been deprived of parental support because of the unemployment of the father, but does not provide such benefits when the mother becomes unemployed. The United States District Court for the District of Massachusetts held that this distinction violates the Due Process Clause of the Fifth Amendment, and ordered that benefits be paid to families deprived of support because of the unemployment of the mother to the same extent they are paid to families deprived of support because of the unemployment of the father.

* * *

As originally enacted in 1935, the AFDC program provided benefits to families whose dependent children were needy because of the death, absence, or incapacity of a parent. This provision, which forms the core of the AFDC program today, is gender neutral: benefits are available to any family so long as one parent of either sex is dead, absent from the home, or incapacitated, and the family otherwise meets the financial requirements of eligibility.

In 1961, and again in 1962, Congress temporarily extended the AFDC program to provide assistance to families whose dependent children were deprived of support because of a parent's unemployment. Again, this provision was gender neutral. A "dependent child," for purposes of determining eligibility for AFDC benefits, was defined to include "a needy child . . . who has been deprived of parental support or care by reason of the unemployment . . . of a parent."

In 1968, as part of a general revision of the Social Security Act, Congress made this extension permanent. In so doing, however, it added a gender qualification to the statute. The definition of "dependent child" in § 407 was amended to include a "needy child . . . who has been deprived of parental support or care by reason of the unemployment . . . of his father." This portion of the AFDC program is known as Aid to Families with Dependent Children, Unemployed Father (AFDC-UF).

* * *

Appellees are two couples who, it is stipulated, satisfy all the requirements for AFDC-UF benefits except for the requirement that the unemployed parent be the father. Cindy and William Westcott are married and have an infant son. They applied to the Massachusetts DPW for public assistance, but were informed that they did not qualify because William, who was unable to find work, had not previously been employed for a sufficient period to qualify as an "unemployed" father under the Act and applicable regulations. Cindy, until her recent unemployment, was the family breadwinner, and would have satisfied the "unemployment" criteria had she been male.

Susan and John Westwood are also married and have an infant son. They applied for Medicaid benefits as a family eligible for, but not receiving, AFDC-UF benefits. They, too, were turned down on the ground that John's prior work history was insufficient. Susan, like Cindy Westcott, had been the family breadwinner before losing her job, and would have qualified the family for benefits had she been male.

Appellees instituted this class action in the United States District Court for the District of Massachusetts, naming as defendants the Secretary of HEW [Health, Education, and Welfare] and the Commissioner of the DPW [Department of Public Welfare]. Appellees alleged that § 407 and its implementing regulations discriminate on the basis of gender in violation of the Fifth and Fourteenth Amendments. They sought declaratory and injunctive relief.

* * *

The Secretary advances two arguments in support of the constitutionality of § 407. First, he contends that although § 407 incorporates a gender distinction, it does not discriminate against women as a class. Second, he urges that the distinction is substantially related to the achievement of an important governmental objective: the need to deter real or pretended desertion by the father in order to make his family eligible for AFDC benefits.

The Secretary readily concedes that § 407 entails a gender distinction. He submits, however, that the Act does not award AFDC benefits to a father where it denies them to a mother. Rather, the grant or denial of aid based on the father's unemployment necessarily affects, to an equal degree, one man, one woman, and one or more children. As the Secretary puts it, even if the statute is "gender-based," it is not "gender-biased."

We are not persuaded by this analysis. For mothers who are the primary providers for their families, and who are unemployed, § 407 is obviously gender biased, for it deprives them and their families of benefits solely on the basis of their sex. The Secretary's argument, at bottom, turns on the fact that the impact of the gender qualification is felt by family units rather than individuals. But this Court has not hesitated to strike down gender classifications that result in benefits being granted or denied to family units on the basis of the sex of the qualifying parent. *See Frontiero v. Richardson*, 411 U.S. 677 (1973) (military quarters allowances and medical and dental benefits); *Weinberger v. Wiesenfeld*, 420 U.S. 636 (1975) (survivor's benefits); *Califano v. Goldfarb*, 430 U.S. 199 (1977) (survivor's benefits); *Califano v. Jablon*, 430 U.S. 924 (1977), *summarily aff'g* 399 F. Supp. 118 (Md. 1975) (spousal benefits). Here, as in those cases, the statute "discriminates against one particular category of family--that in which the female spouse is a wage earner."

The Secretary appears to acknowledge the force of these precedents, but suggests that each involved benefits that either were a form of compensation earned by a woman as a member of the labor force, or were directly related to such compensation. In the present case, in contrast, the benefits are part of a noncontributory welfare program. Thus, the Secretary argues, the gender qualification of § 407 is distinguishable from those contained in the earlier cases, for it does not denigrate "the efforts of women who do work and whose earnings contribute significantly to their families' support."

The distinction between employment-related benefits and other forms of government largesse may be relevant to equal protection analysis. . . . This does not mean, however, that the Constitution is indifferent to a statute that conditions the availability of noncontributory welfare benefits on the basis of gender. The Secretary's argument to the contrary in effect invites a return to the discredited view that welfare benefits are a "privilege" not subject to the guarantee of equal protection. . . . AFDC-UF benefits are not "fringe benefits," nor are they a type of social assistance paid without regard to need. Rather, they are subsistence payments made available as a last resort to families that would otherwise lack basic necessities. The deprivation imposed by § 407, moreover, is not a mere procedural barrier . . . but is an absolute bar to qualification for aid. We therefore reject the contention that the classification imposed by § 407 does not discriminate on the basis of gender.

The Secretary next argues that the gender distinction imposed by § 407 survives constitutional scrutiny because it is substantially related to achievement of an important governmental objective. The Secretary identifies two important objectives served by § 407.

First and most obviously, the statute was intended to provide aid for children deprived of basic sustenance because of a parent's unemployment. As then HEW Secretary Ribicoff put it in testimony before the House Ways and Means Committee, "there is no justification whatsoever for denying to the child of the unemployed parent the food that you give to the child of the parent who deserts or is absent or dead." The appellant Secretary does not contend, however, that the gender qualification of § 407 serves to achieve this goal. Nor could he, since families where the mother is the principal wage earner and is unemployed are often in as much need of AFDC-UF benefits and Medicaid as families where the father is unemployed.

Second, the statute was designed to remedy a structural fault in the original AFDC program. Under that program, a family was eligible for benefits if deprived of parental support because of the "continued absence from the home . . . of a parent." In times of economic adversity, this provision was thought to create an incentive for the father to desert, or to pretend to desert, in order to make the family eligible for assistance. Section 407, by providing AFDC benefits to families rendered needy by parental unemployment, was intended to reduce this incentive and thereby promote the goal of family stability. The Secretary submits that reducing the incentive for the father to desert was an important objective of the AFDC-UF program, and he argues that the gender qualification is substantially related to its achievement.

We perceive, however, at least two flaws in this argument. Although it is relatively clear that Congress was concerned about the problem of parental desertion, there is no evidence that the gender distinction was designed to address this problem. Both the original AFDC program, and the temporary versions of the AFDC-UF program enacted in 1961 and 1962, were gender neutral. The gender qualification added to the permanent version of AFDC-UF in 1968 escaped virtually unnoticed in the hearings and floor debates.

The only explanation for this addition is contained in the following passage, which appears in nearly identical form in both the House and Senate Reports:

> This program was originally conceived by Congress as one to provide aid for the children of unemployed fathers. However, some States make families in which

> the father is working but the mother is unemployed eligible for assistance. The bill would not allow such situations. Under the bill, the program could apply only to the children of unemployed fathers.

This suggests that the gender qualification was part of the general objective of the 1968 amendments to tighten standards for eligibility and reduce program costs. Congress was concerned that certain States were making AFDC-UF assistance available to families where the mother was out of work, but the father remained fully employed and able to support the family. Apparently, Congress was not similarly concerned about States making benefits available where the father was out of work, but the mother remained fully employed. From all that appears, Congress, with an image of the "traditional family" in mind, simply assumed that the father would be the family breadwinner, and that the mother's employment role, if any, would be secondary. In short, the available evidence indicates that the gender distinction was inserted to reduce costs and eliminate what was perceived to be a type of superfluous eligibility for AFDC-UF benefits. There is little to suggest that the gender qualification had anything to do with reducing the father's incentive to desert.

Even if the actual purpose of the gender qualification was to deal with the problem of paternal desertion, it does not appear that the classification is substantially related to the achievement of that goal. The Secretary argues there is "[s]olid statistical evidence" that fathers are more susceptible to pressure to desert than mothers, and thus that Congress was justified in excluding families headed by unemployed mothers from the AFDC-UF program. We may assume, for purposes of discussion, that Congress could legitimately view paternal desertion as a problem separate and distinct from maternal desertion. Even so, the gender qualification of § 407 is not substantially related to the stated purpose. There is no evidence, in the legislative history or elsewhere, that a father has less incentive to desert in a family where the mother is the breadwinner and becomes unemployed, than in a family where the father is the breadwinner and becomes unemployed. In either case, the family's need will be equally great, and the father will be equally subject to pressure to leave the home to make the family eligible for benefits. The Secretary urges that Congress could take "one firm step" toward the goal of eliminating the incentive to desert. But Congress may not legislate "one step at a time" when that step is drawn along the line of gender, and the consequence is to exclude one group of families altogether from badly needed subsistence benefits.

We conclude that the gender classification of § 407 is not substantially related to the attainment of any important and valid statutory goals. It is, rather, part of the "baggage of sexual stereotypes," that presumes the father has the "primary responsibility to provide a home and its essentials," while the mother is the "'center of home and family life.'" Legislation that rests on such presumptions, without more, cannot survive scrutiny under the Due Process Clause of the Fifth Amendment.

Notes and Questions

1. *Family Impact Argument Rejected.* Recall that the Supreme Court in *Dandridge v. Williams* held that the impact of the maximum grant regulation was felt by the entire family unit, rather than by the youngest children in the family. In *Westcott*, however, the Court rejected the government's argument that the impact of the unemployed father regulation was felt by the entire family unit, rather than by female bread-winners. Can you distinguish *Dandridge* and *Westcott*?

2. *Welfare Not a Privilege.* The Court notably rejects the government's purported distinction between employment-related benefits and welfare benefits. The Secretary of Health, Education, and Welfare had attempted to distinguish the gender-based restriction in *Westcott* from a series of other cases in which the Court had invalidated gender-based restrictions in various employment benefit contexts. The majority rejected this distinction, reaffirming the Court's earlier pronouncement that welfare benefits are not a mere privilege but are fully subject to the guarantee of equal protection. The Court uses language similar to that of *Goldberg v. Kelly* in describing welfare benefits "as a last resort to families that would otherwise lack basic necessities."

3. *The Gender Test.* The Court applied its intermediate scrutiny for gender-based equal protection claims, requiring the government to show that its gender-based distinction is substantially related to achievement of an important governmental objective. Consider whether the government failed to convince the Court that the government had an important end, and/or that the chosen means was substantially related to that end.

First, the government apparently argued that the gender restriction served the interest of providing benefits to children with unemployed parents, presumably an important government interest. The Court noted, however, that the gender restriction did not serve that goal. Could the goal be redefined as providing benefits only to children with unemployed fathers? If not, why not?

Second, the government argued that the gender restriction reduces a father's incentive to desert his family. The Court noted that Congress must have assumed that most two-parent families were traditional in the sense that the fathers were the primary breadwinners. Is this assumption rational? Isn't the government's interest in reducing a father's incentive to desert his family an important government interest? If so, why didn't the Court approve the gender distinction based on this interest? Does the Court's rejection of Congress' "traditional family" assumption have any bearing on contemporary welfare reform proposals that seek to limit welfare benefits to families that follow traditional norms?

4. *Rejection of One-Step-At-A-Time.* If the *Dandridge* principle that government may start with solving one part of a problem were applied, couldn't the Court find that meeting the needs of children with unemployed fathers begins to solve part of the problem of meeting the needs of children with unemployed parents? Or couldn't the Court find that reducing a father's incentive to desert when he is unemployed begins to solve part of the problem of reducing a father's incentive to desert when either parent is unemployed? How does the Court respond to this argument? Does the Court's rejection of this argument mean that it will accept the "one step at a time" approach only when it applies rationality review, as compared to any form of heightened scrutiny?

5. *The Role of Pretext.* The Court found that the actual purpose of the gender restriction was to reduce costs. Why didn't the Court defer to the purposes identified by the government? Were the other government interests identified merely pretext? Even if the identified interests were pretext, why didn't the Court analyze, first, whether the actual interest (reducing cost) was an important government interest, and second, whether the gender restriction was substantially related to that interest?

d. Non-Marital Parentage

NEW JERSEY WELFARE RIGHTS ORGANIZATION
v.
CAHILL

411 U.S. 619 (1973)

PER CURIAM.

This case presents the question of the constitutionality under the Equal Protection Clause of the Fourteenth Amendment of the New Jersey "Assistance to Families of the Working Poor" program, that allegedly discriminates against illegitimate children in the provision of financial assistance and other services. Specifically, appellants challenge that aspect of the program that limits benefits to only those otherwise qualified families "which consist of a household composed of two adults of the opposite sex ceremonially married to each other who have at least one minor child . . . of both, the natural child of one and adopted by the other, or a child adopted by both . . . ." Appellants do not challenge the statute's "household" requirement. Rather, they argue that although the challenged classification turns upon the marital status of the parents as well as upon the parent-child relationship, in practical effect it operates almost invariably to deny benefits to illegitimate children while granting benefits to those children who are legitimate. Although apparently conceding the correctness of this position, the United States District Court for the District of New Jersey, sitting as a three-judge court, upheld the statutory scheme on the ground that it was designed "to preserve and strengthen traditional family life."

Confronted with similar arguments in the past, we have specifically declared that:

> The status of illegitimacy has expressed through the ages society's condemnation of irresponsible liaisons beyond the bonds of marriage. But visiting this condemnation on the head of an infant is illogical and unjust. Moreover, imposing disabilities on the illegitimate child is contrary to the basic concept of our system that legal burdens should bear some relationship to individual responsibility or wrongdoing.

> Obviously, no child is responsible for his birth and penalizing the illegitimate child is an ineffectual--as well as an unjust--way of deterring the parent. *Weber v. Aetna Casualty & Surety Co.*, 406 U.S. 164, 175 (1972).

Thus, in *Weber*, we held that under the Equal Protection Clause a State may not exclude illegitimate children from sharing equally with other children in the recovery of workmen's compensation benefits for the death of their parent. Similarly, in *Levy v. Louisiana*, 391 U.S. 68 (1968), we held that a State may not create a right of action in favor of children for the wrongful death of a parent and exclude illegitimate children from the benefit of such a right. And only this Term, in *Gomez v. Perez*, 409 U.S. 535 (1973), we held that once a State posits a judicially enforceable right on behalf of children to needed support from their natural father, there is no constitutionally sufficient justification for denying such an essential right to illegitimate children.

Those decisions compel the conclusion that appellants' claim of the denial of equal protection must be sustained, for there can be no doubt that the benefits extended under the challenged program are as indispensable to the health and well-being of illegitimate children as to those who are legitimate. Accordingly, we grant the motion for leave to proceed in forma pauperis, reverse the judgment of the District Court, and remand for further proceedings consistent with this opinion.

Reversed and remanded.

THE CHIEF JUSTICE concurs in the result.

Justice REHNQUIST, dissenting.

The New Jersey Legislature has enacted a statute entitled "Assistance to Families of the Working Poor," which is designed to provide grants to supplement the income of a discrete class of families with children when independent sources of income are inadequate to support the family unit. The program is completely financed by the State, and therefore need not conform to any of the strictures of the Social Security Act. The New Jersey program for assistance to the working poor does not provide financial grants to classes of children as such, as is the case under various federal plans. Instead, it provides grants to classes of families as units. The Court holds that because benefits are limited to families "which consist of a household composed of two adults of the opposite sex ceremonially married to each other who have at least one minor child . . . of both, the natural child of one and adopted by the other, or a child adopted by both," the legislative scheme violates the Equal Protection Clause of the Fourteenth Amendment.

The Court relies on *Weber v. Aetna Casualty & Surety Co.*, 406 U.S. 164 (1972), where a Louisiana statute that denied workmen's compensation benefits to an illegitimate child was invalidated. But the very language that the Court quotes from *Weber* shows how different this case is from that. There a disability was visited solely on an illegitimate child. Here the statute distinguishes among types of families. While the classification adopted by the New Jersey Legislature undoubtedly results in denying benefits to "families" consisting of a mother and father not ceremonially married who are living with natural children, whatever denial of benefits the classification makes is imposed equally on the parents as well as the children.

Here the New Jersey Legislature has determined that special financial assistance should be given to family units that meet the statutory definition of "working poor." It does not seem to me irrational in establishing such a special program to condition the receipt of such grants on the sort of ceremonial marriage that could quite reasonably be found to be an essential ingredient of the family unit that the New Jersey Legislature is trying to protect from dissolution due to the economic vicissitudes of modern life. The Constitution does not require that special financial assistance designed by the legislature to help poor families be extended to "communes" as well.

In the area of economics and social welfare the Equal Protection Clause does not prohibit a State from taking one step at a time in attempting to overcome a social ill, provided only that the classifications made by the State are rational. Here the classification is based on a particular type of family unit, one of, if not the, core units of our social system. There being a rational basis for the legislative classification, the constitutionality of the law is governed by *Dandridge v. Williams*, 397 U.S. 471 (1970), rather than by *Weber*.

I would affirm the judgment of the District Court.

Notes and Questions

1. *Suspect Class Analysis.* Did the Court consider non-marital children to constitute a suspect class? Have non-marital children suffered historical discrimination? Can they control the circumstances that result in the status of their births? While the answers to these questions support heightened scrutiny, what about the third factor, namely whether non-marital children are politically less powerful or underrepresented?

2. *Level of Scrutiny.* What level of scrutiny did the Court employ, rationality review, intermediate scrutiny, or strict scrutiny? Did the Court accept as legitimate the restriction's purpose of preserving and strengthening traditional family life? When addressing the fit between means and ends, the Court mentioned the purpose of the State assistance program (strengthening the health and well-being of children) rather than the purpose of the restriction (strengthening only traditional families).

3. *Dissent.* Justice Rehnquist in dissent distinguished between regulations that affect only a non-marital child and those that affect types of families. Why would this distinction matter? Is it irrational for a state that wants to assist the working poor to assist only those who live with traditional families?

4. *Families.* Compare *Cahill* to *Lyng v. Castillo*, 477 U.S. 635 (1986), where the Supreme Court upheld the requirement that treated parents, children and siblings who lived together as a single household. The Court explained:

> The disadvantaged class is that comprised by parents, children, and siblings. Close relatives are not a "suspect" or "quasi-suspect" class. As a historical matter, they have not been subjected to discrimination; they do not exhibit obvious, immutable, or distinguishing characteristics that define them as a discrete group; and they are not a minority or politically powerless. In fact, quite the contrary is true.

The Court held that treating close relatives as a household and providing them a lower Food Stamp amount was permissible because Congress could rationally presume that they were likely to purchase and prepare their meals together.

5. *Non-Marital Children as Targets of Welfare Reform.* In the 1996 Personal Responsibility and Work Opportunity

Reconciliation Act which abolished Aid to Families with Dependent Children and created the Temporary Assistance for Needy Families (TANF) block grant program, Congress intended states to "prevent and reduce the incidence of out-of-wedlock pregnancies and establish annual numerical goals for preventing and reducing the incidence of these pregnancies" through their TANF programs. Does such targeting of non-marital children justify heightened scrutiny in an equal protection challenge?

e. (Maybe) Immigrants

All immigrants are persons protected by the language of the Due Process and Equal Protection Clauses. As early as 1886 in *Yick Wo v. Hopkins*, 118 U.S. 356, the Supreme Court applied the Equal Protection Clause to strike down a law that was used to deny laundry business licenses to Chinese nationals.

The Supreme Court's jurisprudence regarding laws affecting immigrants, however, has been less than clear. In some cases, usually when states restricted the rights of immigrants, the Court considered aliens to be a suspect class and applied strict scrutiny. In other cases, usually when the federal government sought to further its foreign or immigration policies, the Court applied less scrutiny and deferred to the federal government. Whether the Court continues to apply different levels of scrutiny depending on whether the states or the federal government took the action harming immigrants remains to be seen.

In 1996, Congress again passed restrictions on the provision of public assistance to both legally documented and undocumented immigrants. These restrictions denied public benefits to undocumented immigrants, and required legally documented immigrants to rely on their sponsors, rather than on public assistance, or face deportation. Challenges to these restrictions will likely be based, in part, on two of the Court's leading immigration decision. In *Plyler v. Doe*, 457 U.S. 202 (1982), excerpted in this chapter, the Supreme Court held that states could not deny public education to undocumented children because, in essence, undocumented children constituted a quasi-suspect class and education constituted a quasi-fundamental right. In *Graham v. Richardson*, which follows, the

Court applied strict scrutiny to state restrictions on immigrants' eligibility for welfare benefits.

GRAHAM v. RICHARDSON

403 U.S. 365 (1971)

[Arizona law imposed a citizenship or fifteen year national durational residency requirement on receipt of disability and old age assistance. Pennsylvania law imposed a citizenship requirement on receipt of general assistance.]

The appellants argue initially that the States, consistent with the Equal Protection Clause, may favor United States citizens over aliens in the distribution of welfare benefits. It is said that this distinction involves no "invidious discrimination" such as was condemned in *King v. Smith*, for the State is not discriminating with respect to race or nationality.

The Fourteenth Amendment provides, "[N]or shall any State deprive any person of life, liberty, or property, without due process of law; nor deny to any person within its jurisdiction the equal protection of the laws." It has long been settled, and it is not disputed here, that the term "person" in this context encompasses lawfully admitted resident aliens as well as citizens of the United States and entitles both citizens and aliens to the equal protection of the laws of the State in which they reside. Nor is it disputed that the Arizona and Pennsylvania statutes in question create two classes of needy persons, indistinguishable except with respect to whether they are or are not citizens of this country. Otherwise qualified United States citizens living in Arizona are entitled to federally funded categorical assistance benefits without regard to length of national residency, but aliens must have lived in this country for 15 years in order to qualify for aid. United States citizens living in Pennsylvania, unable to meet the requirements for federally funded benefits, may be eligible for state-supported general assistance, but resident aliens as a class are precluded from that assistance.

Under traditional equal protection principles, a State retains broad discretion to classify as long as its classification has a reasonable basis. This is so in "the area of economics and social welfare." *Dandridge v. Williams*, 397 U.S. 471, 485 (1970). But the Court's decisions have established that classifications based on alienage, like those based on nationality or race, are inherently suspect and subject to close judicial scrutiny. Aliens as a class are a prime example of a "discrete and insular" minority for whom such heightened judicial solicitude is appropriate.

***

Arizona and Pennsylvania seek to justify their restrictions on the eligibility of aliens for public assistance solely on the basis of a State's "special public interest" in favoring its own citizens over aliens in the distribution of limited resources such as welfare benefits. It is true that this Court on occasion has upheld state statutes that treat citizens and noncitizens differently, the ground for distinction having been that such laws were necessary to protect special interests of the State or its citizens.

***

Whatever may be the contemporary vitality of the special public-interest doctrine . . . we conclude that a State's desire to preserve limited welfare benefits for its own citizens is inadequate to justify Pennsylvania's making noncitizens ineligible for public assistance, and Arizona's restricting benefits to citizens and longtime resident aliens. First, the special public interest doctrine was heavily grounded on the notion that "[w]hatever is a privilege, rather than a right, may be made dependent upon citizenship." But this Court now has rejected the concept that constitutional rights turn upon whether a governmental benefit is characterized as a "right" or as a "privilege." Second, as the Court recognized in *Shapiro [v. Thompson]*: "[A] State has a valid interest in preserving the fiscal integrity of its programs. It may legitimately attempt to limit its expenditures, whether for public assistance, public education, or any other program. But a State may not accomplish such a purpose by invidious distinctions between classes of its citizens. . . . The saving of welfare costs cannot justify an otherwise invidious classification." Since an alien as well as a citizen is a "person" for equal protection purposes, a concern for fiscal integrity is no more compelling a justification for the questioned classification in these cases than it was in *Shapiro*.

Appellants, however, would narrow the application of *Shapiro* to citizens by arguing that the right to travel, relied upon in that decision, extends only to citizens and not to aliens. While many of the Court's opinions do speak in terms of the right of "citizens" to travel, the source of the constitutional right to travel has never been ascribed to any particular constitutional provision. The Court has never decided whether the right applies specifically to aliens, and it is unnecessary to reach that question here. It is enough to say that the classification involved in *Shapiro* was subjected to strict scrutiny under the compelling state interest test, not because it was based on any suspect criterion such as race, nationality, or alienage, but because it impinged upon the fundamental right of interstate movement. . . . The classifications involved in the instant cases, on the other hand, are inherently suspect and are therefore subject to strict judicial scrutiny whether or not a fundamental right is impaired. Appellants' attempted reliance on *Dandridge v. Williams* is also misplaced, since the classification involved in that case (family size) neither impinged upon a fundamental constitutional right nor employed an inherently suspect criterion.

We agree with the three-judge court in the Pennsylvania case that the "justification of limiting expenses is particularly inappropriate and unreasonable when the discriminated class consists of aliens. Aliens like citizens pay taxes and may be called into the armed forces. Unlike the short-term residents in *Shapiro*, aliens may live within a state for many years, work in the state and contribute to the economic growth of the state." There can be no "special public interest" in tax revenues to which aliens have contributed on an equal basis with the residents of the State.

Accordingly, we hold that a state statute that denies welfare benefits to resident aliens and one that denies them to aliens who have not resided in the United States for a specified number of years violate the Equal Protection Clause.

An additional reason why the state statutes at issue in these cases do not withstand constitutional scrutiny emerges from the area of federal-state relations. The National Government has "broad constitutional powers in determining what aliens shall be admitted to the United States, the period they may remain, regulation of their conduct before naturalization, and the terms and conditions of their naturalization." Pursuant to that power, Congress has provided, as part of a comprehensive plan for the regulation of immigration and naturalization, that "(a)liens who are paupers professional beggars, or vagrants" or aliens who "are likely at any time to become public charges" shall be excluded from admission into the United States and that any alien lawfully admitted shall be deported who "has within five years after entry become a public charge from causes not affirmatively shown to have arisen after entry. . . ." Admission of aliens likely to become public charges may be conditioned upon the posting of a bond or cash deposit. But Congress has not seen fit to impose any burden or restriction on aliens who become indigent after their entry into the United States. Rather, it has broadly declared: "All persons within the jurisdiction of the United States shall have the same right in every State and Territory . . . to the full and equal benefit of all laws and proceedings for the security of persons and property as is enjoyed by white citizens. . . ." The protection of this statute has been held to extend to aliens as well as to citizens. . . . Although the Federal Government admittedly has broad constitutional power to determine what aliens shall be admitted to the United States, the period they may remain, and the terms and conditions of their naturalization, Congress does not have the power to authorize the individual States to violate the Equal Protection Clause. Under Art. I, § 8, cl. 4, of the Constitution, Congress' power is to "establish an uniform Rule of Naturalization." A congressional enactment construed so as to permit state legislatures to adopt divergent laws on the subject of citizenship requirements for federally supported welfare programs would appear to contravene this explicit constitutional requirement of uniformity.[14]

Affirmed.

Notes and Questions

1. *Rejection of States' Interests.* Arizona and Pennsylvania argued that their limitations of benefits to citizens or long-term residents served to preserve their limited welfare resources for their own citizens. In rejecting this assertion, the Supreme Court reaffirmed its rejection of two concepts important to the states' argument. First, the Court reaffirmed its rejection of "the concept that constitutional rights turn upon whether a governmental benefit is characterized as a 'right' or as a 'privilege.'" Second, the Court reaffirmed its rejection of the argument that states can save costs by making invidious distinctions between classes of people. How

---

[14]We have no occasion to decide whether Congress, in the exercise of the immigration and naturalization power, could itself enact a statue imposing on aliens a uniform nationwide residency requirement as a condition of federally funded welfare benefits.

fundamental were these concepts to the states' arguments? In other words, if a contemporary court viewed the right/privilege distinction as valid or the interest in cost-saving as overriding, would the states' arguments prevail?

2. *Suspect Class.* The Supreme Court held the citizenship and durational residency requirements to be inherently suspect and applied strict scrutiny. Given the Court's emphasis on the fact that aliens contribute to the economy and to tax revenues, would restrictions prohibiting them from receiving public assistance survive even rationality review?

3. *Mathews v. Diaz.* The Supreme Court held that Congress could impose a five-year national residency requirement as a condition of eligibility for federal medical benefits in *Mathews v. Diaz*, 426 U.S. 67 (1976). The Court noted that temporary aliens or undocumented aliens do not enjoy the right to full government benefits. The Court also deferred to the substantial congressional interest in relations with foreign powers. How is a resident alien's health coverage relevant to the congressional interest in relations with foreign powers?

Immigrants and the 1996 Personal Responsibility Act

In the Personal Responsibility and Work Opportunity Reconciliation Act of 1996, Congress severely restricted immigrant eligibility for various welfare benefits. Congress prohibited legal immigrants from receiving Food Stamps and Supplement Security Income benefits. It also authorized states to deny welfare benefits (funded by the Temporary Assistance for Needy Families block grant program), Medicaid, Title XX Social Services, and state-funded assistance during a legal immigrant's first five years in the United States. After five years, a legal immigrant's sponsor's income would be counted in determining the immigrant's eligibility for benefits. Congress also required states to indicate in their Family Assistance Program plan "whether the State intends to provide assistance under the program to individuals who are not citizens of the United States, and if so, shall include an overview of such assistance."

Recall that the Court in *Graham* invalidated the statutes at issue there, in part because they conflicted with the federal government's power to control immigration policy. States and local governments have no similar constitutional power. Yet Congress left the denial of some welfare benefits to state discretion. May Congress delegate its power to control immigration policy to the states? Should courts defer to state decisions with regard to immigrants?

Congress prohibited states from providing any federal benefits to undocumented immigrants. Congress also prohibited states from providing state or local benefits to undocumented immigrants, unless the state explicitly adopts a law authorizing such benefits. By what authority can Congress control whether a state provides state-funded benefits to its needy residents?

Recall footnote 14 in *Graham* where the Court noted that it did not decide whether Congress had power to enact a nationwide residency requirement as a condition for receipt of welfare benefits. The Court emphasized in the text of the opinion, however, that Congress may not authorize states to violate the Equal Protection Clause. Presumably, neither may Congress itself violate the guarantee of equal protection.

What level of scrutiny would you expect courts to apply to immigrant welfare restrictions passed by Congress? If courts applied mere rationality review, what legitimate government interests would be asserted? If denying government benefits to aliens who contribute to the economy and tax base is irrational, would mere hostility toward aliens constitute a legitimate government interest? How would plaintiffs challenging such laws prove that they were motivated by mere animosity? Recall *United States Department of Agriculture v. Moreno*, excerpted earlier in this chapter, where the Supreme Court invalidated a law which denied food stamps to unrelated household members. The Supreme Court has invalidated other laws that targeted a group due to mere animosity, including *City of Cleburne v. Cleburne Living Center*, 473 U.S. 432 (1985) (holding unsubstantiated negative attitudes and fear and irrational prejudice insufficient to justify special use permit requirement for group home for developmentally disabled persons); *Romer v. Evans*, 116 S. Ct. 1620 (1996) (holding mere animosity toward gays and lesbians insufficient to justify law denying them access to legislative, judicial, or executive branches to seek protection from discrimination).

2. Fundamental Rights

a. The (Very Fundamental) Right to Travel

SHAPIRO v. THOMPSON

394 U.S. 618 (1969)

Justice BRENNAN delivered the opinion of the Court.

These three appeals were restored to the calendar for reargument. Each is an appeal from a decision of a three-judge District Court holding unconstitutional a State or District of Columbia statutory provision which denies welfare assistance to residents of the State or District who have not resided within their jurisdictions for at least one year immediately preceding their applications for such assistance. We affirm the judgments of the District Courts in the three cases.

In No. 9, the Connecticut Welfare Department invoked § 17-2d of the Connecticut General Statutes[2] to deny the application of appellee Vivian Marie Thompson for assistance under the program for Aid to Families with Dependent Children (AFDC). She was a 19-year-old unwed mother of one child and pregnant with her second child when she changed her residence in June 1966 from Dorchester, Massachusetts, to Hartford, Connecticut, to live with her mother, a Hartford resident. She moved to her own apartment in Hartford in August 1966, when her mother was no longer able to support her and her infant son. Because of her pregnancy, she was unable to work or enter a work training program. Her application for AFDC assistance, filed in August, was denied in November solely on the ground that,

---

[2]CONN. GEN. STAT. REV. § 17-2d (1965 Supp.), now § 17-2c, provides:

> When any person comes into this state without visible means of support for the immediate future and applies for aid to dependent children under chapter 301 or general assistance under part I of chapter 308 within one year from his arrival, such person shall be eligible only for temporary aid or care until arrangements are made for his return, provided ineligibility for aid to dependent children shall not continue beyond the maximum federal residence requirement.

An exception is made for those persons who come to Connecticut with a bona fide job offer or are self-supporting upon arrival in the State and for three months thereafter.

as required by § 17-2d, she had not lived in the State for a year before her application was filed. She brought this action in the District Court for the District of Connecticut where a three-judge court, one judge dissenting, declared § 17-2d unconstitutional. The majority held that the waiting-period requirement is unconstitutional because it "has a chilling effect on the right to travel." The majority also held that the provision was a violation of the Equal Protection Clause of the Fourteenth Amendment because the denial of relief to those resident [sic] in the State for less than a year is not based on any permissible purpose but is solely designed as "Connecticut states quite frankly," "to protect its fisc by discouraging entry of those who come needing relief."

* * *

There is no dispute that the effect of the waiting-period requirement in each case is to create two classes of needy resident families indistinguishable from each other except that one is composed of residents who have resided a year or more, and the second of residents who have resided less than a year, in the jurisdiction. On the basis of this sole difference the first class is granted and the second class is denied welfare aid upon which may depend the ability of the families to obtain the very means to subsist--food, shelter, and other necessities of life. In each case, the District Court found that appellees met the test for residence in their jurisdictions, as well as all other eligibility requirements except the requirement of residence for a full year prior to their applications. On reargument, appellees' central contention is that the statutory prohibition of benefits to residents of less than a year creates a classification which constitutes an invidious discrimination denying them equal protection of the laws.[6] We agree. The interests which appellants assert are promoted by the classification either may not constitutionally be promoted by government or are not compelling governmental interests.

Primarily, appellants justify the waiting-period requirement as a protective device to preserve the fiscal integrity of state public assistance programs. It is asserted that people who require welfare

[6]This constitutional challenge cannot be answered by the argument that public assistance benefits are a "privilege" and not a "right."

assistance during their first year of residence in a State are likely to become continuing burdens on state welfare programs. Therefore, the argument runs, if such people can be deterred from entering the jurisdiction by denying them welfare benefits during the first year, state programs to assist long-time residents will not be impaired by a substantial influx of indigent newcomers.[7]

There is weighty evidence that exclusion from the jurisdiction of the poor who need or may need relief was the specific objective of these provisions. In the Congress, sponsors of federal legislation to eliminate all residence requirements have been consistently opposed by representatives of state and local welfare agencies who have stressed the fears of the States that elimination of the requirements would result in a heavy influx of individuals into States providing the most generous benefits. The sponsor of the Connecticut requirement said in its support: "I doubt that Connecticut can and should continue to allow unlimited migration into the state on the basis of offering instant money and permanent income to all who can make their way to the state regardless of their ability to contribute to the economy."

* * *

We do not doubt that the one-year waiting period device is well suited to discourage the influx of poor families in need of assistance. An indigent who desires to migrate, resettle, find a new job, and start a new life will doubtless hesitate if he knows that he must risk making the move without the possibility of falling back on

---

[7]The waiting-period requirement has its antecedents in laws prevalent in England and the American Colonies centuries ago which permitted the ejection of individuals and families if local authorities thought they might become public charges. For example, the preamble of the English Law of Settlement and Removal of 1662 expressly recited the concern, also said to justify the three statutes before us, that large numbers of the poor were moving to parishes where more liberal relief policies were in effect. The 1662 law and the earlier Elizabethan Poor Law of 1601 were the models adopted by the American Colonies. Newcomers to a city, town, or county who might become public charges were "warned out" or "passed on" to the next locality. Initially, the funds for welfare payments were raised by local taxes, and the controversy as to responsibility for particular indigents was between localities in the same State. As States--first alone and then with federal grants--assumed the major responsibility, the contest of nonresponsibility became interstate.

state welfare assistance during his first year of residence, when his need may be most acute. But the purpose of inhibiting migration by needy persons into the State is constitutionally impermissible.

This Court long ago recognized that the nature of our Federal Union and our constitutional concepts of personal liberty unite to require that all citizens be free to travel throughout the length and breadth of our land uninhibited by statutes, rules, or regulations which unreasonably burden or restrict this movement. That proposition was early stated by Chief Justice Taney in the *Passenger Cases*:

> For all the great purposes for which the Federal government was formed, we are one people, with one common country. We are all citizens of the United States; and, as members of the same community, must have the right to pass and repass through every part of it without interruption, as freely as in our own States.

We have no occasion to ascribe the source of this right to travel interstate to a particular constitutional provision. It suffices that, as Mr. Justice Stewart said for the Court in *United States v. Guest*:

> The constitutional right to travel from one State to another . . . occupies a position fundamental to the concept of our Federal Union. It is a right that has been firmly established and repeatedly recognized.
>
> * * *
>
> [T]he right finds no explicit mention in the Constitution. The reason, it has been suggested, is that a right so elementary was conceived from the beginning to be a necessary concomitant of the stronger Union the Constitution created. In any event, freedom to travel throughout the United States has long been recognized as a basic right under the Constitution.

Thus, the purpose of deterring the in-migration of indigents cannot serve as justification for the classification created by the one-year waiting period, since that purpose is constitutionally impermissible. If a law has "no other purpose . . . than to chill the assertion of constitutional rights by penalizing those who choose to exercise them, then it [is] patently unconstitutional."

Alternatively, appellants argue that even if it is impermissible for a State to attempt to deter the entry of all indigents, the challenged classification may be justified as a permissible state attempt to discourage those indigents who would enter the State solely to obtain larger benefits. We observe first that none of the statutes before us is tailored to serve that objective. Rather, the class of barred newcomers is all-inclusive, lumping the great majority who come to the State for other purposes with those who come for the sole purpose of collecting higher benefits. In actual operation, therefore, the three statutes enact what in effect are non-rebuttable presumptions that every applicant for assistance in his first year of residence came to the jurisdiction solely to obtain higher benefits. Nothing whatever in any of these records supplies any basis in fact for such a presumption.

More fundamentally, a State may no more try to fence out those indigents who seek higher welfare benefits than it may try to fence out indigents generally. Implicit in any such distinction is the notion that indigents who enter a State with the hope of securing higher welfare benefits are somehow less deserving than indigents who do not take this consideration into account. But we do not perceive why a mother who is seeking to make a new life for herself and her children should be regarded as less deserving because she considers, among others [sic] factors, the level of a State's public assistance. Surely such a mother is no less deserving than a mother who moves into a particular State in order to take advantage of its better educational facilities.

Appellants argue further that the challenged classification may be sustained as an attempt to distinguish between new and old residents on the basis of the contribution they have made to the community through the payment of taxes. We have difficulty seeing how long-term residents who qualify for welfare are making a greater present contribution to the State in taxes than indigent residents who have recently arrived. . . . Appellants' reasoning would logically permit the State to bar new residents from schools, parks, and libraries or deprive them of police and fire protection. Indeed it would permit the State to apportion all benefits and services according to the past tax contributions of its citizens. The Equal Protection Clause prohibits such an apportionment of state services.

We recognize that a State has a valid interest in preserving the fiscal integrity of its programs. It may legitimately attempt to limit its expenditures, whether for public assistance, public education, or any other program. But a State may not accomplish such a purpose by invidious distinctions between classes of its citizens. It could not, for example, reduce expenditures for education by barring indigent children from its schools. Similarly, in the cases before us, appellants must do more than show that denying welfare benefits to new residents saves money. The saving of welfare costs cannot justify an otherwise invidious classification.

In sum, neither deterrence of indigents from migrating to the State nor limitation of welfare benefits to those regarded as contributing to the State is a constitutionally permissible state objective.

Appellants next advance as justification certain administrative and related governmental objectives allegedly served by the waiting-period requirement. They argue that the requirement (1) facilitates the planning of the welfare budget; (2) provides an objective test of residency; (3) minimizes the opportunity for recipients fraudulently to receive payments from more than one jurisdiction; and (4) encourages early entry of new residents into the labor force.

At the outset, we reject appellants' argument that a mere showing of a rational relationship between the waiting period and these four admittedly permissible state objectives will suffice to justify the classification. The waiting-period provision denies welfare benefits to otherwise eligible applicants solely because they have recently moved into the jurisdiction. But in moving from State to State or to the District of Columbia appellees were exercising a constitutional right, and any classification which serves to penalize the exercise of that right, unless shown to be necessary to promote a *compelling* governmental interest, is unconstitutional.

The argument that the waiting-period requirement facilitates budget predictability is wholly unfounded. The records in all three cases are utterly devoid of evidence that either State or the District of Columbia in fact uses the one-year requirement as a means to predict the number of people who will require assistance in the budget year. None of the appellants takes a census of new residents or collects any other data that would reveal the number of newcomers in the State less than a year. Nor are new residents required to give advance notice of their need for welfare assistance. Thus, the welfare authorities cannot know how many new residents come into the jurisdiction in any year, much less how many of them will require public assistance. In these circumstances, there is simply no basis for the claim that the one-year waiting requirement serves the purpose of making the welfare budget more predictable. In Connecticut and Pennsylvania the irrelevance of the one-year requirement to budgetary planning is further underscored by the fact that temporary, partial assistance is given to some new residents and full assistance is given to other new residents under reciprocal agreements. Finally, the claim that a one-year waiting requirement is used for planning purposes is plainly belied by the fact that the requirement is not also imposed on applicants who are long-term residents, the group that receives the bulk of welfare payments. In short, the States rely on methods other than the one-year requirement to make budget estimates.

* * *

The argument that the waiting period serves as an administratively efficient rule of thumb for determining residency similarly will not withstand scrutiny. The residence requirement and the one-year waiting-period requirement are distinct and independent prerequisites for assistance under these three statutes, and the facts relevant to the determination of each are directly examined by the welfare authorities. Before granting an application, the welfare authorities investigate the applicant's employment, housing, and family situation and in the course of the inquiry necessarily learn the facts upon which to determine whether the applicant is a resident.

Similarly, there is no need for a State to use the one-year waiting period as a safeguard against fraudulent receipt of benefits; for less drastic means are available, and are employed, to minimize that hazard. Of course, a State has a valid interest in preventing fraud by any applicant, whether a newcomer or a long-time resident. It is not denied, however, that the investigations now conducted entail inquiries into facts relevant to that subject. In addition, cooperation among state welfare departments is common. The District of Columbia, for example, provides interim assistance to its former residents who have moved to a State which has a waiting period. As a matter of course, District officials send a letter to the welfare authorities in the recipient's new community "to request the information needed to continue assistance." A like procedure would be an effective safeguard against the hazard of double payments.

Since double payments can be prevented by a letter or a telephone call, it is unreasonable to accomplish this objective by the blunderbuss method of denying assistance to all indigent newcomers for an entire year.

Pennsylvania suggests that the one-year waiting period is justified as a means of encouraging new residents to join the labor force promptly. But this logic would also require a similar waiting period for long-term residents of the State. A state purpose to encourage employment provides no rational basis for imposing a one-year waiting-period restriction on new residents only.

We conclude therefore that appellants in these cases do not use and have no need to use the one-year requirement for the governmental purposes suggested. Thus, even under traditional equal protection tests a classification of welfare applicants according to whether they have lived in the State for one year would seem irrational and unconstitutional. But, of course, the traditional criteria do not apply in these cases. Since the classification here touches on the fundamental right of interstate movement, its constitutionality must be judged by the stricter standard of whether it promotes a compelling state interest. Under this standard, the waiting-period requirement clearly violates the Equal Protection Clause.

* * *

Affirmed.

Chief Justice WARREN, with whom Justice BLACK joins, dissenting.

* * *

Congress has imposed a residence requirement in the District of Columbia and authorized the States to impose similar requirements. The issue before us must therefore be framed in terms of whether Congress may create minimal residence requirements, not whether the States, acting alone, may do so. Appellees insist that a congressionally mandated residence requirement would violate their right to travel. The import of their contention is that Congress, even under its "plenary" power to control interstate commerce, is constitutionally prohibited from imposing residence requirements. I reach a contrary conclusion for I am convinced that the extent of the burden on interstate travel when compared with the justification for its imposition requires the Court to uphold this exertion of federal power.

* * *

The core inquiry is "the extent of the governmental restriction imposed" and the "extent of the necessity for the restriction." As already noted, travel itself is not prohibited. Any burden inheres solely in the fact that a potential welfare recipient might take into consideration the loss of welfare benefits for a limited period of time if he changes his residence. Not only is this burden of uncertain degree, but appellees themselves assert there is evidence that few welfare recipients have in fact been deterred by residence requirements.

The insubstantiality of the restriction imposed by residence requirements must then be evaluated in light of the possible congressional reasons for such requirements. One fact which does emerge with clarity from the legislative history is Congress' belief that a program of cooperative federalism combining federal aid with enhanced state participation would result in an increase in the scope of welfare programs and level of benefits. Given the apprehensions of many States that an increase in benefits without minimal residence requirements would result in an inability to provide an adequate welfare system, Congress deliberately adopted the intermediate course of a cooperative program. Such a program, Congress believed, would encourage the States to assume greater welfare responsibilities and would give the States the necessary financial support for such an undertaking. Our cases require only that Congress have a rational basis for finding that a chosen regulatory scheme is necessary to the furtherance of interstate commerce. Certainly, a congressional finding that residence requirements allowed each State to concentrate its resources upon new and increased programs of rehabilitation ultimately resulting in an enhanced flow of commerce as the economic condition of welfare recipients progressively improved is rational and would justify imposition of residence requirements under the Commerce Clause. And Congress could have also determined that residence requirements fostered personal mobility. An individual no longer dependent upon welfare would be presented with an unfettered range of choices so that a decision to migrate could be made without regard to considerations of possible economic dislocation.

Appellees suggest, however, that Congress was not motivated by rational considerations. Residence requirements are imposed, they insist, for the illegitimate purpose of keeping poor people from migrating. Not only does the legislative history point to an opposite conclusion, but it also must be noted that "[i]nto the motives which induced members of Congress to [act] . . . this Court may not inquire." We do not attribute an impermissible purpose to Congress if the result would be to strike down an otherwise valid statute. Since the congressional decision is rational and the restriction on travel insubstantial, I conclude that residence requirements can be imposed by Congress as an exercise of its power to control interstate commerce consistent with the constitutionally guaranteed right to travel.

* * *

The era is long past when this Court under the rubric of due process has reviewed the wisdom of a congressional decision that interstate commerce will be fostered by the enactment of certain regulations. . . . I am convinced that Congress does have power to enact residence requirements of reasonable duration or to authorize the States to do so and that it has exercised this power.

* * *

I dissent.

Justice HARLAN, dissenting.

* * *

In upholding the equal protection argument, the Court has applied an equal protection doctrine of relatively recent vintage: the rule that statutory classifications which either are based upon certain "suspect" criteria or affect "fundamental rights" will be held to deny equal protection unless justified by a "compelling" governmental interest.

The "compelling interest" doctrine, which today is articulated more explicitly than ever before, constitutes an increasingly significant exception to the long-established rule that a statute does not deny equal protection if it is rationally related to a legitimate governmental objective. The "compelling interest" doctrine has two branches. The branch which requires that classifications based upon "suspect" criteria be supported by a compelling interest apparently had its genesis in cases involving racial classifications, which have, at least since *Korematsu v. United States*, been regarded as inherently "suspect." The criterion of "wealth" apparently was added to the list of "suspects" as an alternative justification for the rationale in *Harper v. Virginia Bd. of Elections*, in which Virginia's poll tax was struck down.

* * *

I think that this branch of the "compelling interest" doctrine is sound when applied to racial classifications, for historically the Equal Protection Clause was largely a product of the desire to eradicate legal distinctions founded upon race. However, I believe that the more recent extensions have been unwise. For the reasons stated in my dissenting opinion in *Harper v. Virginia Bd. of Elections*, I do not consider wealth a "suspect" statutory criterion.

* * *

The second branch of the "compelling interest" principle is even more troublesome. For it has been held that a statutory classification is subject to the "compelling interest" test if the result of the classification may be to affect a "fundamental right," regardless of the basis of the classification.

* * *

I think this branch of the "compelling interest" doctrine particularly unfortunate and unnecessary. It is unfortunate because it creates an exception which threatens to swallow the standard equal protection rule. Virtually every state statute affects important rights. . . . This branch of the doctrine is also unnecessary. When the right affected is one assured by the Federal Constitution, any infringement can be dealt with under the Due Process Clause. But when a statute affects only matters not mentioned in the Federal Constitution and is not arbitrary or irrational, I must reiterate that I know of nothing which entitles this Court to pick out particular human activities, characterize them as "fundamental," and give them added protection under an unusually stringent equal protection test.

* * *

[First, Justice Harlan concludes that the right to travel interstate has its roots in the Due Process Clause of the Fifth Amendment. Next, he identifies four interests served by residence requirements: (1) "to deny welfare benefits to persons who moved into the jurisdiction primarily in order to collect those benefits"; (2) "the prevention of fraud"; (3) "predicting the budgetary amount which will be needed for public assistance in the future"; and (4) "to restrict welfare payments financed in part by state tax funds to persons who have recently made some contribution to the State's economy, through having been employed, having paid taxes, or having spent money in the State."]

The next question is the decisive one: whether the governmental interests served by residence requirements outweigh the burden imposed upon the right to travel. In my view, a number of considerations militate in favor of constitutionality. First, as just shown, four separate, legitimate governmental interests are furthered by residence requirements. Second, the impact of the requirements upon the freedom of individuals to travel interstate is indirect and, according to evidence put forward by the appellees themselves, insubstantial. Third, these are not cases in which a State or States, acting alone, have attempted to interfere with the right of citizens to travel, but one in which the States have acted within the terms of a limited authorization by the National Government, and in which Congress itself has laid down a like rule for the District of Columbia. Fourth, the legislatures which enacted these statutes have been fully exposed to the arguments of the appellees as to why these residence requirements are unwise, and have rejected them. This is not, therefore, an instance in which legislatures have acted without mature deliberation.

Fifth, and of longer-range importance, the field of welfare assistance is one in which there is a widely recognized need for fresh solutions and consequently for experimentation. Invalidation of welfare residence requirements might have the unfortunate consequence of discouraging the Federal and State Governments from establishing unusually generous welfare programs in particular areas on an experimental basis, because of fears that the program would cause an influx of persons seeking higher welfare payments. Sixth and finally, a strong presumption of constitutionality attaches to statutes of the types now before us. Congressional enactments come to this Court with an extremely heavy presumption of validity. A similar presumption of constitutionality attaches to state statutes, particularly when, as here, a State has acted upon a specific authorization from Congress.

I do not consider that the factors which have been urged to outweigh these considerations are sufficient to render unconstitutional these state and federal enactments. It is said, first, that this Court . . . has acknowledged that the right to travel interstate is a "fundamental" freedom. Second, it is contended that the governmental objectives mentioned above either are ephemeral or could be accomplished by means which do not impinge as heavily on the right to travel, and hence that the requirements are unconstitutional because they "sweep unnecessarily broadly and thereby invade the area of protected freedoms." The appellees claim that welfare payments could be denied those who come primarily to collect welfare by means of less restrictive provisions . . . ; that fraud could be prevented by investigation of individual applicants or by a much shorter residence period; that budgetary predictability is a remote and speculative goal; and that assurance of investment in the community could be obtained by a shorter residence period or by taking into account prior intervals of residence in the jurisdiction.

Taking all of these competing considerations into account, I believe that the balance definitely favors constitutionality. In reaching that conclusion, I do not minimize the importance of the right to travel interstate. However, the impact of residence conditions upon that right is indirect and apparently quite insubstantial. On the other hand, the governmental purposes served by the requirements are legitimate and real, and the residence requirements are clearly suited to their accomplishment. To abolish residence requirements might well discourage highly worthwhile experimentation in the welfare field. The statutes come to us clothed with the authority of Congress and attended by a correspondingly heavy presumption of constitutionality. Moreover, although the appellees assert that the same objectives could have been achieved by less restrictive means, this is an area in which the judiciary should be especially slow to fetter the judgment of Congress and of some 46 state legislatures in the choice of methods. Residence requirements have advantages, such as administrative simplicity and relative certainty, which are not shared by the alternative solutions proposed by the appellees. In these circumstances, I cannot find that the burden imposed by residence requirements upon ability to travel outweighs the governmental interests in their continued employment. Nor do I believe that the period of residence required to these cases--one year--is so excessively long as to justify a finding of unconstitutionality on that score.

* * *

Notes and Questions

1. *States Interests.* The states and the District of Columbia identified several interests served by their durational residency requirements, including: (1) preserving fiscal integrity; (2) deterring in-migration of persons seeking higher welfare benefits; (3) distinguishing between new residents and old residents who have contributed to the tax base; (4) planning the welfare budget; (5) testing residency; (6) reducing fraud; and (7) encouraging employment. The Court rejected each of these purposes as insufficient.

The Court seemed to presume the legitimacy of the first interest in preserving fiscal integrity and conceded that the exclusion was "well suited" to the second interest in deterring in-migration of poor families. If the ends were legitimate and the means effectively served those ends, why were these purposes insufficient for upholding the durational residency requirements? On what basis did the Court disapprove the fit between the durational residency requirements and the purposes of deterring poor people from seeking higher benefits and distinguishing between those who have contributed to the tax base and those who have not? On what basis did the Court reject the final four administrative interests?

2. *Reduced Durations.* If the purpose and effect of deterring interstate travel are always impermissible could any durational residency requirement survive the Court's strict scrutiny? What if the duration required was only six months? Three months? Thirty days?

3. *Commerce Clause Authority.* Chief Justice Warren and Justice Black in dissent rejected the Court's focus on the recipients' right to travel, and emphasized instead the authority of Congress to allow states to impose durational residency requirements as encompassed within Congress' power to regulate interstate commerce. If Congress had commerce clause authority to allow exclusions of newly arriving poor families, would that authority protect Congress' action from an equal protection challenge? Or is Congress required to provide equal protection of the laws even if they were otherwise authorized to enact legislation?

4. *Suspect Class Revisited.* Justice Harlan in dissent noted that "[t]he criterion of 'wealth' apparently was added to the list of 'suspects' as an alternative justification for the rationale in *Harper v. Virginia Bd. of Elections*, in which Virginia's poll tax was struck

down." Contrary to Justice Harlan's fears, decisions issued after *Harper* have not followed its reasoning that wealth is a suspect class. For example, in *San Antonio Independent School District v. Rodriguez,* 411 U.S. 1 (1973), the Court noted that it "had never heretofore held that wealth discrimination alone provides an adequate basis for invoking strict scrutiny."

5. *Recent Challenges.* A recent spate of cases have challenged the validity of *Shapiro's* invalidation of durational residency requirements. One of these cases, *Green v. Anderson,* 811 F. Supp. 516 (E.D. Cal. 1993), reached the Supreme Court but was remanded due to lack of ripeness because a lower court had enjoined the State from implementing the requirement. Do you believe the majority's reasoning in *Shapiro* can withstand future challenges?

Migrants and Temporary Assistance For Needy Families

In the Temporary Assistance for Needy Families block grant program, Congress required states to indicate in their Family Assistance Program plan "whether the State intends to treat families moving into the State from another State differently than other families under the program, and if so, how the State intends to treat such families under the program." Congress further authorized states to "apply to a family the rules (including benefit amounts) of the program funded under this part of another State if the family has moved to the State from the other State and has resided in the State for less than 12 months." Will this provision withstand a challenge based on *Shapiro*?

b. The Right to (Some) Access to Criminal Justice

GRIFFIN v. ILLINOIS

351 U.S. 12 (1956)

Justice BLACK announced the judgment of the Court and an opinion in which THE CHIEF JUSTICE, Justice DOUGLAS, and Justice CLARK, join.

* * *

The petitioners Griffin and Crenshaw were tried together and convicted of armed robbery in the Criminal Court of Cook County, Illinois. Immediately after their conviction they filed a motion in the trial court asking that a certified copy of the entire record, including a stenographic transcript of the proceedings, be furnished them without cost. They alleged that they were "poor persons with no means of paying the necessary fees to acquire the Transcript and Court Records needed to prosecute an appeal . . . ." These allegations were not denied. Under Illinois law in order to get full direct appellate review of alleged errors by a writ of error it is necessary for the defendant to furnish the appellate court with a bill of exceptions or report of proceedings at the trial certified by the trial judge. As Illinois concedes, it is sometimes impossible to prepare such bills of exceptions or reports without a stenographic transcript of the trial proceedings. Indigent defendants sentenced to death are provided with a free transcript at the expense of the county where convicted. In all other criminal cases defendants needing a transcript, whether indigent or not, must themselves buy it. The petitioners contended in their motion before the trial court that failure to provide them with the needed transcript would violate the Due Process and Equal Protection Clauses of the Fourteenth Amendment. The trial court denied the motion without a hearing.

* * *

Counsel for Illinois concedes that these petitioners needed a transcript in order to get adequate appellate review of their alleged trial errors. There is no contention that petitioners were dilatory in their efforts to get appellate review, or that the Illinois Supreme Court denied review on the ground that the allegations of trial error were insufficient. We must therefore assume for purposes of this decision that errors were committed in the trial which would merit reversal, but that the petitioners could not get appellate review of those errors solely because they were too poor to buy a stenographic transcript. Counsel for Illinois denies that this violates either the Due Process or the Equal Protection Clause. . . . The sole question for us to decide, therefore, is whether due process or equal protection has been violated.

* * *

[O]ur own constitutional guaranties of due process and equal protection both call for procedures in criminal trials which allow no invidious discriminations between persons and different groups of persons. Both equal protection and due process emphasize the central aim of our entire judicial system--all people charged with crime must, so far as the law is concerned, "stand on an equality before the bar of justice in every American court."

* * *

In criminal trials a State can no more discriminate on account of poverty than on account of religion, race, or color. Plainly the ability to pay costs in advance bears no rational relationship to a defendant's guilt or innocence and could not be used as an excuse to deprive a defendant of a fair trial. Indeed, a provision in the Constitution of Illinois of 1818 provided that every person in Illinois "ought to obtain right and justice freely, and without being obliged to purchase it, completely and without denial, promptly and without delay, conformably to the laws."

There is no meaningful distinction between a rule which would deny the poor the right to defend themselves in a trial court and one which effectively denies the poor an adequate appellate review accorded to all who have money enough to pay the costs in advance. It is true that a State is not required by the Federal Constitution to provide appellate courts or a right to appellate review at all. But that is not to say that a State that does grant appellate review can do so in a way that discriminates against some convicted defendants on account of their poverty. Appellate review has now become an integral part of the Illinois trial system for finally adjudicating the guilt or innocence of a defendant. Consequently at all stages of the proceedings the Due Process and Equal Protection Clauses protect persons like petitioners from invidious discriminations.

* * *

[T]o deny adequate review to the poor means that many of them may lose their life, liberty or property because of unjust convictions which appellate courts would set aside. . . . Destitute defendants must be afforded as adequate appellate review as defendants who have money enough to buy transcripts.

* * *

Vacated and remanded.

Justice FRANKFURTER, concurring in the judgment.

* * *

[N]either the fact that a State may deny the right of appeal altogether nor the right of a State to make an appropriate classification, based on differences in crimes and their punishment, nor the right of a State to lay down conditions it deems appropriate for criminal appeals, sanctions differentiations by a State that have no relation to a rational policy of criminal appeal or authorizes the imposition of conditions that offend the deepest presuppositions of our society.

* * *

Law addresses itself to actualities. It does not face actuality to suggest that Illinois affords every convicted person, financially competent or not, the opportunity to take an appeal, and that it is not Illinois that is responsible for disparity in material circumstances. Of course a State need not equalize economic conditions. . . . But when a State deems it wise and just that convictions be susceptible to review by an appellate court, it cannot by force of its exactions draw a line which precludes convicted indigent persons, forsooth erroneously convicted, from securing such a review merely by disabling them from bringing to the notice of an appellate tribunal errors of the trial court which would upset the conviction were practical opportunity for review not foreclosed.

* * *

The State is not free to produce such a squalid discrimination. If it has a general policy of allowing criminal appeals, it cannot make lack of means an effective bar to the exercise of this opportunity. The State cannot keep the word of promise to the ear of those illegally convicted and break it to their hope.

* * *

Justice BURTON and Justice MINTON, whom Justice REED and Justice HARLAN join, dissenting.

While we do not disagree with the desirability of the policy of supplying an indigent defendant with a free transcript of testimony in a case like this, we do not agree that the Constitution of the United States compels each State to do so with the consequence that, regardless of the State's legislation and practice to the contrary, this Court must hold invalid state appellate proceedings wherever a required transcript has not been provided without cost to an indigent litigant who has requested that it be so provided. It is one thing for Congress and this Court to prescribe such procedure for the federal courts. It is quite another for this Court to hold that the Constitution of the United States has prescribed it for all state courts.

In the administration of local law the Constitution has been interpreted as permitting the several States generally to follow their own familiar procedure and practice. In so doing this Court has recognized the widely differing but locally approved procedures of the several States. Whether approving of the particular procedures or not, this Court has treated them largely as matters reserved to the States and within the broad range of permissible "due process" in a constitutional sense.

Illinois, as the majority admit, could thus deny an appeal altogether in a criminal case without denying due process of law. To allow an appeal at all, but with some difference among convicted persons as to the terms upon which an appeal is exercised does not deny due process. It may present a question of equal protection. The petitioners urge that point here.

* * *

[C]ertainly Illinois does not deny equal protection to convicted defendants when the terms of appeal are open to all, although some may not be able to avail themselves of the full appeal because of their poverty. Illinois is not bound to make the defendants economically equal before its bar of justice. For a State to do so may be a desirable social policy, but what may be a good legislative policy for a State is not necessarily required by the Constitution of the United States.

* * *

The Constitution requires the equal protection of the law, but it does not require the States to provide equal financial means for all defendants to avail themselves of such laws.

Justice HARLAN, dissenting.

* * *

Is an indigent defendant who "needs" a transcript in order to appeal constitutionally entitled, regardless of the nature of the circumstances producing that need, to have the State either furnish a free transcript or take some other action to assure that he does in fact obtain full appellate review?

* * *

In finding an answer to that question in the Equal Protection Clause, the Court has painted with a broad brush. It is said that a

State cannot discriminate between the "rich" and the "poor" in its system of criminal appeals. That statement of course commands support, but it hardly sheds light on the true character of the problem confronting us here. Illinois has not imposed any arbitrary conditions upon the exercise of the right of appeal nor any requirements unnecessary to the effective working of its appellate system. Trial errors cannot be reviewed without an appropriate record of the proceedings below; if a transcript is used, it is surely not unreasonable to require the appellant to bear its cost; and Illinois has not foreclosed any other feasible means of preparing such a record. Nor is this a case where the State's own action has prevented a defendant from appealing. All that Illinois has done is to fail to alleviate the consequences of differences in economic circumstances that exist wholly apart from any state action.

The Court thus holds that, at least in this area of criminal appeals, the Equal Protection Clause imposes on the States an affirmative duty to lift the handicaps flowing from differences in economic circumstances. That holding produces the anomalous result that a constitutional admonition to the States to treat all persons equally means in this instance that Illinois must give to some what it requires others to pay for. Granting that such a classification would be reasonable, it does not follow that a State's failure to make it can be regarded as discrimination. It may as accurately be said that the real issue in this case is not whether Illinois has discriminated but whether it has a duty to discriminate.

I do not understand the Court to dispute either the necessity for a bill of exceptions or the reasonableness of the general requirement that the trial transcript, if used in its preparation, be paid for by the appealing party. The Court finds in the operation of these requirements, however, an invidious classification between the "rich" and the "poor." But no economic burden attendant upon the exercise of a privilege bears equally upon all, and in other circumstances the resulting differentiation is not treated as an invidious classification by the State, even though discrimination against "indigents" by name would be unconstitutional.

* * *

[T]he issue here is not the typical equal protection question of the reasonableness of a "classification" on the basis of which the State has imposed legal disabilities, but rather the reasonableness of the State's failure to remove natural disabilities. The Court holds that the failure of the State to do so is constitutionally unreasonable in this case although it might not be in others. I submit that the basis for that holding is simply an unarticulated conclusion that it violates "fundamental fairness" for a State which provides for appellate review, and thus apparently considers such review necessary to assure justice, not to see to it that such appeals are in fact available to those it would imprison for serious crimes. That of course is the traditional language of due process, and I see no reason to import new substance into the concept of equal protection to dispose of the case, especially when to do so gives rise to the all-too-easy opportunity to ignore the real issue and solve the problem simply by labeling the Illinois practice as invidious "discrimination."

* * *

Notes and Questions

1. *Suspect Class Revisited.* The Court noted that both equal protection and due process protect criminal defendants from invidious discrimination. The Court explained that states can "no more discriminate on account of poverty than on account of religion, race or color." Did the Court mean that poverty is a suspect class? What level of scrutiny did the Court apply? What government interests were served by the transcript fee?

2. *Criminal Context.* The dissent argued that a state is "not bound to make the defendants economically equal before its bar of justice." In his concurrence, Justice Frankfurter responded that, if a state allows a criminal appeal, it cannot condition that appeal on a person's ability to pay for a transcript. Who had the better argument? Is Justice Frankfurter's reasoning limited to criminal appeals, or could it apply to other government benefits?

DOUGLAS v. CALIFORNIA

372 U.S. 353 (1963)

Justice DOUGLAS delivered the opinion of the Court.

Petitioners, Bennie Will Meyes and William Douglas, were jointly tried and convicted in a California court on an information charging them with 13 felonies. A single public defender was appointed to represent them. At the commencement of the trial, the defender moved for a continuance, stating that the case was very complicated, that he was not as prepared as he felt he should be because he was handling a different defense every day, and that there was a conflict of interest between the petitioners requiring the appointment of separate counsel for each of them. This motion was denied. Thereafter, petitioners dismissed the defender, claiming he was unprepared, and again renewed motions for separate counsel and for a continuance. These motions also were denied, and petitioners were ultimately convicted by a jury of all 13 felonies, which included robbery, assault with a deadly weapon, and assault with intent to commit murder. Both were given prison terms. Both appealed as of right to the California District Court of Appeal. That court affirmed their convictions. Both Meyes and Douglas then petitioned for further discretionary review in the California Supreme Court, but their petitions were denied without a hearing. We granted certiorari.

Although several questions are presented in the petition for certiorari, we address ourselves to only one of them. The record shows that petitioners requested, and were denied, the assistance of counsel on appeal, even though it plainly appeared they were indigents. In denying petitioners' requests, the California District Court of Appeal stated that it had "gone through" the record and had come to the conclusion that "no good whatever could be served by appointment of counsel." The District Court of Appeal was acting in accordance with a California rule of criminal procedure which provides that state appellate courts, upon the request of an indigent for counsel, may make "an independent investigation of the record and determine whether it would be of advantage to the defendant or helpful to the appellate court to have counsel appointed. . . . After such investigation, appellate courts should appoint counsel if in their opinion it would be helpful to the defendant or the court, and should deny the appointment of counsel only if in their judgment such appointment would be of no value to either the defendant or the court."

We agree, however, with Justice Traynor of the California Supreme Court, who said that the "[d]enial of counsel on appeal (to an indigent) would seem to be a discrimination at least as invidious as that condemned in *Griffin v. People of State of Illinois* . . . ." In *Griffin v. Illinois*, we held that a State may not grant appellate review in such a way as to discriminate against some convicted defendants on account of their poverty. There, . . . the right to a free transcript on appeal was in issue. Here the issue is whether or not an indigent shall be denied the assistance of counsel on appeal. In either case the evil is the same: discrimination against the indigent. For there can be no equal justice where the kind of an appeal a man enjoys "depends on the amount of money he has."

In spite of California's forward treatment of indigents, under its present practice the type of an appeal a person is afforded in the District Court of Appeal hinges upon whether or not he can pay for the assistance of counsel. If he can the appellate court passes on the merits of his case only after having the full benefit of written briefs and oral argument by counsel. If he cannot the appellate court is forced to prejudge the merits before it can even determine whether counsel should be provided. At this stage in the proceedings only the barren record speaks for the indigent, and, unless the printed pages show that an injustice has been committed, he is forced to go without a champion on appeal. Any real chance he may have had of showing that his appeal has hidden merit is deprived him when the court decides on an ex parte examination of the record that the assistance of counsel is not required.

We are not here concerned with problems that might arise from the denial of counsel for the preparation of a petition for discretionary or mandatory review beyond the stage in the appellate process at which the claims have once been presented by a lawyer and passed upon by an appellate court. We are dealing only with the first appeal, granted as a matter of right to rich and poor alike, from a criminal conviction. . . . Absolute equality is not required; lines can be and are drawn and we often sustain them. But where the merits of the one and only appeal an indigent has as of right are decided without benefit of counsel, we think an unconstitutional line has been drawn between rich and poor.

When an indigent is forced to run this gauntlet of a preliminary showing of merit, the right to appeal does not comport with fair procedure. . . . In California . . . once the court has "gone through" the record and denied counsel, the indigent has no recourse but to prosecute his appeal on his own, as best he can, no matter how meritorious his case may turn out to be. The present case, where counsel was denied petitioners on appeal, shows that the discrimination is not between "possibly good and obviously bad cases," but between cases where the rich man can require the court to listen to argument of counsel before deciding on the merits, but a poor man cannot. There is lacking that equality demanded by the Fourteenth Amendment where the rich man, who appeals as of right, enjoys the benefit of counsel's examination into the record, research of the law, and marshalling of arguments on his behalf, while the indigent, already burdened by a preliminary determination that his case is without merit, is forced to shift for himself. The indigent, where the record is unclear or the errors are hidden, has only the right to a meaningless ritual, while the rich man has a meaningful appeal.

Vacated and remanded.

Justice HARLAN, whom Justice STEWART joins, dissenting.

In holding that an indigent has an absolute right to appointed counsel on appeal of a state criminal conviction, the Court appears to rely both on the Equal Protection Clause and on the guarantees of fair procedure inherent in the Due Process Clause of the Fourteenth Amendment, with obvious emphasis on "equal protection." In my view the Equal Protection Clause is not apposite, and its application to cases like the present one can lead only to mischievous results. This case should be judged solely under the Due Process Clause, and I do not believe that the California procedure violates that provision.

* * *

The States, of course, are prohibited by the Equal Protection Clause from discriminating between "rich" and "poor" as such in the formulation and application of their laws. But it is a far different thing to suggest that this provision prevents the State from adopting a law of general applicability that may affect the poor more harshly than it does the rich, or, on the other hand, from making some effort to redress economic imbalances while not eliminating them entirely.

Every financial exaction which the State imposes on a uniform basis is more easily satisfied by the well-to-do than by the indigent. Yet I take it that no one would dispute the constitutional power of the State to levy a uniform sales tax, to charge tuition at a state university, to fix rates for the purchase of water from a municipal corporation, to impose a standard fine for criminal violations, or to establish minimum bail for various categories of offenses. Nor could it be contended that the State may not classify as crimes acts which the poor are more likely to commit than are the rich. And surely, there would be no basis for attacking a state law which provided benefits for the needy simply because those benefits fell short of the goods or services that others could purchase for themselves.

Laws such as these do not deny equal protection to the less fortunate for one essential reason: the Equal Protection Clause does not impose on the States "an affirmative duty to lift the handicaps flowing from differences in economic circumstances." To so construe it would be to read into the Constitution a philosophy of leveling that would be foreign to many of our basic concepts of the proper relations between government and society. The State may have a moral obligation to eliminate the evils of poverty, but it is not required by the Equal Protection Clause to give to some whatever others can afford.

* * *

Notes and Questions

1. *Suspect Class or Fundamental Right.* The Supreme Court characterized the issue of whether poor defendants had a right to appointed counsel for an appeal as a right involving "discrimination against the indigent." Consider whether the nature of the remedy they sought, avoiding incarceration, influenced the Court's decision.

2. *Redistribution of Wealth.* The dissent argued that the Court's decision forced states to eliminate defendants' poverty. Did it?

3. *No Counsel for Discretionary Appeals.* The Supreme Court limited *Douglas* in its decision in *Ross v. Moffitt,* 417 U.S. 600 (1974). The Court held that states need not appoint counsel for poor defendants' discretionary appeals. The Court described *Douglas* as requiring states to afford poor people minimal access to the appellate system. The Court in *Ross* decided, in effect, that states retained discretion to decide whether to allocate funds for anything more than minimal access. The Court in *Ross* did not follow the *Griffin* and *Douglas* path of focusing on discrimination against the poor.

c. The Right to a (Relatively Underfunded) Education

SAN ANTONIO INDEPENDENT SCHOOL DISTRICT v. RODRIGUEZ

411 U.S. 1 (1973)

Justice POWELL delivered the opinion of the Court.

This suit attacking the Texas system of financing public education was initiated by Mexican-American parents whose children attend the elementary and secondary schools in the Edgewood Independent School District, an urban school district in San Antonio, Texas. They brought a class action on behalf of schoolchildren throughout the State who are members of minority groups or who are poor and reside in school districts having a low property tax base. Named as defendants were the State Board of Education, the Commissioner of Education, the State Attorney General, and the Bexar County (San Antonio) Board of Trustees.

* * *

The [Texas Minimum Foundation School] Program calls for state and local contributions to a fund earmarked specifically for teacher salaries, operating expenses, and transportation costs. The State, supplying funds from its general revenues, finances approximately 80% of the Program, and the school districts are responsible--as a unit--for providing the remaining 20%. The districts' share, known as the Local Fund Assignment, is apportioned among the school districts under a formula designed to reflect each district's relative taxpaying ability. The Assignment is first divided among Texas' 254 counties pursuant to a complicated economic index that takes into account the relative value of each county's contribution to the State's total income from manufacturing, mining, and agricultural activities. It also considers each county's relative share of all payrolls paid within the State and, to a lesser extent, considers each county's share of all property in the State. Each county's assignment is then divided among its school districts on the basis of each district's share of assessable property within the county. The district, in turn, finances its share of the Assignment out of revenues from local property taxation.

The design of this complex system was twofold. First, it was an attempt to assure that the Foundation Program would have an equalizing influence on expenditure levels between school districts by placing the heaviest burden on the school districts most capable of paying. Second, the Program's architects sought to establish a Local Fund Assignment that would force every school district to contribute to the education of its children but that would not by itself exhaust any district's resources. Today every school district does impose a property tax from which it derives locally expendable funds in excess of the amount necessary to satisfy its Local Fund Assignment under the Foundation Program.

* * *

The school district in which appellees reside, the Edgewood Independent School District, has been compared throughout this litigation with the Alamo Heights Independent School District. This comparison between the least and most affluent districts in the San Antonio area serves to illustrate the manner in which the dual system of finance operates and to indicate the extent to which substantial disparities exist despite the State's impressive progress in recent years. Edgewood is one of seven public school districts in the metropolitan area. Approximately 22,000 students are enrolled in its 25 elementary and secondary schools. The district is situated in the core-city sector of San Antonio in a residential neighborhood that has little commercial or industrial property. The residents are predominantly of Mexican-American descent: approximately 90% of the student population is Mexican-American and over 6% is Negro. The average assessed property value per pupil is $5,960--the lowest in the metropolitan area--and the median family income ($4,686) is also the lowest. At an equalized tax rate of $1.05 per $100 of assessed property--the highest in the metropolitan area--the district contributed $26 to the education of each child for the 1967-1968 school year above its Local Fund Assignment for the Minimum Foundation Program. The Foundation Program contributed $222 per pupil for a state-local total of $248. Federal funds added another $108 for a total of $356 per pupil.

Alamo Heights is the most affluent school district in San Antonio. Its six schools, housing approximately 5,000 students, are situated in a residential community quite unlike the Edgewood District. The school population is predominantly "Anglo," having only 18% Mexican-Americans and less than 1% Negroes. The assessed property value per pupil exceeds $49,000, and the median family income is $8,001. In 1967-1968 the local tax rate of $.85 per $100 of valuation yielded $333 per pupil over and above its contribution to the Foundation Program. Coupled with the $225 provided from that Program, the district was able to supply $558 per student. Supplemented by a $36 per-pupil grant from federal sources, Alamo Heights spent $594 per pupil.

* * *

Finding that wealth is a "suspect" classification and that education is a "fundamental" interest, the District Court held that the Texas system could be sustained only if the State could show that it was premised upon some compelling state interest. On this issue the court concluded that "[n]ot only are defendants unable to demonstrate compelling state interests . . . they fail even to establish a reasonable basis for these classifications."

Texas virtually concedes that its historically rooted dual system of financing education could not withstand the strict judicial scrutiny that this Court has found appropriate in reviewing legislative judgments that interfere with fundamental constitutional rights or that involve suspect classifications. If, as previous decisions have indicated, strict scrutiny means that the State's system is not entitled to the usual presumption of validity, that the State rather than the complainants must carry a "heavy burden of justification," that the State must demonstrate that its educational system has been structured with "precision," and is "tailored" narrowly to serve legitimate objectives and that it has selected the "less drastic means" for effectuating its objectives, the Texas financing system and its counterpart in virtually every other State will not pass muster. The State candidly admits that "[n]o one familiar with the Texas system would contend that it has yet achieved perfection." Apart from its concession that educational financing in Texas has "defects" and "imperfections," the State defends the system's rationality with vigor and disputes the District Court's finding that it lacks a "reasonable basis."

This, then, establishes the framework for our analysis. We must decide, first, whether the Texas system of financing public education operates to the disadvantage of some suspect class or impinges upon a fundamental right explicitly or implicitly protected by the Constitution, thereby requiring strict judicial scrutiny. If so, the judgment of the District Court should be affirmed. If not, the Texas scheme must still be examined to determine whether it rationally furthers some legitimate, articulated state purpose and therefore does not constitute an invidious discrimination in violation of the Equal Protection Clause of the Fourteenth Amendment.

The District Court's opinion does not reflect the novelty and complexity of the constitutional questions posed by appellees' challenge to Texas' system of school financing. In concluding that strict judicial scrutiny was required, that court relied on decisions dealing with the rights of indigents to equal treatment in the criminal trial and appellate processes, and on cases disapproving wealth restrictions on the right to vote. Those cases, the District Court concluded, established wealth as a suspect classification. Finding that the local property tax system discriminated on the basis of wealth, it regarded those precedents as controlling. It then reasoned, based on decisions of this Court affirming the undeniable importance of education, that there is a fundamental right to education and that, absent some compelling state justification, the Texas system could not stand.

We are unable to agree that this case, which in significant aspects is *sui generis*, may be so neatly fitted into the conventional mosaic of constitutional analysis under the Equal Protection Clause. Indeed, for the several reasons that follow, we find neither the suspect-classification nor the fundamental-interest analysis persuasive.

The wealth discrimination discovered by the District Court in this case, and by several other courts that have recently struck down school-financing laws in other States, is quite unlike any of the forms of wealth discrimination heretofore reviewed by this Court. Rather than focusing on the unique features of the alleged discrimination, the courts in these cases have virtually assumed their findings of a suspect classification through a simplistic process of analysis: since, under the traditional systems of financing public schools, some poorer people receive less expensive educations than other more affluent people, these systems discriminate on the basis of wealth. This approach largely ignores the hard threshold questions, including whether it makes a difference for purposes of consideration under the Constitution that the class of disadvantaged "poor" cannot be identified or defined in customary equal protection terms, and whether the relative--rather than absolute--nature of the asserted deprivation is of significant consequence. Before a State's laws and the justifications for the classifications they create are subjected to strict judicial scrutiny, we think these threshold considerations must be analyzed more closely than they were in the court below.

The case comes to us with no definitive description of the classifying facts or delineation of the disfavored class. Examination of the District Court's opinion and of appellees' complaint, briefs, and contentions at oral argument suggests, however, at least three ways in which the discrimination claimed here might be described. The Texas system of school financing might be regarded as discriminating (1) against "poor" persons whose incomes fall below some identifiable level of poverty or who might be characterized as functionally "indigent," or (2) against those who are relatively poorer than others, or (3) against all those who, irrespective of their personal incomes, happen to reside in relatively poorer school districts. Our task must be to ascertain whether, in fact, the Texas system has been shown to discriminate on any of these possible bases and, if so, whether the resulting classification may be regarded as suspect.

The precedents of this Court provide the proper starting point. The individuals, or groups of individuals, who constituted the class discriminated against in our prior cases shared two distinguishing characteristics: because of their impecunity they were completely unable to pay for some desired benefit, and as a consequence, they sustained an absolute deprivation of a meaningful opportunity to enjoy that benefit.

* * *

First, in support of their charge that the system discriminates against the "poor," appellees have made no effort to demonstrate that it operates to the peculiar disadvantage of any class fairly definable as indigent, or as composed of persons whose incomes are beneath any designated poverty level. Indeed, there is reason to believe that the poorest families are not necessarily clustered in the poorest property districts. . . . [T]here is no basis on the record in this case for assuming that the poorest people--defined by reference to any level of absolute impecunity--are concentrated in the poorest districts.

Second, neither appellees nor the District Court addressed the fact that, unlike each of the foregoing cases, lack of personal resources has not occasioned an absolute deprivation of the desired benefit. The argument here is not that the children in districts having relatively low assessable property values are receiving no public education; rather, it is that they are receiving a poorer quality education than that available to children in districts having more assessable wealth. Apart from the unsettled and disputed question whether the quality of education may be determined by the amount of money expended for it, a sufficient answer to appellees' argument is that, at least where wealth is involved, the Equal Protection Clause does not require absolute equality or precisely equal advantages. Nor indeed, in view of the infinite variables affecting the educational process, can any system assure equal quality of education except in the most relative sense. . . . The State repeatedly asserted in its briefs . . . that it now assures "every child in every school district an adequate education." No proof was offered at trial persuasively discrediting or refuting the State's assertion.

For these two reasons--the absence of any evidence that the financing system discriminates against any definable category of "poor" people or that it results in the absolute deprivation of education--the disadvantaged class is not susceptible of identification in traditional terms.

As suggested above, appellees and the District Court may have embraced a second or third approach, the second of which might be characterized as a theory of relative or comparative discrimination based on family income. Appellees sought to prove that a direct correlation exists between the wealth of families within each district and the expenditures therein for education. That is, along a continuum, the poorer the family the lower the dollar amount of education received by the family's children.

The principal evidence adduced in support of this comparative-discrimination claim is an affidavit submitted by Professor Joele S. Berke of Syracuse University's Educational Finance Policy Institute. The District Court, relying in major part upon this affidavit and apparently accepting the substance of appellees' theory, noted, first, a positive correlation between the wealth of school districts, measured in terms of assessable property per pupil, and their levels of per-pupil expenditures. Second, the court found a similar correlation between district wealth and the personal wealth of its residents, measured in terms of median family income.

If, in fact, these correlations could be sustained, then it might be argued that expenditures on education--equated by appellees to the quality of education--are dependent on personal wealth. Appellees' comparative-discrimination theory would still face serious unanswered questions, including whether a bare positive correlation or some higher degree of correlation is necessary to provide a basis for concluding that the financing system is designed to operate to the peculiar disadvantage of the comparatively poor, and whether a class of this size and diversity could ever claim the special protection accorded "suspect" classes. These questions need not be addressed in this case, however, since appellees' proof fails to support their allegations or the District Court's conclusions.

Professor Berke's affidavit is based on a survey of approximately 10% of the school districts in Texas. His findings, previously set out in the margin, show only that the wealthiest few districts in the sample have the highest median family incomes and spend the most on education, and that the several poorest districts have the lowest family incomes and devote the least amount of money to education. For the remainder of the districts--96 districts composing almost 90% of the sample--the correlation is inverted, *i.e.*, the districts that spend next to the most money on education are populated by families having next to the lowest median family incomes while the districts spending the least have the highest median family incomes. It is evident that, even if the conceptual questions were answered favorably to appellees, no factual basis exists upon which to found a claim of comparative wealth discrimination.

This brings us, then, to the third way in which the classification scheme might be defined--*district* wealth discrimination. Since the only correlation indicated by the evidence is between district property wealth and expenditures, it may be argued that discrimination might be found without regard to the individual income characteristics of district residents. Assuming a perfect correlation between district property wealth and expenditures from top to bottom, the disadvantaged class might be viewed as encompassing every child in every district except the district that has the most assessable wealth and spends the most on education. Alternatively, as suggested in Justice MARSHALL's dissenting opinion, the class might be defined more restrictively to include children in districts with assessable property which falls below the statewide average, or median, or below some other artificially defined level.

However described, it is clear that appellees' suit asks this Court to extend its most exacting scrutiny to review a system that allegedly discriminates against a large, diverse, and amorphous class, unified only by the common factor of residence in districts that happen to have less taxable wealth than other districts. The system of alleged discrimination and the class it defines have none of the traditional indicia of suspectness: the class is not saddled with such disabilities, or subjected to such a history of purposeful unequal treatment, or relegated to such a position of political powerlessness as to command extraordinary protection from the majoritarian political process.

We thus conclude that the Texas system does not operate to the peculiar disadvantage of any suspect class. But in recognition of the fact that this Court has never heretofore held that wealth discrimination alone provides an adequate basis for invoking strict scrutiny, appellees have not relied solely on this contention. They also assert that the State's system impermissibly interferes with the exercise of a "fundamental" right and that accordingly the prior decisions of this Court require the application of the strict standard of judicial review. It is this question--whether education is a fundamental right, in the sense that it is among the rights and liberties protected by the Constitution--which has so consumed the attention of courts and commentators in recent years.

In *Brown v. Board of Education*, a unanimous Court recognized that "education is perhaps the most important function of state and local governments." What was said there in the context of racial discrimination has lost none of its vitality with the passage of time:

> Compulsory school attendance laws and the great expenditures for education both demonstrate our recognition of the importance of education to our democratic society. It is required in the performance of our most basic public responsibilities, even service in the armed forces. It is the very foundation of good citizenship. Today it is a principal instrument in awakening the child to cultural values, in preparing him for later professional training, and in helping him to adjust normally to his environment. In these days, it is doubtful that any child may reasonably be expected to succeed in life if he is denied the opportunity of an education. Such an opportunity, where the state has undertaken to provide it, is a right which must be made available to all on equal terms.

This theme, expressing an abiding respect for the vital role of education in a free society, may be found in numerous opinions of Justices of this Court writing both before and after *Brown* was decided.

Nothing this Court holds today in any way detracts from our historic dedication to public education. We are in complete agreement with the conclusion of the three-judge panel below that "the grave significance of education both to the individual and to our society" cannot be doubted. But the importance of a service performed by the State does not determine whether it must be regarded as fundamental for purposes of examination under the Equal Protection Clause.

* * *

It is not the province of this Court to create substantive constitutional rights in the name of guaranteeing equal protection of the laws. Thus, the key to discovering whether education is "fundamental" is not to be found in comparisons of the relative societal significance of education as opposed to subsistence or housing. Nor is it to be found by weighing whether education is as important as the right to travel. Rather, the answer lies in assessing whether there is a right to education explicitly or implicitly guaranteed by the Constitution.

Education, of course, is not among the rights afforded explicit protection under our Federal Constitution. Nor do we find any basis for saying it is implicitly so protected. As we have said, the undisputed importance of education will not alone cause this Court to depart from the usual standard for reviewing a State's social and economic legislation. It is appellees' contention, however, that education is distinguishable from other services and benefits provided by the State because it bears a peculiarly close relationship to other rights and liberties accorded protection under the Constitution. Specifically, they insist that education is itself a fundamental personal right because it is essential to the effective exercise of First Amendment freedoms and to intelligent utilization of the right to vote. In asserting a nexus between speech and education, appellees urge that the right to speak is meaningless unless the speaker is capable of articulating his thoughts intelligently and persuasively. The "marketplace of ideas" is an empty forum for those lacking basic communicative tools. Likewise, they argue that the corollary right to receive information becomes little more than a hollow privilege when the recipient has not been taught to read, assimilate, and utilize available knowledge.

A similar line of reasoning is pursued with respect to the right to vote. Exercise of the franchise, it is contended, cannot be divorced from the educational foundation of the voter. The electoral process, if reality is to conform to the democratic ideal, depends on an informed electorate: a voter cannot cast his ballot intelligently unless his reading skills and thought processes have been adequately developed.

We need not dispute any of these propositions. The Court has long afforded zealous protection against unjustifiable governmental interference with the individual's rights to speak and to vote. Yet we have never presumed to possess either the ability or the authority to guarantee to the citizenry the most *effective* speech or the most *informed* electoral choice. That these may be desirable goals of a system of freedom of expression and of a representative form of government is not to be doubted. These are indeed goals to be pursued by a people whose thoughts and beliefs are freed from governmental interference. But they are not values to be implemented by judicial intrusion into otherwise legitimate state activities.

Even if it were conceded that some identifiable quantum of education is a constitutionally protected prerequisite to the meaningful exercise of either right, we have no indication that the present levels of educational expenditures in Texas provide an education that falls short. Whatever merit appellees' argument might have if a State's financing system occasioned an absolute denial of educational opportunities to any of its children, that argument provides no basis for finding an interference with fundamental rights where only relative differences in spending levels are involved and where--as is true in the present case--no charge fairly could be made that the system fails to provide each child with an opportunity to acquire the basic minimal skills necessary for the enjoyment of the rights of speech and of full participation in the political process.

Furthermore, the logical limitations on appellees' nexus theory are difficult to perceive. How, for instance, is education to be distinguished from the significant personal interests in the basics of decent food and shelter? Empirical examination might well buttress an assumption that the ill-fed, ill-clothed, and ill-housed are among the most ineffective participants in the political process, and that they derive the least enjoyment from the benefits of the First Amendment. If so, appellees' thesis would cast serious doubt on the authority of *Dandridge v. Williams* and *Lindsey v. Normet*.

We have carefully considered each of the arguments supportive of the District Court's finding that education is a fundamental right or liberty and have found those arguments unpersuasive. In one further respect we find this a particularly inappropriate case in which to subject state action to strict judicial scrutiny. The present case, in another basic sense, is significantly different from any of the cases in which the Court has applied strict scrutiny to state or federal legislation touching upon constitutionally protected rights. Each of our prior cases involved legislation which "deprived," "infringed," or "interfered" with the free exercise of some such fundamental personal right or liberty. A critical distinction between those cases and the one now before us lies in what Texas is endeavoring to do with respect to education. . . . Every step leading to the establishment of the system Texas utilizes today--including the decisions permitting localities to tax and expend locally, and creating and continuously expanding the state aid--was implemented in an effort to *extend* public education and to improve its quality. Of course, every reform that benefits some more than others may be criticized for what it fails to accomplish. But we think it plain that, in substance, the thrust of the Texas system is affirmative and reformatory and, therefore, should be scrutinized under judicial principles sensitive to the nature of the State's efforts and to the rights reserved to the States under the Constitution.

* * *

We need not rest our decision, however, solely on the inappropriateness of the strict-scrutiny test. A century of Supreme Court adjudication under the Equal Protection Clause affirmatively supports the application of the traditional standard of review, which requires only that the State's system be shown to bear some rational relationship to legitimate state purposes. This case represents far more than a challenge to the manner in which Texas provides for the education of its children. We have here nothing less than a direct attack on the way in which Texas has chosen to raise and disburse state and local tax revenues. We are asked to condemn the State's judgment in conferring on political subdivisions the power to tax local property to supply revenues for local interests. In so doing, appellees would have the Court intrude in an area in which it has traditionally deferred to state legislatures.

* * *

[T]he Justices of this Court lack both the expertise and the familiarity with local problems so necessary to the making of wise decisions with respect to the raising and disposition of public revenues. Yet, we are urged to direct the States either to alter drastically the present system or to throw out the property tax altogether in favor of some other form of taxation. No scheme of taxation, whether the tax is imposed on property, income, or purchases of goods and services, has yet been devised which is free of all discriminatory impact. In such a complex arena in which no perfect alternatives exist, the Court does well not to impose too rigorous a standard of scrutiny lest all local fiscal schemes become subjects of criticism under the Equal Protection Clause.

In addition to matters of fiscal policy, this case also involves the most persistent and difficult questions of educational policy, another area in which this Court's lack of specialized knowledge and experience counsels against premature interference with the informed judgments made at the state and local levels. Education, perhaps even more than welfare assistance, presents a myriad of "intractable economic, social, and even philosophical problems." The very complexity of the problems of financing and managing a statewide public school system suggests that "there will be more than one constitutionally permissible method of solving them," and that, within the limits of rationality, "the legislature's efforts to tackle the problems" should be entitled to respect. On even the most basic questions in this area the scholars and educational experts are divided. Indeed, one of the major sources of controversy concerns the extent to which there is a demonstrable correlation between educational expenditures and the quality of education--an assumed correlation underlying virtually every legal conclusion drawn by the District Court in this case. Related to the questioned relationship between cost and quality is the equally unsettled controversy as to the proper goals of a system of public education. And the question regarding the most effective relationship between state boards of education and local school boards, in terms of their respective responsibilities and degrees of control, is now undergoing searching re-examination. The ultimate wisdom as to these and related problems of education is not likely to be divined for all time even by the scholars who now so earnestly debate the issues. In such circumstances, the judiciary is well advised to refrain from imposing on the States inflexible constitutional restraints that could circumscribe or handicap the continued research and experimentation so vital to finding even partial solutions to educational problems and to keeping abreast of ever-changing conditions.

It must be remembered, also, that every claim arising under the Equal Protection Clause has implications for the relationship between national and state power under our federal system. Questions of federalism are always inherent in the process of determining whether a State's laws are to be accorded the traditional presumption of constitutionality, or are to be subjected instead to rigorous judicial scrutiny. While "[t]he maintenance of the principles of federalism is a foremost consideration in interpreting any of the pertinent constitutional provisions under which this Court examines state action," it would be difficult to imagine a case having a greater potential impact on our federal system than the one now before us, in which we are urged to abrogate systems of financing public education presently in existence in virtually every State.

* * *

While assuring a basic education for every child in the State, [the Texas system of school finance] . . . permits and encourages a large measure of participation in and control of each district's schools at the local level. In an era that has witnessed a consistent trend toward centralization of the functions of government, local sharing of responsibility for public education has survived. . . .

The persistence of attachment to government at the lowest level where education is concerned reflects the depth of commitment of its supporters. In part, local control means . . . the freedom to devote more money to the education of one's children. Equally important, however, is the opportunity it offers for participation in the decisionmaking process that determines how those local tax dollars will be spent. Each locality is free to tailor local programs to local needs. Pluralism also affords some opportunity for experimentation, innovation, and a healthy competition for educational excellence. An analogy to the Nation-State relationship in our federal system seems uniquely appropriate. Justice Brandeis identified as one of the peculiar strengths of our form of government each State's freedom to "serve as a laboratory; and try novel social and economic experiments." No area of social concern stands to profit more from a multiplicity of viewpoints and from a diversity of approaches than does public education.

Appellees do not question the propriety of Texas' dedication to local control of education. To the contrary, they attack the school-financing system precisely because, in their view, it does not provide the same level of local control and fiscal flexibility in all districts. Appellees suggest that local control could be preserved and promoted under other financing systems that resulted in more equality in education expenditures. While it is no doubt true that reliance on local property taxation for school revenues provides less freedom of choice with respect to expenditures for some districts than for others, the existence of "some inequality" in the manner in which the State's rationale is achieved is not alone a sufficient basis for striking down the entire system. It may not be condemned simply because it imperfectly effectuates the State's goals. Nor must the financing system fail because, as appellees suggest, other methods of satisfying the State's interest, which occasion "less drastic" disparities in expenditures, might be conceived. Only where state action impinges on the exercise of fundamental constitutional rights or liberties must it be found to have chosen the least restrictive alternative.

* * *

In sum, to the extent that the Texas system of school financing results in unequal expenditures between children who happen to reside in different districts, we cannot say that such disparities are the product of a system that is so irrational as to be invidiously discriminatory. . . . In its essential characteristics, the Texas plan for financing public education reflects what many educators for a half century have thought was an enlightened approach to a problem for which there is no perfect solution. We are unwilling to assume for ourselves a level of wisdom superior to that of legislators, scholars, and educational authorities in 50 States, especially where the alternatives proposed are only recently conceived and nowhere yet tested.

* * *

Reversed.

Justice MARSHALL, with whom Justice DOUGLAS concurs, dissenting.

The Court today decides, in effect, that a State may constitutionally vary the quality of education which it offers its children in accordance with the amount of taxable wealth located in the school districts within which they reside. The majority's decision represents an abrupt departure from the mainstream of recent state and federal court decisions concerning the unconstitutionality of state educational financing schemes dependent upon taxable local wealth. More unfortunately, though, the majority's holding can only be seen as a retreat from our historic commitment to equality of educational opportunity and as unsupportable acquiescence in a system which deprives children in their earliest years of the chance to reach their full potential as citizens. The Court does this despite the absence of any substantial justification for a scheme which arbitrarily channels educational resources in accordance with the fortuity of the amount of taxable wealth within each district.

In my judgment, the right of every American to an equal start in life, so far as the provision of a state service as important as education is concerned, is far too vital to permit state discrimination on grounds as tenuous as those presented by this record. Nor can I accept the notion that it is sufficient to remit these appellees to the vagaries of the political process which, contrary to the majority's suggestion, has proved singularly unsuited to the task of providing a remedy for this discrimination. I, for one, am unsatisfied with the hope of an ultimate "political" solution sometime in the indefinite future while, in the meantime, countless children unjustifiably receive inferior educations that "may affect their hearts and minds in a way unlikely ever to be undone." I must therefore respectfully dissent.

* * *

I believe it is sufficient that the overarching form of discrimination in this case is between the schoolchildren of Texas on the basis of the taxable property wealth of the districts in which they happen to live. To understand both the precise nature of this discrimination and the parameters of the disadvantaged class it is sufficient to consider the constitutional principle which appellees contend is controlling in the context of educational financing. In their complaint appellees asserted that the Constitution does not permit local district wealth to be determinative of educational opportunity. This is simply another way of saying, as the District Court concluded, that consistent with the guarantee of equal protection of the laws, "the quality of public education may not be a function of wealth, other than the wealth of the state as a whole." Under such a principle, the children of a district are excessively advantaged if that district has more taxable property per pupil than the average amount of taxable property per pupil considering the State as a whole. By contrast, the children of a district are disadvantaged if that district has less taxable property per pupil than the state average. The majority attempts to disparage such a definition of the disadvantaged class as the product of an "artificially defined level" of district wealth. But such is clearly not the case, for this is the definition unmistakably dictated by the constitutional principle for which appellees have argued throughout the course of this litigation. And I do not believe that a clearer definition of either the disadvantaged class of Texas schoolchildren or the allegedly unconstitutional discrimination suffered by the members of that class under the present Texas financing scheme could be asked for, much less needed. Whether this discrimination, against the schoolchildren of property-poor districts, inherent in the Texas financing scheme, is violative of the Equal Protection Clause is the question to which the must now turn.

* * *

[T]he majority today attempts to force this case into the same category for purposes of equal protection analysis as decisions involving discrimination affecting commercial interests. By so doing, the majority singles this case out for analytic treatment at odds with what seems to me to be the clear trend of recent decisions in this Court, and thereby ignores the constitutional importance of the interest at stake and the invidiousness of the particular classification, factors that call for far more than the lenient scrutiny of the Texas financing scheme which the majority pursues. Yet if the discrimination inherent in the Texas scheme is scrutinized with the care demanded by the interest and classification present in this case, the unconstitutionality of that scheme is unmistakable.

* * *

It is true that this Court has never deemed the provision of free public education to be required by the Constitution. . . . Nevertheless, the fundamental importance of education is amply indicated by the prior decisions of this Court, by the unique status accorded public education by our society, and by the close relationship between education and some of our most basic constitutional values.

* * *

Education directly affects the ability of a child to exercise his First Amendment rights, both as a source and as a receiver of information and ideas, whatever interests he may pursue in life. . . . The opportunity for formal education may not necessarily be the essential determinant of an individual's ability to enjoy throughout his life the rights of free speech and association guaranteed to him by the First Amendment. But such an opportunity may enhance the individual's enjoyment of those rights, not only during but also following school attendance. . . .

Of particular importance is the relationship between education and the political process. "Americans regard the public schools as a most vital civic institution for the preservation of a democratic system of government.". . . It is this very sort of intimate relationship between a particular personal interest and specific constitutional guarantees that has heretofore caused the Court to attach special significance, for purposes of equal protection analysis, to individual interests such as procreation and the exercise of the state franchise.[74]

While ultimately disputing little of this, the majority seeks refuge in the fact that the Court has "never presumed to possess either the ability or the authority to guarantee to the citizenry the most

---

[74]I believe that the close nexus between education and our established constitutional values with respect to freedom of speech and participation in the political process makes this a different case from our prior decisions concerning discrimination affecting public welfare, *see, e.g., Dandridge v. Williams*, 397 U.S. 471 (1970), or housing, *see, e.g., Lindsey v. Normet*, 405 U.S. 56 (1972). There can be no question that, as the majority suggests, constitutional rights may be less meaningful for someone without enough to eat or without decent housing. But the crucial difference lies in the closeness of the relationship. Whatever the severity of the impact of insufficient food or inadequate housing on a person's life, they have never been considered to bear the same direct and immediate relationship to constitutional concerns for free speech and for our political processes as education has long been recognized to bear. Perhaps, the best evidence of this fact is the unique status which has been accorded public education as the single public service nearly unanimously guaranteed in the constitutions of our States. Education, in terms of constitutional values, is much more analogous in my judgment, to the right to vote in state elections than to public welfare or public housing. Indeed, it is not without significance that we have long recognized education as an essential step in providing the disadvantaged with the tools necessary to achieve economic self-sufficiency.

effective speech or the most *informed* electoral choice." This serves only to blur what is in fact at stake. With due respect, the issue is neither provision of the most *effective* speech nor of the most *informed* vote. Appellees do not now seek the best education Texas might provide. They do seek, however, an end to state discrimination resulting from the unequal distribution of taxable district property wealth that directly impairs the ability of some districts to provide the same educational opportunity that other districts can provide with the same or even substantially less tax effort. The issue is, in other words, one of discrimination that affects the quality of the education which Texas has chosen to provide its children; and, the precise question here is what importance should attach to education for purposes of equal protection analysis of that discrimination. As this Court held in *Brown v. Board of Education*, the opportunity of education, "where the state has undertaken to provide it, is a right which must be made available to all on equal terms." The factors just considered, including the relationship between education and the social and political interests enshrined within the Constitution, compel us to recognize the fundamentality of education and to scrutinize with appropriate care the bases for state discrimination affecting equality of educational opportunity in Texas' school districts--a conclusion which is only strengthened when we consider the character of the classification in this case.

The District Court found that in discriminating between Texas schoolchildren on the basis of the amount of taxable property wealth located in the district in which they live, the Texas financing scheme created a form of wealth discrimination. This Court has frequently recognized that discrimination on the basis of wealth may create a classification of a suspect character and thereby call for exacting judicial scrutiny. The majority, however, considers any wealth classification in this case to lack certain essential characteristics which it contends are common to the instances of wealth discrimination that this Court has heretofore recognized. We are told that in every prior case involving a wealth classification, the members of the disadvantaged class have "shared two distinguishing characteristics: because of their impecunity they were completely unable to pay for some desired benefit, and as a consequence, they sustained an absolute deprivation of a meaningful opportunity to enjoy that benefit." I cannot agree.

* * *

That wealth classifications alone have not necessarily been considered to bear the same high degree of suspectness as have classifications based on, for instance, race or alienage may be explainable on a number of grounds. The "poor" may not be seen as politically powerless as certain discrete and insular minority groups. Personal poverty may entail much the same social stigma as historically attached to certain racial or ethnic groups. But personal poverty is not a permanent disability; its shackles may be escaped. Perhaps most importantly, though, personal wealth may not necessarily share the general irrelevance as a basis for legislative action that race or nationality is recognized to have. While the "poor" have frequently been a legally disadvantaged group, it cannot be ignored that social legislation must frequently take cognizance of the economic status of our citizens. Thus, we have generally gauged the invidiousness of wealth classifications with an awareness of the importance of the interests being affected and the relevance of personal wealth to those interests.

When evaluated with these considerations in mind, it seems to me that discrimination on the basis of group wealth in this case likewise calls for careful judicial scrutiny. First, it must be recognized that while local district wealth may serve other interests, it bears no relationship whatsoever to the interest of Texas schoolchildren in the educational opportunity afforded them by the State of Texas. Given the importance of that interest, we must be particularly sensitive to the invidious characteristics of any form of discrimination that is not clearly intended to serve it, as opposed to some other distinct state interest. Discrimination on the basis of group wealth may not, to be sure, reflect the social stigma frequently attached to personal poverty. Nevertheless, insofar as group wealth discrimination involves wealth over which the disadvantaged individual has no significant control, it represents in fact a more serious basis of discrimination than does personal wealth. For such discrimination is no reflection of the individual's characteristics or his abilities. And thus--particularly in the context of a disadvantaged class composed of children--we have previously treated discrimination on a basis which the individual cannot control as constitutionally disfavored.

The disability of the disadvantaged class in this case extends as well into the political processes upon which we ordinarily rely as adequate for the protection and promotion of all interests. Here legislative reallocation of the State's property wealth must be sought in the face of inevitable opposition from significantly advantaged districts that have a strong vested interest in the preservation of the status quo, a problem not completely dissimilar to that faced by underrepresented districts prior to the Court's intervention in the process of reapportionment.

Nor can we ignore the extent to which, in contrast to our prior decisions, the State is responsible for the wealth discrimination in this instance. . . . The means for financing public education in Texas are selected and specified by the State. It is the State that has created local school districts, and tied educational funding to the local property tax and thereby to local district wealth. At the same time, governmentally imposed land use controls have undoubtedly encouraged and rigidified natural trends in the allocation of particular areas for residential or commercial use, and thus determined each district's amount of taxable property wealth. In short, this case, in contrast to the Court's previous wealth discrimination decisions, can only be seen as "unusual in the extent to which governmental action *is* the cause of the wealth classifications."

* * *

The nature of our inquiry into the justifications for state discrimination is essentially the same in all equal protection cases: We must consider the substantiality of the state interests sought to be served, and we must scrutinize the reasonableness of the means by which the State has sought to advance its interests. Differences in the application of this test are, in my view, a function of the constitutional importance of the interests at stake and the invidiousness of the particular classification. . . . Here, both the nature of the interest and the classification dictate close judicial scrutiny of the purposes which Texas seeks to serve with its present educational financing scheme and of the means it has selected to serve that purpose.

The only justification offered by appellants to sustain the discrimination in educational opportunity caused by the Texas financing scheme is local educational control. * * *

At the outset, I do not question that local control of public education, as an abstract matter, constitutes a very substantial state interest. . . . The State's interest in local educational control--which certainly includes questions of educational funding--has deep roots in the inherent benefits of community support for public education. Consequently, true state dedication to local control would present, I think, a substantial justification to weigh against simply interdistrict variations in the treatment of a State's schoolchildren. But I need not now decide how I might ultimately strike the balance were we confronted with a situation where the State's sincere concern for local control inevitably produced educational inequality. For, on this record, it is apparent that the State's purported concern with local control is offered primarily as an excuse rather than as a justification for interdistrict inequality.

In Texas, statewide laws regulate in fact the most minute details of local public education. For example, the State prescribes required courses. All textbooks must be submitted for state approval, and only approved textbooks may be used. The State has established the qualifications necessary for teaching in Texas public schools and the procedures for obtaining certification. The State has even legislated on the length of the school day.

* * *

Moreover, even if we accept Texas' general dedication to local control in educational matters, it is difficult to find any evidence of such dedication with respect to fiscal matters. It ignores reality to suggest--as the Court does--that the local property tax element of the Texas financing scheme reflects a conscious legislative effort to provide school districts with local fiscal control. If Texas had a system truly dedicated to local fiscal control, one would expect the quality of the educational opportunity provided in each district to vary with the decision of the voters in that district as to the level of sacrifice they wish to make for public education. In fact, the Texas scheme produces precisely the opposite result. Local school districts cannot choose to have the best education in the State by imposing the highest tax rate. Instead, the quality of the educational opportunity offered by any particular district is largely determined by the amount of taxable property located in the district--a factor over which local voters can exercise no control.

The study introduced in the District Court showed a direct inverse relationship between equalized taxable district property wealth and district tax effort with the result that the property-poor districts making the highest tax effort obtained the lowest per-pupil yield.

The implications of this situation for local choice are illustrated by again comparing the Edgewood and Alamo Heights School Districts. In 1967-1968, Edgewood, after contributing its share to the Local Fund Assignment, raised only $26 per pupil through its local property tax, whereas Alamo Heights was able to raise $333 per pupil. Since the funds received through the Minimum Foundation School Program are to be used only for minimum professional salaries, transportation costs, and operating expenses, it is not hard to see the lack of local choice--with respect to higher teacher salaries to attract more and better teachers, physical facilities, library books, and facilities, special courses, or participation in special state and federal matching funds programs--under which a property-poor district such as Edgewood is forced to labor. In fact, because of the difference in taxable local property wealth, Edgewood would have to tax itself almost nine times as heavily to obtain the same yield as Alamo Heights. At present, then, local control is a myth for many of the local school districts in Texas. As one district court has observed, "rather than reposing in each school district the economic power to fix its own level of per pupil expenditure, the State has so arranged the structure as to guarantee that some districts will spend low (with high taxes) while others will spend high (with low taxes)."

In my judgment, any substantial degree of scrutiny of the operation of the Texas financing scheme reveals that the State has selected means wholly inappropriate to secure its purported interest in assuring its school districts local fiscal control. At the same time, appellees have pointed out a variety of alternative financing schemes which may serve the State's purported interest in local control as well as, if not better than, the present scheme without the current impairment of the educational opportunity of vast numbers of Texas schoolchildren. I see no need, however, to explore the practical or constitutional merits of those suggested alternatives at this time for, whatever their positive or negative features, experience with the present financing scheme impugns any suggestion that it constitutes a serious effort to provide local fiscal control. If, for the sake of local education control, this Court is to sustain interdistrict discrimination in the educational opportunity afforded Texas school children, it should require that the State present something more than the mere sham now before us.

* * *

I would therefore affirm the judgment of the District Court.

Notes and Questions

1. *Government Interests.* What was the government's interest in allowing local property tax wealth to govern a portion of its school financing formula? If, as Justice Marshall asserted, the only government interest was local control of education, was that interest legitimate, substantial, or compelling? Does calculating school financing based on a local property tax basis further the interest of local educational control?

2. *The Purported Fatality of Strict Scrutiny.* The Court focused initially on determining the appropriate level of judicial review. The Court noted that Texas "virtually concedes" that its school financing system could not survive strict scrutiny. Do you agree? The Court then considered whether the classification at issue imparts either a suspect class or a fundamental right.

3. *Suspect Class.* In analyzing whether a suspect class was involved, the Court considered the proper definition of the plaintiff class, thus demonstrating the importance of skillfully defining the class in class action lawsuits.

The Court considered three class definitions, including: (1) objectively poor people; (2) comparatively poor people; and (3) residents of a comparatively poor school district. How did the Court reject the first two class definitions? Did the Court's rejection of both these classes of poor people limit the value of this case with regard to the question of whether poor people constitute a suspect class? Did the Court decide that wealth was not a suspect class?

The Court seemed to place the class in its third category, residents of comparatively poor school districts. Why did the Court decide that this class was not suspect?

4. *Marshall's Analysis.* Justice Marshall in his dissent opined that wealth classifications differed from race classifications. What were his reasons? Did he treat individual wealth classifications as different from group wealth classifications? Did Justice Marshall agree with the majority that a class defined by group wealth was not suspect? What level of scrutiny did Justice Marshall view as appropriate?

5. *Fundamental Rights and Constitutional Interpretation.* How has or should the Supreme Court decide which rights are fundamental? Should the Court try to reconstruct the framers' original intent? Should it look only to the text of the Constitution?

Should it consider which rights serve the underlying values of the Constitution? (If so, what are those values?) Should it consider the needs of contemporary society? (If so, how should it determine those needs?) Which approach did the majority follow? Which approach did Justice Marshall endorse?

Is education fundamental to speech and voting rights? Compare the arguments of the majority and the dissent. Is the majority correct that if education is fundamental to effective political participation, then subsistence must also be a fundamental right?

6. *Notice of Claim.* What was the claim of the plaintiff class? Were they deprived of the best education possible or of an adequate education? Were they, as Justice Marshall asserted, deprived of an equal education?

Do you agree with the majority's assertion that the state's school financing scheme was not a deprivation at all, but an attempt to improve the education offered. If that were true, could any public benefits regulation be considered a deprivation? How would the majority's argument affect other welfare decisions, such as *Goldberg v. Kelly* or *Shapiro v. Thompson*, excerpted in this chapter.

7. *Rationality Review.* The Court discussed the great deference to states in matters of both tax allocation and educational policy. Why? Did the Court mean that it had no business reviewing state or local decisions in this area? Recall the Court's language in *Dandridge v. Williams* that social welfare issues are not the business of the Court. Does the Court in *Dandridge* and *Rodriguez* hold or imply that some matters should not receive even mere rationality review?

8. *Education Policy.* The Court emphasized federalism concerns generally and the importance of decentralized local control specifically, and tied these factors to the complexities and uncertainties among educational experts as to proper educational policies. In particular, the Court questioned: (1) the correlation between dollars spent and educational quality achieved; (2) the lack of consensus about educational goals; and (3) the competing points of control between states and local governments. How do such policy variables affect whether a state has discriminated against some school children? Does the Court's emphasis on the uncertainty in educational policy during the litigation leave the door open for persuading future courts that such uncertainties have been resolved and *Rodriguez* should be revisited?

Following the *Rodriguez* decision, school children, parents, and school districts from around the nation launched challenges of their school financing schemes based on their respective state constitutions. The following decision continues the Texas school financing saga.

EDGEWOOD INDEPENDENT SCHOOL DISTRICT
v.
KIRBY

777 S.W.2d 391 (Tex. 1989)

MAUZY, Justice.

At issue is the constitutionality of the Texas system for financing the education of public school children. Edgewood Independent School District, sixty-seven other school districts, and numerous individual school children and parents filed suit seeking a declaration that the Texas school financing system violates the Texas Constitution. The trial court rendered judgment to that effect and declared that the system violates the Texas Constitution. . . . By a 2-1 vote, the court of appeals reversed that judgment and declared the system constitutional. We reverse the judgment of the court of appeals and, with modification, affirm that of the trial court.

The basic facts of this cause are not in dispute. The only question is whether those facts describe a public school financing system that meets the requirements of the Constitution. As summarized and excerpted, the facts are as follows.

There are approximately three million public school children in Texas. The legislature finances the education of these children through a combination of revenues supplied by the state itself and revenues supplied by local school districts which are governmental subdivisions of the state. Of total education costs, the state provides about forty-two percent, school districts provide about fifty percent, and the remainder comes from various other sources including federal funds. School districts derive revenues from local ad valorem property taxes, and the state raises funds from a variety of sources including the sales tax and various severance and excise taxes.

There are glaring disparities in the abilities of the various school districts to raise revenues from property taxes because taxable property wealth varies greatly from district to district. The wealthiest district has over $14,000,000 of property wealth per student, while the poorest has approximately $20,000; this disparity reflects a 700 to 1 ratio. The 300,000 students in the lowest-wealth schools have less than 3% of the state's property wealth to support their education while the 300,000 students in the highest-wealth schools have over 25% of the state's property wealth; thus the 300,000 students in the wealthiest districts have more than eight times the property value to support their education as the 300,000 students in the poorest districts. The average property wealth in the 100 wealthiest districts is more than twenty times greater than the average property wealth in the 100 poorest districts. Edgewood I.S.D. has $38,854 in property wealth per student; Alamo Heights I.S.D., in the same county, has $570,109 in property wealth per student.

The state has tried for many years to lessen the disparities through various efforts to supplement the poorer districts. Through the Foundation School Program, the state currently attempts to ensure that each district has sufficient funds to provide its students with at least a basic education. Under this program, state aid is distributed to the various districts according to a complex formula such that property-poor districts receive more state aid than do property-rich districts. However, the Foundation School Program does not cover even the cost of meeting the state-mandated minimum requirements. Most importantly, there are no Foundation School Program allotments for school facilities or for debt service. The basic allotment and the transportation allotment understate actual costs, and the career ladder salary supplement for teachers is underfunded. For these reasons and more, almost all school districts spend additional local funds. Low-wealth districts use a significantly greater proportion of their local funds to pay the debt service on construction bonds while high-wealth districts are able to use their funds to pay for a wide array of enrichment programs.

Because of the disparities in district property wealth, spending per student varies widely, ranging from $2,112 to $19,333. Under the existing system, an average of $2,000 more per year is spent on each of the 150,000 students in the wealthiest districts than is spent on the 150,000 students in the poorest districts.

* * *

Property-poor districts are trapped in a cycle of poverty from which there is no opportunity to free themselves. Because of their inadequate tax base, they must tax at significantly higher rates in order to meet minimum requirements for accreditation; yet their educational programs are typically inferior. The location of new industry and development is strongly influenced by tax rates and the quality of local schools. Thus, the property-poor districts with their high tax rates and inferior schools are unable to attract new industry or development and so have little opportunity to improve their tax base.

The amount of money spent on a student's education has a real and meaningful impact on the educational opportunity offered that student. Highwealth districts are able to provide for their students broader educational experiences including more extensive curricula, more up-to-date technological equipment, better libraries and library personnel, teacher aides, counseling services, lower student-teacher ratios, better facilities, parental involvement programs, and drop-out prevention programs. They are also better able to attract and retain experienced teachers and administrators.

The differences in the quality of educational programs offered are dramatic. For example, San Elizario I.S.D. offers no foreign language, no pre-kindergarten program, no chemistry, no physics, no calculus, and no college preparatory or honors program. It also offers virtually no extra-curricular activities such as band, debate, or football. At the time of trial, one-third of Texas school districts did not even meet the state-mandated standards for maximum class size. The great majority of these are low-wealth districts. In many instances, wealthy and poor districts are found contiguous to one another within the same county.

Based on these facts, the trial court concluded that the school financing system violates the Texas Constitution's equal rights guarantee of article I, section 3, the due course of law guarantee of article I, section 19, and the "efficiency" mandate of article VII, section 1. The court of appeals reversed. We reverse the judgment of the court of appeals and, with modification, affirm the judgment of the trial court.

Article VII, section 1 of the Texas Constitution provides:

> A general diffusion of knowledge being essential to the preservation of the liberties and rights of the people, it shall be the duty of the Legislature of the

> State to establish and make suitable provision for the support and maintenance of an efficient system of public free schools.

The court of appeals declined to address petitioners' challenge under this provision and concluded instead that its interpretation was a "political question." Said the court:

> That provision does, of course, require that the school system be "efficient," but the provision provides no guidance as to how this or any other court may arrive at a determination of what is efficient or inefficient. Given the enormous complexity of a school system educating three million children, this Court concludes that which is, or is not, "efficient" is essentially a political question not suitable for judicial review.

We disagree. This is not an area in which the Constitution vests exclusive discretion in the legislature; rather the language of article VII, section 1 imposes on the legislature an affirmative duty to establish and provide for the public free schools. This duty is not committed unconditionally to the legislature's discretion, but instead is accompanied by standards. By express constitutional mandate, the legislature must make "suitable" provision for an "efficient" system for the "essential" purpose of a "general diffusion of knowledge." While these are admittedly not precise terms, they do provide a standard by which this court must, when called upon to do so, measure the constitutionality of the legislature's actions. We do not undertake this responsibility lightly and we begin with a presumption of constitutionality.

* * *

The State argues that, as used in article VII, section 1, the word "efficient" was intended to suggest a simple and inexpensive system.

* * *

While there is some evidence that many delegates wanted an economical school system, there is no persuasive evidence that the delegates used the term "efficient" to achieve that end. It must be recognized that the Constitution requires an "efficient," not an "economical," "inexpensive," or "cheap" system. The language of the Constitution must be presumed to have been carefully selected. The framers used the term "economical" elsewhere and could have done so here had they so intended.

There is no reason to think that "efficient" meant anything different in 1875 from what it now means. "Efficient" conveys the meaning of effective or productive of results and connotes the use of resources so as to produce results with little waste; this meaning does not appear to have changed over time.

* * *

Considering "the general spirit of the times and the prevailing sentiments of the people," it is apparent from the historical record that those who drafted and ratified article VII, section 1 never contemplated the possibility that such gross inequalities could exist within an "efficient" system. At the Constitutional Convention of 1875, delegates spoke at length on the importance of education for *all* the people of this state, rich and poor alike.

* * *

In addition to specific comments in the constitutional debates, the structure of school finance at the time indicates that such gross disparities were not contemplated.

* * *

If our state's population had grown at the same rate in each district and if the taxable wealth in each district had also grown at the same rate, efficiency could probably have been maintained within the structure of the present system. That did not happen. Wealth, in its many forms, has not appeared with geographic symmetry. The economic development of the state has not been uniform. Some cities have grown dramatically, while their sister communities have remained static or have shrunk. Formulas that once fit have been knocked askew. Although local conditions vary, the constitutionally imposed state responsibility for an efficient education system is the same for all citizens regardless of where they live.

We conclude that, in mandating "efficiency," the constitutional framers and ratifiers did not intend a system with such vast disparities as now exist. Instead, they stated clearly that the purpose of an efficient system was to provide for a "*general* diffusion of knowledge." (Emphasis added.) The present system, by contrast, provides not for a diffusion that is general, but for one that is limited and unbalanced. The resultant inequalities are thus directly contrary to the constitutional vision of efficiency.

* * *

We hold that the state's school financing system is neither financially efficient nor efficient in the sense of providing for a "general diffusion of knowledge" statewide, and therefore that it violates article VII, section 1 of the Texas Constitution. Efficiency does not require a per capita distribution, but it also does not allow concentrations of resources in property-rich school districts that are taxing low when property-poor districts that are taxing high cannot generate sufficient revenues to meet even minimum standards. There must be a direct and close correlation between a district's tax effort and the educational resources available to it; in other words, districts must have substantially equal access to similar revenues per pupil at similar levels of tax effort. Children who live in poor districts and children who live in rich districts must be afforded a substantially equal opportunity to have access to educational funds. Certainly, this much is required if the state is to educate its populace efficiently and provide for a general diffusion of knowledge statewide.

* * *

Our decision today is not without precedent. Courts in nine other states with similar school financing systems have ruled those systems to be unconstitutional for varying reasons.

Because we have decided that the school financing system violates the Texas Constitution's "efficiency" provision, we need not consider petitioners' other constitutional arguments. The Texas school financing system as set forth in the Texas Education Code, and as implemented in conjunction with local school districts containing unequal taxable property wealth, is unconstitutional under article VII, section 1 of the Texas Constitution.

* * *

Although we have ruled the school financing system to be unconstitutional, we do not now instruct the legislature as to the specifics of the legislation it should enact; nor do we order it to raise taxes. The legislature has primary responsibility to decide how best to achieve an efficient system. We decide only the nature of the constitutional mandate and whether that mandate has been met. Because we hold that the mandate of efficiency has not been met, we reverse the judgment of the court of appeals. The legislature is duty-bound to provide for an efficient system of education, and only if the legislature fulfills that duty can we launch this great state into a strong economic future with educational opportunity for all. . . .

Notes and Questions

1. *State Constitutions.* The plaintiffs challenged the system under the Texas constitution's equal protection, due process, and efficient education guarantees. The United States Constitution does not explicitly include any education guarantees. It does contain equal protection and due process guarantees. How can a state's equal protection and due process guarantees differ from the Supreme Court's interpretation of the equivalent federal guarantees? Can you argue that state provisions must mean something more than federal provisions?

2. *Political Questions.* The political question doctrine typically prohibits courts from deciding controversial issues better determined through political processes. This doctrine seems to be in tension with the duty of the judiciary to be the final arbiter of its constitution. Consider the nature of constitutional interpretation. Should courts be bound by the intent of the framers, as they typically are when interpreting statutes? Are constitutions designed to allow adaptation as society evolves? Are many, or most, constitutional issues subject to controversy and debate among citizens and politicians?

3. *Efficient as Effective and Equal.* Were you persuaded by the Texas Supreme Court's interpretation of "efficient" as requiring both an economical and effective school system? Do you agree that efficiency requires "substantially equal access to similar revenues per pupil at similar levels of tax effort"?

4. *Implementation.* The Court left implementation of this decision to the state legislature, much as the Supreme Court left implementation of its school integration decree in *Brown v. Board of Education* to the States. The implementation of both decisions is still ongoing.

William Clune

New Answers to Hard Questions Posed by Rodriguez: *Ending the Separation of School Finance and Educational Policy by Bridging the Gap Between Wrong and Remedy*

24 Connecticut Law Review 721 (1992)

* * *

The Remedy of Fiscal Neutrality: Six Hard Questions Posed by *Rodriguez*

The opinion of the Court in *Rodriguez* is an interesting blend of legal reasoning and policy analysis. Legally, the case holds that, under the Fourteenth Amendment, educational spending above the minimum foundation level (supported by the state) is not a fundamental interest, and also that linking local wealth and spending does not harm a suspect class. But much of the opinion is, in fact, a probing policy analysis of the uncertain effects of fiscal neutrality as a remedy. Uncertainties about the remedy, magnified by the distance of federal courts from state policy, seemed to weigh heavily on the Court. Such uncertainties easily could explain the Court's reluctance to proceed with a massive, court-sponsored reform of state school finance.

The *Rodriguez* criticisms of fiscal neutrality, each suggesting a gap between wrong and remedy, can be classified conveniently as follows. Each criticism includes a discussion of historical experience relevant to the validity of the criticism.

The Cost/Quality Problem

The cost/quality problem is perhaps the most obscure criticism of fiscal neutrality, but also the most fundamental. It suggests that any reallocation of resources to poorer districts cannot possibly help the students in those districts because money above the minimum foundation level is unlikely to improve student achievement or other important educational outcomes. The Supreme Court in *Rodriguez* did not seem to doubt the theoretical power of extra educational dollars to provide meaningful educational opportunities and to bring about gains in student achievement, but the remedy of fiscal neutrality offered no guarantee, or even increased probability, of such effective spending. The Court observed that most educational spending is absorbed by inputs with an uncertain effect on achievement--teacher salaries and class size. Thus, while the essence of the complaint alleged a diminished opportunity for a good education in poor districts, the remedy would not necessarily improve education in these districts.

In the time since *Rodriguez,* the theoretical problem of cost/quality has been considerably clarified. The heavy influence of student and family inputs on achievement, revealed in the once-shocking Coleman report, is now accepted as obvious and considered no obstacle to the educational policy goal of improving student achievement. The focus now is not on making students absolutely equal with each other but rather on providing a gain in achievement from particular kinds of schools, classrooms, teaching, and educational programs. And the *possibility* of gain is actually quite clear. Certain kinds of schools, classrooms, teachers, and programs produce *substantial* gains in student achievement, as well as other valuable educational outcomes (like staying in school). While the *Rodriguez* Court was accurate in questioning the potency of the inputs of reduced class sizes and increased salaries, as these inputs typically are used in schools, research clearly shows that these same inputs produce exceptional gains in well-conceived programs. . . . Clearly, more resources means a greater *opportunity* to make improvements. In one sense, the problem is that dollars and gross inputs, like salaries and class size, are very crude indicators of effective education. Effective education requires effective process and management as well as resources.

Yet the cost/quality problem remains serious in exactly the practical sense in which it is most relevant to a school finance remedy: available evidence suggests that substantial increases in funding produce only modest gains in most schools. Apparently these schools make poor use of the most expensive and typical inputs. The lack of a prospect for substantial gains in achievement is especially serious at a time when many school reforms are being stalled by budgetary limits and crises. The essential indeterminacy of the cost/quality relationship--its dependence on quality of process and management--never can be completely eliminated. For example, the exact amount of gain in achievement that might be expected from any given increase in resources cannot be specified. Nevertheless, a means of improving the odds of success would be most welcome as an addition to any school finance remedy.

The Indeterminacy of a Just Equalization Level

Even if a strong, reliable relationship between cost and quality were presumed, there remains a problem of how *much* equalization, either through foundation spending or tax base adjustment, to guarantee. Assume that the most basic and expensive educational inputs are used efficiently: for example, reductions in class size are used to create effective tutoring and increases in teacher salaries are used to hire and retain more genuinely qualified teachers. Under these circumstances, positive returns from increased educational spending probably run the whole range up to the fiscally unattainable "English Nanny" level of giving every child a full-time, highly qualified teacher/tutor. The *Rodriguez* Court seemed to have nothing to choose from along a continuum of spending where at the low end the most poorly-financed student got something important and at the high end the best-financed student could always use more. Under these circumstances, the minimum provided by the state for a "basic" education might seem reasonable enough.

Solving the level of equalization problem was probably the greatest strength of fiscal neutrality (and thus, logically, the adverse holding of *Rodriguez* must flow more from the other problems). Because there really is no spending level that can be specified as "correct" in either a constitutional or a policy sense, the rule of fiscal neutrality states simply that the same kind of decision be made for all the children in the state--a decision free from the influence of local wealth. The core of the wrong identified in school finance litigation is not the deprivation of any particular level of education but the deprivation of a fair decision about the spending level.

Historical experience has generated two serious remedial problems on this point of obtaining a fair decision. First, getting a fair decision out of legislatures, and sometimes getting *any* decision, has been quite difficult and time-consuming. School finance litigation seems to go on forever; legislatures seem to suffer from a problem of political instability in creating fiscally neutral systems. Second, part of the problem of legislative solutions is the special difficulty of limiting spending in wealthier districts--this is the recapture problem discussed below.

Variations in Spending Due to Variable Local Taxes

Although the essence of the complaint in *Rodriguez* was the unavailability of resources to children in poor districts, the financial benefit of the remedy of fiscal neutrality to students was unclear because of the unpredictability of local tax rates. If legislatures adopted district power equalization (or a guaranteed tax base) as a form of fiscal neutrality that preserved local control of taxing and spending, students would receive what school districts decided to give them. The possible shift (in a given district) from low spending because of low wealth to low spending because of local tax politics seems of little value to students and would require a massive incursion by federal courts into state and local taxation.

* * *

Concern about the variability of local tax rates has proven historically justified. . . . In short, power equalization--the equalization of local tax bases--did not enjoy wide popularity as a main element of state aid and has given way to a strong trend toward equalization of spending.

Resource Availability to Students from Poor Families

The plaintiffs in *Rodriguez* argued that poverty should be a suspect classification. Yet the impact of fiscal neutrality on poor students was (and is) dependent on accidents of demographics and was, therefore, highly uncertain. The Court gave close attention to the probable impact of school finance reform on poor children and clearly was not satisfied. Critics of school finance litigation continue to point to the possibility that poor students might predominantly live in urban districts of above-average wealth and would be harmed by a redistribution of state aid toward poorer districts. What occurred was a disjuncture between the alleged constitutional wrong--the low spending and political powerlessness of poor districts--and the responsiveness of the proposed remedy to the group of students most clearly deserving of special protection. Thus, the Court wondered if, in eliminating one kind of discrimination, it might be creating a more serious one.

In retrospect, the concern about poor students was justified. Although fiscal neutrality has left legislatures free to provide compensatory aid, and almost all legislatures do provide some such aid, many districts with concentrations of poor students lose money under fiscally neutral remedies. Disadvantaged students, therefore, do not get what they need because there is often a redistribution of state aid from wealthier urban districts and a lack of any special, constitutional status for their needs in the turmoil of legislative planning.

Impact on Local Control

Equal spending throughout the state could satisfy fiscal neutrality and eliminate the problem of spending variations due to local tax rates. The cost, however, would be diminished local control over the level of educational spending--at least for those relatively few wealthy districts that could afford to spend substantially above the average. The essence of the argument for power equalization of local tax resources--the fiscally neutral system least restrictive of local control in the sense of local freedom to set spending levels--was that the state did not provide meaningful local control to the poorer districts, and, therefore, under a redistributive remedy, any freedom of spending lost by rich districts would be exactly compensated by the increased freedom of poorer districts. But the remedy was not clear about *how* the spending of wealthy districts might be constrained. Would the state give aid to every district (implying a vast increase in the state budget), take property taxes from wealthier districts (an alternative with uncertain significance under state constitutions), or put caps on local spending? Each of these possibilities seemed to raise complex and poorly understood questions of fiscal, intergovernmental and educational policy, and much of the Court's opinion in *Rodriguez* is directed at loss of local control.

Local control is probably the area with the greatest irony of historical experience in the saga of school finance litigation. At the time of the early cases, it was argued and widely accepted that the appeal of fiscal neutrality rested in large part on the cleverness of the remedy of power equalization in removing wealth biases and achieving a high degree of spending equalization while at the same time retaining a high degree of local control. History has demonstrated that a specific issue of local control--recapture of local tax revenues from local districts--has been the single greatest practical problem with judicial decrees of fiscal neutrality. It would not be overstating the case to say that fiscal neutrality encountered the "nightmare of recapture." Wealthier districts have proven the most determined foes of fiscal neutrality in constitutional litigation. Much of the delay and uncertainty in reaching stable legislative solutions has revolved around the rich districts. Recapture led to at least two state supreme court cases that held equalization through recapture unconstitutional. The great irony of this turbulence is that it is all for nothing. Because states lack the fiscal resources to raise all districts up to the level of the wealthiest districts, equalization through recapture may be of little benefit to poorer districts.

Judicial Role in a Complex Reform Process

Because of the immense size and complexity of public education, and the major uncertainties just discussed, the Court's concern about lack of judicial expertise is understandable. Ideally, the Court would like to resolve a constitutional problem through a simple, effective, and manageable remedy. In the reapportionment cases, the simplicity and manageability of the remedy of one-person/-one-vote allowed the Court to enter, and then quickly vacate, the "political thicket" of representative government. Perhaps the greatest strength argued on behalf of fiscal neutrality was its simplicity and manageability. A decree of fiscal neutrality would require the state to remove the influence of wealth and otherwise leave to the legislature the greatest possible amount of legislative discretion; rather than making educational policy, the Court would tell the state only what *not* to do. But this guarantee of simplicity might seem unreliable to any court that could foresee the possibility of complications, such as the nature of limitations on spending in the wealthy districts.

Given the complexities in this analysis, the Court in *Rodriguez* seems correct in its suspicions that the remedial task was more complicated than argued by the plaintiffs. Equalization of tax resources proved to be a devilishly complicated exercise of intergovernmental management, both with respect to spending limits and recapture from the wealthiest districts. If equalization of spending seemed more manageable, what level of spending should occur (given different needs), and how should a court give guidance to a legislature? How could a court possibly play a manageable role in setting the amount of compensatory aid for poor children and the development of more effective spending policies?

* * *

The Recommended Three-Part Remedy

1. A Base Program of Substantial Equality of Spending Throughout the State

The state would guarantee a base program of substantially equal spending for at least ninety-five percent of the state's students, with that level of equalization maintained from year to year. The base program could be implemented through a high foundation program with appropriate cost adjustments, or through a slightly lower foundation program with a second tier of guaranteed tax bases, also designed to reflect cost differences. In principle, the foundation program should include all instructional costs and costs with an impact on instruction, such as expenditures for facilities and debt repayment to the extent they affect instruction.

2. A Substantial Amount of Compensatory Aid Based on a Realistic Needs Assessment of Children in Poverty

State courts should require legislatures to adopt a substantial program of compensatory aid for children affected by poverty, for example $1000 per pupil, fully proportional to the number of disadvantaged students in a school.

The compensatory aid should be added to the base program for purposes of calculating state aid, even when this means that state aid would go to urban districts that are wealthier than average. The point is that each disadvantaged student should be guaranteed the base program plus the compensatory amount. When special needs overlap, for example, where a student is both handicapped and disadvantaged, the cumulative amount of aid should cover the cumulative cost factors. The compensatory aid should be fully proportional to the number of disadvantaged students with no cap on the total amount of aid. Research shows that schools with many disadvantaged students do not achieve economies of scale, but, if anything, experience diseconomies of scale because of the need for costly structural changes. For example, flexible schedules, often recommended for the at-risk, are more disruptive to the basic schedule as more students are involved.

3. Performance-Oriented Policies Designed to Increase the Effectiveness of Educational Spending

Courts should require legislatures to develop a set of performance-oriented policies designed to increase the probability that educational resources will result in more effective education and gains in student achievement. Modern educational policy has provided several alternatives to the older, unmanageable approach of detailed standards for educational inputs and processes such as detailed certification standards. The "systemic" approach employs radically upgraded goals for curriculum content and pedagogy, relying on state policy to enrich and coordinate the parts of the system that are most important to that kind of educational change--specifically, curriculum frameworks, student assessments, and teacher training. The "accountability" approach combines careful measurements of gains in student achievement with selected rewards, punishments, and technical assistance for schools performing above or below acceptable levels. An "organizational" approach gives new kinds of decision-making authority to agents with a comparative advantage in pursuing educational objectives and with superior information about the local scene. Examples of this approach are parental choice, private practice schools (run by teachers under contract with a district), and local democratic control. Experimentation and flexibility must be built into the performance system because such performance-oriented policies are new to education and will require time to be evaluated and refined.

* * *

Notes and Questions

1. *Policy Questions Today.* Does Clune's synthesis of the problems that troubled the Supreme Court in *Rodriguez* provide guidance for future solutions? For example, do we now know, or is it more reasonable to assume, that educational cost and quality are related? Is fiscal neutrality the best or the only means to equalization? Can we achieve equalization as long as school financing is tied to local taxes? How do we supplement support for poor students, regardless of the wealth of their school district? Can we achieve equalization as long as great value is placed on local control of education? Can equalization be achieved by the judiciary?

2. *The Substance and Procedure of Merit.* Clune proposed that schools be financed by a state guaranteed equalized base grant with supplemental funds for poor students and be monitored according to performance standards. Would wealthier school districts be allowed to add financing to their local schools under Clune's proposal? Should they be allowed to do so? Which performance approach do you prefer: (1) the systemic approach (increasing educational input); (2) the accountability approach (measuring educational output); or (3) the organizational approach (parental choice, privatization, or local democratic control)? Much recent experimentation followed the choice, privatization, and local democratic control models. Have these solved or lessened the equalization problem?

PLYLER v. DOE

457 U.S. 202 (1982)

Justice BRENNAN delivered the opinion of the Court.

The question presented by these cases is whether, consistent with the Equal Protection Clause of the Fourteenth Amendment, Texas may deny to undocumented school-age children the free public education that it provides to children who are citizens of the United States or legally admitted aliens.

Since the late 19th century, the United States has restricted immigration into this country. Unsanctioned entry into the United States is a crime, and those who have entered unlawfully are subject to deportation. But despite the existence of these legal restrictions, a substantial number of persons have succeeded in unlawfully entering the United States, and now live within various States, including the State of Texas.

In May 1975, the Texas Legislature revised its education laws to withhold from local school districts any state funds for the education of children who were not "legally admitted" into the United States. The 1975 revision [§ 21.031] also authorized local school districts to deny enrollment in their public schools to children not "legally admitted" to the country.

* * *

This is a class action, filed in the United States District Court for the Eastern District of Texas in September 1977, on behalf of certain school-age children of Mexican origin residing in Smith County, Tex., who could not establish that they had been legally admitted into the United States. The action complained of the exclusion of plaintiff children from the public schools of the Tyler Independent School District.[2] . . . After certifying a class consisting of all undocumented school-age children of Mexican origin residing within the School District, the District Court preliminarily enjoined defendants from denying a free education to members of the plaintiff class. In December 1977, the court conducted an extensive hearing on plaintiffs' motion for permanent injunctive relief.

---

[2]Despite the enactment of § 21.031 in 1975, the School District had continued to enroll undocumented children free of charge until the 1977-1978 school year. In July 1977, it adopted a policy requiring undocumented children to pay a "full tuition fee" in order to enroll. . . .

* * *

The Fourteenth Amendment provides that "[n]o State shall . . . deprive any person of life, liberty, or property, without due process of law; nor deny to any person within its jurisdiction the equal protection of the laws." Appellants argue at the outset that undocumented aliens, because of their immigration status, are not "persons within the jurisdiction" of the State of Texas, and that they therefore have no right to the equal protection of Texas law. We reject this argument. Whatever his status under the immigration laws, an alien is surely a "person" in any ordinary sense of that term. Aliens, even aliens whose presence in this country is unlawful, have long been recognized as "persons" guaranteed due process of law by the Fifth and Fourteenth Amendments.

* * *

Appellants seek to distinguish our prior cases, emphasizing that the Equal Protection Clause directs a State to afford its protection to persons within its jurisdiction while the Due Process Clauses of the Fifth and Fourteenth Amendments contain no such assertedly limiting phrase.

* * *

That a person's initial entry into a State, or into the United States, was unlawful, and that he may for that reason be expelled, cannot negate the simple fact of his presence within the State's territorial perimeter. Given such presence, he is subject to the full range of obligations imposed by the State's civil and criminal laws. And until he leaves the jurisdiction--either voluntarily, or involuntarily in accordance with the Constitution and laws of the United States--he is entitled to the equal protection of the laws that a State may choose to establish.

Our conclusion that the illegal aliens who are plaintiffs . . . may claim the benefit of the Fourteenth Amendment's guarantee of equal protection only begins the inquiry. The more difficult question is whether the Equal Protection Clause has been violated by the refusal of the State of Texas to reimburse local school boards for the education of children who cannot demonstrate that their presence within the United States is lawful, or by the imposition by those school boards of the burden of tuition on those children. It is to this question that we now turn.

The Equal Protection Clause directs that "all persons similarly circumstanced shall be treated alike." But so too, "[t]he Constitution does not require things which are different in fact or opinion to be treated in law as though they were the same." The initial discretion to determine what is "different" and what is "the same" resides in the legislatures of the States. A legislature must have substantial latitude to establish classifications that roughly approximate the nature of the problem perceived, that accommodate competing concerns both public and private, and that account for limitations on the practical ability of the State to remedy every ill. In applying the Equal Protection Clause to most forms of state action, we thus seek only the assurance that the classification at issue bears some fair relationship to a legitimate public purpose.

But we would not be faithful to our obligations under the Fourteenth Amendment if we applied so deferential a standard to every classification. The Equal Protection Clause was intended as a restriction on state legislative action inconsistent with elemental constitutional premises. Thus we have treated as presumptively invidious those classifications that disadvantage a "suspect class,"[14] or that impinge upon the exercise of a "fundamental right."[15] With

---

[14]Several formulations might explain our treatment of certain classifications as "suspect." Some classifications are more likely than others to reflect deep-seated prejudice rather than legislative rationality in pursuit of some legitimate objective. Legislation predicated on such prejudice is easily recognized as incompatible with the constitutional understanding that each person is to be judged individually and is entitled to equal justice under the law. Classifications treated as suspect tend to be irrelevant to any proper legislative goal. Finally, certain groups, indeed largely the same groups, have historically been "relegated to such a position of political powerlessness as to command extraordinary protection from the majoritarian political process." The experience of our Nation has shown that prejudice may manifest itself in the treatment of some groups. Our response to that experience is reflected in the Equal Protection Clause of the Fourteenth Amendment. Legislation imposing special disabilities upon groups disfavored by virtue of circumstances beyond their control suggests the kind of "class or caste" treatment that the Fourteenth Amendment was designed to abolish.

[15]In determining whether a class-based denial of a particular right is deserving of strict scrutiny under the Equal Protection Clause, we look to the Constitution to see if the right infringed has its source, explicitly or implicitly, therein. But we have also recognized the fundamentality of participation in state "elections on an equal basis with other citizens in the jurisdiction," even though "the right to vote,

respect to such classifications, it is appropriate to enforce the mandate of equal protection by requiring the State to demonstrate that its classification has been precisely tailored to serve a compelling governmental interest. In addition, we have recognized that certain forms of legislative classification, while not facially invidious, nonetheless give rise to recurring constitutional difficulties; in these limited circumstances we have sought the assurance that the classification reflects a reasoned judgment consistent with the ideal of equal protection by inquiring whether it may fairly be viewed as furthering a substantial interest of the State.[16] We turn to a consideration of the standard appropriate for the evaluation of § 21.031.

Sheer incapability or lax enforcement of the laws barring entry into this country, coupled with the failure to establish an effective bar to the employment of undocumented aliens, has resulted in the creation of a substantial "shadow population" of illegal migrants--numbering in the millions--within our borders. This situation raises the specter of a permanent caste of undocumented resident aliens, encouraged by some to remain here as a source of cheap labor, but nevertheless denied the benefits that our society makes available to citizens and lawful residents. The existence of such an underclass presents most difficult problems for a Nation that prides itself on adherence to principles of equality under law.[19]

The children who are plaintiffs in these cases are special members of this underclass. Persuasive arguments support the view

---

per se, is not a constitutionally protected right." With respect to suffrage, we have explained the need for strict scrutiny as arising from the significance of the franchise as the guardian of all other rights.

[16]This technique of "intermediate" scrutiny permits us to evaluate the rationality of the legislative judgment with reference to well-settled constitutional principles. . . . Only when concerns sufficiently absolute and enduring can be clearly ascertained from the Constitution and our cases do we employ this standard to aid us in determining the rationality of the legislative choice.

[19]We reject the claim that "illegal aliens" are a "suspect class." No case in which we have attempted to define a suspect class has addressed the status of persons unlawfully in our country. Unlike most of the classifications that we have recognized as suspect, entry into this class, by virtue of entry into this country, is the product of voluntary action. Indeed, entry into the class is itself a crime. . . .

that a State may withhold its beneficence from those whose very presence within the United States is the product of their own unlawful conduct. These arguments do not apply with the same force to classifications imposing disabilities on the minor children of such illegal entrants. At the least, those who elect to enter our territory by stealth and in violation of our law should be prepared to bear the consequences, including, but not limited to, deportation. But the children of those illegal entrants are not comparably situated. Their "parents have the ability to conform their conduct to societal norms," and presumably the ability to remove themselves from the State's jurisdiction; but the children who are plaintiffs in these cases "can affect neither their parents' conduct nor their own status." Even if the State found it expedient to control the conduct of adults by acting against their children, legislation directing the onus of a parent's misconduct against his children does not comport with fundamental conceptions of justice.

* * *

Of course, undocumented status is not irrelevant to any proper legislative goal. Nor is undocumented status an absolutely immutable characteristic since it is the product of conscious, indeed unlawful, action. But § 21.031 is directed against children, and imposes its discriminatory burden on the basis of a legal characteristic over which children can have little control. It is thus difficult to conceive of a rational justification for penalizing these children for their presence within the United States. Yet that appears to be precisely the effect of § 21.031.

Public education is not a "right" granted to individuals by the Constitution. But neither is it merely some governmental "benefit" indistinguishable from other forms of social welfare legislation. Both the importance of education in maintaining our basic institutions, and the lasting impact of its deprivation on the life of the child, mark the distinction. . . . [E]ducation has a fundamental role in maintaining the fabric of our society. We cannot ignore the significant social costs borne by our Nation when select groups are denied the means to absorb the values and skills upon which our social order rests.

In addition to the pivotal role of education in sustaining our political and cultural heritage, denial of education to some isolated group of children poses an affront to one of the goals of the Equal Protection Clause: the abolition of governmental barriers presenting unreasonable obstacles to advancement on the basis of individual merit. Paradoxically, by depriving the children of any disfavored group of an education, we foreclose the means by which that group might raise the level of esteem in which it is held by the majority. But more directly, "education prepares individuals to be self-reliant and self-sufficient participants in society." Illiteracy is an enduring disability. The inability to read and write will handicap the individual deprived of a basic education each and every day of his life. The inestimable toll of that deprivation on the social economic, intellectual, and psychological well-being of the individual, and the obstacle it poses to individual achievement, make it most difficult to reconcile the cost or the principle of a status-based denial of basic education with the framework of equality embodied in the Equal Protection Clause.

* * *

These well-settled principles allow us to determine the proper level of deference to be afforded § 21.031. Undocumented aliens cannot be treated as a suspect class because their presence in this country in violation of federal law is not a "constitutional irrelevancy." Nor is education a fundamental right; a State need not justify by compelling necessity every variation in the manner in which education is provided to its population. But more is involved in these cases than the abstract question whether § 21.031 discriminates against a suspect class, or whether education is a fundamental right. Section 21.031 imposes a lifetime hardship on a discrete class of children not accountable for their disabling status. The stigma of illiteracy will mark them for the rest of their lives. By denying these children a basic education, we deny them the ability to live within the structure of our civic institutions, and foreclose any realistic possibility that they will contribute in even the smallest way to the progress of our Nation. In determining the rationality of § 21.031, we may appropriately take into account its costs to the Nation and to the innocent children who are its victims. In light of these countervailing costs, the discrimination contained in § 21.031 can hardly be considered rational unless it furthers some substantial goal of the State.

* * *

[W]e perceive no national policy that supports the State in denying these children an elementary education. The State may borrow the federal classification. But to justify its use as a criterion for its own discriminatory policy, the State must demonstrate that the classification is reasonably adapted to "the purposes for which the state desires to use it." We therefore turn to the state objectives that are said to support § 21.031.

Appellants argue that the classification at issue furthers an interest in the "preservation of the state's limited resources for the education of its lawful residents." Of course, a concern for the preservation of resources standing alone can hardly justify the classification used in allocating those resources. The State must do more than justify its classification with a concise expression of an intention to discriminate. Apart from the asserted state prerogative to act against undocumented children solely on the basis of their undocumented status--an asserted prerogative that carries only minimal force in the circumstances of these cases--we discern three colorable state interests that might support § 21.031.

First, appellants appear to suggest that the State may seek to protect itself from an influx of illegal immigrants. While a State might have an interest in mitigating the potentially harsh economic effects of sudden shifts in population, § 21.031 hardly offers an effective method of dealing with an urgent demographic or economic problem. There is no evidence in the record suggesting that illegal entrants impose any significant burden on the State's economy. To the contrary, the available evidence suggests that illegal aliens underutilize public services, while contributing their labor to the local economy and tax money to the state fisc. The dominant incentive for illegal entry into the State of Texas is the availability of employment; few if any illegal immigrants come to this country, or presumably to the State of Texas, in order to avail themselves of a free education. Thus, even making the doubtful assumption that the net impact of illegal aliens on the economy of the State is negative, we think it clear that "[c]harging tuition to undocumented children constitutes a ludicrously ineffectual attempt to stem the tide of illegal immigration," at least when compared with the alternative of prohibiting the employment of illegal aliens.

Second, while it is apparent that a State may "not . . . reduce expenditures for education by barring [some arbitrarily chosen class of] children from its schools," appellants suggest that undocumented children are appropriately singled out for exclusion because of the special burdens they impose on the State's ability to provide high-quality public education. But the record in no way supports the claim that exclusion of undocumented children is likely to improve the overall quality of education in the State. . . . In terms of educational cost and need, . . . undocumented children are "basically indistinguishable" from legally resident alien children.

Finally, appellants suggest that undocumented children are appropriately singled out because their unlawful presence within the United States renders them less likely than other children to remain within the boundaries of the State, and to put their education to productive social or political use within the State. Even assuming that such an interest is legitimate, it is an interest that is most difficult to quantify. The State has no assurance that any child, citizen or not, will employ the education provided by the State within the confines of the State's borders. In any event, the record is clear that many of the undocumented children disabled by this classification will remain in this country indefinitely, and that some will become lawful residents or citizens of the United States. It is difficult to understand precisely what the State hopes to achieve by promoting the creation and perpetuation of a subclass of illiterates within our boundaries, surely adding to the problems and costs of unemployment, welfare, and crime. It is thus clear that whatever savings might be achieved by denying these children an education, they are wholly insubstantial in light of the costs involved to these children, the State, and the Nation.

If the State is to deny a discrete group of innocent children the free public education that it offers to other children residing within its borders, that denial must be justified by a showing that it furthers some substantial state interest. No such showing was made here.

* * *

Affirmed.

Chief Justice BURGER, with whom Justice WHITE, Justice REHNQUIST, and Justice O'CONNOR join, dissenting.

Were it our business to set the Nation's social policy, I would agree without hesitation that it is senseless for an enlightened society to deprive any children--including illegal aliens--of an elementary education. I fully agree that it would be folly--and wrong--to tolerate creation of a segment of society made up of illiterate persons, many having a limited or no command of our language. However, the

Constitution does not constitute us as "Platonic Guardians" nor does it vest in this Court the authority to strike down laws because they do not meet our standards of desirable social policy, "wisdom," or "common sense." We trespass on the assigned function of the political branches under our structure of limited and separated powers when we assume a policymaking role as the Court does today.

* * *

Once it is conceded--as the Court does--that illegal aliens are not a suspect class, and that education is not a fundamental right, our inquiry should focus on and be limited to whether the legislative classification at issue bears a rational relationship to a legitimate state purpose.

The State contends primarily that § 21.031 serves to prevent undue depletion of its limited revenues available for education, and to preserve the fiscal integrity of the State's school-financing system against an ever-increasing flood of illegal aliens--aliens over whose entry or continued presence it has no control. Of course such fiscal concerns alone could not justify discrimination against a suspect class or an arbitrary and irrational denial of benefits to a particular group of persons. Yet I assume no Member of this Court would argue that prudent conservation of finite state revenues is per se an illegitimate goal. . . . The significant question here is whether the requirement of tuition from illegal aliens who attend the public schools--as well as from residents of other states, for example--is a rational and reasonable means of furthering the State's legitimate fiscal ends.

Without laboring what will undoubtedly seem obvious to many, it simply is not "irrational" for a state to conclude that it does not have the same responsibility to provide benefits for persons whose very presence in the state and this country is illegal as it does to provide for persons lawfully present. By definition, illegal aliens have no right whatever to be here, and the state may reasonably, and constitutionally, elect not to provide them with governmental services at the expense of those who are lawfully in the state.

* * *

It is significant that the Federal Government has seen fit to exclude illegal aliens from numerous social welfare programs, such as the food stamp program, the old-age assistance, aid to families with dependent children, aid to the blind, aid to the permanently and totally disabled, and supplemental security income programs, the Medicare hospital insurance benefits program, and the Medicaid hospital insurance benefits for the aged and disabled program. Although these exclusions do not conclusively demonstrate the constitutionality of the State's use of the same classification for comparable purposes, at the very least they tend to support the rationality of excluding illegal alien residents of a state from such programs so as to preserve the state's finite revenues for the benefit of lawful residents.

* * *

In the absence of a constitutional imperative to provide for the education of illegal aliens, the State may "rationally" choose to take advantage of whatever savings will accrue from limiting access to the tuition-free public schools to its own lawful residents, excluding even citizens of neighboring States.

Denying a free education to illegal alien children is not a choice I would make were I a legislator. Apart from compassionate considerations, the long-range costs of excluding any children from the public schools may well outweigh the costs of educating them. But that is not the issue; the fact that there are sound policy arguments against the Texas Legislature's choice does not render that choice an unconstitutional one.

The Constitution does not provide a cure for every social ill, nor does it vest judges with a mandate to try to remedy every social problem. Moreover, when this Court rushes in to remedy what it perceives to be the failings of the political processes, it deprives those processes of an opportunity to function. When the political institutions are not forced to exercise constitutionally allocated powers and responsibilities, those powers, like muscles not used, tend to atrophy. Today's cases, I regret to say, present yet another example of unwarranted judicial action which in the long run tends to contribute to the weakening of our political processes.

* * *

Notes and Questions

1. *Quasi-Heightened or Intermediate Scrutiny.* The Court conceded in footnote 19 that undocumented aliens are not a suspect class. They also conceded that education is not a fundamental right. Yet they seem to treat undocumented children as quasi-suspect and education as quasi-fundamental. Based on these factors, the Court applied intermediate scrutiny, requiring the state to prove that the

education of undocumented children fairly furthers a substantial government interest. Do you agree that intermediate scrutiny was appropriate? Does this intermediate review advance the purposes of equal protection?

2. *Government Interests.* The Court summarily rejected the State's interest in preserving its limited educational resources. Why? The Court seemed to assume that the other interests advanced by the State were legitimate. Why were they not sufficiently substantial to survive intermediate scrutiny? Why did the Court view the exclusion of undocumented children as ineffective to serve each state interest, including preventing an influx of aliens, protecting against the special burdens imposed, and ensuring that educational dollars benefit the state? Were the means overinclusive or underinclusive or both?

3. *Discerning Discrimination.* The dissent accused the Court of making policy. Do you agree? Chief Justice Burger argued that once the majority considered that no suspect class or fundamental right was involved, they should have employed mere rationality review and upheld the classification because lawful residents are rationally different from unlawful residents. How can courts detect when one's documentation status is properly relevant and when it operates as a shorthand for prejudice?

4. *Other Challenges.* Could the exclusion of Mexican or Mexican-American children have been challenged on other grounds, such as race, nationality, or alienage?

5. *Implications for Welfare.* If courts must apply intermediate scrutiny to undocumented children, will the exclusion of these children from other government benefits such as welfare survive this scrutiny?

6. *Contemporary Restrictions.* Immigrants have re-emerged as a prime target of restrictive welfare reform proposals that restrict noncitizens from receiving most government benefits, such as welfare benefits, social services, health care services, and public education. Will such restrictions survive a challenge based on *Plyler*?

d. (No) Right to Housing

LINDSEY v. NORMET

405 U.S. 56 (1972)

Justice WHITE delivered the opinion of the Court.

This case presents the question of whether Oregon's judicial procedure for eviction of tenants after nonpayment of rent violates either the Equal Protection Clause or the Due Process Clause of the Fourteenth Amendment. .

* * *

Before a tenant is forcibly evicted from property the Oregon statute requires a judicial determination that he is not legally entitled to possession. . . . The objective of achieving rapid and peaceful settlement of possessory disputes between landlord and tenant has ample historical explanation and support. It is not beyond the State's power to implement that purpose by enacting special provisions applicable only to possessory disputes between landlord and tenant.

There are unique factual and legal characteristics of the landlord-tenant relationship that justify special statutory treatment inapplicable to other litigants. The tenant is, by definition, in possession of the property of the landlord; unless a judicially supervised mechanism is provided for what would otherwise be swift repossession by the landlord himself, the tenant would be able to deny the landlord the rights of income incident to ownership by refusing to pay rent and by preventing sale or rental to someone else. Many expenses of the landlord, continue to accrue whether a tenant pays his rent or not. Speedy adjudication is desirable to prevent subjecting the landlord to undeserved economic loss and the tenant to unmerited harassment and dispossession when his lease or rental agreement gives him the right to peaceful and undisturbed possession of the property. Holding over by the tenant beyond the term of his agreement or holding without payment of rent has proved a virulent source of friction and dispute. We think Oregon was well within its constitutional powers in providing for rapid and peaceful settlement of these disputes.

Appellants argue, however, that a more stringent standard than mere rationality should be applied both to the challenged classification and its stated purpose. They contend that the "need for decent shelter" and the "right to retain peaceful possession of one's home" are fundamental interests which are particularly important to the poor and which may be trenched upon only after the State demonstrates some superior interest. They invoke those cases holding that certain classifications based on unalterable traits such as race and lineage are inherently suspect and must be justified by some "overriding statutory purpose." They also rely on cases where classifications burdening or infringing constitutionally protected rights were required to be justified as "necessary to promote a compelling governmental interest."

We do not denigrate the importance of decent, safe, and sanitary housing. But the Constitution does not provide judicial remedies for every social and economic ill. We are unable to perceive in that document any constitutional guarantee of access to dwellings of a particular quality, or any recognition of the right of a tenant to occupy the real property of his landlord beyond the term of his lease without the payment of rent or otherwise contrary to the terms of the relevant agreement. Absent constitutional mandate, the assurance of adequate housing and the definition of landlord-tenant relationships are legislative, not judicial, functions. Nor should we forget that the Constitution expressly protects against confiscation of private property or the income therefrom.

Since the purpose of the Oregon Forcible Entry and Wrongful Detainer Statute is constitutionally permissible and since the classification under attack is rationally related to that purpose, the statute is not repugnant to the Equal Protection Clause of the Fourteenth Amendment.

* * *

Notes and Questions

1. *Fundamental Rights.* The tenants argued that housing is a fundamental right, deserving heightened scrutiny. Why did the Court reject that argument? Do you agree with the Court's reasoning?

If housing is not by itself fundamental, could adequate shelter be necessary prerequisites to one's ability to exercise other fundamental rights, such as voting or political participation?

2. *State Constitutions or Statutes.* Although housing is not a fundamental right recognized in the United States Constitution, it might be recognized in state constitutions in a manner similar to how

the Texas constitution established a right to an efficient education in *Edgewood Independent School District v. Kirby*, 777 S.W.2d 391 (Tex. 1989), excerpted in this chapter.

e. The (Gridlocked and Underfunded) Right to Health Care

LEWIS v. GRINKER

965 F.2d 1206 (2d Cir. 1992)

WALKER, Circuit Judge:

Eleven years ago, plaintiffs, a group of aliens living in New York, initiated this lawsuit on behalf of themselves and all similarly situated persons seeking to enjoin the Secretary of Health and Human Services (the Secretary) from denying them Medicaid coverage based on their alienage status. Since the suit was filed, the Medicaid statute has been amended in relevant ways five times, the district court has issued three different injunctions and four separate opinions, the Secretary has announced a host of new regulations, and yet questions persist about the precise contours of aliens' entitlement to Medicaid coverage.

In this appeal, we are called upon to decide only a single narrow question. Did Congress, in enacting the Omnibus Budget Reconciliation Act of 1986 (OBRA '86), intend to prevent otherwise eligible pregnant women who are residing in this country without the approval of the Immigration and Naturalization Service (INS) from receiving Medicaid sponsored prenatal care, even though their children, if born in the United States, will become United States citizens? After reviewing the language of the statute, the legislative and statutory background, and the relevant administrative interpretations, we conclude that Congress did not intend to bar these women from receiving Medicaid sponsored prenatal care. Accordingly, we affirm the permanent injunction issued by the district court.

In order to understand the complex question presented by this appeal, it is necessary to explore in some depth the structure of the Medicaid statute, the development of Medicaid coverage for prenatal care, and the origins of the alienage restriction at issue here.

Originally enacted in 1965, Medicaid is a "cooperative federal/state cost-sharing program designed to enable participating states to furnish medical assistance to persons whose income and resources are insufficient to meet the costs of necessary medical care and services." In order to provide Medicaid coverage to its citizens, a state must first adopt a state Medicaid plan and submit the plan for approval by the Secretary. Once the state plan is approved, the federal government will partially reimburse the state for expenditures made pursuant to the state plan.

The Act authorizes state plans to extend coverage to two basic categories of individuals, the categorically needy and the medically needy. As the district court explained, . . . "[r]oughly speaking, the categorically needy are those who earn no more than that necessary to cover the necessities of life; the medically needy differ in that it is only the expense of necessary medical care that strains their ability to pay for basic necessities." The Medicaid statute provides a complex set of standards for the way that participating states must provide coverage to categorically and medically needy individuals.

First, 42 U.S.C. § 1396a(a)(10)(A)(i) requires participating states to provide Medicaid to a sub-group of the categorically needy, the "mandatory categorically needy." This group is mostly made up of those already receiving some other government benefit, such as aid to families with dependent children (AFDC), or supplemental security income (SSI). Women who meet the statutory definition of "qualified pregnant women" are also considered mandatory categorically needy.

Second, § 1396d(a)(i) defines a group of categorically needy individuals to whom the state may, at the state's option, choose to provide Medicaid coverage. "Generally speaking . . . the optionally needy subgroup includes minors, the elderly, the blind, the disabled, pregnant women, [and] the spouses of SSI recipients or AFDC-related caretaker relatives, if they are 'needy' according to the income and resource requirements of the AFDC and SSI cash benefit programs."

Third, the medically needy category includes the same groups of individuals that the states may cover as optional categorically needy, but applies less stringent financial and resource requirements. While medically needy coverage is generally optional with the states, once a state chooses to provide coverage to some medically needy individuals, it must provide, *inter alia*, prenatal and delivery services to medically needy pregnant women.

Under current law, pregnant women seeking prenatal care may be eligible for Medicaid under any of the three categories, depending on their financial status. However, this was not always the case. Before 1981, pregnant women were not even identified as a special eligibility group under the Medicaid statute. Instead, states simply had the option to extend prenatal care directly to the fetus, under the assumption that fetuses were optional categorically needy as "persons under the age of 21."

[After a lengthy discussion of the history of the Medicaid amendments, the court returned to the issue at hand.]

The Secretary makes little effort to justify denying, pursuant to an alien restriction, care that will, in all likelihood, benefit future citizens. The Secretary does not dispute that prenatal care is cost effective or that a significant number of citizen children will suffer birth defects as a direct result of the denial of prenatal care to their non-PRUCOL [permanently residing under color of law] mothers. The Secretary suggests only that denying Medicaid coverage to poor, pregnant, non-PRUCOL women will somehow inspire them to return to their native land for prenatal care. . . . [W]e must determine whether Congress intended that result or some other, and, if it did, whether Congress' choice was constitutional.

The Secretary relies principally on the plain language of OBRA '86. . . . Plaintiffs concede that prenatal care does not come within the definition of an emergency condition in § 1396b(v).[1]

---

[1][Editors' note: The Court explained and excerpted the relevant statutes as follows:

> On October 21, 1986, Congress passed the Omnibus Budget Reconciliation Act of 1986 (OBRA '86). OBRA '86 added to § 1396a of the Medicaid act the provision that:
>
> [n]otwithstanding paragraph 10(B) or any other provision of this subsection, a State plan shall provide medical assistance with respect to an alien who is not lawfully admitted for permanent residence or otherwise permanently residing in the United States under color of law only in accordance with section 1396b(v) of this title.
>
> § 1396b(v) provides that:
>
> (2) Payments shall be made under this section for care and services that are furnished to an alien . . . only if--
>
> (A) such care and services are necessary for the treatment of an emergency medical condition of the alien, and
>
> (B) such alien otherwise meets the eligibility requirements for medical assistance under the State plan . . .

Clearly, the Secretary's position is consistent with the plain language of the statute.

In the usual case, where the language of the statute is clear, that is the end of the analysis. But, we can never forget that what we are searching for is Congressional intent. . . . We must bear in mind Learned Hand's admonition that "it is one of the surest indexes of a mature and developed jurisprudence not to make a fortress out of the dictionary; but to remember that statutes always have some purpose or object to accomplish, whose sympathetic and imaginative discovery is the surest guide to their meaning."

This advice is particularly pertinent when construing a recent amendment to a complex statute that produces an unexpected result and when there is strong reason to doubt that Congress intended that result.

* * *

Here, although we agree with the Secretary that the plain language of the statute appears to require denying prenatal care to non-PRUCOL women, for the reasons discussed below we are convinced that Congress did not realize this result would follow from the blanket alienage restriction of OBRA '86 and that had Congress foreseen this problem, it would not have enacted the statute as written. Accordingly, . . . recognizing an exception to the alienage restriction of OBRA '86 for non-PRUCOL pregnant women would further, not undermine, Congressional purpose.

There are several reasons to believe that Congress did not realize that OBRA '86 would result in denying non-PRUCOL women access to Medicaid sponsored prenatal care. First, the Medicaid Act is a statute of "unparalleled complexity" among the "most intricate ever drafted by Congress." Its provisions are "almost unintelligible to the uninitiated.". . . It simply is unwise to blindly assume that Congress will always fully anticipate every implication of the plain meaning of a particular amendment to such a convoluted statute. This seems particularly true when the Congressional enactment comes in the form of a section of an end-of-session, omnibus budget reconciliation bill.

---

(3) For purposes of this subsection, the term "emergency medical condition" means a medical condition (including emergency labor and delivery) manifesting itself by acute symptoms of sufficient severity.]

Within this contorted scheme, few areas are more complex than the coverage of prenatal care. . . . [I]n the years preceding OBRA '86, Congress had radically expanded the basis for determining eligibility for prenatal care and had gradually moved from a fetal centered to a maternal centered approach. In doing so, Congress frequently tripped over the statute's complexities. . . . Both the complexity of the area and the history of mistakes as Congress strove to expand pre-natal benefits to future citizens raise doubts about whether Congress realized the implications of OBRA '86.

* * *

Further, construing OBRA '86 to terminate prenatal care for non-PRUCOL pregnant women creates an anomaly in another section of the statute. Newborn children are automatically eligible for Medicaid in their own name if their mothers were eligible for Medicaid sponsored prenatal care. If non-PRUCOL pregnant women are ineligible for Medicaid, then the child of an alien would not automatically be eligible for Medicaid while the child of a citizen would. Yet both children are United States citizens. Such discrimination against the citizen child on the basis of the alien status of the parent would raise serious equal protection questions.

* * *

This potential constitutional infirmity raises further doubt as to Congress' intent to exclude non-PRUCOL aliens from prenatal care. It also highlights the irrationality, which Congress doubtless would have perceived if it had focused on the issue, of treating the fetus of a non-PRUCOL woman as an alien when, upon birth, the child will become eligible for the full panoply of protections afforded citizens.

* * *

In the ordinary case, we would be reluctant to conclude that even an unexpected result conflicted with Congressional purpose. Here, however, the purpose of Congress in enacting OBRA '86 and the long history of Congressional treatment of prenatal care point decisively in a direction opposite to the one the Secretary urges. Accordingly, here we can confidently state that denying prenatal care to non-PRUCOL women conflicts with Congress' intent.

OBRA '86 was a budget reconciliation act. Congress' basic purpose was to "achieve net expenditure reductions" while "achiev[-ing] certain program improvements." The Secretary does not deny that providing prenatal care is cost effective. Indeed, that conclusion is intuitive. Studies have shown that every dollar spent on prenatal care saves between two and ten dollars in future medical care costs. Indeed, in other parts of OBRA '86, Congress relied on the cost effectiveness of prenatal care in its decision to expand Medicaid coverage for prenatal care. In short, there can be little question that denying prenatal care to non-PRUCOL aliens undermines the clearly expressed Congressional purpose of curbing expenditures.

Our conclusion that the Secretary's policy conflicts with Congressional purpose is further solidified by the fact that Congress has over the years unequivocally expressed its desire to continue to expand access to prenatal care.

* * *

In reaching this conclusion, we necessarily reject the claim that Congress, had it realized the implications of the alienage restriction, would have concluded that immigration policy required barring the provision of prenatal care to non-PRUCOL aliens. While we express no view on whether Congress could, constitutionally, make such a choice, we do note that "legislation directing the onus of a parent's misconduct against his children does not comport with fundamental conceptions of justice."

* * *

The Secretary contends, however, that even if we disagree that the plain language compels the course that the Secretary has taken, and even if we discern an intent contrary to the one that the Secretary has found, nonetheless the Secretary's interpretation of the statute must be affirmed so long as it is a permissible construction of the statute.

However, it is not clear here precisely what position of the Secretary this court ought to defer to. The Secretary points to a response to a comment published in the federal register. The commentator asked whether non-PRUCOL pregnant women could receive Medicaid benefits for prenatal care, and the Secretary responded that they could not. However, this response, coming while plaintiff's motion for a permanent injunction was pending, is the sort of *post hoc* litigation posture that is entitled to no deference.

* * *

Finally, while we are mindful of the general rule that in interpreting a statute of this complexity, the agency's position carries special weight, here the agency's position is not based on any expertise in the statute's realm. Rather, the only justification that this health agency offers is that "immigration policy" requires precluding non-PRUCOL pregnant women from receiving prenatal care. Surely the Secretary of Health and Human Services has no special expertise in deciding what makes good immigration policy, the province of a wholly separate executive department.

* * *

After examining the legislative history and the statutory context of OBRA '86, we conclude that Congress did not intend to prevent otherwise eligible pregnant women from receiving prenatal care to benefit their future citizen children. Further, we conclude that the Secretary's determination to the contrary is not entitled to deference. Finally, since the case can be resolved on statutory grounds, we express no opinion on plaintiffs' constitutional challenge. Accordingly, the decision of the district court is affirmed.

Notes and Questions

1. *Statutory Interpretation.* The Second Circuit Court of Appeals' decision began with an interpretation of the Medicaid Statute. The court's analysis focused on discerning the intent of Congress as revealed through: (1) the coverage of the Medicaid program; (2) the plain language of the Medicaid statute; (3) the compliance structure of the Medicaid scheme; (4) the legislative history; and (5) potential constitutional ramifications.

The court conceded that the Secretary of Health and Human Services' position was consistent with the plain language of the statute. Should that conclusion have ended the Court's inquiry?

The court suggested that the complexity of the pre-natal coverage provisions of the Medicaid statute may have caused either an error by Congress or a failure to anticipate the consequences of omitting authorization of coverage for undocumented pregnant women. Which judicial assumption seems more justified, assuming a Congressional error or an unintended omission?

2. *The Constitutional Shadow in Statutory Interpretation.* The court did not reach the constitutional question whether "discrimination against the citizen child on the basis of the alien status of the parent" violated equal protection. Yet the court noted that such discrimination "would raise serious equal protection questions." The court implied that Congress would not have intended to violate the

Equal Protection Clause and presumably did not intend to deny Medicaid coverage to undocumented pregnant women. Thus, the court relied on the potential unconstitutionality of the exclusion, without deciding it, to influence its interpretation of the statute. The Supreme Court has employed this technique in other contexts. For example, the Court sometimes interprets statutes so as to avoid a challenge that Congress improperly delegated its authority. *See Industrial Union Department, AFL-CIO v. American Petroleum Institute*, 448 U.S. 607 (1980).

3. *Cost Effectiveness.* Congress intended its OBRA '86 statute, like many others, to reduce federal expenditures. The Court apparently refused to interpret this purpose as merely reducing short-run costs. It noted instead the cost-effectiveness of pre-natal coverage and presumed that providing pre-natal coverage to undocumented women would serve the statute's purpose. Could this argument apply to other cost-cutting laws enacted by Congress?

4. *Deference to the Administrator.* The Secretary of Health and Human Services was responsible for interpreting and implementing the Medicaid statute. Courts generally defer to the expertise of the administrator. In this case, the court departed from this rule of deference because the Secretary's justification emerged after the litigation began and was not based on agency expertise and because the Secretary of HHS was not an expert on immigration policy. Consider whether similar arguments could apply to agency interpretations of other welfare provisions.

5. *Health Care as Fundamental Right.* As noted above the Court did not reach the equal protection issue and thus did not decide whether either fetuses or children of undocumented women had a right to pre-natal care. The court suggested, however, that citizen children of undocumented parents might receive heightened judicial scrutiny. (The court also implied that the exclusion would fail mere rationality review.) The court made no mention of whether health care is a fundamental right. What arguments could be made to support, and to attack, the proposition that health care is a fundamental right? Would the government's interest in encouraging undocumented women to leave the United States be considered legitimate, substantial, or compelling? Would exclusion of pre-natal coverage rationally, substantially, or indispensably further that interest?

6. *Tension with Roe v. Wade.* In its landmark decision in *Roe v. Wade*, 410 U.S. 113 (1974), the Supreme Court held that a

woman's right to privacy includes the right to abort a fetus in some circumstances. In *Lewis*, the court discussed the rights of the "citizen child" when health coverage excludes fetuses of undocumented women prior to their birth. Do the arguments supporting the right to health care of a fetus in *Lewis* conflict with the arguments supporting a right to abortion in *Roe*? Could the same lawyer have represented both the *Lewis* and *Roe* plaintiffs? Could the government consistently argue that fetuses have rights in *Roe* but that they have no rights in *Lewis*?

HARRIS v. McRAE

448 U.S. 297 (1980)

Justicc STEWART delivered the opinion of the Court.

This case presents statutory and constitutional questions concerning the public funding of abortions under Title XIX of the Social Security Act, commonly known as the "Medicaid" Act, and recent annual Appropriations Acts containing the so-called "Hyde Amendment." The statutory question is whether Title XIX requires a State that participates in the Medicaid program to fund the cost of medically necessary abortions for which federal reimbursement is unavailable under the Hyde Amendment. The constitutional question, which arises only if Title XIX imposes no such requirement, is whether the Hyde Amendment, by denying public funding for certain medically necessary abortions, contravenes the liberty or equal protection guarantees of the Due Process Clause of the Fifth Amendment, or either of the Religion Clauses of the First Amendment.

The Medicaid program was created in 1965, when Congress added Title XIX to the Social Security Act, for the purpose of providing federal financial assistance to States that choose to reimburse certain costs of medical treatment for needy persons. Although participation in the Medicaid program is entirely optional, once a State elects to participate, it must comply with the requirements of Title XIX.

One such requirement is that a participating State agree to provide financial assistance to the "categorically needy"[1] with respect to five general areas of medical treatment: (1) inpatient hospital services, (2) outpatient hospital services, (3) other laboratory and X-ray services, (4) skilled nursing facilities services, periodic screening and diagnosis of children, and family planning services, and (5) services of physicians. Although a participating State need not "provide funding for all medical treatment falling within the five general categories, [Title XIX] does require that [a] state Medicaid pla[n] establish 'reasonable standards . . . for determining . . . the extent of medical assistance under the plan which . . . are consistent with the objectives of [Title XIX].'"

Since September 1976, Congress has prohibited--either by an amendment to the annual appropriations bill for the Department of Health, Education, and Welfare[2] or by a joint resolution--the use of any federal funds to reimburse the cost of abortions under the Medicaid program except under certain specified circumstances. This funding restriction is commonly known as the "Hyde Amendment," after its original congressional sponsor, Representative Hyde.

* * *

It is well settled that if a case may be decided on either statutory or constitutional grounds, this Court, for sound jurisprudential reasons, will inquire first into the statutory question. This practice reflects the deeply rooted doctrine "that we ought not to pass on questions of constitutionality . . . unless such adjudication is unavoidable." Accordingly, we turn first to the question whether Title XIX requires a State that participates in the Medicaid program to continue to fund those medically necessary abortions for which federal reimbursement is unavailable under the Hyde Amendment.

---

[1]The "categorically needy" include families with dependent children eligible for public assistance under the Aid to Families with Dependent Children program, and the aged, blind, and disabled eligible for benefits under the Supplemental Security Income program. Title XIX also permits a State to extend Medicaid benefits to other needy persons, termed "medically needy." If a State elects to include the medically needy in its Medicaid plan, it has the option of providing somewhat different coverage from that required for the categorically needy.

[2]The Department of Health, Education, and Welfare was recently reorganized and divided into the Department of Health and Human Services and the Department of Education. The original designation is retained for purposes of this opinion.

If a participating State is under such an obligation, the constitutionality of the Hyde Amendment need not be drawn into question in the present case, for the availability of medically necessary abortions under Medicaid would continue, with the participating State shouldering the total cost of funding such abortions.

The appellees assert that a participating State has an independent funding obligation under Title XIX because (1) the Hyde Amendment is, by its own terms, only a limitation on federal reimbursement for certain medically necessary abortions, and (2) Title XIX does not permit a participating State to exclude from its Medicaid plan any medically necessary service solely on the basis of diagnosis or condition, even if federal reimbursement is unavailable for that service. It is thus the appellees' view that the effect of the Hyde Amendment is to withhold federal reimbursement for certain medically necessary abortions, but not to relieve a participating State of its duty under Title XIX to provide for such abortions in its Medicaid plan.

* * *

The Medicaid program created by Title XIX is a cooperative endeavor in which the Federal Government provides financial assistance to participating States to aid them in furnishing health care to needy persons. Under this system of "cooperative federalism," if a State agrees to establish a Medicaid plan that satisfies the requirements of Title XIX, which include several mandatory categories of health services, the Federal Government agrees to pay a specified percentage of "the total amount expended . . . as medical assistance under the State plan . . . ." The cornerstone of Medicaid is financial contribution by both the Federal Government and the participating State. Nothing in Title XIX as originally enacted, or in its legislative history, suggests that Congress intended to require a participating State to assume the full costs of providing any health services in its Medicaid plan. Quite the contrary, the purpose of Congress in enacting Title XIX was to provide federal financial assistance for all legitimate state expenditures under an approved Medicaid plan.

Since the Congress that enacted Title XIX did not intend a participating State to assume a unilateral funding obligation for any health service in an approved Medicaid plan, it follows that Title XIX does not require a participating State to include in its plan any services for which a subsequent Congress has withheld federal funding. Title XIX was designed as a cooperative program of shared financial responsibility, not as a device for the Federal Government to compel a State to provide services that Congress itself is unwilling to fund. Thus, if Congress chooses to withdraw federal funding for a particular service, a State is not obliged to continue to pay for that service as a condition of continued federal financial support of other services. This is not to say that Congress may not now depart from the original design of Title XIX under which the Federal Government shares the financial responsibility for expenses incurred under an approved Medicaid plan. It is only to say that, absent an indication of contrary legislative intent by a subsequent Congress, Title XIX does not obligate a participating State to pay for those medical services for which federal reimbursement is unavailable.

Thus, by the normal operation of Title XIX, even if a State were otherwise required to include medically necessary abortions in its Medicaid plan, the withdrawal of federal funding under the Hyde Amendment would operate to relieve the State of that obligation for those abortions for which federal reimbursement is unavailable. The legislative history of the Hyde Amendment contains no indication whatsoever that Congress intended to shift the entire cost of such services to the participating States. Rather, the legislative history suggests that Congress has always assumed that a participating State would not be required to fund medically necessary abortions once federal funding was withdrawn pursuant to the Hyde Amendment. Accordingly, we conclude that Title XIX does not require a participating State to pay for those medically necessary abortions for which federal reimbursement is unavailable under the Hyde Amendment.[16]

Having determined that Title XIX does not obligate a participating State to pay for those medically necessary abortions for which Congress has withheld federal funding, we must consider the constitutional validity of the Hyde Amendment. The appellees assert that the funding restrictions of the Hyde Amendment violate several rights secured by the Constitution--(1) the right of a woman, implicit in the Due Process Clause of the Fifth Amendment, to decide whether to terminate a pregnancy, (2) the prohibition under the Establishment

---

[16]A participating State is free, if it so chooses, to include in its Medicaid plan those medically necessary abortions for which federal reimbursement is unavailable. We hold only that a State need not include such abortions in its Medicaid plan.

Clause of the First Amendment against any "law respecting an establishment of religion," and (3) the right to freedom of religion protected by the Free Exercise Clause of the First Amendment. The appellees also contend that, quite apart from substantive constitutional rights, the Hyde Amendment violates the equal protection component of the Fifth Amendment.

It is well settled that, quite apart from the guarantee of equal protection, if a law "impinges upon a fundamental right explicitly or implicitly secured by the Constitution [it] is presumptively unconstitutional." Accordingly, before turning to the equal protection issue in this case, we examine whether the Hyde Amendment violates any substantive rights secured by the Constitution.

We address first the appellees' argument that the Hyde Amendment, by restricting the availability of certain medically necessary abortions under Medicaid, impinges on the "liberty" protected by the Due Process Clause as recognized in *Roe v. Wade*, 410 U.S. 113, and its progeny.

In the *Wade* case, this Court held unconstitutional a Texas statute making it a crime to procure or attempt an abortion except on medical advice for the purpose of saving the mother's life. The constitutional underpinning of *Wade* was a recognition that the "liberty" protected by the Due Process Clause of the Fourteenth Amendment includes not only the freedoms explicitly mentioned in the Bill of Rights, but also a freedom of personal choice in certain matters of marriage and family life. This implicit constitutional liberty, the Court in *Wade* held, includes the freedom of a woman to decide whether to terminate a pregnancy.

But the Court in *Wade* also recognized that a State has legitimate interests during a pregnancy in both ensuring the health of the mother and protecting potential human life. These state interests, which were found to be "separate and distinct" and to "gro[w] in substantiality as the woman approaches term," pose a conflict with a woman's untrammeled freedom of choice. In resolving this conflict, the Court held that before the end of the first trimester of pregnancy, neither state interest is sufficiently substantial to justify any intrusion on the woman's freedom of choice. In the second trimester, the state interest in maternal health was found to be sufficiently substantial to justify regulation reasonably related to that concern. And at viability, usually in the third trimester, the state interest in protecting the potential life of the fetus was found to justify a criminal prohibition against abortions, except where necessary for the preservation of the life or health of the mother. Thus, inasmuch as the Texas criminal statute allowed abortions only where necessary to save the life of the mother and without regard to the stage of the pregnancy, the Court held in *Wade* that the statute violated the Due Process Clause of the Fourteenth Amendment.

In *Maher v. Roe*, 432 U.S. 464, the Court was presented with the question whether the scope of personal constitutional freedom recognized in *Roe v. Wade* included an entitlement to Medicaid payments for abortions that are not medically necessary. At issue in *Maher* was a Connecticut welfare regulation under which Medicaid recipients received payments for medical services incident to childbirth, but not for medical services incident to nontherapeutic abortions.

* * *

The doctrine of *Roe v. Wade*, the Court held in *Maher*, "protects the woman from unduly burdensome interference with her freedom to decide whether to terminate her pregnancy," such as the severe criminal sanctions at issue in *Roe v. Wade*, *supra*, or the absolute requirement of spousal consent for an abortion challenged in *Planned Parenthood of Central Missouri v. Danforth*, 428 U.S. 52.

But the constitutional freedom recognized in *Wade* and its progeny, the *Maher* Court explained, did not prevent Connecticut from making "a value judgment favoring childbirth over abortion, and . . . implement[ing] that judgment by the allocation of public funds."

* * *

The Court in *Maher* noted that its description of the doctrine recognized in *Wade* and its progeny signaled "no retreat" from those decisions. In explaining why the constitutional principle recognized in *Wade* and later cases--protecting a woman's freedom of choice---did not translate into a constitutional obligation of Connecticut to subsidize abortions, the Court cited the "basic difference between direct state interference with a protected activity and state encouragement of an alternative activity consonant with legislative policy. Constitutional concerns are greatest when the State attempts to impose its will by force of law; the State's power to encourage actions deemed to be in the public interest is necessarily far broader." Thus, even though the Connecticut regulation favored childbirth over abortion by means of subsidization of one and not the other, the

Court in *Maher* concluded that the regulation did not impinge on the constitutional freedom recognized in *Wade* because it imposed no governmental restriction on access to abortions.

The Hyde Amendment, like the Connecticut welfare regulation at issue in *Maher*, places no governmental obstacle in the path of a woman who chooses to terminate her pregnancy, but rather, by means of unequal subsidization of abortion and other medical services, encourages alternative activity deemed in the public interest. The present case does differ factually from *Maher* insofar as that case involved a failure to fund nontherapeutic abortions, whereas the Hyde Amendment withholds funding of certain medically necessary abortions. Accordingly, the appellees argue that because the Hyde Amendment affects a significant interest not present or asserted in *Maher*--the interest of a woman in protecting her health during pregnancy--and because that interest lies at the core of the personal constitutional freedom recognized in *Wade*, the present case is constitutionally different from *Maher*. It is the appellees' view that to the extent that the Hyde Amendment withholds funding for certain medically necessary abortions, it clearly impinges on the constitutional principle recognized in *Wade*.

It is evident that a woman's interest in protecting her health was an important theme in *Wade*. In concluding that the freedom of a woman to decide whether to terminate her pregnancy falls within the personal liberty protected by the Due Process Clause, the Court in *Wade* emphasized the fact that the woman's decision carries with it significant personal health implications--both physical and psychological. In fact, although the Court in *Wade* recognized that the state interest in protecting potential life becomes sufficiently compelling in the period after fetal viability to justify an absolute criminal prohibition of nontherapeutic abortions, the Court held that even after fetal viability a State may not prohibit abortions "necessary to preserve the life or health of the mother." Because even the compelling interest of the State in protecting potential life after fetal viability was held to be insufficient to outweigh a woman's decision to protect her life or health, it could be argued that the freedom of a woman to decide whether to terminate her pregnancy for health reasons does in fact lie at the core of the constitutional liberty identified in *Wade*.

But, regardless of whether the freedom of a woman to choose to terminate her pregnancy for health reasons lies at the core or the periphery of the due process liberty recognized in *Wade*, it simply does not follow that a woman's freedom of choice carries with it a constitutional entitlement to the financial resources to avail herself of the full range of protected choices. The reason why was explained in *Maher*: although government may not place obstacles in the path of a woman's exercise of her freedom of choice, it need not remove those not of its own creation. Indigency falls in the latter category. The financial constraints that restrict an indigent woman's ability to enjoy the full range of constitutionally protected freedom of choice are the product not of governmental restrictions on access to abortions, but rather of her indigency. Although Congress has opted to subsidize medically necessary services generally, but not certain medically necessary abortions, the fact remains that the Hyde Amendment leaves an indigent woman with at least the same range of choice in deciding whether to obtain a medically necessary abortion as she would have had if Congress had chosen to subsidize no health care costs at all. We are thus not persuaded that the Hyde Amendment impinges on the constitutionally protected freedom of choice recognized in *Wade*.

Although the liberty protected by the Due Process Clause affords protection against unwarranted government interference with freedom of choice in the context of certain personal decisions, it does not confer an entitlement to such funds as may be necessary to realize all the advantages of that freedom. To hold otherwise would mark a drastic change in our understanding of the Constitution. It cannot be that because government may not prohibit the use of contraceptives, or prevent parents from sending their child to a private school, government, therefore, has an affirmative constitutional obligation to ensure that all persons have the financial resources to obtain contraceptives or send their children to private schools. To translate the limitation on governmental power implicit in the Due Process Clause into an affirmative funding obligation would require Congress to subsidize the medically necessary abortion of an indigent woman even if Congress had not enacted a Medicaid program to subsidize other medically necessary services. Nothing in the Due Process Clause supports such an extraordinary result. Whether freedom of choice that is constitutionally protected warrants federal subsidization is a question for Congress to answer, not a matter of constitutional entitlement. Accordingly, we conclude that the Hyde Amendment does not impinge on the due process liberty recognized in *Wade*.

[The Court held that the Hyde Amendment did not violate the Establishment Clause and that plaintiffs lacked standing to challenge it under the Free Exercise Clause.]

* * *

It remains to be determined whether the Hyde Amendment violates the equal protection component of the Fifth Amendment. This challenge is premised on the fact that, although federal reimbursement is available under Medicaid for medically necessary services generally, the Hyde Amendment does not permit federal reimbursement of all medically necessary abortions. The District Court held, and the appellees argue here, that this selective subsidization violates the constitutional guarantee of equal protection.

The guarantee of equal protection under the Fifth Amendment is not a source of substantive rights or liberties, but rather a right to be free from invidious discrimination in statutory classifications and other governmental activity. It is well settled that where a statutory classification does not itself impinge on a right or liberty protected by the Constitution, the validity of classification must be sustained unless "the classification rests on grounds wholly irrelevant to the achievement of [any legitimate governmental] objective." This presumption of constitutional validity, however, disappears if a statutory classification is predicated on criteria that are, in a constitutional sense, "suspect," the principal example of which is a classification based on race, e. g., *Brown v. Board of Education*, 347 U.S. 483.

For the reasons stated above, we have already concluded that the Hyde Amendment violates no constitutionally protected substantive rights. We now conclude as well that it is not predicated on a constitutionally suspect classification. In reaching this conclusion, we again draw guidance from the Court's decision in *Maher v. Roe*. As to whether the Connecticut welfare regulation providing funds for childbirth but not for nontherapeutic abortions discriminated against a suspect class, the Court in *Maher* observed: "An indigent woman desiring an abortion does not come within the limited category of disadvantaged classes so recognized by our cases. Nor does the fact that the impact of the regulation falls upon those who cannot pay lead to a different conclusion. In a sense, every denial of welfare to an indigent creates a wealth classification as compared to nonindigents who are able to pay for the desired goods or services. But this Court has never held that financial need alone identifies a suspect class for purposes of equal protection analysis." Thus, the Court in *Maher* found no basis for concluding that the Connecticut regulation was predicated on a suspect classification.

It is our view that the present case is indistinguishable from *Maher* in this respect. Here, as in *Maher*, the principal impact of the Hyde Amendment falls on the indigent. But that fact does not itself render the funding restriction constitutionally invalid, for this Court has held repeatedly that poverty, standing alone, is not a suspect classification. That *Maher* involved the refusal to fund nontherapeutic abortions, whereas the present case involves the refusal to fund medically necessary abortions, has no bearing on the factors that render a classification "suspect" within the meaning of the constitutional guarantee of equal protection.

The remaining question then is whether the Hyde Amendment is rationally related to a legitimate governmental objective. It is the Government's position that the Hyde Amendment bears a rational relationship to its legitimate interest in protecting the potential life of the fetus. We agree.

* * *

[T]he Hyde Amendment, by encouraging childbirth except in the most urgent circumstances, is rationally related to the legitimate governmental objective of protecting potential life. By subsidizing the medical expenses of indigent women who carry their pregnancies to term while not subsidizing the comparable expenses of women who undergo abortions (except those whose lives are threatened), Congress has established incentives that make childbirth a more attractive alternative than abortion for persons eligible for Medicaid. These incentives bear a direct relationship to the legitimate congressional interest in protecting potential life. Nor is it irrational that Congress has authorized federal reimbursement for medically necessary services generally, but not for certain medically necessary abortions. Abortion is inherently different from other medical procedures, because no other procedure involves the purposeful termination of a potential life.

* * *

Where, as here, the Congress has neither invaded a substantive constitutional right or freedom, nor enacted legislation that purposefully operates to the detriment of a suspect class, the only requirement of equal protection is that congressional action be rationally related to a legitimate governmental interest. The Hyde Amendment satisfies that standard. It is not the mission of this Court or any other to decide whether the balance of competing interests reflected in the Hyde Amendment is wise social policy. If that were our mission, not every Justice who has subscribed to the judgment of the Court today could have done so. But we cannot, in the name of the Constitution, overturn duly enacted statutes simply "because they may be unwise, improvident, or out of harmony with a particular school of thought." Rather, "when an issue involves policy choices as sensitive as those implicated [here] . . . , the appropriate forum for their resolution in a democracy is the legislature."

For the reasons stated in this opinion, we hold that a State that participates in the Medicaid program is not obligated under Title XIX to continue to fund those medically necessary abortions for which federal reimbursement is unavailable under the Hyde Amendment. We further hold that the funding restrictions of the Hyde Amendment violate neither the Fifth Amendment nor the Establishment Clause of the First Amendment.

* * *

It is so ordered.

Notes and Questions

1. *Nature of the Claim.* The plaintiffs challenged the Hyde Amendment on the grounds that it funded all childbirth of poor women but limited abortion funding to those necessary to save a poor woman's life. What legal claims could have been used to bring this challenge?

2. *Federalism and Unfunded Mandates.* Why did the Supreme Court refuse to presume that Congress intended to require states to provide medical services that Congress refused to fund? Could Congress explicitly have required such coverage without providing funding? In other words, does Congress have the authority, as a condition of receiving federal funds, to direct how states spend their own funds?

3. *Substantive Due Process.* The plaintiffs claimed that the government's refusal to fund certain abortions deprived poor women of their privacy protected within the liberty component of the Due Process Clause. Should courts interpret the Constitution to protect poor women's health? The Court answered in the negative, explaining that "although government may not place obstacles in the path of

a woman's exercise of her freedom of choice, it need not remove those not of its own creation. Indigency falls in the latter category." Does government play a role in creating indigency? Should it play a role in eliminating indigency?

4. *Heightened Scrutiny.* The Court refused to apply heightened scrutiny because poverty alone was not a suspect classification. Did poverty "stand alone" in *Harris*? Should the Court have blended various indicia, including poverty and gender classifications and privacy as a fundamental right, to justify heightening its scrutiny?

5. *Rationality.* The Court held that the Hyde Amendment rationally served the government's legislative interest in protecting life. Can the government consistently justify protecting life by refusing to fund abortions, as in *Harris*, and refusing to protect life by refusing to fund pre-natal care to undocumented pregnant women in *Lewis*?

Health Care Reform

After President Clinton took office in 1993, his administration devoted much of its early energy to investigating and evaluating the health care system, and designing its reform. The President presented his plan to Congress in September, 1993. One year later, his plan died. For a discussion of the demise of the Clinton health care plan, *see* Manish C. Shah and Judith M. Rosenberg, *Health Care Reform in the 103d Congress--A Congressional Analysis*, 33 HARVARD JOURNAL ON LEGISLATION 585 (1996). But the issues raised during the national debate remain the subject of both considerable attention and piecemeal legislation. In the excerpts that follow, Professors Louise Trubek and Vernellia Randall explore important issues relating to creating an entitlement to health care, and ensuring equality for racial minorities and poor people in health care programs.

Louise Trubek

IS HEALTH CARE A RIGHT? PASSAGE OF THIS PROPOSAL WILL MAKE IT SO

MILWAUKEE JOURNAL, April 3, 1994

Should there be a right to health care? President Clinton and those who support his plan seem to think so. They believe that coverage must be universal and benefits guaranteed for all. The president has spoken of a "right to health care," and one supporter described the Clinton plan as "making health care coverage a right of citizenship rather than a fringe benefit of employment."

It would be a bold move for the United States to proclaim that health care is a right of citizenship. No such right exists today. Most Americans receive health care coverage through the workplace. Employees may secure rights to coverage through contract, and the poor and elderly have some rights under Medicaid and Medicare, but neither the Constitution nor the laws mandate coverage for most citizens of the U.S.

The Clinton plan would change all this, for it will create both statutory and constitutional guarantees. The plan creates a universal and comprehensive program of health care for all citizens, thus creating a statutory right to health care. Moreover, once such a right exists, citizens will also become entitled to certain constitutional guarantees.

It may sound strange to some that a statute can create a constitutional right where none existed before, but this is a familiar process. The Supreme Court has never held that Americans have a right to health care, and it is not likely to do so in the near future. But [it] has ruled that when the Congress provides a social benefit such as health care or Social Security or welfare, it must follow certain constitutional norms that effect all actions taken by government. This doctrine has provided constitutional protections for those with statutory rights to benefits similar to health care, and it is likely to affect the operation of the health care plan proposed by the president.

The Clinton plan [makes a] bold step toward the creation of a statutory right to health care. Supporters of the plan call for "privately provided, publicly guaranteed" health care for all Americans. By making the state the guarantor of health care coverage, the plan brings health care within the scope of constitutional protections against arbitrary state action.

It will ensure that citizens are not only entitled to coverage but also to fair treatment. These protections now are available only to those who have enrolled in government-run programs such as Medicare and Medicaid, but not to the vast majority who are covered through the workplace or the significant minority who have no coverage whatsoever.

The creation of the statutory right to universal coverage for all Americans as proposed in the Clinton plan (and several others under consideration) opens up constitutional protections based on both the due process clause, which guarantees fair procedure, and the equal protection clause, which protects minorities against discriminatory treatment. Due process is likely to require some type of hearing for a denial of coverage. So, for example, if you are denied coverage of a procedure that you and your doctor think is medically necessary and is covered under the plan, you will be able to have some type of hearing and review under the Clinton plan. This would give citizens a right to have an impartial judge take a second look at the health system's initial decision and permit reversal if the decision was unreasonable or illegal.

The Equal Protection Clause of the U.S. Constitution may also come into play. This provision allows the court to review decisions in situations in which the interests of disadvantaged groups may be affected by the health care system. For example, the Clinton plan requires that pools of enrollees be created. If pools were set up in a way that had a disparate impact on a disadvantaged group such as a racial minority, the pools could be challenged.

Imagine that separate pools were created for the City of Milwaukee and the suburbs. Since the population of racial minorities is so much higher in the city than in the suburbs, a successful Constitutional challenge might be made on the grounds of disparate impact. Another disadvantaged group that might be able to raise a challenge would be women who are not receiving appropriate health care (e.g., mammography at regular intervals). Plans that symmetrically ignore such appropriate treatment while providing preventive care for the groups might be subject to constitutional review based on the lack of equal treatment for women. It might even be possible that the courts would treat children as a protected class, and strike down health care programs that create disadvantage for children in some specific fashion.

The Clinton proposals on health care have dramatically shifted the attitude of the American people and the policy-makers. The widespread acceptance of the concept of universal coverage and health care as a right is revolutionary. If the legislation is enacted to express this societal goal, the courts can play a significant role in interpreting constitutional principles that will guarantee protection for health care for all Americans. To create a mixed statutory and constitutional right to health care would be a bold step, but one long overdue and well worth taking.

Vernellia R. Randall

DOES CLINTON'S HEALTH CARE REFORM PROPOSAL ENSURE [E]QUALITY OF HEALTH CARE FOR ETHNIC AMERICANS AND THE POOR?

60 BROOKLYN LAW REVIEW 167 (1994)

On September 22, 1993, President Clinton appeared before the American people to discuss his plans to reform the health care system. On November 20, 1993, the Health Security Act (the "Act" or "HSA") was introduced into Congress. The Act responded to concerns about the uninsured and underinsured, about uncompensated care and about cost containment. An implicit assumption has been that economic access is the most significant barrier to health care; and, in fact, it may be. However, there are many other barriers to access.

If equitable access means, or is defined as, the actual receipt of the quality and quantity of services needed, then access in America has been inequitable. Many individuals receive different health care (both quantity and quality) based on characteristics other than medical need. The care received by the wealthy is different than the care received by the poor; the care received by European Americans is different than the care received by ethnic Americans; and the care received by men is different than the care received by women.

Has the HSA designed a system that removes or minimizes inequities? Or will it provide the wealthy with one level of care and the poor with another? Does the HSA fashion a system that distributes health care resources so that ethnic Americans receive the same quantity and quality of care as European Americans? Will the system envisioned result in improved health status for ethnic Americans?

* * *

[This] article concludes that health care reform will fail ethnic Americans and the poor because it maintains a structurally and ideologically flawed system; it perpetuates a fragmented system with inadequate infrastructure; it maintains a culturally incompetent system based on illness care; it rations health care through a tiered system based on private interests; and it inadequately protects against health care discrimination.

* * *

Of the industrialized nations, only two, the United States and South Africa, do not have a national system of health care for their citizens. The Health Security Act sets the framework for a national health care system.

* * *

According to the HSA, the federal government sets the basic framework for the system, including national standards on benefits, quality and access to care. States are given flexibility to implement health care reform within the federal framework, including designing and monitoring the system. That flexibility extends to designing a single-payer plan if a state desires.

The Act, however, clearly lays out each player's responsibilities under the health care plan. States must identify one or more regional alliances to serve as purchasing agents for health care insurance. The board of each regional alliance consists of employers and consumers, but providers are specifically prohibited from sitting on a regional alliance. Employers with more than 5000 employees may opt out of the regional alliance and develop their own corporate alliance. Those that do not are required to pay 80% of the average premium of a full-time employee's health care premium. Health plans that are selected by the alliances may market their product in the alliance. But, ultimately health plans are responsible for guaranteeing coverage for a basic comprehensive benefits package by contracting with providers to provide services. Providers may choose to participate in as many or as few health plans as they desire. Consumers are required to enroll in a health care plan, to obtain a health care card, and to make premium payments, co-payments and deductible payments. No eligible individual can be disenrolled from a health plan until that individual is enrolled in another health plan or becomes Medicare-eligible.

* * *

Eligible individuals include citizens or nationals of the United States; an alien permanently residing in the United States under color of law; or a long-term nonimmigrant. A Medicare-eligible individual is entitled to health benefits under the Medicare program. Military personnel and families, veterans and Indians have a choice of health plan coverage. Prisoners and undocumented aliens, however, are ineligible for benefits through enrollment in a health plan.

* * *

Unfortunately, for ethnic Americans and the poor, the ethical foundations of health reform are "ideological, financial and legalistic terms." By framing the need for health care reform in terms designed to appeal to middle-class European Americans, the Clinton administration denies the existence of the health crisis among ethnic Americans and the poor. In particular, it fails to place the issues of race, class or culture at the forefront of health care reform.

Ethnic Americans need a health system that is structurally and ideologically focused on improving health status. Thus, for ethnic Americans, the reformed health care system proposed by the Act is structurally and ideologically flawed because its ethical foundations are incomplete and inadequate; it focuses on states' rights; it continues an employment-based health insurance system; it expands the "private sector" role in health care delivery; and it does not insure representation of ethnic Americans in policy-level decisions.

* * *

One of the major problems with the current system is that it is a fragmented system. The current health care system is a puffed-up system providing unnecessary, indulgent services for the privileged, while basic critically needed services for the disadvantaged are rationed and often unavailable. Unfortunately, the Health Security Act continues the fragmentation of an inadequate infrastructure. Such inadequate infrastructure might not be so bad if the Health Security Act delivered on the Clinton administration's promises of universal coverage for comprehensive benefits. However, for ethnic Americans the Act provides less than universal coverage, and the benefits are not comprehensive enough.

* * *

Despite the apparent importance of economics as a barrier to access to health care, the unavailability of providers and facilities from which to obtain health care is equally as devastating. Even persons with the ability to pay may not have quality health care. In fact, the more inaccessible the providers and facilities, the more likely the person will, at a minimum, delay seeking care.

Certainly, providers and facilities are not accessible if they are not located near the population they are intended to serve. Moreover, even if they are located in the community, they are unavailable if they refuse to accept patients. Both rural communities and inner city communities have significant problems with access due to inadequate infrastructure.

* * *

Nothing in the HSA indicates that the public health structure for delivery of services will be preserved, expanded or revitalized. In fact, health reform shifts the emphasis away from the direct delivery of health services. Instead, it redirects the emphasis of public health to health-related data collection, surveillance and outcomes monitoring; protection of environment, housing, food and water; investigation and control of diseases and injuries; public information and education; accountability and quality assurance; laboratory services; training and education; and leadership, policy development and administration.

While these are important and necessary functions of public health, so is service delivery. The public health system developed as a result of the failure of the private sector to provide health services to the poor, to the underserved and to ethnic Americans. It is improbable that private corporations and voluntary health care organizations will build health care infrastructures in ethnic American, poor or rural communities. Thus, it is unlikely that private corporations and voluntary health care organizations can replace health care provided by the existing public health infrastructure.

* * *

Access to health care requires actual services provided by physicians and hospitals. But, many physicians and hospitals are reluctant to serve ethnic Americans. Within a professional culture that is reluctant to serve ethnic Americans and poor communities, universal coverage, by itself, will not "appreciably redistribute the physician supply" in a way that would significantly improve access. In sum, infrastructure barriers, separate and distinct from the issue of financing, are not adequately addressed, and the promise of universal coverage is not a promise of equality of care.

* * *

The plan maintains a fragmented system by excluding large segments of the population, keeping them outside of the main system. Specifically, undocumented aliens, Medicare recipients, prison populations, employees of eligible corporate alliance sponsors, military personnel and families, veterans and Indians are all either excluded or kept outside of the main system.

These exclusions are problematic for several reasons. First, the exclusion of a large number of individuals threatens the financial integrity of the main health system by producing inefficiencies and duplications. Second, the exclusion of some individuals inevitably causes discrimination, because someone must determine who is not covered. Consequently, providers and facilities may use skin color or language as a de facto method of determining eligibility for citizens who do not have health security cards. Finally, a significant portion of ethnic American males will not be in the system since prison populations are specifically excluded and military personnel and veterans may opt out. This is particularly troubling because the HSA does not assure that individuals in alternative systems will receive at least the same comprehensive services.

* * *

A person does not have meaningful access to health care if that person is not provided health care within the context of his or her cultural background. Merely providing a person with a piece of paper (insurance) or a provider does not mean that that person will receive health care that assists in improving the person's health status. For centuries, Americans indulged in the fantasy that all persons (native Americans, immigrants and slaves) blended into one great "melting pot" to become Americans. While it is true that there are unique American cultural similarities that cut across all groups, this country has always had a diverse population of races, ethnic groups, subcultures and religions.

That diverse mix will continue. By the end of this century, 39% of the population will be from foreign-born parents. At the same time, 50% of all Americans will be either African American, Hispanic American, Asian American or Native American. America is a "micro-world reflecting [the] cultural diversity of the entire world."

* * *

Merely providing financial coverage for health care does nothing to assure that ethnic Americans will have access to care that is culturally competent. One barrier to culturally competent care is physicians' own negative perceptions about ethnic Americans. This barrier exists in part because the health care system is designed around the cultural needs of middle-class European Americans. Ethnic Americans and poor individuals seem less compliant and more difficult to care for because they have differing needs and problems in accessing care. The problem, however, is not poor patients or ethnic Americans, but the health care system's inability to provide effective care to diverse populations. If increased compliance and improved health status are the goals, then the health care system must be flexible enough to match a community's cultural, ethnic, lifestyle and socioeconomic needs.

The HSA does little to address the issue of assuring culturally competent care. For instance, despite the fact that ethnic Americans respond well to community-based health education programs, the Act fails to require health plans to provide such activities. Furthermore, it fails to require removal of the barriers to the effective utilization of such services. Rather, the Act permits, but does not require, states to provide financial incentives to ensure that health plans provide for extra services such as interpreting services. Finally, since the HSA never explicitly defines "disadvantaged groups," the scope of the incentives is indeterminate.

Health care requires interaction between the patient seeking care and the provider. When individuals do not understand, speak or read English, they may avoid contact with the health care system. Although some Americans do not understand English well enough to be able to talk with their physicians, the Act does not require that health care plans address these language barriers. Language barriers can defeat the provision of health care if essential information cannot be conveyed. Consequently, although universal coverage makes it easier for many ethnic Americans to seek and obtain effective health services, language barriers will continue to inhibit their use of the health care system, unless the system is required to restructure itself to address those concerns.

* * *

The HSA's universal coverage does not cover many of the services needed by poor Americans. For instance, it does not cover eyeglasses or hearing aids, and provides that no person 18 years or older can receive prevention, diagnosis or treatment of dental disease before January 1, 2001. These items may be of marginal expense to middle-income persons, but to the poor they are not only expensive but they are also essential corrective treatment.

The Act also provides insufficient "comprehensive coverage" for mental health and substance abuse. Although the Act covers inpatient and residential mental illness and substance abuse treatment, intensive nonresidential mental illness and substance abuse treatment, and outpatient mental illness and substance abuse treatment, these services are available subject to significant limitations. Given the serious significant mental health and substance abuse problems in ethnic American and poor communities, basic mental health services are inadequate. In addition, the proposal to phase-in mental health benefits over five years is particularly troubling since political changes may result in the non-delivery of benefits.

* * *

It is only recently that the need for reform was characterized as a need for universal access. Health care reform was motivated not by the desire or need to provide better access, but by a concern for cost containment. More specifically, they were motivated by problems associated with uncompensated care and the cost of health care to employers and the government. To control costs, individuals, providers or health insurance plans will need to ration care. The Act places the rationing function in the hands of managed care plans owned by private enterprise. Private enterprise, however, will not be able to control cost if the majority of Americans do not elect managed care plans.

* * *

Sadly, the HSA envisions not across-the-board rationing, but the continuation of a tiered health care system with rationing only for some. The reformed health care system will continue to ration health care based on economics. It will continue to ration health care based on race. It will continue to ration health care based on class.

* * *

It is clear that the potential for continuing discrimination is significant. Any effort to create a just health care system will depend on the ability of advocates to litigate and prevent discrimination. Advocates' effectiveness will depend on the anti-discrimination provisions of the HSA. The Act contains express anti-discrimination enforcement provisions, but they are insufficient.

* * *

Ethnic Americans have always had to contend with discrimination in health care. That discrimination was based on the behavior of providers. Now individuals will have to contend with not only provider discrimination, but regional alliance and health plan discrimination. This is a significant change which has the potential of completely undermining access to care. As greater pressure is placed on physicians to curtail treatment services, physicians may not ration across the board. Rather, they may more strictly ration services to vulnerable populations (i.e., ethnic Americans). As health care plans find their premiums caps insufficient, not only will they place increasingly strict gatekeeping requirements on physicians, they may also significantly increase their utilization review denials and they may do so in a discriminatory manner. The Act will not prevent these practices.

* * *

The HSA fails generally in several respects. First, it forbids only limited discrimination by states and alliances and contains no direct prohibition against discrimination by providers. Because of the historical problems with determining to whom a discrimination law is applicable, the prohibition should be applicable to both public and private organizations and for profit and not-for-profit organizations. It should also be applicable both to an individual person and to a broad range of organizational forms including private organizations, sole proprietorship, partnerships, associations and corporations. Furthermore, health care providers should be specifically responsible for their discrimination.

Second, the Act takes an inconsistent approach to banning discrimination. On the one hand, it significantly broadens equal access by prohibiting discrimination based not only on race, national origin, age and disability but also on language, socioeconomic status, health status, affiliation, mix of health professionals or anticipated need for services. Unfortunately, the listing of protected groups is not consistent throughout the HSA. For instance, prohibiting activities by health plans has the effect of attracting or limiting enrollees on the basis of personal characteristics. Only the following characteristics are identified: health status, anticipated need for health care, age, occupation, or affiliation with any person or entity. In the same section, in prohibiting health care discrimination the characteristics identified are: race, national origin, sex, language, socioeconomic status, age, disability, health status, or anticipated need for health services. Furthermore, while alliances are required to ensure enrollment of all eligible individuals, the anti-discrimination provisions include only race, sex, national origin, religion, mix of health professionals, location of the plan's headquarters, or organizational arrangement, but not language, socioeconomic status, age, disability, health status, or anticipated need for health services. To ensure the civil rights of individuals under the complex reformed system, the listing of protected groups should be broad and uniform throughout the Act.

Third, the HSA only uses the "effects" test to measure discrimination by health plans. While it specifically addresses forms of discrimination to the activities of the states and Alliance, the Act does not explicitly apply the "effects test" to those activities. By including the "effects test" in the health plan's prohibition against discrimination, some may argue that only intentional discrimination is prohibited in all other areas of the Act. This is a substantial problem since, in all likelihood, the type of discrimination which will be most prevalent by the National Health Board, States, Alliances (Regional and Corporate) and providers is "effects" discrimination.

Finally, the HSA also fails to provide comprehensive protection based on language discrimination. For instance, neither the National Health Board, alliances nor health plans are forbidden from discriminating based on language. This is important to a large number of ethnic Americans who are most likely to be incorrectly denied service as a direct result of the HSA's failure to cover undocumented aliens.

* * *

The current health care system is flawed in a number of ways. There are significant economic barriers, including no insurance, no money, co-payments and deductibles. People do not have universal portable health care coverage. Moreover, even the massive financing reforms of the Health Security Act that are aimed at increasing coverage do not automatically translate into broadened access and improved services. After some years, when government and private institutions encounter budgetary stringency, it is likely that they will economize by decertifying persons and placing limits on benefits.

Furthermore, the reformed system lacks adequate infrastructure to provide culturally competent care. Instead, it perpetuates a middle-class European American focus for the delivery of health care. Where services do exist, there is significant fragmentation with ill-defined or inadequately defined community health or public health programs. Furthermore, the Act permits different population groups to receive different health care treatment. This is due in part to the institutional racism in the system but also to the insufficient or nonexistent health research data that is race or culture-specific (including quality assurance or utilization review data). Given the focus of cost containment on middle-class health care needs, there exists the potential for significant health care discrimination. The existing anti-discrimination laws will not effectively combat this discrimination. For these reasons, the Health Care Security Act is only a partial answer and, in many ways, an inadequate answer to the need for health care reform.

Notes and Questions

1. *Federalism.* One irony of the movement to reform health care was that it attempted to create for health care what was being dismantled for welfare, namely a system based on national standards of eligibility with state flexibility in implementation. Do you think nationalization of standards was part of the reason Congress rejected the Health Security Act?

2. *Exclusions.* Does it make sense to exclude prisoners and undocumented aliens from a nationalized health care plan?

3. *Diversity.* Professor Randall argued that health care reform proposals perpetuate the dominance of white culture by failing to account for the different needs of ethnic Americans. What are those different needs? How can they be addressed in the future?

4. *Fragmentation.* Randall noted that poor people in both rural and inner-city communities face enormous obstacles blocking their access to health care. How should those obstacles be addressed? Should government assume responsibility for delivery of health care to poor people? If so, should it do so by direct provision of benefits or indirectly by providing incentives for the private sector to increase service to poor people?

5. *Rationing and Discrimination.* Professor Randall argued that health care reform efforts were motivated primarily by cost-cutting desire, rather than by a wish to improve the quality of care. She further argued that a system of rationing care would disadvantage people based on their race and class. Do you agree? How could anti-discrimination provisions be structured to better prevent discrimination and enforce sanctions?

6. *Fundamental Right.* Professor Trubek argued that health care reform proposed universal coverage which would create a statutory right to health care. Why didn't Professor Randall share her optimism?

7. *Medicare.* Many elderly and disabled people receive health care through the Medicare program. Like Medicaid, Medicare is projected to grow at rate of about 10% per year as we approach and surpass the turn of the century. Unlike Medicaid, Medicare enjoys widespread public support. For a defense of Medicare, *see* William G. Dauster, *Protecting Social Security and Medicare*, 33 HARVARD JOURNAL ON LEGISLATION 461 (1996).

8. *State Flexibility and Social HMOs.* Some states have experimented with variations on a new social health maintenance organization model for low-income people. According to Professor Louise Trubek, these social HMOs follow one of two approaches, the workplace approach which merges Medicaid into workplace policies or the Medicaid approach which merges low-income working families into Medicaid. *See* Louise G. Trubek, *The Social HMO for Low-Income Families: Consumer Protection and Community Participation,* 26 SETON HALL LAW REVIEW 1143 (1996). Professor Trubek concludes, "Success in either system can be achieved only when regulation and oversight are combined with client voice, community participation, and sufficient funding." *Id.* at 1162.

CHAPTER 7: THE UNCONSTITUTIONAL CONDITIONS DILEMMA

One question repeatedly surfaces from judicial decisions involving constitutional challenges brought by poor people: do recipients waive their constitutional rights when they seek government welfare benefits? For an example of this problem, consider the following cases involving, first, the Fourth Amendment right to be free from unreasonable government searches and, second, the Fifth Amendment right to be free from uncompensated government taking of property.

WYMAN v. JAMES

400 U.S. 309 (1971)

Justice BLACKMUN delivered the opinion of the Court.

This appeal presents the issue whether a beneficiary of the program for Aid to Families with Dependent Children (AFDC) may refuse a home visit by the caseworker without risking the termination of benefits.

* * *

Plaintiff Barbara James is the mother of a son, Maurice, who was born in May 1967. They reside in New York City. Mrs. James first applied for AFDC assistance shortly before Maurice's birth. A caseworker made a visit to her apartment at that time without objection. The assistance was authorized.

Two years later, on May 8, 1969, a caseworker wrote Mrs. James that she would visit her home on May 14. Upon receipt of this advice, Mrs. James telephoned the worker that, although she was willing to supply information "reasonable and relevant" to her need for public assistance, any discussion was not to take place at her home. The worker told Mrs. James that she was required by law to visit in her home and that refusal to permit the visit would result in the termination of assistance. Permission was still denied.

On May 13 the City Department of Social Services sent Mrs. James a notice of intent to discontinue assistance because of the visitation refusal. The notice advised the beneficiary of her right to a hearing before a review officer. The hearing was requested and was held on May 27. Mrs. James appeared with an attorney at that hearing. They continued to refuse permission for a worker to visit the James home, but again expressed willingness to cooperate and to permit visits elsewhere. The review officer ruled that the refusal was a proper ground for the termination of assistance. His written decision stated:

> The home visit which Mrs. James refuses to permit is for the purpose of determining if there are any changes in her situation that might affect her eligibility to continue to receive Public Assistance, or that might affect the amount of such assistance, and to see if there are any social services which the Department of Social Services can provide to the family.

A notice of termination issued on June 2.

Thereupon, without seeking a hearing at the state level, Mrs. James, individually and on behalf of Maurice, and purporting to act on behalf of all other persons similarly situated, instituted the present civil rights suit under 42 U.S.C. § 1983. She alleged the denial of rights guaranteed to her under the First, Third, Fourth, Fifth, Sixth, Ninth, Tenth, and Fourteenth Amendments, and under Subchapters IV and XVI of the Social Security Act and regulations issued thereunder. She further alleged that she and her son have no income, resources, or support other than the benefits received under the AFDC program. She asked for declaratory and injunctive relief.

* * *

When a case involves a home and some type of official intrusion into that home, as this case appears to do, an immediate and natural reaction is one of concern about Fourth Amendment rights and the protection which that Amendment is intended to afford. Its emphasis indeed is upon one of the most precious aspects of personal security in the home: "The right of the people to be secure in their persons, houses, papers, and effects . . . ." This Court has characterized that right as "basic to a free society." And over the years the Court consistently has been most protective of the privacy of the dwelling.

* * *

This natural and quite proper protective attitude, however, is not a factor in this case, for the seemingly obvious and simple reason that we are not concerned here with any search by the New York social service agency in the Fourth Amendment meaning of that term.

It is true that the governing statute and regulations appear to make mandatory the initial home visit and the subsequent periodic "contacts" (which may include home visits) for the inception and continuance of aid. It is also true that the caseworker's posture in the home visit is perhaps, in a sense, both rehabilitative and investigative. But this latter aspect, we think, is given too broad a character and far more emphasis than it deserves if it is equated with a search in the traditional criminal law context. We note, too, that the visitation in itself is not forced or compelled, and that the beneficiary's denial of permission is not a criminal act. If consent to the visitation is withheld, no visitation takes place. The aid then never begins or merely ceases, as the case may be. There is no entry of the home and there is no search.

If however, we were to assume that a caseworker's home visit, before or subsequent to the beneficiary's initial qualification for benefits, somehow (perhaps because the average beneficiary might feel she is in no position to refuse consent to the visit), and despite its interview nature, does possess some of the characteristics of a search in the traditional sense, we nevertheless conclude that the visit does not fall within the Fourth Amendment's proscription. This is because it does not descend to the level of unreasonableness. It is unreasonableness which is the Fourth Amendment's standard.

* * *

There are a number of factors that compel us to conclude that the home visit proposed for Mrs. James is not unreasonable:

1. The public's interest in this particular segment of the area of assistance to the unfortunate is protection and aid for the dependent child whose family requires such aid for that child. The focus is on the *child* and, further, it is on the child who is *dependent*. There is no more worthy object of the public's concern. The dependent child's needs are paramount, and only with hesitancy would we relegate those needs, in the scale of comparative values, to a position secondary to what the mother claims as her rights.

2. The agency, with tax funds provided from federal as well as from state sources, is fulfilling a public trust. The State, working through its qualified welfare agency, has appropriate and paramount interest and concern in seeing and assuring that the intended and proper objects of that tax-produced assistance are the ones who benefit from the aid it dispenses. Surely it is not unreasonable, in the

Fourth Amendment sense or in any other sense of that term, that the State have at its command a gentle means, of limited extent and of practical and considerate application, of achieving that assurance.

3. One who dispenses purely private charity naturally has an interest in and expects to know how his charitable funds are utilized and put to work. The public, when it is the provider, rightly expects the same.

* * *

4. The emphasis of the New York statutes and regulations is upon the home, upon "close contact" with the beneficiary, upon restoring the aid recipient "to a condition of self-support," and upon the relief of his distress. The federal emphasis is no different. It is upon "assistance and rehabilitation," upon maintaining and strengthening family life, and upon "maximum self-support and personal independence consistent with the maintenance of continuing parental care and protection . . . ." It requires cooperation from the state agency upon specified standards and in specified ways. And it is concerned about any possible exploitation of the child.

5. The home visit, it is true, is not required by federal statute or regulation. But it has been noted that the visit is "the heart of welfare administration"; that it affords "a personal, rehabilitative orientation, unlike that of most federal programs"; and that the "more pronounced service orientation" effected by Congress with the 1956 amendments to the Social Security Act "gave redoubled importance to the practice of home visiting." The home visit is an established routine in States besides New York.

6. The means employed by the New York agency are significant. Mrs. James received written notice several days in advance of the intended home visit.[8] The date was specified. . . . Privacy is emphasized. The applicant-recipient is made the primary source of information as to eligibility. Outside informational sources, other than public records, are to be consulted only with the

[8] It is true that the record contains 12 affidavits, all essentially identical, of aid recipients (other than Mrs. James) which recite that a caseworker "most often" comes without notice; that when he does, the plans the recipient had for that time cannot be carried out; that the visit is "very embarrassing to me if the caseworker comes when I have company"; and that the caseworker "sometimes asks very personal questions" in front of children.

beneficiary's consent. Forcible entry or entry under false pretenses or visitation outside working hours or snooping in the home are forbidden. All this minimizes any "burden" upon the homeowner's right against unreasonable intrusion.

7. Mrs. James, in fact, on this record presents no specific complaint of any unreasonable intrusion of her home and nothing that supports an inference that the desired home visit had as its purpose the obtaining of information as to criminal activity. She complains of no proposed visitation at an awkward or retirement hour. She suggests no forcible entry. She refers to no snooping. She describes no impolite or reprehensible conduct of any kind. She alleges only, in general and nonspecific terms, that on previous visits and, on information and belief, on visitation at the home of other aid recipients, "questions concerning personal relationships, beliefs and behavior are raised and pressed which are unnecessary for a determination of continuing eligibility." Paradoxically, this same complaint could be made of a conference held elsewhere than in the home, and yet this is what is sought by Mrs. James. The same complaint could be made of the census taker's questions. What Mrs. James appears to want from the agency that provides her and her infant son with the necessities for life is the right to receive those necessities upon her own informational terms, to utilize the Fourth Amendment as a wedge for imposing those terms, and to avoid questions of any kind.[9]

8. We are not persuaded, as Mrs. James would have us be, that all information pertinent to the issue of eligibility can be obtained by the agency through an interview at a place other than the home, or, as the District Court majority suggested, by examining a lease or a birth certificate, or by periodic medical examinations, or by

---

[9]We have examined Mrs. James' case record with the New York City Department of Social Services, which, as an exhibit, accompanied defendant Wyman's answer. It discloses numerous interviews from the time of the initial one on April 27, 1967, until the attempted termination in June 1969. The record is revealing as to Mrs. James' failure ever really to satisfy the requirements for eligibility; as to constant and repeated demands; as to attitude toward the caseworker; as to reluctance to cooperate; as to evasiveness; and as to occasional belligerency. There are indications that all was not always well with the infant Maurice (skull fracture, a dent in the head, a possible rat bite). The picture is a sad and unhappy one.

interviews with school personnel. Although these secondary sources might be helpful, they would not always assure verification of actual residence or of actual physical presence in the home, which are requisites for AFDC benefits, or of impending medical needs. And, of course, little children, such as Maurice James, are not yet registered in school.

9. The visit is not one by police or uniformed authority. It is made by a caseworker of some training[11] whose primary objective is, or should be, the welfare, not the prosecution, of the aid recipient for whom the worker has profound responsibility. . . . The caseworker is not a sleuth but rather, we trust, is a friend to one in need.

10. The home visit is not a criminal investigation, does not equate with a criminal investigation, and despite the announced fears of Mrs. James and those who would join her, is not in aid of any criminal proceeding. If the visitation serves to discourage misrepresentation or fraud, such a byproduct of that visit does not impress upon the visit itself a dominant criminal investigative aspect. And if the visit should, by chance, lead to the discovery of fraud and a criminal prosecution should follow, then, even assuming that the evidence discovered upon the home visitation is admissible, an issue upon which we express no opinion, that is a routine and expected fact of life and a consequence no greater than that which necessarily ensues upon any other discovery by a citizen of criminal conduct.

11. The warrant procedure, which the plaintiff appears to claim to be so precious to her, even if civil in nature, is not without its seriously objectionable features in the welfare context. If a warrant could be obtained (the plaintiff affords us little help as to how it would be obtained), it presumably could be applied for *ex parte*, its execution would require no notice, it would justify entry by force, and its hours for execution would not be so limited as those

[11]The *amicus* brief submitted on behalf of the Social Services Employees Union . . . recites that "caseworkers are either badly trained or untrained" and that "[g]enerally, a caseworker is not only poorly trained, but also young and inexperienced. . . ." Despite this astonishing description by the union of the lack of qualification of its own members for the work they are employed to do, we must assume that the caseworker possesses at least some qualifications and some dedication to duty.

prescribed for home visitation. The warrant necessarily would imply conduct either criminal or out of compliance with an asserted governing standard. Of course, the force behind the warrant argument, welcome to the one asserting it, is the fact that it would have to rest upon probable cause, and probable cause in the welfare context, as Mrs. James concedes, requires more than the mere need of the caseworker to see the child in the home and to have assurance that the child is there and is receiving the benefit of the aid that has been authorized for it. In this setting the warrant argument is out of place.

It seems to us that the situation is akin to that where an Internal Revenue Service agent, in making a routine civil audit of a taxpayer's income tax return, asks that the taxpayer produce for the agent's review some proof of a deduction the taxpayer has asserted to his benefit in the computation of his tax. If the taxpayer refuses, there is, absent fraud, only a disallowance of the claimed deduction and a consequent additional tax. The taxpayer is fully within his "rights" in refusing to produce the proof, but in maintaining and asserting those rights a tax detriment results and it is a detriment of the taxpayer's own making. So here Mrs. James has the "right" to refuse the home visit, but a consequence in the form of cessation of aid, similar to the taxpayer's resultant additional tax, flows from that refusal. The choice is entirely hers, and nothing of constitutional magnitude is involved.

* * *

Mrs. James is not being prosecuted for her refusal to permit the home visit and is not about to be so prosecuted. Her wishes in that respect are fully honored. We have not been told, and have not found, that her refusal is made a criminal act by any applicable New York or federal statute. The only consequence of her refusal is that the payment of benefits ceases. Important and serious as this is, the situation is no different than if she had exercised a similar negative choice initially and refrained from applying for AFDC benefits.

* * *

Our holding today does not mean, of course, that a termination of benefits upon refusal of a home visit is to be upheld against constitutional challenge under all conceivable circumstances. The early morning mass raid upon homes of welfare recipients is not unknown. But that is not this case. Facts of that kind present another case for another day.

* * *

Justice DOUGLAS, dissenting.

We are living in a society where one of the most important forms of property is government largesse which some call the "new property." The payrolls of government are but one aspect of that "new property." Defense contracts, highway contracts, and the other multifarious forms of contracts are another part. So are subsidies to air, rail, and other carriers. So are disbursements by government for scientific research. So are TV and radio licenses to use the air space which of course is part of the public domain. Our concern here is not with those subsidies but with grants that directly or indirectly implicate the *home life* of the recipients.

In 1969 roughly 127 billion dollars were spent by the federal, state, and local governments on "social welfare." To farmers alone almost four billion dollars were paid, in part, for not growing certain crops. Almost 129,000 farmers received $5,000 or more, their total benefits exceeding $1,450,000,000. Those payments were in some instances very large, a few running a million or more a year. But the majority were payments under $5,000 each.

Yet almost every beneficiary whether rich or poor, rural or urban, has a "house"--one of the places protected by the Fourth Amendment against "unreasonable searches and seizures."[5] The question in this case is whether receipt of largesse from the government makes the *home* of the beneficiary subject to access by an inspector of the agency of oversight, even though the beneficiary objects to the intrusion and even though the Fourth Amendment's procedure for access to one's *house* or *home* is not followed. The penalty here is not, of course, invasion of the privacy of Barbara James, only her loss of federal or state largesse. That, however, is merely rephrasing the problem. Whatever the semantics, the central question is whether the government by force of its largesse has the

[5]"The right of the people to be secure in their persons, houses, papers, and effects, against unreasonable searches and seizures, shall not be violated, and no Warrants shall issue, but upon probable cause, supported by Oath or affirmation, and particularly describing the place to be searched, and the persons or things to be seized."

power to "buy up" rights guaranteed by the Constitution. But for the assertion of her constitutional right, Barbara James in this case would have received the welfare benefit.

* * *

"[T]he rule is that the right to continue the exercise of a privilege granted by the state cannot be made to depend upon the grantee's submission to a condition prescribed by the state which is hostile to the provisions of the federal Constitution."

* * *

If the regime under which Barbara James lives were enterprise capitalism as, for example, if she ran a small factory geared into the Pentagon's procurement program, she certainly would have a right to deny inspectors access to her home unless they came with a warrant.

* * *

Is a search of her home without a warrant made "reasonable" merely because she is dependent on government largesse?

Judge Skelly Wright has stated the problem succinctly:

> Welfare has long been considered the equivalent of charity and its recipients have been subjected to all kinds of dehumanizing experiences in the government's effort to police its welfare payments. In fact, over half a billion dollars are expended annually for administration and policing in connection with the Aid to Families with Dependent Children program. Why such large sums are necessary for administration and policing has never been adequately explained. No such sums are spent policing the government subsidies granted to farmers, airlines, steamship companies, and junk mail dealers, to name but a few. The truth is that in this subsidy area society has simply adopted a double standard, one for aid to business and the farmer and a different one for welfare.

If the welfare recipient was not Barbara James but a prominent, affluent cotton or wheat farmer receiving benefit payments for not growing crops, would not the approach be different? Welfare in aid of dependent children, like social security and unemployment benefits, has an aura of suspicion. There doubtless are frauds in every sector of public welfare whether the recipient be a Barbara James or someone who is prominent or influential. But constitutional rights--here the privacy of the *home*--are obviously not dependent on the poverty or on the affluence of the beneficiary. It is the precincts of the *home* that the Fourth Amendment protects; and their privacy is as important to the lowly as to the mighty.

* * *

Justice MARSHALL, whom Justice BRENNAN joins, dissenting.

* * *

Conceding for the sake of argument that someone might view the 'visitation' as a search, the majority nonetheless concludes that such a search is not unreasonable. . . . An unbroken line of cases holds that, subject to a few narrowly drawn exceptions, any search without a warrant is constitutionally unreasonable. In this case, no suggestion that evidence will disappear, that a criminal will escape, or that an officer will be injured, justifies the failure to obtain a warrant. Instead, the majority asserts what amounts to three state interests that allegedly render this search reasonable. None of these interests is sufficient to carve out a new exception to the warrant requirement.

First, it is argued that the home visit is justified to protect dependent children from "abuse" and "exploitation." These are heinous crimes, but they are not confined to indigent households. Would the majority sanction, in the absence of probable cause, compulsory visits to all American homes for the purpose of discovering child abuse? Or is this Court prepared to hold as a matter of constitutional law that a mother, merely because she is poor, is substantially more likely to injure or exploit her children? Such a categorical approach to an entire class of citizens would be dangerously at odds with the tenets of our democracy.

Second, the Court contends that caseworkers must enter the homes of AFDC beneficiaries to determine eligibility. Interestingly, federal regulations do not require the home visit. In fact, the regulations specify the recipient himself as the primary source of eligibility information thereby rendering an inspection of the home only one of several alternative secondary sources. The majority's implication that a biannual home visit somehow assures the verification of actual residence or actual physical presence in the home strains credulity in the context of urban poverty. Despite the caseworker's responsibility for dependent children, he is not even required to see the children as a part of the home visit. Appellants offer scant explanation for their refusal even to attempt to utilize public records, expenditure receipts, documents such as leases, non-home interviews, personal financial records, sworn declarations, etc.--all sources that governmental agencies regularly accept as adequate to establish eligibility for other public benefits. In this setting, it ill behooves appellants to refuse to utilize informational sources less drastic than an invasion of the privacy of the home.

We are told that the plight of Mrs. James is no different from that of a taxpayer who is required to document his right to a tax deduction, but this analogy is seriously flawed. The record shows that Mrs. James has offered to be interviewed anywhere other than her home, to answer any questions, and to provide any documentation that the welfare agency desires. The agency curtly refused all these offers and insisted on its "right" to pry into appellee's home. Tax exemptions are also governmental "bounty." A true analogy would be an Internal Revenue Service requirement that in order to claim a dependency exemption, a taxpayer *must* allow a specially trained IRS agent to invade the home for the purpose of questioning the occupants and looking for evidence that the exemption is being properly utilized for the benefit of the dependent. If such a system were even proposed, the cries of constitutional outrage would be unanimous.

Appellants offer a third state interest that the Court seems to accept as partial justification for this search. We are told that the visit is designed to rehabilitate, to provide aid. This is strange doctrine indeed. A paternalistic notion that a complaining citizen's constitutional rights can be violated so long as the State is somehow helping him is alien to our Nation's philosophy. More than 40 years ago, Justice Brandeis warned: "Experience should teach us to be most on our guard to protect liberty when the Government's purposes are beneficent."

* * *

Surely the majority cannot believe that valid Fourth Amendment consent can be given under the threat of the loss of one's sole means of support. Nor has Mrs. James waived her rights. Had the Court squarely faced the question of whether the State can condition welfare payments on the waiver of clear constitutional rights, the answer would be plain. The decisions of this Court do not support the notion that a State can use welfare benefits as a wedge to coerce "waiver" of Fourth Amendment rights.

* * *

I find no little irony in the fact that the burden of today's departure from principled adjudication is placed upon the lowly poor. Perhaps the majority has explained why a commercial warehouse deserves more protection than does this poor woman's home. I am not convinced; and, therefore, I must respectfully dissent.

Notes and Questions

1. *Ms. James' Choice.* The Supreme Court held that a required home visit by an AFDC caseworker was not a search within the meaning of the Fourth Amendment because it was not forced or compelled. Did Ms. James have a choice to deny the visit?

2. *Waiver of Constitutional Rights.* The Court then held that, even if the home visit constituted a search, it was not unreasonable. The first handful of reasons cited by the Court involved the public's interest in conducting the home visit. The other reasons defended the method by which the visit was to be conducted. But the Court returned several times to the argument that Ms. James was not forced to consent to the visit because she could choose instead to forego welfare benefits. The court noted that Ms. James wanted to use the Fourth Amendment to receive welfare on her own terms. If the Court had concluded that the home visit constituted an unreasonable search, would the resulting terms have been those of Ms. James or of the Constitution? Did Ms. James waive her right to Fourth Amendment or other constitutional protection when she applied for and accepted welfare benefits?

3. *Discrimination.* Justice Douglas in dissent was troubled by the discrimination between Ms. James and wealthier recipients of government benefits. Could an equal protection argument be made between different types of government benefits?

4. *Recipients of Government Interests.* Justices Marshall and Brennan in dissent argued that the government's interests were insufficient to justify the visit. How persuasive were their arguments? Did the majority respond to these arguments effectively?

BOWEN v. GILLIARD

483 U.S. 587 (1987)

Justice STEVENS delivered the opinion of the Court.

As part of its major effort to reduce the federal deficit through the Deficit Reduction Act of 1984, (DEFRA) Congress amended the statute authorizing Federal Aid to Families with Dependent Children (AFDC) to require that a family's eligibility for benefits must take into account, with certain specified exceptions, the income of all parents, brothers, and sisters living in the same home. The principal question presented in this litigation is whether that requirement violates the Fifth Amendment to the United States Constitution when it is applied to require a family wishing to receive AFDC benefits to include within its unit a child for whom child support payments are being made by a noncustodial parent.

* * *

[The net effect of DEFRA resulted in three changes:] (1) the addition of the child receiving support would enlarge the filing unit and entitle the family to a somewhat larger benefit; (2) child support would be treated as family income and would be assigned to the State, thereby reducing the AFDC benefits by that amount; and (3) the reduction would be offset by $50 if that amount was collected from an absent parent. In sum, if the assigned support exceeded $50 plus the difference in the benefit level caused by adding the child or children receiving support, the family would suffer; if less than $50 and the difference in the benefit level was collected as support, it would not.

* * *

The District Court was undoubtedly correct in its perception that a number of needy families have suffered, and will suffer, as a result of the implementation of the DEFRA amendments to the AFDC program. Such suffering is frequently the tragic byproduct of a decision to reduce or to modify benefits to a class of needy recipients. Under our structure of government, however, it is the function of Congress--not the courts--to determine whether the savings realized, and presumably used for other critical governmental functions, are significant enough to justify the costs to the individuals affected by such reductions. The Fifth Amendment "gives the federal courts no power to impose upon [Congress] their views of what constitutes wise economic or social policy," by telling it how "to reconcile the demands of . . . needy citizens with the finite resources available to meet those demands." *Dandridge v. Williams.* Unless the Legislative Branch's decisions run afoul of some constitutional edict, any inequities created by such decisions must be remedied by the democratic processes. The District Court believed that the amendment at issue did conflict with both the Due Process Clause and the Takings Clause of the Fifth Amendment. We consider these arguments in turn, and reject them.

The precepts that govern our review of appellees' due process and equal protection challenges to this program are similar to those we have applied in reviewing challenges to other parts of the Social Security Act: "[O]ur review is deferential. 'Governmental decisions to spend money to improve the general public welfare in one way and not another are "not confided to the courts. The discretion belongs to Congress unless the choice is clearly wrong, a display of arbitrary power, not an exercise of judgment.'" This standard of review is premised on Congress' "plenary power to define the scope and the duration of the entitlement to . . . benefits, and to increase, to decrease, or to terminate those benefits based on its appraisal of the relative importance of the recipients' needs and the resources available to fund the program."

The District Court had before it evidence that the DEFRA amendment was severely impacting some families. For example, some noncustodial parents stopped making their support payments because they believed that their payments were helping only the State, and not their children. It is clear, however, that in the administration of a fund that is large enough to have a significant impact on the Nation's deficit, general rules must be examined in light of the broad purposes they are intended to serve. The challenged amendment unquestionably serves Congress' goal of decreasing federal expenditures. The evidence that a few noncustodial parents were willing to violate the law by not making court-ordered support payments does not alter the fact that the entire program has resulted in saving huge sums of money.

The rationality of the amendment denying a family the right to exclude a supported child from the filing unit is also supported by the Government's separate interest in distributing benefits among competing needy families in a fair way. Given its perceived need to make cuts in the AFDC budget, Congress obviously sought to identify a group that would suffer less than others as a result of a reduction in benefits. When considering the plight of two five-person families, one of which receives no income at all while the other receives regular support payments for some of the minor children, it is surely reasonable for Congress to conclude that the former is in greater need than the latter. This conclusion is amply supported by Congress' assumption that child support payments received are generally beneficial to the entire family unit, and by "the common sense proposition that individuals living with others usually have reduced per capita costs because many of their expenses are shared."

It was therefore rational for Congress to adjust the AFDC program to reflect the fact that support money generally provides significant benefits for entire family units. This conclusion is not undermined by the fact that there are no doubt many families in which some--or perhaps all--of the support money is spent in a way that does not benefit the rest of the family. In determining how best to allocate limited funds among the extremely large class of needy families eligible for AFDC benefits, Congress is entitled to rely on a classwide presumption that custodial parents have used, and may legitimately use, support funds in a way that is beneficial to entire family units. As we have repeatedly explained: "If the classification has some 'reasonable basis,' it does not offend the Constitution simply because the classification 'is not made with mathematical nicety or because in practice it results in some inequality.'" "The problems of government are practical ones and may justify, if they do not require, rough accommodations--illogical, it may be, and unscientific." "A statutory discrimination will not be set aside if any state of facts reasonably may be conceived to justify it." We have no doubt that the DEFRA amendment satisfies this test.

* * *

Aside from holding that the amendment violated the Due Process Clause of the Fifth Amendment and its equal protection component, the District Court invalidated the DEFRA amendments as a taking of private property without just compensation. The court based this holding on the premise that a child for whom support payments are made has a right to have the support money used exclusively in his or her "best interest." Yet, the court reasoned, the requirements (1) that a custodial parent who applies for AFDC must include a child's support money in computing family income, and (2) that the support must be assigned to the State, effectively converts the support funds that were once to be used exclusively for the child's best interests into an AFDC check which, under federal law, must be used for the benefit of all the children. Therefore, the District Court held that the State was "taking" that child's right to exclusive use of the support money. In addressing this issue, it is helpful to look first at whether the State "takes" the child's property when it considers the support payments as part of the family's income in computing AFDC eligibility. We will then consider whether the requirement that support payments be assigned to the State requires a finding that the amendments violate the taking prohibition.

Some perspective on the issue is helpful here. Had no AFDC program ever existed until 1984, and had Congress then instituted a program that took into account support payments that a family receives, it is hard to believe that we would seriously entertain an argument that the new benefit program constituted a taking. Yet, somehow, once benefits are in place and Congress sees a need to reduce them in order to save money and to distribute limited resources more fairly, the "takings" label seems to have a bit more plausibility. For legal purposes though, the two situations are identical. Congress is not, by virtue of having instituted a social welfare program, bound to continue it at all, much less at the same benefit level. Thus, notwithstanding the technical legal arguments that have been advanced, it is imperative to recognize that the amendments at issue merely incorporate a definitional element into an entitlement program. It would be quite strange indeed if, by virtue of an offer to provide benefits to needy families through the entirely voluntary AFDC program, Congress or the States were deemed to have taken some of those very family members' property.

The basic requirement that the AFDC filing unit must include all family members living in the home, and therefore that support payments made on behalf of a member of the family must be considered in determining that family's level of benefits, does not even arguably take anyone's property. The family members other than the child for whom the support is being paid certainly have no takings claim, since it is clear that they have no protected property rights to continued benefits at the same level. Nor does the simple inclusion of the support income in the benefit calculation have any legal effect on the child's right to have it used for his or her benefit. To the extent that a child has the right to have the support payments used in his or her "best interest," he or she fully retains that right. Of course, the effect of counting the support payments as part of the filing unit's income often reduces the family's resources, and hence increases the chances that sharing of the support money will be appropriate. But given the unquestioned premise that the Government has a right to reduce AFDC benefits generally, that result does not constitute a taking of private property without just compensation.

The only possible legal basis for appellees' takings claim, therefore, is the requirement that an applicant for AFDC benefits must assign the support payments to the State, which then will remit the amount collected to the custodial parent to be used for the benefit of the entire family. This legal transformation in the status of the funds, the argument goes, modifies the child's interest in the use of the money so dramatically that it constitutes a taking of the child's property. As a practical matter, this argument places form over substance, and labels over reality. Although it is true that money which was earmarked for a specific child's or children's "best interest" becomes a part of a larger fund available for all of the children, the difference between these concepts is, as we have discussed, more theoretical than practical.[20]

In evaluating whether governmental regulation of property constitutes a "taking" we have "eschewed the development of any set formula . . . and have relied instead on ad hoc, factual inquiries into the circumstances of each particular case." "To aid in this determination, however, we have identified three factors which have

[20]In analyzing the effect of the assignment it is again instructive to ask what would happen to the support payments if there were no AFDC program at all. In that case, it would appear that custodial parents would have to use a much greater portion of the support payments to sustain the family unit, since it could hardly be deemed in the child's best interest for his custodial parent and siblings to have no funds whatsoever. The overall practical effect of the AFDC program (even after the 1984 amendments), therefore, is to enhance the probability that a child whose custodial parent is receiving support payments in the child's behalf will obtain direct economic benefit from those funds, in addition to the benefits that result from preserving the family unit. A reduction in that enhancement is no more a taking than any other reduction in a Social Security program.

'particular significance': (1) 'the economic impact of the regulation on the claimant'; (2) 'the extent to which the regulation has interfered with distinct investment-backed expectations'; and (3) 'the character of the governmental action.'" Here, each of these three factors refutes the conclusion that there has been a taking.

First, in evaluating the economic impact of the assignment, it is important to remember that it is the impact on the child, not on the entire family unit, that is relevant. Thus, the fact that the entire family's net income may be reduced does not necessarily mean that the amount of money spent for the benefit of a supported child will be any less than the amount of the noncustodial parent's support payments. The reality is that the money will usually continue to be used in the same manner that it was previously since the typical AFDC parent will have used the support money as part of the general family fund even without its being transferred through AFDC. Moreover, any diminution in the value of the support payments for the child is mitigated by the extra $50 that the family receives as a result of the assignment, by the extra AFDC benefits that are received by the inclusion of an additional family member in the unit, and by the fact that the State is using its own enforcement power to collect the support payments, and is bearing the risk of nonpayment in any given month. Whatever the diminution in value of the child's right to have support funds used for his or her "exclusive" benefit may be, it is not so substantial as to constitute a taking under our precedents.

Second, the child receiving support payments holds no vested protectable expectation that his or her parent will continue to receive identical support payments on the child's behalf, and that the child will enjoy the same rights with respect to them. The prospective right to support payments, and the child's expectations with respect to the use of such funds, are clearly subject to modification by law, be it through judicial decree, state legislation, or congressional enactment. For example, one of the chief criteria in assessing a child support obligation is the noncustodial parent's ability to make payments, and an adverse change in that parent's ability may, of course, require a modification of the decree. Any right to have the State force a noncustodial parent to make payments is, like so many other legal rights (including AFDC payments themselves), subject to modification by "the public acts of government." As the District Court explained, Congress, and the States, through their implementing statutes and regulations, have modified those rights through passage of (and the States' compliance with) the DEFRA amendments. This prospective change in the child's expectations concerning future use of support payments is far from anything we have ever deemed a taking.

Finally, the character of the governmental action here militates against a finding that the States or Federal Government unconstitutionally take property through the AFDC program. It is obviously necessary for the Government to make hard choices and to balance various incentives in deciding how to allocate benefits in this type of program. But a decision to include child support as part of the family income certainly does not implicate the type of concerns that the Takings Clause protects. This is by no means an enactment that forces "some people alone to bear public burdens which, in all fairness and justice, should be borne by the public as a whole."

The law does not require any custodial parent to apply for AFDC benefits. Surely it is reasonable to presume that a parent who does make such an application does so because she or he is convinced that the family as a whole--as well as each child committed to her or his custody--will be better off with the benefits than without. In making such a decision, the parent is not taking a child's property without just compensation; nor is the State doing so when it responds to that decision by supplementing the collections of support money with additional AFDC benefits.

* * *

The judgment of the District Court is reversed.

Justice BRENNAN, with whom Justice MARSHALL joins, dissenting.

Government in the modern age has assumed increasing responsibility for the welfare of its citizens. This expansion of responsibility has been accompanied by an increase in the scale and complexity of the activities that government conducts. Respect for the enormity of the administrative task that confronts the modern welfare state, as well as for the scarcity of government resources, counsels that public officials enjoy discretion in determining the most effective means of fulfilling their responsibilities.

The very pervasiveness of modern government, however, creates an unparalleled opportunity for intrusion on personal life. In a society in which most persons receive some form of government benefit, government has considerable leverage in shaping individual behavior. In most cases, we acknowledge that government may wield its power even when its actions likely influence choices involving personal behavior. On certain occasions, however, government intrusion into private life is so direct and substantial that we must deem it intolerable if we are to be true to our belief that there is a boundary between the public citizen and the private person.

This is such a case. The Government has told a child who lives with a mother receiving public assistance that it cannot both live with its mother and be supported by its father. The child must either leave the care and custody of the mother, or forgo the support of the father and become a Government client. The child is put to this choice not because it seeks Government benefits for itsclf, but because of a fact over which it has no control: the need of other household members for public assistance. A child who lives with one parent has, under the best of circumstances, a difficult time sustaining a relationship with both its parents. A crucial bond between a child and its parent outside the home, usually the father, is the father's commitment to care for the material needs of the child, and the expectation of the child that it may look to its father for such care. The Government has thus decreed that a condition of welfare eligibility for a mother is that her child surrender a vital connection with either the father or the mother.

The Court holds that the Government need only show a rational basis for such action. This standard of review has regularly been used in evaluating the claims of applicants for Government benefits, since "a noncontractual claim to receive funds from the public treasury enjoys no constitutionally protected status." Plaintiff child support recipients in this case, however, are children who wish not to receive public assistance, but to continue to be supported by their noncustodial parent. Their claim is not that the Government has unfairly denied them benefits, but that it has intruded deeply into their relationship with their parents. More than a mere rational basis is required to withstand this challenge, and, as the following analysis shows, the Government can offer no adequate justification for doing such damage to the parent-child relationship.

* * *

Julie A. Nice

MAKING CONDITIONS CONSTITUTIONAL BY ATTACHING THEM TO WELFARE: THE DANGERS OF SELECTIVE CONTEXTUAL IGNORANCE OF THE UNCONSTITUTIONAL CONDITIONS DOCTRINE

72 DENVER UNIVERSITY LAW REVIEW 971 (1995)

* * *

The Fifth Amendment's Takings Clause prohibits government from taking private property for public use without just compensation. In recent years, the Supreme Court has applied heightened scrutiny to regulatory takings made by the government. Specifically, in *Nollan v. California Coastal Commission*,[72] the Court established heightened scrutiny as the proper standard of review and struck down the government's condition that a homeowner provide a public access easement along a beach because the condition bore an insufficient relation to a legitimate government interest.

***Nollan*'s (and *Dolan*'s) Heightened Scrutiny**

The Supreme Court in *Nollan* established heightened scrutiny as the proper standard for reviewing the California Coastal Commission's condition that the Nollans provide a public easement along their beach-front property in exchange for a building permit to replace a bungalow with a three-bedroom home. Writing for the majority, Justice Scalia invoked the "long recognized" requirement that the government prove that its taking substantially advances legitimate state interests. He acknowledged that the government held the greater power to prohibit construction of the house, and that it might have held the lesser power to condition construction upon some concession by the owner. Justice Scalia's analysis did not end, however, with the "greater power includes the lesser power" concession. He further required that, in order for the condition to not constitute extortion, it had to survive his "essential nexus" test, meaning that the condition must further the same end served by the outright prohibition. Because the Court found that the public access

[72]483 U.S. 825 (1987). I focus on *Nollan*, rather than *Dolan* [*v. City of Tigard*, 114 S. Ct. 2309 (1994)], because it was decided in such close proximity (the day after) to the welfare benefits case I use for comparison, *Bowen v. Gilliard*, 483 U.S. 587 (1987).

easement condition did not serve the same ends as prohibition of construction, it struck down the easement condition as a violation of the Takings Clause.

Later, in *Dolan v. City of Tigard*, the Court explicitly adopted the unconstitutional conditions doctrine, reaffirmed *Nollan*'s heightened scrutiny for takings conditions, and required the government to prove that its condition served its justification with "rough proportionality."

***Gilliard*'s Mere Rationality**

The day before it applied strict scrutiny to strike down a condition on use of real property in *Nollan*, the Court decided *Bowen v. Gilliard*. In *Gilliard*, the Court applied mere rationality to uphold against a takings challenge two related government conditions to welfare benefits. The first condition required inclusion of a child not in need of welfare into the welfare family unit. The second condition required assignment of that child's parental support payments to the state to repay the family's welfare benefits. The relevant issue in *Gilliard* was whether the government's taking of these parental support payments that belonged to the non-needy child violated the Fifth Amendment's Takings Clause.

The majority in *Gilliard* rejected heightened scrutiny and went to some lengths to establish mere rationality as the appropriate level of review. They purportedly invoked rationality review in deference to Congress' authority to determine how to allocate government benefits enacted pursuant to its plenary power to make spending decisions. They also reiterated a string-cite from *Dandridge v. Williams* that sets out various statements of the rationality standard. Applying this rationality review, they concluded that the provision requiring assignment of a child's parental support payments to the government unquestionably served Congress' goal of decreasing federal expenditures, and rationally served the government's interest in allocating benefits among needy families.

When the Court examined whether the *inclusion* of a child's parental support payments in computing the rest of the family's income constituted a taking, it adopted a no-benefits baseline, applied the "greater power includes the lesser power" argument, then upheld the inclusion requirement. After finding that the government's greater power to deny welfare includes the lesser power to condition it, the Court did not subject the inclusion requirement to any additional scrutiny similar to the heightened scrutiny for regulatory takings it established in *Nollan* the following day.

When considering *assignment* of the child support payments to the government, however, the Court considered the three factors it normally evaluates for takings analysis: the economic impact of the taking, the expectation in the property interest, and the character of the government action. First, the Court minimized the economic impact of the assignment on the child by assuming that AFDC parents would spread all available income to support the family, no matter its source. Second, the Court minimized the child's expectation of continued receipt of support payments, reasoning that support payments are not fixed but may be modified by law.

In analyzing the third factor, the Court's view of welfare again played the pivotal role. Regarding the character of the government's action in requiring assignment of child support payments, the Court opined that welfare requires government "to make hard choices and to balance various incentives" in allocating funds. More importantly, the Court again invoked the choice argument, stating,

> [t]he law does not require any custodial parent to apply for AFDC benefits. Surely it is reasonable to presume that a parent who does make such an application does so because she or he is convinced that the family as a whole—as well as each child committed to her or his custody—will be better off with the benefits than without.

Although the Court appeared to apply takings analysis to the assignment condition, it jettisoned normal scrutiny midstream, again relying on the nature of welfare to justify lower scrutiny. The Court then concluded its decision as it had begun, by reiterating its commitment to mere rationality for conditions affecting welfare because "the intractable economic, social, and even philosophical problems presented by public welfare assistance programs are not the business of this Court."

Comparing *Nollan/Dolan* with *Gilliard*

How are building permits different than welfare benefits for the purpose of scrutinizing arguably unconstitutional conditions? First, the government has the greater power to deny both building permits and welfare benefits, so neither benefit is an absolute right. In both instances, government acts indirectly, rather than directly. Second, both applicants have a choice of whether to request the benefit or not. Third, both conditions are neutral insofar as they do not target any subset of applicants, but apply to all. Fourth, *Nollan* and *Dolan* did not involve any more affirmative compulsion by the government than did *Gilliard.* Fifth, courts typically give great deference to the legislatures in both land use regulation and welfare administration. Finally, both involve legitimate government interests: environmental protection and cost-saving. Thus, they seem to present similar unconstitutional conditions problems. Yet the Court treated them differently. Again, perhaps the reason is that building permits are popular and welfare benefits are not.

The votes in *Nollan* and *Gilliard* turned on whether (popular) property rights, or (unpopular) welfare benefits were at issue. Now-Chief Justice Rehnquist, and Justices White, Powell, O'Connor, and Scalia applied heightened scrutiny to invalidate the public access easement condition in *Nollan.* These same justices applied only rationality review to uphold the parental support assignment condition in *Gilliard.* Similarly, Justices Brennan, Marshall, and Blackmun would have applied rationality review and would have upheld the public access easement condition in *Nollan.* These same justices would have applied heightened scrutiny and would have invalidated the parental support assignment condition in *Gilliard.*

The primary differences between *Nollan* and *Gilliard* were (1) the property at issue—real property as compared to child support payments, and (2) the benefit at issue—building permits as compared to welfare grants. The Court's analyses in the two cases, however, turned not on the difference in the property at issue, but rather on the difference in benefits at issue. Building permit conditions received strict scrutiny while welfare benefit conditions received mere rationality review. But both involved takings challenges, so the same test should have applied.

Comparing *Nollan* and *Gilliard* reveals the Court's context-driven dichotomy that disadvantages welfare benefits but not other government benefits. In *Nollan*, the Court applied heightened scrutiny to a building permit condition and determined that it was invalid. But when reviewing a condition attached to welfare, the Court refused to apply the unconstitutional conditions doctrine (as it was urged to do, in effect, by Justice Brennan in dissent), and instead invoked its antithesis, the "greater power includes the lesser power" argument, to first circumvent and then dispose of normal takings analysis. The Court insisted, both at the beginning and at the end of *Gilliard*, that, for welfare benefits, the context necessarily limits judicial scrutiny to mere rationality, regardless of the constitutional doctrine at issue.

* * *

Notes and Questions

1. *Unconstitutional Conditions Doctrine.* In many decisions involving conditions attached to government benefits, the Supreme Court emphasizes that the government has no obligation to provide the benefit at all, but voluntarily chooses to do so, and that recipients do not have to apply for the benefit, but voluntarily choose to do so. Thus, the offer and acceptance of benefits results from a voluntary exchange on both sides. Should the voluntariness of the exchange render the Constitution inapplicable? Or, in other words, when the government acts as a party to a contract, is it immune from normal constitutional restrictions on its conduct?

2. *Spending Power.* When the federal government spends money, it acts pursuant to the power granted to Congress by the Spending Clause. Does the Spending Clause give Congress plenary power to attach any strings it desires to federal funds? Consider the Spending Clause test established in *South Dakota v. Dole*, 483 U.S. 203 (1987) requiring that Congressional spending must: 1) further the general welfare; 2) unambiguously state the conditions so that states can exercise an informed choice; 3) be related to the federal interest in national projects or programs; and 4) not violate other constitutional provisions. Does the final requirement, that spending not violate other constitutional provisions, have the same effect as the Unconstitutional Conditions Doctrine?

Exercises

1. *Workfare.* In the Temporary Assistance for Needy Families block grant program, Congress mandates that states require parents to participate in "community service employment" after receiving 2 months of benefits, unless a state opts out. Congress also mandates that states require parents to "engage in work" once they are ready or have received benefits for 2 years, whichever comes first. Can the government require welfare recipients to engage in certain work as a condition of receiving welfare benefits? For an argument

that workfare violates the Thirteenth Amendment's prohibition against involuntary servitude, *see* Julie A. Nice, *Welfare Servitude,* 1 GEORGETOWN JOURNAL ON FIGHTING POVERTY 340 (1994)(excerpted in Chapter 10).

2. *Reproductive Restrictions.*

a) *Norplant.* Proposals to encourage or require women receiving welfare benefits to use the contraceptive Norplant have received considerable attention in both mainstream media and law review articles. Determine the constitutionality of the various proposals which follow.

> i) *Mandates.* Suppose that a state restricts welfare benefits to women who agree to use Norplant to prevent pregnancy. Can the government require recipients to surrender their constitutional right to reproductive choice in exchange for welfare benefits? *See* Susan Frelich Appleton, *Standards for Constitutional Review of Privacy-Invading Welfare Reforms: Distinguishing the Abortion-Funding Cases and Redeeming the Undue-Burden Test,* 49 VANDERBILT LAW REVIEW 1 (1996); Catherine R. Albiston and Laura Beth Nielsen, *Welfare Queens and Other Fairy Tales: Welfare Reform and Unconstitutional Reproductive Controls,* 38 HOWARD LAW JOURNAL 473 (1995); Laurence C. Nolan, *The Unconstitutional Conditions Doctrine and Mandating Norplant for Women on Welfare*, 3 AMERICAN UNIVERSITY JOURNAL ON GENDER AND THE LAW 15 (1994); Linda M. Merritt, *Birth Control Incentives for Welfare Mothers,* 3 KANSAS JOURNAL OF LAW & PUBLIC POLICY 171 (1994). Compare a denial of welfare, unless the recipient uses Norplant, to a denial of marriage license, unless the recipient pays child support, discussed in Chapter 9.
>
> ii) *Benefit Bonuses.* Suppose that a state merely offers a bonus to recipients who agree to use Norplant. Is that constitutional? *See* David S. Coale, *Norplant Bonuses and the Unconstitutional Conditions Doctrine,* 71 TEXAS LAW REVIEW 189 (1992); John Robert Hand, *Buying Fertility: The Constitutionality of Welfare Bonuses for Welfare Mothers Who Submit to Norplant Insertion*, 46 VANDERBILT LAW REVIEW 715 (1993).

iii) *Cost Subsidies.* Suppose instead that a state offers Norplant to welfare recipients for free, or for a nominal fee. Is that constitutional? *See* Anne-Marie Funk, *Norplant Use in Conjunction with the Welfare System,* 2 SOUTHERN CALIFORNIA INTERDISCIPLINARY LAW JOURNAL 147 (1993). Compare cost subsidies of Norplant to refusals to fund abortion discussed in Chapter 9.

b) *Child Exclusion.* Suppose a state simply refuses to provide benefits when a child is born into a family on welfare. Is that constitutional? *See* Laura M. Friedman, *Family Cap and the Unconstitutional Conditions Doctrine: Scrutinizing a Welfare Woman's Right to Bear Children,* 56 OHIO STATE LAW JOURNAL 637 (1995). Consider the discussion of Child Exclusion in Chapter 9.

3. *Other Welfare Reform Programs.* What other rules or programs devised as part of federal or state welfare reform might present unconstitutional conditions challenges?

SECTION III: INTEGRATING THEORY AND PRACTICE

CHAPTER 8: WELFARE REFORM

For sixty years, the basic structure of welfare remained largely unchanged. Although critics never ceased lamenting various problems with welfare, no radical restructuring resulted. Then along came Charles Murray in 1984 with his bold proposal that government welfare be eliminated. Murray dared to write what many others believed beyond reasonable debate: that survival of the fittest should run its course, leaving poor people with only private alternatives to meet their subsistence needs.

Murray's proposal spawned more than a decade of ongoing debate, no longer about whether, but now about how, to reform welfare. Congress responded with the Family Support Act (FSA) of 1988, designed to provide support for its requirements that recipients move from welfare to work. Another round of Congressional reform in 1995 and 1996 culminated in the Personal Responsibility and Work Opportunity Reconciliation Act (PRA) of 1996. In this legislation, Congress continued its commitment to moving recipients from welfare to work by requiring that recipients engage in work as soon as the state determines they are ready, or once they have received benefits for 2 years, whichever happens first. Congress did not stop there. It completely abolished Aid to Families with Dependent Children (AFDC), ended the federally-based entitlement of welfare benefits to all eligible applicants, replaced it with the Temporary Assistance for Needy Families (TANF) block grant system of providing lump sums of federal dollars to states, authorized states to use the funds in any manner "reasonably calculated" to accomplish the purposes of the statute, and prohibited recipients from receiving benefits for more than 5 years.

To understand contemporary welfare reform, one must begin with the first strike, Charles Murray's proposal to end welfare.

A. PERSPECTIVES ON WELFARE REFORM

1. The Debate

Charles Murray

LOSING GROUND: AMERICAN SOCIAL POLICY 1950-1980 (1984)

A Proposal for Public Welfare

I begin with the proposition that it is within our resources to do enormous good for some people quickly. We have available to us a program that would convert a large proportion of the younger generation of hardcore unemployed into steady workers making a living wage. The same program would drastically reduce births to single teenage girls. It would reverse the trendline in the breakup of poor families. It would measurably increase the upward socioeconomic mobility of poor families. These improvements would affect some millions of persons.

All these are results that have eluded the efforts of the social programs installed since 1965, yet, from everything we know, there is no real question about whether they would occur under the program I propose. A wide variety of persuasive evidence from our own culture and around the world, from experimental data and longitudinal studies, from theory and practice, suggests that the program would achieve such results.

The proposed program, our final and most ambitious thought experiment, consists of scrapping the entire federal welfare and income-support structure for working-aged persons, including AFDC, Medicaid, Food Stamps, Unemployment Insurance, Worker's Compensation, subsidized housing, disability insurance, and the rest. It would leave the working-aged person with no recourse whatsoever except the job market, family members, friends, and public or private locally funded services. It is the Alexandrian solution: cut the knot, for there is no way to untie it.

It is difficult to examine such a proposal dispassionately. Those who dislike paying for welfare are for it without thinking. Others reflexively imagine bread lines and people starving in the streets. But as a means of gaining fresh perspective on the problem of effective reform, let us consider what this hypothetical society might look like.

A large majority of the population is unaffected. A surprising number of the huge American middle and working classes go from birth to grave without using any social welfare benefits until they receive their first Social Security check. Another portion of the population is technically affected, but the change in income is so small or so sporadic that it makes no difference in quality of life. A third group comprises persons who have to make new arrangements and behave in different ways. Sons and daughters who fail to find work continue to live with their parents or relatives or friends. Teenaged mothers have to rely on support from their parents or the father of the child and perhaps work as well. People laid off from work have to use their own savings or borrow from others to make do until the next job is found. All these changes involve great disruption in expectations and accustomed roles.

Along with the disruptions go other changes in behavior. Some parents do not want their young adult children continuing to live off their income, and become quite insistent about their children learning skills and getting jobs. This attitude is most prevalent among single mothers who have to depend most critically on the earning power of their offspring.

Parents tend to become upset at the prospect of a daughter's bringing home a baby that must be entirely supported on an already inadequate income. Some become so upset that they spend considerable parental energy avoiding such an eventuality. Potential fathers of such babies find themselves under more pressure not to cause such a problem, or to help with its solution if it occurs.

Adolescents who were not job-ready find they are job-ready after all. It turns out that they can work for low wages and accept the discipline of the workplace if the alternative is grim enough. After a few years, many--not all, but many--find that they have acquired salable skills, or that they are at the right place at the right time, or otherwise find that the original entry-level job has gradually been transformed into a secure job paying a decent wage. A few--not a lot, but a few--find that the process leads to affluence.

Perhaps the most rightful, deserved benefit goes to the much larger population of low-income families who have been doing things right all along and have been punished for it: the young man who has taken responsibility for his wife and child even though his friends with the same choice have called him a fool; the single mother who has worked full time and forfeited her right to welfare for very little extra money; the parents who have set an example for their children even as the rules of the game have taught their children that the example is outmoded. For these millions of people, the instantaneous result is that no one makes fun of them any longer. The longer-term result will be that they regain the status that is properly theirs. They will not only be the bedrock upon which the community is founded (which they always have been), they will be recognized as such. The process whereby they regain their position is not magical, but a matter of logic. When it becomes highly dysfunctional for a person to be dependent, status will accrue to being independent, and in fairly short order. Noneconomic rewards will once again reinforce the economic rewards of being a good parent and provider.

The prospective advantages are real and extremely plausible. In fact, if a government program of the traditional sort (one that would "do" something rather than simply get out of the way) could *as plausibly* promise these advantages, its passage would be a foregone conclusion. Congress, yearning for programs that are not retreads of failures, would be prepared to spend billions. Negative side-effects (as long as they were the traditionally acceptable negative side-effects) would be brushed aside as trivial in return for the benefits. For let me be quite clear: I am not suggesting that we dismantle income support for the working-aged to balance the budget or punish welfare cheats. I am hypothesizing, with the advantage of powerful collateral evidence, that the lives of large numbers of poor people would be radically changed for the better.

There is, however, a fourth segment of the population yet to be considered, those who are pauperized by the withdrawal of government supports and unable to make alternate arrangements: the teenaged mother who has no one to turn to; the incapacitated or the inept who are thrown out of the house; those to whom economic conditions have brought long periods in which there is no work to be had; those with illnesses not covered by insurance. What of these situations?

The first resort is the network of local services. Poor communities in our hypothetical society are still dotted with storefront health clinics, emergency relief agencies, employment services, legal services. They depend for support on local taxes or local philanthropy, and the local taxpayers and philanthropists tend to scrutinize them rather closely. But, by the same token, they also receive considerably more resources than they formerly did. The dismantling of the federal services has poured tens of billions of dollars back into the private economy. Some of that money no doubt has been spent on Mercedes and summer homes on the Cape. But some has been spent on capital investments that generate new jobs. And some has been spent on increased local services to the poor, voluntarily or as decreed by the municipality. In many cities, the coverage provided by this network of agencies is more generous, more humane, more wisely distributed, and more effective in its results than the services formerly subsidized by the federal government.

But we must expect that a large number of people will fall between the cracks. How might we go about trying to retain the advantages of a zero-level welfare system and still address the residual needs?

As we think about the nature of the population still in need, it becomes apparent that their basic problem in the vast majority of cases is the lack of a job, and this problem is temporary. What they need is something to tide them over while finding a new place in the economy. So our first step is to re-install the Unemployment Insurance program in more or less its previous form. Properly administered, unemployment insurance makes sense. Even if it is restored with all the defects of current practice, the negative effects of Unemployment Insurance *alone* are relatively minor. Our objective is not to wipe out chicanery or to construct a theoretically unblemished system, but to meet legitimate human needs without doing more harm than good. Unemployment Insurance is one of the least harmful ways of contributing to such ends. Thus the system has been amended to take care of the victims of short-term swings in the economy.

Who is left? We are now down to the hardest of the hard core of the welfare-dependent. They have no jobs. They have been unable to find jobs (or have not tried to find jobs) for a longer period of time than the unemployment benefits cover. They have no families who will help. They have no friends who will help. For some reason, they cannot get help from local services or private charities except for the soup kitchen and a bed in the Salvation Army hall.

What will be the size of this population? We have never tried a zero-level federal welfare system under conditions of late-twentieth-century national wealth, so we cannot do more than speculate. But we may speculate. Let us ask of whom the population might consist and how they might fare.

For any category of "needy" we may name, we find ourselves driven to one of two lines of thought. Either the person is in a category that is going to be at the top of the list of services that localities vote for themselves, and at the top of the list of private services, or the person is in a category where help really is not all that essential or desirable. The burden of the conclusion is not that every single person will be taken care of, but that the extent of resources to deal with needs is likely to be very great--not based on wishful thinking, but on extrapolations from reality.

To illustrate, let us consider the plight of the stereotypical welfare mother--never married, no skills, small children, no steady help from a man. It is safe to say that, now as in the 1950s, there is no one who has less sympathy from the white middle class, which is to be the source of most of the money for the private and local services we envision. Yet this same white middle class is a soft touch for people trying to make it on their own, and a soft touch for "deserving" needy mothers--AFDC was one of the most widely popular of the New Deal welfare measures, intended as it was for widows with small children. Thus we may envision two quite different scenarios.

In one scenario, the woman is presenting the local or private service with this proposition: "Help me find a job and day-care for my children, and I will take care of the rest." In effect, she puts herself into the same category as the widow and the deserted wife--identifies herself as one of the most obviously deserving of the deserving poor. Welfare mothers who want to get into the labor force are likely to find a wide range of help. In the other scenario, she asks for an outright and indefinite cash grant--in effect, a private or local version of AFDC--so that she can stay with the children and not hold a job. In the latter case, it is very easy to imagine situations in which she will not be able to find a local service or a private philanthropy to provide the help she seeks. The question we must now ask is: What's so bad about that? If children were always better off being with their mother all day and if, by the act of giving birth, a mother acquired the inalienable right to be with the child, then her situation would be unjust to her and injurious to her children. Neither assertion can be defended, however--especially not in the 1980s, when more mothers of all classes work away from the home

Grand specul.

than ever before, and even more especially not in view of the empirical record for the children growing up under the current welfare system. Why should the mother be exempted by the system from the pressures that must affect everyone else's decision to work?

As we survey these prospects, important questions remain unresolved. The first of these is why, if federal social transfers are treacherous, should locally mandated transfers be less so? Why should a municipality be permitted to legislate its own AFDC or Food Stamp program if their results are so inherently bad?

Part of the answer lies in conceptions of freedom. I have deliberately avoided raising them--the discussion is about how to help the disadvantaged, not about how to help the advantaged cut their taxes, to which arguments for personal freedom somehow always get diverted. Nonetheless, the point is valid: Local or even state systems leave much more room than a federal system for everyone, donors and recipients alike, to exercise freedom of choice about the kind of system they live under. Laws are more easily made and changed, and people who find them unacceptable have much more latitude in going somewhere more to their liking.

But the freedom of choice argument, while legitimate, is not necessary. We may put the advantages of local systems in terms of the Law of Imperfect Selection. A federal system must inherently employ very crude, inaccurate rules for deciding who gets what kind of help. . . . At the opposite extreme--a neighbor helping a neighbor, a family member helping another family member--the law loses its validity nearly altogether. Very fine-grained judgments based on personal knowledge are being made about specific people and changing situations. In neighborhoods and small cities, the procedures can still bring much individualized information to bear on decisions. Even systems in large cities and states can do much better than a national system; a decaying industrial city in the Northeast and a booming sunbelt city of the same size can and probably should adopt much different rules about who gets what and how much.

A final and equally powerful argument for not impeding local systems is diversity. We know much more in the 1980s than we knew in the 1960s about what does not work. We have a lot to learn about what *does* work. Localities have been a rich source of experiments. Marva Collins in Chicago gives us an example of how a school can bring inner-city students up to national norms. Sister

Falaka Fattah in Philadelphia shows us how homeless youths can be rescued from the streets. There are numberless such lessons waiting to be learned from the diversity of local efforts. By all means, let a hundred flowers bloom, and if the federal government can play a useful role in lending a hand and spreading the word of successes, so much the better.

The ultimate unresolved question about our proposal to abolish income maintenance for the working-aged is how many people will fall through the cracks. In whatever detail we try to foresee the consequences, the objection may always be raised: We cannot be *sure* that everyone will be taken care of in the degree to which we would wish. But this observation by no means settles the question. If one may point in objection to the child now fed by Food Stamps who would go hungry, one may also point with satisfaction to the child who would have an entirely different and better future. Hungry children should be fed; there is no argument about that. It is no less urgent that children be allowed to grow up in a system free of the forces that encourage them to remain poor and dependent. If a strategy reasonably promises to remove those forces, after so many attempts to "help the poor" have failed, it is worth thinking about.

But that rationale is too vague. Let me step outside the persona I have employed and put the issue in terms of one last intensely personal hypothetical example. Let us suppose that you, a parent, could know that tomorrow your own child would be made an orphan. You have a choice. You may put your child with an extremely poor family, so poor that your child will be badly clothed and will indeed sometimes be hungry. But you also know that the parents have worked hard all their lives, will make sure your child goes to school and studies, and will teach your child that independence is a primary value. Or you may put your child with a family with parents who have never worked, who will be incapable of overseeing your child's education--but who have plenty of food and good clothes, provided by others. If the choice about where one would put one's own child is as clear to you as it is to me, on what grounds does one justify support of a system that, indirectly but without doubt, makes the other choice for other children? The answer that "What we really want is a world where that choice is not forced upon us" is no answer. We have tried to have it that way. We failed. Everything we know about why we failed tells us that more of the same will not make the dilemma go away.

Notes and Questions

1. *Behavior Modification.* Charles Murray painted a utopian vision of how people will respond to a social system requiring self-sufficiency. Can government policy effectively modify individual behavior? Consider the perspective of Lucy Williams in her article on The Ideology of Division: Behavior Modification Welfare Reform Proposal, 102 Yale. L. J. 719 (1992) (excerpted in Chapter 8). Williams argues that empirical data show that economic incentives have failed to achieve their desired results. Does Murray offer any empirical or other evidence to support his view that behavior modification will work?

2. *Retaining Unemployment Insurance.* Murray conceded that we need to retain Unemployment Insurance. Why? How is it different from welfare? How will unemployment benefits keep laid-off workers from becoming as lazy as Murray believes welfare recipients have become?

3. *Race.* Murray first mentions race in this excerpt when he distinguishes the "stereotypical welfare mother" from the "white middle class." How do these categories define the race of welfare recipients for Murray's reader?

4. *Gender and Motherhood.* Murray claimed the historic justification for AFDC was that mothers should stay home to provide care to young children, and he offered two reasons why this justification can no longer be defended. First, he asserted that mothers of all classes now work away from the home. Second, he suggested that welfare mothers fail to properly care for children. Can, or should, either of these propositions be subjected to empirical proof? If either proposition were proved or presumed to be more likely true than not, is requiring a woman receiving AFDC to work outside the home an effective remedy?

5. *Federalism.* Murray suggested that local or state programs would be more effective than federal programs in assisting poor people because they leave more room for freedom of choice about program design and to account for more individualized information. Because the federal government allows states to obtain waivers from program requirements, states have already achieved some freedom of choice in designing their programs. Why do you suspect Murray considered the waiver option insufficient? For a discussion of

waivers, see Susan Bennett and Kathleen Sullivan, *Disentitling the Poor: Waivers and Welfare "Reform,"* 26 U. Mich. J. L. Reform 741 (1993), (excerpted in this chapter). How would local or state government programs account for individualized information in a away not possible at the federal level?

6. *Failure of Welfare.* Murray grounded his proposal on the assumption that the welfare system had failed. He then argued that society had nothing to lose by considering his proposal. And he strengthened his appeal by personalizing each reader's hypothetical choice to have their children raised either with sufficient funds but without good values, or without sufficient funds but with good values. He assumed that readers would choose the latter. Do you agree? Why did Murray's proposal appeal to so many readers, pundits, and politicians?

Marilyn A. Friedman
WOMEN IN POVERTY AND WELFARE EQUITY
From George R. Lucas, Jr.,
POVERTY, JUSTICE AND THE LAW (1986)

A new and controversial book has recommended that we eliminate "the entire federal welfare and income-support structure for working-aged persons" with the sole exception of unemployment insurance. The author is Charles Murray; the book is *Losing Ground.* Murray's suggestion would apply to "AFDC (Aid to Families with Dependent Children), Medicaid, Food Stamps, . . . Worker's Compensation, subsidized housing, disability insurance, and the rest." Murray's proposal is aimed equally at both men and women; both sexes would be subjected to his suggested changes.

"Thought experiments" and hypothetical anecdotes frequently take the place of argument in Murray's book. For example, at one point he asks us to think about whether income transfers from the haves to the have-nots are justified at all. He invites us to answer that they are not by asking us to contrast the "case of a man who has worked steadily for many years and, in his fifties, is thrown out of his job because the factory closes" with the case of

> A second man, healthy and in the prime of life, [who] refuses to work. I offer him a job, and he still refuses to work. I am called upon to answer the question again: Why should I transfer money to him? Why

> should I not let him starve, considering it a form of suicide?

Murray neglects to consider the case in which the "man" is really a *woman*, and her "refusal to work" is really a refusal to *work outside the home*. She refuses to work outside the home because she has young children to care for; the wage she would make in the only job she could get, as a domestic servant, would not pay the day-care costs for her children while she worked; and the biological father of her children, who deserted her long ago, has paid not a penny of his court-ordered child support money. In short, this woman is a victim of what has recently come to be called the "feminization of poverty," a plight which Murray's draconian proposal entirely disregards.

Murray is not the only theorist who advocates a welfare policy that is aimed equivalently at men and women and thereby disregards the feminization of poverty. Nor is this view confined to a "right-wing" or libertarian perspective on welfare. Among philosophers who *defend* federal welfare programs in one form or another, Carl Wellman and Richard Brandt have also advocated what they consider to be sexual equity in welfare policy. Says Brandt, "there is no reason grounded in utility for the tax-welfare system to treat males and females differently. " . . .In particular, he asserts, if work is made a condition for single male parents to obtain welfare assistance, so, too, should it be for single female parents. Carl Wellman, in a section entitled "The Right to Equitable Welfare Treatment" in his book, *Welfare Rights*, claims that it would be unfair to deny to unemployed fathers benefits that were available to unemployed mothers. The call for a sex-neutral welfare policy, shared by Brandt, Wellman, and Murray, is a central target of my paper.

THESIS: My position is that impoverished single mothers of dependent children form a special category of welfare recipients which ought to be treated differently from other categories of working-aged adults--just as the blind and the disabled would continue to be, even in Murray's proposal. I am not, of course, suggesting that motherhood is a kind of physical impairment. However, it is not inappropriate to think of being a poor, single mother as a kind of *economic* impairment, a condition that disables a person from earning as much as she otherwise might, were she not affected by the combination of those conditions. The traditional socialization of women, combined with ongoing constraints on the earning potential of women in the workplace . . . make women significantly less able than men, as single parents, to earn enough income outside the home to be able to care adequately for their families. For women whose income forces them, together with their dependent children, below the poverty line, what is needed is *not* a federal welfare policy that treats them "identically" to men, for the consequences of such treatment are not identical at all. What is needed is a welfare policy that takes account of the distinctive economic vulnerability of this group, for example, a policy of income supplements that affords these mothers the option of choosing either to work outside the home or to work in the full-time care of their own children.

* * *

The "feminization of poverty"[8] is generally understood to refer to the increasing percentage of people below the poverty line who are women or their dependent children. Just under one-third of households headed by a female with no male present live in poverty. This compares to a ratio of about one in nine for male single parents and about one in nineteen for families with both male and female householders present. The percentage of families headed by a single female living in poverty has remained about the same over the past decade. But because the number of households headed by single women has increased, the absolute numbers of such poverty families has increased as well: by about 100,000 annually between 1969 and 1978 and by about 150,000 annually between 1978 and 1980.

The decline in poverty that occurred during the 1970s was almost entirely in families with a male householder present. Says the National Advisory Council on Economic Opportunity:

> In 1979, there were over 1 million fewer poor children in families with a male householder than a decade earlier. But there were more than 1.2 million *more* poor children in families with a female householder [i.e., single female head of household.]

Even families with *single* male adults experience a 23 percent decline in poverty between 1969 and 1978. The result is that the *proportion* of poor families which are headed by single women has increased from 36 percent to more than 50 percent during the decade of the

[8]The earliest article of which I am aware that uses the expression is Diana M. Pearce's "The Feminization of Poverty: Women, Work and Welfare," *The Urban and Social Change Review*, v. 11 (1978), 28-36.

1970s. . . . This recent trend, due, in part, to an increasing frequency of marital disruption, is usually what is meant by the "feminization of poverty."

But, in another sense, the feminization of poverty is not new at all. Or, rather: what is not new is the *poverty of feminization.* Women have always been poor, in the sense that they have always formed an economically dependent class. The structural causes of the economic dependency of women are to be found in the combined effects of their gender socialization and the economic, legal, governmental, and social systems which, in our society until recent times, deprived women of virtually all property ownership or access to governmental, economic, or educational opportunities in the larger social order outside the home. Women have traditionally been socialized, pressured, and coerced into solving the economic problems of caring for their own material needs and those of their potential and actual dependent children by seeking to marry, and remain married to, men. Women who did not marry, or whose husbands died or deserted the family unit, either solved their economic problems in some other way or became impoverished and fell back on whatever charitable resources were available in the community.

In the nineteenth century, the institutions which characteristically dealt with people in poverty were organized private philanthropies, neighborhood organizations, and settlement houses. In our century, poverty has more characteristically been dealt with by the state. Federal legislation dealing with poverty has been group based; it has typically been directed at specific groups of persons whose poverty was assumed to have some identifiable systematic connection with the category to which they belonged and thus, *not* to have been a function of their own individual failures. Poverty categories used in the Social Security Act of 1935, such as the handicapped and the elderly, refer to groups of persons whose socio-economic histories and future prospects explain their poverty in different ways and provide a correspondingly different basis for potential rights claims to which they are legitimately entitled.

The civil rights movement of the 1950s and 1960s inspired us to conceive of poverty in terms of the categories of ethnic minorities. White Americans came to recognize, for example, how a history of explicit, legalized slavery, denial of voting rights, exclusion from adequate public schools, and exclusion from housing in non-poor neighborhoods each contributed, along with a litany of other harms, to a distinctive and systematic impoverishment of Black Americans. Along with an improved understanding of the history of Black people in America and the causes of their contemporary social and economic predicament came an appreciation of the claims to which Blacks were entitled, as a matter of right, by virtue of those historical experiences.

Only very recently has the notion of a "feminization of poverty" become parlance. The real significance of this notion seems to me to lie in the alternative conceptual framework which invokes for understanding the causes of poverty and the legitimate social claims to which those causes give rise. Of course, the histories of certain ethnic minorities in this culture are still as vitally relevant as ever to understanding the causes of poverty. But the notion of the "feminization of poverty" draws our attention to additional factors which an "ethnicization of poverty" overlooks. We are invited to recognize, for example, that the recent increase in marital disruption would have no relevance to poverty whatsoever were it not for certain chronic economic conditions which have traditionally structured women's lives. The *significant* causes of poverty must be understood as including the age-old conditions of women's economic dependence and deprivation.

I have been suggesting that the significance of the "feminization of poverty" really lies in the feminization of the *concept* of its causes and of the legitimate rights claims to which it gives rise. There is a curious sense in which the feminization of the concept of poverty is not new. From their inception, certain welfare programs were aimed specifically at a certain class of impoverished *women*. Aid to Dependent Children, the original ADC under the Social Security Act of 1935, was tailored essentially for those mothers of dependent children who lived without a husband in the house. The program was conceived as providing benefits for women whose husbands had died or deserted them and who were left with dependent children to support on their own. At that time, it was not expected that such women should seek income-producing work outside the home. In those depression-ridden years, ADC was also perhaps conceived as an incentive to lure women back into their homes so that they would not compete against men for scarce jobs. Thus, ADC mothers were not originally required to work for income, or to seek income-producing jobs, in exchange for their ADC benefits. The sociologist Guida West has used the expressions "maternal ethic" to characterize ADC (and its later metamorphosis, Aid to Families with Dependent Children, or AFDC) in those early decades, prior to 1967. The program was governed by norms about the traditional female role, and the appropriateness of full-time parenting and the inappropriateness of income-producing work for women who filled the role. I call this the "old" feminization of the concept of poverty.

By 1967, the old feminization of the concept of poverty had begun to disappear at the federal level. Recipients of AFDC were no longer regarded as innocent, involuntary victims of poverty. Already by the early 1960s, their status as single mothers was recognized to have come about more through divorce and illegitimacy of offspring than through spousal death or desertion. In 1967, new AFDC programs required all persons receiving AFDC (still primarily women) to register for work and training as a condition for receiving public assistance. West characterizes the change as a shift from the "maternal ethic" to a "work ethic," by which she means, of course, a "work-outside-the-home-for-pay ethic." In particular, the new 1967 Work Incentive Program, originally known by the acronym WIP (which was later changed, for obvious reasons, to WIN) required all AFDC recipients to register for work and job training. Since that time, welfare proposals under all successive administrations have incorporated such work availability requirements and have been progressively tightened over time in the degree to which they have been enforced against women.

The old feminization of the concept of poverty differs very significantly from the new. The old perspective did not incorporate the view that feminization was systematically impoverishing, and it presumed the thorough-going legitimacy of the female role norms on which it was based. The old "feminizing" of the concept of poverty amounted to nothing more than a sense that there were a number of otherwise unrelated individual cases in which women experienced the (presumed) misfortune of losing their men.

The new feminization of the concept of poverty is radically subversive of the presumptions underpinning the old. The new perspective is based on the assumption that "feminization," as traditionally constituted and enforced, is fundamentally structured on a basis of economic dependency. It is also based on a clear recognition that parental responsibilities still intersect the options to

New feminiz. of poverty

earn income in this culture in ways that are different for women than for men. When parents separate or divorce, the children of those couples are very likely to remain in the care of their female parents. When unmarried couples produce offspring, the resulting children are overwhelmingly likely to end up in the care of the parents of whom they sprang, namely, their mothers. As seen from the new perspective, the female role norms and the social, economic, legal, and governmental practices and policies which supported them, are problematic, at best, and morally outrageous, at worst.

* * *

Contemporary social analysts are providing us with a detailed understanding of what the feminization of poverty, as it is now understood, actually means. Some of the major contributing conditions are: (1) relatively inadequate wages and salaries that are paid to women; (2) overrepresentation in occupational categories with relatively inferior wages, benefits, and job security; (3) welfare programs that are unable to boost women out of poverty; and (4) the absence of legal provisions to ensure that nonresident fathers of dependent children share in the income support of their children. I shall discuss these points briefly.

In the labor market, according to data from the U.S. Bureau of Census, women average approximately 60 percent of the wages and salaries earned, on average, by men. Some of this discrepancy is due to ongoing sexual discrimination within job categories in which women earn less than men with equivalent levels of education, training, and experience. Some of the discrepancy is due to the occupational segregation of women into "pink collar ghettoes," job categories which, as a whole, are relatively low-paying. Many of these jobs are in what sociologists call the "secondary" sector of the labor market, a sector defined by jobs that are often temporary, part-time, low-paying, seldom unionized, and that offer inadequate health and retirement benefits, if any at all. Females predominate in this sector of the economy. By contrast, males predominate in the so-called "primary" sector of the labor market, a sector characterized by jobs with relatively better pay, job security, health benefits, retirement benefits, and a significant level of unionization.

When people in the primary sector of the labor market lose their jobs, they are generally eligible for such income support programs as Unemployment Insurance, programs in which eligibility is determined by past contributions which were based on earnings.

"primary" welfare sector

One need not demonstrate poverty or the lack of all other possible financial resources in order to qualify for benefits. Benefits are comparatively generous, often with minimum levels established by the federal government. Some authors have referred to these sorts of income support programs as the "primary sector" of the welfare system. In 1978, according to the U.S. Census Bureau, males were the recipients of 89 percent of all benefits dispensed by the primary welfare system. The poverty rate among this group was a low 4 percent.

There is also a "secondary" welfare sector, a sector consisting of programs in which benefits are lower than in the primary welfare sector. These programs include AFDC, food stamps, and Medicaid. Eligibility for benefits is based on a person's having exhausted all other financial resources. In 1978, according to the U.S. Census Bureau, a majority of the benefits from the secondary welfare sector went to single mothers--a welfare group with a disheartening poverty rate of 71 percent. Says the sociologist Diana M. Pearce:

> The stubborn obsession with getting women off welfare and into jobs as quickly as possible, with no attention to their special needs (e.g., for child care or fringe benefits that include adequate health insurance), has long-term results that are counterproductive. Those who accept or are forced to take economically marginal jobs in the secondary sector quickly find that they do not have access to the primary welfare sector when they lose or are laid off from these jobs. They are then forced to depend on impoverished secondary-welfare-sector programs. Thus, the interlocking secondary welfare system and secondary labor market reinforce a vicious circle of welfare dependency and marginal work.

Recognizing that the sources of income for women are inadequate, whether in the labor market or in the welfare system, is a significant part of the feminization of the concept of poverty. Another important insight pertains to the lack of an effective social or legal mechanism to ensure that nonresident fathers contribute to the income-support of their children. Researchers have estimated that in any given year, 34 percent of mothers who have been awarded child support payments by the courts are likely to receive no payments whatsoever. There is no automatic legal mechanism which ensures that a divorced father who has been ordered by a court to provide income support for his children actually does so. To summarize, the feminization of the concept of poverty illuminates policies and practices such as these which are major causes of contemporary impoverishment of single mothers and their dependent children.

Any theory of welfare rights must be formulated with a proper appreciation of the circumstances and vulnerabilities of different groups of impoverished people. I have noted the persistent average wage discrepancy between women and men; the preponderance of women in occupations that are low in pay, fringe benefits, and job security; and the fact that single mothers frequently receive little or no child support from the nonresident biological fathers of their dependent children. In virtue of these economic discrepancies, welfare policies that treat women and men identically would have a greatly disparate economic impact upon them. Genuine equality calls for *differential* treatment of at least certain categories of women, relative to other potential welfare clients. Since Wellman and Brandt defend existing welfare programs, their calls for the sex-neutral administration of such programs are sufficiently refuted by pointing out, as I have done, that such policies would provide a substantially *lesser* degree of real welfare support for single mothers than for other groups. In other words, the issue with Wellman and Brandt is simply one of equitable treatment.

However, the call for equity alone is not enough to refute Murray's proposals. Recall that Murray has proposed that we eliminate all federal welfare programs for working age people, with the exception of Unemployment Insurance, a program which, as noted earlier, services primarily male clients. All of the programs that have high percentages of working-age women among their clients, such as AFDC, would be scrapped. Let us not forget that many of the beneficiaries of the programs that Murray would cut are not of working age at all: namely, the dependent *children* who benefit from AFDC, food stamps, Medicaid, and so forth. Young children are surely among the "deserving poor," the poor who deserve aid in virtue of the nonvoluntary nature of their poverty and their nonvoluntary inability to break out of their poverty and attain economic self-sufficiency.

vs Murray

Murray argues throughout his book that poor parents are better off working income-producing jobs, and poor children are better off having parents who work at income-producing jobs, than any of them would be if those parents did not work at such jobs and received welfare benefits instead--even in cases where the income level was lower from a job than from welfare. His argument is, thus, based largely on his assessment of the *consequences* to the poor themselves of various policies. The apparent assumption behind such reasoning is that welfare policy should be guided by consideration of what is *best* for the poor. To show that Murray's proposal is not justifiable for single mothers and their dependent children, it is necessary to show not only that that population group would suffer more than others if his recommendations were implements, but that the conditions and prospects of those people would be *worse* without welfare support than it would be with that support. In the remaining paragraphs, I shall begin to sketch a consequentialist counterargument to Murray's proposal.

One step in constructing such an argument is to consider, in further detail, what the consequences would be of eliminating income support that such programs as AFDC provide. We can get some idea of this by looking to historical times and places when welfare benefits for single mothers were even less adequate than they are now. In the southern states, prior to the 1960s, the benefits paid to ADC recipients were very low compared to the rest of the country. Furthermore, the "maternal ethic" began to disappear in these states quite soon after the federal implementation of the program. Louisiana was the first state, in 1943, to enact employable mother rules requiring that all ADC families with children seven years old or older be refused assistance as long as the mother was presumed to be employable in agricultural labor. It has been suggested by Frances Fox Piven and Richard A. Cloward that these measures were designed to ensure workers for low-paid, seasonal jobs as farm laborers. Parenthetically, it is worth noting that the rules were enforced more heavily against blacks than against whites in the two states that enacted such explicit rules, Louisiana and Georgia. And in other southern states, suggest Piven and Cloward, informal practices of racial discrimination served to keep many otherwise eligible impoverished Black mothers off the welfare rolls and, therefore, desperately in need of whatever jobs they could find.

Thus, it *has* been possible to get significant numbers of impoverished women off welfare rolls and out into the income-producing workforce: just pay them inadequate benefits or no benefits at all. Where agricultural labor is not available, such women can always find work as domestic servants--or in any of the other occupations with low pay, few fringe benefits, or little job security that welfare mothers typically obtain when they work outside the home.

Abolishing all federally funded welfare programs for working-aged adults, with the exception of Unemployment Insurance, would have the effect of providing a relatively cheap supply of workers for secondary labor market jobs. It is unlikely that the lives of women or children in families headed by single mothers would be improved by such a policy. Consider the actual consequences for such a family: The only job that the mother can obtain is low in wages and low in benefits. If she can afford any child care at all, it will be of inferior quality and no substitute for parental care. Her job does not provide health insurance to cover the medical costs of her growing family. And her lack of job security makes the prospect of even a steady *meager* wage uncertain. The condition of such a family could hardly be improved by withdrawing the governmental income support which the mother currently falls back on when there is no income from other sources.

Murray ignores the extra burdens faced by single parents, the economically inferior status of women as compared to that of men, and the substantial likelihood of poverty when these conditions coincide in particular cases. Because he neglects such data, Murray fails to make his case that the abolition of federally funded welfare programs would improve the condition of impoverished single mothers and their dependent children. Indeed, the evidence overwhelmingly suggests otherwise.

* * *

Notes and Questions

1. *Sameness versus Difference.* Feminist scholars have debated whether women would be better served by laws that treat them the same as men, or laws that treat them differently. Marilyn Friedman described the new feminization of poverty as including inadequate wages for women, inferior jobs for women, insufficient welfare, and insufficient child support enforcement. She argued that poor women therefore should be treated differently than poor men.

Charles Murray took the argument a step further: women are now treated the same as men with regard to work outside the home, and poor women should be treated the same as other women. Marilyn Friedman disagrees. Both authors purport to care about what is best for poor people. Which approach will be more likely to benefit poor women? Why?

2. *Lessons from History.* Friedman argued that history teaches how disastrous Murray's proposal will be. She described welfare rules in Louisiana and Georgia that ensured available laborers for low-paid seasonal agricultural work and that were enforced more heavily against African-Americans. She seemed to concede that Murray's proposal would succeed in forcing poor people into low-paid labor. But she argued that their lives would not be improved. What factors did Friedman consider that Murray did not?

2. The Compromise

Charles Murray struck a chord among conservatives who took up the call to end welfare with considerable vigor. Perhaps more surprising was the response of traditional liberals. Rather than defending the need for welfare, many liberals seemed to view the attack on welfare as an opportunity to explore the flaws in the welfare system. One scholar, David Ellwood, considered the "conundrums" of how to assist poor people without interfering with what he viewed as basic American values. After President Clinton's election, Ellwood worked for a time as a key advisor to the President on welfare issues.

David Ellwood
POOR SUPPORT (1988)

The history of social policy can be seen as a series of attempts to help people without interfering too seriously with the basic values of autonomy, work, family, and community. Until recently, social policy succeeded in avoiding the dilemmas [conundrums] to a remarkable degree. But it did so by eschewing pure welfare forms that should offer generous benefits to all needy applicants, choosing instead to rely chiefly on nonwelfare forms of support linked to specific problems. . . .

The Foundation: 1930-60

* * *

The mission was clear: help only those who cannot work through no fault of their own. Protection was offered at three levels: Social Security, employment-related benefits, and means-tested benefits.

Social Security was brilliant in its conception, for it managed to reinforce the values of autonomy, work, family, and community.

* * *

Social Security was designed as a universal system to cover all working Americans and it remains in place today. No groups are targeted, so none is isolated. In Social Security, benefits are linked directly to past earnings: the more one earned in the past, the higher the benefits in the event of retirement, disability, or death. (The decision to avoid targeting and to tie the program to work had been a conscious one. In response to pressures to focus benefits on the poor President Franklin D. Roosevelt replied: "We put those payroll contributions there so as to give the contributors a legal, moral, and political right to collect their pensions.")

* * *

By being universal, by linking benefits to past work, by giving support only to those who demonstrably have work-inhibiting conditions, by being explicitly supportive of families, the Social Security system has seemed to avoid the conundrums. There are complaints that the elderly work less because of their benefits and that some people who could do some work get into the disability program. And the system probably has diminished the responsibility of extended families to care for each other and the need for workers to save for their retirement. But such complaints have never generated any real enthusiasm.

Few minded if the old wanted to retire. Indeed, such behavior was welcomed in the depression of the 1930s. Then, as now, workers did not object to contributing to a fund that they thought of as offering insurance and pension benefits. People believed they were getting back only what they had put in.

In fact, Social Security is much more than a pension-insurance plan, and contributions are not actually saved. Current workers pay for current retirees. When the system started up, retirees who contributed little got back a great deal. Even today, retirees receive far more in benefits than they ever contributed. And the system has a strong redistributive element; the structure of the benefit formula actually means that low-income workers get considerably higher benefits per dollar contributed than do high-income workers. But the program has always been considered to be for middle Americans, and the overwhelming majority of resources have gone to the nonpoor.

* * *

Unemployment insurance is different. Some people clearly lose their jobs through no fault of their own and they often have troubles finding new ones. The problem is that it is hard to determine whether unemployment is voluntary. Any system that gives benefits to the unemployed may discourage them from working, may isolate them, and may cause them to become dependent. Unemployment insurance is a clever way to provide help while avoiding the most serious worries. Benefits are given only to those who have had work experience and whose former employers certify that they neither quit nor were fired for misbehavior. Like Social Security, benefits are available to workers at all levels, and benefits are higher for upper-income workers. To ensure that the unemployed do not become dependent, unemployment insurance is limited in duration usually to twenty-six weeks or less. Additional benefits cannot be collected until the person has accumulated enough work experience to be eligible again.

* * *

During this period, a third tier of support--*means-tested benefits*--was available mainly to the aged, the disabled, and single-parent families (or two-parent families in which the fathers were disabled). These families were protected by federally sponsored but state-administered programs which were available only to people of limited means. Virtually no welfare money was available for healthy two-parent families, single individuals, childless couples, or working families. The single-parent, elderly, and disabled household who received benefits typically got little money and they were subject to severe restrictions on their assets, on the presence of an able-bodied man in the house, and so forth. Caseworkers had considerable discretion over these benefits. They were allowed to make unannounced searches and sometimes could cut off benefits if the family had so much as a telephone!

When these programs were first designed, they were seen as temporary or transitional programs that would end once Social

Security was phased in and expanded. The elderly and disabled were expected to be covered by Social Security, not welfare. AFDC was viewed as a program to protect families in which the father was dead, incapacitated, or, in rare instances, had abandoned them. The consequences of either the death or the incapacity of a breadwinner were to be eased by Social Security. Abandonment was a small problem. "Welfare" programs were thus for the small group who were not expected to work but who got so little protection from Social Security and employment-related benefits that they were still destitute.

* * *

Thus, the policies of 1960 were generally compatible with the values of autonomy, work, family and community. The vast majority of money was going to universal insurance-type programs. Welfare was only a tiny expenditure, and what little was spent went to single mothers, who still were not expected to work. The conundrums were hardly evident. They had been avoided by emphasizing universal programs that were targeted to specific and clearly recognizable impediments to work.

* * *

Takeoff: 1960-76

The satisfaction would not last. America discovered its hungry. It discovered discrimination and prejudice. It fought an unpopular war that galvanized its young people. And it did all these things in one of the most remarkable periods of economic growth in the history of the United States. It was easy to see the poor as victims when they were so clearly hungry and when discrimination so blatantly held people back--especially at a time when the government was worrying about how it would spend all the surplus taxes that kept rolling in.

By the end of the 1960s, the debate about poverty had been dramatically transformed. A revolution in thinking had occurred--a revolution led by intellectuals. . . . Potent and troubling books like Michael Harrington's *The Other America* and Kenneth Clark's *Dark Ghetto* stirred the hearts and minds of the increasingly professional policy analysts by describing the dehumanizing environment of the poor and the consequences of their isolation. And the media began to portray images of hungry children living in shacks.

At first, most of the attention was focused on policies that sought to remove the barriers that prevented people from advancing.

After its adoption in 1964, the Job Corps trained out-of-school youths by moving them to separate residential training centers. Head Start was adopted to help disadvantaged preschoolers in the same year. The Elementary and Secondary Education Act of 1965 provided money for the educationally disadvantaged who were already in school. Affirmative action and anti-discrimination efforts ballooned. Busing and desegregation of housing were supposed to offer blacks a route out of their neighborhoods and give both races a chance to understand each other better. Urban development and community action organizations were designed to rebuild the cities.

Insurance and protection policies also expanded dramatically. Significant medical protection was added through medicare for the elderly and through Medicaid for those who qualified for public assistance (impoverished aged and disabled persons and those in single-parent families). Social Security benefits were raised dramatically as the rapid growth in wages raised contributions far above the benefit payments. Unemployment insurance was extended to far more workers.

* * *

Unfortunately, it soon became clear that Social Security, employment-related benefits, medical protection, and human investment strategies would not be nearly enough to ensure the security of the employable and healthy poor. The early programs showed that these groups could not dramatically transform their lives with a modest bit of training or services. Academics and policy makers concluded that if the poor were really to be pushed out of poverty, cash transfers had to be expanded.

During the takeoff period, welfare started to be viewed in a new light. Welfare rights advocates argued that the degrading and dehumanizing treatment of welfare recipients was part of the problem. Welfare robbed people of their self-esteem. It stigmatized and brutalized them. The distinctions in the welfare system between the "deserving poor" (who got public assistance) and the "undeserving poor" (who got nothing) seemed arbitrary .

* * *

By the late 1960s, a new goal seemed to be emerging for social policy: the government should guarantee that everyone achieved a minimum standard of living. The goal translated into more than just investing in people and protecting them from old age or disability. It implied that government should also provide a guaranteed annual income. In policy circles, the guaranteed annual income was called the negative income tax, since policy makers hoped that it could be implemented through the tax system. . . . It represented a sort of noblesse oblige of the American Government toward the poor.

This new policy goal was a radical departure from the previous goal of supporting those who could not work. Indeed, advocates of the negative income tax repeatedly emphasized that it was a way of supplementing the income of the working poor--a group who had, until then, been left out of the social welfare net.

* * *

AFDC was expanded, both by court cases and by social planners. Courts essentially forced many states to raise their benefits and eliminate the man-in-the-house rule. Legislation introduced "work incentives" so that single mothers who worked would not lose $1 in benefits for every $1 they earned. . . . And there was a changed attitude about welfare. Welfare now was seen as more of a right than an embarrassment.

* * *

The only really major change in the structure of assistance came in the form of the Food Stamp program, which became a kind of mini negative income tax. Any poor person could get at least some food stamps. But the benefits started low and were cut as income rose. To a family with no other income, they offered the 1986 equivalent of seventy-five cents per person per meal. For a family whose income was half the poverty line, benefits were about thirty-eight cents. Thus, there was guaranteed income, but it was in the form of food stamps that were worth at most $3,300 per year (in 1986 dollars). To get any kind of serious income support, families usually still had to be aged, disabled, or headed by a single parent.

* * *

[T]hese changes pushed up means-tested benefits from $16 billion in 1960 to almost $54 billion in 1976. The level and ease of collecting benefits had been expanded for the groups who had been getting them earlier (the aged, the disabled, and single mothers). In many states, some two-parent families with an unemployed worker could collect AFDC. Medicaid protection had been added for these same groups. And every poor person was at least eligible for food stamps.

* * *

Retrenchment: 1976-87

[B]y the mid-seventies, the world had changed. The strongest ally of the War on Poverty was probably the booming economy. A growing economy typically generates higher wages, lower employment, and increased opportunities--all good friends of the poor and of programs that attempt to improve their economic condition. A growing economy also generates greater tax revenues and a more generous public. But in the early 1970s, wages stopped growing. Adjusted for inflation, even as late as 1986, the median wage of full-year full-time workers was still well below the peak it reached in 1973.

Families coped by sending more workers into the labor market and by doing with less. In this more austere environment, it seemed increasingly hard to justify expanded aid to the poor. The means-tested programs seemed to gall those Americans who were trying hard just to break even. Why should some people live off the government's largess while others were struggling to survive?

* * *

[T]here was no increase in means-tested programs after 1976. Indeed, AFDC benefits were not even adjusted for inflation, so in the next decade in most states, their real value per family fell by 30-50 percent. Eligibility rules were retightened, and workfare became more acceptable. Advocates tried mostly to protect means-tested programs, not expand them.

* * *

The public harbored deep-seated fears that social policies, particularly welfare, were counterproductive. In one survey, 59 percent of the public believed that welfare made "poor people dependent and encourage[d] them to stay poor." Only 19 percent thought it gave people a chance to "stand on their own two feet and get started again," and almost two thirds believed that welfare encouraged irresponsibility by fathers. A large majority believed that welfare often encouraged divorce and illegitimacy. For the public, welfare policies seems to have trapped the poor in a quagmire. The poor, they thought, were different from other Americans. Thus, when America's ghettos became front-page news again in the mid-eighties, as they had been in the mid-sixties, Americans seemed far less willing to blame the environment, discrimination, or the economy.

* * *

So helping the poor increasingly has come to look like a no-win proposition. At least until recently, there has been no clear vision. Society could not accept the old goal that only those who were unable to work should be helped. It could not even agree on who was unable to work (surely the aged and disabled should not work, but what about single mothers?). Nor could it accept the view that the government should guarantee security for all. So, for over a decade, social policies for the poor have languished, seemingly trapped between Scylla and Charybdis, wanting to help the poor but skeptical that the government would only encourage dependence and aid the irresponsible. Thus, we are left with a set of social policies for the poor that everyone hates.

Looking over the history of social policy, I am struck by the fact that the further we move toward a system that makes judgments about the causes of poverty, that tries to link benefits to work, and that avoids excessive targeting, the less bothersome the conundrums seem to be. Conversely, the closer we move to time-unlimited, cashlike, income-tested assistance--that is, the closer we move to pure welfare programs--the more difficult the value dilemmas become. By turning to welfare, we are actually turning away from our values and ignoring the causes of poverty. In giving welfare to the healthy, the government and citizens can avoid making judgements about the expectations that society may have of its citizens. They can also avoid deciding what opportunities society ought to guarantee its citizens. Instead, they are retreating to a "neutral" world of income guarantees.

Welfare should be the perfect policy if poverty was caused only by the lack of money. But poverty is never simply a matter of limited income. Poverty is the result of other problems. When people are poor because they are too sick to work, it is their disability that prevents them from working. When people work but are still poor, they are poor because their wages are too low. When the unemployed are poor, the problem is that they cannot find work they are willing to take. When single mothers are poor, they may be poor because they are trying to balance two responsibilities--that of nurturing their children and providing for them--without outside support. When people are poor in the ghetto, they may lack the education, the opportunity, or the vision to make it.

The most practical and politically viable policies of the past have always reflected society's expectations and sought to link benefits and treatments to the causes of deprivation. Social Security goes to the disabled, the widowed, and the old. Unemployment insurance goes to those who had been working, and it is limited in duration because society believes people ought eventually to find work for themselves.

Conversely, welfare programs like AFDC cannot decide what their goals should be. Should programs be generous in recognition of the dignity of the recipients and the problems they face or punitive to discourage dependence and encourage people to make it on their own? Should welfare mothers be required to "work off" their checks, or do such policies only serve to damage further the self-esteem of a group who already feels powerless and inadequate? Should welfare be a source of embarrassment or seen as a right? Welfare represents a failure, but no one is quite sure whose failure it is. Either the recipients failed to do enough for themselves or society failed to provide enough opportunities.

These issues cannot easily be resolved in a program that is designed only to provide income to those who lack it. The answers can be found only by looking deeper at the causes of poverty and the responsibilities of both the society and its citizens. If we look at the *why* rather than the *who* of poverty, we ought to be able to come far closer to the American ideal--not of guaranteed income, but of a guarantee that people who strive and who meet reasonable social responsibilities will be able to achieve at least a modest level of dignity and security. Ideally, social policy would be used to further the American dreams of opportunity, prosperity, and independence, rather than to pick up the pieces when the dreams are shattered.

* * *

Notes and Questions

1. *Basic Values.* Just as Charles Murray focused on values, David Ellwood structured his telling of welfare history around what he called the basic values of autonomy, work, family, and community. How basic are these values in American life? Did

Ellwood account for tensions among these values, for example, between autonomy and community or between work and family?

2. *Failure of Welfare.* Also like Charles Murray, Ellwood assumed that welfare "represents a failure." Is Ellwood's view of the failure of welfare the same as Murray's?

3. *Shift to Responsibility.* Ellwood, again like Murray, proposed that welfare be modified away from guaranteeing income and toward guaranteeing that people who satisfy their "responsibilities" will achieve "modest" security. How should we determine what constitutes responsibility? Can welfare be reformed to encourage or require greater responsibility on the part of recipients? If so, how?

4. *From Policy to Proposals.* Ellwood was not alone in his call for a shift to responsibility in the welfare system. For example, Judith Gueron, head of the Manpower Demonstration Research Corporation and one of the nation's foremost analysts of welfare employment programs, called for similar welfare reform. *See* Judith M. Gueron, *Welfare and Poverty: The Elements of Reform,* 11 YALE LAW AND POLICY REVIEW 113 (1993). Gueron wrote:

> For the last thirty years, there has been widespread agreement that the nation's welfare system should be reformed to make it more consistent with basic public values endorsing the primacy of family and the importance of work. There has been disagreement, however, about specific proposals, and resistance to providing the funds needed for large-scale reform. This Article discusses the three approaches state and federal governments can use to reduce welfare and encourage work: (1) making welfare less attractive; (2) making welfare a reciprocal obligation; and (3) making work more attractive. It concludes that a combined strategy, which links welfare-to-work program mandates with increased rewards for low-wage work, offers promise. As a new Administration committed to change shapes and implements its agenda, the trade-offs and lessons from the past provide guidance on how to translate a vision of reform into a concrete program that will better meet multiple policy objectives and produce institutional change.

Id. In addition to analysts such as Gueron, Ellwood's colleagues at the Department of Health and Human Services supported the shift toward greater responsibility. *See, e.g.*, Wendell E. Primus & Marcia J. Carlson, The Need for Welfare Reform and the Role of Government in Promoting Parental Responsibility, Work, and Child Well-Being, 3 Kansas Journal of Law & Public Policy 77 (1994). For an interesting account of how the Clinton administration formulated its welfare policies, *see* Jason DeParle, *The Clinton Welfare Bill Begins Trek in Congress,* N.Y. TIMES, July 15, 1994, at A1. For a description of the role of Republican moderates in Congressional reform, *see* Jeffrey L. Katz, *GOP Moderates Central to Welfare Overhaul,* CONGRESSIONAL QUARTERLY 813 (March 18, 1995).

5. *Welfare Reform Consensus.* In the late 1980s, conservatives like Murray and liberals like Ellwood seemed to agree that the welfare system had failed because it conflicted with basic American values. They agreed that requiring more individual responsibility was the key to welfare reform. Does this consensus between conservatives and liberals surprise you? Do they agree on both the means and the ends?

6. *Material versus Behavioral Poverty.* Robert Rector, a welfare analyst at the Heritage Foundation, based his welfare reform ideas in the distinction between material and behavioral poverty. *See* Robert Rector, *Fighting Behavioral Poverty,* 1 GEORGETOWN JOURNAL ON FIGHTING POVERTY 69 (1993). Rector defined material poverty as "having insufficient resources to meet basic physical needs." *Id.* According to Rector, "[b]ehavioral poverty incorporates a cluster of social pathologies including an eroded work ethic; a lack of educational aspiration and achievement; an inability or unwillingness to control one's children; and increased levels of single parenthood and illegitimacy, criminal activity, and drug and alcohol abuse. *Id.* In order to fight behavioral poverty, Rector recommended a welfare reform package that would: 1) reduce benefits; 2) establish work requirements; 3) enforce education requirements; 4) establish paternity and enforce child support payments; 5) provide tax credits or vouchers for medical coverage to all working families; 6) provide tax relief to all families with children. *Id.* How does Rector's distinction between material and behavioral poverty compare to Ellwood's focus on values, including responsibility? To what extent are each of their ideas reflected in the Personal Responsibility and Work Opportunity Reconciliation Act of 1996? To what extent can

government rules, whether incentives or disincentives, change human behavior?

3. The Critique

Lucy Williams
THE IDEOLOGY OF DIVISION:
BEHAVIOR MODIFICATION WELFARE REFORM PROPOSALS
102 YALE LAW JOURNAL 719 (1992)

* * *

The rhetoric of the current "welfare reform" debate goes something like this: Aid to Families with Dependent Children (AFDC) recipients are themselves responsible for their poverty because they have not "pulled themselves up by their bootstraps"; they are dysfunctional mothers incapable of fitting into mainstream society, and they are economically and emotionally atrophied because of their "dependence" on welfare. Proponents of "welfare reform" further argue that by withholding AFDC benefits, the government can transform present recipients into productive members of society, thereby solving the intractable problems of poverty. Consistent with this rhetoric, the current "welfare reform" proposals condition AFDC eligibility on conformity with putative moral norms of society. Underlying the proposals is the belief that the receipt of assistance is debilitating.

These concepts, always an undercurrent in American history, surfaced with new vigor in the work of conservative scholars in the early 1980's. The conservatives' ideas engendered several state demonstration projects, including Learnfare (loss of benefits if a child misses a certain number of days of school or fails to average a certain grade), Family Cap (loss of benefits for additional children), Bridefare or Wedfare (small monetary incentives given to a mother to marry the father of her child combined with the loss of benefits for additional children), incentives for recipients to use Norplant contraception, and benefit reductions if the mother pays her rent irregularly or fails to obtain medical treatment for her children. The idea behind all of these projects is the same: only those women and children who conform to majoritarian middle-class values deserve government subsistence benefits.

* * *

Learnfare

In July 1987, at the request of newly elected Governor Tommy G. Thompson, the Wisconsin Legislature passed the first Learnfare statute. Learnfare programs condition AFDC eligibility on dependent children's regular school attendance. As originally enacted, the statute targeted only teens who were themselves parents (as opposed to all teens who were part of an AFDC family unit) and provided that teens could not be sanctioned until after they had been given an opportunity to participate in a school program for "children at risk" or "school-age parents." Governor Thompson used his line-item veto power to reshape the program: by deleting critical words and provisions, he effectively expanded Learnfare to cover all teens receiving AFDC and eliminated the requirement that teens be referred to special school programs before sanctions would be imposed against them. The Department of Health and Human Services [HHS] approved the federal waivers requested for the Learnfare portion of the Wisconsin Welfare Reform Demonstration on October 20, 1987.

In March 1988, Wisconsin began to enforce the program against teens under fifteen and against all teen parents. At the beginning of the 1988-89 school year the State expanded the program to include all teen dependents living with a parent.

Under the program, a teen on AFDC who misses ten unexcused full days of school in a semester is monitored monthly thereafter, and is "sanctioned" if she or he misses two unexcused full days of school in any month. A sanction reduces the family's AFDC grant by the entire amount designated for the teen. For example, for a family consisting of a mother and two children, this sanction results in a reduction of $77.60 a month from a total grant of $517.60. During the 1988-89 and 1989-90 school years, an average of 2,125 students were sanctioned each month. AFDC families lost $3,080,000 during 1989 alone.

There are two official goals of the Wisconsin program. First, the program is intended to ensure that more teenagers on AFDC complete high school or its equivalent and thereby acquire the minimum level of education needed to become productive citizens. Second, the program seeks to establish a relationship of mutual responsibility between the State and AFDC recipients: the State provides assistance to recipients in getting off, and recipients undertake education, training, and job searches that will help them become self-sufficient. At first glance, these goals seem benign; indeed, the notions that children should stay in school and that parents should be responsible for their children are hardly controversial. However, in historical context and in actual operation, Learnfare reinforces the myth that social problems such as truancy are caused by the deviant behavior of welfare recipients.

Why did this program, at this time, emerge to respond to this perceived crisis? The answer to this question requires an examination of the underlying premises of Learnfare. Such an examination reveals that Learnfare is based on a series of empirically faulty assumptions. Consequently, it is not surprising that the Wisconsin program--and for that matter any Learnfare program--will fail to achieve its goals. In recent years national high school dropout rates have declined dramatically: the percentage of white adults between twenty-five and twenty-nine years old who have not completed high school dropped from 36.3% in 1960 to 13.2% in 1985; for African Americans the figure dropped from 60% in 1960 to 17.6% in 1985. Ninety-two percent of the AFDC teens subject to Learnfare are meeting the school attendance requirements; only 8% are sanctioned. Moreover, Wisconsin's AFDC rolls had begun to decline in mid-1986. Nevertheless, this data neither dampened the support for a punitive program for AFDC recipients nor altered the perception of a welfare or underclass crisis.

Learnfare as a Method to Reduce High School Dropout Rates

If Learnfare is to achieve its first stated goal, curbing the high school dropout rate, several assumptions must be made: (1) the mother whose teenager skips school is exercising her free choice within a wide range of options in allowing the child to be truant; (2) the reason for the failure to attend school is endemic to the child's family, not to external causes; and (3) teens are motivated by economic incentives targeted at the family.

These assumptions ignore both the psychology of teenagers and the realities of poverty. Many of the choices that middle-class families make are inconceivable to poor women who do not have the option of sending their rebellious children to a different school system or to a parochial or private school. They cannot simply move to a less drug-infested neighborhood or put their children into therapy or other specialized counseling. They may not have the money to travel to school for parent-teacher conferences, or to pay for child care for other children while attending them. Even if a mother can ensure that a teen gets to school every morning, she cannot stay there all day, every day, to enforce attendance. As a Milwaukee assistant principal stated, sanctioned students "are not going to realize the value of an education by docking their parents. We've had youngsters brought here by their Learnfare parents at 8 o'clock, and at 9 o'clock they're gone. It's in one door and out the other." Moreover, Learnfare ignores both the wealth of literature demonstrating why teens drop out of school and the many existing programs and strategies to get them to return or remain in school. The motivations for dropping out of school are complex and do not disappear with a simple solution, however politically attractive.

* * *

Learnfare as a Tool for Social Contract

The second articulated goal of Learnfare is to create a "social contract" between the government and the welfare family. In other words, in exchange for receiving assistance, the family must comply with certain values or modify its behavior in ways deemed appropriate by policymakers. Once again, this goal is predicated on faulty assumptions. The first is that welfare families are different than average families, that is, that AFDC teens are more likely to be truant than teens in non-AFDC poor families and that an AFDC mother is less responsible for her children's school attendance, less of a parent than the average parent, and does not want the best for her children. Another faulty assumption is that the average non-AFDC family whose child is truant is not receiving "assistance" and therefore should not be required to fulfill a "social contract" with the state.

Available data confirms that children in AFDC families do not miss significantly more days of school than other children.

* * *

AFDC mothers place a strong emphasis on education for their children. In a recent study of AFDC recipients, 82% stated that education was what it "would take for their children to get ahead." AFDC mothers agreed with both the general public and members of Congress that improvement of public schools should be either the first or second priority among mechanisms to solve poverty.

Learnfare, however, blames the mother, assuming that she is at fault for her child's behavior, regardless of the availability of needed services.

* * *

Contrast the relationship the government has with non-AFDC parents whose children are truant. Non-AFDC families receive a major tax break for each dependent; no one questions their continued right to receive this dependency allowance or suggests conditioning that right on the child's school attendance record.

* * *

Learnfare's failure seriously challenges the notion that using threats to cut subsistence programs influences the behavior of those who depend on them. Designed to serve political rhetoric, the program was never supported by empirical data, but rather, was premised on superficial notions about the psychology of poor families.

Family Cap

Building on the historic biases reflected in the suitable home and "man-in-the-house" rules, the Family Cap demonstration proposals attempt to influence poor women's decisions about procreation. They are inherently flawed because they are based on the assumption that the value systems of AFDC mothers are fundamentally alien to those of the rest of the population. The proposals . . . eliminate or reduce additional AFDC benefits for the support of additional children conceived after a mother begins receiving AFDC.

* * *

The underlying goal of Family Cap programs is for people to plan for their children; the assumption is that middle-class people are intelligent enough to refrain from having children when they cannot support them and that poor women should do likewise. The unspoken motivation is far less racially benign: the stereotypical AFDC mother is African American, urban, lazy, and a "bad mother" who gets pregnant to obtain more AFDC benefits. It follows, according to the argument, that the denial of these additional benefits will curb the pregnancies that the policymakers find so troubling.

As was the case with the Learnfare programs, the underlying assumptions of Family Cap proposals--that AFDC mothers have many children, that they have free access to medical options for family planning, and that they get pregnant in order to receive additional benefits--are unsound. In fact, as of 1990, the average AFDC family, including adults, had 2.9 members; 72.5% of all families on AFDC had only one or two children, and almost 90% had three or fewer children. These figures are no larger than those found among two-parent families in the general population. Moreover, AFDC family size has declined substantially; in 1969, 32.5% of AFDC families had four or more children, and in 1990, only 9.9% had four or more children. Contrary to the commonly held perception that teen pregnancies are skyrocketing, teen birthrates have dropped dramatically over the last three decades.[118]

Furthermore, for those women who wish to terminate their pregnancies, neither abortion facilities nor government funding are necessarily available. Title X of the Public Health Service Act, the only federal program targeted for the provision of family planning services, was cut by 16% during the 1980's. In addition, even when a woman does obtain birth control, the failure rates for the most reliable forms of contraceptives (i.e., the pill, diaphragms, condoms) range from 6% to 16% per year.

There are many reasons why AFDC mothers become pregnant or choose to remain pregnant. These reasons include occurrences of unplanned pregnancies (whether due to a lack of information, money, or forethought), the belief that a child solidifies a relationship with the father, the assumption that children represent an economic value (e.g., to serve as agricultural workers, to support parents in their old age), the belief that the significant health problems and infant

---

[118]The teen birthrate per 1000 females aged 15-19 was 89.1 in 1960, 68.3 in 1970, and 58.1 in 1989. 1992 GREEN BOOK; CHILD TRENDS, INC., FACTS AT A GLANCE 1 (Jan. 1992). Although the birth rate for African- American teens has always been higher than for white teens, the Birth Rate for African-American teens has fallen with some fluctuation over the longterm, from 156.1 births per 1000 in 1960 to 115.0 births in 1989. 1992 GREEN BOOK. Further, although pregnancy rates for white women have been increasing since 1986 and for African-American women since 1984, id. at 1093, this rise cannot be credited to an increase in the economic incentive of AFDC benefits, since the value of AFDC benefits has been substantially declining since 1972. The average monthly payment per recipient in 1972 was $170.32 in 1990 dollars, but only $136 in 1990. U.S. DEPARTMENT OF HEALTH AND HUMAN SERVICES, SOCIAL SECURITY ADMINISTRATION, SOCIAL SECURITY BULLETIN, ANNUAL STATISTICAL SUPPLEMENT 108 (1992) [hereinafter SOCIAL SECURITY BULLETIN].

mortality rates associated with poverty increase the risk that a single woman with only one child will become childless, a sense that one's life is so hopeless that having a child gives it value and meaning, and the desire to give a grandchild to one's own mother. Many of these reasons are equally applicable to non-AFDC, middle-class women.

"Normal" women allegedly have children only when they are economically able to support them. This is not true. Most people do not view having a baby as the prize for having made it economically, nor do they have a child to gain an additional tax deduction for a dependent. Just like AFDC recipients, they want to be parents and to share their lives with a child. Of course, some families decide not to have an additional child because they believe that they cannot afford it, but the dollar value placed on whether they can afford it varies widely. Therefore, many upper-income families may have a small number of children because they believe it is critical to provide the child with certain advantages, such as piano lessons or private school education, that never enter the minds of a working class family with more children.

Empirical studies have consistently documented the lack of a correlation between the receipt of AFDC benefits and the child-bearing decisions of unmarried women-even for young, unmarried women. In a recent study of AFDC recipients by the Center for Urban Affairs and Policy Research, 100% of the mothers said their ability to receive AFDC had no effect on the decision to have a child. In addition, AFDC families are not larger in those states with larger AFDC grants, and teen birth rates are not higher in the states with higher AFDC grants. The number of female-headed families has continued to grow since the early 1970's, even though AFDC benefits, adjusted for inflation, have decreased by 30%. Women receiving AFDC are less likely than non-AFDC recipients to want an additional child, less likely to have multiple pregnancies, and more likely to practice contraception.

* * *

The Method Behind the Madness

In the face of uniform data that Learnfare, Family Cap, and other behavioral modification "welfare reform" proposals will not accomplish their articulated goals, why do policymakers, politicians, and the American public continue to espouse and support them? Why does American society cling to the myth that unlike the majority, welfare recipients have deviant values that can be manipulated solely by the economics of a meager AFDC grant? What has changed since the passage of the Social Security Act during the New Deal? Have those changes affected our historical ambivalence toward and perceptions of poor women and children? The answer to these questions lies in a New Right agenda, which I call an ideology of division, playing to America's deepest racial fears and to resentment of the poor, single, unemployed mother.

Beginning in the early 1980's, the New Right's economic strategy was to privilege the rich, thereby causing the "trickle down" of largesse from the wealthy to the poor. The articulated ideology was that by investing, the wealthy would create opportunities for those less fortunate. However, the result of supply-side economics has been redistribution of money to the rich, increased poverty, and a decline of the buying power of wages. To legitimate the failure of their economic agenda, the New Right sought to divert workers' justified anger from the wealthy and to focus it on welfare recipients, those who, it was argued, had not seized the offered opportunity, did not share the national work ethic, and whose values seemed to deviate dramatically from the national ideology.

The articulation of the "otherness" of the poor--their amorality and depravity--is longstanding. But the unique contribution of the American New Right has been to manipulate public attitudes through the subtle use of racism, scapegoating and stereotypes. It is no accident that the bulk of conservative scholarship about public assistance has focused on AFDC, the social welfare program that highlights most graphically race and gender distinctions. Thus the New Right has achieved popular acceptance for the misuse of AFDC laws, shifting our attention from national structural problems to the purported social deviance of individual women of color.

* * *

Contrary to the myth, empirical data does not support the stereotype of welfare recipients as African Americans living in urban ghettos. Only 39.7% of all AFDC recipients in 1990 were African American. Non-Hispanic whites comprised 38.1% of AFDC recipients in 1990. The percentage of African-American recipients has in fact decreased from 45.8% since 1973. Moreover, only 8.9% of the total poor live in "ghettos." The median stay on AFDC in 1990 was twenty-three months. Under any of prevailing definitions, the urban "underclass" is but a small percentage of the AFDC population.

Nevertheless, by focusing on images of the underclass welfare mother, the New Right has reduced the entire poverty debate to the AFDC program. The New Right advocates have transformed the increase of minorities on AFDC rolls in the 1960's and 1970's into a racially dependent definition of poverty. The New Right inflames outrage at the lack of individual responsibility in the African-American community, thus making it acceptable to express blatantly racist concepts without fear or shame.

* * *

This attempt to use economic motivation to create changed behavior in AFDC mothers and children leads to "solutions" that are contrary to empirical evidence and thus cannot solve the problems for which they are ostensibly designed. "Welfare reform" programs such as Learnfare and Family Cap do not solve burgeoning social problems; they reflect only political expedience and culturally biased mythology.

Notes and Questions

1. *False Assumptions.* Professor Williams argued that the assumptions underlying Family Cap proposals were false. What were those assumptions, and how were they false?

2. *Other Purposes.* If Williams' data are sound, why do Learnfare and Family Cap proposals and regulations persist? What other purposes might they serve for their proponents? In a later section of her article, Williams argued:

> To legitimate the failure of their economic agenda, the New Right sought to divert workers' justified anger from the wealthy and to focus it on welfare recipients, those who, it was argued, had not seized the offered opportunity, did not share the national work ethic, and whose values seemed to deviate dramatically from the national idealogy.

Do you agree? Why or why not?

3. *Critiques of Welfare Reform.* Professor Williams was not alone in her critique of welfare reform. In Congress, Senator Daniel Patrick Moynihan, who had been instrumental in leading the passage of the Family Support Act of 1988, firmly opposed the various versions of the Personal Responsibility Act and its abolition of the

federal commitment to poor children. *See, e.g.,* Ian Fisher, *A Senator Stands Alone in the Debate on Welfare,* N.Y. TIMES, Sept. 27, 1995, at A12. In the popular press, scholars wrote op-ed pieces defending the importance of a federal welfare safety net. *See, e.g.,* Richard P. Nathan, Reform Welfare? What For?, N.Y. Times, Oct. 7, 1993, at A19; Susan Mayer and Christopher Jencks, *War on Poverty: No Apologies, Please,* N.Y. TIMES, Nov. 9, 1995. Columnists joined in as well. *See, e.g.,* Clarence Page, *Welfare As We Know It May Not Be All That Bad,* ROCKY MOUNTAIN NEWS, Mar. 17, 1994, at 45A; Bob Herbert, *Scapegoat Time,* N.Y. TIMES, Nov. 16, 1994, at A19.

In scholarly journals, other legal scholars criticized the reform. *See, e.g.,* Joel F. Handler, *"Ending Welfare As We Know It"--Wrong For Welfare, Wrong For Poverty,* 2 GEORGETOWN JOURNAL ON FIGHTING POVERTY 3 (1994) (concluding "Wclfare reform by itself does nothing to improve the job market. Unless we can create more jobs that pay more income, we will have done nothing to lessen poverty or reduce the need for welfare."); Dorothy E. Roberts, *Irrationality and Sacrifice in the Welfare Reform Consensus,* 81 VIRGINIA LAW REVIEW 2607 (1995) (placing "far more hope in the possibility of forming progressive coalitions to achieve economic, racial and gender justice than I would in any welfare 'consensus' reached between liberals and conservatives"); Larry Catá Backer, *Welfare Reform at the Limit: The Futility of "Ending Welfare As We Know It,"* 30 HARVARD CIVIL RIGHTS-CIVIL LIBERTIES LAW REVIEW 339 (1995) (describing contemporary reform efforts as giving "some people more or less poor relief in the hope that they will adopt certain basic social and economic norms" and fighting "about the manner and extent to which we can compel the adoption of these norms or show disapproval for failure to adopt them") ; Lucie White, *Searching for the Logic Behind Welfare Reform,* 6 UCLA WOMEN'S LAW JOURNAL 427 (1996) (proposing disengaging from welfare reform and recentering efforts in "transnational feminist activism, particularly at the grassroots level"). Even economists weighed in on the effects of the reform efforts. *See, e.g.,* Robert Moffitt, *Welfare Reform: An Economist's Perspective,* 11 YALE LAW & POLICY REVIEW 126 (1993) (arguing that the assumptions underlying the behavioral reforms lack statistical support, and that expanded education, training, and work programs are the "best hope for a long-run solution to the welfare problem").

4. The Targets

As Lucy Williams explained, the primary goal of welfare reform seems to be to modify the behavior of poor people. To accomplish this aim, specific welfare reform proposals target certain groups of recipients, particularly unemployed adults, single mothers, children, and immigrants.

a. Unemployed Adults

According to the contemporary orthodoxy of welfare reform, all people must work outside of the home. Those who do not participate in the labor market should be forced to work as a condition of receiving welfare. While work requirements will be explored in more detail in Chapter 10, their role in welfare reform will be briefly examined here.

Recall from Chapter 1 that over 40% of AFDC recipients worked outside of the home in the early 1990s. Recipients typically complain that they cannot find jobs. States historically required welfare recipients to seek work and accept offered employment. And most recipients had to work because their welfare benefits were inadequate to support them. Congress enacted the first national work requirement for "employable" recipients in 1967. During the 1970s and 1980s, Congress toughened the work requirements while it simultaneously reduced funding for work programs. The 1988 Family Support Act's Job Opportunities and Basic Skills (JOBS) program imposed sanctions on recipients who failed to comply with work requirements, but promised additional funding for programs which support work requirements, such as child care. Congress failed to allocate funds to cover the entire cost of the JOBS program, and instead required that states meet matching fund requirements. One-third of the federal funds that were allocated for 1991 went unused because the states could not afford to meet the matching fund requirements. As a result, less than 7% of adult AFDC recipients participated in more than twenty hours of JOBS activities per week in 1992.

The truth behind work programs is that they cost money. While they may prove cost-effective in the long run, they prove quite costly in the short run. The question remains: if government has been unable to afford mandatory work programs for the vast majority of welfare recipients, how can they require every recipient to work? This question has not proved troublesome to the politicians. President Clinton's 1992 pledge to "end welfare as we know it" meant to move recipients from welfare to work. Both of the vetoed welfare reform bills in late 1995 and early 1996, and the Personal Responsibility and Work Opportunity Reconciliation Act enacted in the summer of 1996 required states to place a steadily increasing percentage of welfare recipients in work programs. Neither the vetoed bills nor the final legislation provided adequate funding to implement these work requirements.

What assumptions underlie the current reform effort to move recipients from welfare to work? Can policymakers justify supporting work requirements without the requisite funding for programs designed to move recipients to work? If so, how? Who will be affected most adversely by unfunded work requirements?

b. Single Mothers

According to Charles Murray, single motherhood is either the worst cause or the worst effect of poverty, or perhaps both. As we will explore in Chapter 9, single mothers have been a persistent target of welfare reform. Single mothers are adversely affected by the unfunded work requirements because of their need to either provide care for their children themselves or ensure other affordable, quality child care. Unlike earlier times where society preferred some single mothers to remain at home, most politicians assume that society today prefers single mothers to work. Should single mothers work outside the home? Reformers presume the answer is yes. Do single mothers work on their own initiatives? Reformers presume the answer is no. Yet some studies have shown that single mothers do work, but that their work does not substantially reduce their poverty. *See, e.g.*, Kathleen Mullan Harris, *Work and Welfare among Single Mothers in Poverty*, 99 AMERICAN JOURNAL OF SOCIOLOGY 317 (1993) (reporting results which "reveal substantial labor market activity among single mothers on welfare not previously found"); NATIONAL NETWORK FOR WOMEN'S EMPLOYMENT, WOMEN WORK, POVERTY PERSISTS: A STATUS REPORT ON DISPLACED HOMEMAKERS & SINGLE MOTHERS IN THE UNITED STATES.

Presumptions are wrong

Single mothers historically have been the special targets of moral regulation through welfare requirements. Government has regulated the sexuality of low-income single mothers through the suitable home, man-in-the-house, and substitute father rules, as well as contemporary family cap or child exclusion programs which prohibit benefits for children born during receipt of welfare.

Single mothers were the particular target of the 1996 welfare reform legislation. Consider the following Congressional findings for the Temporary Assistance for Needy Families block grant program:

> (1) Marriage is the foundation of a successful society.
>
> (2) Marriage is an essential institution of a successful society which promotes the interests of children.
>
> (3) Promotion of responsible fatherhood and motherhood is integral to successful child rearing and the well-being of children.
>
> (4) In 1992, only 54% of single-parent families with children had a child support order established and, of that 54%, only about one-half received the full amount due. . . .
>
> (5) The number of individuals receiving Aid to Families with Dependent Children . . . has more than tripled since 1965. More than two-thirds of these recipients are children. 89% of children receiving AFDC benefits now live in homes in which no father is present. . . .
>
> (6) The increase of out-of-wedlock pregnancies and births is well documented . . . .
>
> (7) An effective strategy to combat teenage pregnancy must address the issue of male responsibility, including statutory rape culpability and prevention. . . .
>
> (8) The negative consequences of an out-of-wedlock birth on the mother, the child, the family, and society are well documented . . . .
>
> (9) Currently 35% of children in single-parent homes were born out-of-wedlock, nearly the same percentage as that of children in single-parent homes whose parents are divorced (37%). . . . [T]he negative consequences of raising children in single-parent homes are well documented . . . .
>
> (10) Therefore, in light of this demonstration of the crisis in our Nation, it is the sense of the Congress that prevention of out-of-wedlock pregnancy and reduction in out-of-wedlock

> birth are very important Government interests and the policy contained [in this statute] is intended to address the crisis.

According to one legal activist, "[t]he challenge that the New Paternalism poses to poor people's advocates is . . . to use legal theories to educate as well as to litigate, and to use law to unmask the underlying roots of programs that rest on sexist and racist assumptions about poor women." Martha F. Davis, *The New Paternalism: War on Poverty or War on Women?* 1 GEORGETOWN JOURNAL ON FIGHTING POVERTY 88, 93 (1993). How could advocates for the poor use Congress' findings as Davis suggests?

c. Children

While few proponents of welfare reform publicize that their efforts will harm children, they cannot deny the serious effect of contemporary welfare reform proposals on children. For example, the family cap/child exclusion programs which deny benefits to children born during receipt of welfare deny any additional income to a family trying to absorb the costs of a new infant. Moreover, the 1996 federal welfare reform legislation cut $54 billion from various welfare programs, including over $23 billion from Food Stamps. Commentators estimated that half of the Food Stamps cut would fall on the 70% of families with children who live below half of the poverty line. Critics of the 1996 legislation warned that it would especially increase poverty among children, and deepen the extent of poverty suffered by children already poor. According to the Children's Defense Fund, the 1996 legislation will cause 1.1 million children to fall into poverty.

d. Immigrants

Hardest Hit

Immigrants may experience the most thorough suffering as a result of the summer 1996 welfare reform legislation which denies most types of benefits to immigrants, even if they are legal residents. The federal legislation prohibits states from providing Food Stamps or Supplemental Security Income to new legal immigrants. It allows states to decide whether also to deny legal immigrants benefits funded by the Temporary Assistance for Needy Families block grant program, Medicaid, and Title XX Social Services. It prohibits states from providing any federal benefits to undocumented immigrants, and prohibits states from providing their own state funds to undocumented immigrants unless the state passes explicit legislation authorizing such benefits.

e. Disabled and Elderly Persons

Federal benefits programs that provide benefits to disabled and elderly people have reduced the extent of poverty among these populations. While the programs designed to benefit disabled and elderly people had enjoyed relatively stable political support since they were nationalized, the 1996 welfare reform legislation targets them for some loss of benefits. They will suffer from the nearly 20% cuts in Food Stamp amounts, the denial of benefits to some disabled children, and the denial of benefits such as Food Stamps and Supplemental Security Income to disabled or elderly immigrants.

B. Changes in Welfare Structure and Administration

While the Personal Responsibility and Work Opportunity Reconciliation Act of 1996 created larger holes in the safety net for certain segments of the poor population, other changes accomplished by the federal legislation were structural. In particular, Congress replaced Aid to Families with Dependent Children with the Temporary Assistance for Needy Families block grant program, abolished the federal entitlement to welfare benefits, and imposed a time limit on receipt of federal welfare benefits during an individual's lifetime. Congress also imposed more stringent fraud control responsibilities on the states.

1996 Welfare structured changes

1. "Cooperative Federalism"

The welfare system is frequently described as a scheme of "cooperative federalism," a phrase popularized by the Supreme Court in *King v. Smith*. Most basic welfare programs involve concurrent federal and state oversight. Aid to Families with Dependent Children was funded jointly by federal and state governments, and administered by the state governments. Medicaid still follows this structure. (These programs are subject to regulation by Congress, the

United States Department of Health and Social Services, each state legislature, and each state welfare agency.) The Food Stamps program is funded by the federal government and administered by the states. The Supplemental Security Income program is funded and administered by the federal government. Most General Assistance programs are funded and administered by state governments. Not surprisingly, concurrent federal and state regulation of the creation, participation, regulation, and administration of many welfare programs causes poverty lawyers to develop considerable expertise in administrative law.

In addition to the practical effects of concurrent federal and state regulation of welfare, the rhetoric of federalism permeates much of the debate about the proper structure of welfare. Commentators commonly ask what level of government (national, state, or local) can best create and implement welfare programs?

Which level of government is in the best position to understand the causes of poverty? Which level of government best understands how systemic economic factors cause poverty? For example, is the national government in the best position to design anti-poverty programs that reflect its control of national economic policies, including setting interest rates so as to maintain a desired level of unemployment in order to control inflation? Or are local or state governments more likely to have knowledge about the specific strengths and weaknesses of local labor markets? Which level of government best understands how individual factors cause poverty? Can individual factors be understood in a local, regional, or national sense? Do they vary by location? Are local officials more likely to know the characteristics and behaviors of particular recipients than state or national officials?

Which level of government is in the best position to implement welfare programs? Can any level of government take better advantage of possible economies of scale? Should welfare regulations be rule-based (with less official discretion) or standard-based (with more official discretion)? What is the proper role of a welfare caseworker? Should welfare workers be effective social workers, and/or efficient managers, and/or fraud control experts?

Which level of government is more responsive to the needs of welfare recipients? Which is more responsive to the wishes of taxpayers? Which level of government is in the best position to experiment with relationships between welfare programs and their effects?

Should the question of whether welfare is the responsibility of the federal government or the states be resolved on a philosophical or historical basis? In a New York Times op-ed piece on November 15, 1995, Charles Murray claimed: "The heart of the American project was that government's powers should be limited and exercised as close to home as possible. The federalization of American life in the last half-century, not the prospect of devolution in 1995, is the historical aberration." Is Murray's claim accurate?

2. Block Grants

The Personal Responsibility and Work Opportunity Reconciliation Act of 1996 (PRA) abolished AFDC and replaced it with Temporary Assistance for Needy Families block grants to the states. Through the block grant device, the federal government provides welfare funds to states. These funds are now fixed lump sums, and states are allowed to establish their own systems for designing block grant benefits, determining eligibility for such benefits, and delivering benefits.

Block grants are not new. Several well-known programs have been funded through block grants to the states, including Comprehensive Training and Employment Act (CETA), Community Development Block Grant (CDBG), and Job Training Partnership Act (JTPA). What do we know about how block grants operate in these other programs? Block grant programs have varied greatly depending on the specific language and intent of Congress in creating the programs. According to the General Accounting Office, most block grants existing in 1995:

1) authorized federal aid for a wide range of activities within a broadly defined functional area;
2) granted states substantial discretion to identify problems, design programs, and allocate resources;
3) limited administrative, fiscal reporting, planning, and other federally imposed requirements to those necessary to ensure that national goals are being accomplished; and
4) distributed federal aid on the basis of a statutory formula

> with few, if any, matching requirements, but with federal spending caps.[1]

With regard to the effects of block grant systems, one thing is certain: federal block grant programs tend to cut, or at least limit, federal costs, because they fix expenditures.

The Personal Responsibility and Reconcilation Act of 1996 (PRA) created the Temporary Assistance for Needy Families (TANF) block grant program for welfare benefits. TANF allows states to design their own welfare systems. The federal law imposes many requirements on the states, such as putting designated percentages of their welfare recipients to work, prohibiting recipients from receiving more than 5 years of benefits, and prohibiting benefits for certain immigrants. Congress generally authorized the states to use the block grant funds in any manner "reasonably calculated" to further the purposes of the statute. Congress specified the purposes of the statute are to increase flexibility for state welfare programs to: 1) provide assistance to needy children in their homes; 2) end the dependence of needy parents on government; 3) prevent and reduce the incidence of out-of-wedlock pregnancies; and 4) encourage the formation and maintenance of two-parent families.

a. Use of Funds.

The PRA does not require states to use the block grant funds to provide cash assistance to low-income people. How will each state handle the block grant funds it receives? Will states terminate their programs that provide grants directly to poor people? What will prevent states from using welfare block grants to indirectly assist the poor, such as through funding highway improvement projects that are designed to increase economic development and jobs?

b. Insufficiency of Funds.

What will happen in states that do not allocate sufficient funds to meet the matching fund requirements? Most importantly, what

---

[1] UNITED STATES GENERAL ACCOUNTING OFFICE, REPORT TO THE CHAIRMAN, COMMITTEE ON FINANCE, U.S. SENATE, BLOCK GRANTS: ISSUES IN DESIGNING ACCOUNTABILITY PROVISIONS, September 1, 1995 [GAO/AIMD-95-226].

will happen if states use up their block grant funds without providing aid to all poor applicants? Will state or local governments create their own safety nets to care for impoverished people?

To what extent will poor people be protected from claims by state, county, or local government administrators that they have no funds available for assistance? For example, if advocates for the poor can argue that state laws created a mandate for particular welfare obligations, could they prevent a state from claiming a lack of funds? For a review of the caselaw relating to the government's defense of fiscal impossibility, *see* Anson B. Levitan, *What Does It Mean When They Say They Can't Afford It?: Defining the Fiscal Defense,* 29 Clearinghouse Review 854 (January 1996).

c. Administration.

Will states do a better job of administering welfare under a block grant system? For a veritable horror story of block grant mismanagement, *see* Robert Frank, *No Quick Fix: Proposed Block Grants Seem Unlikely to Cure Management Problems,* THE WALL STREET JOURNAL, May 1, 1995 (reporting results of a state audit which found Mississippi had "squandered" its $8.3 million child care block grant on "such things as personal furniture and designer salt and pepper shakers"). Who will control state allocation of block grants, the state legislature or the state welfare agency? How will each state's constitutional, statutory, and administrative law affect allocation and implementation of block grant programs? Will states redirect the funds as block grants to their counties or municipalities for allocation? How will state's balance the needs of rural poor people with inner city poor people? *See, e.g.,* James Dao, *Welfare Rules Created for Cities Cause Trouble in the Countryside,* N.Y. TIMES, Aug. 9, 1995, at A1. How will states interpret the language in the PRA which requires states "to serve all political subdivisions in the State (not necessarily in a uniform manner)"?

The PRA creates the possibility of increased privatization of welfare administration. It explicitly authorizes states to contract with charitable, religious, or other private organizations to administer their welfare program. News reports revealed that corporations view the overhaul and administration of welfare programs as a new marketplace. *See* Nina Bernstein, *Businesses See Big Bucks in*

Welfare, THE DENVER POST, Sept. 15, 1996, at 2A. For example, companies such as Lockheed Information Services (a division of Lockheed Martin), Electronic Data Systems (founded by perennial pundit and presidential candidate Ross Perot), and Andersen Consulting were competing in bids to operate Texas' welfare system. *Id.* Will private companies bring needed cost-effectiveness to the administration of welfare? Will they sacrifice the needs of the poor in the interest of the bottom line?

d. Discretion and Accountability.

The federalization of welfare benefits in the AFDC program was based in part on the abuse of discretion states had demonstrated when they controlled welfare programs. For a discussion of the role of discretion, *see* Joel F. Handler, *Discretion in Social Welfare: The Uneasy Position in the Rule of Law,* 92 YALE LAW JOURNAL 1270 (1983). How will recipients ensure reasonable and fair administration of the block grant funds? The PRA requires that states "set forth objective criteria for the delivery of benefits and the determination of eligibility and for fair and equitable treatment, including an explanation of how the State will provide opportunities for recipients who have been adversely affected to be heard in a State administrative or appeal process." Recipients may have a difficult time, however, demonstrating a sufficient basis for an action to enforce requirements imposed on the states by the federal legislation. Moreover, the statute expressly prohibits any officer or employee of the federal government from regulating the conduct of the states or enforcing the federal legislation, except as otherwise authorized in the statute. See Chapters 4 and 5 for a discussion of these issues.

3. Entitlement Status

On a theoretical level, welfare benefits were conceived as entitlements beginning with Charles Reich's *The New Property*, 73 YALE LAW REVIEW 733 (1964). Professor Reich argued that all government benefits on which recipients rely should be treated as entitlements. In cases brought by legal services lawyers and other poverty advocates, the Supreme Court repeatedly and explicitly reaffirmed its adoption of Reich's entitlement theory, and its rejection of the argument that receipt of welfare benefits was a mere privilege or gratuity, rather than a right. Although the Court adopted Reich's theory that benefits created by government's legislative or executive branches should be treated as entitlements, recall that the Court has never held that the constitution itself creates any entitlement or right to minimum subsistence.

The federal government established eligibility requirements for welfare programs when it began funding them in the mid 1930s. Until the 1960s, the federal government allowed states great discretion to interpret and apply these requirements. This discretion resulted in restrictive state rules such as the suitable home, man in the house, and substitute father rules.[1] These rules, which denied benefits to recipients deemed immoral and excluded racial minorities in disproportionate numbers, were invalidated by the Supreme Court.

From the 1960s to the mid 1990s, federal welfare benefits were consistently treated as federal entitlements. In the mid 1990s, welfare reformers across the political spectrum agreed to end the entitlement status of welfare benefits. Congress abolished the federal entitlement explicitly in the Personal Responsibility and Work Opportunity Reconciliation Act of 1996. Is legislative intent dispositive of the question whether a statute creates an entitlement? Review the discussion of due process in chapter 5.

4. Time Limits

In the Personal Responsibility and Work Opportunity Reconciliation Act of 1996, Congress imposed a five year lifetime cap on receipt of welfare benefits. This time limit, by ending a recipient's entitlement to welfare benefits, was intended to force poor people to move from welfare to work.

What effects will the time limit have on poor people? *See, e.g.,* Christopher Jencks, *Can We Put a Time Limit on Welfare?,* 11 THE AMERICAN PROSPECT 32 (1992). Will poor adults find work, or will homelessness and hunger increase? Can time limits be

---

[1]For a description of this early history, read Winifred Bell's book, AID TO DEPENDENT CHILDREN (1965).

challenged in court? What clients would pose the strongest challenge to time limits? What claims would they raise?

5. Fraud Control

Most discussions about welfare fraud are based on pure speculation. Many people simply assume that welfare recipients frequently commit fraud. The media produces high-profile news reports whenever welfare fraud is disclosed. We hear much less frequently about fraud in other government programs, such as income tax fraud or farm subsidy fraud. The federal and state governments nevertheless devote welfare dollars to fraud control. Is the extent of fraud in the welfare system an empirical question? Should government devote resources to determining the level of fraud in welfare programs? Does it matter whether people commit fraud more frequently in welfare programs than in other government programs?

Most welfare agencies rely on recipients' Social Security numbers to identify them. Recently some states have experimented with electronic food stamp cards designed to reduce the sale of food stamps. Others have begun to use electronic imaging machines to read fingerprints before processing welfare applications and issuing welfare checks. These systems raise issues of both cost and civil liberties. On what should government base its decision about how many welfare dollars it should spend on fraud control? What claims might be raised by recipients to argue fraud control methods go too far?

C. STATE EXPERIMENTATION

Susan Bennett & Kathleen Sullivan

DISENTITLING THE POOR: WAIVERS AND WELFARE "REFORM"

26 UNIVERSITY OF MICHIGANJOURNAL OF LAW REFORM 741 (1993)

* * *

Since 1962, the Social Security Act has included a provision permitting the Secretary of HHS to grant waivers from the requirements of the statute to states for "experimental, pilot, or demonstration project[s]" that would promote the objectives of the Act.

* * *

There is considerable evidence that waiver requests are not being scrutinized sufficiently. From 1990 through mid-1993, HHS had denied no state approval to conduct a demonstration project and to date has disapproved only one state project. Waivers also are granted relatively quickly, sometimes within thirty days of a state request. Waivers sometimes have been approved before a state has obtained the necessary state legislative approval. Although the state projects approved by HHS invariably are characterized as welfare reform experiments, the agency requires little articulation of the hypotheses a state intends to test, or the procedures by which it will evaluate those hypotheses. The agency does not generate a written record of the standards by which it evaluated the proposal, nor the reasons for its approval, other than standard approval letters and agreements. The agency even has approved waivers for states to undertake demonstration projects which imposed conditions that subsequently were held to be unconstitutional. The combination of these factors raises serious doubts about the quality of HHS decisionmaking.

Some features of the approved state projects depart drastically from the core values of the AFDC program.[16] Projects have been approved which impose residency requirements or lower benefits for recent state entrants, limit the amount of time that a recipient can collect AFDC benefits, authorize the reduction of assistance to families whose children are truant, implement across-the-board reductions in benefits to AFDC recipients, and eliminate procedures designed to assure fair process to recipients before the imposition of sanctions.

The current surge of AFDC waivers has been undertaken without regard to standards or discernible procedures ordinarily featured in administrative agency decisionmaking. Waivers have been granted without any attempt by HHS to define the types of projects

---

[16]Included among the core values of the AFDC program as expressed in the Social Security Act and interpreted by HHS and the courts are the following: that dependent children be cared for in their own homes, that children should not be penalized for the behavior of their parents, that administration be uniform within each jurisdiction, that recipients be treated equitably, and that benefit reductions be accompanied by fair process.

that promote the objectives of the public assistance titles of the Social Security Act. Furthermore, aspects of some of the state reform projects appear merely to be attempts to reduce benefits under the guise of experimentation.

* * *

Recent Reform Experiments and the Sacrifice of National Standards

The desire for cost containment drives, and indeed always has driven, much of welfare reform. The perception that welfare costs are spiraling out of control lies close to the heart of reform proposals. Some states have responded to this perception by instituting across-the-board percentage cuts in AFDC, which do not require federal approval. States also may control entry into the program by failing to increase their standard of need, the largely hypothetical figure for the actual cost of living which states must articulate, but which their payment levels need not meet. Between 1991 and 1992, six states actually lowered their AFDC payment levels and thirty-five states effectively lowered them by not increasing them, while only eleven states raised them.

It is the fear of loss of control, rather than of simple fiscal distress, that seems to inspire the desire for the kind of changes for which states must ask permission. The tenor of the proposals results from popular hypotheses for the causes of the increasing costs and growing caseloads. Central among these is the thesis that transfer payments motivate behavior that swells caseloads: migration across state lines to get bigger benefits; entry into the status of single parenthood, through either unwed motherhood or marital separation, to qualify initially for the benefit; and production of more babies to qualify for incremental increases in benefits. The thesis implicitly acknowledges that the legacy of the loose federalized structure of AFDC and of the program's history of extreme deference to the states is one of serious systemic weakness--benefits are penurious, and vary enormously from state to state. Of course, the thesis blames the recipient, not the system, for the behavior purportedly induced by the systemic weaknesses.

Of the punitive waiver-based programs born of the behavioral thesis, the most controversial program is the family cap, which withholds increases in the basic grant for children born after the family has entered the AFDC program. Four states applied to HHS in 1992 and 1993 for approval of some version of the family cap; three proposals have been approved, with action on another one pending.

* * *

The Supreme Court has long prohibited states from penalizing children because of accidents of birth. Illegitimacy and parental immigration status are two conditions for which children obviously cannot answer and for which states cannot make them suffer. When the Court has viewed disparate treatment of children as the result of birth status, it has accorded children with protections that it withheld when it chose to view similar discriminations as mere relative deprivations of needs.

Put differently, children should not suffer for their status, or for the status or behavior of their parents.

* * *

New Jersey's Family Development Act contains, among other elements, the first family cap program to receive federal waiver approval. The family cap provision of the act is one of the few enacted and approved welfare experimentation packages which has met with any litigative challenge. Here the challenge came in two forms. First, an administrative complaint filed shortly after the passage of the act with HHS's Department of Civil Rights Enforcement which as of the date of this writing, still is awaiting resolution. Second, a class action filed in federal district court to enjoin the "Child Exclusion" as violating the Act's guarantees of equal treatment, the Administrative Procedure Act, and the federal and state constitutions.

The New Jersey cap excludes from the AFDC household, and thus denies benefits to any child born to an adult woman receiving AFDC. The provision clearly is aimed at deterring pregnancy, by denying to the afterborn child and her family benefits that the child would have enjoyed had she been conceived before her family began receiving assistance.

* * *

Any constitutional justification for a family cap can be based only on the most superficial reading of the limited applicable law. In *Dandridge v. Williams*, the Supreme Court upheld Maryland's own version of the family cap, a limitation on incremental increases in AFDC payments for children born into large families. The case is cited constantly, one might say tiresomely, for the propositions that the Constitution provides no guarantee of economic rights and that states are free to set their own benefit levels. It also is cited to justify the imposition of the most minimal review of any classifications which states make in the process of administering their welfare programs. *Dandridge* constitutes the last word on judicial scrutiny of most states' welfare decisions; indeed, so final a last word that the judiciary seems to have treated it as a eulogy.

Dandridge should not be read, however, as an endorsement of the constitutionality of family caps. The *Dandridge* Court never dealt with the issue of whether the withholding of additional benefits from children born after the capped limit impermissibly penalized children by dint of their birth order. Nor did the majority opinion address the question of whether Maryland's AFDC cap violated the corresponding statutory provision that requires states to afford every eligible potential recipient of the benefit the opportunity to apply. Rather, the Court framed the issue in terms of the states' rights to spread out welfare benefits as they wished among large and small families, which are constitutionally unprotected groups. This approach allowed the Court to avoid the problem of a scheme that withheld funding from a dependent child simply because she had the misfortune of being born after seven equally dependent siblings.

This issue may be less avoidable in the litigation challenging the current cap in New Jersey. Whereas the Supreme Court in *Dandridge* could characterize the cap at issue as having the relatively benign purpose of apportioning benefits equally between larger and smaller families, the New Jersey provision penalizes welfare recipients who have additional children while on welfare, regardless of the size of their families. It thus penalizes children born to such families.

* * *

Notes and Questions

1. *State Waivers.* The AFDC statue allowed waivers to encourage state experimentation. Many reforms adopted by Congress were firsty approved by the Secretary of Health and Human Services in the form of a state waiver from compliance with federal rules. for example, States experimented with time limits, workfare, and learnfare before these requirements were adopted in the Personal

Responsibility and Work Opportunity Reconciliation Act of 1996. The reality has been, unfortunately, that states do not experiment carefully. States typically fail to alter only one variable at a time, and do not monitor the results of an experimental group compared to the results of a control group. Yet federal reform proposals frequently copy the states' experiments. Do the states' reform projects constitute true experimentation? If not, what purposes do they serve?

2. *Departure from Statutory Values.* Professors Bennett and Sullivan argued that many state waiver programs departed from "core values" of AFDC. What were those values? How did state waiver programs depart from them? Can we identify core values from a statute born of legislative compromise? Are there any "statutory norms" in the Personal Responsibility and Work Opportunity Reconciliation Act of 1996, where provision of assistance to needy families is only one of four major goals of the statute? The other goals are to end the dependence of needy parents on government benefits, to prevent and reduce the incident of out-of-wedlock pregnancies, and to encourage the formation and maintenance of two-parent families.

3. *Empirical Research.* Could some welfare reform questions be answered by empirical research? What can we learn from the literature which assesses the performance of state welfare experiments? For example, can we learn whether strengthened work requirements increase the likelihood that recipients will train, seek, obtain, and retain employment? Consider the conclusions of one scholar:

> Realistic assessment of the current debate reveals how little it is informed by the body of literature regarding the determinants of work and welfare, and how much it is a reflection of a purely political and philosophical clash between competing values that have always characterized the tensions in American social policy. The outcomes of these political decisions will be devastating if real opportunities for poor women to support their families decently through the regular labor market are absent. These policies will exacerbate growing patterns of income inequality and threats to social cohesion. A review of the significant

> discussion between what is proposed and what the research suggests will be needed to reduce poverty and welfare dependence.

Mary Bryna Sanger, *Welfare Reform Within A Changing Context: Redefining the Terms of the Debate*, 23 FORDHAM URBAN LAW JOURNAL 273 (1996).

4. *Other Critiques.* Professors Bennett and Sullivan were not alone in their critique of waivers. *See, e.g.*, Lucy A. Williams, *The Abuse of Section 1115 Waivers: Welfare Reform in Search of a Standard,* 12 YALE LAW & POLICY REVIEW 8 (1994) (concluding that "[b]road-based state experimentation without adequate evaluative processes and protections for those whose lives are being disrupted is little more than a simplistic political response to the electorate's hostility to welfare recipients"); Vernellia Randall, Sally Giess, Gabrielle Boller, Cornelia Tinkler, Shalonda Bayless, Andrew Romero, Stacey Henry, and Charles Whipple, *Section 1115 Medicaid Waivers: Critiquing the State Applications,* 26 SETON HALL LAW REVIEW 1069 (1996) (arguing that waiver applications fail to assure access to health care, especially for minority communities, and fail to assure high quality health care, but do provide for cost containment).

5. *Post-PRA State Waivers.* The Personal Responsibility and Work Opportunity Reconciliation Act of 1996 allowed states to continue waiver programs in effect as of October 1, 1996. The federal government had approved waiver applications for all but five states as of September, 1996. The PRA provided for further approval of waivers prior to July 1, 1996, providing that those waivers comply with the PRA's mandatory work requirements and do not require federal expenditures greater than those provided by the PRA. Current waiver programs depart from the requirements imposed by the PRA in numerous ways. For example, waivers in effect may provide for different time limits with different exceptions than those required by the PRA.

In the PRA, Congress authorized each state to terminate its waiver, but directed the Secretary of Health and Human Services to "encourage any State operating a waiver . . . to continue the waiver and to evaluate, using random sampling and other characteristics of accepted scientific evaluations, the result or effect of the waiver." Will this language provide a basis for identifying possible statutory standards discussed by Bennett and Sullivan?

Implementation of Temporary Assistance for Needy Families State Block Grants

The biggest fear of critics of the 1996 welfare reform is that states will engage in a race to the bottom. They fear that to ensure that a state will not attract recipients from other states, each state will attempt to make its program less attractive than those of other states. Because the Temporary Assistance for Needy Families block grant program allows each state to set its own system for eligibility, benefit levels, and delivery of benefits, no uniform federal standards will protect against a race to the bottom. The only limit to this race may be the level of human suffering each state can tolerate.

As Governor of Massachusetts, William Weld praised the unanimous vote of the nation's governors to support transferring control of welfare from the federal to the state governments. *See* William Weld, *The States Won't Be Cruel,* N.Y. TIMES, Feb. 9 1996, at A15. Governor Weld explained, "The unanimous vote ought to allay fears about returning power to the states. Clearly, the proposals are not part of a hard-hearted conservative plot. Critics suggest that our bipartisan agreement simply means that governors of both parties are more interested in balancing their budgets than in protecting the most vulnerable. This view holds that fiscal prudence and good social services are opposing goals. This fallacy was born in Washington." *Id.* He argued that most states offered more benefits than the federal government required, and that increased flexibility would allow states to deliver welfare "more efficiently and compassionately." *Id.* If state politicians are more directly accountable to the citizens of their states, how will this ensure compassionate policies? What factors are likely to influence the average voter's level of compassion? What protections exist to prevent the race to the bottom?

CHAPTER 9: THE FOCUS ON THE FAMILY

A. REGULATION OF SEXUALITY

1. Punishing "Immoral" Behavior

Yvette Marie Barksdale
AND THE POOR HAVE CHILDREN
14 LAW & INEQUALITY 1 (1995)

A Fable

Once upon a time, in a land far away, there was a swamp. This swamp was dank, dismal, and infested with crocodiles, poisonous snakes and other vermin. A whirlpool pulled people unfortunate enough to fall into the swamp deeper and deeper into its vortex, until they drowned or were destroyed by the vermin. This was not a place into which any sane person would wish to venture. Unfortunately, every so often a hapless traveller would stumble by and find herself pulled into the quagmire.

Not far from the swamp there lived a man. The man, having grown up near the swamp, knew its eddies and currents, its ebbs and flows, its pitfalls and escape routes. He knew how to save hapless travellers who might stumble into the swamp. However, he was also an ideologue. His mission in life was to reform the world according to his personal vision of morality and right. He considered each traveller who stumbled by a page onto which he might write his particular vision of morality and justice. Each time he heard the horrified screams of a traveller in distress, he thought, "Aha, someone I can save." However, his rescue always had a price. The price was that the traveller agree to forfeit her freedom, to live within the rescuer's homestead, and to abide by his moral requirements. If she did not agree, or if at any later time she departed from the ethical code, she was simply thrown back into the swamp. Indeed, these rescue rejects were the primary source of nourishment for the vermin within.

Was this Samaritan good?

* * *

The more things change, the more they stay the same. The regulation of poor women's sexuality has been consistently a central aim of American welfare policy. Consider the rules restricting sexual conduct developed by states as a limitation on Aid to Families with Dependent Children eligibility, including the suitable home rules, the man-in-the-house rules, and the substitute father rules. Each of these rules, in effect, required termination of the family's benefits if the mother was suspected of having sex with a man. They are discussed in the opinions in *King v. Smith* below, which is rich in analysis relating to the regulation of poor women's sexuality.

KING v. SMITH

392 U.S. 309 (1968)

CHIEF JUSTICE WARREN delivered the opinion of the Court.

Alabama, together with every other State, Puerto Rico, the Virgin Islands, the District of Columbia, and Guam, participates in the Federal Government's Aid to Families With Dependent Children (AFDC) program, which was established by the Social Security Act of 1935. This appeal presents the question whether a regulation of the Alabama Department of Pensions and Security, employed in that Department's administration of the State's federally funded AFDC program, is consistent with Subchapter IV of the Social Security Act, 42 U.S.C. §§ 601-609, and with the Equal Protection Clause of the Fourteenth Amendment. At issue is the validity of Alabama's so-called "substitute father" regulation which denies AFDC payments to the children of a mother who "cohabits" in or outside her home with any single or married able-bodied man. Appellees brought this class action against appellants, officers, and members of the Alabama Board of Pensions and Security, in the United States District Court for the Middle District of Alabama, under 42 U.S.C. § 1983,[2] seeking declaratory and injunctive relief. . . .

---

[2]"Every person who, under color of any statute, ordinance, regulation, custom, or usage, of any State or Territory, subjects or causes to be subjected, any citizen of the United States or other person within the jurisdiction thereof to the deprivation of any rights, privileges, or immunities secured by the Constitution and laws, shall be liable to the party injured in an action at law, suit in equity, or other proper proceeding for redress."

The AFDC program is one of three major categorical public assistance programs established by the Social Security Act of 1935. The category singled out for welfare assistance by AFDC is the "dependent child," who is defined as an age-qualified "needy child . . . who has been deprived of parental support or care by reason of the death, continued absence from the home or physical or mental incapacity of a parent, and who is living with" any one of several listed relatives. Under this provision, and, insofar as relevant here, aid can be granted only if "a parent" of the needy child is continually absent from the home. Alabama considers a man who qualifies as a "substitute father" under its regulation to be a nonabsent parent within the federal statute. The State therefore denies aid to an otherwise eligible needy child on the basis that his substitute parent is not absent from the home.

Under the Alabama regulation, an "able-bodied man, married or single, is considered a substitute father of *all the children of the applicant* . . . mother" in three different situations: (1) if "he lives in the home with the child's natural or adoptive mother for the purpose of cohabitation"; or (2) if "he visits [the home] frequently for the purpose of cohabiting with the child's natural or adoptive mother"; or (3) if "he does not frequent the home but cohabits with the child's natural or adoptive mother elsewhere." Whether the substitute father is actually the father of the children is irrelevant. It is also irrelevant whether he is legally obligated to support the children, and whether he does in fact contribute to their support. What is determinative is simply whether he "cohabits" with the mother.[9]

The testimony below by officials responsible for the administration of Alabama's AFDC program establishes that "cohabitation," as used in the regulation, means essentially that the man and woman have "frequent" or "continuing" sexual relations.

---

[9]Under the regulation, when "there appears to be a substitute father," the mother bears the burden of proving that she has discontinued her relationship with the man before her AFDC assistance will be resumed. The mother's claim of discontinuance must be "corroborated by at least two acceptable references in a position to know. Examples of acceptable references are: law-enforcement officials; ministers; neighbors; grocers." There is no hearing prior to the termination of aid, but an applicant denied aid may secure state administrative review.

With regard to how frequent or continual these relations must be, the testimony is conflicting. One state official testified that the regulation applied only if the parties had sex at least once a week; another thought once every three months would suffice; and still another believed once every six months sufficient. The regulation itself provides that pregnancy or a baby under six months of age is prima facie evidence of a substitute father.

Between June 1964, when Alabama's substitute father regulation became effective, and January 1967, the total number of AFDC recipients in the State declined by about 20,000 persons, and the number of children recipients by about 16,000 or 22%. As applied in this case, the regulation has caused the termination of all AFDC payments to the appellees, Mrs. Sylvester Smith and her four minor children.

Mrs. Smith and her four children, ages 14, 12, 11, and 9, reside in Dallas County, Alabama. For several years prior to October 1, 1966, they had received aid under the AFDC program. By notice dated October 11, 1966, they were removed from the list of persons eligible to receive such aid. This action was taken by the Dallas County welfare authorities pursuant to the substitute father regulation, on the ground that a Mr. Williams came to her home on weekends and had sexual relations with her.

Three of Mrs. Smith's children have not received parental support or care from a father since their natural father's death in 1955. The fourth child's father left home in 1963, and the child has not received the support or care of his father since then. All the children live in the home of their mother, and except for the substitute father regulation are eligible for aid. The family is not receiving any other type of public assistance, and has been living, since the termination of AFDC payments, on Mrs. Smith's salary of between $16 and $20 per week which she earns working from 3:30 a.m. to 12 noon as a cook and waitress.

Mr. Williams, the alleged "substitute father" of Mrs. Smith's children, has nine children of his own and lives with his wife and family, all of whom are dependent upon him for support. Mr. Williams is not the father of any of Mrs. Smith's children. He is not legally obligated, under Alabama law, to support any of Mrs. Smith's children. Further, he is not willing or able to support the Smith children, and does not in fact support them. His wife is required to work to help support the Williams household.

The AFDC program is based on a scheme of cooperative federalism. It is financed largely by the Federal Government, on a matching fund basis, and is administered by the States. States are not required to participate in the program, but those which desire to take advantage of the substantial federal funds available for distribution to needy children are required to submit an AFDC plan for the approval of the Secretary of Health, Education, and Welfare (HEW). The plan must conform with several requirements of the Social Security Act and with rules and regulations promulgated by HEW.

One of the statutory requirements is that "aid to families with dependent children . . . shall be furnished with reasonable promptness to all eligible individuals. . . ." As noted above, § 406(a) of the Act defines a "dependent child" as one who has been deprived of "parental" support or care by reason of the death, continued absence, or incapacity of a "parent." In combination, these two provisions of the Act clearly require participating States to furnish aid to families with children who have a parent absent from the home, if such families are in other respects eligible.

The State argues that its substitute father regulation simply defines who is a nonabsent "parent" under § 406(a) of the Social Security Act. The State submits that the regulation is a legitimate way of allocating its limited resources available for AFDC assistance, in that it reduces the caseload of its social workers and provides increased benefits to those still eligible for assistance. Two state interests are asserted in support of the allocation of AFDC assistance achieved by the regulation: first, it discourages illicit sexual relationships and illegitimate births; second, it puts families in which there is an informal "marital" relationship on a par with those in which there is an ordinary marital relationship, because families of the latter sort are not eligible for AFDC assistance.

We think it well to note at the outset what is *not* involved in this case. There is no question that States have considerable latitude in allocating their AFDC resources, since each State is free to set its own standard of need and to determine the level of benefits by the amount of funds it devotes to the program.[15] Further, there is no question that regular and actual contributions to a needy child, including contributions from the kind of person Alabama calls a substitute father, can be taken into account in determining whether the child is needy. In other words, if by reason of such a man's contribution, the child is not in financial need, the child would be ineligible for AFDC assistance without regard to the substitute father rule. The appellees here, however, meet Alabama's need requirements; their alleged substitute father makes no contribution to their support; and they have been denied assistance solely on the basis of the substitute father regulation. Further, the regulation itself is unrelated to need, because the actual financial situation of the family is irrelevant in determining the existence of a substitute father.

Also not involved in this case is the question of Alabama's general power to deal with conduct it regards as immoral and with the problem of illegitimacy. This appeal raises only the question whether the State may deal with these problems in the manner that it has here--by flatly denying AFDC assistance to otherwise eligible dependent children.

Alabama's argument based on its interests in discouraging immorality and illegitimacy would have been quite relevant at one time in the history of the AFDC program. However, subsequent developments clearly establish that these state interests are not presently legitimate justifications for AFDC disqualification. Insofar as this or any similar regulation is based on the State's asserted interest in discouraging illicit sexual behavior and illegitimacy, it plainly conflicts with federal law and policy.

A significant characteristic of public welfare programs during the last half of the 19th century in this country was their preference for the "worthy" poor. Some poor persons were thought worthy of public assistance, and others were thought unworthy because of their

---

[15]The rather complicated formula for federal funding is contained in 42 U.S.C. § 603. The level of benefits is within the State's discretion, but the Federal Government's contribution is a varying percentage of the total AFDC expenditures within each State. The benefit levels vary greatly from State to State. For example, for May 1967, the average payment to a family under AFDC was about $224 in New Jersey, $221 in New York, $39 in Mississippi, $20 in Puerto Rico, and $53 in Alabama.

supposed incapacity for "moral regeneration." This worthy-person concept characterized the mothers' pension welfare programs, which were the precursors of AFDC. Benefits under the mothers' pension programs, accordingly, were customarily restricted to widows who were considered morally fit.

In this social context it is not surprising that both the House and Senate Committee Reports on the Social Security Act of 1935 indicate that States participating in AFDC were free to impose eligibility requirements relating to the "moral character" of applicants. During the following years, many state AFDC plans included provisions making ineligible for assistance dependent children not living in "suitable homes." As applied, these suitable home provisions frequently disqualified children on the basis of the alleged immoral behavior of their mothers.[18]

In the 1940's, suitable home provisions came under increasing attack. Critics argued, for example, that such disqualification provisions undermined a mother's confidence and authority, thereby promoting continued dependency; that they forced destitute mothers into increased immorality as a means of earning money; that they were habitually used to disguise systematic racial discrimination; and that they senselessly punished impoverished children on the basis of their mothers' behavior, while inconsistently permitting them to remain in the allegedly unsuitable homes. In 1945, the predecessor of HEW produced a state letter arguing against suitable home provisions and recommending their abolition. Although 15 States abolished their provisions during the following decade, numerous other States retained them.

In the 1950's, matters became further complicated by pressures in numerous States to disqualify illegitimate children from AFDC assistance. Attempts were made in at least 18 States to enact laws excluding children on the basis of their own or their siblings' birth status. All but three attempts failed to pass the state

---

[18]Bell quotes a case record, for example, where a mother whose conduct with men displeased a social worker was required, as a condition of continued assistance, to sign an affidavit stating that, "I . . . do hereby promise and agree that until such time as the following agreement is rescinded, I will not have any male callers coming to my home nor meeting me elsewhere under improper conditions." W. BELL, AID TO DEPENDENT CHILDREN 48 (1965).

legislatures, and two of the three successful bills were vetoed by the governors of the States involved. In 1960, the federal agency strongly disapproved of illegitimacy disqualifications.

Nonetheless, in 1960, Louisiana enacted legislation requiring, as a condition precedent for AFDC eligibility, that the home of a dependent child be "suitable," and specifying that any home in which an illegitimate child had been born subsequent to the receipt of public assistance would be considered unsuitable. In the summer of 1960, approximately 23,000 children were dropped from Louisiana's AFDC rolls. In disapproving this legislation, then Secretary of Health, Education, and Welfare Flemming issued what is now known as the Flemming Ruling, stating that as of July 1, 1961,:

> *A State plan . . . may not impose an eligibility condition that would deny assistance with respect to a needy child on the basis that the home conditions in which the child lives are unsuitable, while the child continues to reside in the home.* Assistance will therefore be continued during the time efforts are being made either to improve the home conditions or to make arrangements for the child elsewhere.

Congress quickly approved the Flemming Ruling, while extending until September 1, 1962, the time for state compliance. At the same time, Congress acted to implement the ruling by providing, on a temporary basis, that dependent children could receive AFDC assistance if they were placed in foster homes after a court determination that their former homes were, as the Senate Report stated, "unsuitable because of the immoral or negligent behavior of the parent."

In 1962, Congress made permanent the provision for AFDC assistance to children placed in foster homes and intended such coverage to include children placed in child-care institutions. At the same time, Congress modified the Flemming Ruling by amending § 404(b) of the Act. As amended, the statute permits States to disqualify from AFDC aid children who live in unsuitable homes, provided they are granted other "adequate care and assistance."

Thus, under the 1961 and 1962 amendments to the Social Security Act, the States are permitted to remove a child from a home that is judicially determined to be so unsuitable as to "be contrary to the welfare of such child." The States are also permitted to terminate

AFDC assistance to a child living in an unsuitable home, if they provide other adequate care and assistance for the child under a general welfare program. The statutory approval of the Flemming Ruling, however, precludes the States from otherwise denying AFDC assistance to dependent children on the basis of their mothers' alleged immorality or to discourage illegitimate births.

The most recent congressional amendments to the Social Security Act further corroborate that federal public welfare policy now rests on a basis considerably more sophisticated and enlightened than the "worthy-person" concept of earlier times. State plans are now required to provide for a rehabilitative program of improving and correcting unsuitable homes; to provide voluntary family planning services for the purpose of reducing illegitimate births; and to provide a program for establishing the paternity of illegitimate children and securing support for them.

In sum, Congress has determined that immorality and illegitimacy should be dealt with through rehabilitative measures rather than measures that punish dependent children, and that protection of such children is the paramount goal of AFDC. In light of the Flemming Ruling and the 1961, 1962, and 1968 amendments to the Social Security Act, it is simply inconceivable, as HEW has recognized, that Alabama is free to discourage immorality and illegitimacy by the device of absolute disqualification of needy children. Alabama may deal with these problems by several different methods under the Social Security Act. But the method it has chosen plainly conflicts with the Act.

Alabama's second justification for its substitute father regulation is that "there is a public interest in a State not undertaking the payment of these funds to families who because of their living arrangements would be in the same situation as if the parents were married, except for the marriage." In other words, the State argues that since in Alabama the needy children of married couples are not eligible for AFDC aid so long as their father is in the home, it is only fair that children of a mother who cohabits with a man not her husband and not their father be treated similarly. The difficulty with this argument is that it fails to take account of the circumstance that children of fathers living in the home are in a very different position from children of mothers who cohabit with men not their fathers: the child's father has a legal duty to support him, while the unrelated substitute father, at least in Alabama, does not. We believe Congress intended the term "parent" to include only those persons with a legal duty of support.

The Social Security Act of 1935 was part of a broad legislative program to counteract the depression. Congress was deeply concerned with the dire straits in which all needy children in the Nation then found themselves. . . . The AFDC program, however, was not designed to aid all needy children. The plight of most children was caused simply by the unemployment of their fathers. With respect to these children, Congress planned that "the work relief program and . . . the revival of private industry" would provide employment for their fathers. As the Senate Committee Report stated: "Many of the children included in relief families present no other problem than that of providing work for the breadwinner of the family." Implicit in this statement is the assumption that children would in fact be supported by the family "breadwinner."

The AFDC program was designed to meet a need unmet by programs providing employment for breadwinners. It was designed to protect what the House Report characterized as "[o]ne clearly distinguishable group of children." This group was composed of children in families without a "breadwinner," "wage earner," or "father," as the repeated use of these terms throughout the Report of the President's Committee, Committee Hearings and Reports, and the floor debates makes perfectly clear. To describe the sort of breadwinner that it had in mind, Congress employed the word "parent." A child would be eligible for assistance if his parent was deceased, incapacitated or continually absent.

The question for decision here is whether Congress could have intended that a man was to be regarded as a child's parent so as to deprive the child of AFDC eligibility despite the circumstances: (1) that the man did not in fact support the child; and (2) that he was not legally obligated to support the child. The State correctly observes that the fact that the man in question does not actually support the child cannot be determinative, because a natural father at home may fail actually to support his child but his presence will still render the child ineligible for assistance. On the question whether the man must be legally obligated to provide support before he can be regarded as the child's parent, the State has no such cogent answer. We think the answer is quite clear: Congress must have meant by the term "parent" an individual who owed to the child a state-imposed legal duty of support.

It is clear, as we have noted, that Congress expected "breadwinners" who secured employment would support their children. This congressional expectation is most reasonably explained on the basis that the kind of breadwinner Congress had in mind was one who was legally obligated to support his children. We think it beyond reason to believe that Congress would have considered that providing employment for the paramour of a deserted mother would benefit the mother's children whom he was not obligated to support.

By a parity of reasoning, we think that Congress must have intended that the children in such a situation remain eligible for AFDC assistance notwithstanding their mother's impropriety. . . . We think it apparent that neither Congress nor any reasonable person would believe that providing employment for some man who is under no legal duty to support a child would in any way provide meaningful economic security for that child.

* * *

Our interpretation of the term "parent" is strongly supported by the way the term is used in other sections of the Act.

* * *

We think that these provisions corroborate the intent of Congress that the only kind of "parent," under § 406(a), whose presence in the home would provide adequate economic protection for a dependent child is one who is legally obligated to support him. Consequently, if Alabama believes it necessary that it be able to disqualify a child on the basis of a man who is not under such a duty of support, its arguments should be addressed to Congress and not this Court.

* * *

In denying AFDC assistance to appellees on the basis of this invalid regulation, Alabama has breached its federally imposed obligation to furnish "aid to families with dependent children . . . with reasonable promptness to all eligible individuals. . . ." Our conclusion makes unnecessary consideration of appellees' equal-protection claim, upon which we intimate no views.

We think it well, in concluding, to emphasize that no legitimate interest of the State of Alabama is defeated by the decision we announce today. The State's interest in discouraging illicit sexual behavior and illegitimacy may be protected by other means, subject to constitutional limitations, including state participation in AFDC rehabilitative programs. Its interest in economically allocating its limited AFDC resources may be protected by its undisputed power to set the level of benefits and the standard of need, and by its taking into account in determining whether a child is needy all actual and regular contributions to his support.

All responsible governmental agencies in the Nation today recognize the enormity and pervasiveness of social ills caused by poverty. The causes of and cures for poverty are currently the subject of much debate. We hold today only that Congress has made at least this one determination: that destitute children who are legally fatherless cannot be flatly denied federally funded assistance on the transparent fiction that they have a substitute father.

Affirmed.

Justice DOUGLAS (concurring).

The Court follows the statutory route in reaching the result that I reach on constitutional grounds. It is, of course, traditional that our disposition of cases should, if possible, be on statutory rather than constitutional grounds, unless problems of statutory construction are insurmountable. We do have, however, in this case a long-standing administrative construction that approves state AFDC plans containing a man-in-the-house provision. Certainly that early administrative construction, which so far as I can ascertain has been a consistent one, is entitled to great weight.

The Department of Health, Education, and Welfare balked at the Alabama provision only because it reached all nonmarital sexual relations of the mother, not just nonmarital relations on a regular basis in the mother's house. Since I cannot distinguish between the two categories, I reach the constitutional question.

The Alabama regulation describes three situations in which needy children, otherwise eligible for relief, are to be denied financial assistance. In none of these is the child to blame. The disqualification of the family, and hence the needy child, turns upon the "sin" of the mother.[4]

First, if a man not married to the mother and not the father of the children lives in her home for purposes of cohabitating with her, the children are cast into the outer darkness.

Second, if a man who is not married to the mother and is not the father of the children visits her home for the purpose of cohabitating with her, the needy children meet the same fate.

Third, if a man not married to the mother and not the father of the children cohabits with her outside the home, then the needy children are likewise denied relief. In each of these three situations the needy family is wholly cut off from AFDC assistance without considering whether the mother's paramour is in fact aiding the family, is financially able to do so, or is legally required to do so. Since there is "sin," the paramour's wealth or indigency is irrelevant.

In other words, the Alabama regulation is aimed at punishing mothers who have nonmarital sexual relations. The economic need of the children, their age, their other means of support, are all irrelevant. The standard is the so-called immorality of the mother.

The other day in a comparable situation we held that the Equal Protection Clause of the Fourteenth Amendment barred discrimination against illegitimate children. We held that they cannot be denied a cause of action because they were conceived in "sin," that the making of such a disqualification was an invidious discrimination. I would think precisely the same result should be reached here. I would say that the immorality of the mother has no rational connection with the need of her children under any welfare program.

Notes and Questions

1. *The Development and Interpretation of Rules.* Notice how the Alabama regulations evolved. The federal statute limited

---

[4]Whether the mother alone could constitutionally be cut off from assistance because of her "sin" is a question not presented. The aid is to the needy family, and without removing the children from their mother because of her unfitness--action not contemplated here, as far as the record indicates--there is no existing means by which Alabama can assist the children while ensuring that the mother does not benefit.

eligibility for AFDC benefits to children with an absent "parent." Alabama took it from there. First, Alabama, like other states, issued a regulation that deemed a "substitute father" to be a nonabsent parent. Second, Alabama defined a substitute father to be any man who "lives," "visits," or "cohabits" with the mother. At this point, officials' interpretations of the state's regulations took over. These officials interpreted cohabitation to mean "frequent" or "continuing" sexual relations. Officials' interpretations then differed as to whether frequent or continuing sexual relations meant once every week, every three months, or every six months. Were Alabama's interpretations of the federal statute's meaning of "parent" reasonable? Were the state agency officials' interpretations of the Alabama regulations reasonable? How did the plaintiffs challenge the reasonableness of these interpretations? Did welfare recipients have fair notice of what behavior was prohibited?

2. *Statutory Interpretation.* The Supreme Court faced the same challenge addressed by Alabama's substitute father rule -- it had to interpret what Congress meant in limiting benefits to children suffering the absence of a parent. How did the Court arrive at its conclusion that only an individual who has a legal obligation to support a child is a parent within the meaning of the statute? Was the Court's interpretation of Congress' intent reasonable? Did the state's interpretation actually conflict with the federal statute? On what would that depend?

3. *State's Interests.* Alabama argued that it was merely interpreting the federal statute to allocate its limited resources in such a manner as to discourage immorality and to treat equally informal and formal marital relationships.

Regarding immorality, the Supreme Court relied in part on the federal government's rejection of punitive suitable home rules in favor of rehabilitative requirements. What if Congress instead had adopted suitable home and/or substitute father rules? Would that have changed the Court's analysis and the outcome?

On what basis did the Court conclude that informal and formal marital relationships should be treated differently, at least for purposes of AFDC eligibility?

4. *The Fairness of Process.* As a procedural matter, the welfare agency's presumption of the existence of a substitute father prevailed unless the mother rebutted the presumption with

corroboration from two witnesses such as law enforcement officials, ministers, neighbors, or grocers. Moreover, pregnancy or a baby under six months old were deemed prima face evidence of a substitute father. Also, recipients received no prior hearing but suffered termination of benefits unless and until the state reversed its decision. Would these procedures survive a due process challenge?

5. *The Role of Ideology.* Review the excerpt from Martha Fineman's article, The Images of Mothers in Poverty Discourses (excerpted in Chapter 1). Did Alabama's substitute father rule reflect patriarchal ideology? If so, how? Does the Supreme Court's reasoning also reflect that ideology? Many commentators criticize the impact of personal political views on judicial decisions, although the centrality of politics is well accepted in the legislative and executive arenas. How could judges separate their decision-making from the influence of prevailing ideology? When a judge's own morality conforms to prevailing norms, how should that judge resolve any conflict between her individual moral ideology and her duty to protect minorities from any oppression dictated by that ideology? Would a judge be likely to decide that a policy she finds to be moral could be oppressive?

Regulation of Sexuality in Temporary Assistance For Needy Families Block Grants

In the 1996 Personal Responsibility and Work Opportunity Reconciliation Act of 1996, Congress replaced AFDC with the Temporary Assistance for Needy Families block grants. In what ways does this legislation continue the historical focus on the regulation of poor women's sexuality? For example, one of the principle goals of the legislation is to prevent and reduce the incidence of out-of-wedlock pregnancies. States retain broad discretion to determine how to meet this goal. Would a state's denial of TANF benefits to women who have male visitors survive a challenge similar to *King v. Smith*? May the government constitutionally limit a woman's procreation?

The TANF block grant legislation requires states to take certain actions with regard to young parents. For example, it specifically prohibits states from providing assistance to unmarried teenage parents who have not completed, and are not working toward, the equivalent of a high school education. It also prohibits states from providing assistance to unmarried teenage parents who do not reside with an approved adult supervisor. Are these provisions constitutional?

For a discussion calling for better formulation of policies designed to reduce teen pregnancies, *see* Deborah Jones Merritt, *Ending Poverty by Cutting Teenaged Births: Promise, Failure, and Paths to the Future*, 57 OHIO STATE LAW JOURNAL 441 (1996); Deborah L. Rhode, *Politics and Pregnancy: Adolescent Mothers and Public Policy,* 1 REVIEW OF LAW AND WOMEN'S STUDIES 99 (1992). For a broader discussion about welfare reforms aimed at controlling the reproduction of poor women, *see* Linda C. McClain, *"Irresponsible" Reproduction,* 47 HASTINGS LAW JOURNAL 339 (1996); Dorothy E. Roberts, *The Future of Reproductive Choice for Poor Women and Women of Color*, 14 WOMEN'S RIGHTS LAW REPORTER 305 (1992). Consider Linda McClain's conclusion:

> An assumption in much of the rhetoric of reproductive irresponsibility is that a particular family form -- the marital, heterosexual two-parent family -- is morally superior to other forms and best suited for important tasks of social reproduction. Too little serious conversation takes place, however, about precisely what the functions of families are and how the state should support and facilitate families in performing those functions. The appeal to inscribe personal responsibility into law and policy raises significant questions about what kind of responsibility government will promote and who will be included and excluded from such campaigns. I have suggested that current rhetoric stresses the need for responsibility as accountability; insufficient attention is given to providing or respecting the preconditions for responsibility as autonomy. As the keen attention to steering the reproductive behavior of welfare recipients suggests, people dependent on government for the means of subsistence may be more subject to and vulnerable to such campaigns than other citizens, even though the rhetoric of irresponsibility at its broadest implicates the lives of many other persons. This selectivity warrants close attention.

McLain at 453. What implications do McClain's arguments raise for policy, and for potential legal challenges to restrictions on poor women's reproductive activity?

What if a state conditions receipt of welfare on sterilization or use of the contraceptive Norplant? Would such restrictions be constitutional? For a discussion of these issues, *see* Meredith Blake, *Welfare and Coerced Contraception: Morality Implications of State Sponsored Reproductive Control,* 34 UNIVERSITY OF LOUISVILLE JOURNAL OF FAMILY LAW 311 (1995-96). Also, review Chapter 7 on Unconstitutional Conditions. In the next section, we revisit the unconstitutional conditions dilemma with regard to another popular welfare reform proposal, the so-called family cap or child exclusion.

2. Excluding Children From Benefits

Yvette Marie Barksdale
AND THE POOR HAVE CHILDREN
14 LAW & INEQUALITY 1

* * *

Family cap plans are an increasingly popular form of so-called welfare reform. The plans generally deny new birth benefit increases for children born or conceived while the mother is receiving Aid for Dependent Children (AFDC). Arkansas, Georgia, New Jersey, and Wisconsin were the four earliest states to adopt such welfare programs. Subsequently, several other states have passed or introduced legislation to do the same.

* * *

The first Wisconsin program was a five year pilot program called the Parental and Family Responsibility Demonstration Project (PFR), which applied only to a limited target population (primarily teenage parents) in certain Wisconsin counties. Wisconsin has subsequently adopted a "Work Not Welfare" proposal that also includes a child limitation proposal. Most recently, Wisconsin adopted a statewide AFDC Benefit Cap program, which would eliminate the additional birth increment for children born to welfare recipients on or after November 1, 1996.

According to the State of Wisconsin, the PFR plan is designed to promote families by removing disincentives in the welfare system that may discourage young couples from marrying and working. The Wisconsin PFR plan reduces the normal benefit increase for additional children by half when a second child is born and eliminates the increase entirely for the third child and subsequent children. The plan permits working welfare recipients to "earn back" some of the lost benefits by increasing the "earned income disregards." The earned income disregard provides that certain limited amounts of earned income may be disregarded in calculating welfare recipient income for purposes of determining welfare eligibility, and thus permits working recipients to earn more money yet still remain eligible for welfare. Thus, if a person whose income exceeds $6,000 per year is ineligible for welfare, the "income disregard" permits the recipient to "disregard" certain earned income in determining whether her total income exceeds $6,000.

* * *

[T]he Wisconsin PFR pilot program specifically states that two of its goals are to reduce the number of children born to teenage welfare mothers and to promote marriage among pregnant teenagers.

* * *

The proposed federal legislation adopting family caps is also based upon moral and value judgments about procreative choices. For example, the express purpose of the bill passed by the House of Representatives is to promote marriage and reduce illegitimacy. The welfare reform bill states that marriage is "the foundation of a successful society" and an "essential social institution," and that a goal of the welfare program is "promoting work and marriage and discourag[ing] out of wedlock births."

These policies handicap welfare recipients by denying their children eligibility for welfare, even though the children would have been eligible if born to non-recipients. Family cap policies substitute the government's own model of appropriate behavior for that of the welfare recipient, and accordingly substitute the government's value choice concerning childbearing for that of the individual. The question that thus arises is whether it is appropriate for the government to intrude into the childbearing choices of poor women merely because they are dependent upon government aid.

* * *

The Supreme Court has clearly established that the right to decide whether to bear or beget children is part of an individual's constitutionally protected fundamental right of privacy. The Court grounded the right in the general due process protection of the freedom to make intimate decisions concerning family life, including decisions regarding contraception, abortion, and childbearing. Accordingly, government intrusions upon the right are traditionally subject to strict scrutiny and are thus permissible only if narrowly tailored to further a compelling state interest. The Supreme Court has struck down state statutes authorizing forced sterilization of criminals, banning or restricting access to contraception, and prohibiting abortion. The Supreme Court has upheld state restrictions on the right to decide whether to bear or beget children primarily in the abortion cases based upon the state's considerable interest in protecting life. Yet even here the Supreme Court upheld only limited government restrictions on the right to an abortion. In circumstances other than the decision to abort, the Court has rarely recognized any state interest as sufficient to justify restricting the individual's childbearing decisions. Obviously, the state's interest in protecting life would not justify governmental restrictions on an individual's decision to bear children. Government restrictions on decisions to bear children burden rather than advance the state interest in protecting life. Other lesser government interests, such as the state's interests in protecting security and deterring crime, are sometimes asserted to support sterilization or contraception restrictions. However, these interests also rarely pass muster, except in the context of persons considered to have less constitutional protection, such as convicted persons, prisoners, or in some cases the mentally incompetent.

Accordingly, a government welfare plan that simply forbids welfare mothers to have children while receiving welfare would violate welfare mothers' fundamental constitutional right to bear children. Such a plan might not be as intrusive as forced sterilization of welfare recipients and would only apply during the limited duration of a mother's status as a welfare beneficiary, yet even such a limited prohibition on the childbearing rights of a welfare mother would infringe upon her fundamental right to decide whether to bear children. Such a plan would be subjected to heightened scrutiny, under which the supporting interests that the government might assert, such as an interest in lowering welfare costs or in enforcing the government's standards of moral decency or responsibility, would not justify the plan's impairment of welfare mothers' right to bear and beget children.

Moreover, even as to funding decisions, the government probably could not constitutionally eliminate welfare recipients' right to all benefits or even reduce recipients' prior entitlement on the birth of an additional child. Supreme Court doctrine provides that the government may not burden or penalize the exercise of a fundamental right, even if the government does not prohibit the exercise of the right altogether. For example, the state may not impose improper regulatory requirements upon the right, or, as applied to funding decisions, completely deny persons eligibility for government entitlements because of the exercise of the right. Under this view, depriving welfare recipients of eligibility for all support or reducing benefit payments upon the birth of a child would burden the exercise of the right, and thus would violate the right.

Under traditional fundamental rights analysis, the government could not constitutionally forbid people, whether welfare recipients or not, from having children or otherwise penalize them for having additional children by eliminating or reducing their welfare entitlement. However, current Supreme Court doctrine suggests that the government may indirectly influence or encourage the welfare recipient to choose not to have additional children by refusing to fund the additional child.

* * *

The Court's distinction between benefit allocations that are impermissible burdens or penalties and those that are permissible refusals to subsidize is fairly clear. The Supreme Court considers a government benefits allocation to be a burden or penalty on the exercise of a constitutional right if the benefit allocation permits individuals to exercise the constitutional right only by forfeiting either another constitutional right, a property right, or a statutory entitlement to something other than direct funding of the constitutional right at stake. If, in contrast, the government simply "refuses" to extend funding to the particular constitutional right at stake and does not otherwise require a forfeiture by the individual as a cost of exercising the right, the allocation is not a penalty or a burden on the right, but is merely a permissible refusal to subsidize. The Supreme Court's position, pursuant to its negative rights view of the Constitution, is that the Constitution places few--if any--limits on government's ability to refuse to subsidize the exercise of a constitutional right, even if government expressly excludes the constitutional right from otherwise available government funding. Such refusals to subsidize may in fact substantially harm a recipient because of her exercise of a constitutional right, but the Court concludes that such programs are permissible as long as the funding allocation does not penalize or burden the right.

Under this analysis welfare plans that refuse to fund children born to welfare recipients while funding children born to non-welfare recipients are constitutionally valid legislative allocations of government welfare benefits among different classes of welfare recipients. They are subject only to the minimal rational relations scrutiny accorded economic regulation and not to the strict scrutiny otherwise applicable to government intrusions on childbearing choices. The fact that such plans would obviously influence, or even be designed to influence, the childbearing choices of welfare recipients would be immaterial on the ground that the plans merely refused to subsidize rather than penalized the woman's childbearing choices.

* * *

This view fails to recognize the harm inflicted by government decisions to exclude constitutional rights from funding. Family cap plans eliminate assistance for the increased need that results from the birth of an additional child and consign poor families to an even more desperate existence than they otherwise would have. This constitutional structure, with its privileging of regulatory government benefit allocations, unleashes the power of the legislature to oppressively control the constitutional rights of the poor who depend upon government largesse for survival. In contrast, the constitutional rights of those fortunate enough not to depend upon government benefits for their subsistence are protected because, to inflict harm upon them, the government cannot merely refuse to give to them but instead must take away something that they have. This confiscation constitutes an unconstitutional burden or penalty on the constitutional rights. Consequently, the rights of the "haves" are protected because the government lacks constitutional weapons to affect their rights. In contrast, the rights of the "have-nots" are jeopardized because the government constitutionally retains weapons to affect their rights, namely, the deprivation of subsistence government aid.

Government use of benefits to attack constitutional rights is also more likely to pass legislatively when it affects only a small and unpopular segment of the population, such as the poor or other disfavored classes. For example, child limitation proposals would probably never pass if applied to the general public. Imagine the uproar if the government were to condition dependent-child tax exemptions on passing a means test to prove that taxpayers were able to adequately support their children, or a parenting test to prove that they were capable parents, were lawfully wed, or could provide a stable two-parent home. The public furor would almost certainly defeat any such proposal.

* * *

A proper view of the Constitution should see this type of government action as at least problematic and thus subject to heightened constitutional scrutiny. In particular, decisions of legislative majorities to use benefit-allocating authority to prey upon the poor--to use poverty itself as leverage to affect constitutionally protected behavior and value choices--should not be an automatically legitimate use of government power.

Heightened scrutiny would not mean that the government could not seek to influence individuals, including poor people, to make beneficial reproductive choices that would help them to become more economically self-sufficient or that would generally benefit the community. Rather, heightened scrutiny would recognize that the means the government uses to accomplish these goals may be problematic, even if the goal itself is not. While some means of encouraging socially productive behavior may be appropriate, e.g., public information campaigns or educational programs, harmful and oppressive means are not.

Additionally, heightened scrutiny would not constitutionally obligate the government to provide minimum levels of benefits. Rather, once the government decides to award benefits, the Constitution should place fairness limits on the government's distribution of those benefits and restrain government from using benefits to harm persons because of their exercise of their constitutional rights. Government denials of funding of an individual's constitutional right expressly because the individual exercised it in a government-disfavored way, and particularly government use of funding decisions to influence constitutionally-protected value and lifestyle choices, are not merely minimally-rational legislative distributions of public resources. Rather, government use of benefits as a club to harm the individual because of her exercise of constitutional rights is as much a burden or penalty on the exercise of the constitutional right as a direct prohibition or fine would be. In both cases, government harms the individual because of her exercise of a constitutional right. Although the government goal of reducing the number of children born into poverty may be laudable, means used to achieve that goal must not impair the right of benefit recipients to autonomous constitutionally protected value choices. Otherwise, the government violates basic, underlying constitutional limits on government power, which are the essence of constitutional protection for fundamental rights.

* * *

Notes and Questions

1. *Legitimacy of Child Exclusion Goals.* Are the government's interests in promoting marriage and discouraging non-marital births legitimate, important, and/or compelling? Most lawmakers, judges, and commentators concede at least the legitimacy of these interests. What makes them legitimate? What interest does government have in regulating people's intimate lives?

2. *The Due Process Analysis.* According to constitutional jurisprudence, the due process clauses' protection of liberty establishes a fundamental right of privacy which encompasses the right to decide whether to have children. In the context of abortion, however, the Court has been increasingly tolerant of restrictions placed on a woman's process of deciding whether to carry a pregnancy to term. *See Planned Parenthood v. Casey*, 112 S.Ct. 2791 (1992) (upholding requirements that women receive specified information about their fetuses followed by 24 hour waiting period and that they give their informed consent prior to abortion and that minors obtain either parental or judicial consent, but rejecting spousal consent requirement). If the Constitution protects decisional autonomy, what justifies government interference with either the decisional process or the decision?

3. *An Equal Protection Comparison.* Could the government deny public education to non-marital children? Even if the courts

applied intermediate scrutiny (on the basis either that non-marital children are a quasi-suspect class or that education is a quasi-fundamental right), would denial of public education to non-marital children be substantially related to any important government interest? How strong is the government's interest in discouraging non-marital births--legitimate, important/significant, or compelling?

4. *The Unconstitutional Conditions Dilemma Revisited.* Yvette Marie Barksdale argued that the Supreme Court has distinguished between direct burdens (such as criminal prohibitions) and indirect incentives (such as refusals to subsidize). Because refusal to provide welfare benefits is a type of refusal to subsidize, the courts might find that the government had not interfered with any constitutional right.

Reconsider the arguments in Chapter 7 on Unconstitutional Conditions. Is the distinction between direct burdens and indirect refusals to subsidize a meaningful one? If you think so, how would you answer Professor Barksdale's queries--for example, could the government "condition dependent-child tax exemptions on passing a means test to prove that taxpayers were able to adequately support their children"?

5. *State Option to Exclude Children.* In its 1996 Personal Responsibility and Work Opportunity Reconciliation Act, Congress did not require the exclusion of children born during the family's receipt of Temporary Assistance for Needy Families block grant funds. It did not prohibit states from excluding such children, however, and it authorized the continuance of approved federal waivers, some of which include a child exclusion provision. How can child exclusion rules be challenged? Consider the following complaint in a lawsuit challenging the Child Exclusion (or Family Cap) adopted in New Jersey.

UNITED STATES DISTRICT COURT
DISTRICT OF NEW JERSEY

C.K., *et al.*,
Plaintiff,

Case No. 93-5354

v.

SHALALA,
Defendant

CLASS ACTION
COMPLAINT FOR
DECLARATORY AND
INJUNCTIVE RELIEF

PRELIMINARY STATEMENT

1. This action seeks to enjoin the United States Department of Health and Human Services (HHS), the New Jersey Department of Human Services (DHS), and the officials in charge of those agencies from subjecting women and their needy dependent children to a substantial cut in Aid to Families with Dependent Children (AFDC) grants under a statewide program change, in the guise of a research experiment, referred to herein as the "Child Exclusion" or "Exclusion."

2. In an express attempt to reduce the number of child births in AFDC families, the Child Exclusion denies any grant increase when an additional child is born to a family on AFDC. This Child Exclusion penalty constitutes an unprecedented and improper intrusion of the state into the most personal of decisions: whether or not to have children. Under the Exclusion, which became effective on October 1, 1992, dependent children conceived by AFDC recipients are barred from receiving an AFDC grant amount for their care, maintenance, support and protection.

3. The Child Exclusion harms innocent infant children by cutting off resources for their most basic needs, in an attempt to penalize or deter conduct of their mothers over which these children have absolutely no control. The Child Exclusion also penalizes all family members by substantially reducing their AFDC grant without any regard to whether the mother is able to find work or secure income in an amount sufficient to offset the amount of the grant cut, and thereby provide for at least some of her family's most basic needs. The Exclusion imposes these penalties without regard to

whether the mother took reasonable steps to prevent her pregnancy, or became pregnant under circumstances, such as rape or incest, that were beyond her ability to control.

* * *

7. The notification and implementation of the Child Exclusion have caused plaintiff mothers great stress, anxiety, humiliation and other psychological trauma directly attributable to the uncertainty over how they would feed, clothe and shelter their babies and other children if they gave birth, and to their separation and stigmatization as a targeted class--mothers who conceive and give birth while on welfare--for whom the state has indicated its disfavor. As a result, some arranged for an abortion but later decided not to go through with it for health and other personal reasons. One plaintiff would have had an abortion if she had been informed earlier in her pregnancy that her new child would be barred from receiving AFDC. Another was misinformed by AFDC officials that the Child Exclusion would not apply to her children, a mistake not corrected until it was too late to have an abortion.

8. Solely because of the Child Exclusion, plaintiffs are or will be denied the same level of assistance that the State of New Jersey provides to other families of identical size. More specifically, they are or will be denied between 10% and 32% of the basic AFDC grant, depending on the size of the family.

9. Due to the lower grant resulting from the Child Exclusion, plaintiffs experience much greater hardship in securing adequate housing, food and clothing for their children.

* * *

10. This gap between grant and need has dire effects, as demonstrated by plaintiffs' current circumstances. Plaintiff H.K., who just had triplets, has no housing of her own, lives crammed into one room in her sister's apartment with her three babies and two other children, and could be evicted at any time. L.W. was recently homeless and is now living in one room that costs her entire AFDC grant, leaving her without resources to obtain other essential items needed by her baby and her two-year-old son. Plaintiffs C.K. and E.M. could be evicted from their homes at anytime because they cannot pay their rent. . . . Because their rent consumes all or nearly all of their AFDC grant, plaintiff mothers simply have no funds left to obtain adequate food, diapers, baby formula, clothes, laundry,

transportation, toilet paper, soap, toothpaste, nonprescription medicines, cribs, furniture, and other essentials for their babies and families. The Child Exclusion substantially deepens plaintiffs' poverty, thereby significantly increasing their risk and exposure to hunger, illness, inadequate housing, homelessness, and other physical and psychological harm.

11. This deprivation and resulting harm violates plaintiffs' rights under the Social Security Act and AFDC regulations; the Human Subjects protections contained in 42 U.S.C. § 3515b, 42 U.S.C. § 289, and implementing regulations; the federal Administrative Procedure Act, 5 U.S.C. § 702; the right to equal protection and due process under the United States and New Jersey Constitutions; and the right to privacy under the New Jersey Constitution.

JURISDICTION AND VENUE

12. This Court has subject matter jurisdiction pursuant to 28 U.S.C. § 1331, as a case arising under the Constitution and laws of the United States; under 28 U.S.C. § 1343(a)(3), as an action to redress the deprivation, under color of state law, of rights, privileges and immunities secured by the Constitution and laws of the United States providing for equal rights of persons; under 28 U.S.C. § 1361, as a mandamus action to compel an officer or employee of the United States or one of its agencies to perform a duty owed to the plaintiff; and under 28 U.S.C. § 1367, as state constitutional claims warranting the exercise of this Court's supplemental jurisdiction.

13. Venue lies in this district pursuant to 28 U.S.C. § 1391 (b).

PARTIES

14. Plaintiff C.K., a twenty-eight year-old AFDC recipient, resides in Somerville, New Jersey, with her seven-year-old daughter, J.M. C.K. was receiving AFDC in January 1993 when she became pregnant. On October 27, 1993, C.K. gave birth to her second child, S.B., a baby girl. C.K. has been advised by DHS, through the Somerset County Board of Social Services, that her baby is subject to the Child Exclusion and will not receive AFDC. Plaintiff C.K. brings this action on her own behalf and as guardian *ad litem* for her baby girl S.B. and her daughter J.M.

* * *

22. Defendant Donna Shalala is the Secretary of HHS. In that capacity, she has overall responsibility for the formulation and implementation of the AFDC program. The Secretary of HHS must assure that each state which participates in the AFDC program and the Medicaid program and receives matching funds complies with the Social Security Act, 42 U.S.C. §§ 601-84, and its implementing regulations. In defined circumstances, the Secretary under 42 U.S.C. § 1315 may waive compliance with certain of those provisions, if a state requests a waiver to conduct a research experiment involving the AFDC program. Defendant Shalala's predecessor granted such a waiver for the Child Exclusion and FDP [Family Development Program, a package of legislative reform]. Defendant Shalala subsequently denied the request of plaintiffs' counsel to withdraw or rescind the waiver for the Child Exclusion issued by her predecessor, and she has allowed DHS to implement the Child Exclusion in accordance with the terms and conditions of the waiver. Defendant Shalala is sued in her official capacity, along with her successor, employees, agents or other representatives.

23. Defendant United States Department Health and Human Services is the federal agency responsible for providing federal funding to states for the AFDC program and for ensuring that each state fully complies with the Social Security Act and regulations promulgated by the agency in implementing the AFDC program.

24. Defendant New Jersey Department of Human Services (DHS) is the single state agency in New Jersey responsible for the administration and operation of the AFDC program, including the AFDC Child Exclusion and the FDP.

25. Defendant William Waldman is the Commissioner of DHS. As DHS Commissioner, defendant Waldman is the state official directly responsible for the operation of the AFDC program and for the implementation of the Child Exclusion. Defendant Waldman is sued in his official capacity.

CLASS ACTION ALLEGATIONS

26. Plaintiffs bring this action as a class action pursuant to Rules 23(a) and (b)(2) of the Federal Rules of Civil Procedure.

27. Plaintiffs' class consists of all individuals in AFDC recipient families in New Jersey (a) in which an adult member of the family has conceived or will conceive a child anytime after October 1, 1992; (b) which were receiving AFDC at the time the child was

conceived; and (c) in which an adult member (i) has given or will give birth to a child after August 1, 1993, (ii) has had her pregnancy terminated or will have her pregnancy terminated because her child, if born, would be subject to the Child Exclusion, or (iii) is still pregnant.

28. Plaintiffs' class of individuals is divided into three subclasses: (1) adult family members who become pregnant, (2) children born after August 1, 1993 who are subject to the Child Exclusion, and (3) all other children of the family. Subclass (1) is further divided into those who (a) have given or will give birth to a child after August 1, 1993, (b) have had or will have their pregnancies terminated because their child would have been subject to the Child Exclusion, or (c) are still pregnant.

29. Plaintiffs' class is so numerous that joinder of all members is impracticable. DHS reports that at least 470 babies born in August and September 1993 did not receive AFDC because they were subject to the Child Exclusion. In its waiver application, DHS estimated that each year approximately 3,600 babies will not receive AFDC under the Child Exclusion because they will be born to women who became pregnant while they were receiving AFDC.

30. Questions of law and fact common to all members of subclasses (1)(a), (1)(b), (1)(c), (2), and (3) predominate over questions about individual members of each subclass, in that the claims set forth in this complaint apply to all members of each subclass and these claims do not vary with individual factual circumstances of the subclass members.

31. The claims of the named plaintiffs are typical of the claims of the subclasses which they represent. The named plaintiffs have no claims that are adverse to the claims of the subclass which they represent.

32. The named plaintiffs and their class are represented by Legal Services of New Jersey, attorneys from individual Legal Services programs in New Jersey, the NOW Legal Defense and Education Fund, and the American Civil Liberties Union of New Jersey, through its attorneys Crummy, Del Deo, Dolan, Griffinger & Vecchione. These attorneys are experienced in class action litigation and will adequately represent the interests of the class.

33. Defendants have acted or failed to act on grounds generally applicable to the class, thereby making appropriate final injunctive and declaratory relief with respect to the class as a whole.

34. The prosecution of separate actions by individual class members would unduly burden the courts and create the possibility of conflicting decisions.

FACTUAL ALLEGATIONS

35. AFDC consists of money payments to needy children who are dependent as a result of the absence, death, unemployment or incapacity of a parent. The purpose of AFDC is to provide assistance to needy dependent children so that the parents of such children can care for them in their homes, to maintain and strengthen the lives of such children in their families, and to help the parents of such children become self-sufficient as they provide parental care and continuing protection for such children.

36. AFDC is a joint federal and state program established by Title IV-A of the Social Security Act. States are not required to participate in the AFDC program, but if they choose to do so, they must provide aid in accordance with federal law. Participating states must have an AFDC state plan that meets the requirements of 42 U.S.C. § 602 and is approved by HHS.

37. The Social Security Act, 42 U.S.C. § 1315, authorizes the Secretary of HHS to waive compliance with the requirements of 42 U.S.C. § 602 so that states can implement "experimental, pilot, or demonstration projects[s]" that "promot[es] the objectives" of the AFDC program. Under this section, the Secretary can grant waivers for AFDC experiments only "to the extent and for the period he finds necessary" to allow the state to carry out the experiment.

38. Under federal and state law, New Jersey is required to establish a standard of need for the AFDC program. The standard of need is the amount needed to maintain a safe and decent life. The standard of need serves as a benchmark against which to measure whether the benefits actually paid to recipients are sufficient to enable those recipients to secure adequate food, shelter, clothing and other basic necessities of daily living.

39. New Jersey's standard of need was determined by DHS in 1992, based on a 1990 study of living costs. The standard of need for a single parent and one child is $819, for a single parent and two children $985, and for a single parent and three children $1,127. The

standard of need continues to increase with family size. If there are more than eight in a family, $112 is added for each person.

40. Under federal law, states can establish their own grant levels for AFDC, and thus set the amounts of assistance paid monthly to eligible recipients.

41. New Jersey's AFDC grant levels are set by DHS regulation. An eligible family consisting of a single parent and one child currently receives $322 per month; a single parent and two children receive $424 per month; and a single parent and three children receive $488 per month. Grant levels continue to increase as family size increases; if there are more than eight in the family, $50 is provided for each additional family member.

42. AFDC benefits in New Jersey, even when food stamp allotments are included, are far below what is necessary for needy families to obtain food, shelter, clothing and other essentials of daily living, as determined by DHS in its standard of need. For example, a mother with one child receives $322 per month in AFDC benefits, and may be eligible for a maximum monthly food stamp allotment of $206. Added together, these benefits are merely 64% of DHS' standard of need for a family of this size.

43. In January 1992, the New Jersey Legislature enacted five separate bills collectively known as the Family Development Program (FDP). Taken as a whole, the FDP is a permanent, statewide change in New Jersey's AFDC program.

44. The centerpiece of the FDP is a job training, education and employment program for AFDC recipients, intended to serve as New Jersey's program of education, employment and training (JOBS) that the state must establish pursuant to 42 U.S.C. § 681.

* * *

47. The FDP also includes the Child Exclusion. This provision changes existing law by withholding the standard AFDC grant increase for any child conceived by and born to an AFDC recipient. Families subject to the Child Exclusion are permitted to retain more earned income than is permitted for other AFDC families.

48. The declared purpose of the Child Exclusion is to discourage women on AFDC from becoming pregnant and having additional children, thereby reducing fertility and birth rates among these women.

49. The legislative history makes it clear that the Child

Exclusion was intended to be implemented as part of the overall FDP and not independent of it.

50. Many of the FDP's provisions, including the AFDC Child Exclusion, do not comply with federal law and regulations governing the AFDC program. As a result, DHS requested that the Secretary of HHS issue a waiver of these requirements so that the Child Exclusion could be implemented as a research experiment under 42 U.S.C. § 1315.

51. DHS' waiver request, filed with the HHS on June 5, 1992, conceded that depriving children of AFDC under the Child Exclusion may be "harsh," but asserted that the purpose of the Child Exclusion is to "encourage" women to "be responsible" in their decision to "have another child while receiving welfare." DHS also stated that it would offer "financial incentives" to "encourage" women subjected to the Child Exclusion to "offset the benefit they would have otherwise received" through the increased income earnings disregard and "priority for employment and training services" in the FDP jobs training program.

* * *

54. On July 20, 1992, the Secretary of HHS approved the waiver to allow the FDP, including the Child Exclusion, to be implemented as a five-year research experiment under 42 U.S.C. § 1315.

* * *

66. Plaintiff mothers E.S., L.W. and E.M. became pregnant even though they were utilizing birth control regularly. . . .

67. When plaintiff C.K. became pregnant, she expected to marry the father of her baby. Her relationship with the baby's father broke off after her pregnancy was confirmed.

68. Plaintiffs L.W. and E.P. gave serious consideration to terminating their pregnancy by abortion when they were informed by DHS of the Child Exclusion . . . .

* * *

71. Plaintiff families headed by C.K., *[et al.,]* receive $322 per month in AFDC, the amount for a single dependent child and his or her mother. These plaintiffs also receive approximately $200 per month in food stamps. Plaintiffs have no other income.

72. The newborn babies of plaintiff mothers C.K., *[et al.,]* are subject to the Child Exclusion. As a result, these plaintiffs will

not receive $102 per month in AFDC for these babies. This amount would have increased their total AFDC grant to $424 per month, the AFDC grant amount for a parent with two dependent children. Instead, plaintiffs will get no grant increase to take care of their new baby, and must provide for the care and support of their two children with $322 AFDC per month, the AFDC grant amount DHS provides for a parent with one child. The Exclusion results in a 24% overall reduction in AFDC to these plaintiffs' families.

73. When combined, the AFDC and food stamps received by plaintiffs C.K., *[et al.,]* are only 54% of DHS' standard of need for a family of one parent and two children, although plaintiffs will receive some increase in food stamps for their newborn babies.

* * *

85. None of the plaintiffs receives permanent housing or rental assistance from any federal, state or local housing program, although plaintiffs have sought such assistance. Without such assistance, plaintiffs must try to find decent housing that they can rent with their monthly AFDC grant.

* * *

92. Plaintiffs C.K., *[et al.,]* have been enrolled in various educational and job training programs offered by DHS, or have been employed, during the past three years. These plaintiffs have been unable to continue participation in these programs or have stopped working because they are homeless or imminently homeless, because they had physical problems related to their pregnancies, or because they must stay at home to care for their infant children. . . .

96. At current AFDC grant levels, plaintiffs have no realistic capacity to rent housing and purchase utilities, food, clothing and other necessities. The birth of their babies imposes upon each plaintiff mother additional burdens to ensure that the newborn and the other children are properly fed, housed, and clothed in an atmosphere conducive to healthy child development. The Child Exclusion deprives plaintiffs of the AFDC grant necessary to meet these additional needs. The Exclusion thus has caused and will continue to cause plaintiffs and their children homelessness, hunger, psychological trauma, and other physical and emotional harm to their health, safety and welfare.

CLAIMS FOR RELIEF

FIRST COUNT
VIOLATION OF DUTY TO
PROVIDE ASSISTANCE TO ALL ELIGIBLE INDIVIDUALS

97. Plaintiff children subject to the Child Exclusion meet, in all respects, the definition of "dependent child" under 42 U.S.C. § 606(a) and, but for the Child Exclusion, meet all criteria for "need" and financial and other eligibility as promulgated within the framework set forth in 42 U.S.C. § 602(a)(7) and (8).

98. The State defendants have a duty under 42 U.S.C. § 602(a) (10)(a) to provide aid to "all eligible individuals."

99. The Child Exclusion is not a permissible ground for excluding a child from AFDC eligibility under any provision of the Social Security Act and, by denying plaintiff children the AFDC assistance necessary for a minimally decent life, contravenes the fundamental purpose of the Act as set forth in 42 U.S.C. § 601.

100. This requirement to furnish AFDC assistance to all eligible individuals, contained in 42 U.S.C. § 602(a)(10), was not waived by the Secretary of HHS in approving the Child Exclusion. Further, the provisions of 42 U.S.C. §§ 601, 606(a) are not waivable, and were not in fact waived by the Secretary.

101. The Child Exclusion thus violates the duty to provide assistance to all eligible individuals, as set forth in 42 U.S.C. § 602(a)(10), drawing upon the provisions in 42 U.S.C. §§ 601, 606 (a).

* * *

THIRD COUNT
VIOLATION OF DUTY TO DETERMINE
NEED AND AMOUNT
OF ASSISTANCE ON AN OBJECTIVE AND
EQUITABLE BASIS

105. Under 45 C.F.R. § 233.20(a)(1), the State defendants are under an obligation to "[p]rovide that the determination of need and amount of assistance for all applicants and recipients will be made on an objective and equitable basis . . . except where otherwise specifically authorized by Federal statute."

106. Different treatment, in the form of different AFDC grant amounts, of families of identical size and composition, based solely upon the timing of a child's birth, is not equitable. Furthermore, denial of a critically important grant amount based solely upon such timing is not an "objective" determination of need and amount of assistance. Under the Child Exclusion, a different amount of assistance is provided even though the objective need--and the family size--is the same.

107. The Child Exclusion therefore violates 45 C.F.R. § 233.20(a)(1), to the great harm of plaintiffs. The requirements of 45 C.F.R. § 233.20(a)(1) were not waived by the Secretary of HHS in approving the Child Exclusion.

* * *

NINTH COUNT
VIOLATIONS OF THE UNITED STATES CONSTITUTION

130. By approving the Child Exclusion, HHS has deprived plaintiffs and members of their class of their rights to equal protection and due process of law, in violation of the Fifth Amendment to the United States Constitution. These deprivations include, but are not limited to: (1) the differential treatment of AFDC families of identical size based solely on when a child is conceived and born; (2) the burden placed on women recipients of AFDC in the exercise of their fundamental rights to make decisions about family composition, conception and childbirth without undue governmental intrusion; (3) the approval of a program motivated, in whole or in part, by the impermissible governmental purpose of deterring conception and childbirth among women on AFDC; (4) cutting plaintiffs' AFDC income without regard to whether adult plaintiffs and their subclass members have the actual ability to make up for that lost income by working and retaining a portion of their earnings; (5) excluding plaintiff newborns and their subclass members from the AFDC grant, but in a contradictory fashion including them in the AFDC household for the limited purpose of attributing child support received on their behalf to the entire household, and thereby reducing to $50 monthly the amount of such child support that can actually be retained by the AFDC household; and (6) unnecessarily imposing the punitive and harmful Child Exclusion on over 130,000 families which are not part of either the "treatment" or "control" groups and whose

inclusion serves no legitimate research purpose. Similarly, by implementing the Child Exclusion, the State defendants, acting under color of state law, have deprived plaintiffs of their rights to due process and equal protection of the law, as set out above, in violation of the Fifth and Fourteenth Amendments to the United States Constitution, for which a cause of action against a state agency is afforded by 42 U.S.C. § 1983.

* * *

PRAYER FOR RELIEF

WHEREFORE, plaintiffs respectfully request that this Court:

A. Assume jurisdiction of this case;

B. Certify this action as a class action;

C. On the First . . . and Third Counts for violation of the Social Security Act and implementing regulations,

(1) find and declare that the Child Exclusion violates:

(a) 42 U.S.C. 602 (a)(10)(A), by denying AFDC to eligible dependent plaintiff children and members of their subclass;

* * *

(c) 45 C.F.R. § 233.20(a)(1), by failing to provide plaintiffs an AFDC grant which is determined on an objective and equitable basis, as necessary for the proper care, maintenance and support of plaintiffs and the members of their class; and

(2) enter a preliminary and permanent injunction barring HHS and DHS from implementing the Child Exclusion; . . .

I. On the Ninth Count for violation of the United States Constitution and 42 U.S.C. § 1983,

(1) find and declare that the Child Exclusion violates plaintiffs' rights under the equal protection and due process clauses of the United States Constitution; and

(2) enter a preliminary and permanent injunction reversing the approval and waiver for the Child Exclusion and barring defendants from its further implementation;

* * *

K. Pursuant to 42 U.S.C. § 1988, allow plaintiffs reasonable attorneys fees and their costs and disbursements;

L. Grant plaintiffs such other and further relief as the Court may deem just and proper; and

M. If an order granting plaintiffs' preliminary and permanent injunctive relief is entered, issue notice to all class members at HHS and DHS' expense regarding this ruling and plaintiffs' right to pursue retroactive relief through the state administrative hearing process.

LEGAL SERVICES OF NEW JERSEY, Inc.
HUDSON COUNTY LEGAL SERVICES
SOMERSET-SUSSEX LEGAL SERVICES
PASSAIC COUNTY LEGAL AID SOCIETY
UNION COUNTY LEGAL SERVICES
NOW LEGAL DEFENSE AND EDUCATION FUND
AMERICAN CIVIL LIBERTIES UNION--NEW JERSEY

Exercises

1. *Answer.* Draft an Answer to the Complaint in C.K. v. Shalala.

2. *Memorandum.* Draft a Memorandum of Law for the Secretary of Health and Human Services analyzing the strengths and weaknesses of Plaintiffs' and Defendants' arguments.

3. *Evidence Strategy.* Draft a plan for the Plaintiffs' introduction of evidence at hearings to be held on their requests for preliminary and permanent injunctions. How would plaintiffs and defendants handle preliminary reports from Rutgers University showing that New Jersey's "family cap" did not reduce the likelihood of procreation?

4. *Summary Judgment Motions.* Draft a Motion and Memorandum of Law in Support of either Plaintiffs' or Defendants' requests for Summary Judgment.

5. *Decision.* Draft a decision for the United States District Court Judge on either the Plaintiffs' request for a Preliminary Injunction or the Plaintiffs' and Defendants' Cross-Motions for Summary Judgment.

6. *TANF Complaint.* Draft a complaint on behalf of C.K. and the other plaintiffs based not on the AFDC statute, but on its replacement, the 1996 Personal Responsibility and Work Opportunity Act's Temporary Assistance for Needy Families block grant program. The TANF statute does not include any requirement that states provide benefits to all eligible individuals, or that states base their benefit levels on standards of need. How could plaintiffs use the TANF statute's requirement that each state's Family Assistance Program plan "shall set forth objective criteria for the delivery of benefits and the determination of eligibility and for fair and equitable treatment"?

3. Not Funding Abortion

HARRIS v. McRAE
448 U.S. 297 (1980)

* * *

Mr. Justice STEWART delivered the opinion of the Court.

This case presents statutory and constitutional questions concerning the public funding of abortions under Title XIX of the Social Security Act, commonly known as the "Medicaid" Act, and recent annual Appropriations Acts containing the so-called "Hyde Amendment." The statutory question is whether Title XIX requires a State that participates in the Medicaid program to fund the cost of medically necessary abortions for which federal reimbursement is unavailable under the Hyde Amendment. The constitutional question, which arises only if Title XIX imposes no such requirement, is whether the Hyde Amendment, by denying public funding for certain medically necessary abortions, contravenes the liberty or equal protection guarantees of the Due Process Clause of the Fifth Amendment, or either of the Religion Clauses of the First Amendment.

The Medicaid program was created in 1965, when Congress added Title XIX to the Social Security Act, 42 U.S.C. § 1396 et seq. for the purpose of providing federal financial assistance to States that choose to reimburse certain costs of medical treatment for needy persons. Although participation in the Medicaid program is entirely optional, once a State elects to participate, it must comply with the requirements of Title XIX.

One such requirement is that a participating State agree to provide financial assistance to the "categorically needy" with respect to five general areas of medical treatment: (1) inpatient hospital services, (2) outpatient hospital services, (3) other laboratory and X-ray services, (4) skilled nursing facilities services, periodic screening and diagnosis of children, and family planning services, and (5) services of physicians. Although a participating State need not "provide funding for all medical treatment falling within the five general categories, [Title XIX] does require that [a] state Medicaid pla[n] establish 'reasonable standards . . . for determining . . . the extent of medical assistance under the plan which . . . are consistent with the objectives of [Title XIX].'

Since September 1976, Congress has prohibited--either by an amendment to the annual appropriations bill for the Department of Health, Education, and Welfare or by a joint resolution--the use of any federal funds to reimburse the cost of abortions under the Medicaid program except under certain specified circumstances. This funding restriction is commonly known as the "Hyde Amendment," after its original congressional sponsor, Representative Hyde. . . .

On September 30, 1976, the day on which Congress enacted the initial version of the Hyde Amendment, these consolidated cases were filed in the District Court for the Eastern District of New York. The plaintiffs--Cora McRae, a New York Medicaid recipient then in the first trimester of a pregnancy that she wished to terminate, the New York City Health and Hospitals Corp., a public benefit corporation that operates 16 hospitals, 12 of which provide abortion services, and others--sought to enjoin the enforcement of the funding restriction on abortions. They alleged that the Hyde Amendment violated the First, Fourth, Fifth, and Ninth Amendments of the Constitution insofar as it limited the funding of abortions to those necessary to save the life of the mother, while permitting the funding of costs associated with childbirth. Although the sole named defendant was the Secretary of Health, Education, and Welfare, the District Court permitted Senators James L. Buckley and Jesse A. Helms and Representative Henry J. Hyde to intervene as defendants.

* * *

After a hearing, the District Court entered a preliminary injunction prohibiting the Secretary from enforcing the Hyde Amendment and requiring him to continue to provide federal reimbursement for abortions under the standards applicable before the funding restriction had been enacted. Although stating that it had not expressly held that the funding restriction was unconstitutional, since the preliminary injunction was not its final judgment, the District Court noted that such a holding was "implicit" in its decision granting the injunction. The District Court also certified the McRae case as a class action on behalf of all pregnant or potentially pregnant women in the State of New York eligible for Medicaid and who decide to have an abortion within the first 24 weeks of pregnancy, and of all authorized providers of abortion services to such women.

The Secretary then brought an appeal to this Court. After deciding *Beal v. Doe*, and *Maher v. Roe*, we vacated the injunction of the District Court and remanded the case for reconsideration in light of those decisions.

* * *

After a lengthy trial, which inquired into the medical reasons for abortions and the diverse religious views on the subject, the District Court filed an opinion and entered a judgment invalidating all versions of the Hyde Amendment on constitutional grounds. The District Court rejected the plaintiffs' statutory argument, concluding that even though Title XIX would otherwise have required a participating State to fund medically necessary abortions, the Hyde Amendment had substantively amended Title XIX to relieve a State of that funding obligation. Turning then to the constitutional issues, the District Court concluded that the Hyde Amendment, though valid under the Establishment Clause, violates the equal protection component of the Fifth Amendment's Due Process Clause and the Free Exercise Clause of the First Amendment. With regard to the Fifth Amendment, the District Court noted that when an abortion is "medically necessary to safeguard the pregnant woman's health, . . . the disentitlement to [M]edicaid assistance impinges directly on the woman's right to decide, in consultation with her physician and in reliance on his judgment, to terminate her pregnancy in order to preserve her health." The court concluded that the Hyde Amendment violates the equal protection guarantee because, in its view, the decision of Congress to fund medically necessary services generally but only certain medically necessary abortions serves no legitimate governmental interest. As to the Free Exercise Clause of the First Amendment, the court held that insofar as a woman's decision to seek a medically necessary abortion may be a product of her religious beliefs under certain Protestant and Jewish tenets, the funding restrictions of the Hyde Amendment violate that constitutional guarantee as well.

Accordingly, the District Court ordered the Secretary to "[c]ease to give effect" to the various versions of the Hyde Amendment insofar as they forbid payments for medically necessary abortions. It further directed the Secretary to "[c]ontinue to authorize the expenditure of federal matching funds [for such abortions]." In addition, the court recertified the McRae case as a nationwide class action on behalf of all pregnant and potentially pregnant women eligible for Medicaid who wish to have medically necessary abortions, and of all authorized providers of abortions for such women.

The Secretary then applied to this Court for a stay of the judgment pending direct appeal of the District Court's decision. We denied the stay, but noted probable jurisdiction of this appeal.

It is well settled that if a case may be decided on either statutory or constitutional grounds, this Court, for sound jurisprudential reasons, will inquire first into the statutory question. This practice reflects the deeply rooted doctrine "that we ought not to pass on questions of constitutionality . . . unless such adjudication is unavoidable."

* * *

The Medicaid program created by Title XIX is a cooperative endeavor in which the Federal Government provides financial assistance to participating States to aid them in furnishing health care to needy persons. Under this system of "cooperative federalism," *King v. Smith*, if a State agrees to establish a Medicaid plan that satisfies the requirements of Title XIX, which include several mandatory categories of health services, the Federal Government agrees to pay a specified percentage of "the total amount expended . . . as medical assistance under the State plan . . . ." The cornerstone of Medicaid is financial contribution by both the Federal Government and the participating State. Nothing in Title XIX as originally enacted, or in its legislative history, suggests that Congress intended to require a participating State to assume the full costs of providing any health services in its Medicaid plan. Quite the contrary, the purpose of Congress in enacting Title XIX was to provide federal financial assistance for all legitimate state expenditures under an approved Medicaid plan.

Since the Congress that enacted Title XIX did not intend a participating State to assume a unilateral funding obligation for any health service in an approved Medicaid plan, it follows that Title XIX does not require a participating State to include in its plan any services for which a subsequent Congress has withheld federal funding. Title XIX was dcsigned as a cooperative program of shared financial responsibility, not as a device for the Federal Government to compel a State to provide services that Congress itself is unwilling to fund. Thus, if Congress chooses to withdraw federal funding for a particular service, a State is not obliged to continue to pay for that service as a condition of continued federal financial support of other services. This is not to say that Congress may not now depart from the original design of Title XIX under which the Federal Government shares the financial responsibility for expenses incurred under an approved Medicaid plan. It is only to say that, absent an indication of contrary legislative intent by a subsequent Congress, Title XIX does not obligate a participating State to pay for those medical services for which federal reimbursement is unavailable.

* * *

Having determined that Title XIX does not obligate a participating State to pay for those medically necessary abortions for which Congress has withheld federal funding, we must consider the constitutional validity of the Hyde Amendment. The appellees assert that the funding restrictions of the Hyde Amendment violate several rights secured by the Constitution--(1) the right of a woman, implicit in the Due Process Clause of the Fifth Amendment, to decide whether to terminate a pregnancy, (2) the prohibition under the Establishment Clause of the First Amendment against any "law respecting an establishment of religion," and (3) the right to freedom of religion protected by the Free Exercise Clause of the First Amendment. The appellees also contend that, quite apart from substantive constitutional rights, the Hyde Amendment violates the equal protection component of the Fifth Amendment.

* * *

It is well settled that, quite apart from the guarantee of equal protection, if a law "impinges upon a fundamental right explicitly or implicitly secured by the Constitution [it] is presumptively unconstitutional." Accordingly, before turning to the equal protection issue in this case, we examine whether the Hyde Amendment violates any substantive rights secured by the Constitution.

We address first the appellees' argument that the Hyde Amendment, by restricting the availability of certain medically necessary abortions under Medicaid, impinges on the "liberty" protected by the Due Process Clause as recognized in *Roe v. Wade*, and its progeny.

In the *Wade* case, this Court held unconstitutional a Texas statute making it a crime to procure or attempt an abortion except on medical advice for the purpose of saving the mother's life. The constitutional underpinning of *Wade* was a recognition that the "liberty" protected by the Due Process Clause of the Fourteenth Amendment includes not only the freedoms explicitly mentioned in the Bill of Rights, but also a freedom of personal choice in certain matters of marriage and family life. This implicit constitutional liberty, the Court in *Wade* held, includes the freedom of a woman to decide whether to terminate a pregnancy.

* * *

In *Maher v. Roe*, the Court was presented with the question whether the scope of personal constitutional freedom recognized in *Roe v. Wade* included an entitlement to Medicaid payments for abortions that are not medically necessary. At issue in *Maher* was a Connecticut welfare regulation under which Medicaid recipients received payments for medical services incident to childbirth, but not for medical services incident to nontherapeutic abortions. The District Court held that the regulation violated the Equal Protection Clause of the Fourteenth Amendment because the unequal subsidization of childbirth and abortion impinged on the "fundamental right to abortion" recognized in *Wade* and its progeny.

It was the view of this Court that "the District Court misconceived the nature and scope of the fundamental right recognized in *Roe*." The doctrine of *Roe v. Wade*, the Court held in *Maher*, "protects the woman from unduly burdensome interference with her freedom to decide whether to terminate her pregnancy," such as the severe criminal sanctions at issue in *Roe v. Wade*, or the absolute requirement of spousal consent for an abortion challenged in *Planned Parenthood of Central Missouri v. Danforth.*

But the constitutional freedom recognized in *Wade* and its progeny, the *Maher* Court explained, did not prevent Connecticut from making "a value judgment favoring childbirth over abortion, and . . . implement[ing] that judgment by the allocation of public funds." As the Court elaborated: "The Connecticut regulation before us is different in kind from the laws invalidated in our previous abortion decisions. The Connecticut regulation places no obstacles--absolute or otherwise--in the pregnant woman's path to an abortion. An indigent woman who desires an abortion suffers no disadvantage as a consequence of Connecticut's decision to fund childbirth; she continues as before to be dependent on private sources for the service she desires. The State may have made childbirth a more attractive alternative, thereby influencing the woman's decision, but it has imposed no restriction on access to abortions that was not already there. The indigency that may make it difficult--and in some cases, perhaps, impossible--for some women to have abortions is neither created nor in any way affected by the Connecticut regulation."

The Court in *Maher* noted that its description of the doctrine recognized in *Wade* and its progeny signaled "no retreat" from those decisions. In explaining why the constitutional principle recognized in *Wade* and later cases--protecting a woman's freedom of choice--did not translate into a constitutional obligation of Connecticut to subsidize abortions, the Court cited the "basic difference between direct state interference with a protected activity and state encouragement of an alternative activity consonant with legislative policy. Constitutional concerns are greatest when the State attempts to impose its will by force of law; the State's power to encourage actions deemed to be in the public interest is necessarily far broader." Thus, even though the Connecticut regulation favored childbirth over abortion by means of subsidization of one and not the other, the Court in *Maher* concluded that the regulation did not impinge on the constitutional freedom recognized in *Wade* because it imposed no governmental restriction on access to abortions.

The Hyde Amendment, like the Connecticut welfare regulation at issue in *Maher*, places no governmental obstacle in the path of a woman who chooses to terminate her pregnancy, but rather, by means of unequal subsidization of abortion and other medical services, encourages alternative activity deemed in the public interest. The present case does differ factually from *Maher* insofar as that case involved a failure to fund nontherapeutic abortions, whereas the Hyde Amendment withholds funding of certain medically necessary abortions. Accordingly, the appellees argue that because the Hyde Amendment affects a significant interest not present or asserted in *Maher*--the interest of a woman in protecting her health during pregnancy--and because that interest lies at the core of the personal constitutional freedom recognized in *Wade*, the present case is constitutionally different from *Maher*. It is the appellees' view that to the extent that the Hyde Amendment withholds funding for certain medically necessary abortions, it clearly impinges on the constitutional principle recognized in *Wade*.

It is evident that a woman's interest in protecting her health was an important theme in *Wade*. In concluding that the freedom of a woman to decide whether to terminate her pregnancy falls within the personal liberty protected by the Due Process Clause, the Court in *Wade* emphasized the fact that the woman's decision carries with it significant personal health implications--both physical and psychological. In fact, although the Court in *Wade* recognized that the state interest in protecting potential life becomes sufficiently compelling in the period after fetal viability to justify an absolute criminal prohibition of nontherapeutic abortions, the Court held that even after fetal viability a State may not prohibit abortions "necessary to preserve the life or health of the mother." Because even the compelling interest of the State in protecting potential life after fetal viability was held to be insufficient to outweigh a woman's decision to protect her life or health, it could be argued that the freedom of a woman to decide whether to terminate her pregnancy for health reasons does in fact lie at the core of the constitutional liberty identified in *Wade*.

But, regardless of whether the freedom of a woman to choose to terminate her pregnancy for health reasons lies at the core or the periphery of the due process liberty recognized in *Wade*, it simply does not follow that a woman's freedom of choice carries with it a constitutional entitlement to the financial resources to avail herself of the full range of protected choices. The reason why was explained in *Maher*: although government may not place obstacles in the path of a woman's exercise of her freedom of choice, it need not remove those not of its own creation. Indigency falls in the latter category. The financial constraints that restrict an indigent woman's ability to enjoy the full range of constitutionally protected freedom of choice are the product not of governmental restrictions on access to abortions, but rather of her indigency. Although Congress has opted to subsidize medically necessary services generally, but not certain medically necessary abortions, the fact remains that the Hyde Amendment leaves an indigent woman with at least the same range of choice in deciding whether to obtain a medically necessary abortion as she would have had if Congress had chosen to subsidize no health care costs at all. We are thus not persuaded that the Hyde Amendment impinges on the constitutionally protected freedom of choice recognized in *Wade*.

* * *

Although the liberty protected by the Due Process Clause affords protection against unwarranted government interference with freedom of choice in the context of certain personal decisions, it does not confer an entitlement to such funds as may be necessary to realize all the advantages of that freedom. To hold otherwise would mark a drastic change in our understanding of the Constitution. It cannot be that because government may not prohibit the use of contraceptives, *Griswold v. Connecticut*, or prevent parents from sending their child to a private school, *Pierce v. Society of Sisters*, government, therefore, has an affirmative constitutional obligation to ensure that all persons have the financial resources to obtain contraceptives or send their children to private schools. To translate the limitation on governmental power implicit in the Due Process Clause into an affirmative funding obligation would require Congress to subsidize the medically necessary abortion of an indigent woman even if Congress had not enacted a Medicaid program to subsidize other medically necessary services. Nothing in the Due Process Clause supports such an extraordinary result. Whether freedom of choice that is constitutionally protected warrants federal subsidization is a question for Congress to answer, not a matter of constitutional entitlement. Accordingly, we conclude that the Hyde Amendment does not impinge on the due process liberty recognized in *Wade*.

* * *

The appellees also argue that the Hyde Amendment contravenes rights secured by the Religion Clauses of the First

Amendment. It is the appellees' view that the Hyde Amendment violates the Establishment Clause because it incorporates into law the doctrines of the Roman Catholic Church concerning the sinfulness of abortion and the time at which life commences. Moreover, insofar as a woman's decision to seek a medically necessary abortion may be a product of her religious beliefs under certain Protestant and Jewish tenets, the appellees assert that the funding limitations of the Hyde Amendment impinge on the freedom of religion guaranteed by the Free Exercise Clause.

It is well settled that "a legislative enactment does not contravene the Establishment Clause if it has a secular legislative purpose, if its principal or primary effect neither advances nor inhibits religion, and if it does not foster an excessive governmental entanglement with religion." Applying this standard, the District Court properly concluded that the Hyde Amendment does not run afoul of the Establishment Clause. Although neither a State nor the Federal Government can constitutionally "pass laws which aid one religion, aid all religions, or prefer one religion over another," it does not follow that a statute violates the Establishment Clause because it "happens to coincide or harmonize with the tenets of some or all religions." That the Judaeo-Christian religions oppose stealing does not mean that a State or the Federal Government may not, consistent with the Establishment Clause, enact laws prohibiting larceny. The Hyde Amendment, as the District Court noted, is as much a reflection of "traditionalist" values towards abortion, as it is an embodiment of the views of any particular religion. In sum, we are convinced that the fact that the funding restrictions in the Hyde Amendment may coincide with the religious tenets of the Roman Catholic Church does not, without more, contravene the Establishment Clause.

We need not address the merits of the appellees' arguments concerning the Free Exercise Clause, because the appellees lack standing to raise a free exercise challenge to the Hyde Amendment. [Plaintiffs failed to allege that they sought abortions under compulsion of their religious beliefs.]

* * *

It remains to be determined whether the Hyde Amendment violates the equal protection component of the Fifth Amendment. This challenge is premised on the fact that, although federal reimbursement is available under Medicaid for medically necessary services generally, the Hyde Amendment does not permit federal reimbursement of all medically necessary abortions. The District Court held, and the appellees argue here, that this selective subsidization violates the constitutional guarantee of equal protection.

The guarantee of equal protection under the Fifth Amendment is not a source of substantive rights or liberties, but rather a right to be free from invidious discrimination in statutory classifications and other governmental activity. It is well settled that where a statutory classification does not itself impinge on a right or liberty protected by the Constitution, the validity of classification must be sustained unless "the classification rests on grounds wholly irrelevant to the achievement of [any legitimate governmental] objective." This presumption of constitutional validity, however, disappears if a statutory classification is predicated on criteria that are, in a constitutional sense, "suspect," the principal example of which is a classification based on race.

* * *

For the reasons stated above, we have already concluded that the Hyde Amendment violates no constitutionally protected substantive rights. We now conclude as well that it is not predicated on a constitutionally suspect classification. In reaching this conclusion, we again draw guidance from the Court's decision in *Maher v. Roe*. As to whether the Connecticut welfare regulation providing funds for childbirth but not for nontherapeutic abortions discriminated against a suspect class, the Court in *Maher* observed: "An indigent woman desiring an abortion does not come within the limited category of disadvantaged classes so recognized by our cases. Nor does the fact that the impact of the regulation falls upon those who cannot pay lead to a different conclusion. In a sense, every denial of welfare to an indigent creates a wealth classification as compared to nonindigents who are able to pay for the desired goods or services. But this Court has never held that financial need alone identifies a suspect class for purposes of equal protection analysis." Thus, the Court in *Maher* found no basis for concluding that the Connecticut regulation was predicated on a suspect classification.

It is our view that the present case is indistinguishable from *Maher* in this respect. Here, as in *Maher*, the principal impact of the Hyde Amendment falls on the indigent. But that fact does not itself render the funding restriction constitutionally invalid, for this Court has held repeatedly that poverty, standing alone is not a suspect classification. That *Maher* involved the refusal to fund nontherapeutic abortions, whereas the present case involves the refusal to fund medically necessary abortions, has no bearing on the factors that render a classification "suspect" within the meaning of the constitutional guarantee of equal protection.

* * *

The remaining question then is whether the Hyde Amendment is rationally related to a legitimate governmental objective. It is the Government's position that the Hyde Amendment bears a rational relationship to its legitimate interest in protecting the potential life of the fetus. We agree.

In *Wade*, the Court recognized that the State has an "important and legitimate interest in protecting the potentiality of human life." That interest was found to exist throughout a pregnancy, "grow[ing] in substantiality as the woman approaches term." Moreover, in *Maher*, the Court held that Connecticut's decision to fund the costs associated with childbirth but not those associated with nontherapeutic abortions was a rational means of advancing the legitimate state interest in protecting potential life by encouraging childbirth.

It follows that the Hyde Amendment, by encouraging childbirth except in the most urgent circumstances, is rationally related to the legitimate governmental objective of protecting potential life. By subsidizing the medical expenses of indigent women who carry their pregnancies to term while not subsidizing the comparable expenses of women who undergo abortions (except those whose lives are threatened), Congress has established incentives that make childbirth a more attractive alternative than abortion for persons eligible for Medicaid. These incentives bear a direct relationship to the legitimate congressional interest in protecting potential life. Nor is it irrational that Congress has authorized federal reimbursement for medically necessary services generally, but not for certain medically necessary abortions. Abortion is inherently different from other medical procedures, because no other procedure involves the purposeful termination of a potential life.

* * *

After conducting an extensive evidentiary hearing into issues surrounding the public funding of abortions, the District Court concluded that "[t]he interests of . . . the federal government . . . in the fetus and in preserving it are not sufficient, weighed in the balance with the woman's threatened health, to justify withdrawing medical assistance unless the woman consents . . . to carry the fetus to term." In making an independent appraisal of the competing interests involved here, the District Court went beyond the judicial function. Such decisions are entrusted under the Constitution to Congress, not the courts. It is the role of the courts only to ensure that congressional decisions comport with the Constitution.

Where, as here, the Congress has neither invaded a substantive constitutional right or freedom, nor enacted legislation that purposefully operates to the detriment of a suspect class, the only requirement of equal protection is that congressional action be rationally related to a legitimate governmental interest. The Hyde Amendment satisfies that standard. It is not the mission of this Court or any other to decide whether the balance of competing interests reflected in the Hyde Amendment is wise social policy. If that were our mission, not every Justice who has subscribed to the judgment of the Court today could have done so. But we cannot, in the name of the Constitution, overturn duly enacted statutes simply "because they may be unwise, improvident, or out of harmony with a particular school of thought." Rather, "when an issue involves policy choices as sensitive as those implicated [here] . . ., the appropriate forum for their resolution in a democracy is the legislature."

For the reasons stated in this opinion, we hold that a State that participates in the Medicaid program is not obligated under Title XIX to continue to fund those medically necessary abortions for which federal reimbursement is unavailable under the Hyde Amendment. We further hold that the funding restrictions of the Hyde Amendment violate neither the Fifth Amendment nor the Establishment Clause of the First Amendment. It is also our view that the appellees lack standing to raise a challenge to the Hyde Amendment under the Free Exercise Clause of the First Amendment. Accordingly, the judgment of the District Court is reversed, and the case is remanded to that court for further proceedings consistent with this opinion.

* * *

Notes and Questions

1. *Encouragement v. Obstacle.* The Supreme Court ruled that states may favor childbirth over abortion, by subsidizing childbirth but not abortion, without violating a woman's liberty of reproductive choice, because the encouragement of childbirth did not constitute an obstacle to abortion. According to the Court, the obstacle to abortion was caused by the poor woman's poverty. The government had no duty to remove the obstacle of poverty that it did not create. For an argument that the courts consistently have applied similar reasoning with regard to welfare benefits, *see* Lynn A. Baker, *The Prices of Rights: Toward a Positive Theory of Unconstitutional Conditions,* 75 CORNELL LAW REVIEW 1185 (1990); Lynn A. Baker, *Bargaining for Public Assistance,* 72 DENVER UNIVERSITY LAW REVIEW 949 (1995).

Are there any flaws in, or limits to, this reasoning? Won't the government's failure to fund particular types of health care for poor people effectively deny that health care to poor people? Recall the discussion of unconstitutional conditions in Chapter 7. According to Professor Kathleen Sullivan, government has a special duty to avoid pressuring certain types of recipients to surrender certain constitutional rights. *See* Kathleen Sullivan, *Unconstitutional Conditions,* 102 HARVARD LAW REVIEW 1415 (1989). In particular, Professor Sullivan argues that government should be prohibited from overreaching, that it should be held to a standard of evenhandedness, and that it should not be allowed to create hierarchies among rightholders. Does the Court's reasoning in *Harris v. McRae* violate any of these norms? Does it matter whether government enjoys monopoly power over a benefit? If so, does the government hold monopoly power over the provision of welfare? Does it matter whether the government has created the dependency? If so, has government helped to create welfare dependency? Does it matter whether the constitutional right at issue protects the rightholder's decisional autonomy? If so, does the right to freedom of reproductive choice protect decisional autonomy? *Id.* at 1451-54, 1486-87.

What constitutes an "obstacle"? Does government create obstacles only by taking action? Can government create obstacles through its inaction? Can government create obstacles in effect, by treating groups of potential beneficiaries differently?

2. *Traditional Values, Not Religious Values.* The Court seems to conclude that traditional values are not necessarily religious values. If so, then what forms the basis for "traditional" values? Can you identify any values that are unique to religion generally, or to certain religions specifically?

3. *No Suspect Class of Poor Women.* On what basis did the Court decline to apply heightened scrutiny for the class of poor women affected by the statute?

4. *The Effect of the Undue Burden Test.* The standard applied in abortion cases has evolved since the Court decided *Harris v. McRae*. The Court has since applied an "undue burden" standard. As the Court explained in *Planned Parenthood of Southeastern Pennsylvania v. Casey*, 112 S.Ct. 2791 (1992), "an undue burden is a shorthand for the conclusion that a state regulation has the purpose or effect of placing a substantial obstacle in the path of a woman seeking an abortion of a nonviable fetus." Would the denial of government funding for medically necessary abortions for poor women survive the undue burden standard? Do you expect that the legislators who enacted the Hyde Amendment intended that it would deter poor women from obtaining such abortions? Do you expect that, as an empirical matter, the denial of funding has had the effect of denying abortions to poor women?

4. Encouraging Marriage.

In its 1996 Personal Responsibility and Work Opportunity Act, Congress made the encouragement of marriage one of the primary goals of the Temporary Assistance for Needy Families (TANF) block grant program. The first Congressional finding in the statute was that "[m]arriage is the foundation of a successful society." What makes this a "finding"? Is it possible to challenge Congressional findings and purposes? If so, how? What federal constitutional challenges might be possible? Does the government's encouragement of marriage constitute the establishment of one religious viewpoint as the law of the land? Does Congress' encouragement of marriage infringe on the fundamental right to privacy, which includes the right to decide whether to marry? How would the Court's reasoning in *Harris v. McRae* affect such establishment clause and privacy claims? Does Congress' encouragement of marriage deny equal protection? What similarly situated groups does it treat differently? How strong is the government's interest in encouraging marriage: legitimate, important, or compelling? To what extent are the provisions of the TANF statute tailored to achieve the government's purpose: rationally tailored, substantially tailored, or narrowly tailored? Could state constitutional claims be raised? Are statutory challenges possible? For example, what if other federal or state laws prohibited discrimination based on marital status?

B. CHILD SUPPORT

1. Child Support Enforcement and Its Limits

One of the most popular components of the much touted welfare reform consensus of the mid 1990s was the commitment to strengthen child support enforcement. Both feminists and proponents of family values shared the desire to increase child support requirements, as did both Democrat and Republican officials.

Child Support, Federalism, and the Personal Responsibility Act

Prior to the Personal Responsibility and Work Opportunity Reconciliation Act of 1996, Congress had been gradually strengthening child support enforcement requirements. Critics complained, however, that states simply had not collected sufficient child support payments. According to an independent analysis of data compiled by the federal Office of Child Support Enforcement, the Center for Law and Social Policy found that less than 20 percent of families using the state child support collection system received any payments in 1993, the same percentage as received payments in 1989. *See* TINA MARIE PERRY, PAULA ROBERTS, CENTER FOR LAW AND SOCIAL POLICY, THE STATE OF THE STATES: WHAT THE OCSE ANNUAL REPORT TO CONGRESS DOESN'T TELL YOU (1995).

Some commentators and legislators have called for full federalization of child support enforcement, with federal officials establishing paternity, setting child support orders, and enforcing those orders. Others proposed that the federal government establish minimum support guidelines, but leave implementation to the states. The Personal Responsibility and Work Opportunity Reconciliation

Act of 1996 took partial steps toward federalizing child support. The PRA requires states to follow uniform procedures, including adopting the Uniform Interstate Family Support Act. Congress also specified uniform requirements for state collection of data to be reported to the federal government. Although Congress increased some oversight functions of the Secretary of Health and Human Services, it left the implementation of child support enforcement to the states. Should Congress continue this cooperative federalism arrangement for child support enforcement, or should it increase or decrease federal involvement?

Costs versus Benefits

Some recent research suggests that, while enormous sums are spent on the government's child support enforcement bureaucracy, collected child support payments add little to the average poor family's income. Researchers at the Institute for Women's Policy Research, for example, found that child support contributed no more than 2% on average to families receiving AFDC.[1] What prevents the government from collecting more child support? Could the private sector collect child support more efficiently, and/or more effectively? What are the government's interests in collecting child support, especially if it fails to increase poor children's income?

Child Support and the Takings Clause

Part of the reason child support does not substantially increase poor families' incomes is because the government uses child support to reimbursement itself for welfare benefits paid. For example, under the prior AFDC "pass through" system, government forwarded only the first $50 of collected support to poor families.

To whom does child support belong? Whose support is it? Review *Bowen v. Gilliard* in Chapter 7 and recall the Supreme Court's holding that government's taking of support payments made by non-custodial parents does not violate children's rights under the takings clause.

---

[1] Roberta M. Spalter-Roth, Heidi I. Hartmann and Linda Andrews, Report to the Ford Foundation from the Institute for Women's Policy Research, Combining Work and Welfare: An Alternative Anti-Poverty Strategy (1992).

In the 1996 Personal Responsibility and Work Opportunity Reconciliation Act (PRA), Congress continued its requirement that welfare recipients assign their support rights to the state. Congress ended, however, the pass through system of forwarding the first $50 of collected child support to children. For families receiving welfare assistance, Congress required the states to use collected child support to first pay back the federal share of welfare benefits and then to either pay back the state share of welfare benefits or distribute that amount to the family. Are these requirements likely to affect a court's judgment whether the government's taking of support payments violates the takings clause?

Child Support and Privacy

How far can the government go to encourage payment of child support? The Personal Responsibility and Work Opportunity Act of 1996 includes many requirements that arguably invade the privacy of us all. For example, Congress required that states document the social security numbers of all persons who apply for professional, occupational, driver's or marriage licenses, and those subject to a divorce decree, support order, or paternity determination. Employers must report the name, address, and Social Security number of every new employee in the state within 20 days of their employment to the State Directory of New Hires. States then must report this information to the new Federal Directory of New Hires.

With regard to parents, state agencies must be able to order genetic testing, issue subpoenas, and access both public and private records to obtain information for establishing paternity. Congress required states to maintain an automated State Case Registry that contains the names, Social Security numbers, and other identifying information about both parents. States must report this information to the new Federal Case Registry. Consumer credit agencies and states must share information regarding delinquent parents. Financial institutions must provide names, addresses, and Social Security numbers of their delinquent accountholders (for which Congress relieves financial institutions of any liability), and states must have procedures to impose liens against bank accounts or other property.

The statute allows states to contract with private entities to administer the state's system, and requires that such private entities have access to collected information. Congress requires states, however, to adopt safeguards to ensure the privacy of individuals. Are these provisions constitutional? Consider how the Supreme Court's analysis in the following case might affect a constitutional challenge to the Personal Responsibility Act's child support provisions.

ZABLOCKI v. REDHAIL

434 U.S. 374 (1978)

Justice MARSHALL delivered the opinion of the Court.

At issue in this case is the constitutionality of a Wisconsin statute which provides that members of a certain class of Wisconsin residents may not marry, within the State or elsewhere, without first obtaining a court order granting permission to marry. The class is defined by the statute to include any "Wisconsin resident having minor issue not in his custody and which he is under obligation to support by any court order or judgment." The statute specifies that court permission cannot be granted unless the marriage applicant submits proof of compliance with the support obligation and, in addition, demonstrates that the children covered by the support order "are not then and are not likely thereafter to become public charges." No marriage license may lawfully be issued in Wisconsin to a person covered by the statute, except upon court order; any marriage entered into without compliance with § 245.10 is declared void; and persons acquiring marriage licenses in violation of the section are subject to criminal penalties.

* * *

Appellee Redhail is a Wisconsin resident who, under the terms of § 245.10, is unable to enter into a lawful marriage in Wisconsin or elsewhere so long as he maintains his Wisconsin residency. The facts, according to the stipulation filed by the parties in the District Court, are as follows. In January 1972, when appellee was a minor and a high school student, a paternity action was instituted against him in Milwaukee County Court, alleging that he was the father of a baby girl born out of wedlock on July 5, 1971. After he appeared and admitted that he was the child's father, the court entered an order on May 12, 1972, adjudging appellee the father and ordering him to pay $109 per month as support for the child until she reached 18 years of age. From May 1972 until August 1974, appellee was unemployed and indigent, and consequently was unable to make any support payments.

On September 27, 1974, appellee filed an application for a marriage license with appellant Zablocki, the County Clerk of Milwaukee County, and a few days later the application was denied on the sole ground that appellee had not obtained a court order granting him permission to marry, as required by § 245.10. Although appellee did not petition a state court thereafter, it is stipulated that he would not have been able to satisfy either of the statutory prerequisites for an order granting permission to marry. First, he had not satisfied his support obligations to his illegitimate child, and as of December 1974 there was an arrearage in excess of $3,700. Second, the child had been a public charge since her birth, receiving benefits under the Aid to Families with Dependent Children program. It is stipulated that the child's benefit payments were such that she would have been a public charge even if appellee had been current in his support payments.

* * *

In evaluating §§ 245.10(1), (4), (5) under the Equal Protection Clause, "we must first determine what burden of justification the classification created thereby must meet, by looking to the nature of the classification and the individual interests affected." Since our past decisions make clear that the right to marry is of fundamental importance, and since the classification at issue here significantly interferes with the exercise of that right, we believe that "critical examination" of the state interests advanced in support of the classification is required.

The leading decision of this Court on the right to marry is *Loving v. Virginia*, 388 U.S. 1 (1967). In that case, an interracial couple who had been convicted of violating Virginia's miscegenation laws challenged the statutory scheme on both equal protection and due process grounds. The Court's opinion could have rested solely on the ground that the statutes discriminated on the basis of race in violation of the Equal Protection Clause. But the Court went on to hold that the laws arbitrarily deprived the couple of a fundamental liberty protected by the Due Process Clause, the freedom to marry.

* * *

When a statutory classification significantly interferes with the exercise of a fundamental right, it cannot be upheld unless it is supported by sufficiently important state interests and is closely tailored to effectuate only those interests. Appellant asserts that two interests are served by the challenged statute: the permission-to-marry proceeding furnishes an opportunity to counsel the applicant as to the necessity of fulfilling his prior support obligations; and the welfare of the out-of-custody children is protected. We may accept for present purposes that these are legitimate and substantial interests, but, since the means selected by the State for achieving these interests unnecessarily impinge on the right to marry, the statute cannot be sustained.

There is evidence that the challenged statute, as originally introduced in the Wisconsin Legislature, was intended merely to establish a mechanism whereby persons with support obligations to children from prior marriages could be counseled before they entered into new marital relationships and incurred further support obligations. Court permission to marry was to be required, but apparently permission was automatically to be granted after counseling was completed. The statute actually enacted, however, does not expressly require or provide for any counseling whatsoever, nor for any automatic granting of permission to marry by the court, and thus it can hardly be justified as a means for ensuring counseling of the persons within its coverage. Even assuming that counseling does take place--a fact as to which there is no evidence in the record--this interest obviously cannot support the withholding of court permission to marry once counseling is completed.

With regard to safeguarding the welfare of the out-of-custody children, appellant's brief does not make clear the connection between the State's interest and the statute's requirements. At argument, appellant's counsel suggested that, since permission to marry cannot be granted unless the applicant shows that he has satisfied his court-determined support obligations to the prior children and that those children will not become public charges, the statute provides incentive for the applicant to make support payments to his children. This "collection device" rationale cannot justify the statute's broad infringement on the right to marry.

First, with respect to individuals who are unable to meet the statutory requirements, the statute merely prevents the applicant from getting married, without delivering any money at all into the hands of the applicant's prior children. More importantly, regardless of the applicant's ability or willingness to meet the statutory requirements, the State already has numerous other means for exacting compliance with support obligations, means that are at least as effective as the instant statute's and yet do not impinge upon the right to marry. Under Wisconsin law, whether the children are from a prior marriage or were born out of wedlock, court-determined support obligations may be enforced directly via wage assignments, civil contempt proceedings, and criminal penalties. And, if the State believes that parents of children out of their custody should be responsible for ensuring that those children do not become public charges, this interest can be achieved by adjusting the criteria used for determining the amounts to be paid under their support orders.

There is also some suggestion that § 245.10 protects the ability of marriage applicants to meet support obligations to prior children by preventing the applicants from incurring new support obligations. But the challenged provisions of § 245.10 are grossly underinclusive with respect to this purpose, since they do not limit in any way new financial commitments by the applicant other than those arising out of the contemplated marriage. The statutory classification is substantially overinclusive as well: Given the possibility that the new spouse will actually better the applicant's financial situation, by contributing income from a job or otherwise, the statute in many cases may prevent affected individuals from improving their ability to satisfy their prior support obligations. And, although it is true that the applicant will incur support obligations to any children born during the contemplated marriage, preventing the marriage may only result in the children being born out of wedlock, as in fact occurred in appellee's case. Since the support obligation is the same whether the child is born in or out of wedlock, the net result of preventing the marriage is simply more illegitimate children.

The statutory classification created by §§ 245.10(1), (4), (5) thus cannot be justified by the interests advanced in support of it. The judgment of the District Court is, accordingly,

Affirmed.

Justice REHNQUIST, dissenting.

* * *

Earlier this Term the traditional standard of review was applied in *Califano v. Jobst*, 434 U.S. 47 (1977), despite the claim that the statute there in question burdened the exercise of the right to marry. The extreme situation considered there involved a permanently disabled appellee whose benefits under the Social Security Act had been terminated because of his marriage to an equally disabled woman who was not, however, a beneficiary under the Act. This Court recognized that Congress, in granting the original benefit, could reasonably assume that a disabled adult child remained dependent upon his parents for support. The Court concluded that, upon a beneficiary's marriage, Congress could terminate his benefits, because "there can be no question about the validity of the assumption that a married person is less likely to be dependent on his parents for support than one who is unmarried." Although that assumption had been proved false as applied in that individual case, the statute was nevertheless rational. "The broad legislative classification must be judged by reference to characteristics typical of the affected classes rather than by focusing on selected, atypical examples."

* * *

[T]he Wisconsin Legislature has "adopted this rule in the course of constructing a complex social welfare system that necessarily deals with the intimacies of family life." Because of the limited amount of funds available for the support of needy children, the State has an exceptionally strong interest in securing as much support as their parents are able to pay. . . . I conclude that the statute, despite its imperfections, is sufficiently rational to satisfy the demands of the Fourteenth Amendment.

* * *

Notes and Questions

1. *Government's Interest in Collecting Child Support.* The government provides collection services for child support, regardless of whether the children receive welfare benefits. What are the government's interests in collecting child support? How strong are these interests -- legitimate, important/significant, or compelling? Does the government have a stronger interest to collect support as reimbursement for welfare benefits? In part of Justice Rehnquist's dissent in *Zablocki* omitted from the preceding excerpt, he concluded that "the State has an exceptionally strong interest in securing as much support as their parents are able to pay." Do you agree?

2. *Some Privacy Rights May Be More Fundamental Than Others.* The Supreme Court in *Zablocki* treats the right to marry as

a fundamental right which enjoys protection through the Court's strictest scrutiny. Recall the discussion of Why does a non-custodial parent who has failed to support his children but wants to marry enjoy a more fundamental right of privacy than a woman who lacks income to support a child but wants to bear a child?

3. *Alternatives.* What other methods might the government use to ensure adequate support for children?

2. Child Support Alternatives

Stephen D. Sugarman

FINANCIAL SUPPORT OF CHILDREN AND THE END OF WELFARE AS WE KNOW IT

81 VIRGINIA LAW REVIEW 2523 (1995)

Introduction

Who should financially support America's children? Our nation is badly divided over which fundamental principles we should use to answer this question. In the discussion that follows, I set forth what I understand to be competing conservative and liberal visions of individual and collective obligations to provide for children. . . . I finally consider whether some sort of "child support assurance" scheme might garner widespread support; in particular, I propose an expanded role for our Social Security system.

The conservative view I have in mind rests on the principle that although having and raising a child can be a wonderful thing, moral obligations attach to that decision; until one can financially afford to provide adequate food, shelter, clothing and the like for a child, it is morally irresponsible to have one. To be financially ready to raise children typically requires job security or clear employment options and some savings. Although it is not always essential for both parents to have reliable earnings opportunities, if a woman is not readily able to support her child without financial assistance, she needs to be especially careful. In those circumstances, it is morally reckless for her to bear a child unless she is confident that the child's father has made, and can be counted on to honor, a genuine financial commitment to the child. Because marriage is seen as a way of maximizing that prospect, choosing to become a single parent (or deciding to become pregnant when one's marriage is on the rocks) is very often morally culpable behavior.

The morally responsible husband honors his financial obligation to his child even if there is a breakdown in his marital relationship--perhaps remaining with his wife for the sake of the child, but in any event dutifully paying child support even if he becomes the noncustodial parent. Men who knowingly or carelessly impregnate women to whom they are not married are usually morally irresponsible for doing so and in any case should take responsibility for the resultant child's financial needs regardless of their actual intentions at the time the sexual relation occurs.

* * *

The contrasting liberal vision I have in mind rests on very different principles. First, because having and raising a child can be a wonderful thing and an expression of one's identity, everyone in our society who wants to do it should be enabled to do so--at least if they are emotionally mature enough. This implies a collective moral obligation to aid those would-be parents among us who would otherwise be too poor to support their children on their own. Second, this vision recognizes from the outset that, short of mass sterilization, most women will bear children. It further holds that the resulting innocent children are entitled to a decent life regardless of what one might think of the morality of their parents. Moreover, although liberals agree that parents have a duty to support their children when they are financially able to do so, they are not committed to the belief that it is routinely better for children to be raised in a traditional family. For example, a woman should be enabled to raise her children without marrying a man if that is her preference; likewise, both same-sex couples and unmarried couples are quite acceptable as "parents."

Liberals, too, praise those who take on responsibility for other people's children, but in their vision, a man's first children have no greater claim to support from their father than do later-acquired step-children or newborn children with a different mother. In short, earlier children have no more priority than do older siblings within a traditional family.

Liberals believe needy children are not to be punished for the sins of their parents. Thus, even if the mother engages in morally questionable conduct, such conduct should not to lead to any loss of the household's welfare benefit. Of course, if the conduct is so bad as to render the mother unfit, the children must be removed from her custody and made wards of the state. Perhaps it is unwise for a poor woman already on welfare to have (or risk having) more children, but this decision is best left to the mother, aided by government-provided education and voluntary birth control programs, but free from threats of financial penalties that, if imposed, would simply punish the newborn and his or her sibling(s).

* * *

[T]here appear to be only two areas of real overlap between liberals and conservatives concerning the functions of government with respect to the financial support of children. First, there is general agreement on the desirability of an active state role in the imposition and collection of child support in settings where parents live apart because they are either divorced or were never married to each other. Second, there is general support for Social Security child and caretaker benefits where the breadwinner parent is deceased or disabled.

* * *

When Social Security child benefits were first introduced in 1939, the main category of AFDC recipients at that time were widowed mothers and their children. The clear goal of the reformers was to move the lion's share of these claimants off one program and onto the other, and they have largely succeeded. Today, nearly two million children with a deceased parent receive Social Security benefits, and fewer than 200,000 such children are on AFDC. At the end of the 1950s, when Social Security benefits for disabled workers were adopted, the provision of additional benefits for those workers' children represented a second important step in the same direction, once more moving families off AFDC and onto Social Security. This aspiration too has largely been attained. Indeed, at that time there were many who envisioned a gradual withering of AFDC because families of "deceased" and "incapacitated" fathers would receive more favored Social Security treatment. But these visionaries did not reckon with the coming explosion in both marital dissolution and child-bearing outside of marriage. Divorced and never-married cases, which comprised a tiny share of the AFDC load in the 1930s, overwhelmingly dominate the plan today. Is it now time for a third step? In short, just as Social Security now provides children with life insurance and disability insurance, should it also deliver what would, in effect, be child support insurance?

In recent years, others have proposed, in varying forms, a completely separate, new "child support assurance" program. Representatives from both political parties have provided early backing for Irwin Garfinkel's plan, the scheme that has been discussed most extensively. In its widest formulation, child support assurance would guarantee any single parent a specified level of child support regardless whether that amount of money were actually obtained from the absent parent. The guarantor, of course, would be the government.

Garfinkel's proposition should be distinguished from children's allowance schemes of the sort that exist in many countries and are proposed as an American solution by some advocates. First, whereas children's allowances are typically paid across the board to all parents, Garfinkel's plan focuses solely on single-parent households. Second, the child support assurance approach promises only a guarantee which the absent parent must reimburse to the extent of his child support obligation. The children's allowance, by contrast, is unconditional and would be supplemented by the full extent of child support payments from absent parents. Although some liberals would undoubtedly prefer a generous children's allowance, Garfinkel's plan has captured the attention of politicians and analysts because, by being far more closely tailored to need, it would be much less expensive.

Probably the most critical question in child support assurance plans is the level of the guarantee. It could be the poverty level or greater, which would, of course, make the proposal most appealing to liberals. In practice, most of the discussion so far seems to envision a somewhat lower sum (on cost grounds). Still, a single parent could try to escape poverty by earning wages on top of the guaranteed support amount. Under most versions, she could keep all outside earnings (or, under some proposals, she would have to give back only a small proportion of the support guarantee, such as fifteen or twenty cents per dollar earned). The upshot is that it would make good economic sense to combine work and the child support guarantee in ways that combining work and welfare currently does not.

* * *

I propose a different sort of child support assurance, one that would cover children of "absent" parents under Social Security. More precisely, I argue that we should entitle a child and his or her caretaker parent to the same Social Security benefits when the caretaker is a single parent owing to absence as they would have obtained if single parenthood had arisen from the death of the other parent.

* * *

[M]any young mothers, especially teen mothers, would be unable to claim these new Social Security benefits for themselves and their children. This is because the fathers of those children would be much less likely to be "insured" for Social Security purposes. Although many liberals might wince at the exclusion of some poor mothers, it is probably essential for conservative support. Moreover, there is a possible silver lining here. Once we move a significant share of current AFDC recipients onto Social Security, AFDC would become a much smaller program and, as such, a less appealing target for those who are prone to bash the poor. Furthermore, although younger women remaining on AFDC and most at risk of long-term dependency may receive even worse treatment than they receive today, that need not be the case. Rather, by restricting AFDC, society could focus on other social intervention strategies that are too daunting today when they must fulfill the needs of so many recipients. I return to these possibilities at the conclusion of my discussion.

* * *

Although both liberals and conservatives say they want to "end welfare as we know it," because they have such divergent starting points regarding the role of government in the financial support of children the commonly proposed solutions of either side are even more unacceptable to the other side than is the current system. This makes welfare a continuing thorn in the side of the body politic despite its relatively trivial cost relative to the entire federal budget. I propose a compromise solution that splits today's welfare population. To simplify, women who now come into AFDC because of divorce (and in some cases unmarried women because of abandonment) would instead be able to turn to Social Security for themselves and their children, just as widows do. New approaches could then focus particularly on never married teen mothers, the

AFDC beneficiaries who create the greatest uproar and who are now most at risk of long-term dependency on welfare. If a social consensus were reached to support this plan, an economic consensus could be achieved to support the necessary increase in the Social Security payroll tax, which, after all, would be substantially offset by reductions in the rest of the budget for current state and federal welfare costs.

Notes and Questions

1. *Politics Again.* With respect to child support, what areas of agreement and disagreement between conservatives and liberals are identified by Stephen Sugarman?

2. *Child Support Alternatives.* Child support enforcement and welfare benefits are the two main methods currently used by government to support children. Professor Sugarman distinguishes between other alternatives, including Child Allowances (unconditional payments to all parents, as provided by most other industrialized nations), Child Support Assurance (guarantees of child support payments to all single parents, as proposed by Irwin Garfinkel), and Sugarman's proposal of Social Security Child Support Insurance (child support payments made to children whose absent parent qualified for Social Security benefits). How do these alternatives compare in terms of goals, political support, financial feasibility, and comprehension of coverage? What other criteria might be relevant to evaluating these alternatives? What other alternatives for supporting children might be possible?

3. *Critiques.* Commentators have been critical of Professor Sugarman's Social Security Child Support Insurance proposal. David Chambers argues that Professor Sugarman's proposal underestimates the extent to which conservatives, employers, and Congress are concerned with cutting costs. *See* David L. Chambers, *Fathers, the Welfare System, and the Virtues and Perils of Child-Support Enforcement*, 81 VIRGINIA LAW REVIEW 2575 (1995). Professor Chambers also points out that the insurance proposal would not provide benefits for children who do not have qualifying wage-earners as parents, thus leaving us with the problem of providing some sort of welfare benefits to these children. *Id.* Professor Dorothy Roberts also criticizes the insurance proposal:

> The objective of welfare reform should not be to reach a consensus by adopting irrational conservative

> policies that sacrifice the interests of the neediest children. What would an agenda that refused to compromise with conservatives look like? It would abolish the stratification based on notions of "earned" entitlements and "undeserved" handouts. It would place individual welfare programs in the larger context of the entire welfare state and its role in fostering citizenship. It would rely on a collective obligation to poor families, rather than on fathers' private interest in their own children. And it would provide public financial assistance as part of a broader program to restructure economic, social and political institutions to make them more egalitarian, democratic and just.

Dorothy E. Roberts, *Irrationality and Sacrifice in the Welfare Reform Consensus*, 81 VIRGINIA LAW REVIEW 2607, 2622 (1995).

C. CHILD CARE

Another popular part of the mid 1990s consensus on welfare reform was the expectation that poor mothers must participate in the paid labor force. The primary obstacle to satisfying this expectation for many poor mothers is the difficulty in finding affordable, high quality child care. A patchwork of federal programs provide direct or subsidized child care, as the following articles describe.

1. A History of Child Care

Dorothy Miller
WOMEN AND SOCIAL WELFARE

Day nurseries for working mothers were first established in the United States by wealthy women for the benefit of poor mothers who needed to be in the labor force. The first center was opened in 1838. Centers expanded after the Civil War to provide for children of war widows. Social reformers during the Progressive Era at the turn of the century also established nurseries in poor neighborhoods for employed mothers. Day care was seen primarily as a social service for poor and troubled families and was primarily funded through private donation. Kindergarten, in contrast, begun in this country in the second half of the nineteenth century, stressed the social and educational needs of young children and operated on a part-day basis for the children of middle- and upper-income parents who could afford it.

It was not until the Depression that the federal government began to subsidize day care, and then it was for the purpose of employing school personnel who were out of work. Later, during World War II the Lanham Act provided for day care centers to be established near industrial centers that needed to employ women in the defense industry. It was assumed, however, even among advocates for these centers, that day care should be used only in extenuating circumstances. Federal Children's Bureau staff even fought against making the centers too convenient because women might be tempted to keep their children in care after the war.

After the war federal support was withdrawn and publicly supported day care remained in the few states and localities that chose to subsidize them. Women were encouraged to leave their jobs and return home to their rightful place. Many women did not make this retreat, however, and Congress finally acknowledged their need for child care by passing a tax deduction for child care expenses in 1954. Since then there have been three types of federal subsidies for child care: tax-related provisions, subsidies for direct provision, and Head Start.

In the 1960s, Head Start, a developmental program for poor children, was launched. It was based on the belief that poor children started school already behind their middle-class counterparts and needed enrichment programs to bring them up to par before they began. Head Start was created in the tradition of developmental preschool kindergartens and adapted for disadvantaged children. However, it was never intended to serve the function of child care for employed mothers. Indeed, only 10 percent of children in Head Start today are in full-day programs.

Simultaneous with their concern about bringing poor children up to par with their middle-class counterparts, Congress was faced with increasing welfare rolls and seemingly became desirous of getting welfare mothers into the labor force. Day care for poor mothers had to be a component of any such project. Thus the Public Welfare Amendments of 1962 included an authorization of day care funds to facilitate the employment of welfare mothers, and day care was included as a support service when the WIN program was established in 1967.

It is noteworthy that Head Start followed the kindergarten model and did not incorporate the day nursery model as well. It was designed in such a way that parental involvement in center activities was integral to the program and timed in such a way that employed parents could not participate and in many cases could not enroll their children. It's as if the policy makers and planners thought of the Head Start population and the children of those welfare mothers who were to be prodded into working as *different* people. To this day, Head Start remains a very popular, but limited program for some lucky poor children, some of whose mothers are presented with a kind of catch-22: go to work and better your family and settle for what day care you can get, or remain on welfare and let your children reap the benefits of Head Start.

* * *

2. Contemporary Programs and Critiques

Peter Pitegoff

CHILD CARE ENTERPRISE,
COMMUNITY DEVELOPMENT,AND WORK

81 GEO. L.J. 1897

* * *

The United States has no comprehensive child care system, but has instead a patchwork of public policies and private initiatives. Licensed day care centers . . . include both not-for-profit enterprises . . . . There is extensive variation within the category of licensed centers, from small proprietary businesses to large for-profit chains or franchise networks, from union-sponsored programs to work-site centers for employees of corporate businesses, and from independent not-for-profit organizations to day care groups based in churches or schools, or sponsored by other community organizations. Relatively few corporate employers provide child care support to employees, although an increasing number of initiatives sponsored by large corporations have received media attention.

Completing the spectrum of regulated child care alternatives are family day care services, ordinarily provided by women in their own homes for a small number of children. These micro-enterprises are popular as a child care alternative for children under six and as a means of self-employment for women. Although they are subject to increasing regulation and licensure, many such operations remain informal and unlicensed and vary in quality.

Much of the child care for preschool children, in fact, is outside of the regulatory spectrum of licensed day care centers and home-based day care. Private and informal arrangements, essentially unregulated by the state, together involve a larger number of preschool children than licensed centers and home-based services. For example, some working parents who can afford private child care hire providers for regular full-time care in their own homes. Networks of friends and extended families make up another informal child care system that enables many parents to work. Some of these arrangements essentially mirror the regulated centers and home-based day care services, without being subject to government over-sight. But within this informal system, a number of young children are simply left to care for themselves or are cared for by an older child. Finally, many parents manage to provide full-time parental care to their preschool children, sometimes by choice--when affordable or with staggered job hours by two working parents--but increasingly due to involuntary unemployment by one or both parents.

The private market alone cannot support the array of day care providers currently operating, or the additional services that are needed. Fee-based child care is supplemented to some degree by charitable funding and by public subsidies for service to low-income families. Governments intervene at the state and local level with some financial support to providers, along with regulatory standards. The system of state support is quite fragmented, however, and there is wide variation among states in both standards and subsidy levels. Dozens of separate federal programs provide some form of child care assistance, with billions of dollars spent annually. The federal government subsidizes a portion of consumer costs for child care through tax policy and social welfare allowances, and it channels money to providers primarily through block grants to local governments and food subsidies to child care centers via state agencies. The federal government is most directly involved with early childhood in the Head Start program, which is essentially a part-time educational and family development program not a child care program that frees parents for full-time work. Aside from Head Start, most child care subsidies for low-income recipients are aimed at reducing welfare dependency of poor parents, rather than at meeting the developmental needs of children.

The federal government provides limited tax relief for child care to parents through the Child and Dependent Care Tax Credit. This consumer subsidy, largely to the benefit of middle class taxpayers, amounts to the single largest federal expenditure on child care. The primary federal subsidy to low-income consumers of child care is through Aid to Families with Dependent Children (AFDC), a legacy of the Depression-era Aid to Dependent Children. AFDC includes a child care allowance, which remains the most widespread form of child care assistance for low-income families. Employed recipients of AFDC can disregard the costs of child care from their earnings when computing their benefits. Other federal child care initiatives from the 1960s and 1970s have been consolidated in Title XX of the Social Security Act. Under Title XX, Social Services Block Grants are channeled to states, and local governments are given discretion for allocation among different needed services including child care.

While the system, such as it is, cannot meet current demand, the need for affordable child care is steadily growing. Labor force participation by mothers of young children has dramatically increased in recent decades, due to both choice and economic necessity. The U.S. Department of Labor reported in 1988 that fifty-seven percent of all women with children under six years old worked outside the home, compared with twelve percent in 1950. By 1995, an estimated two-thirds of all preschool children will have mothers in the work force, a fifty percent increase from just ten years earlier.

Demand for child care cuts across class lines has dramatically grown among middle class families. The high cost of quality care forces many middle-income families into lower quality care, or even out of the work force. Despite government and philanthropic subsidies, funding for child care efforts in low-income neighborhoods fails to provide families with sufficient affordable day care. In these situations in particular, child care providers are sorely underfunded and, as a consequence, their institutional stability and quality of care suffer. Child care options for the working poor are extremely limited and, with cruel irony, many child care providers count among these working poor.

The 1990 National Child Care Survey highlights the vulnerability of low-income working mothers, whose jobs typically provide little flexibility in work schedules. This lack of flexibility results in a higher incidence of absenteeism among low-income workers duc to child sickness or child care problems, such as the unavailability of the regular provider. Only three out of ten working parents reported the availability of part-time work, unpaid leave, or flextime. Low-income working parents often have little choice but to lose a day of work and pay in the event of a family emergency. The working poor face a disadvantage because employer benefits for child care are often less available to them, and they havc limited disposable income to pay for child care in the absence of targeted benefits.

The Family and Medical Leave Act, enacted in February 1993, provides some limited benefit to the working poor. The Act requires private employers with fifty or more employees, and certain government employers, to provide eligible employees with up to twelve weeks of unpaid leave for birth or adoption of a child; for care of a seriously ill child, spouse, or parent; or for the employee's own serious illness. Employers must guarantee the employee a right to return to his or her previous job or an equivalent position after the leave and must maintain any existing health benefits during the leave.

This Act represents a significant victory for its advocates after eight years of effort in Congress. Many low-income workers, however, cannot afford to take unpaid leave and have few, if any, existing health benefits to extend during a leave. The definition of "eligible employee," moreover, will exclude from coverage many of the working poor, who work part-time or on a temporary basis, or for an employer with less than fifty employees.

For those persons covered by the Act, the right to reinstatement after a leave provides an important element of job security. Half of all mothers surveyed in 1990, before enactment of the 1993 Act, took some leave after the birth of their youngest child, seventy percent without pay. Paid parental leave remains rare, and those who are paid during such leaves ordinarily use a combination of vacation, sick, and disability pay, and their own resources. These options are generally not available to low-income workers. The limitations of family leave policies, by legislation or in private enterprise practice, fall hardest upon the working poor, a class of individuals consisting disproportionately of women and racial minorities.

Trends in federal funding during the 1980s illustrate the class-based structure of child care policy. In 1977, Title XX funds, used to subsidize day care for children of low-income families, accounted for forty percent of total federal child care spending. Also in 1977, twenty-five percent of federal spending consisted of the tax cost of the Dependent Care Tax Credit, used by middle and upper middle class taxpayers. By 1986, Title XX comprised only about seven percent of federal child care spending, while the Dependent Care Tax Credit accounted for more than sixty percent of the total. Thus, although total federal spending on child care rose during this period, most of the increase came via tax subsidies, with a disproportionate share of the tax benefits going to middle- and upper middle-income families, rather than to the working poor.

Especially for poor women, the lack of affordable child care is a frequent obstacle to employment. Federal subsidies to poor families for child care--primarily through Head Start, Title XX Social Services Block Grants, Aid to Families with Dependent Children, and the National School Lunch Program--are insufficient to subsidize all eligible families and fail to reach working class families whose income makes them ineligible despite their critical need. A 1987 government estimate showed child care costs consuming up to twenty-six percent of family income among poor families, compared with ten percent among families generally. In that same year, 16.4% of families with children were in poverty, a rise of nearly thirty-five percent in less than a decade. Nearly half of all female headed households with children live in poverty. Inadequate funding limits child care assistance to the population most in need and, even when child care is available, seriously undermines the quality of care.

* * *

Mary L. Heen

Welfare Reform, Child Care Costs, and Taxes

13 Yale Law & Policy Review 173 (1995)

The current system of work-related child care assistance includes both direct federal child care expenditure programs and various income tax provisions relating to child care expenses. At first glance, the current federal approach to child care assistance appears in need of reform: the largest single source of child care assistance, estimated to total approximately $2.7 billion in forgone revenue in fiscal year 1995, is delivered through the tax system in the form of a nonrefundable credit utilized mostly by middle- and upper-income taxpayers; and another set of programs, totalling just over $2 billion, is delivered to low-income families through a patchwork of direct assistance programs designed to serve various political and social goals.

* * *

Key direct assistance programs include child care provided under the Family Support Act of 1988 to AFDC and former AFDC recipients, the At-Risk Child Care Program, the Child Care and Development Block Grant Program, various expenditures under the Social Services Block Grant Program of Title XX of the Social Security Act, and to a limited extent, the Head Start program. Not counting federal expenditures for Head Start, federal child care assistance from these programs totalled roughly $2.05 billion for fiscal year 1993.

Several design features of federal direct assistance programs affect the availability and quality of work-related child care. First, some of the federal program funding structures require states to provide their own funds as a prerequisite for receiving federal money. The states' failure to allocate sufficient funds, as well as federal limitations on certain federal matching funds, have resulted in deficiencies in implementation of the programs. Second, some of the federal funding programs, especially the block grant programs, have required expenditures to improve the quality of the child care services. The possibility of losing child care improvement funding in the current round of welfare reform, along with any resulting relaxation of minimum standards, is worrisome. Even at current funding levels, the child care received by many low-income children has raised concerns about their health and safety. In addition, the block grant programs have provided child care assistance to low-income families that do not receive welfare. The increased child care needs of welfare recipients under new work requirements, without increased funding levels, may prevent these other low-income families from receiving the assistance they need.

* * *

The major entitlement-type federal matching fund programs are provided under the Family Support Act of 1988 (FSA), which was enacted during the last major reform of the welfare system. The FSA created the Job Opportunity and Basic Skills (JOBS) program to replace the Work Incentive Program (WIN), established in 1967. It also mandated improved procedures for child support enforcement and the establishment of paternity, guaranteed federal assistance for child care during participation in education, training, and employment (AFDC-related child care), and provided transitional eligibility for a year of extended child care and medical assistance for former AFDC recipients who become ineligible for AFDC because of increased income from employment (transitional child care).

The JOBS program is funded through a capped federal entitlement under which states are partially reimbursed (pursuant to a federal matching rate) for each dollar spent on JOBS until they reach the maximum amount allocated to them. Few states, however, have fully utilized their allotment. Budget constraints on the states as well as the cost of child care are among the reasons identified for the less than full implementation of the JOBS program. In many states, the same amount was spent on AFDC and transitional child care as on the JOBS program itself.

In contrast to the capped entitlement funding for the JOBS program, the federally mandated child care assistance for JOBS participants is an open-ended entitlement for which the states receive federal matching funds at the Medicaid rate. State welfare agencies administer the program, and may provide child care directly, arrange for care through providers by purchase of service contracts or vouchers, provide families with advance cash or vouchers, reimburse families, or use other appropriate arrangements. Under a method of providing assistance referred to as a child care "disregard," states may also exempt a certain amount of the value of child care services from the income of a family in determining the amount of AFDC benefits to which they are entitled. Reimbursement for child care costs are subject to certain limits. States vary in the mix of AFDC child care arrangements provided to JOBS recipients. On the whole, however, about forty percent of the children are in child care centers, about twenty-five percent in non-relative family day care, and about eighteen percent are provided care by a relative.

As stated above, the FSA also guarantees time-limited Transitional Child Care (TCC), to the extent that child care is necessary for employment, in the case of families no longer eligible for AFDC support because of increased hours or increased income from employment, or because of the loss of the child care disregard due to time limitations. Families are eligible for TCC "for a period of 12 months after the last month for which the family received [AFDC]," if they "have received [AFDC] in at least 3 of the 6 months immediately preceding the month in which the family became ineligible for [AFDC]." They must contribute to the cost of child care under a sliding scale formula established by the state. The federal share of TCC is based on the state's Medicaid matching rate, and the program generally operates under the same rules as the child care program for AFDC recipients. The limited data available show that the mix of TCC child care arrangements used by the states roughly echoes that of the child care provided to AFDC JOBS recipients, with a slightly greater percentage in center-based care and a smaller percentage receiving care from relatives.

In addition to the FSA child care programs, a capped entitlement program established in 1990, the At-Risk Child Care Program, provides federal matching funds for states to provide child care services for low-income families who are "at risk" of becoming welfare recipients if they do not receive work-related child care. Families are required to contribute to the cost of care on a sliding fee schedule based on the family's ability to pay. The At-Risk Child Care program is otherwise structured similarly to the AFDC and TCC child care programs. Child care providers, except those providing care solely to family members, must be licensed, regulated, or registered. States are allocated limits based on an allocation formula (with allocation amounts carried over to the following year if not utilized), and the amount received by the state is based on the state's Medicaid matching rate. However, the shortage of state child care matching funds has made it difficult for states to draw their full allotment of federal At-Risk Program funds.

The Child Care and Development Block Grant (CCDBG) program, also created in 1990, provides funding for child care services to low-income families, as well as for efforts to improve the quality and supply of child care in general. Federal funds are distributed to states, territories, and tribes under a formula, and no matching funds are required. States are required to use twenty-five percent of their allotments for activities to improve the quality of child care and to increase the availability of early child development and before- and after- school programs. Child care services are funded from a portion of the remaining seventy-five percent of the state's allotment. Payment rates for child care services provided under the program must be "sufficient to ensure equal access for eligible children to comparable child care services . . . that are provided to children whose parents are not eligible to receive" federal or state child care assistance.

States are required to give eligible families the option of enrolling their children with an eligible provider or receiving a child care certificate with which they can purchase child care. Providers must meet all state or local licensing or regulatory requirements, and must meet certain health and safety requirements. In addition, states are required to conduct a review of their child care licensing and regulatory requirements and policies, unless they have done so in the last three years.

In addition to the CCDBG program, some child care funds are available through the Social Services Block Grant Program of Title XX of the Social Security Act. Title XX block grants operate as a capped entitlement, with no state matching requirement, under which states are allocated funds pursuant to a formula based on their relative population. The program gives the states flexibility in designing their social services programs. Most states spend some portion of their block grants on child care services, and some but not all states determine eligibility for child care services based on income standards.

The Internal Revenue Code provisions specifically addressing child care expenses are § 21, the child and dependent care tax credit, and § 129, the exclusion from income for certain employer-provided child care benefits. These provisions provide tax benefits to all working parents, but upper- and middle-income taxpayers utilize them the most for reasons explained below. The following subsection describes in greater detail how the child care credit and employer-provided child care exclusion provisions work, and how the current design of these provisions makes it difficult for low-income taxpayers to benefit from them.

Section 21 provides a nonrefundable tax credit, the amount of which is equal to an "applicable percentage" of the eligible employment-related child care expenses paid by the taxpayer during the year. The applicable percentage, which ranges on a sliding scale of twenty to thirty percent, varies with adjusted gross income. The amount of child care expenses that may be taken into account depends upon the number of children included in the taxpayer's household. Eligible expenses are limited to $2,400 per year for one child, and $4,800 per year for two or more children. A taxpayer with adjusted gross income of $10,000 or less receives a credit of thirty percent of employment-related expenses. The credit percentage declines by one percentage point for each $2,000 (or fraction thereof) in adjusted gross income above $10,000, but in no case is the applicable percentage reduced below twenty percent. For taxpayers with adjusted gross incomes greater than $28,000, therefore, the applicable percentage is twenty percent. For taxpayers with adjusted gross income of $10,000 or less, thus qualifying for the highest applicable percentage of thirty percent, the maximum credit is $720 for one child, and $1,440 for two or more children. For taxpayers with incomes in excess of $28,000, thus qualifying for the lowest applicable percentage of twenty percent, the maximum credit is $480 for one child, and $960 for two or more children.

The amount of the dependent care credit and the applicable percentage income phase-down schedule have not changed since 1981. Income tax thresholds, however, have substantially increased since then. Thus, although § 21 appears to target low-income taxpayers, the relationship between the credit percentage income phase-down and current income tax thresholds makes it unlikely that poor taxpayers receive any benefit from the credit. The Tax Reform Act of 1986 removed a large number of poor families from the tax rolls by increasing standard deduction and personal exemption amounts, and adjusting those amounts on a yearly basis for inflation. In 1995, for example, a family of four (two parents and two children) would owe no taxes on up to $16,550 of adjusted gross income, which is above the federal poverty threshold for a family of four. Although the family would be entitled to a tax credit of twenty-six percent of up to $4,800 of child care expenses, for a credit of $1,248, they would have no income tax liability to offset through use of the credit. A single head of household with one child would owe no taxes up to $10,750 of income, which is above the poverty level for a family of two. Although such a taxpayer would be entitled to a child care credit of twenty-nine percent of up to $2,400 of expenses, for a maximum credit of $696, the credit could not be utilized if no taxes are owed on that amount of income. The current thresholds for tax liability combined with the nonrefundability of the credit thus make it unlikely that poor families benefit from the child and dependent care tax credit.

Section 129 provides an exclusion from the gross income of employees of amounts up to $5,000 paid by the employer under a dependent care assistance program. The dependent care assistance program must be a separate written plan of the employer for the exclusive benefit of employees and must meet certain other requirements. The amount of the exclusion may not exceed the lesser of the earned income of the employee or the earned income of the employee's spouse. Payments for child care made to the employee's spouse or certain other related individuals (another child of the employee, for example) are ineligible for exclusion.

Employers most frequently provide the dependent care assistance benefit through reimbursement accounts, sometimes referred to as flexible spending accounts, which may also cover other types of expenses, such as out-of-pocket health care expenses. Up to $5,000 may be paid into a dependent care assistance account (through a salary reduction plan) from which child care expenses of the employee are reimbursed. The effect of such a program is that the employee may pay child care expenses (or out-of-pocket health care expenses) with pre-tax dollars. About one-third of full-time employees at large and medium-sized private firms were eligible for such accounts in 1991, compared to nearly one tenth of such workers who were eligible for child care benefits provided by the employer in the form of child care facilities provided at or near the workplace, or through direct reimbursement of employee expenses.

Generally, taxpayers choose whether to claim eligible child care expenses under the § 21 credit or the § 129 exclusion. Double dipping is not permitted. For most middle- or upper-income taxpayers, the § 129 exclusion provides the largest benefit. For example, for taxpayers subject to the current highest marginal tax rate, the § 129 exclusion is worth $1,980, compared to the maximum § 21 credit of $480 for one child or $960 for two or more children.

Although some kind of federal work requirement has been imposed on welfare recipients for nearly thirty years, recent welfare reform proposals emphasize more stringent time limits on benefits without work and impose such requirements on mothers with younger children. The historical shift in the welfare paradigm toward mandatory work for mothers with young children has not been accompanied, however, by universal child care.

The child care now provided AFDC children by their mothers must be replaced if they are at work. Inadequate funding for work-related childcare for low-income families raises serious concerns. Without increased federal or state support of work-related child care, new work requirements cannot succeed in reducing dependence on welfare by mothers of young children. In addition, low-income children will be placed in increased danger of receiving inadequate or unsafe care. The following subsections discuss the inadequacies of current funding levels, and the failure of welfare reform proposals to fund necessary child care support.

Under current federal funding levels, the states have been unable to meet the need for child care assistance for low-income families. Between five and six percent of the AFDC caseload received AFDC child care subsidies, and only about one out of three JOBS participants received JOBS-related child care. About 20 percent of those eligible received Transitional Child Care (TCC) assistance for the first year after leaving welfare for work. Surveys conducted in 1993 and 1994 found that most states either had lengthy waiting lists for child care assistance or had stopped accepting new applications. In addition, the competition for slots has resulted in the shifting of scarce state child care funds from low-income working families to families receiving AFDC. Families that have used up their one year of guaranteed TCC assistance after leaving welfare have to compete with other low-income, non-AFDC families for child care assistance. If they do not receive assistance, many have no choice but to go back on the welfare rolls because they cannot afford the full cost of child care.

The cost of child care remains a significant obstacle for low-income families making the transition from welfare to work. In general, the type of child care purchased and the amount spent on care varies by the family's economic situation and the type of care used. Lower-income families spend on average about twenty-three percent of their incomes on child care even though they spend significantly less, in absolute terms, on child care than families with higher incomes. Without subsidized child care, low-income families will likely rely on lower-quality child care or informal arrangements and relative-provided care. Those who pay for relatives to care for their children pay the lowest average weekly costs, with increasingly higher weekly average costs for family child care, center care, and in-home care by a non-relative. The family and relative care received by children from low-income families and the center-based care for very young children raise developmental concerns.

Although the federal block grant programs have made improvements in the states' quality control of center-based or licensed family day care homes, many low-income children are enrolled in unregulated, informal child care settings. Many states do not require care-givers to meet even minimal standards and few states conduct inspections of family child care homes that are exempt from licensing requirements.

* * *

Notes and Questions

1. *The Ideology of Child Care.* If the general consensus on welfare reform believes that poor mothers must work, and if care for their children is necessary to allow them to work, then why isn't there greater support for providing child care to low income families? Are any ideological conflicts reflected in the debate about the extent to which the federal government should provide and/or subsidize child care for poor children? In her book, WOMEN AND SOCIAL WELFARE, Dorothy Miller argues that child care threatens basic patriarchal and capitalist tenets. She writes:

> Day care is a threat to patriarchy in that it is a threat to male control -- it promotes women's independence. It strikes at the heart of the patriarchal definition of

> mothering as the only acceptable source of child care. It is a threat to conventional marriage, since it aids women's advancement in the world of work. It is a threat to capitalism, in that it removes one additional excuse to keep women in low-paying positions. Insofar as it might allow women to work longer hours with less worry, it is a threat to male supremacy in the work force.

Do you agree? If not, what do you believe explains the difficulty in obtaining child care for poor children?

2. *Supply, Demand, and Cost.* We know that the demand for child care has been rising steadily with the rate of labor force participation of women. Estimating the supply of child care providers is quite difficult due to the extent of care provided by unlicensed caretakers. Most estimates have concluded that supply is insufficient for the carc of babies and preschool children. Not surprisingly, with high demand and short supply for segments of that demand, the cost of day care has risen. As the cost of child care rises for all parents, this increase inflicts greater harm on low income parents who pay a disproportionate percentage of their income toward child care costs.

Two sets of losers emerge from the child-care picture: poor children and child care workers. From an economic perspective, it is not surprising that young, poor children suffer from their parents' inability to obtain adequate affordable child care. But why do wages of child care workers remain so low, given the strong demand for their services?

3. *Direct Financing v. Indirect Subsidizing.* Compare the relative advantages and disadvantages of direct government financing of child care programs and indirect subsidies through tax credits and income exclusions. Assuming the federal government chooses to continue funding child care, is one of these methods superior? If so, which one?

4. *Block Grants: Flexibility versus Funding.* Many of the federal government's child care programs required states to match federal funds at a particular level and to maintain specified quality in child care. The 1996 Personal Responsibility and Work Opportunity Act gave states greater control of their child care programs by channeling federal funds for low income child care through block

grants. States may achieve greater flexibility in designing their programs, but have fewer federal dollars to operate these programs. Is this trade-off worth it?

Child Care and Development Block Grant Amendments of 1996

In the 1996 Personal Responsibility and Work Opportunity Act, Congress enacted the Child Care and Development Block Grant Amendments of 1996. The block grant program caps federal spending for child care and eliminates the state obligation to provide child care for welfare recipients participating in work. Congress established the following goals for the block grant program:

> (1) to allow each State maximum flexibility in developing child care programs and policies that best suit the needs of children and parents within such State;
> (2) to promote parental choice to empower working parents to make their own decisions on the child care that best suits their family's needs;
> (3) to encourage States to provide consumer education information to help parents make informed choices about child care;
> (4) to assist States to provide child care to parents trying to achieve independence from public assistance;
> (5) to assist States in implementing the health, safety, licensing, and registration standards established in State regulations.

Congress allows states to use the child care block grant funds in any manner designed to achieve these goals. Congress specifically eliminated federal review of state licensing requirements, but required states to make particular certifications, including that they have child care licensing requirements in effect, that they require child care providers to comply with state health and safety requirements, that they maintain records of parental complaints, and that they provide parental access to their children in child care.

The Center for Law and Social Policy reports that the 1996 legislation provides a single child care block grant with three components:

> The Act repeals current authority for three child care programs, which are sometimes referred to together as IV-A Child Care: AFDC Child Care (for AFDC

> recipients in work and work-related activities); Transitional Child Care (which provides up to one year of child care assistance for families leaving AFDC due to employment); and At-Risk Child Care (funding for child care assistance to families who would otherwise be at risk of AFDC receipt). Instead, states will receive federal child care funding under a Child Care and Development Block Grant with three components: each state will receive a share of $1 billion in discretionary funding; each state will qualify for "general entitlement" funds, set at the higher of 1992-94 average, 1994, or 1995 federal spending for the IV-A Child Care programs; and each state that maintains its prior level of state spending for the IV-A Child Care programs can qualify to receive additional federal funds above its historic level of spending, subject to state match.

CENTER FOR LAW AND SOCIAL POLICY, A SUMMARY OF KEY CHILD CARE PROVISIONS OF H.R. 3734, THE PERSONAL RESPONSIBILITY AND WORK OPPORTUNITY RECONCILIATION ACT OF 1996 (August 1996).

What values underlie these goals and requirements? What directions do these goals and requirements show Congress to be heading with respect to child care policy? Will these changes increase the availability of affordable, high quality child care for low-income families?

D. CHILD PROTECTION

Logically a child's likelihood of suffering abuse and neglect bears no relation to the family's income status. Low income children, however, seem to have greater contact with state child protection systems than their middle and upper class counterparts. This may be due in part to several poverty-related factors: 1) protective service workers may deem the characteristics of poverty to be neglect; 2) poor families may have greater contact with government institutions, thereby subjecting them to greater scrutiny and the accompanying risk of being reported to protective services agencies; and, 3) poor families lack resources for legal representation to resist regulation by state protective services agencies. Whatever factors contribute to the cause, poor children are frequently the subject of the child protection system's attention. The following sections explore, first, government's power but lack of duty to protect children from abuse and neglect, second, some forms of alternative care for poor children, and third, the potential emergence of human rights protection for poor children.

1. States' Power, Without Duty, to Protect Children

Tension abounds between the government's twin, and sometimes competing, obligations to protect liberty relating to family life, and to protect children from abuse and neglect by family members. While the Due Process Clauses of the United States Constitution's Fifth and Fourteenth Amendments protect families from intrusion by the government, what protects children from abuse and neglect? The federal Adoption Assistance and Child Welfare Act provides assistance for abused, neglected, and dependent children. Does the Constitution require states to protect children from abuse? Consider the following decision in *DeShaney v. Winnebago County Department of Social Services*.

DeSHANEY
v.
WINNEBAGO COUNTY DEPARTMENT OF SOCIAL SERVICES

489 U.S. 189 (1989)

CHIEF JUSTICE REHNQUIST delivered the opinion of the Court.

Petitioner is a boy who was beaten and permanently injured by his father, with whom he lived. Respondents are social workers and other local officials who received complaints that petitioner was being abused by his father and had reason to believe that this was the case, but nonetheless did not act to remove petitioner from his father's custody. Petitioner sued respondents claiming that their failure to act deprived him of his liberty in violation of the Due Process Clause of the Fourteenth Amendment to the United States Constitution. We hold that it did not.

The facts of this case are undeniably tragic. Petitioner Joshua DeShaney was born in 1979. In 1980, a Wyoming court granted his parents a divorce and awarded custody of Joshua to his father, Randy DeShaney. The father shortly thereafter moved to Neenah, a city located in Winnebago County, Wisconsin, taking the infant Joshua with him. There he entered into a second marriage, which also ended in divorce.

The Winnebago County authorities first learned that Joshua DeShaney might be a victim of child abuse in January 1982, when his father's second wife complained to the police, at the time of their divorce, that he had previously "hit the boy causing marks and [was] a prime case for child abuse." The Winnebago County Department of Social Services (DSS) interviewed the father, but he denied the accusations, and DSS did not pursue them further. In January 1983, Joshua was admitted to a local hospital with multiple bruises and abrasions. The examining physician suspected child abuse and notified DSS, which immediately obtained an order from a Wisconsin juvenile court placing Joshua in the temporary custody of the hospital. Three days later, the county convened an ad hoc "Child Protection Team"--consisting of a pediatrician, a psychologist, a police detective, the county's lawyer, several DSS caseworkers, and various hospital personnel--to consider Joshua's situation. At this meeting, the Team decided that there was insufficient evidence of child abuse to retain Joshua in the custody of the court. The Team did, however, decide to recommend several measures to protect Joshua, including enrolling him in a preschool program, providing his father with certain counselling services, and encouraging his father's girlfriend to move out of the home. Randy DeShaney entered into a voluntary agreement with DSS in which he promised to cooperate with them in accomplishing these goals.

Based on the recommendation of the Child Protection Team, the juvenile court dismissed the child protection case and returned Joshua to the custody of his father. A month later, emergency room personnel called the DSS caseworker handling Joshua's case to report that he had once again been treated for suspicious injuries. The caseworker concluded that there was no basis for action. For the next six months, the caseworker made monthly visits to the DeShaney home, during which she observed a number of suspicious injuries on Joshua's head; she also noticed that he had not been enrolled in school, and that the girlfriend had not moved out. The caseworker dutifully recorded these incidents in her files, along with her continuing suspicions that someone in the DeShaney household was physically abusing Joshua, but she did nothing more. In November 1983, the emergency room notified DSS that Joshua had been treated once again for injuries that they believed to be caused by child abuse. On the caseworker's next two visits to the DeShaney home, she was told that Joshua was too ill to see her. Still DSS took no action.

In March 1984, Randy DeShaney beat 4-year-old Joshua so severely that he fell into a life-threatening coma. Emergency brain surgery revealed a series of hemorrhages caused by traumatic injuries to the head inflicted over a long period of time. Joshua did not die, but he suffered brain damage so severe that he is expected to spend the rest of his life confined to an institution for the profoundly retarded. Randy DeShaney was subsequently tried and convicted of child abuse.

Joshua and his mother brought this action under 42 U.S.C. § 1983 in the United States District Court for the Eastern District of Wisconsin against respondents Winnebago County, DSS, and various individual employees of DSS. The complaint alleged that respondents had deprived Joshua of his liberty without due process of law, in violation of his rights under the Fourteenth Amendment, by failing to intervene to protect him against a risk of violence at his father's hands of which they knew or should have known. The District Court granted summary judgment for respondents.

The Court of Appeals for the Seventh Circuit affirmed, holding that petitioners had not made out an actionable § 1983 claim for two alternative reasons. First, the court held that the Due Process Clause of the Fourteenth Amendment does not require a state or local governmental entity to protect its citizens from "private violence, or other mishaps not attributable to the conduct of its employees." . . . Second, the court held, in reliance on our decision in *Martinez v. California*, 444 U.S. 277, 285 (1980), that the causal connection between respondents' conduct and Joshua's injuries was too attenuated to establish a deprivation of constitutional rights actionable under § 1983.

* * *

The Due Process Clause of the Fourteenth Amendment provides that "[n]o State shall . . . deprive any person of life, liberty, or property, without due process of law." Petitioners contend that the State deprived Joshua of his liberty interest in "free[dom] from . . . unjustified intrusions on personal security," by failing to provide him with adequate protection against his father's violence. The claim is one invoking the substantive rather than the procedural component of the Due Process Clause; petitioners do not claim that the State denied Joshua protection without according him appropriate procedural safeguards, but that it was categorically obligated to protect him in these circumstances.

But nothing in the language of the Due Process Clause itself requires the State to protect the life, liberty, and property of its citizens against invasion by private actors. The Clause is phrased as a limitation on the State's power to act, not as a guarantee of certain minimal levels of safety and security. It forbids the State itself to deprive individuals of life, liberty, or property without "due process of law," but its language cannot fairly be extended to impose an affirmative obligation on the State to ensure that those interests do not come to harm through other means. Nor does history support such an expansive reading of the constitutional text. Like its counterpart in the Fifth Amendment, the Due Process Clause of the Fourteenth Amendment was intended to prevent government "from abusing [its] power, or employing it as an instrument of oppression." Its purpose was to protect the people from the State, not to ensure that the State protected them from each other. The Framers were content to leave the extent of governmental obligation in the latter area to the democratic political processes.

Consistent with these principles, our cases have recognized that the Due Process Clauses generally confer no affirmative right to governmental aid, even where such aid may be necessary to secure life, liberty, or property interests of which the government itself may not deprive the individual. As we said in *Harris v. McRae*: "Although the liberty protected by the Due Process Clause affords protection against unwarranted government interference . . ., it does not confer an entitlement to such [governmental aid] as may be necessary to realize all the advantages of that freedom." If the Due Process Clause does not require the State to provide its citizens with particular protective services, it follows that the State cannot be held liable under the Clause for injuries that could have been averted had it chosen to provide them. As a general matter, then, we conclude that a State's failure to protect an individual against private violence simply does not constitute a violation of the Due Process Clause.

Petitioners contend, however, that even if the Due Process Clause imposes no affirmative obligation on the State to provide the general public with adequate protective services, such a duty may arise out of certain "special relationships" created or assumed by the State with respect to particular individuals. Petitioners argue that such a "special relationship" existed here because the State knew that Joshua faced a special danger of abuse at his father's hands, and specifically proclaimed, by word and by deed, its intention to protect him against that danger. Having actually undertaken to protect Joshua from this danger--which petitioners concede the State played no part in creating--the State acquired an affirmative "duty," enforceable through the Due Process Clause, to do so in a reasonably competent fashion. Its failure to discharge that duty, so the argument goes, was an abuse of governmental power that so "shocks the conscience," as to constitute a substantive due process violation.

We reject this argument. It is true that in certain limited circumstances the Constitution imposes upon the State affirmative duties of care and protection with respect to particular individuals. In *Estelle v. Gamble*, 429 U.S. 97 (1976), we recognized that the Eighth Amendment's prohibition against cruel and unusual punishment, made applicable to the States through the Fourteenth Amendment's Due Process Clause, requires the State to provide adequate medical care to incarcerated prisoners. We reasoned that because the prisoner is unable "by reason of the deprivation of his liberty [to] care for himself," it is only "just" that the State be required to care for him.

In *Youngberg v. Romeo*, 457 U.S. 307 (1982), we extended this analysis beyond the Eighth Amendment setting, holding that the substantive component of the Fourteenth Amendment's Due Process Clause requires the State to provide involuntarily committed mental patients with such services as are necessary to ensure their "reasonable safety" from themselves and others. As we explained: "If it is cruel and unusual punishment to hold convicted criminals in unsafe conditions, it must be unconstitutional [under the Due Process Clause] to confine the involuntarily committed--who may not be punished at all--in unsafe conditions."

But these cases afford petitioners no help. Taken together, they stand only for the proposition that when the State takes a person into its custody and holds him there against his will, the Constitution imposes upon it a corresponding duty to assume some responsibility for his safety and general well-being. The rationale for this principle is simple enough: when the State by the affirmative exercise of its power so restrains an individual's liberty that it renders him unable to care for himself, and at the same time fails to provide for his basic human needs--e.g., food, clothing, shelter, medical care, and reasonable safety--it transgresses the substantive limits on state action set by the Eighth Amendment and the Due Process Clause. The affirmative duty to protect arises not from the State's knowledge of the individual's predicament or from its expressions of intent to help him, but from the limitation which it has imposed on his freedom to act on his own behalf. In the substantive due process analysis, it is the State's affirmative act of restraining the individual's freedom to act on his own behalf--through incarceration, institutionalization, or other similar restraint of personal liberty--which is the "deprivation of liberty" triggering the protections of the Due Process Clause, not its failure to act to protect his liberty interests against harms inflicted by other means.

The *Estelle-Youngberg* analysis simply has no applicability in the present case. Petitioners concede that the harms Joshua suffered occurred not while he was in the State's custody, but while he was in the custody of his natural father, who was in no sense a state actor. While the State may have been aware of the dangers that Joshua faced in the free world, it played no part in their creation, nor did it do anything to render him any more vulnerable to them. That the State once took temporary custody of Joshua does not alter the analysis, for when it returned him to his father's custody, it placed him in no worse position than that in which he would have been had it not acted at all; the State does not become the permanent guarantor of an individual's safety by having once offered him shelter. Under these circumstances, the State had no constitutional duty to protect Joshua.

* * *

Justice BRENNAN, with whom Justice MARSHALL and Justice BLACKMUN join, dissenting.

* * *

I would begin from the opposite direction. I would focus first on the action that Wisconsin has taken with respect to Joshua and children like him, rather than on the actions that the State failed to take.

* * *

I would recognize, as the Court apparently cannot, that "the State's knowledge of [an] individual's predicament [and] its expressions of intent to help him" can amount to a "limitation . . . on his freedom to act on his own behalf" or to obtain help from others.

* * *

Wisconsin has established a child-welfare system specifically designed to help children like Joshua. Wisconsin law places upon the local departments of social services such as respondent (DSS or Department) a duty to investigate reported instances of child abuse. While other governmental bodies and private persons are largely responsible for the reporting of possible cases of child abuse, Wisconsin law channels all such reports to the local departments of social services for evaluation and, if necessary, further action. Even when it is the sheriff's office or police department that receives a report of suspected child abuse, that report is referred to local social services departments for action, the only exception to this occurs when the reporter fears for the child's immediate safety. In this way, Wisconsin law invites--indeed, directs--citizens and other governmental entities to depend on local departments of social services such as respondent to protect children from abuse.

The specific facts before us bear out this view of Wisconsin's system of protecting children. Each time someone voiced a suspicion that Joshua was being abused, that information was relayed to the Department for investigation and possible action. When Randy DeShaney's second wife told the police that he had "hit the boy causing marks and [was] a prime case for child abuse," the police referred her complaint to DSS. When, on three separate occasions, emergency room personnel noticed suspicious injuries on Joshua's body, they went to DSS with this information. When neighbors informed the police that they had seen or heard Joshua's father or his father's lover beating or otherwise abusing Joshua, the police brought these reports to the attention of DSS. And when respondent

Kemmeter, through these reports and through her own observations in the course of nearly 20 visits to the DeShaney home, compiled growing evidence that Joshua was being abused, that information stayed within the Department--chronicled by the social worker in detail that seems almost eerie in light of her failure to act upon it. (As to the extent of the social worker's involvement in, and knowledge of, Joshua's predicament, her reaction to the news of Joshua's last and most devastating injuries is illuminating: "I just knew the phone would ring some day and Joshua would be dead.")

Even more telling than these examples is the Department's control over the decision whether to take steps to protect a particular child from suspected abuse. While many different people contributed information and advice to this decision, it was up to the people at DSS to make the ultimate decision (subject to the approval of the local government's Corporation Counsel) whether to disturb the family's current arrangements. When Joshua first appeared at a local hospital with injuries signaling physical abuse, for example, it was DSS that made the decision to take him into temporary custody for the purpose of studying his situation--and it was DSS, acting in conjunction with the corporation counsel, that returned him to his father. Unfortunately for Joshua DeShaney, the buck effectively stopped with the Department.

In these circumstances, a private citizen, or even a person working in a government agency other than DSS, would doubtless feel that her job was done as soon as she had reported her suspicions of child abuse to DSS. Through its child-welfare program, in other words, the State of Wisconsin has relieved ordinary citizens and governmental bodies other than the Department of any sense of obligation to do anything more than report their suspicions of child abuse to DSS. If DSS ignores or dismisses these suspicions, no one will step in to fill the gap. Wisconsin's child-protection program thus effectively confined Joshua DeShaney within the walls of Randy DeShaney's violent home until such time as DSS took action to remove him. Conceivably, then, children like Joshua are made worse off by the existence of this program when the persons and entities charged with carrying it out fail to do their jobs.

It simply belies reality, therefore, to contend that the State "stood by and did nothing" with respect to Joshua. Through its child-protection program, the State actively intervened in Joshua's life and, by virtue of this intervention, acquired ever more certain knowledge that Joshua was in grave danger.

* * *

As the Court today reminds us, "the Due Process Clause of the Fourteenth Amendment was intended to prevent government 'from abusing [its] power, or employing it as an instrument of oppression.'" My disagreement with the Court arises from its failure to see that inaction can be every bit as abusive of power as action, that oppression can result when a State undertakes a vital duty and then ignores it. Today's opinion construes the Due Process Clause to permit a State to displace private sources of protection and then, at the critical moment, to shrug its shoulders and turn away from the harm that it has promised to try to prevent. Because I cannot agree that our Constitution is indifferent to such indifference, I respectfully dissent.

Justice BLACKMUN, dissenting.

* * *

Poor Joshua! Victim of repeated attacks by an irresponsible, bullying, cowardly, and intemperate father, and abandoned by respondents who placed him in a dangerous predicament and who knew or learned what was going on, and yet did essentially nothing except, as the Court revealingly observes, "dutifully recorded these incidents in [their] files." It is a sad commentary upon American life, and constitutional principles--so full of late of patriotic fervor and proud proclamations about "liberty and justice for all"--that this child, Joshua DeShaney, now is assigned to live out the remainder of his life profoundly retarded. Joshua and his mother, as petitioners here, deserve--but now are denied by this Court--the opportunity to have the facts of their case considered in the light of the constitutional protection that 42 U.S.C. § 1983 is meant to provide.

Notes and Questions

1. *The Baseline Question.* The primary disagreement between the majority and the dissents stemmed from the different baselines from which they assessed Joshua's claim. According to Justice Brennan, the majority's baseline was that states have no general duty to protect citizens from harm, and therefore, no specific

duty to protect Joshua from harm inflicted by his father. Justices Brennan, Marshall, and Blackmun assessed the case instead from the baseline that Wisconsin's knowledge, intent, and actions which purported to help Joshua gave rise to a duty to take further action to protect him from harm.

Only government possesses legitimate power to intervene in families. How will states exercise this power after *DeShaney*? Will states be subject to any constitutional check, now that they enjoy power to intervene in families to protect children without any concomitant obligation to intervene?

2. *Parental Rights.* What rights protect parents involved in abuse or neglect petitions? Recall *Lassiter v. Department of Social Services*, 452 U.S. 16 (1981) (excerpted in Chapter 5) which held that indigent parents have no general right to appointment of counsel when a state threatens to terminate their parental rights.

3. *Prevention.* Given that the Supreme Court has held states have no duty to take action to protect children from abuse, it seems unlikely that the Court would require states to take action to prevent the likelihood of abuse or neglect. Is it not surprising then that few support services are available to families, typically until they become subjects of ongoing investigations or enforcement actions?

4. *Block Grants.* Welfare reformers have proposed giving states more flexibility to run their child protection programs by replacing the federal programs which regulate states and provide open-ended federal assistance with block grant funds which would cap the federal funds. Are states likely to be better able to handle child protection with the greater flexibility they gain at the expense of receiving limited federal dollars?

2. Alternative Care for Children

State law and officials determine whether a child suffers from neglect. Most states require parents to remedy the problems causing the neglect within a specified period of time in order to retain or regain custody of their children. If a state concludes that a family's poverty is causing their children to be neglected, then logically parents must succeed in raising their income above the poverty level in order to remedy their situation. If parents previously lacked motivation to work, as conservatives typically argue, then perhaps the state's intervention will inspire them to become self-reliant. If, however, parents' difficulty in obtaining living wage employment caused the family's poverty in the first place, then the state's intervention and assertion of control over their children seems likely to be ineffective in changing the family's circumstances. When a family fails to improve its circumstances, states sometimes remove children from their homes and place them in alternative care.

Foster care arrangements remain controversial in several respects. First, families with foster care children typically receive greater financial support from the government than the child's own family would receive from welfare grants. The child remains the same person with the same financial needs in both families. Why do the benefit levels differ? Second, critics complain that states fail to make every effort to keep children with their parents, relatives, or family friends. The following article explores the latter issue.

Randi Mandelbaum

TRYING TO FIT SQUARE PEGS INTO ROUND HOLES: THE NEED FOR A NEW FUNDING SCHEME FOR KINSHIP CAREGIVERS

22 FORDHAM URBAN LAW JOURNAL 907 (1995)

Ms. Jones is a fifty-nine year-old woman. She also is the paternal grandmother of Brenda, age three, and Johnnie, age four. Ms. Jones's son, the father of the children, is deceased. The children's mother has a serious substance abuse addiction and is unable to care for the children. She visits the children every few months (she just drops by); otherwise, Ms. Jones has no contact with the mother. The children have been living with Ms. Jones for the past two years. They view her as "Mom."

Ms. Jones worked for many years as a janitor in an office building, but for the past year she has been supported by social security disability benefits on account of severe arthritis. She has been a widow for many years. The disability benefits would be sufficient income for her to live on, but she is having trouble supporting both herself and her grandchildren. When she could no longer work, she applied for public assistance through the Aid to Families with Dependent Children program, but was found to be ineligible. Because her son's name is not on the children's birth certificates, she was unable to prove that she was related to the children, one criteria of eligibility.

Obtaining medical care for the children has been another problem because Ms. Jones has no legal authority to consent to such care. She finally found a clinic that will treat the children, but it is across town and only handles routine medical concerns.

In addition, Johnnie is due to start kindergarten in September, and Ms. Jones is worried that she will not be able to enroll him in school. Her neighbor who is caring for a nephew experienced this problem. This child had to wait six months before he could enter school.

Ms. Smith is a divorced, single mother of three children who for the last year also has been raising her nephew, Matthew. Matthew is six years old. Matthew's mother, Ms. Smith's sister, died six months ago of an AIDS-related illness. Ms. Smith does not know who Matthew's father is.

Ms. Smith was barely scraping by on her income from her job as a cashier in a department store (her ex-husband does not provide any child support) when Matthew came to live with the family. Now, the bills have begun to pile up, and she is at risk of having her phone and utilities terminated.

Ms. Smith receives public assistance ("welfare") for Matthew, but it does not cover the costs of even his basic needs. When Matthew came to live with Ms. Smith, he came with virtually no clothes that fit him and none of the belongings or toys that little boys usually have. Ms. Smith also had to buy him a bed, a dresser and one other small piece of furniture. She still has not paid off the bill for these things. She often wonders if the little bit of money the welfare agency gives her is worth all the time and fuss. It is such a degrading and humiliating process.

In addition, Matthew has recently taken to having some violent tantrums where he ends up destroying many of Ms. Smith's belongings. She understands, from the therapist Matthew is seeing, that he is acting out his anger over losing his mother. However, she does not know how long she can endure the emotional and financial strain that the addition of Matthew in her home has caused.

Ms. Watkins is a forty-nine year-old woman who has five adult children of her own and who is currently raising six children who are not her natural children. Three are her grandchildren, one is the step-sibling of one of her grandchildren, but is not related to her by blood, one is the nephew of her husband and the sixth is the child of a friend. One mother is incarcerated on a long-term sentence. Another has a serious substance abuse addiction. It is difficult to ascertain where some of the other parents are. All the children who are old enough to talk call Ms. Watkins "Grandma" and thrive in her warmth and nurturing.

For nearly two years, Mr. and Ms. Watkins and the six children have lived in a transitional shelter. Mr. and Ms. Watkins lost their home in New Jersey when they moved to Maryland to take on the care of two of the children. They are slowly getting back on their feet. Ms. Watkins was finally able to obtain public assistance for the three children that are her grandchildren. She is not eligible for AFDC for the two children to whom she is not related, and she does not have the necessary verification to receive any kind of assistance for the nephew of her husband.

The family recently obtained public housing and Mr. Watkins is about to start a permanent job. Still, every month is a struggle as Ms. Watkins wonders whether the food stamps will last until the end of the month.

Ms. Anderson must leave her job as a receptionist fifteen minutes early every day so that she can pick up her godchild, Anthony, at day care by 5:30 p.m. Fortunately, her boss is understanding. Anthony came to live with her two years ago after his mother was hospitalized for the fifth time with a mental illness. He never left. Anthony is now eight years old. Ms. Anderson, a single woman, is prepared to raise Anthony, but worries how she will be able to provide for him on her very limited income.

Because Ms. Anderson is not related to Anthony, she is not eligible for any public assistance ("welfare") for him. She twice inquired about becoming a foster parent to Anthony. The first time she called she was told that Anthony would have to be removed from her home while she underwent a month-long foster care licensing process. This seemed ridiculous to her.

The second time she called, she was informed by the child welfare agency that she could not pursue these benefits at all. Because Anthony was already living with her at the time she contacted the child welfare agency, the agency took the position that he was safe and no longer at risk of abuse or neglect. Therefore, the agency would not initiate any court actions to place Anthony in the custody of the state, a situation that must occur before Ms. Anderson could apply to become his foster parent. Ms. Anderson knows of several friends and neighbors who have left the children they are raising on the doorstep of the child welfare agency. When the children are returned the next morning--after spending the night in the child welfare agency offices because there are insufficient foster care placements--the agency promises to pursue the necessary steps to bring the children before the attention of the court. Despite desperately needing financial assistance, Ms. Anderson cannot bring herself to put Anthony through that.

Listening to the news media today, one might conclude that the only persons receiving welfare are lazy, often very young, unwed mothers. Similarly, the term "foster care" has become synonymous with orphanages or children living in the homes of licensed strangers. Yet, as these stories illustrate, welfare recipients and foster parents are frequently loving grandmothers, aunts or godparents who want to assume the responsibility of caring for--even raising--their kin, but who need some financial assistance to support the children. This Article will refer to these caregivers as kinship caregivers and will define kinship care broadly to include anyone who is caring for a child, either temporarily or permanently, who is not the child's biological or adoptive parent. Under this interpretation, non-relative caregivers would be considered kinship caregivers. Approximately 15% of all Aid to Families with Dependent Children cases are kinship care families and roughly 31% of all foster parents who receive foster care payments under the federal foster care program are kinship caregivers.

Despite their large and growing presence, kinship caregivers are a forgotten group in the debate over welfare reform and in the analyses of public policies concerning the Aid to Families with Dependent Children and foster care programs. Studying the experiences of this group of people and how they fare in our social service system helps to elucidate the themes and larger problems being discussed in the controversy over welfare reform. It also clearly demonstrates that the two financial assistance programs available to kinship caregivers are not responsive to the needs of these families.

Currently, kinship caregivers must rely on one of two federal funding programs: Aid to Families with Dependent Children (AFDC) or foster care through the Adoption Assistance and Child Welfare Act of 1980 (AACWA). In order to be reimbursed by the federal government, state programs must adhere to federal program requirements. Neither program, however, was designed to meet the needs of this group of caregivers, and therefore the caregivers and public agencies that administer these programs run into enormous problems when they attempt to adapt these programs to the needs of kinship caregivers. Trying to "fit" kinship caregivers into these programs leads to a myriad of problems for the kinship caregivers while simultaneously creating troubling social policy dilemmas.

. . . AFDC is the oldest federal public assistance program, enacted in 1935 as Title IV of the larger Social Security Act. It is a public assistance program for children who are deprived of the care of at least one parent, on account of absence, illness, death, incapacity or unemployment, and is colloquially known as "welfare." AFDC is available to single or unemployed parents and to relative caretakers to the fifth degree of relationship. Both must apply for assistance at local income maintenance offices (welfare offices). The only significant difference in the way the program treats parents versus relative caretakers is that the income and resources of the parents must be considered in determining eligibility while the income and resources of the relative caretakers do not.

* * *

[T]here are some other very significant inconsistencies between the requirements and characteristics of the AFDC program and the needs of kinship caregivers and the children they are raising.

The AFDC program has as its major goal the eventual self-sufficiency of its recipients. It is intended as a short-term, temporary program to assist single parents caring for children. The goal is to aid the parent in getting back on her/his feet. This is incompatible with kinship care situations where it may be in the best interest of the children that the kinship care arrangement be long-term or even permanent, and where ongoing assistance may be necessary. When children go to live with relatives because their mother has died of AIDS, is a substance abuser, or is incarcerated on a long-term sentence, one hopes that they will remain with those relatives for many years, if not their entire childhoods.

As the opening vignettes illustrate, the kinship caregivers' resources, without supplemental benefits, are often strained to the breaking point. At times, these economic straits force kinship caregivers to turn over the children to the child welfare agency for placement into foster care. Kinship caregivers are not the parents of these children and are not legally responsible for the care and support of the children they are raising. Yet, the current systems force kinship care families to choose between unfair impoverishment and disintegration, and do so heedless of manifest legislative intent to the contrary.

For similar reasons, it is inappropriate to require kinship caregivers to participate in job training, education and employment activities in order to be eligible to receive financial assistance.

* * *

These objectives are in conflict with the realities of most kinship care situations. Requiring aging or retired kinship caregivers to participate in job training or readiness programs is both impractical and pointless.

Kinship caregivers also experience problems when they attempt to apply for AFDC. Traditional AFDC applicants must meet many procedural requirements that are more difficult, if not impossible, for kinship caregivers to fulfill. For example, relative caregivers frequently cannot produce the documents needed to verify their applications for assistance. Birth certificates, social security cards, school records and immunization records are often in the possession of the absent parents and difficult to reproduce without the absent parents' consent.

Paternal relatives often have a particularly onerous time. For example, proving their relationship to the child, as required by the statute and regulations, is difficult when the father's name is not on the child's birth certificate. In such cases, it may be impossible for the relative caregiver to receive aid.

The federal foster care statute, the Adoption Assistance and Child Welfare Act of 1980, does not even mention relative or kinship caregivers, much less promote placement with relatives as the best foster care option. Kinship caregivers are not contemplated in the statutory description of either case plan requirements or case review assessments. Additionally, attempts to place children with kinship caregivers have never been considered to be part of the "reasonable efforts" requirement, under which the state agency must demonstrate that efforts were made both to avoid removing children from the parental home and to promote reunification of any children so removed. The AACWA also does not require the state child welfare agency to notify kin that their relative children needed to be removed from their parents and placed in foster care. Frequently, kin never know that the relative children were placed into foster care until the children have spent months or years in foster care.

For a child to be eligible to receive foster care benefits and for the state to be partially reimbursed by the federal government for the cost of the child's care, custody of the child must be with the state. In other words, a court must determine that the child cannot remain in the parental home without risk of further abuse or neglect, and that the child must be removed, if even temporarily, from the care of his or her parent(s).

This "removal" or "state custody" requirement has been interpreted in such a way that a child is not considered to be in state custody unless the child has been physically removed from the parental home. A change in legal custody alone does not constitute removal. Consequently, federal reimbursement would not be available, for example, to a grandmother caring for a grandchild, if the child came to stay at the grandmother's home before legal custody was transferred to the state and the child was formally placed with the grandmother through the child welfare system.

The U.S. Supreme Court decision of *Miller v. Youakim* ensures that kinship caregivers not be prevented from receiving the same financial benefits as other foster care providers, as long as they meet state licensing requirements for foster care homes and are providing care for a child who was receiving AFDC or who would have been eligible to receive AFDC. In practice, however, both the licensing and eligibility requirements are very difficult for them to meet. To be eligible for federal reimbursement of foster care payments, states must license all foster homes. Policies vary from state to state as to whether the child will be permitted to remain with the kinship caregiver during the licensing process. Often distinctions are based on whether the kinship caregiver is a blood relative. Very few states will permit a child to be placed with a godparent or "friend of the family" unless the caregiver is licensed. Consequently, the child is often uprooted from his family and loved ones and placed with strangers while the kinship caregiver pursues the often laborious and lengthy foster care licensing process.

To qualify for foster care benefits, a foster parent must satisfy a multitude of licensing requirements. These requirements seek to ensure that the child will be living in a safe, secure and appropriate home environment. Many of the child protection and safety requirements for licensure, however, are unduly formalistic and formulaic. Low-income kinship caregivers are often unable to meet these requirements and are thus prohibited from participating in the foster care program. The fact that there is a loving and established relationship between a kinship caregiver and child and that certifying the kinship caregiver as a foster parent might allow the child to remain with this caregiver are not factors typically considered. There is a need for family assessments and home studies of kinship caregivers as potential foster parents to ensure the protection and safety of the children, and, at the same time, to recognize the strengths of kinship care situations and the importance of family.

Another problem with the structure of the foster care program concerns permanency for the child. Even when a kinship caregiver has met the licensing requirements, there is no guarantee that the child will be permitted to stay in her care on a long-term basis. A child in foster care is, by definition, in state custody. Accordingly, the state child welfare agency determines issues of physical custody. Thus, the kinship caregiver and the child face the constant risk that the child will be removed from the family. No sense of permanency exists for either the kinship foster child or the kinship foster family.

Permanency planning is problematic from another standpoint as well. Once a child is in the care of a kinship caregiver who is receiving foster care benefits, the only mechanism in the federal statute that provides both ongoing financial assistance and permanency for the child is the adoption assistance or subsidy program. Yet, adoption as a permanency choice is unsuitable in the majority of kinship care situations. Adoption requires the severing of all parental rights and ties. This is ill-suited to situations where, for example, a grandmother has assumed the care of her daughter's children. For emotional and psychological, as well as other reasons, the grandmother is usually unwilling to participate in the petition to terminate the parental rights of her own daughter or in the subsequent adoption proceedings of her grandchildren. Consequently, children in kinship care arrangements often remain in kinship foster care indefinitely, without the permanency or stability offered by adoption, just so the kinship caregiver can continue to receive the higher public assistance benefits offered by the foster care program.

* * *

Kinship caregivers are different from parents; the law does not impose on them the same responsibilities and obligations to the child. Accordingly, kinship caregivers should not be forced to participate in programs designed to promote and instill this sense of duty and accountability in order to receive assistance for the care of someone else's children. Kinship caregivers do, however, exemplify responsibility. They have agreed to provide care for children whose parents cannot do so. They do more than provide substitute care; kinship caregivers also impart a sense of family and familial ties to the children. Without them, these children would be alone and completely dependent on the state.

* * *

What is needed is a multi-faceted solution that either revises the two existing federal programs, or alternatively replaces these programs with a new one that directly addresses the needs of kinship caregivers and the children they are raising. Reform, however implemented, should emphasize support for these families, not only through providing assistance, but through creating options and educating the caregivers about these options. There is a need for the laws and accompanying regulations to be more flexible and responsive to the concerns of kinship caregivers and for these caregivers to be both assisted and empowered by the process.

If revising the existing programs is the chosen method of reform, kinship caregivers should be excluded or exempted from all current and proposed restrictions concerning the AFDC program. As explained above, these procedural requirements, which are designed to reduce dependency and promote self-sufficiency, are unnecessary and inappropriate in the kinship care context. The rationales behind these programs and the incentives they create conflict with the realities of kinship care arrangements. Kinship caregivers are surrogate or substitute caregivers. They are not obligated to care for or support the children they have taken in and chosen to raise. They should be rewarded for this decision, not punished and forced to confront a labyrinth of bureaucratic obstacles in order to receive assistance.

[The foster care statute] also needs to be amended in several significant ways in order to encompass the needs of kinship caregivers. First, Congress should amend the statute to create a preference for placement with relatives. Unless a state child welfare caseworker has reason to believe otherwise, placement with a relative caregiver should be considered the best initial, temporary and permanent option for a child if the child cannot be placed with his or her parents. To some extent, this would be legislating what is current practice in many states. In 1992, twenty-nine states had policies that required child welfare workers to give preference to relatives as foster care providers for their kin. Another fifteen states placed children with relatives routinely.

Additional legislative changes also could help promote the kinship caregiver preference. Congress could incorporate an acknowledgement of the importance of kin and placement with kin throughout the statute. For example, the availability of a kinship caretaker could be added to the list of required considerations for case plans and case reviews. Efforts to place a child with kin could become a mandatory component of the "reasonable efforts" requirement. Likewise, an initial and periodic kin notification system could be created. Precedent for such legislative requirements can be found in the Indian Child Welfare Act of 1978 (ICWA). ICWA was enacted, in large part, to put a halt to the rampant separation of Native American children from their families and tribes. A significant portion of the legislation focuses on the preservation of the ethnic heritage of Native American children in foster care through a variety of protections emphasizing preferences for placements with extended family or tribal custodians whenever Native American children need to be placed in foster, preadoptive or adoptive homes. Thus, while the focus of ICWA is somewhat different than the concerns of kinship caregivers, it acknowledges a similar need for children to remain with family whenever possible. To accomplish this goal, ICWA authorizes grants for Native American child and family service programs and establishes standards and guidelines for the placement of Native American children in foster or adoptive homes. Specifically, the statute creates a stringent and detailed notification system and sets forth priorities for substitute care.

The second area of needed reform with regard to the current federal foster care statute concerns the licensing requirements for foster parents. The licensing requirements for kin should be modified to eliminate arbitrary criteria that do not reinforce safety and protection standards. This would enable more kin to become kinship foster parents.

Just as states have already implemented relative caregiver preference systems, some jurisdictions have relaxed licensing requirements either through explicit state laws and policies, or through formal and informal waivers of federal or state policies. In 1985, the United States Department of Heath and Human Services issued a policy interpretation stating that all foster care facilities must meet licensing standards but that, in special situations, states may vary or waive certain standards when licensing or approving the homes of individual relatives as foster family homes. Some states exempt relative caregivers from some of the licensing requirements.

A third significant way that the foster care statute must be revised concerns the need for permanency. Permanency planning for children in kinship care families differs significantly from permanency planning for children in traditional foster care situations. There also is evidence that children placed with relatives by the state remain the legal responsibility of the state longer than children in other alternative care arrangements. Thus, there is a need for the creation of another option whereby permanent placement with the kinship caregiver could be countenanced, yet the kinship caregiver could continue to receive ongoing foster care payments or the equivalent.

One option, endorsed by the Child Welfare League of America, is subsidized guardianship. Under this proposed system, once a child has been placed with a kinship foster parent and efforts to rehabilitate the child's natural parents have failed, the kinship caregiver could become the child's legal guardian and continue to receive foster care payments. Under this program, there would no longer be a need for ongoing supervision by the child welfare agency and the court. Several states have been experimenting with this model on the state and local levels. The Inspector General has recommended a study on the costs and benefits of providing subsidies to relatives who assume guardianship for special-needs children. He noted that, as proponents for the adoption subsidy program successfully argued, the increased costs of such subsidies may be offset by the long-term savings in court and administrative costs of keeping children in foster care.

An alternative to amending and revising the AFDC and foster care programs would be to replace one or both of them with a separate kinship care program that would provide benefits, at a rate somewhere in between AFDC and foster care, as well as supportive services such as subsidized child care, respite care, support groups and transportation services. This new program would attempt to establish one program that caters to all kinship caregivers regardless of the legal status of the children in their care. The custodial status of the child would not be a determining factor in the decision concerning a caregiver's eligibility for benefits under this plan. Whether a child is in the legal custody of the state, the kinship caregiver, or even the parent would be irrelevant to the decision of whether a caregiver is eligible for kinship care benefits. The only relevant question with respect to eligibility would concern where the child is residing.

The focus of the program would be on the legal, financial and emotional needs of children living in extended families. It would recognize that children need their families and "that it is in families that children thrive, are loved and educated, and are taught family values."

* * *

Notes and Questions

1. *Reforming Foster Care.* Randi Mandelbaum proposes overhauling the foster care system to better enable kinship caregivers to provide care for children. Do you expect opposition to her proposal? If so, from whom, and on what basis?

2. *Orphanages and Welfare Reform.* Some proponents of welfare reform urged that poor children be removed from their homes and sent to orphanages. From a budget perspective alone, of course, supporting children in orphanages costs more than assisting families to care for children at home. Assuming that poor children will not be sent away to orphanages, what will happen to poor children if the welfare system is dismantled? If time limits prevent families from receiving welfare after they reach the mandated limit, what will happen to those children and their parents who remain in poverty?

If block grants allow states to spend their federal welfare dollars on trickle-down-development projects rather than welfare grants, what will support those children and their parents who remain in poverty?

3. Human Rights for Children

If tensions persist between the values of compassion and economic justice, on the one hand, and individual responsibility and market philosophy, on the other, will society ever develop a consensus in favor of providing for the needs of poor families? Some commentators have begun to use human rights rhetoric to reframe the ugly pictures of poverty. Martha Minow argues below that human rights rhetoric offers renewed hope for poor children.

Martha Minow

WHAT EVER HAPPENED TO CHILDREN'S RIGHTS?

80 MINNESOTA LAW REVIEW 267

* * *

I have no plan or even hope for mobilizing public support for children, especially poor children, at this point in American history. Each of the four rhetorics -- child protection, children's liberation, children's rights as potential adults, and redistribution -- have failed to find a strong constituency. Instead, political figures win strong support by invoking conventional authority structures, family privacy, and self-reliance, and by attacking a social welfare state. It is tempting to look at other Western industrialized countries and to wonder why state-subsidized health care, day care, child allowances, and other programs are so well-established elsewhere but so politically infeasible here. The failure of the varied rhetorics for children, however, can be only a symptom of and not an explanation for the failure of initiatives for children here.

What, then, might explain the failure of children's initiatives? History suggests four. First, children do not vote, and no other lobby has appeared on their behalf. Second, we have seen cycles of reform and disillusionment, epitomized by changes in juvenile court. The reforms of one generation become the problems to be reformed by a later generation; the earlier reforms and subsequent problems then caution against further reform. Third, children's needs are connected to larger, intractable issues, such as the economy's failure to provide good jobs for many people, the presence of women in the paid labor force without reallocation of some of child care from mothers to fathers and others, negative views of poor parents, misallocated health care expenditures, failures of public education, and divisive conflicts over abortion and crime control. Finally, our culture and ideology produce great resistance to state intervention in families; a resistance articulated both by the political left and the right. Conceptions of personal responsibility and privacy, government bungling and individual freedom, and cultural diversity and mutual distrust fuel this resistance. The cultural resistance to rights for children thus reflects a fear that such public rights would disrupt private traditions and fail to meet children's needs compared with reliance on private families. As a result, we treat other people's children as beyond public concern. Perhaps because of our troubled heterogeneity, with historic racism and intergroup distrust, we do not view other people's children as ours in many important ways.

Given these reasons, rhetoric alone will not alter the situation of children. Yet it is tempting to seek yet another rhetoric, such as the emerging human rights rhetoric . . . . The human rights rhetoric has much appeal to those who believed in any prior version of rights for children. More practically, an occasion for political mobilization has arisen now that the United States has signed but not yet ratified the Convention. Because of the international framework, the United States signing could become an occasion to look beyond the parochial and idiosyncratic views that undermine children's legal protections in this country and consider the standards for treating children developed elsewhere.

* * *

The human rights argument seeks to treat children as candidates not for "children's rights," "child protections," or "adult rights," but instead for "human rights." As human beings, children deserve the kind of dignity, respect, and freedom from arbitrary treatment that rights signal. This dignity, respect, and freedom does not displace or undermine parents, but instead reminds parents and other adults of their fundamental responsibilities toward children.

Unlike children's liberation, the human rights formulation rejects the pretense that children are just like adults in all respects relevant to the law. Thus, the Convention calls for development rights--rights to education, cultural activities, play and leisure, and freedom of thought--to meet children's needs in reaching their full potential. More comprehensive than child protection, the human rights formulation underscores that the absence of rights exposes children to risks of abuse both by their parents and by government actors such as teachers, social workers, and judges. Unlike the social resource redistribution rhetoric, this formulation focuses specifically on children and affords a point for evaluating the entire range of legal treatments of children, not only those dealing with access to resources. Thus, as human beings, children deserve economic and social benefits appropriate to their needs.

Human rights in the international sphere depend upon the development of a community that believes in them rather than an authority--court or legislature--that will enforce them.

The vulnerability of international human rights for children to the willingness and commitments of adults at first seems like a weakness, a failure to secure something with force. This vulnerability in another sense, however, becomes a strength because it reveals how dependent and interdependent children are upon adults. Organizing to influence and shape such a community may line up means and ends in precisely the way most important for children. Without adults who believe in the importance and entitlements of children, no phrase, judicial order, or legislative statement will alter their conditions.

In a basic sense, all rights--for adults as well as for children--require a commitment by others to recognize the claims of others and to behave accordingly. Freedoms of association and religion, rights to marry and to procreate, and rights to maintain relationships with family members all depend upon community commitments to include the rights-bearers in the group deserving respect and attention.

Rights rhetorics in the past have tended too often to imply only freedom from--freedom from state control, freedom from interference by others. Children may need some forms of such freedoms but they also need guidance, involvement, support, and even control to protect them from harms against which they cannot protect themselves. I suggest that nothing inherent in rights rhetorics prevents acknowledging these needs of children. At the same time, the rhetoric of rights is the coin of the realm in national, and increasingly in international, law and politics. Not only does invoking this language put children on the map of public concern, it also crucially "impl[ies] a respect which places one in the referential range of self and others, which elevates one's status from human body to social being."

Many may ask whether it is practical to press for human rights on behalf of children. A negative answer might arise given the considerable resources right-wing groups muster in opposing such rights as interference in their privacy. The history of the children's rights movements throughout this century casts further doubt on the practicality of a human rights effort for children. By the 1980s, children's rights, as a phrase in search of a program, encompassed many contrasting and even conflicting commitments to children without a notable improvement of circumstances for many, many children. Whether styled as children's liberation or child protection, or as social welfare redistribution programs, each effort found powerful opponents poised against it. Moreover, the conventional conception of rights as implying an autonomous person who needs freedom from interference seems ill-suited to meeting the needs of most children.

Yet the past does not determine our future, but instead offers a set of lessons about the relationship between ideals and contingent realities. Powerful concepts like rights are amenable to new interpretations and applications that may in turn make good on their earlier promise and deeper meanings. So I suggest we roll up our sleeves and work on every front--our own workplaces, schools, communities, and states, our Congress, our medical care, our world--to explore what it would mean to view children as human beings entitled to human rights, or else find a better way to summon attention and resources on their behalf.

E. DOMESTIC VIOLENCE

As with problems of child abuse and neglect, domestic violence does not discriminate based on class; it affects people of every socio-economic class. What challenges might domestic violence present for poverty policy? Consider two primary factors that link domestic violence and poverty. First, if victims of abuse have no private or public safety net on which to rely if they desire to escape abusive spouses, they will face the dilemma of either remaining in an abusive home or facing severe poverty when they flee that home. This is true regardless whether the victim is fully dependent on another wage earner or not, because even wage-earning victims who have to flee their locale may have to leave their job as well. Second, both poverty and domestic violence discriminate based on gender. In other words, both poverty and domestic violence affect women at disproportionate rates. Policies dealing with poverty and domestic violence share the strictures dictated by the ideology of patriarchy, which often defines the terms available to those who seek relief.

One of the greatest successes of the women's movement has been its domestic violence movement. Advocates have achieved great success in changing how law deals with domestic violence, as Naomi Cahn and Joan Meier explain:

> In the last twenty years, litigation, legislation, activism, and, to a lesser extent, social services for battered women have proliferated. In that time society has moved from virtual denial of the existence of domestic violence to a somewhat grudging acknowledgment that it is a pervasive and serious problem with legal, sociological, and psychological dimensions. Fundamental changes in civil and criminal law and practice have resulted in battered women becoming more visible in the legal system: protective restraining orders are now available in every state; many states have amended their custody statutes to provide for consideration of domestic violence in custody cases; policies for arrest of batterers are increasingly common; prosecutors' offices have begun to prosecute domestic violence cases; and public

defenders have begun to recognize the relevance of battering to some of their client's defenses.[1]

Has society made more progress in responding to domestic violence than we have in responding to poverty? If so, why? Given all these improvements in the legal system's response to domestic violence, why has the prevalence of domestic violence persisted? What does this teach us about the role of law in society?

If the legal system's response to violence remains insufficient, could advocates bring any constitutional challenges? Remember that most other provisions of the constitution require some form of state action. Do the police have a constitutional duty to protect people from domestic violence? Consider how *DeShaney v. Winnebago County Department of Social Services*, 489 U.S. 189 (1989) (excerpted in this chapter) might apply to a substantive due process analysis of this question. What if the intervention of the police could be proved to increase the danger to the victim? Could women raise an equal protection claim against the police, perhaps based on gender-based inequality in how law enforcement officials respond to alleged violations of various laws? Even if no state action exists, could advocates bring a claim against perpetrators for violating the Thirteenth Amendment's prohibition against involuntary servitude? Are there statutory or administrative challenges that could be brought? Check whether the Violence Against Women Act of 1994 creates any rights for victims of domestic violence. Consider also whether the right to be free from domestic violence is a human right.

Domestic Violence and the Personal Responsibility Act

In the Personal Responsibility and Work Opportunity Act of 1996, Congress provided a limited exception to its five-year time limit on receipt of federal welfare assistance for victims of domestic violence. It allowed states to continue to provide benefits to families that include an individual who has been battered or subjected to extreme cruelty. Congress prohibited the states, however, from making such domestic violence exceptions to the time limit in more

---

[1]Naomi Cahn and Joan Meier, *Domestic Violence and Feminist Jurisprudence: Towards A New Agenda*, 4 BOSTON UNIVERSITY PUBLIC INTEREST LAW JOURNAL 339 (1995).

than 20% of cases. Moreover, Congress failed to require states to screen for domestic violence, but allowed states to conduct such screening at their option. Will these provisions allow poor people subjected to domestic violence to be terminated from federal welfare assistance? For an examination of related issues, *see* Jody Raphael, *Domestic Violence and Welfare Receipt: Toward a New Feminist Theory of Welfare Dependency,* 19 HARVARD WOMEN'S LAW JOURNAL 201 (1996).

CHAPTER 10: THE FIGHT FOR WORK

A. A HISTORY OF WORK AND WELFARE

Larry L. Orr & Felicity Skidmore
THE EVOLUTION OF THE WORK ISSUE IN WELFARE REFORM
in **WELFARE REFORM IN AMERICA,** edited by Paul M. Sommers

Any receipt of cash or goods that is not a reward for work by definition makes work less necessary, because the recipient can enjoy a given level of consumption while working less than would otherwise be the case. Any program whose benefits fall as other income rises--as indeed they must in any program designed to aid low-income families--intensifies this disincentive by reducing the net reward for work.

That this matters is attested to by thc prominence of the work issue and efforts to deal with it throughout the history of federal welfare policy. On the moral level, work is considered to have intrinsic value in our society. Thus, having a job or being supported by someone who is earning can be expected to be important to the self-esteem of society's members. In addition, since work is valued, those who feel that society has a responsibility to ensure certain minimum living standards, and are working and paying taxes to fulfill this responsibility, are likely to feel that those benefitting from society's help also have a responsibility to work. On the economic level, work is important, in that any reduction in earnings means that the cost to the taxpayers of providing a given standard of living is increased. It is also important because any reduction in work reduces the nations's production--reducing the amount of goods and services that society as a whole can consume and, thus, the standard of living of us all. On the political level, work is important because these moral and economic considerations are not lost on the voting public, who are therefore less likely to support generous income support programs that do not take these considerations into account.

The federal government entered the welfare policy arena in 1935 with the passage of the original Social Security Act. In the four and a half decades since, efforts to deal with the work issue in welfare and welfare reform have gone from a relatively straightforward concern to ensure that those expected to work did in fact work by denying them eligibility for cash transfers, to the recent realization that cash transfers, combined with jobs in an integrated income support system, can achieve more effectively than cash alone the "uneasy triangle" of income support policy objectives: (1) adequacy, (2) desired incentives, and (3) economy.

The Social Security Act of 1935 marked the beginning of federal income support policy and its contours can still be seen in the basic structure of our income support system. The act was based on the following perception of the work issue: most individuals are either capable of and thus expected to work, or they belong to families that include such a worker. They can, therefore, be expected to command adequate living standards from private earnings.

Certain groups or categories are not expected to work, however, for various socially acceptable reasons, and these are deserving of help. In 1935, the categories defined as not expected to earn their own way were the aged, mothers of dependent children (i.e., children with no father in the house), and the blind. The Social Security Act thus included three welfare programs: Aid to the Blind (AB), Aid to the Aged (OAA), and Aid to Dependent Children (ADC). It should be noted, however, that these were considered short-term programs for residual groups rather than the mainstay of the act. The central programs were designed on the assumption that even the deserving categories had been workers or dependents of workers. Thus, the elderly were assumed to have had a lifetime of gainful employment, mothers of dependent children were assumed to be the widows of former workers, and the unemployed were assumed to have fallen on hard times that were temporary. These circumstances were provided for by a series of social insurance programs that, when in full operation, were to be self-financing in the form of payroll deductions during the breadwinner's working life: Old Age Insurance, Unemployment Insurance, and (in 1938) Survivor's Insurance.

In 1950, a set of amendments added to the categories of the deserving--by introducing Aid to the Permanently and Totally Disabled (APTD) and including benefits to the caretaker (usually the mother) of dependent children in the ADC (now AFDC) program, as well as to the children themselves--but did not change the basic approach to the work issue. The addition in 1956 of the Disability Insurance program followed the same pattern.

By the 1960s, however, it was clear that dealing with the work issue simply by separating the workers from the nonworkers and only providing income support for the latter was causing distortions that were in fact defeating the objectives of encouraging work. The AFDC program was the focus of the criticism. In spite of the establishment of Survivor's Insurance, the AFDC caseload had grown steadily. It was increasingly recognized, in consequence, that women on AFDC were not predominantly widows, but women who had been left by the fathers of their children. The suspicion was also growing that the categorical division that led to only single parents with children being eligible for support was causing men to leave their wives and children simply in order to qualify them for public support. In addition, views had changed somewhat since 1935 with respect to whether women should stay home with their children at public expense or whether they should, rather, work to contribute to their own support.

All this led in the 1960s to a new scrutiny of AFDC and the work issue, and three major new initiatives to deal with it. The first came in 1961, when the AFDC program was expanded, at state option, to cover two-parent families when the breadwinner was unemployed. The explicit objective of such a step was, in the words of the Secretary of Health, Education, and Welfare, to "keep families together." However, concern lest this money would allow fathers to be idle who would otherwise be gainfully employed led to such restrictions on eligibility with respect to prior attachment to the labor force that few families at any one time were able to qualify.

The second major change came in 1962, with the recognition that regulations governing the benefits could themselves be a factor in inhibiting work. Up to this point, recipients could in fact become worse off by working if expenses were incurred in connection with that work, because the grant was reduced by the total amount of the recipient's earnings. The 1962 amendments allowed the deduction of work-related expenses from the income offset against the welfare benefit. There was, in addition, some seed money for day care and some provision (not much used) for federal matching funds for employment and training programs.

The year 1967 saw the third change--basically a substantial

extension of the 1962 beginnings with respect both to deductibility from earnings as an incentive to work, and training and services to increase the employability of AFDC mothers. The work incentive (WIN) program was passed as part of the 1967 amendments, to provide training, work experience, and jobs. And the 30 and 1/3 rule was introduced, whereby the first $30 of earnings (in addition to the work expenses) and one-third of each additional dollar earned was to be disregarded in computing the benefit. The belief that recipients differed in their suitability for work, and that this difference should be recognized, was still evident in the 1967 legislation in the provision requiring only AFDC recipients judged appropriate to be referred to WIN. By 1972, views about the responsibility of AFDC recipients to work had hardened, and the so-called Talmadge Amendment was passed, requiring all AFDC recipients to register for work or training.

As these Social Security Amendments were changing the legislative approach to the work issue, in the late 1960s the war on poverty was leading to a parallel development that was very important in its influence on the treatment of the work issue in the 1970s. Policy planners in the Office of Economic Opportunity began to favor a concept espoused by a variety of academic economists throughout the 1960s: a universal noncategorical negative income tax. The universal negative income tax proposal was a direct response to the recognition that a categorical system that treated different groups differently created incentives to change categories, that a substantial group of families was poor even though they contained an able-bodied breadwinner working full-time and not covered by any significant transfer option, and that any feasible transfer option for that group had to pay careful attention to work incentives.

The OEO group was concerned, however, that public fear of the work-disincentive consequences of providing a negative income tax for the working poor would defeat any such proposal. A series of income maintenance experiments was therefore funded, in the expectation that the work disincentive resulting from an experimental negative income tax would turn out to be small and that this evidence would further the cause of reform.

As it turned out, just two years after the first experiment was initiated, a negative income tax proposal was introduced in Congress--the Family Assistance Plan (FAP), designed to replace AFDC and extend benefits to all poor families with children. It had no jobs component, but it did have a work requirement specifying that employable family members who refused to accept training or employment would forfeit their share of the benefit; and some additional funding for training under WIN was provided. FAP failed to pass for many reasons, but probably crucial to its defeat was the unrelenting concern with work incentives displayed by the Senate Finance Committee and the damage done to the FAP cause by the demonstration that, when combined with existing programs, FAP recipients could make themselves actually worse off by working. Concern was also expressed by the committee about the absence of a jobs component. A revised version of FAP (H.R. 1) was introduced in 1971, transferring the administration of payments to employable families from HEW to the Department of Labor and including some better integration of its tax rate provisions with those of existing programs. Criticism of its incentive features, again, was a prominent factor in its defeat.

That the crux of the problem was cash assistance for the working poor is supported by examination of the successful legislation that did flow from the FAP-H.R. 1 effort. The Supplemental Security Income Program--originally proposed in the FAP legislation--was passed in 1972, to replace the categorical programs for the aged, blind, and disabled with a uniform federal negative income tax. The Food Stamp Program was reformed by executive action in 1970 and legislative amendments in 1971 and 1973 into a national, universal negative income tax program, with a work test, but no categorical exclusions from eligibility. It was thus the first guaranteed income program to include all families headed by able-bodied working age males--but the currency was earmarked vouchers rather than cash. And in 1974, the Earned Income Tax Credit (EITC) was passed, the effect of which was to raise the incomes of the poor families who worked by supplementing earnings up to $8,000 a year.

Whatever its legislative success, the introduction of FAP was a landmark event in welfare policy with respect to the work issue, signaling a shift from the exclusionary, categorical policies that had been followed since the 1930s to a principle of universal coverage with reliance on work requirements and incentives (primarily, "low" tax rates) to mitigate reductions in work effort. As we have seen, the policy shift did not go so far as to attempt to actually increase work effort or employability in any major way. But during the same period, seemingly unrelated policy developments were under way in the areas of employment and training, which in the 1970s would come together with the movement for a universal negative income tax and culminate in a second major shift in welfare policy.

Unlike the Social Security Act, which formed the basis of transfer policy, the major employment and training programs of the 1930s--the Works Progress Administration (WPA), Public Works Administration (PWA), Civilian Conservation Corps (CCC), National Youth Administration (NYA), and Civil Works Administration (CWA), among others--did not outlive the immediate urgent needs of the Depression. Except for some relatively modest public works programs intended to combat the recessions of the late 1940s and 1950s, the use of direct provision of employment and training to alleviate economic hardship was largely nonexistent until the early 1960s. The return to these policies took form largely in response to the steady decline of the dominant industries in certain areas. The key pieces of legislation that made up this initiative were the Area Redevelopment Act and the Public Works Acceleration Act. These were both designed to address structural unemployment on a regional basis, rather than defining and focusing on the employment problems of particular types of individuals. The passage in 1962 of the Manpower Development and Training Act (MDTA)--although its focus was still on structural unemployment and the consequences of technological change--marked the beginning of efforts to enhance the employment opportunities of individuals.

In the mid-1960s, the nation's training and employment policy again shifted, this time from workers unemployed (or in danger of losing their jobs) because of technological change to individuals who had few skills and in many cases little education or training of any kind. The Equal Opportunity Act of 1964 and the establishment of the Office of Economic Opportunity led to a series of job assistance and training programs for the disadvantaged. In keeping with the times, the emphasis of MDTA was also shifted in 1967 from retraining to initial skill development and remedial education for people with few labor market skills.

In 1973, the various employment and training programs stemming from MDTA and the antipoverty initiatives of the mid and late sixties became, under the Comprehensive Employment and Training Act (CETA), a single decentralized, decategorized program. National guidelines contained in federal program regulations, however, as well as strong local program support, helped to maintain the emphasis on services to disadvantaged populations in spite of the change in the service delivery system.

Concomitant with the increased targeting of employment and training programs on the poor with few labor market skills as an antipoverty strategy was the macroeconomic concern with the difficulty of keeping unemployment low without running in unacceptably high rates of inflation. This search for ways to "cheat on the Phillips curve" provided an additional reason for interest in public service employment (PSE) as a cure for structural unemployment--the hope that the hard-to-employ who are not reached by macroeconomic stimuli can be placed into jobs that do not compete with the private sector and therefore do not drive up wages and prices.

Acting on these concerns, in 1978 Congress moved to substantially tighten eligibility provisions in the CETA Reauthorization Act. The act defined separate titles (and appropriations) for the structurally and cyclically unemployed, made more stringent the income and unemployment requirements for eligibility, and placed stricter restrictions on CETA PSE wage rates. The effects on eligibility were dramatic: in 1978, almost 19 million persons met the CETA PSE eligibility requirements; in 1979, only about 4 million persons qualified for CETA PSE jobs under Title II (the title covering the structurally unemployed).

There was still, however, no direct link between CETA and the income transfer programs. The increasing targeting of employment and training programs on hard-to-employ, disadvantaged workers mcant that these two sets of programs were increasingly serving the same clientele. Because of the categorical nature of cash assistance and the continued exclusion of most of the working poor, even with the 1978 CETA amendments only about 15% of CETA enrollees actually received cash assistance. But in 1979, over 90% of new CETA PSE enrollees were economically disadvantaged (Committee on Evaluation 1979). Extension of cash assistance to all low-income families would therefore result in a near-identity between the two target populations.

Recognition of the convergence of objectives and clientele in these two policy areas, together with the inherent difficulties of designing cash transfer programs that would enhance--or even preserve--work incentives, led in the late 1970s to the second major shift in welfare policy since the 1930s: innovative attempts to design an integrated income support/employment system that would combine CETA-type employment and training opportunities with universal cash assistance. The first was the unsuccessful Program for Better Jobs and Income (PBJI), introduced in Congress in 1978. The second, a scaled-down version of PBJI, was introduced in 1979 as two separate bills, the Social Welfare Reform Amendments of 1979 and the Work and Training Opportunities Act.

The basic approach of the two now-defunct proposals was the same. They again preserved the distinction between those expected and not expected to work, but were designed to provide income support to both groups. The latter were eligible for a cash transfer program with no work component. For the former, the work concern was addressed by providing a combined cash and jobs program for the principal earners in welfare eligible families, and welfare eligibility was significantly expanded by mandating AFDC-UP in all states.

* * *

Notes and Questions

1. *Moral Values.* Larry Orr & Felicity Skidmore describe the societal view of work as encompassing several moral imperatives. First, American society values work as being essential to the sustenance of healthy self-esteem. Second, work discharges our mutual responsibilities to one another; each of us is required to contribute to the common good, usually through tax contributions from earnings.

How do these basic principles help us resolve more complex questions about what constitutes work, for example, whether the time, knowledge, skill, and energy expended in caring for children or other dependent members of society count as work? Do those who care for dependent children or adults contribute to the common good? If we measure contribution to the common good through the tax system, should law require that the value provided by caretakers be both compensated and taxed?

Also, do we apply these basic principles evenhandedly to all members of society? For example, do we evaluate the work effort of financially dependent spouses who do not contribute to caretaking? Do we evaluate the work effort of persons who derive their sustenance from inherited wealth? Neither of these groups rely directly on government benefits for their sustenance; does the government nevertheless subsidize their activities through tax or other policies?

2. *Categorization.* Professors Orr and Skidmore explain that welfare policy draws its primary distinction between those who are expected to work and those who are not expected to work. What criteria govern whether a group is required to work? Prior to the 1930s, elderly and disabled people and single parents were not exempted from work force participation. What factors may have caused these groups to be exempted from work requirements in the 1930s?

Do we truly exempt any category of people from working? Do we provide government benefits adequate to support the actual minimal economic needs of families receiving Aid to Families with Dependent Children? How does the adequacy of AFDC benefit amounts compare to the amounts received by the elderly or the disabled? Remember that elderly and disabled people receive benefits from different government programs depending on whether they worked steadily enough to draw from the earnings-based Social Security system or, if not, from the need-based programs.

3. *Shifts to Work Requirements and Employment Opportunities.* Professors Orr & Skidmore describe two primary shifts in welfare work policy. First, in the 1960s and early 1970s, welfare policy shifted away from categorization toward more universal coverage combined with work requirements. Second, in the late 1970s, lawmakers began to combine cash welfare benefits with training and employment programs.

Regarding the first shift, has categorization been eliminated from welfare policy? Were work requirements added only as a payback for more universal coverage? What other factors might have contributed to the addition of work requirements? Consider how the racial composition of the AFDC rolls changed during the 1960s.

Regarding the second shift, we have not fully combined our welfare and job training programs. Many job training opportunities remain limited to people more advantaged than welfare recipients. For example, welfare recipients typically do not receive the same job training and employment opportunities offered to the recently unemployed. Why do we continue to separate the job training offered to recently unemployed persons and the job training offered to welfare recipients?

4. *The Economy.* Macroeconomic concerns play a critical role in shaping welfare work policy. Because many economists believe that lower unemployment causes higher inflation, economic policymakers attempt to manage the economy so as to maintain a stable level of unemployment. What implications does this policy have for welfare recipients? Are our politicians guilty of inconsistency when they decry the unemployment of the poor, but support maintaining a level of unemployment healthy for our macro-economy? Do welfare recipients contribute to the common good by helping to limit inflation?

Joanna Weinberg

THE DILEMMA OF WELFARE REFORM: "WORKFARE" PROGRAMS AND POOR WOMEN

26 NEW ENGLAND LAW REVIEW 415 (1991)

In 1988, Congress passed what many have called the most sweeping welfare reform effort since the creation of federal welfare programs, an act known as the Family Support Act of 1988. The overall thrust of the reform was to initiate a trend toward requiring Aid to Families with Dependent Children (AFDC) recipients to participate in mandatory work/training programs. The statute mandates that states add to their public assistance programs a provision that requires some recipients of public assistance to participate in "workfare"--mandatory work requirements that are imposed as a condition of receiving public assistance payments. . . . These changes have substantially restructured the design of public benefit programs in ideological as well as substantive ways.

What is unique about the reforms are two important ideological shifts. First, a surprising coalition of liberal and conservative forces united on the nature of the connection between welfare benefits and workforce participation. Second, the reforms incorporated values of the women's movement that emphasize autonomy and full workplace participation, but they do so in a way that fails to account for the often inadequate preparation for and availability of appropriate work settings. . . . The Family Support Act represents a clear signal that work requirements will be mandated on a national basis, for the first time for a population that is primarily composed of women with children.

* * *

Welfare has never been a popular program; some say that it is a perpetual scapegoat. American society has traditionally assessed a person's value to society on the basis of one's ability to perform paid work, and allows the free market to determine the worth of a person's work. Not all women have benefitted from the advances of the last twenty-five years. Most of the new jobs created during the economic boom of the eighties, when so many women moved into the workforce, are at the lowest end of the wage scale--minimum wage, often part-time, without benefits. At a time when more women are working single mothers, much of the traditional work of women--caregiving, homemaking, child care--is still not considered "work," in the context of a market economy.

Public policy has failed to consider adequately these limitations. As mandatory work requirements become the model for the next generation of public assistance programs, it is important to understand whether such requirements are an effective means of restructuring welfare in order to reduce continuing cycles of welfare dependency. It is also necessary to look at the intended beneficiaries, in order to determine how the restructuring of public benefits affects their lives.

* * *

States have been permitted to institute work requirements in some form since 1967, first through the WIN program, which merely required registering for work and emphasized education and training. An amendment to WIN in 1971 toughened the work registration requirement. WIN, however, was not a successful program; only about 40% of public assistance recipients were required to participate, only half of these actually did participate, and most of those who did participate found jobs on their own. The 1981 Omnibus Budget Reconciliation Act (OBRA) shifted considerable discretion and authority in the policymaking area to states and local government agencies, and the 1988 Act continued the trend toward localization of policymaking authority. However, while OBRA did not mandate work requirements, its goal was to make public assistance less attractive for recipients than work, and to shift much of the policymaking authority for program structure to local agencies and private industry. After OBRA, the CETA program, under which the federal government had heavily subsidized local community service work/training programs, was phased out and replaced with the Job Training Partnership Act (JTPA). JTPA encouraged local governments to link public assistance recipients with private employers, but provided minimal federal subsidies for such activity. OBRA permitted states and local governments to experiment with imposing work requirements as a condition of receiving AFDC.

* * *

The Family Support Act Provisions

Title I contains broad changes in collection procedures for child support (which will apply for the first time to all child support orders, not just those where a family receives AFDC). These include a provision for attachment of a delinquent parent's wages, a mandated change in the mechanisms for establishing paternity, and automation of child support enforcement systems in every state so that inter- and intra-state collection rates can be improved.

Title II established a new employment, education and training program for AFDC and AFDC-U recipients, called the JOBS program. Rather than spreading responsibility for work requirement programs among the five existing programs--(The Work Incentive (WIN), the WIN demonstration project, Community Work Experience (CWEP), work supplementation and job search programs)--these programs were consolidated under the JOBS program into one administrative umbrella. The purpose of the program is "to assure that needy families with children obtain the education, training and employment that will help them avoid long term welfare dependence."

Title II also mandated a higher level of federal funding for work-related training and education services than previously existed: between 1989 and 1995, total expenditures were to rise from the existing $500 million in the present WIN program to about $3 billion. The legislation also required that states spend 55% of their federal funding on programs for hard-core public assistance recipients, those who have been on welfare rolls for over two years, or who are frequent repeaters, in order to avoid the common practice of "creaming" the most motivated recipients and ignoring long-term recipients. Finally the legislation required that participants in work programs receive one year of transitional medical and child care subsidies.

Another change from present policy relates to exemptions from participation in work-related programs. Under the old law, which applied to exemptions from the WIN program, authorized exceptions included the following provisions: individuals who were ill, incapacitated or over 65; needed in the home because of the illness or incapacity of another family member; a caretaker parent of children under 6; a person employed 30 hours or more; women in the last trimester of pregnancy; and non-principal-earner parents in a two-parent family. Under the new legislation, parents of children under 3 (in AFDC-U families) will also be exempt. The House version of the bill would also have exempted parents of children between the ages of 3 and 6 unless day care was guaranteed and participation was limited to 20 hours a week or less. In the final version, the day care guarantee provision was eliminated, and states are permitted to require participation in educational activities for no more than 20 hours a week. Again, however, there is an inherent pitfall; because exemptions are discretionary, the effective participation of women with young children may be undermined because of lack of child care or other support services. In districts that are short-funded, this provides a ready excuse to limit training and education opportunities.

The mandated minimum wage rate is relatively low, aimed at moving people into entry level jobs. Job search activities are required only in combination with some additional educational, training or employment activity designed to improve the participant's qualifications for employment. Title II also contains a provision for teenage parents who have not completed high school; states must require a custodial parent under age 20 to participate in high school or equivalent education, remedial education, or English as a second language, for up to 24 hours a week, regardless of the age of the child. Another modification from the existing WIN regulations stipulates that parents participating in work requirement programs cannot be required to travel "an unreasonable distance" from home for work assignments, a change from the two-hour commuting limitation in present law.

Title III, Supportive Services for Families, contains provisions relating to training and education. It does not significantly increase availability of federal programming or funding for these services, but it does contain important mandates for state initiated services. All states must guarantee child care for participants in work, training or educational programs, to the extent that such care is deemed reasonable and necessary for an individual's employment. No one can be required to participate in work requirement programs unless such care is available. As indicated earlier, one year of transitional medical and child care is also required for participants who enter the workforce. States must also cover transportation and other work-related expenses that are necessary to enable participation in the JOBS program. There are also provisions to improve the standardization and delivery of child care services, and to limit the cost of child care to the local market rate.

In sum, the 1988 Act contains significant features that will affect the administration of public assistance programs in states that have heretofore not served two-parent families. Its most far-reaching reform, however, is likely to be the commitment of the federal government to find means to move people off of public assistance by reducing benefits, increasing mandatory requirements such as work provisions, or assisting in the collection of child support from absent parents.

The Impact of the Family Support Act

* * *

It should be remembered that while the aim of a work requirement is to make public assistance less profitable than low-wage work, in practice this is not always the effect. The underlying ideology of the work requirement is that performance of work is not fee-for-service based, as are most wage-based jobs, but is a form of repayment for services rendered, a reciprocal contract in which one party has very little bargaining power. This ideology has two fundamental effects. First, it underscores the tenuous connection between the work performed and the employment market. In many cases, the work performed has little inherent market value; because unions object to work requirements that replace private market labor with public assistance recipients, participants often perform work that would not otherwise be done. Second, and more fundamentally, workfare participants are not paid through valuation of what their work is worth; they are paid using an arbitrary wage rate formula based upon hours worked multiplied by the minimum wage. "True" workfare is simply a requirement that welfare recipients "work-off" benefits. But because of minimum wage rules and restrictions on the earnings of recipients, participants can earn only up to the amount of their grant; otherwise, they would lose benefits. In and of itself, this limitation may not be objectionable. However, the hourly rate of payment, when based upon a minimum wage calculation, is often considerably less than the wage rate for a comparable job in the economy of a particular area. The Act does mandate that after nine months, the calculation must be made on the basis of the wage rate for other people employed at the same site, but this does not apply where work assignments are performed exclusively by public assistance recipients. Unless there is an added benefit, such as education, training or some form of subsidy, this method of calculation might set an artificially low wage rate, which would then become the baseline when the participant leaves public assistance.

Women as a Target of Work/Training Programs

To date there has not been a great deal of attention to issues of gender in development and implementation of work/training programs. However, during the 1980s, the mandatory programs have increasingly come to focus on AFDC recipients, a population that is largely female.

* * *

Targeting work/training programs at a female population is, of course, not necessarily a bad thing. Most public assistance recipients prefer jobs to welfare, and the majority of AFDC recipients leave the welfare rolls on their own in under two years. Long-term AFDC recipients tend to share certain characteristics: they are young women, never married, who begin to receive AFDC when their first child is less than three years old, and have minimal education and work experience. Over 40% of this group will receive AFDC for 10 years or more. The reasons for this are obvious: many jobs, including many of the early work/training programs, are not tailored to the needs of custodial single parents of very young children. Inflexibility of time commitments, low availability of affordable child care, and failure to provide medical benefits for the entire family, are the major reasons that it is often more economical for these AFDC recipients to remain on welfare. In addition, many of the recipients are very young, with poor education and little skill training, so that they are the last to be hired in a buyer's job market.

* * *

As presently constituted, mandatory work programs tend to perpetuate many of the gender-based inequities that already exist in the workplace. Rather than enabling women to enter the workplace with a full earnings potential, these programs are often structured so as to tie women to low-end jobs, at low pay, and often of temporary duration. Three trends are of particular concern. First, services such as child care, education, and social services for women with children have in reality been quite limited, and have limited both the type of jobs that can be obtained and the ability of women to remain in those jobs. Moreover, the new generation of "workfare" support services provisions do not address caretaking responsibilities for persons other than young children. Second, the present generation of work programs, by tying into an existing gender-segregated job market, may be creating a new tier of low-paid workers doing "women's jobs" at "women's pay." Finally, the emphasis on work/training only through AFDC programs means that little attention is being paid to jobs and training for older displaced women workers. These women, who may only be in their thirties or forties, no longer qualify for AFDC benefits once their youngest turns eighteen.

The studies of "workfare" programs . . . suggest that work requirement participants average income only slightly above the average welfare grant, about $400 additional income per year. Even a full-time job at minimum wage leaves most recipients with income substantially below the poverty line.[104] But an additional danger of mandatory work-requirements is that most of the jobs seem to be clustered in traditional areas of "women's work," for example as caretakers for children and the elderly in day care centers and nursing

---

[104]Benefit levels under entitlement programs are significantly lower than the cost of living; for example, the average grant for a single person supported under the federal disability program is about $6000 annually. AFDC benefits range from a high of $5900 annually in Wisconsin to $1380 annually in Alabama, for a mother with two children. The Bureau of Labor Standards says that the income needed to remain above the poverty line is $8740 for a family of three.

homes, food service work, and cleaning services. Moreover, many of the service-oriented features such as child care, educational programs, and medical benefits are limited and underfunded, and designed to provide services cheaply, but are not necessarily designed for the women recipients' needs. The findings, which are preliminary but compelling, suggest that merely transferring people from "welfare" to "workfare" does little to counteract the problems of the feminization of poverty; woman-headed single-parent families comprise almost 50% of all poor families in the United States.

In short, the quality and character of the promised "work," the subsistence nature of the income, and the tentative commitment to support services such as medical assistance and child care, suggest that public benefit recipients are being sold down the river. Analysis of the work/training programs that form the background of the new generation of entitlement programs suggests that while job training and education for the workplace is indeed a desired end, the current programs perpetuate the gender inequities of the workplace, and will have the long term effect of cementing those inequities.

* * *

Conclusion

The success of workfare programs ultimately depends on whether permanent full-time jobs are available, not on whether mandatory work requirements succeed. Mandatory work requirements are only as good as the jobs behind them. On-the-job training can be a cost-effective way of providing education and training, as long as private sector employers provide jobs at fair wages with permanency potential. A disturbing trend in recent statistics suggests, however, that many of the new jobs created during the 1980s paid substantially lower wages than the jobs lost, with minimum-wage service sector jobs replacing higher paying factory and industrial work. . . . This raises the concern that an effect of work requirement programs on the employment sector has been to encourage businesses to create a second class tier of low-paying jobs and services, and that these jobs will permanently imprison former welfare recipients below the poverty line.

Moreover, analysis of the initial phase of many of the work/welfare programs' implementation shows serious problems that significantly disadvantage the primarily female AFDC population. First, there has been a low level of active participation even in the mandatory programs, . . . and a broad use of exemptions, especially for the most vulnerable AFDC recipients: very young women and mothers of young children. Second, only a small number of participants have actually found permanent employment enabling them to leave AFDC, and of these, men are vastly overrepresented. Third, most participants have received little or no child care services, often having to make arrangements on their own, and only a small number received vocational training. Finally, there has been no attempt to work with employers to structure a job market geared toward permanent meaningful employment. The programs have concentrated on filling temporary gaps in the workplace, and on low-level, traditionally "women's work" jobs. Finally, the work/welfare programs were not designed to address the needs of women who are not AFDC recipients but those who have similar needs, particularly women who have been out of the workforce raising children (or who never were in the workforce), but whose children have grown. These "displaced homemakers" need a similar focus on educational and employment skills, but remain outside the range of most work/training programs. It is therefore unclear whether such programs, as structured, can meaningfully address the economic self-sufficiency of AFDC recipients and thereby reduce poverty. The current assumption seems to be that welfare, not poverty, is the root of the problem, and the program has not addressed the more fundamental economic and social context: low wages, gender-segregated workplace, and unemployment.

* * *

Finally, there is a growing concern that public assistance programs will only provide subsistence benefits that least drain public resources. Because the focus of the FSA is on entry-level work, the danger is that the legislation will do no more than perpetuate a permanent class of partially-employed workers doing work that is marginal to the job market. As those jobs cease to exist, workers will return to public assistance, and the cycle begins again.

There is an additional concern that the work requirement programs are weighted toward creation of underclasses of child care, medical care, and educational institutions--programs paid for out of public funds, in which only public assistance recipients will participate, because they alone will have no other choice.

In order to stress coordination of job skills, education, and other supportive services, with entry into the workforce, there must be incentives to participants as well as to private employers. The incentives to the participant will be contingent on employers' willingness to provide leave time for participation in supportive or educational activities, and on the government's willingness to make those services available on a voluntary basis.

The new ideology of a reciprocal contract, with a work requirement as its cornerstone, runs the danger of not serving the people who most need the training, particularly mothers with young children and older displaced workers--and may in fact undermine the autonomy of women and their ultimate ability to enter the permanent workforce. Unless careful attention is given to the structure of the work requirements and the provision of meaningful support services and jobs in the mainstream economy, the trend toward a two-class workplace ethic will intensify. In short, work requirements are not a panacea for the dependency cycle of welfare; work is.

Notes and Questions

1. *Work as the Orthodoxy of Welfare Reform.* From the 1960s until it abolished Aid to Families with Dependent Children in 1996, Congress imposed nationally mandated work requirements as a condition of receiving AFDC. (Congress increased welfare work requirements in the Personal Responsibility and Work Opportunity Act of 1996.) The strong bipartisan consensus that passed and praised this legislation revealed a renewed orthodoxy in welfare reform, the dedication to moving recipients from welfare to work. What factors contributed to the success of the work-not-welfare campaign? To what extent can the success of the work-not-welfare movement be attributed to the societal change in gender roles reflected by more women working outside the home across class lines?

The program spawned in 1988 by the work-not-welfare orthodoxy was the Job Opportunities and Basic Skills (JOBS) work-requirement program. Does current research evaluate whether JOBS or similar programs have been successful in moving recipients from welfare to work? What percentage of recipients moved from welfare to work would count as successful? Would the measure of success depend on how long these recipients stayed off welfare? Would it depend on whether workers could fully support their families from their income?

2. *Gender-Based Inequities.* From the early work of Diana Pearce, scholars have criticized what Pearce called "the feminization of poverty." *See* Diana M. Pearce, *The Feminization of Poverty: Women, Work, and Welfare,* 11 URBAN AND SOCIAL CHANGE REVIEW 28 (1978). Indeed, Professor Weinberg argued that the JOBS program likely would place women in temporary, low-end, low-pay jobs, thus perpetuating gender discrimination. If this result occurred, would the program survive a gender-based equal protection challenge? How should work programs be structured to avoid such gender inequities?

3. *Work Requirements versus Jobs.* What if the factor most causing the percentage of long-term welfare dependency was lack of jobs, rather than lack of an incentive to work, as Professor Weinberg suggests? How should, or could, welfare work policy change to address a lack of jobs?

4. *Non-Market Work.* Joanna Weinberg explained that much of the work performed by welfare recipients is not valued in the private market. Why not? She also noted that welfare recipients are paid government-controlled wages which are limited by the recipient's benefit amounts, rather than the market wages received by workers in comparable jobs. Weinberg characterizes this system as "a reciprocal contract in which one party has very little bargaining power." Is this system legal? Does it violate any contract law principles? Is it constitutional? Does it violate the Thirteenth Amendment's prohibition against involuntary servitude?

5. *Workfare.* Few commentators question the ability of government to require welfare recipients to work. Consider the following analysis which, relying on a historical line of cases construing the Thirteenth Amendment's prohibition against involuntary servitude, argues that work-in-exchange-for-welfare violates the Thirteenth Amendment.

Julie A. Nice

WELFARE SERVITUDE

3 GEORGETOWN JOURNAL ON FIGHTING POVERTY 340 (1994)

Much of the current welfare system and the national debate about reforming that system revolve around mandatory work for welfare, which I term "welfare servitude." During the 1992 presidential campaign, candidate Bill Clinton promised to "end welfare as we know it" by requiring welfare recipients to work after they had received benefits for two years. Although President Clinton has not yet finalized his proposal for Congress, his administration has granted several states permission to require welfare recipients to work by terminating their benefits after two years.

President Clinton's proposal follows a widespread trend toward increasing welfare work requirements. A broad-based public and political consensus supports this trend, and appears to include the presumption that the government has the authority to require welfare recipients to work as a condition for receipt of benefits. To date, neither the courts nor the commentators have adequately analyzed the constitutionality of mandatory work for welfare, particularly the question of whether it violates the Thirteenth Amendment's prohibition of involuntary servitude.

A Thirteenth Amendment analysis of welfare servitude confronts two immediate obstacles. The first is the misconception that the Thirteenth Amendment was limited to the abolition of American slavery, a system of coerced labor marked by property ownership of primarily African-American laborers. Since slavery as we knew it has been largely abolished, this argument goes, the Thirteenth Amendment has been rendered obsolete. In fact, however, the Thirteenth Amendment has been applied repeatedly to forms of coerced labor that do not involve physical force against the laborer. For example, it has been applied to invalidate indentured apprenticeships, the padrone system (servitude of immigrant children), peonage (servitude required to discharge a debt), and the criminal surety system (servitude to discharge debt to a surety who paid a convict's criminal fine).

* * *

Thirteenth Amendment Doctrine

The Thirteenth Amendment prohibits at least three types of labor conditions: 1) labor akin to slavery; 2) labor compelled by physical coercion; 3) labor compelled by legal coercion. Welfare servitude meets each of these tests. Welfare servitude, like slavery, disproportionately affects people of color, especially African-Americans. It also directly affects physical survival. Termination of welfare benefits as a penalty for failure to work is a legal sanction.

Contemporary destitute persons have no actual means other than welfare to support themselves. They have no practical choice but to accept welfare benefits on the condition that they participate in a welfare work program.

* * *

Work as an Unconstitutional Condition for Welfare

Proponents of work for welfare may defend its constitutionality with a "voluntariness" argument. This argument separates into two related assertions, both of which rely on the premise that welfare is not a right/entitlement, but a privilege/gratuity. One prong centers on the government's voluntary role in distributing welfare, while the other prong focuses on purported voluntary participation by the recipient.

First, proponents of welfare servitude argue that because government is not obligated to provide welfare, its provision of welfare is "voluntary." If the government may terminate all benefits, they reason, it may offer benefits only if the recipient satisfies conditions imposed by the government. Second, they contend that since recipients choose to participate in the welfare program, their receipt of benefits is "voluntary." If they do not wish to comply with any condition attached to the benefits, they may choose to terminate their welfare participation. Under this reasoning, work for welfare cannot violate the Thirteenth Amendment because it is not coercive on either end of the exchange.

The voluntariness argument, however, is seriously flawed. Even if welfare is a mere privilege or gratuity, neither government nor recipient "voluntariness" precludes application of Thirteenth Amendment doctrine to welfare servitude. Moreover, welfare ceases to appear "voluntary" when one considers the alternatives to subsistence.

Government Voluntariness

According to widespread constitutional interpretation, the government is under no obligation to provide welfare benefits. Proponents of welfare servitude rely on this interpretation to contend that government's greater power to eliminate welfare benefits includes the lesser power to grant benefits on any condition that serves governmental interests. I refer to this as the "greater-includes-the-lesser" argument. Under this reasoning, government may condition receipt of welfare benefits on the surrender of the Thirteenth Amendment right to be free from involuntary servitude, or presumably, any other right.

Commentators across the political spectrum agree that the logic of the greater-includes-the-lesser defense fails. Its fatal weakness is that government may not do indirectly what it is forbidden from doing directly. Government may not directly interfere with constitutional rights. Government likewise may not indirectly interfere with constitutional rights by requiring the surrender of the right as a condition for a government benefit. This principle is known as the doctrine of unconstitutional conditions. Applied to welfare, it holds that government may not condition receipt of welfare on surrender of any constitutional right, including the right to be free from involuntary servitude.

Although courts have acknowledged the unconstitutional conditions doctrine for most of the twentieth century, their decisions regarding the doctrine reveal remarkable inconsistency and unpredictability. The doctrine, nonetheless, "tenaciously endures." Commentators have proposed various revisions of the doctrine. Professor Kathleen Sullivan has thoroughly reviewed the doctrine, its justifications, and its applications, exploring "*why* conditions on government benefits that 'indirectly' pressure preferred liberties should be as suspect as 'direct' burdens on those same rights, such as the threat of criminal punishment."[268]

The unconstitutional conditions doctrine has been justified traditionally as a technique to avoid the harm of coercion which occurs when a beneficiary is pressured to surrender a right in order

---

[268][*See* Kathleen Sullivan, *Unconstitutional Conditions*, 102 HARVARD LAW REVIEW 1415, 1419 (1989)].

to obtain a benefit. Although Professor Sullivan argues that coercion is only a partial justification for the doctrine, she emphasizes the great danger created by government coercion. Among the circumstances which pose this greater danger of government coercion, she identified three which relate to welfare servitude.

First, Professor Sullivan argues that coercion by the government is inappropriate when the government enjoys monopoly power over a benefit. She identifies historical displacement of private alternatives as one situation in which the government enjoys monopoly power. She further identifies minimal subsistence provision in the welfare state as a case in point. Because the government holds a near monopoly over the provision of welfare, government enjoys substantial coercive power vis a vis welfare recipients. Second, she argues that coercion by the government is inappropriate when the government has itself created a dependency, since government has a duty not to exploit a dependency which it created. Commentators across the political spectrum have criticized government welfare programs for creating such a dependency. Third, she argues that government interference with a decision about the exercise of a constitutional right is inappropriate when that right protects the right-holder's decisional autonomy. She cites the Thirteenth Amendment's inalienable right to free labor as an example of a right designed to protect decisional autonomy. Any government interference with the decision about whether to exercise the right to free labor improperly disregards the fundamental value underlying the right. Each of these arguments bolsters the application of the unconstitutional conditions doctrine to welfare servitude.

The unconstitutional conditions doctrine protects beneficiaries from pressure to surrender rights in order to obtain government benefits. Some commentators argue that the importance of the threatened constitutional right, rather than the unconstitutional conditions doctrine, should decide the question. In the case of welfare servitude, the threatened constitutional right is the Thirteenth Amendment right to be free from involuntary servitude. This right itself protects people from coercion to labor against their will.

Recipient Voluntariness

Defenders of welfare servitude are likely to resist Thirteenth Amendment analysis by arguing that recipients are not compelled to accept welfare. Rather, they contend, recipients choose to accept welfare. Under this reasoning, any recipient who does not want to work can simply stop receiving welfare benefits and escape the work requirement. This argument defends a Thirteenth Amendment challenge by denying the existence of coercion. It suffers, however, several significant flaws.

First, the voluntariness of an agreement to work is doctrinally irrelevant to the Thirteenth Amendment question. Recall that the Supreme Court has rejected any distinction between voluntary and involuntary peonage, holding that the Thirteenth Amendment "denounces a status or condition, irrespective of the manner or authority by which it is created." An appearance of voluntariness is doctrinally irrelevant.

Second, welfare servitude exposes the actual limits of both consent and coercion. Scholars may debate whether freedom is inalienable, but the Thirteenth Amendment, rather than the philosophical debate, settles the question. The Thirteenth Amendment establishes that freedom of contract to labor is inalienable. Thus, the right to one's labor may be bought and sold subject only to the volition of the worker. The Thirteenth Amendment is violated the moment a person is compelled to work against his or her will. The problem with welfare servitude is that it impermissibly compels those who are destitute to perform specific labor in exchange for financial assistance necessary to prevent destitution. Because welfare is an income source of last resort, recipients must either accept welfare and all its conditions or face destitution. When work is required as a condition for welfare, the recipient's "choice" is destitution or welfare with "coercive work." This is not a choice at all, but coercion. Labelling such a dilemma either "choice" or "coercion" does not advance the analysis properly concerned with the degree of coercion involved.

The problem arises when the law presumes consent to work because policymakers do not want welfare recipients to get something for nothing. Comparing the options of persons in the peonage era to that of welfare recipients illustrates the "sham" nature of this "consent." Destitute persons in the peonage era obtained advances from private employers, in exchange for an agreement to work off the advance. To free themselves from their debt, they faced three alternatives: 1) obtain funds sufficient to subsist and pay back the advance; 2) refuse to work and face the legal presumption that they took the advance with the intent to commit fraud; or 3) perform specific labor to work off the advance. The first alternative was unavailable because of their inability to obtain the necessary funds. Because the law presumes that they either intended to repay the advance or committed fraud, the second alternative imposes a legal penalty, in this case criminal prosecution and likely imprisonment. The Supreme Court's holdings prohibited this legal penalty because it coerced destitute persons into the only remaining alternative, working off the advance. The court held that coercion to work by such a legal mechanism violates the Thirteenth Amendment.

Similarly, when contemporary destitute persons lack sufficient resources to provide for their subsistence, they obtain welfare benefits from the government. To free themselves from welfare, they face three similar alternatives: 1) obtain funds to provide for their ongoing subsistence; 2) refuse to work and face termination of benefits; or 3) perform specific labor to work off the welfare. The first alternative is unavailable because they are unable to obtain subsistence funding. Because the law presumes either that they consented to work when they accepted welfare or that they are undeserving of benefits, the second alternative imposes a legal penalty, in this case termination of subsistence benefits. This legal penalty coerces destitute persons into the only remaining alternative, working against their will for welfare. Coercion to work by such a legal mechanism violates the Thirteenth Amendment.

This analysis reveals that the nature of deprivation increases the degree of coercion. For example, most people view welfare as a form of property at best. But termination of welfare benefits deprives recipients of physical liberty because of their inability to care for their physical subsistence needs. Termination of benefits may also be life-threatening. Thus, welfare recipients are vulnerable to coercion because their physical liberty and life may be at stake. In addition, because of the history of racial subjugation and the ongoing reduction of opportunities suffered by people of color, the disproportionate racial impact of welfare termination increases the degree of coercion.

In short, as either a practical or doctrinal matter, the voluntariness argument does not save welfare servitude from Thirteenth Amendment invalidation. Participation in mandatory work that alone stands between welfare recipients and total destitution is neither practically nor legally voluntary. Thus, welfare servitude forces destitute persons to work in violation of the Thirteenth Amendment.

Notes and Questions

1. *Unconstitutional Conditions.* Recall the Unconstitutional Conditions doctrine examined in Chapter 7. The doctrine holds that government may not do indirectly what it may not do directly. Certainly government may not directly compel poor people to work. Can government indirectly compel poor people to work, by requiring such work as a condition of welfare benefits? Why or why not?

2. *Coercion.* To what extent does your view of the constitutionality of work-for-welfare depend on your view of the level of coercion involved? First, is government coercing welfare recipients to perform particular work? Does it matter whether welfare recipients have exhausted every other possible remedy for their financial straits? Second, if coercion is involved, does government have the constitutional power to engage in such coercion? Are you persuaded by the arguments that government's monopoly power over the provision of welfare, and its arguable creation of the poor's government-dependency, make government coercion over poor people inappropriate? Are you persuaded by the argument that the Thirteenth Amendment's protection of decisional autonomy in the context of labor forbids any government interference with any decision about whether to perform particular work?

3. *Work and the Personal Responsibility Act.* The Personal Responsibility and Work Opportunity Reconciliation Act of 1996 imposed a variety of work requirements. Its general work requirement in the Temporary Assistance for Needy Families (TANF) block grant welfare program requires parents to engage in work as soon as the state deems them ready, or no later than after receiving 2 years of benefits. States also are authorized to impose an optional work requirement for TANF recipients to engage in "community service employment" after receiving 2 months of benefits. In the section on child support, Congress authorized states to order an individual who fails to pay child support to participate in such work activities as the state deems appropriate. Do any of these requirements violate the Thirteenth Amendment's prohibition against involuntary servitude?

4. *Commentators on Workfare.* Other commentators have analyzed the wisdom and constitutionality of workfare. *See, e.g.*, James W. Fox, Jr., Liberalism, Democratic Citizenship, and Welfare Reform: The Troubling Case of Workfare, 74 WASHINGTON UNIVERSITY LAW QUARTERLY 103 (1996); Cynthia A. Bailey, *Workfare and Involuntary Servitude--What You Wanted To Know But Were Afraid To Ask,* 15 BOSTON COLLEGE THIRD WORLD LAW JOURNAL 285 (1995).

B. THE LABOR MARKET

1. Discrimination

Teresa L. Amott & Julie A. Matthaei
RACE, GENDER, AND WORK (1991)

The Transformation of Women's Wage Work

The transformation of women's jobs must be viewed within the larger framework of the growth of the U.S. economy. Through a combination of immigration and childbearing, the total U.S. population grew more than seven-fold between 1870 and 1980, from almost 40 million to over 225 million. This population growth helped fuel the rapidly industrializing economy, as the labor force grew from 13 to 98 million. Productivity increases in agriculture, combined with growing employment opportunities in the manufacturing and service sectors, meant that the labor force increasingly shifted from the former to the latter. Totally new jobs were created such as automobile worker and word processor, while others, such as buggy maker and livery-stable keeper, disappeared. Meanwhile, as a growing share of women entered the paid labor force, the workforce became less of a white male preserve. In 1900, white men made up 72 percent of all workers, but by 1980, their share had fallen to less than 50 percent. (See Table 10-1.)

How has the growing participation of white women and people of color in the paid labor force affected racial-ethnic and gender hierarchies? While this movement into paid work brought white women, women of color, and men of color into the same economic arena as white men, as free workers exchanging their labor time for a wage, it did not bring these groups into equality. Even though by 1980 they constituted a minority relative to other groups, white men have continued to monopolize most highly paid and powerful jobs.

Table 10-1
Racial-Ethnic and Gender Composition of the Labor Force, 1900 and 1980

	1900		1980	
	Number	*Percent of Labor Force*	*Number*	*Percent of Labor Force*
Total	29,285,922	100.0	97,639,355	100.0
White Men	21,041,792	71.8	46,916,660	48.1
Men of Color	2,914,323	10.0	9,088,030	9.3
White Women	3,992,797	13.6	33,875,824	34.7
Women of Color	1,337,010	4.6	7,758,841	7.9
White people	25,034,589	85.5	80,792,484	82.7
People of Color	4,251,333	14.5	16,846,871	17.3
Men	23,956,115	81.8	56,004,690	57.4
Women	5,329,807	18.2	41,634,665	42.6

NOTES: 1900 data is gainfully employed persons; 1980 is persons in the labor force. In 1900, whites and people of color include Latinas/os, as racially classified; in 1980, all Latinas/os are counted as people of color. Island Puerto Ricans are not included in these calculations. . . .

As white women and people of color entered the labor market from other labor systems, they found themselves engaged in a struggle for earnings and power in which they were at a disadvantage. Employers commonly used them as a low-wage labor force, often as replacements for or strikebreakers against existing workers. The threatened workers, usually white and/or male, fought to defend their jobs by attacking these less powerful workers. In other instances, when people of color had established a foothold in areas not directly competing with whites, whites reacted with attempts to exclude them, such as the "Great Driving Out" of Chinese in the 1870s, Irish immigrants' displacement of free Black servants and construction workers in the mid-1800s, and southern whites' post-bellum attacks on Black crafts workers and tenant farmers. Whites and men also used their power to maintain their privileged access to education and training, further solidifying their claim on elite jobs.

The operation of gender, class, and racial-ethnic power in the labor market has had two main consequences. First, disempowered groups have been concentrated in jobs with lower pay, less job security, and more difficult and dangerous working conditions. Second, work places have been places of extreme segregation, in which workers have worked in jobs only with members of their same racial-ethnic, gender, and class group, even though the particular racial-ethnic group and gender assigned to a job may have varied across firms and regions.

Within this context, oppressed groups have had to fight, individually and collectively, for economic survival. They have battled for higher wages for their jobs and for access to better jobs, struggling to advance within an inherently unequal structure. In the 1960s and 1970s, for example, the civil rights movement of African Americans, the Chicano student and Red Power movements, and the white feminist movement all incorporated demands for the elimination of discrimination in hiring, promotion, and access to education and training. Struggles to acquire education have been central to both individual and group efforts to break through labor market barriers, and white women and people of color with income and educational privilege have been the first to advance in the hierarchy.

Macroeconomic Changes and the Sex-Race-Typing of Jobs

Macroeconomic cycles--changes in the level of economic activity as a whole--have played an important role in racial-ethnic and gender struggles over jobs. While the U.S. economy has expanded dramatically over the past four centuries, growth has not been stable or smooth, since, like all capitalist economies, the United States experiences cycles of economic activity. During the twentieth century, the U.S. economy has experienced over 15 recessions and two periods of economic crisis. Recessions are short downturns in the economy when unemployment rises and remains at a high level for between one and three years. Longer-term downturns are called depressions or, equivalently, crises of profitability; during a crisis, the profitability of capitalist firms falls. After a recession, the economy recovers, economic growth and production resume, and unemployment falls. A crisis, on the other hand, forces a restructuring of key economic and political institutions before profitability can be restored. After the crisis of the Great Depression, for instance, the U.S. government assumed a more extensive role in regulating employment, banking, and social welfare. The increased spending of World War II also helped the economy emerge from the crisis. The post-war period was a time of nearly unprecedented economic growth, which continued until a new period of crisis set in during the 1970s. Since then, wages have failed to grow and unemployment has remained at high levels.

Those who lose their jobs during downturns function as a cyclical "reserve army of the unemployed." Members of this reserve army are available to be drawn into the labor force during periods of expansion, but can be readily expelled when they are no longer needed. Those who are not in the wage labor force actively looking for work, but who can be drawn into it during economic upturns, constitute a latent reserve army. Because members of the reserve army can be called upon whenever wages threaten to rise, their existence protects the profits of capitalist employers.

White women and people of color have been disproportionately represented in both parts of the reserve army. Their weak political and economic status has meant that they have had more difficulty than white men protecting themselves from expulsion during economic downturns. Further, married women working as full-time homemakers have been an important part of the latent reserve army, drawn into the labor force, for example, during the two World Wars; and expelled at peace time. Finally, foreign workers, most of them of color and male, have been an important part of the reserve army--for example, Mexican workers brought into the U.S. economy by the Bracero Program, and Asians and Puerto Ricans who travelled to the U.S. and Hawaii on contracts as agricultural workers. One recent example from the 1970s was the importation of Filipina workers. Hospitals recruited Filipina nurses under a program which required them to return home after two years.

Thus, job loss during recessions and depressions has not affected all workers, or all occupations, equally. For instance, during the Great Depression, employers fired their domestic servants to save money; since immigrant women and women of color, especially Black women, were disproportionately employed in domestic service, they were hardest hit. Also during that era, falling cotton prices and the collapse of credit pushed many tenant farmer families, again disproportionately Black, off the land. Many employers adopted or strengthened bars against the employment of married women. In contrast, when the recession of the early-1980s decimated the midwestern steel and automobile industries, men, especially men of color, were disproportionately affected. However, in the context of the post-World War II era--characterized by greater labor force participation of married women and the end of the marriage bar--wives increasingly entered the labor force to take up the slack. Indeed, British economist Jane Humphries found that women's employment has been less affected by economic downswings since World War II than it was in the first part of the twentieth century.

Often the process of job loss has been institutionalized in labor market practices that protect those workers with the most seniority. In general the last hired have been the first laid off. During the twentieth century, white women and people of color have gradually gained entrance to occupations from which they previously had been excluded. Since they are thus more likely to be the "last hired" in these jobs than are white men, white women and people of color are more likely to be the "first fired" during an economic downturn.

Furthermore, in severe downturns, as people have lost their jobs, they have searched for work further down the occupational hierarchy, pushing out those beneath them. Often this has meant taking the jobs of a subordinate race or class--although, thus far, job displacement rarely appears to have crossed gender lines. That is, white men have displaced men of color, and white women have displaced women of color. For example, during the 1930s, white women who lost their jobs took the jobs of women of color in domestic service and sales. Already at the bottom of the job hierarchy, Black women had few choices other than to apply for government relief.

If recessions and depressions have tended to be especially hard on white women and people of color, have periods of rapid growth boosted their fortunes? . . . [E]mployers have often made exceptions to their racist and sexist hiring policies during times of rapid employment growth and scarce labor. And, since discrimination has kept oppressed peoples from being employed at levels consistent with their education and training, they represent a reserve of workers who can be drawn out of lower-paid jobs during economic upturns. During wars, military service has taken many men from their usual jobs, and created additional jobs in war industries. Employers' needs for labor, combined with efforts by white women and people of color, sometimes have overruled prejudice by bosses and workers alike. During the Civil War, many women went into teaching, previously a male-dominated profession, to replace men who had been drawn into combat. World War I was a watershed for the employment of Black men and women and white married women. World War II facilitated the entry of Chinese and Filipina/o Americans into white-collar jobs, broke down more barriers against Black employment in industrial and clerical work, and drew more white married women into paid work. While returning servicemen pushed out some of these new workers, these groups had gained many footholds which they were able to maintain in the postwar period. These historical patterns suggest the centrality of a full employment policy--the guarantee of paid work for all who seek it--to an agenda for economic justice in the 1990s.

* * *

[Professors Amott & Matthaei explored the experiences of white women and people of color in several work contexts, including domestic service, new service (such as childcare, food service, and health care assistance), agriculture, manufacturing, clerical work, and professional service. Their analysis of the history of inequality in manufacturing, which follows, explores their broader arguments in specific context.]

Manufacturing Inequality

As capitalism developed in the United States, labor shifted out of agriculture and domestic service into manufacturing. Manufacturing itself gradually changed from predominantly skilled craft and artisan work to unskilled and semi-skilled factory work.

By 1900, manufacturing made up approximately one-fourth of total employment. There was great variation in the proportions of women and men workers of the different racial-ethnic groups who were employed in manufacturing occupations. Among women, more than one-fourth of European American, American Indian, and Chinese American women held manufacturing jobs, while for Japanese American, island Puerto Rican, and African American women, the share in manufacturing was much lower, as shown in Table 10-8. Among men, only European Americans held more than their labor market share of manufacturing jobs; men of color remained relatively concentrated in agriculture. Thus, in 1900, manufacturing jobs sill represented a white preserve from which most men and women of color were excluded.

Table 10-8
Share of Employed Women Working in Manufacturing, by Racial-Ethnic Group, 1900-1980

	1900	1930	1960	1980
African American	2.6	8.4	15.5	18.4
European American	32.6	21.2	18.5	12.6
American Indian	24.9	37.6	18.1	17.0
Chinese American	41.1	20.8	24.0	20.8
Japanese American	7.7	12.2	19.0	12.5
Filipina American	n.a.	15.3	17.4	13.8
Chicana	n.a.	24.7	29.1	26.0
U.S. Puerto Rican	n.a.	n.a.	69.3	29.1
Island Puerto Rican	14.6	52.4	31.3	22.0

NOTES: Asian American data include Hawaii for all years; 1980 data for American Indians include Eskimo and Aleut peoples; for 1900-1960, African American and European American include Latinas.

Particular manufacturing occupations were typed by gender and/or by race-ethnicity. For example, skilled garment making--performed by dressmakers, seamstresses, shirt collar and cuff makers, tailors and tailoresses--was a job undertaken by women of all racial-ethnic groups, often in their own homes. Women made up 78 percent of these workers in 1900, and only African American women had less than their labor market share. European American women had five times their share (with immigrant women more likely to be so employed than U.S.-born), American Indian women four times, and Japanese American and Chinese American at least twice. Needlework jobs were also important for Puerto Rican and Chicana women.

In contrast, in 1900, textile mill operatives were almost exclusively white, and about half men and half women. White men held less than their labor market share of these jobs (since they could find more lucrative jobs), while white women held more than three times their labor market share. Within the mills, jobs were typed according to sex and ethnicity. European immigrants, especially Irish, Italian, English, and Welsh, had relative concentrations in mill jobs higher than did U.S. born whites. On the other hand, no group of men or women of color had achieved more than one-twentieth of their labor market share of textile mill jobs, which paid considerably more than the agricultural and domestic service jobs into which they were crowded.

A third set of jobs was monopolized by white males: traditional masculine crafts, such as carpentry, masonry, plumbing, blacksmithing, cabinet-making, and machine-making (machinists). In all these jobs, European American men maintained a near monopoly.

* * *

[M]any slave men, trained in these crafts, were prevented by white men from practicing their trades by white men after Emancipation. However, this exclusion worked unevenly: in 1900, African American men held about their labor market share of masonry and plastering jobs, a little less than half their share of carpentry and blacksmithing, and only about one-tenth their share of plumbing and machinist jobs. No other group of men held even half its labor market share, although Chinese American, Japanese American and American Indian men had a significant part of their shares in carpentry and blacksmithing. Women of all racial-ethnic groups were the most excluded from the crafts, with none receiving more than six percent of their labor market share. Exclusion was costly since the crafts were generally much higher-paid than other manufacturing jobs.

Between 1900 and 1980, as the economy grew and changed, the number of manufacturing jobs quadrupled and manufacturing's share of total employment increased. Women's manufacturing employment also quadrupled, but women's total employment grew even faster, so the share of women in manufacturing fell. However, the decline in women's manufacturing employment was very uneven across racial-ethnic groups. Only among white women was there a smooth decline, as white women found better-paid jobs as sales, clerical, and professional and managerial workers. Not until the mid-twentieth century did Black women gain entry to manufacturing, as a result of organizing, war-time labor shortages, and white women's exodus. Very high percentages of Puerto Rican women have been employed in manufacturing, both in Puerto Rico and in the United States, at rates which have fluctuated widely with the movement of firms in and out of Puerto Rico or New York.

If we look at the overall pattern, an interesting change is clear. In 1900, when manufacturing represented a relatively good job, white women's share was greater than that of most women of color. In contrast, in 1980, most women of color, other than Japanese Americans, had higher participation in manufacturing than white women. This signifies not a reversal of the racial-ethnic hierarchy, but the movement of white women into higher-paid, higher-status jobs such as clerical and professional work.

Since 1970, overall U.S. employment in manufacturing (excluding construction) has fallen in absolute terms as a result of a combination of factors, including productivity increases, the transfer of plants abroad, and competition from foreign producers. The decline has taken a disproportionate toll on women of color, for many of whom unionized manufacturing jobs offered steady income. New immigrant women, speaking Spanish or other languages, are particularly affected by the loss of manufacturing jobs, since white-collar work demands English-language proficiency.

With factory jobs in decline, employers have increasingly relied on two forms of manufacturing work common in the nineteenth and early twentieth century, sweatshops and industrial homework. Now, as then, these jobs employ a disproportionate number of immigrant women. . . . [M]any Southeast Asian refugee women, undocumented Mexican immigrant women, and recent Chinese immigrant women are finding employment in the newly resurgent sweatshops. Industrial homework--manufacturing work contracted out to workers in their own homes--has also been on the rise. For employers, homework offers freedom from unionization, government regulations, and overhead costs. Women, on the other hand, turn to homework in the hopes of combining work and family, or because no other work is available. Under the Reagan administration, regulations prohibiting homework were disbanded. As a result, capitalists are opting to locate more work in workers' homes and have expanded the range of manufacturing jobs contracted out to homeworkers, including electronic component assembly as well as the traditional garment work.

Today, as in the past, women of different racial-ethnic groups are unevenly represented in different manufacturing jobs. Garment work--both by dressmakers and by sewing machine operators--continues to be female-dominated. However, Black women are no longer excluded and now hold more than twice their labor market share of these jobs; Asian American women and Latinas each have five to six times their labor market share, while white women have twice theirs.

On the other hand, as a result of the anti-discrimination struggles of the past twenty years, women and people of color are gaining entrance into craft occupations. The most significant improvement has been for men of color. For example, in the three white male crafts we looked at in 1900, plumbing, carpentry, and machine-making, Black, American Indian, and Latino men all now have more than their labor market share, as do white men. On the other hand, women of all racial-ethnic groups have no more than one-third of their labor market share; these crafts, then, shifted from white-male-dominated to male-dominated. Women of color are doing better than white women in the crafts: Chicana, Japanese American, Puerto Rican, Filipina, and American Indian women have the highest proportion of their labor market share in craft work, ranging from 31 to 24 percent respectively, with white women at 17 percent of their labor market share. Since craft work offers relatively high-paying and secure employment to people who cannot afford higher education, it is not surprising that women of color, who have less access to education, choose this route to economic security.

The Persistence of Racial-Ethnic, Gender, and Class Hierarchies in the Labor Market

One way to quantify the persistence of racial-ethnic and gender hierarchies is to look at earnings and income inequality. Table 10-13 presents median incomes for 1980. Unfortunately, earnings data are not available in detailed racial-ethnic categories; the best data available are median incomes of full-time, full-year workers (which do closely approximate earnings). The striking progress of Asian Americans, who now surpass whites in many income categories, is evident.

Table 10-13
Median Incomes of Full-Time, Full-Year Workers, by Gender and Race-Ethnicity, 1980

	Women	Men	W/M	W/EAM
European American	$10,564	$18,157	58%	58%
African American	9,589	12,677	76	53
Chicana/o	8,616	12,623	68	47
U.S. Puerto Rican	9,390	12,108	78	52
Island Puerto Rican	6,452	7,218	89	36
American Indian	9,350	14,034	67	51
Japanese American	11,916	20,262	59	66
Chinese American	11,891	17,945	66	65
Filipina/o American	12,007	15,101	80	66

NOTES: EAM equals European American men. American Indian includes Eskimo and Aleut peoples.

Women workers' incomes ranged from 58 percent to 89 percent of men's, according to racial-ethnic group. The male-female gap is the largest for European American and Japanese American women because the men in these groups earn such high incomes. Racial-ethnic differences in median incomes for full-time, full-year workers were also substantial in 1980: island Puerto Rican men's median incomes stood at only 36 percent of Japanese American men's. When race, ethnicity, and gender are combined, the full import of the labor market hierarchy on workers' incomes is clear: the highest median income (Japanese American men) was over three times the lowest (island Puerto Rican women).

Even these data underestimate the full extent of gender and racial-ethnic inequality in incomes because they ignore the role of part-time work and unemployment. In each racial-ethnic group, fewer women worked full-time than did men, largely as a result of women's continuing responsibility for unpaid work. Comparing median incomes of all women and men with incomes (not just full-time, full-year workers), we find that the incomes of island Puerto Rican women stood at a meager one-fifth that of white men and Japanese American men. Unemployment rates also varied substantially across groups, as shown in Table 10-14, and were highest for those racial-ethnic groups on the bottom of the income hierarchy. Unemployment rates for Chicanas/os, African Americans, American Indians, and Puerto Ricans all ranged from one and one-half to over five times higher than those for Asian American and white men and women.

Table 10-14
Unemployment Rates, by Race-Ethnicity and Gender, 1980

	Women	Men
American Indian	11.9%	14.1%
European American	5.6	5.8
African American	11.3	12.3
Chicana/o	9.9	8.7
Chinese American	4.1	3.2
Japanese American	3.3	2.7
Filipina/o American	4.6	5.1
U.S. Puerto Rican	12.7	11.1
Island Puerto Rican	16.4	14.4
Highest/Lowest	5.0	4.5

NOTE: American Indian includes Eskimo and Aleut peoples.

Together, lower earnings and higher unemployment rates created shocking differences in per capita income and poverty rates across racial-ethnic groups in 1980, as shown in Table 10-15. Among American Indians, African Americans, Chicanas/os, and both U.S. and island Puerto Ricans, incomes per person were less than three-fifths those of European Americans. Poverty rates varied widely, from a low of 6.5 percent to a high of 62 percent; for non-Asian people of color, the share which lived in poverty was from two and one-half to seven times higher than that for whites. At least 6 percent of each racial-ethnic group, and one-quarter or more of non-Asian people of color, live in poverty. Since these data represent the share in poverty at one time, a much larger share experiences poverty at some time in their lives.

The twentieth century has been a time of significant movement in the direction of greater economic justice, particularly during the 1960s and 1970s. However, our progress has been countered by a strong reaction from the wealthy and powerful, who wish to leave the economy to the "invisible hand" of the market, with its legacy of race, class, and gender oppression. If we are to defend past gains, and move further towards economic justice, we must "seek beyond history" for a truly inclusive movement for economic justice.

* * *

Table 10-15
Per Capita Income and Poverty Rates, by Racial-Ethnic Group, 1980

	Per Capita Income	Poverty Rates
Japanese American	$9,068	6.5%
European American	7,942	8.9
Chinese American	7,476	13.5
Filipina/o American	6,915	7.1
American Indian	4,618	27.6
African American	4,556	29.8
Chicana/o	4,231	23.3
U.S. Puerto Rican	3,905	36.3
Island Puerto Rican	2,126	62.4

NOTE: American Indian includes Eskimo and Aleut peoples.

Notes and Questions

1. *Inferior Working Conditions.* Teresa Amott & Julie Matthaei argued that, despite enormous changes in the American job market, historically disadvantaged groups remained "concentrated in jobs with lower pay, less job security, and more difficult and dangerous working conditions." What factors caused this concentration of disadvantaged groups in jobs with inferior working conditions? How did this concentration occur in the manufacturing industry?

2. *Segregation.* Professors Amott & Matthaei also argued that employees worked in jobs with members of their same racial-ethnic, gender, and class group, even though the group performing a job sometimes changed over time. What factors caused this segregation of workers? How did this segregation occur in the manufacturing industry?

3. *Full Employment.* Should the economic policies implemented through various laws be aimed toward full employment, meaning "the guarantee of paid work for all who seek it," as Amott & Matthaei suggest.

4. *Income Inequality.* According to data from the United States Census Bureau, income varied greatly by gender and race due to markedly different earnings and unemployment rates. The lower earnings and higher unemployment rates of people of color as compared to whites, and of women as compared to men, reflect what Professors Amott & Matthaei call "the persistence of racial-ethnic, gender, and class hierarchies in the labor market." Given that these data are from full-time, full-year workers, can they be explained by differing work efforts? Do these data reveal intentional efforts to advantage some workers at the expense of others? Perhaps more to the point, of what relevance is the debate over whether these results stemmed from intentional effort, if the market continues to produce such unequal results? If these data merely reveal the current effects of discriminatory past practices, how should law take the continuing inequality into account? What implications do these data raise for the debate about whether equal opportunity includes an ongoing need for affirmative action for disadvantaged groups?

5. *The Impact of Economic Downturns.* Recessions and depressions do not impact workers equally, but hit the workers at the lowest echelons the hardest, causing their temporary or chronic unemployment. White women and people of color tend to be overrepresented among the lowest status workers, resulting in disproportionate harm to these groups during economic downturns. What implications does this information raise for economic policy? Is it fair for legal policy to treat workers equally if economic forces treat them unequally? Should law account for the unequal harm suffered by various workers?

2. Economic Instability

Fran Ansley

STANDING RUSTY AND ROLLING EMPTY:
LAW, POVERTY AND AMERICA'S ERODING INDUSTRIAL BASE
81 GEORGETOWN LAW JOURNAL 1757, 1763-84 (1993)

* * *

Plant closings are not a new phenomenon. Businesses fail and relocate all the time; such is and has been a normal and expected fact of life in our economic system. Old jobs disappear. New and different ones replace them.

The recent spate of plant closings, however, is both quantitatively and qualitatively different. The number and size of closings, as well as their frequency (what some have called the "velocity" of change) have all increased rapidly. Further, there are disturbing patterns in the types of jobs lost and the types of jobs gained. These trends and a number of other potent interrelated characteristics distinguish today's plant closings from those of the past.

First, new technologies and information systems, coupled with the increasingly concentrated and transnational character of many business enterprises, have resulted in an astonishing level of global interconnection and interdependence. Corporate management can oversee far-flung operations and stay in close touch with outposts that are only a fax away. Investments can be altered, and capital redirected, with an ease and dispatch that was barely thinkable only a few years ago. Meanwhile, the long-term trend toward greater concentration of corporate ownership has continued and accelerated. One report noted, "By 1980 more than 70 percent of all private economic activity was controlled and operated by eight hundred conglomerate firms, while the remaining 30 percent was shared by 14 million firms."

Along with the ability to move capital fast and far has come the will to do so. A powerful tendency has emerged for managers and investors to seek the highest possible short-term returns on investment, and to display less and less commitment to any underlying product, place, or group of employees. Many plants are closed not because they fail to make a profit, but because they fail to make *enough* profit to hold the decisionmaker's interest when compared to some other marginally more profitable opportunity. When management fails to reinvest and modernize, productivity and profit margins most often *do* decline, thereby reinforcing the initial, casual decisions whose rhetoric often either places blame at the feet of labor, or speaks of these developments as if they constituted some natural and inevitable evolutionary path beyond anyone's control.

Fueling and being fueled by this trend is the related explosion of mergers and acquisitions, many of which are quickly followed by downsizings, mass layoffs, and plant closings. More profit can often be made in less time by orchestrating a leveraged buyout than by managing the concrete manufacture of an actual product. The managerial culture of this merger "frenzy," with its emphasis on deal-driven profits over productivity or equity, has been noted with dismay and alarm by observers as diverse as the presidents of the United Auto Workers and of Harvard University. While there are signs that the frenzy may have slowed somewhat, concern and debate about its significance continue.

Another new feature of the wave of present plant closings that distinguishes it from closings of the past is direction. The nature of economic investment and activity within the United States has dramatically shifted away from industrial production and toward service-based enterprises. The pool of blue-collar jobs in traditionally unionized sectors is shrinking, while the pool of white-collar and service jobs is expanding. Union membership has declined from a postwar high of nearly forty percent in the mid-1950s, to its present startling level close to fifteen percent, leaving the vast majority of the U.S. work force unorganized. One projection has U.S. union membership falling to five percent by the year 2000.

Entire regions of the country whose economic and cultural personalities had been identified with particular industries for decades have stood in shock while owners shut down and pulled out. Social activist and labor attorney Staughton Lynd recalls the aftermath of the massive steel mill closings in Ohio and Pennsylvania:

> The collapse of the steel industry in Youngstown, Pittsburgh and other communities of the industrial heartland disrupted the implicit social contract that had existed in these towns for a generation. . . . The [union] vice-president . . . said: "Most people couldn't

> believe it. It was so huge and had operated so long and so many people depended on it for their livelihood." More than one steelworker in Youngstown indicated that the only thing they had experienced like it was Pearl Harbor.

This pattern of national deindustrialization leads to a more severe impact of today's plant closings upon both workers and communities, than if the closings took place in an environment of continued industrial vigor. If entire occupations and industries are disappearing, then finding a new job or revitalizing a local tax base after a plant closing become risky propositions at best. Thus, present economic trends work both to increase the number of plant closings and to make their impact on workers and communities more severe.

A third feature of current economic developments that affects the impact and meaning of plant closings is the growth of what some observers are calling the "contingent work force." Increasing numbers of workers do not enjoy the relatively thick and stable set of obligations and expectations that we have come to associate with a "regular job" in this society. Although such relationships have never been available to all workers, it is fair to say that the presumed workplace norm for white male wage earners has been full-time, relatively long-term, and accompanied by a cluster of inadequate, but still quite meaningful, protections. Some of these protections, such as unemployment and workers' compensation, pension regulation, health and safety standards, and antidiscrimination rules, were mandated by law. Others, such as good cause requirements for termination, seniority benefits, and retirement, were generally won through collective bargaining. General market and societal pressures yielded still other protections (such as sick leave and vacation, certain weaker forms of seniority, and health insurance) even at unorganized job sites.

Shifts in the economy and management strategies have begun to throw into question whether traditional notions of "a steady job" accurately describe most workers' relationship to paid employment today. Even ignoring those who are unemployed, the proportion of workers who have what we might call a "core" employment relationship to their employer has significantly declined in recent years. At the same time, the proportion of those involved in part-time work, temporary work, employee leasing arrangements, and independent contracting relationships is on the rise. Whether this trend is good or bad for the U.S. economy is subject to dispute. Some see it as providing a desirable flexibility for employers and employees alike. Others are highly critical, pointing to decreased benefits, wages, and job security for employees and to a general deterioration in the social fabric.

Another important segment of the contingent work force is made up of undocumented workers, a group whose outlines are defined by the Immigration Reform and Control Act of 1986 (IRCA). Although examination of that statute is well beyond the scope of this article, it is worth noting IRCA's role in creating a new subclass of undocumented workers, starkly unprotected and excluded on most fronts from the norms of aboveground employment relationships. Such employees often lack even the most rudimentary understanding of their legal rights, are vulnerable to exploitation, and are all but invisible to most of the citizenry. Moreover, the group represents one more element in the growing group of workers who are given a place not quite inside the employment circle, but rather in the anterooms, the kitchens, the backyards, the bordellos, the shanty towns, the hideouts of the fringe.

A fourth distinctive feature of the economic environment that surrounds plant closings today is the high degree of competition and division that exists among different workers struggling for jobs or for enhanced job security, and among different governmental bodies struggling for a more stable and prosperous economic base. As prior foundations of economic security erode, and managers call for increased management flexibility and mobility, workers and communities that want to keep or attract jobs are told they must compete with fellow workers next door and halfway around the world, as well as compete with other towns, counties, or nations. Many other reform efforts directed at corporate behavior are met with the same threat.

Although the legal ability to move investments at will has value in its own right for management, in the current climate it also is fast becoming a powerful source of leverage in employers' dealings with employees and communities on a whole range of issues. For instance, the threat of plant shutdowns has become one of the hottest tools in management's arsenal of employment relations strategies. It can serve as a club to force concessions from an established union, or the bugaboo with which to chill and defeat a union election campaign.

In today's economy, such threats are often not idle ones. Given the relative openness of the U.S. economy, American corporations are under pressure from competitors (both foreign and domestic) who are taking advantage of low-cost labor in other countries. Workers are well aware of the real possibility of capital redeployment. Fear and grudging subservience are often the result.

The threat of a plant closing sometimes pits workers at one of the company's plants against fellow workers at another in a race to see which is able to concede the most or increase productivity the fastest in order to avoid a shutdown. Whether or not management actually bases its eventual closing decision on the concessions won during this hotbox phase, it is usually happy to reap the benefits of the dynamic. On other occasions, a company may move (or threaten to move) work to a nonunion plant, thus pitting union workers against nonunion workers and making the implicit statement that the union should stop representing its members so aggressively. In still other instances, the workers who are pitted against each other are from different countries. The contradictions and inequities of the global division of labor and resources come home to roost as American workers are told they must compete against employees receiving third world wages or fail to make the grade and lose the work.

In all these situations, the relative immobility of workers and unions as compared with the increasing mobility of capital puts workers at a severe disadvantage, a disadvantage that management has been quick to exploit. Such corporate behavior can, of course, be characterized in different ways. What some see as brutal and destructive greed, others see as a necessary, even desperate, response to competitive pressure, and still others would characterize as a welcome, rational set of decisions that will help to move the economy toward a freer and more efficient market.

In addition to workers and their organizations, governments as well are often pressured to join a race to the bottom in order to hold or attract industrial investment. Governmental actors at the federal level worry about economic competition with other jurisdictions and demonstrate concern about holding and attracting investment capital within geopolitical boundaries. For instance, during debates on the federal Worker Adjustment and Retraining Notification Act (WARN), which requires employers to give sixty days advance notice of plant closings under certain circumstances, opponents of mandatory notice argued that it was important to maintain a national "proinvestment" climate in order to keep and increase investment in the United States. Interestingly, these opponents must have presumed that our "peers" in this competition for capital are third world countries, because other industrialized nations have overwhelmingly embraced the mandatory notice idea.

The picture at the federal level is made more complex by the fact that federal government actors pursue political and military foreign policy objectives, not just economic ones. The United States assumption of the role of international superpower, with the accompanying pressure for it to play a stabilizing role in the global economy, and the associated blurring of "national" and "global" interests, has complicated the calculus. Federal decisionmakers must take more into account in policy development than the health of the domestic economy.

There is the further complication that many U.S. companies now function multinationally and are no longer tied to the fortunes of any particular nation, although they are nevertheless interested in "their" government's aid in pursuing extraterritorial investment on favorable terms. Numerous federal statutes and regulations function to allow and sometimes reward U.S. investment *outside* the United States. These programs are sometimes defended as benevolence toward underdeveloped nations; at other times they may be depicted as part of a strategy for enhancing the competitiveness of "our" corporations.

* * *

The federal government displays a similar schizophrenia with regard to direct foreign investment in the United States. On the one hand, leaders are hungry for investment capital, regardless of its source. On the other hand, many are queasy about the potential impact on national sovereignty. The extent to which direct foreign investment by multinationals headquartered abroad is significantly different from investment by multinationals headquartered in the United States is a question that has only begun to be explored. Although the federal government's role in the international competition to attract investment capital is in some ways analogous to the role of state and local governments in the national competition for plants, there are differences as well.

State and local governments are subject to severe competitive pressures in the struggle to attract and retain capital investment. The "globalization" of the economy coupled with a precipitously declining role in development activities by the federal government has left states and municipalities unshielded and unfettered on a stage that is increasingly international. As one commentator has observed, "State, county and municipal governments increasingly are on their own in assisting . . . local economies to compete directly in the world economy. Regions of the United States used to see themselves in competition with other regions of the country. Now, they are also in competition with regions throughout the world."

This competition can be fierce whether it is across municipal, state, or national boundaries. As state and local governments have scrambled to join the "development" game, many of them have struggled to outbid each other in making attractive offers to industry. Governments typically are authorized by statute to assemble incentive packages, which may include tax breaks, industrial development bonds, infrastructure improvements, and more. The volume of such public contributions to corporate welfare has been on the rise, even while their effectiveness at generating or maintaining employment has been challenged with increasing sophistication from within and without the development establishment.

The most flamboyant examples of local competition for economic development involve the public courtship of a large out-of-state or out-of-country manufacturer. If the courting is successful, then with much fanfare and hoopla the lucky governmental winner of the bidding war ushers the corporate bridegroom into its new home, amid rosy promises of future employment and economic growth, and with ample photo opportunities for the players who count. After the honeymoon, many localities unfortunately find the marriage falls short of their original hopes and expectations.

Too many states and localities are currently engaged in the "race to the bottom." They are competing for how much they can arrange for their local citizens to give away in subsidies, lower wages, and damage to the environment, not how much they can be sure of gaining in return; they are competing for how fearful and meagerly paid, not how skilled and secure, the work force of their state or area is going to be. Admittedly, local governments are often responding to forces over which they have little control. Nevertheless, even within current parameters, a more democratic and egalitarian understanding of development, both as a goal and as a process, would suggest a very different approach.

The changes taking place in our national and global economies are open-ended and fraught with possibilities. Traditional American economic dominance and popular isolationism are being challenged in new and powerful ways, and such challenges can sometimes produce ugly results. Given the increased hate group activity and xenophobia that exist, it is not fanciful to worry that deindustrialization might feed a backlash against those pushing for more opportunities for the poor; more access for the excluded; and other changes in racial, ethnic, and gender hierarchies.

The recent rise in violence directed against various target groups is well- documented. Such outbreaks frequently track in time and place the declining economic fortunes of working class whites, as well as other cultural and economic shifts that cause people to feel threatened by forces that seem beyond their control. The epidemic of family violence directed primarily against women and children also seems to bear at least some significant relationship to the economic climate.

Despite the dangers, the changes in our national and global economies also open up opportunities. A global economy creates all kinds of opportunity for greater understanding and solidarity across many boundaries of race, gender, language, culture, and geography. American and Third World workers are increasingly employed by the same entities, confronted with the same explanations for the hardships they experience in daily life, and are in a position to see more clearly than ever before their common problems and interests.

Interpenetrations are occurring on many levels. American capital flows abroad. Foreign investments flow into the United States. American jobs go to super-exploited Third World workers. Super-exploited Third World workers come to American jobs. These kinds of changes are disorienting and can produce fearful reactions, but may also create new friends. Much will depend on whether those interested in the welfare of poor and working people can develop and communicate an effective critique of economic arrangements and policies, and can convincingly articulate an alternative to them.

* * *

Notes and Questions

1. *The Changing Economy.* Fran Ansley provides a provocative critique of changes currently sweeping our economy. First, she argued that capital is increasingly mobile, allowing buy-outs, downsizings, and closings with ease. Second, she noted the shift from an industrial to a service-based economy. Third, she observed the growth of the contingent work force, remarkable for the instability of workers. Fourth, she decries the competitive race to the bottom among governments attempting to appease companies seeking the lowest worker costs. Finally, she compares the rising xenophobia and violence with the emerging opportunities for greater connection and solidarity, both resulting from the increasing globalization of the economy. How persuasive are Professor Ansley's argument that the economy is undergoing fundamental changes? What implications do these changes have for workers generally, and for poor people in particular?

2. *An Alternative Vision.* Professor Ansley suggests "a more democratic and egalitarian understanding of development"--what might that entail? Have advocates for the poor and working classes articulated a feasible alternative vision of economic relationships? If so, what is it? If not, how should such a task be approached? Consider the following remarks of the Clinton Administration's Secretary of Labor.

Robert B. Reich
THE REVOLT OF THE ANXIOUS CLASS
SPEECH TO DEMOCRATIC LEADERSHIP COUNCIL (1994)

What so many Americans find shocking about today's economy is the seeming randomness of their fates. On a recent national poll, 55 percent of American adults said they no longer believe that you can build a better life for yourself and your family by working hard and playing by the rules. Of those without college degrees, fully 68 percent no longer believe it--because they have been working hard, and they are still falling behind.

This isn't the way it's supposed to be in America. Unlike more fatalistic cultures, Americans have always had a deep faith that effort will be rewarded, that you reap what you sow--in other words, that you earn your fate. If you work hard and play by the rules, you'll get ahead. That was the bargain. For generations, Americans have believed in that bargain, guided their lives by it, passed it on to their children. It's woven deep into the fabric of our culture. It sounds like an economic equation, but it's more than that: It's an implicit moral compact. The conviction that you earn your own fate forms the bedrock for the American ethic of individual worth and accountability.

In the years after World War Two, America built the biggest middle class in history on the foundation of that bargain. We turned our hard work into homes and cars, health care and pensions. The middle class grew, enlarged and enriched still further, as the barriers of race and class and gender slowly began to fall. Poverty reached an historic low. And the sense of possibility grew stronger.

But then something happened. Around 15 years ago, this American dream began to fade. And as it faded, middle class families tried every means of holding on: spouses went to work; both parents worked longer hours or took multiple jobs; they decided to have fewer kids and have them later; they drew down their savings. But as economist Frank Levy has pointed out, middle class families have pushed these coping mechanisms about as far as they can go. And they still feel they are losing the dream.

We are on the way to becoming a two-tiered society composed of a few winners and a larger group left behind, whose anger and disillusionment is easily manipulated. Once unbottled, mass resentment can poison the moral integrity of a nation, replacing ambition with envy, tolerance with hate. Today the targets of rage are immigrants, welfare mothers, government officials, gays, and an ill-defined "counter-culture." As the middle class continues to erode, who will be the targets tomorrow?

All of which raises the central question: Why is it no longer the case that working hard and playing by the rules reaps a just reward? Why is the middle class fragmenting? Simply this: hard work is not enough any more, because two emerging forces have rewritten the rules. The first is technology--largely computer based--which has either eradicated or devalued every routine job which can be done by a software program, and simultaneously enriched every job utilizing the problem-solving skills of the human brain. The second force is global competition, which has reinforced the same trends, imperiling the jobs of those who must compete with low-wage workers elsewhere on the planet, while rewarding those better equipped to take advantage of new markets for American insights and skills. And we cannot overlook labor unions, whose decline accounts for as much as 20 percent of the increase in wage inequality among American men.

There is another reason, more difficult to quantify but probably no less important: the breaching of the postwar bargain between companies and their employees. It used to be that as companies became more productive and more profitable, employees who worked hard and proved their loyalty could count on steady jobs with rising pay and better benefits. No more.

All the old bargains, it seems, have been breached. The economic bargain was that if you worked hard and your company prospered, you would share the fruits of success. There was a cultural bargain, too, echoing the same strong themes of responsibility and its rewards: live by the norms of your community--take care of your family, obey the law, treat your neighbors with respect, love your country--and you'd feel secure in the certainty that everyone else would behave the same way.

How can we get it back? How can we reconstruct our basic bargains? How can we reverse the erosion of the middle class and the meltdown of our moral core?

It cannot be done by trying to turn back the tides of history--stopping technological advances or seceding from the global economy. Even were such a neo-Luddite strategy possible, it wouldn't rescue those who are falling behind, only drag everyone down with them.

* * *

Another choice is conceding that more and more of our wealth will be created by a shrinking number of economic superstars, and then trying to save the middle class by redistributing some of the winners' bounty to the also-rans. Nations have pursued this path for a time, but it is hard to follow forever, and it has never been comfortable for Americans.

Others say the solution is far simpler: cut taxes and lift the burden of a government which is stifling the middle class. There is no dispute that taxes should be as low as possible, and that government should not spend a single citizen's dollar more than it must. The American voter wants a leaner government, to be sure. But let's not delude ourselves or attempt to delude the nation: federal income taxes cannot account for the decline of the middle class. Federal taxes--even including the growing social-security burden on average workers--took 19.8 percent of middle-income families' earnings in 1980, and take 19.6 percent today.

Some argue similarly that massive tax cuts for the rich will somehow restore the middle class. The claim is that while they may not lift middle-class incomes directly, trickle-down tax cuts, even on the sale of assets that investors already own, will ignite an economic surge that will boost profits and incomes. We have heard this before. In the 1980s, this country ran one of history's most expensive experiments to test this theory. We learned that public deficits can spur a temporary boom, at the price of long-term indebtedness. The rich got richer. Everyone else's income stagnated or declined. And to this day we are paying the bill. Interest on the debt America accumulated under the prior two Presidents alone accounts for $162 billion a year. The dead weight of this burden claims 28 cents of every dollar individuals pay in taxes today.

* * *

The only enduring solution is to equip every American to succeed through hard work--under the new rules. It used to be enough to keep your shoulder to the wheel and be loyal to your employer. But the rules have changed. Now you need to make your own way in the economy, learn new skills throughout your career, be ready to apply them in new ways and in new settings.

Can you get ahead if you play by these new rules? Absolutely. Do the new rules define enough good jobs to support a new middle class? Without a doubt. There is no limit to the ingenuity of Americans, no limit to the opportunities for creating value. A salesclerk who taps PCs to monitor sales and replenish inventories, and who advises customers on the variety of ways to meet the customers' needs, adds substantial value; as does an auto mechanic who can repair the electronic gadgetry under the hood, or the operator of a desktop publishing program who devises new graphic layouts, or the factory worker who reprograms a computer-controlled machine tool for finer tolerances and quicker setups, or the secretary who orchestrates a sophisticated spreadsheet program. In the emerging economy, every job can become more valuable; every person, more valued.

Contrary to some theorists, our destinies do not reside in our genes. Study after study shows that skills can be learned. Every year of education or job training beyond high school--whenever it occurs in one's life--increases average future earnings by 6 to 12 percent. GNP is not simply a matter of DNA. Most Americans are on a downward slide not because of some genetic deficiencies, but because they lack the learnable skills to prosper in an economy convulsing with change.

We know we cannot resurrect the old middle class of the first decades after World War Two. The economy has changed forever. What we can do is clear the way for a new middle class -- a middle class equipped to master the realities of the new economy, at least as large but more inclusive than the vast middle class of our younger days. A new middle class with plenty of room for people who play by the rules, without requiring a four-year college degree as the entry ticket. A new middle class that rests on a refinement of the old American bargain: You take responsibility for working hard, you get a chance to work smart.

The private sector has a critical role to play in creating this new middle class. It won't happen unless companies invest heavily in training their workers to use new technologies, and give them authority to make decisions. This is not a matter of charity. The best companies in America, large and small . . . are treating their employees as assets to be developed rather than as costs to be cut. Some are also sharing with their workers the upside gains of the enterprise as well as the downside risks, converting a portion of wages into a share of the profits.

* * *

Mark my words: If American industry fails to forge such a compact with their workers, it will jeopardize American competitiveness in decades to come. If American business continues to pursue short-term profits at the price of insecurity and falling living standards for a large portion of our society, it will sooner or later reap the bitter harvest of popular rage. The American public is basically pro-business. But that support rests on an implicit bargain. And business betrays that bargain every time it fires an older worker in order to hire a younger one at a lower wage, provides gold-plated health insurance to top executives while denying its workers health coverage, labels employees independent contractors in order to avoid paying them full-time wages and benefits, or discards its workers rather than invest in them when profits are booming.

But it's not realistic--it's not even responsible--to expect business to carry the whole burden. All of us have a stake in rebuilding the middle class, creating ladders into it from the underclass, and restoring the reward for working hard and playing by the rules. If the rules have changed because of advanced technologies and global competitors, then this nation has a moral obligation to help all Americans who are willing to work hard prosper under the new rules.

* * *

If this society is to reverse the long decline in living standards of American workers, a far bolder strategy is necessary. First, to be sure, let's accelerate the agenda of reform: streamline and consolidate the current clutter of adult education and job-training programs, and pull the plug on programs that don't work. But reform is no longer enough--we need to reinvent lifelong learning. Instead of feeding the budgets of bureaucracies--federal or state--let's channel resources directly into the pockets of ordinary Americans so they can get the skills they need -- at the time, in the place, and in the way that makes sense for them. In other words, let's put people first. And finally, let's make sure that Americans have up-to-date information on what skills are in demand and likely to stay in demand, and where they can get those skills.

How to pay for this, on the scale required to reverse the downward slide? The federal budget is already strained. The DLC's Progressive Policy Institute has suggested at least one possibility--one that squares with the voters' distaste for halfway approaches. It has compiled a formidable list of special tax benefits for particular industries, totaling over $111 billion over 5 years. Since we are committed to moving the disadvantaged from welfare to work, why not target corporate welfare as well, and use the savings to help all Americans get better work? Ending corporate welfare as we know it is a worthy goal, made all the worthier if it frees funds for investments in workers. "Welfare to work," in the fullest meaning of this phrase--including cuts in corporate welfare to pave the way to better work--offers a powerful theme for the 104th Congress.

Notes and Questions

1. *Politics.* Robert Reich was President Clinton's Secretary of Labor when he delivered this speech to the Democratic Leadership Council. To what broader constituency did Secretary Reich address his remarks? Who are the good and bad players in Reich's view? Does he sound moderate and mainstream? Do you think that was his intent?

2. *Reasons for the Revolt.* Secretary Reich lamented the anxiety suffered by the hard-working middle class. He cited several factors contributing to their sense of insecurity, including shifts in technology, global competition, and the breach of the business sector's duty to invest in loyal workers. Do you think his belief in the bargain between business and workers is shared widely?

3. *Solutions.* Does Secretary Reich propose any solutions? If so, which ones? Does he adopt the political left's solution of redistributing wealth? Does he adopt the political right's solution of cutting taxes? What do you think he has in mind when he endorses treating employees as assets to be developed? How does he propose channeling "resources directly into the pockets of ordinary Americans"?

4. *Corporate Welfare.* Secretary Reich's suggestion of ending corporate welfare as we know it departed from the national norm of supporting or ignoring subsidies and handouts to corporations, at least compared to the attention showered on welfare recipients. Another exception was provided by writer James Donahue's essay in The Washington Post. In ridiculing corporate welfare recipients, Mr. Donahue criticized the "culture of dependency that has encouraged certain industries to live off the taxpayers." He proposed a two years and out time limit for businesses dependent on corporate entitlements to support their activities, such as below-market fees for cattle grazing and mineral extraction on public lands, grants for advertising products such as American soybeans and candy bars abroad, and exclusive marketing rights for private companies developing drugs with government research dollars. See James P. Donahue, *The Fat Cat Freeloaders: When American Big Business*

Bellys Up to the Public Trough, THE WASHINGTON POST, March 6, 1994. *See also,* Lars-Erik Nelson, *Ending Corporate Welfare: A Worthy Goal,* THE DENVER POST, Nov. 29, 1994, at 9B; Steven Craig and James Taranto, *Slash Welfare Benefits--For Bureaucrats,* N.Y. TIMES, Feb. 27, 1995, at A11; *Go After Corporate Welfare,* N.Y. TIMES, Jan. 17, 1995, at A14.

3. Unemployment

Most people probably agree that it would be better to have poor people working than receiving welfare. Do you think most people understand that the Federal Reserve Board attempts to maintain a certain level of unemployment so as to keep inflation from rising? *See, e.g.,* James Risen, *Fed Adjusts Interest Rates Based on 6% Jobless Rate,* THE DENVER POST, Aug. 29, 1994, at 2A; Jim Hoagland, *Why Keep Employment Down?,* THE DENVER POST, June 26, 1994, at 5D; Louis Uchitelle, *Is The Fed Promoting Unemployment?,* THE DENVER POST, April 24, 1994. Is there any inconsistency in government policies that both blame welfare recipients for not working and attempt to keep a certain percentage of potential workers from finding work?

The unemployment insurance system provides some relief for workers who cannot find jobs. The articles which follow explore emerging issues related to unemployment insurance, including how the system generally handles "contingent" workers, and how it specifically handles women workers.

Deborah Maranville

CHANGING ECONOMY, CHANGING LIVES: UNEMPLOYMENT INSURANCE AND THE CONTINGENT WORKFORCE

4 BOSTON UNIVERSITY PUBLIC INTEREST LAW JOURNAL 291 (1995)

I. Introduction

* * *

First, many gender-based assumptions underlying the unemployment insurance system are no longer valid. The world contemplated by the architects of the American social welfare system, including unemployment insurance, consisted mostly of white, male breadwinners and their full-time, homemaker wives. With that social framework in mind, the unemployment insurance system in the United States intended to provide the best protection to workers who were available for work on a full-time, year round basis. In addition, unemployment insurance targeted workers in relatively stable jobs structured around the traditional employer-employee relationships. But because workers and jobs in the United States economy increasingly fail to reflect the assumptions underlying the program as originally designed, the protection afforded by the unemployment insurance system has become increasingly inadequate.

With the entry of a substantial number of women into the workforce, fewer workers fit the traditional male breadwinner script. Yet women continue to bear greater responsibility for family care, and thus are more likely to drop out of the labor force with greater frequency, and for longer time periods than men. Women also are more likely to take part-time employment and to place limits on their availability for work on weekends or for particular shifts. Moreover, labor market segregation continues to result in women holding lower-paying jobs with less security and fewer benefits than men. As this paper will demonstrate, each of these factors results in women receiving less favorable treatment under the unemployment insurance system.

Second, the American economy in recent decades has undergone a major transformation away from the assumption of job stability contemplated by those who designed the nation's unemployment insurance system. This transformation has had four primary components: a shift from manufacturing jobs to service jobs, with an accompanying decline in the percentage of the workforce that is unionized; an increasing gap between high-paying jobs requiring significant educational prerequisites and low-paying unskilled jobs; a growing disparity in income, marked by a decrease in the real value of the minimum wage, and a rising differential between average wages and executive salaries; and a trend away from job security and long-term employment toward increased reliance on contract, temporary, and part-time workers. These changes have had a pervasive effect on unemployment insurance, including a steadily decreasing percentage of unemployed workers who receive benefits, an increasing fixation with job training programs, and a rise in eligibility issues affecting contingent workers.

Third, legislative efforts during the 1980's have exacerbated the effects of economic and social changes on the number of workers covered by the unemployment compensation system. Rapid inflation in the 1970's, combined with high unemployment, strained the solvency of many state unemployment programs, forcing many states to borrow from the federal loan fund available in such emergencies.

* * *

Unemployment insurance typically imposes four requirements that can create eligibility problems for contingent workers. First, all states make eligibility for unemployment benefits contingent upon satisfying a "work test," whereby a claimant must have worked in statutorily approved employment for a specified number of hours or weeks, or must have earned a prescribed sum during a specified period before becoming unemployed. Thus, the system excludes women following the traditional homemaker script who are forced into the labor market by unexpected necessities until they can satisfy the work test. Similarly, many individuals who combine work and caretaking activities are likely, at times, to fail the "work test" requirement, either because they move in and out of the work force, or because of insufficient part-time earnings. In addition, the number of part-time, seasonal, and temporary workers who qualify for unemployment insurance will vary greatly depending on the specifics of the work test, particularly the requirements covering the number of weeks worked, earnings, and the period(s) of employment.

Second, in all states, workers who "voluntarily quit" their employment without good cause are disqualified from receiving unemployment benefits. To the extent that family reasons are not considered good cause, workers who leave their employment either due to family emergencies or because they are unable to comply with a change in their work schedule are disadvantaged by this requirement. Women, of course, still perform the bulk of family care and disproportionately comprise those quitting for family reasons.

Third, all states require that an individual be "able and available for work" in order to qualify for unemployment benefits. Typically, availability is defined according to standards fitting the male breadwinner script. In other words, an individual is likely to face legal obstacles in receiving benefits unless he or she is available for employment on a full-time, year-round basis, regardless of the assigned shift. A fourth requirement, closely related to the third, is that a worker receiving benefits who refuses an offer of "suitable" employment will be disqualified from receiving further benefits. In addition to monitoring the effect of these specific eligibility requirements, advocates for the poor must also consider the ways in which the legal system in general, and unemployment insurance statutes in particular, create unnecessary incentives for employers to rely on contingent workers.

A fourth requirement, closely related to the third, is that a worker receiving benefits who refuses an offer of "suitable" employment will be disqualified from receiving further benefits. .

Research conducted by the Institute for Women's Policy provides a particularly relevant source of information. The Institute's 1994 report on the effects of combining work and welfare on poor women's lives demonstrates that even though a substantial portion of women who receive AFDC also engage in paid employment, few receive any unemployment compensation benefits if they lose their jobs. The Institute's preliminary research suggests that women who combine unemployment compensation with their income from work and welfare ("cyclers") have slightly higher income over the long-term than those who combine only work and AFDC ("combiners"). Yet the total work effort of cyclers is not significantly greater than the work effort of women who receive no unemployment compensation benefits. Rather "cyclers" tend to work more intensively while they work, often at multiple jobs, and at higher average wages, while "combiners" work more weeks, but average fewer hours per week.

These data highlight two important policy concerns. First, because AFDC functions as a substitute for unemployment compensation, current proposals to limit AFDC eligibility to two years again illustrate how the gendered structure of our social welfare system disadvantages women. Second, while the income advantage for cyclers is small, the data reinforce the argument in favor of reducing those barriers that prevent women from receiving unemployment insurance. The attachment to the labor force requirements, the voluntary quit disqualification, and the availability requirement discussed in the previous section all undoubtedly exclude many AFDC recipients from receiving unemployment benefits.

* * *

The distinction between benefits obtained through attachment to the labor force ("earned benefits") and benefits obtained on the basis of need ("welfare") is central to the public perception of the American social welfare system. This distinction also marks the difference between the programs with firm public support and those that fall under less-popular ambit of "welfare."

Historically, unemployment compensation programs remained securely in the "earned benefits" camp. However, this notion may soon need reconsideration in light of recently adopted federal regulations which require states to engage in "worker profiling" as a precondition to receiving funds for their unemployment insurance programs. "Worker profiling" involves identifying claimants who are particularly appropriate candidates for retraining because of their likelihood to remain unemployed for long periods and "exhaust" their benefits. The process raises three important concerns: First, what criteria will be used to identify likely candidates for retraining? Second, will the retraining opportunities offered to workers identified through profiling be desirable, or will they merely create additional barriers to overcome in order to remain eligible for benefits? Third, if the training opportunities are desirable, will worker profiling result in a two-tiered training system with the best assistance available only to those identified through profiling?

The rise of "worker profiling" has led some advocates to foresee one of two shifts in the future character of the unemployment insurance system. Under one view, need concepts, as well as more stringent conditions on eligibility, will gradually take over the unemployment compensation system. In the alternative, a two-tiered system will develop for unemployment insurance replicating the inequities that characterize our social welfare system as a whole. Under this scenario, the most generous benefits will wind up going to the "ideal male" workers in the form of funding for training and education, while other workers will receive only minimal, time-limited cash payments and routine job-search assistance.

Research on the characteristics of the long-term unemployed has identified two major, and quite different, groups who risk exhausting their unemployment insurance. The first group consists of less-educated workers permanently laid off from a long-term job. These workers, consisting disproportionately of male union-members accustomed to earning above-average wages, are unlikely to return to the same industry or occupation due to structural changes in the economy. The second group, composed disproportionately of white women, and men and women of color, includes workers with limited education who have held a series of short-term jobs with different employers. Recent Labor Department directives provide that workers identified through profiling should automatically qualify as "dislocated" workers as defined by the Economic Dislocated Worker Adjustment Assistance Act. The directives also adopt a profiling methodology that seeks to identify the former group exclusively.

[T]hree factors exist to cast doubt on the prospective quality of those [job training] opportunities. First, job training is meaningful only if jobs are available when training is complete. Many observers are skeptical about the Clinton Administration's emphasis on job training precisely because of doubts that high quality jobs will be available for those who undergo training. As federal job training programs begin to use worker profiling as a "gatekeeper" for entry into employment and training programs, the implications for workers extend beyond the confines of the unemployment compensation program. A distinct possibility exists that a two-tier job training system will emerge which provides quality services to profiled workers but nothing for the rest. In this scenario, the criteria relied on for worker profiling becomes crucial. If less educated workers accustomed to intermittent employment are excluded from quality training programs, then the economic, racial, and gender-based inequities characterizing our current social welfare system will be reproduced in the employment training context. * * *

To ensure that attachment to the labor force requirements do not exclude "contingent workers," advocates will need to rely on legislation at both the state and federal levels, administrative rulemaking efforts, and major law reform litigation. The definition of "good cause" in voluntary quit cases, as well as the definition of "availability" can be expanded through individual casework in states having only broad statutory provisions. However, efforts at the legislative and agency level will be needed in states with restrictive statutes, and may both affect more claimants and be necessary in order to preserve gains achieved through individual case work. Major efforts to reform the job training and welfare systems are likely to take place primarily in Congress, but the administrative agencies and the states will also play a critical role, and advocates concerned with unemployment insurance must not overlook developments in those areas.

Notes and Questions

1. *Race and Gender Based Origins.* Farm and domestic workers were excluded from the original unemployment system, but have since been included. What group of people were disproportionately likely to be farm and domestic workers? Some employers, especially of domestic workers, fail to pay their payroll taxes to the unemployment system on behalf of their employees. What group of people disproportionately continue to perform domestic work?

2. *Eligibility for Unemployment Benefits.* Deborah Maranville outlined the four basic eligibility requirements for unemployment benefits, including: 1) documentation of sufficient recent employment; 2) certification that the worker did not voluntarily quit his or her employment without good cause; 3) demonstration that the worker is able and available for work; and 4) compliance with the requirement that the worker accept suitable work offered.

Unemployment benefits are time-limited, typically for twenty-six weeks. As a result, the chronically unemployed lose their eligibility for unemployment benefits. How might these requirements otherwise affect poor people? Consider, for example, what constitutes good cause for leaving employment, why workers must be available for full-time work, and what counts as a suitable work offer.

3. *Comparing Unemployment and Welfare.* Professor Maranville recounted the research conducted by the Institute for Women's Policy Research revealing an income advantage for women who cycle between work, unemployment, and welfare, compared to those who combine only work and welfare. This is not surprising given that unemployment benefit amounts frequently exceed welfare benefit amounts. Women who receive unemployment rather than welfare benefits also enjoy greater social acceptance. Because unemployment benefits are perceived to be earned, recipients do not suffer from the moral stigma associated with receipt of welfare. As more workers become contingent, Professor Maranville fears that unemployment benefits will be redesignated as need-based (with the accompanying stigma that entails), or will be divided into two-tiers

of benefits for the ideal male workers and for everyone else. What types of actions could advocates for contingent workers take to prevent these dangers from becoming reality?

Stephen Bingham

REPLACE WELFARE FOR CONTINGENT WORKERS WITH UNEMPLOYMENT COMPENSATION

22 FORDHAM URBAN LAW JOURNAL 937 (1995)

Richard V. worked seven years for General Motors in Detroit. Unable to continue because of ruptured discs, he received disability benefits before actively seeking work again. After his extended UI benefits expired, he survived on a $345 General Assistance grant, living in a church rent-free in return for light housekeeping chores.

Jerome L. worked as a ramp agent for nine years at San Francisco Airport for Pacific Southwest Airlines and its successor US Air. Because of several absences from work on account of serious personal problems, he was fired for misconduct, thus becoming ineligible for UI benefits. Because state unemployment was over 9% at the time, he was only able to find a $310 per month job on Sundays running a city community center. He lived in his father's van for a while.

The current American welfare reform debate ignores a fundamental reason why so many low-income persons rely on income-maintenance programs ("welfare"): the ineligibility of over half of the work force for Unemployment Insurance Benefits (UI).

* * *

All attempts at welfare reform will fail unless they result from a comprehensive understanding of why people are poor. Aside from the inadequacy of benefits, poverty also results from the lack of available jobs, particularly full-time jobs paying above the federal poverty line. Hysterical claims about welfare recipients refusing to look for work and preferring AFDC should be tempered by several ignored realities.

First, the Federal Reserve Board asserts that at least 6% of the workforce must be unemployed at any given time to prevent inflationary wage pressure from overheating the economy. This TUR, which the Federal Reserve Bank considers the minimum unemployment rate that would have no adverse effect on the national inflation rate, is known by some economists as the "nonaccelerating inflation rate of unemployment" or the "natural unemployment rate."

The TUR, as defined above, however, underestimates the Hidden Unemployment Rate by about one half. In other words, because Federal Reserve Bank considers a stable TUR to be roughly 6%, our economic system today requires that approximately 12% of the entire workforce, or one in eight workers, be effectively unemployed. A recent San Francisco Examiner headline, declaring, "Jobless rise sends markets soaring," dramatically illustrates the degree to which Wall Street considers higher unemployment economically beneficial.

Second, the percentage of unemployed persons who receive unemployment compensation has dropped dramatically. The New Deal social compact that led to passage of the 1935 Social Security Act guaranteed that unemployed workers be entitled to Unemployment Insurance Benefits. As the memory fades of how close the Nation came to social revolution when millions were unemployed and totally destitute, so too does this national commitment.

The consequence of these (and many other) gaping holes in the UI safety net is that many ineligible workers have no choice but to apply for welfare. Others who do receive UI must often also rely on welfare benefits because the UI level is so low for low-wage workers. Increasingly restrictive UI eligibility rules exclude the sector of the economy that is expanding relative to other groups: the contingent and part-time work force. Women and people of color form a disproportionate share of this segment of the work force.

National policymakers ignore these truths. Instead, political rhetoric blames the poor for their unemployment and demands that they be weaned from welfare and told to find nonexistent jobs. While the welfare debate has stalled on behavior modification strategies and queries whether the federal government should play any anti-poverty role at all, productive debate on developing a national anti-poverty strategy involving both the private and public sectors has been stifled.

The goal of welfare reform should be not to reduce the availability of AFDC--or any other income maintenance entitlement program--to those who must rely on it. Rather, reform efforts should attempt to reduce the need for such programs through the development of different anti-poverty tools.

* * *

Millions who work full-time at the minimum wage remain poor. The current $4.25 minimum wage is nearly $1.75 below what it would be had the 1975 level been adjusted for inflation. In fact, the real value of the minimum wage is now at its second lowest level since 1955. For minimum wage workers without health insurance, complete destitution is only an illness away. For single parents, that disaster is almost inevitable, because rent and childcare can absorb an entire paycheck, leaving nothing for any other expenses.

The misinformed public would be surprised to learn that AFDC parents are typically part of the labor force. Nearly three-quarters of AFDC recipients have recent work experience and less than a third continue to receive AFDC for as long as twenty-four months. They often receive AFDC benefits while they work because they earn extremely low wages, and frequently work part-time. Over one quarter of the new jobs created in the March 1991-July 1993 recovery period were part-time; 75% of those jobs were filled involuntarily by people who would have preferred full-time work. Other AFDC recipients are laid-off workers who fail to meet the earnings threshold for Unemployment Compensation and must therefore fall back entirely on AFDC until they find new employment. Because of the high frequency of lay-off from low-wage jobs, people often move in and out of the workforce, never accumulating a work history sufficient to entitle them to UI benefits.

* * *

Among the most important reasons that so few unemployed workers receive benefits are the various ways that federal and state law restrict UI eligibility. First, federal law excludes certain types of workers, such as those who are self-employed, regardless of the amount of money they earn or the length of time that they work. Federal law permits states to exclude other categories as well. States may exclude agricultural workers, domestic workers, independent contractors and casual workers. As a consequence, approximately 12% of the work force works in employment not covered by unemployment compensation. Additionally, these exclusions provide employers with the opportunity to misclassify workers as independent contractors or consultants to avoid UI costs. Various states have considered legislation that would prohibit this practice but to date, no such legislation has passed.

States have also limited eligibility to UI by imposing restrictions based on earnings levels and workforce connection requirements. These requirements base eligibility upon a combination of total earnings and amount of time in the workforce. The earnings tests in at least half of the states would disqualify an average part-time worker. A worker's ability to satisfy these tests is further limited by the "lag quarter" rule. Under this rule, neither income earned in the calendar quarter within which one is applying, nor that earned in the immediately preceding calendar quarter, is counted in determining UI eligibility. For instance, a Californian applying on June 29 would have all earnings in the April-June quarter excluded from consideration, as well as all money earned in the lag quarter, January-March, a total of six months of earnings. The original justification for the lag quarter rule was that it was not possible to process a worker's hour and wage information from the most recent quarter quickly enough to include it in eligibility calculations. Today, however, that justification is no longer valid on account of advances in information technology.

A third mechanism states apply in order to disqualify applicants is the "voluntary quit" rule. States generally define "voluntary" broadly. In 1993, for example, only nine states did not define voluntary to include quitting a job because of sexual harassment. Additionally, most states define voluntary to include leaving because of family or medical emergencies. Also, many states consider that leaving work because of an emergency child care problem is a voluntary quit.

A fourth limitation on UI eligibility is the "able and available to work" requirement. Forty-four states maintain these requirements, which disqualify workers who are looking only for part-time work. This disqualification applies regardless of the applicant's previous work history and is particularly harmful to permanently employed part-time workers. It ignores the importance of part-time workers to the economy, both from the standpoint of persons such as working mothers who cannot work full-time, and from the standpoint of small businesses who need part-time workers to fill their varying needs.

A final way that states limit eligibility is through "durational disqualification." . . . [S]tates have always penalized workers who have been discharged for misconduct, those who have left a job voluntarily and those who have refused suitable work. Originally, these penalties would disqualify such persons from UI for a fixed number of weeks. Today, however, most states disqualify affected persons until they work again for enough time and earnings to reestablish a connection to the workforce. For instance, in South Dakota, a disqualified claimant must work six weeks and earn wages equal to or greater than his or her weekly benefit amount in each of those weeks before he can be eligible for UI benefits again. Persons disqualified under these provisions have no alternative but to turn to welfare.

The above restrictions affect those in poverty most profoundly. On account of such restrictions, those living under the federal poverty index form one-third of the unemployed, but they form only one-fifth of those receiving UI benefits.

* * *

Federal and state changes in the unemployment compensation system would significantly improve its ability to help the unemployed, and thereby reduce dependency on welfare and housing programs. Such a shift in strategy is politically urgent in today's climate of welfare-bashing. It would go far in reducing the number of people forced to survive on meager welfare benefits, thereby making continued benefits to the unemployable AFDC population more acceptable politically. The public, frustrated with the perception that employable persons are responsible for burgeoning welfare rolls, would likely be more willing to support adequate unemployment benefits. Someone receiving UI is not "on the dole." Rather, the UI recipient is receiving money deducted from his pay under the Federal Unemployment Tax Act (FUTA), and is therefore receiving his due.

In February 1994, the Advisory Council on Unemployment Compensation (ACUC) made several important recommendations that would help repair the UI safety net. First, the Council recommended that Congress eliminate the exemption of agricultural workers on small farms from Unemployment Insurance coverage. Second, the Council urged states to adopt a "movable base period" to eliminate the harsh effects of the "lag quarter" rule. Under the moveable base approach, when a claimant has not earned sufficient wages during four of the five previous quarters that are used to determine eligibility, the state would reassess the claim based on wages earned in the fifth or "lag" quarter. Additionally, the Council directed that states should not set base requirements any higher than 800 times the minimum wage, and that they should eliminate seasonal exclusions and the practice of denying benefits to workers who seek only part-time work. Finally, the Council urged that benefit levels be set that would replace at least 50% of lost earnings over a six-month period.

The Council also urged reform of the extended benefit system. Extended benefits are intended to stabilize the economy in periods of particularly long-term unemployment, by providing an additional thirteen weeks of benefits to persons who have exhausted their basic twenty-six week grant of benefits without finding work. The Council suggested that a new program should be developed that would ensure that a significantly greater proportion of "exhaustees" of regular twenty-six week benefits become entitled to extended benefits. Receipt of extended benefits is low because currently, in order to offer extended benefits, a state's rate of unemployment must exceed a certain level and must be worsening. In 1981, the Omnibus Budget and Reconciliation Act raised the unemployment level at which extended benefits would be triggered. The new standard severely limited the ability of states to offer extended benefits. As a result, the formula used to determine when extended benefits would apply, qualifying states for the 50% matching federal share to pay extended benefits, was unresponsive to high unemployment rates. Under that formula, only eight states activated extended benefits during the 1991 recession. Although 1992 federal legislation offered states the option of reforming the state formula, few states did so. Instead, the states pressured Congress, which passed the Emergency Unemployment Compensation ("EUC") Act. Unfortunately, federal political will was exhausted last year and the EUC program was not extended. The practice of setting extended benefit trigger points so high, and thereby being forced to resort to EUC legislation, has been more costly and less effective economically as a counter-cyclical tool than a more easily-triggered EB system would have been. Congress spent approximately 40% more on emergency unemployment benefits between 1991 and 1994 than it would have spent on a more comprehensive extended benefit program.

The cost of limiting extended benefits so strictly is high. The Center on Budget Policies and Priorities (CBPP) has noted that during the height of the 1993 California recession, the long-term unemployed constituted 25% of the total unemployment rate, resulting in approximately 50,000 California workers per month who exhausted their regular UI benefits without finding work. In a state that lost nearly 800,000 jobs in the early 1990s, many of those workers have not been reemployed and must rely on welfare instead.

* * *

A major reason for trust fund solvency problems is that employers pay a smaller and smaller percentage of wages into the funds. At the inception of the Unemployment Compensation program in 1935, the taxable wage base was 100% of payrolls. That percentage has fallen since then because legislation has capped the amount of workers' wages for which an employer must pay a tax. The current cap, $7,000, was significantly below the average annual wage of $25,500 in 1992. By 1992, the ratio of taxable wages to covered wages had fallen to the lowest level yet, 36%. One proposal would link the cap to the earnings base for Old Age Security and Disability Insurance (OASDI), currently $61,200. The current $56 cost per worker of the Federal Unemployment Tax Act (FUTA) tax in 1992 was close to its lowest historic level.

Comparisons with the Group of Seven ("G7") nations' unemployment compensation systems dramatically illustrate how out-of-line the United States taxable wage base has become. A 1992 congressional report places the U.S. at the very bottom. The median U.S. state base of $8,250 is over 30% less than that of the next lowest country, Canada. The United States national average tax rate applied to taxable wages in covered employment is 1.9% state and 0.8% federal. The total of 2.7% compares to rates of 4.3% (Germany), 5.4% (Canada), 6.95% (France). That report also illustrates that the United States is very close to the bottom of the G7 countries in public expenditures for UI as a percent of Gross Domestic Product.

Amending the Unemployment Compensation program is not the entire answer to ensuring replacement income for unemployed workers. Political reality requires that employer-financed benefits must be of limited duration and cover only those persons with a significant labor-force connection. Employable but unemployed persons without a minimal connection to the labor force need some other form of protection.

The inherent inadequacy of the unemployment compensation program even as originally conceived, has long been recognized. In 1980, for example, the Federal Government's National Commission on Unemployment Compensation ("NCUC"), was "deeply concerned about the substantial number of unemployed individuals who exhaust all UC benefits to which they are entitled" and believed that "every effort must be made to limit the extent to which unemployed persons must apply for and receive welfare." The NCUC consequently recommended, by a vote of 11-0-1, the establishment of "a program of income-tested benefits, administered completely separately from unemployment compensation, to provide some minimum protection for all unemployed persons exhausting or not eligible for unemployment compensation benefits and for whom no other job or program is available."

Such a program could still be enacted at the federal level, but preserve a degree of control for the states. It would cover unemployed persons who have exhausted their benefits or are ineligible for UI benefits for the many different reasons discussed earlier. The income would replace current welfare benefits and, ideally, would be sufficient to raise a person or family above the official federal poverty line. Requirements for receiving unemployment assistance would include participation in a job search program, as currently required by the UC program. The program would also be "means tested," but would not necessarily require a complete "spend-down" of assets for eligibility. Those unable to find regular employment after a certain period of time could move into a public service job or continue training.

Such Unemployment Assistance programs exist in several European countries. The congressional report cited earlier notes that France, Germany and the United Kingdom provide such assistance to unemployed individuals irrespective of their attachment to the work force. Financed by national treasuries rather than through employer-funded insurance, such unemployment assistance insures that employable persons are readily connected to local employment agencies, have access to job training programs and receive a minimum stipend to survive. Currently, most recipients of public assistance have little or no access to job training programs.

The program would be funded mainly by the federal government, but would include contributions from employers, primarily those who hire largely contingent workers, such as part-time employees of fast-food restaurants. The program would be administered by the Department of Labor through its UI division.

* * *

A new program of unemployment assistance to protect those persons most likely to be ineligible for UI under the current system is needed to keep those persons from turning to public assistance. Such a program would provide economic stimulus and would protect unemployed persons from falling into poverty. The new system would protect persons who currently slip through the safety net, those who are ineligible to receive UI benefits but who cannot receive public assistance either. Instead of blaming persons for their unemployment or poverty, this system would admit that a certain degree of unemployment is inevitable and help those persons continue to contribute to the economy until they can find more work.

Notes and Questions

1. *Rhetoric versus Reality.* Stephen Bingham deplored the gap between the rhetoric of the lazy poor and the reality of the many hardworking poor who lack full-time jobs which pay wages sufficient to maintain a family above the poverty line. (Does this theme sound familiar by now?) Would information about the actual work effort and the lack of jobs more effectively reach the public if explained in the context of unemployment, rather than welfare?

2. *Reforming Unemployment Insurance.* Professor Bingham endorsed various reform proposals, including: 1) eliminating exclusions of workers; 2) eliminating technical disqualifications resulting from rules governing calculations of eligible periods of work; 3) increasing unemployment benefit levels to replace 50% of each unemployed person's lost earnings; and 4) making it easier to extend time-limitation for receipt of benefits in regions experiencing high unemployment. How politically feasible are these proposals? How costly are they? Who would lobby for their passage?

3. *Creating Unemployment Assistance.* Professor Bingham proposed creating an Unemployment Assistance program that would

provide need-based, time-limited benefits to people experiencing long-term unemployment. These benefits, ideally, would enjoy widespread popular support because they would be based on societal recognition that unemployment is an inevitable byproduct of our economic system. How could support for such a program be built? Is it likely to be succeed?

Deborah Maranville

FEMINIST THEORY AND LEGAL PRACTICE: A CASE STUDY ON UNEMPLOYMENT COMPENSATION BENEFITS AND THE MALE NORM

43 HASTINGS LAW JOURNAL 1081 (1992)

A broad view of legal theory is that it encompasses any effort to think about, struggle with, and shed light on the intractable problems of our time. A doctrinal approach, by contrast, operates in a middle level of abstraction, neither practical nor truly theoretical, in the sense of attempting to provide explanations or insight into the multiplicity of lives that we lead.

At the most basic level, theory can refer to any attempt to generalize from experience. In this sense, the process of linking language to events virtually always can be described as one implicating theory. Even three-year-olds engage in theory as they attempt to learn about the world, and all attorneys engage in theory, however, unreflective or unsophisticated. At a second level, we engage in theory when we attempt to critique or challenge those initial generalizations and assumptions. A third, and in some academic circles dominant, view is that theory consists of detached and objective explanations for the world-generalizations from which we deduce the appropriate response in particular cases.

The concept of legal practice is equally complex, including activities ranging from interacting with clients and legal institutions to developing legal strategies and arguments. Thus, theories about legal practice can be directed at understanding the ways in which acting the role of the lawyer restricts the lawyer's freedom in relating to both clients and legal institutions, the effects on the lawyer-client relationship of different approaches to lawyering skills, the implications of gender differences for lawyering, and the ways in which new legal arguments can be developed with the assistance of critical social theories that change our understanding of the world.

The difficulty in sorting out the different meanings of the terms theory and practice helps explain why calls to integrate theory and practice are often accompanied by expressions of concern that theory should not become too remote from practice. To the extent that theory implies Grand Theory deductively applied, or even abstract doctrine deductively applied, such theory often seems impervious to correction by reference to reality. Even efforts made at the second level of theory to challenge our underlying assumptions become ossified and pejoratively "theoretical," unless we treat our generalizations merely as working hypotheses and constantly revisit seemingly settled issues as the world changes around us.

This case study addresses but one of the many intersections between theory and practice: the way in which a legal practitioner can recognize the potential for new legal arguments through a familiarity with feminist theory's insights concerning the gendered effects of our legal institutions. The case studied here is by no means unique. Rather, it provides an "everyday" illustration of a process that underlies a wide range of legal change during recent decades. That process reflects a constant interaction between feminist theory and legal practice.

The feminist movement was founded on consciousness raising--an attempt to move from concrete personal experience to broader theoretical insights into the political implications of everyday experience. Because of that foundation, many feminists contest the validity of the dichotomies that traditionally characterize Western thought, including the dichotomy between theory and practice. Not surprisingly, therefore, many leading feminist theoreticians also have been actively involved in feminist legal practice--whether developing strategies for new legal claims, writing amicus briefs, or representing individual women.

Sustained theoretical attention to questions of gender, as well as the legal response to difference generally, has accompanied the increase in women entering legal academia during the past decade and a half. A new generation of theorists has struggled with the inadequacies of equal protection and discrimination analysis, traditionally premised on the norm of formal equality, to recognize or remedy the real inequalities in women's lives. At the same time practitioners have fought for legal change in such areas as fetal protection polices, maternity or parental leave policies, sexual harassment, the legal response to pornography, and the battered woman syndrome defense.

The unemployment compensation case of Ms. H, handled by interns at the University of Washington Law School's Civil Law Clinic, provides a classic illustration of this theory/practice interaction. Feminist theory's efforts to name or rename the social world helped Ms. H's representatives transform their understanding of social life and develop legal theories based on that new understanding.

In Ms. H's case, the Clinic challenged a policy of the Employment Security Department that limited benefits to individuals seeking full-time work (the "full-time work rule"). The Clinic built its legal strategy on two key insights of feminist jurisprudence. The first is that our current legal system often affects women differently, and less favorably, than men, and especially disadvantages the majority of women whose lives are significantly affected by their roles as mothers. This understanding allowed us to question whether the full-time work rule had a differential impact on women and thus to identify a potential challenge to that rule.

The second insight is that the disfavored situation of women often results because laws implicitly have been structured to fit male life patterns--male norms that are not stated as such, but are instead mistaken for the inevitable, natural state of being. This insight provided a basis for contending that because the existing interpretation of the statute was based on such a male norm, a more inclusive understanding of work patterns could lead to an interpretation of the statute that accommodated both women's and men's experience.

As currently interpreted by the Washington Employment Security Department, the unemployment compensation system is structured to fit a worklife more typical of male than female workers. In that typical worklife, a worker is employed full-time, without breaks except for periods of involuntary unemployment, needs the pay that accompanies full-time employment, and has no domestic responsibilities that limit the worker's availability for all shifts. In contrast, Ms. H, along with a significant portion of American women today, faces a quite different reality. Because the daily realities of adult work lives remain heavily gendered, many women are significantly disadvantaged by the structure of the Washington unemployment compensation laws.

The following sections describe in more detail the structure of the Washington unemployment compensation statutes, the responsibilities faced by Ms. H, and the impact of the statutory scheme on Ms. H and the many women (and some men) with similar work and family lives.

A claimant seeking unemployment benefits in Washington must meet a series of requirements. First, the individual must have worked at a job covered by the unemployment insurance system for the equivalent of seventeen weeks of full- time work during the fifteen months before becoming unemployed and applying for benefits. Second, the claimant must be unemployed in accordance with the statutory definition. Third, the person must meet a series of basic eligibility conditions, including being "able to work, and . . . available for work in any . . . occupation . . . for which he or she is reasonably fitted," which means "ready, able, and willing, immediately to accept any suitable work." Fourth, the individual must avoid disqualification from benefits under the statutory provisions that, among other things, deny benefits to claimants who voluntarily quit work, are fired for misconduct, or are on strike.

Under this statutory scheme, a woman who works steadily at a part-time job, say for twenty hours per week, easily will meet the first requirement of having worked and paid into the system for the equivalent of seventeen full-time work weeks. Upon becoming unemployed, however, she will not qualify for benefits if she plans to continue working part-time and limits her job search to such work. This is because the Employment Security Department has interpreted . . . the statute requiring a claimant to be available for work, to mean that a claimant must be available for full-time work. The Department claims that by restricting her availability to part-time work, the worker materially and impermissibly restricts her availability for employment.

The Department also considers domestic responsibilities an impermissible reason for the part-time worker to restrict her availability for employment. Although the statute does not explicitly state that a worker may not limit work availability based on her responsibilities at home, such a position is implicit in [the statute], which provides that domestic responsibilities do not constitute good cause for voluntarily leaving employment.

The Clinic's opportunity to challenge these restrictions began, of course, with a client: Ms. H. A single parent of a special needs child, Ms. H had worked part-time as an assembly line piece-worker making buttons used for political campaigns. The workload fluctuated and during a slow period before the December holidays, Ms. H's hours were reduced by more than a third. She continued working these reduced hours, but applied for unemployment compensation benefits and began looking for other, more stable, part-time employment. During the process of applying for unemployment benefits, Ms. H explained to the Employment Security Department that she was not seeking full-time employment and was not available to work full-time. As justification for this decision, Ms. H referred to pending judicial proceedings concerning residential care of her son, in which a Family Law Commissioner had suggested that the son's needs could not be met adequately if the parents were both working full-time. The Department denied Ms. H's application for benefits on the ground that she was not "available for work."

The two Clinic interns initially assigned to the case began their challenge to the full-time work requirement by pursuing the feminist insight that the law often works a differential, negative impact on women. The students quickly gathered data to support our (fairly obvious) intuition that such a process was at work here.

That research demonstrated that the Department's full-time work requirement has a differential, negative impact on women for three related reasons. First, women continue to bear significantly greater domestic responsibilities than men for both child-care and caring for elderly relatives. Second, as a consequence of their greater domestic responsibilities, far more women than men work part-time. Third, part-time workers fare significantly worse financially than full-time workers. The availability of part-time employment has increased primarily in the lower paying sectors that traditionally hire women. Part-time workers also suffer higher levels of involuntary unemployment.

Because women currently are more likely to work part-time and to need to work part-time, a policy that disqualifies part-time workers from receiving unemployment compensation benefits unless they are available for full-time work disadvantages women. And that disproportionate effect magnifies the disadvantages inherent in a context in which women earn lower wages than men, have a lower standard of living than men after divorce, and make up a disproportionate percentage of the American poor.

Recognizing and demonstrating that the Department's "full-time work" requirement differentially affects women was not too difficult. The next step--challenging the Department's anticipated defense of the requirement-was not as easy. That step required recognizing and unmasking the male norm underlying the unemployment compensation statutes.

The Department's argument--that a claimant who seeks only part-time employment materially limits her availability for work --initially seems well-founded. The policy is not based on an explicitly gender-based classification, and it seems justified by the ways in which part-time workers differ from full-time workers. A worker who is available only for part-time work presumably decreases the pool of jobs for which he or she might qualify, and consequently increases the likelihood of extended unemployment.

One could argue, however, that the old saw applies here: What's good for the goose is good for the gander. If the part-time worker must be available for full-time work in order to increase the pool of jobs for which she will qualify, why not apply the same analysis to full-time workers? Full-time workers would also have more job opportunities if they were required to be available for part-time work. I suspect most readers would view such a requirement as ridiculous, and, indeed, the Department does not extend this apparently logical requirement to the would-be full-time worker. Such workers are permitted to look only for full-time work. Why?

Underlying the Department's full-time requirement is a classic, unstated male norm: that of the male "head-of-household," whose primary domestic responsibility consists of providing economic support to a wife and children. The unemployment compensation system was enacted in response to unprecedented levels of unemployment among such males during the Great Depression of the 1930s. As "primary wage earners" with wives at home to handle the domestic responsibilities, those men wanted and needed full-time work.

In Washington, the need of the male norm worker for full-time work is implicitly accommodated under the availability requirement of [the statute]. Under that statute claimants are required only to be available to accept "suitable" work. In practice, however, a worker seeking full-time work is not required also to seek part-time work. Though never articulated, the logic is apparently as follows: The typical full-time worker (male or female) requires full-time work for self-support and, often, to support additional family members. Part-time work will not be sufficient to pay the bills, or at least will be insufficient to support the desired lifestyle. For such workers, therefore, part-time work does not constitute "suitable" work because it conflicts with their economic needs.

Yet the need for full-time work can be conceptualized as a "domestic" need or responsibility, as well as an "economic" need. The traditional family responsibilities of women are viewed as "domestic," and the corresponding family responsibilities of men as "economic," because of a "separate spheres" ideology and practice in the white middle class during the nineteenth and early twentieth centuries. The separate spheres ideology allocates the world of work to males and the world of family and home to females. Once we recognize that the male norm worker's need for full-time work is a domestic need and that the unemployment compensation statute implicitly accommodates that domestic need, we can make a similar "suitability" argument on behalf of part-time workers. For workers who have heavy child-care, elder-care, or other domestic responsibilities, full-time work is not suitable work because it conflicts with their need to satisfy domestic obligations.

The ultimate question is not whether workers seeking only full-time, or only part-time, work limit their availability for work. Of course they do. Nor is the question whether male norm workers seeking only full-time work and part- time workers with child-care duties limit their availability for employment based on "domestic responsibilities." Clearly they do. Rather, within the framework of the unemployment compensation system, the question is whether such limitations should place the workers beyond the purview of the unemployment compensation system--a system that provides benefits only to individuals who are genuinely attached to the labor market. Within that framework, it makes sense to require that a worker be available for a wide enough range of job openings that she has a reasonable chance of obtaining a job. Such a requirement, however, need not encompass a full-time work rule.

Applying the insights of feminist theory provided an opportunity for a classic "Aha!" reaction. The feminist insight that unstated male norms often underlie statutes that disadvantage women allowed us to say, "Hey, I see what's going on here," by providing a conceptual framework for recognizing and naming the way the unemployment compensation statute operates. From this understanding, we could then develop a traditional combination of statutory and constitutional arguments. Our primary contention was that the existing statute could be interpreted to authorize benefits for individuals who were seeking part-time work. We hoped to make that argument more palatable by highlighting constitutional problems with the Department's "full-time work" rule. Given developments in constitutional equal protection doctrine, an effort to mount a federal challenge to the state statute would have been problematic because we were forced to rely on the statute's differential impact on women. Fortunately, Washington state law, although unsettled on this point, leaves room for argument.

As it happened, Ms. H won the first round of her case. But she did not win because the challenge outlined above was successful. Instead, and ironically, Ms. H benefitted from a special statutory provision that is apparently targeted at one group of male norm workers--hourly paid individuals in industries subject to seasonal reductions in available work. The Washington statute provides that an individual is considered unemployed if working less than full-time and earning less than the payable weekly unemployment compensation benefit amount. Department regulations permit such "partially unemployed individuals" to collect unemployment compensation benefits without requiring them to be "available" for other work. Although the statute and regulations are not targeted at individuals who were employed part-time prior to a reduction in hours, they do not exclude such persons. Thus, because Ms. H was still employed part-time, she was eligible for benefits.

Ms. H's saga did not end there, however. Her employers were angry at her receipt of benefits and demanded that Ms. H quit or agree that she would not apply for unemployment benefits while she worked for their firm. She refused their condition. Now out of work, she again applied for unemployment compensation benefits.

Predictably, she became embroiled in another hearing that considered both whether she voluntarily quit or was fired, and whether she was "available for work" given her restriction to part-time employment. The employer defaulted and an Administrative Law Judge ruled that full-time work did not constitute "suitable work" for Ms. H.

Apart from the result in Ms. H's case, the broader problem is likely to remain, and we will face the choice of whether to pursue litigation, administrative change, a legislative strategy, or perhaps all of the above. In any event, the insights of feminist jurisprudence remain and may affect future cases.

Attorneys often discount legal theory as abstract and irrelevant to the practice of law, and indeed it can be. Good theory, however, has intrinsic, inspirational, and instrumental value. Thus, as illustrated by Ms. H's case, successful theory not only can help develop new categories and new strategies for thinking about old problems, but it also can help us recognize that "the way things are" is neither natural, necessary, nor in some cases desirable.

Notes and Questions

1. *Theory and Practice.* Deborah Maranville explained that attorneys engage in theory when they link language to events, create generalizations, and challenge assumptions and norms. She noted that the practicing attorney's use of theory may be unreflective. Do you agree? Do we need to be conscious of our theoretical assumptions, generalizations, and critiques in order to use theory effectively in the practice of law? Or, to put the question another way, what might be gained if attorneys engaged in a more theoretically reflective practice?

2. *The Full-Time Employment Norm.* Professor Maranville's and her students' client, Ms. H, was limited to part-time employment so that she could adequately care for her special needs child. Her circumstances were unusual, compared to the experiences of parents of children without special needs. So how were the students able to use feminist theory's ideas about gender-based assumptions, which apply generally to women and men, to specifically help Ms. H.?

4. Minimum Wage

Economists continue to debate whether a minimum wage affects the demand for labor. Some economists argue that increases in the minimum wage result in fewer jobs being available for workers. Others argue that the number of jobs have grown following each increase in the minimum wage. As this economic debate continues, workers in minimum wage jobs endure hourly wages far below the amount needed to support a family above the federal poverty line. From 1991 to 1996, the federal minimum wage was $4.25 an hour. In July of 1996, Congress finally increased the federal minimum wage to $4.75, and to $5.15 as of July 1, 1997. Although most states have their own minimum wage laws, few of those surpass the federal minimum wage level. Some states have minimum wages below the federal level which apply to employees not covered by the federal wage, such as agricultural workers. For an analysis of the issues related to the minimum wage, *see* William P. Quigley, *"A Fair Day's Pay For A Fair Day's Work": Time To Raise and Index the Minimum Wage,* 27 ST. MARY'S LAW JOURNAL 513 (1996).

5. Earned Income Tax Credit

In the early 1970s, policy makers debated enacting a negative income tax. A pure negative income tax would transfer cash to low income families. The amount of the transfer would decrease as the family's income increases. Although a negative income tax was not adopted, Congress approved an alternative tax-based program, the Earned Income Tax Credit (EITC), which provides an increasing tax credit to low-wage earners as their earnings grow (up to the income level at which the credit begins to be phased out). Opponents of the EITC regard it as welfare in disguise. Critics of the EITC complain that low-wage earners underutilize it due to their lack of knowledge about eligibility requirements and their apprehension of the tax system. Supporters of the EITC tout its effects of encouraging both work and marriage, propositions explored by Anne Alstott below.

Anne L. Alstott
The Earned Income Tax Credit and the Limitations of Tax-based Welfare Reform
108 HARVARD LAW REVIEW 533 (1995)

The federal earned income tax credit (EITC), which provides cash payments to low-income workers, has recently assumed a central role in U.S. social welfare policy. Under legislation enacted in 1993, by 1997 the EITC will pay annual aggregate benefits as large as those paid under Aid to Families with Dependent Children (AFDC), the nation's principal cash welfare program. The 1993 expansion of the EITC is a key feature of President Clinton's plan for welfare reform.

Although the EITC is styled a "refundable tax credit," in fact it is a kind of welfare program--or, in economists' terms, an income-transfer program. It uses the rules and procedures of the federal income tax system to make payments to low-income workers based on their earnings and total income. As a refundable tax credit, the EITC not only reduces or eliminates federal income tax liability, but also pays cash to low-income taxpayers whose EITC exceeds the tax they owe.

For many years, the EITC was a relatively small program, viewed principally as a means of offsetting the adverse distributional and incentive effects of federal income and payroll taxes on low-income workers. In recent years, however, the EITC's advocates have increasingly promoted the EITC as a solution to two central and recurring concerns of welfare policy. First, proponents claim, the EITC promotes work and family responsibility among the poor, unlike traditional welfare programs, which have long attracted criticism for their putative effects on work and family structure. Second, advocates argue, because the EITC is part of the federal tax system, it is simpler and cheaper to administer than programs run by the welfare bureaucracy and affords greater dignity and privacy to beneficiaries.

A close examination of the two central claims made for the EITC reveals that the EITC is neither the radical departure from welfare that its advocates claim, nor the duplicate of welfare that its opponents depict. . . . [C]urrent debates over the EITC are seriously incomplete in two ways. First, both advocates and opponents of the program give undue weight to its potential effects on work and marriage among EITC recipients. The EITC's advocates exaggerate the program's effectiveness in encouraging work. Opponents emphasize the program's potential work disincentives, arguing that the EITC is welfare all over again. This conventional debate is too narrowly framed. It relies on an incomplete economic analysis and reflects important but unacknowledged normative tensions. Debates over the EITC's effects on marriage are also flawed: they typically lack empirical foundation and ignore important realities of institutional design.

Second, both proponents and opponents of the EITC have overlooked the important point that, because the EITC is a tax-based transfer program, it faces significant institutional constraints that are not present in traditional welfare programs. Tax-based transfer programs may be cheaper and less stigmatizing than welfare, although advocates typically assert these claims without empirical support. Nevertheless, . . .[t]he tax system's limitations render the EITC inherently inaccurate, unresponsive, and vulnerable to fraud and error in ways that traditional welfare programs are not. More empirical evidence is needed to evaluate the magnitude of these structural flaws and to make a quantitative comparison of tax-based and traditional programs. The central point, however, is that improving the performance of the EITC or other tax-based transfer programs requires either compromising the benefits of tax-based administration or undertaking a major restructuring of basic institutions of the federal tax system. Absent large-scale (and politically unlikely) reform of the federal income tax, the EITC and similar tax-based transfer programs are likely to prove acceptable only if we radically revise our expectations about accuracy, responsiveness, and compliance in income-transfer programs.

* * *

In one respect, the EITC represents an important liberalization of American social welfare policy. The EITC embodies a recognition that hard work may not lift a family out of poverty when wages are low and that the working poor as well as the nonworking poor need and deserve income transfers to support their families. Traditional welfare programs provide little aid to the working poor. Categorical eligibility restrictions exclude many families, and high benefit reduction rates quickly deny benefits even to workers with low earnings. In contrast, the EITC has grown in recent years to provide substantial levels of assistance to the working poor.

* * *

The case for the EITC, however, reflects the uneasy state of current welfare politics, in which the EITC's redistributive function is cloaked in anti-welfare rhetoric to attract maximum political support. This strategy could potentially turn anti-welfare sentiment to political advantage, but it is also risky. Promoting the EITC as the answer to the problems of welfare feeds inflated expectations about the capabilities of redistributive programs and reinforces negative attitudes about welfare that, in the long run, may jeopardize the cause of the EITC and of poverty relief more generally. Recent attacks on the EITC that condemn it as "welfare" and as a "handout" suggest that this danger is more than theoretical.

Thus far, the EITC has found a secure niche in welfare policy by responding to two strong themes in current debates: a bipartisan consensus on work-based welfare reform and widespread dissatisfaction with traditional welfare administration. One familiar critique of welfare is that it allows and encourages recipients to violate important norms of individual responsibility. . . . Another common criticism is that the current welfare system is miserly, stigmatizing, and uneven in coverage--that it rewards the "dependent" poor but provides too little assistance to the working poor. These views reflect widely varying normative premises and support different policy prescriptions. . . . Nevertheless, there is an apparent political consensus in support of reforms that in some way link welfare and work.

* * *

In the current political climate, then, work and responsibility are "in" and traditional welfare is "out." It may appear to those committed to providing public assistance that there is little to lose--and much to gain for the poor--by promoting the EITC as the "pro work" and "pro family" solution to welfare's perceived disincentives and administrative failures .

* * *

Some commentators oppose work requirements in welfare programs on the grounds that mandatory work (or "workfare") programs are more expensive, less effective, and harsher than voluntary work programs. But the EITC, unlike workfare, has no mandatory work feature. It provides income transfers to people who choose to work, and it does not deny current welfare benefits to nonworkers. Thus, some opponents of mandatory work requirements in welfare programs do not criticize the EITC. The EITC has also garnered additional political support as a program of tax relief and even child care, which appeal to political constituencies that may not be concerned with welfare reform per se.

How does the EITC achieve its ostensible advantages over welfare? The EITC is a complex hybrid of an earnings subsidy, a traditional income-transfer program, and a tax credit program. Understanding these features and the tensions they create lays the groundwork for the subsequent analysis of the EITC's effects on behavior and its institutional limitations.

Traditional income transfers provide a useful benchmark for comprehending the EITC. A traditional income-transfer program that tailors benefits to need pays the largest benefits to families with the lowest incomes and reduces benefits as income rises. Thus, a family with $5000 of outside income typically receives smaller income-transfer benefits than a family of the same size with no outside income. As outside income increases, benefits fall, and at some level of income--the income cutoff point--benefits fall to zero. The reduction in benefits as income rises can be termed the "income test."

The EITC produces a pattern of benefits that at first seems entirely different. For workers with earnings and total income between one dollar and $8425, the EITC provides an earnings subsidy equal to an extra forty cents for every dollar of earnings. In this income range, the EITC appears to be a "backwards" income-transfer program, because it provides greater dollar benefits to those with higher earnings and no benefits at all to those without wages, regardless of need.

The EITC begins to tailor benefits to need through an income test at slightly higher levels of earnings. When earnings reach $8425, the earnings subsidy is capped. Above that threshold, the dollar amount of EITC benefits remains constant up to an earnings level of $11,000 and then is reduced by twenty-one cents for every dollar of earnings over $11,000. Under this schedule, EITC benefits are reduced to zero at $27,000 of earnings. Thus, between $11,000 and $27,000 in earnings, the EITC resembles a traditional income-transfer program, which reduces benefits as earnings increase. . . . Initially, an increase in earnings results in higher EITC benefits; as earnings increase above $8425, however, the EITC benefit first remains constant and then declines, ultimately to zero.

The EITC also differs from traditional transfers in administration. Traditional welfare programs use government workers to collect and verify information about applicants and recipients. In contrast, the EITC is administered through the federal income tax system as a refundable tax credit. In theory, workers eligible for the EITC need never see a bureaucratic face. They simply attach a special schedule to their federal income tax returns.

The IRS awards the EITC based on the information provided in the tax return. The EITC first offsets federal income tax liability (if any), and the balance is refunded in cash. The unusual refund feature makes it possible for the EITC to provide cash benefits to workers who are too poor to owe any tax or whose tax liability is less than their EITC benefit. The Code allows workers to claim projected EITC benefits from their employers throughout the year rather than as an annual lump sum, but virtually no EITC recipients choose this option.

Conventional policy debates over the EITC, like debates over welfare policy, are dominated by economic analyses that focus on potential disincentives for work and marriage. . . .[T]hese narrowly focused debates are analytically incomplete and reflect considerable normative confusion. Although advocates of the EITC have probably exaggerated its positive effects on labor supply, critics of the EITC give undue weight to potential negative effects on work effort. They rely on an "economic" analysis that departs significantly from both the analytic conventions and the standard normative underpinnings of traditional economic theory.

* * *

In the following discussion, it is essential to distinguish disincentives from the effects of those disincentives on behavior. Economic theory can establish the existence of disincentives to work or to marry, but empirical study is needed to establish whether and how those disincentives actually affect people's decisions to work or to marry. For example, whether work disincentives actually reduce work effort depends on the strength of people's preferences for work and the extra income work generates compared to leisure or other activities. Those preferences may be shaped by a variety of forces, including the availability of incrementally longer or shorter work hours, and family responsibilities. There is a wealth of empirical evidence on traditional welfare programs' impact on work, but that evidence is both difficult to interpret and uneven in its coverage of different types of workers. To be as clear as possible for all readers, and at the cost of deviating from standard economic terminology, I will refer to "potential" disincentives to emphasize the tentative nature of theoretical predictions.

One classic dilemma of redistribution is the potential trade off between redistribution and labor supply. Redistributive programs may decrease total economic output if they reduce work effort by income-transfer recipients or by taxpayers who finance the program. Thus, reductions in work effort raise the economic cost of redistributive programs. Even those analysts most committed to distributive justice for the least advantaged have grappled with this economic constraint. Empirical studies suggest that redistributive programs on balance probably have a small but nontrivial negative effect on work effort and that specific transfer programs can vary in their effects, but analysts differ on the magnitude of the actual work disincentives found.

* * *

The standard analysis assumes that workers and potential workers understand how the EITC, the tax system, and the welfare system affect their earnings. Because the EITC is complex, however, EITC recipients may not understand the connection between work and the EITC benefits they receive. This informational gap may blunt both the EITC's potential incentives and its potential disincentives.

Standard economic analysis suggests that the EITC creates competing potential work incentives and disincentives that vary among groups of workers. . . . [T]he EITC combines three distinct elements: an earnings subsidy, a "stationary" range, and a "phase-out" or income test. For workers with earnings in the earnings subsidy range, the EITC acts as a proportional pay increase, which provides up to four dollars for every ten dollars of earnings. A casual observer might suppose that a pay raise necessarily increases work effort, but economic theory suggests that the earnings subsidy may either increase or decrease work by a worker who is already employed. The earnings subsidy increases the return to work relative to other activities (for example, leisure), and this "substitution effect" may increase people's proclivity to work rather than to consume leisure. On the other hand, EITC benefits provide extra money, which allows the worker to consume as much as before with less work. This "income effect" may lead the worker to consume more leisure, depending on her preferences. The net impact on work depends on the relative magnitudes of these competing effects. Importantly, however, the EITC's potential incentives are different for a nonworker contemplating entering the workforce. For her, the EITC is an unambiguous potential work incentive; she receives no income support from the EITC unless she goes to work and so the income effect is absent.

In contrast, workers with incomes in the stationary range, who receive an EITC benefit that does not vary with earnings, face a potential work disincentive. The earnings subsidy is no longer available with respect to extra earnings, so the EITC substitution effect neither encourages nor discourages work relative to leisure. Further, the income effect (or the feeling of being better off with less work) may discourage work.

For workers with earnings in the EITC phase-out range, additional earnings reduce EITC benefits, just as in a traditional income-transfer program. This incremental benefit reduction as income rises is analogous to a tax on income: although the tax does not add to the government's coffers, the worker keeps less than a dollar for each additional dollar earned. This benefit reduction, like any actual tax, reduces the net monetary reward for extra work.

* * *

Although microeconomic theory can make limited predictions about the EITC's potential effects on different groups of workers, only empirical evidence can determine whether the EITC on balance encourages or discourages work. In theory, the EITC might do either. Early estimates of the EITC's impact on work effort suggest that the EITC reduces work effort in the aggregate, but probably by a smaller amount than do traditional welfare programs.

* * *

Debates over the EITC also reflect concerns about potential marital disincentives in income-transfer programs. Single-parent families, particularly those headed by women, tend to be disproportionately poor and constitute a growing segment of the population. The causes of poverty among female-headed families are complex, as are the causes of the declining marriage rate. However, if redistributive programs bolster an existing social trend that contributes to pre-transfer poverty, once again behavioral effects may raise the cost of redistribution. Despite popular stereotypes, empirical studies suggest that welfare has contributed little to the growth in the number of single-parent families. Nevertheless, the perceived effects of marital disincentives in welfare programs continue to play a significant role in both popular and academic discussions of welfare policy.

EITC advocates point out that, unlike welfare, the EITC is fully available to two-parent families. Critics of the EITC argue that the program, is nevertheless biased against marriage, because it creates "marriage penalties" that may discourage poor workers from marrying (or may encourage them to divorce). Although understanding potential disincentives is useful, it is crucial to remember that they do not translate automatically into behavior. A firm conclusion must await empirical evidence, but at the outset it seems at least as plausible to expect that the EITC (like welfare) has little effect on family structure as to predict a dramatic impact.

* * *

Further, critiques of the EITC's marital disincentives fail to confront the policy trade offs inherent in designing the EITC or any other redistributive program. Marriage penalties are a virtually unavoidable characteristic of income transfers that tailor benefits to need. Although it is in theory possible to redesign income-tested transfer programs to avoid penalizing marriage, the necessary changes would compromise policy goals that many may find more important than marriage neutrality.

* * *

This Article raises serious questions about the validity of the over-simplified claims made for--and against--the EITC. Claims that the EITC promotes work and responsibility are exaggerated, but EITC opponents' attempts to equate the EITC with welfare are equally unsound. The EITC may have certain advantages as a tax-based program, including greater accessibility, cheaper administration, and reduced stigma for recipients. But policy analysts should also consider the inherent disadvantages of a tax-based program: less accurate targeting, less responsiveness to changing needs, and vulnerability to noncompliance. Although the magnitude of these costs requires empirical study, they are qualitatively important. Legislation in the 1990s has transformed the EITC into a major income support program without acknowledging that tax-based administration imposes these potentially significant institutional constraints.

Understanding these trade offs does not require a rejection of the EITC or tax-based administration. The challenge for EITC advocates is to strengthen the case for the EITC by acknowledging these limitations and then explaining why the EITC is still worthwhile. Future research could extend the analysis begun here to compare more fully the strengths and weaknesses of the EITC with those of existing alternative institutions and potential new programs--for example, family allowances or wage subsidies--each of which might be tax-based or administered through traditional expenditure programs.

* * *

Notes and Questions

1. *Comparing EITC and Welfare.* To what extent does the EITC serve the same functions as welfare? The EITC provides tax credits only for people who have jobs; it does nothing for those without jobs. Insofar as it provides an incentive for unemployed people to seek jobs, it attempts to correct any deficiencies in work ethic. But what about those who have a strong work ethic, but cannot find jobs?

2. *Tax System Administration.* The Internal Revenue Service administers the EITC through the tax system. What advantages and disadvantages stem from administration through the tax system?

3. *Theory versus Evidence.* Anne Alstott emphasizes that commentators with different perspectives on economic theory make different predictions of the EITC's incentives and disincentives, but that only empirical evidence will demonstrate its actual effects. What kind of empirical evidence would we need to evaluate the effects of the EITC? Is empirical evidence merely factual and objective, or subject to different interpretations? Could all welfare policy debates profit from recognition of the limitations of theory and the need for empirical evidence?

A Note on Taxation of Public Assistance Benefits

Internal Revenue Service policies exclude from gross income such public assistance benefits as Welfare (Aid to Families with Dependent Children or its Temporary Assistance for Needy Families block grant replacements), Supplemental Security Income, Food Stamps, Medicaid, Medicare, and Housing Assistance. Beginning in 1979, Congress required partial taxation of unemployment benefits, which have been fully taxed since 1987. Since 1983, Congress has required taxation of portions of Social Security benefits received by taxpayers earning in excess of designated amounts. Professor Jonathan Barry Forman has argued that logical arguments relating to income definition support full taxation of public benefits, as does the federal government's need for revenues. *See* Jonathan Barry Forman, *The Income Tax Treatment of Social Welfare Benefits*, 26 UNIVERSITY OF MICHIGAN JOURNAL OF LAW REFORM 785 (1993). Professor Forman explained the arguments for and against taxation of public assistance benefits:

> Standard deductions and personal exemptions already ensure that almost no low-income taxpayers actually pay any income tax. A taxpayer's standard deduction and personal exemptions combine to establish a simple income tax threshold; a taxpayer owes no income tax unless the taxpayer's income exceeds the applicable income tax threshold.
>
> * * *
>
> Thus, because standard deductions and personal exemptions already protect low-income taxpayers from virtually any income tax liability, the current exclusion of public assistance benefits does almost nothing more to help them. Instead, virtually all of the tax savings from the exclusion of public assistance benefits inure to taxpayers who are decidedly not low-income. Put simply, the exclusion of public assistance benefits does not help the most needy individuals and greater equity could be achieved by taxing the public assistance benefits received by higher-income taxpayers and redistributing those revenues to lower-income taxpayers.

On the other hand, public assistance benefits already are targeted to the most needy through means testing by way of benefit-reduction formulae. If public assistance benefits were subject to income taxation, the combination of income taxes, Social Security taxes, and benefit-reduction rates would result in an extraordinarily high cumulative marginal tax rate for some individuals. Such high marginal tax rates can and assuredly do discourage people from working and offer the most compelling reason not to tax public assistance benefits, or at least to figure out how to better synchronize the tax and welfare systems.

The failure to tax public assistance benefits, however, itself results in disincentives to work. . . . [W]ork disincentives arise any time the value of tax-free benefits approach the after-tax value of the wages that an individual can earn. For example, many recipients of AFDC and food stamps actually fare worse economically if they work at low-wage jobs than if they remain on welfare. After paying income and Social Security taxes, some low-wage workers will have less after-tax income than welfare will provide, and leaving welfare results in the termination of valuable Medicaid benefits for the worker and the worker's family. Consequently, taxing AFDC and Medicaid benefits might help to avoid such work disincentives.

Moreover, the low participation rates associated with most forms of public assistance raise another important equity question. Only about sixty percent of the poor participate in the food stamp program; only about sixty percent of poor children are covered by AFDC; and only about sixty percent of the elderly poor participate in SSI. Thus, the failure to tax public assistance tends to increase the differences between the disposable incomes of welfare program participants and nonparticipants who struggle in low-paying jobs to earn a living. Consequently, taxing public assistance benefits would temper that inequity.

> Unfortunately, taxing public assistance benefits would increase the complexity of the tax laws. In addition, taxing in-kind benefits such as Medicaid, food stamps, and housing assistance would require valuation and thus could create administrative difficulties. There has been a good deal of research on valuation of social welfare benefits, and the problems of valuation may not be insurmountable. One solution would be to replace most in-kind benefits with equivalent cash benefits. Alternatively, in-kind benefits like food stamps could simply be valued according to their face amounts.

What are the strengths and weaknesses of Professor Forman's arguments for taxing public assistance benefits?

C. COMMUNITY ECONOMIC DEVELOPMENT

Peter Pitegoff

CHILD CARE ENTERPRISE, COMMUNITY DEVELOPMENT, AND WORK

81 GEORGETOWN LAW JOURNAL 1897 (1993)

* * *

Henrietta Keenan had a dream. Standing before a two-story frame house on the east side of Buffalo, New York, she saw a potential child care center. Others saw a house in need of substantial repair, in one of the poorest inner-city neighborhoods in western New York. But Ms. Keenan had grown up in this house, and she knew firsthand the critical need for day care for children in that community. Years ago, affordable child care had eased her struggle to balance work and school while she raised two children. Now, as a foster care counselor at the New York State Division of Youth, her clients--many of them young parents--remind her daily that affordable child care might enable parents to work or attend school.

Precious Jewels Day Care Center, Inc. opened its doors at the start of 1993. Five years earlier Ms. Keenan's mother, no longer able to maintain the house, transferred title to Ms. Keenan. What followed were intensive and persistent efforts to renovate the house; meet licensing standards for a child care center; obtain the adjacent lot for a play area; acquire furniture, equipment, supplies, and toys; hire teachers and staff; contract for needed services; obtain financing; negotiate through a maze of legal requirements and transactions; develop an early childhood development program; and, finally, market the center and enroll children. Important to this process was building organization within the new shell of a tax-exempt corporation, with establishment of governance and management policies and informal norms of doing business and relating to one another. In Precious Jewels, one woman's dream was evolving into a community-based institution.

The saga of Precious Jewels Day Care Center is an allegory for issues in child care and community economic development generally, both the constraints and the potential. It reads like a dream come true, of a woman drawing upon a deep spiritual strength to create a desperately needed enterprise in her old neighborhood. A new not-for-profit corporation will employ local residents and enable parents to find work or further their education. Renovated housing stock will be maintained, while the daily activity at the Center will help to revitalize one small part of the distressed inner city. In a city plagued by racism, Precious Jewels demonstrates effective collaboration across racial lines. A host of both public and private institutions, including the Community Economic Development Law Clinic at the State University of New York at Buffalo, came together and brought their resources to bear upon an often-neglected urban agenda. Ms. Keenan and the Law Clinic envision Precious Jewels, potentially, as a model for others and part of a network of child care centers and related enterprises.

Yet, the flip side of this story is the tremendous effort required "simply" to create a day care center for less than two dozen inner-city children. Precious Jewels reached the starting gate only after thousands of hours of volunteer effort by its founder, community leaders, and technical experts, hard work by the initial director and staff, and financial and political support from government officials, local businesses, church organizations, and friends. The economics of operating a child care center in a low-income community will require Precious Jewels continually to supplement basic operating revenue with substantial subsidies from government and charitable sources. Wages and benefits for the staff will be limited, despite ongoing subsidies. The industry norm for wages ranks child care among the poorest paid of the human service professions, and, at least at the outset, Precious Jewels has insufficient resources to escape this norm. As an operating entity, early on, the Center struggles to survive.

The challenges facing Precious Jewels reflect the reality for thousands of child care centers, particularly in inner-city communities. Absent sufficient subsidies, the economics of child care demand impossible trade-offs that undermine the stability and quality of care.

* * *

Concerned with social goals and not just growth, a community-based approach to economic development directly supports labor and community interests and does not assume that increased business profits necessarily benefit the locale. It attempts to change the way a local economy relates to external market and political forces by mobilizing local resources and reinforcing local control to better capture broader opportunities, rather than passively relying on beneficence of government or private enterprise.

The notion of linkage is critical for effective community economic development. Collaboration among local groups can provide economies of scale in doing business, a regional perspective, and needed political clout. Intermediary institutions that link local groups can serve as a repository of technical expertise and access to resources. In the context of capital mobility in the private sector, and budget pressures in the public sector, self-sufficiency for local enterprises is more feasible if enterprises are linked with global markets and resources. In recent decades, community development corporations (CDCs) have served as one vehicle for linkages.

* * *

CDCs are typically not-for-profit corporations governed by selected community leaders, with a goal of stimulating a range of locally controlled development activities. They engage in various combinations of housing development, commercial revitalization, business financing, social service delivery, cultural activity, technical assistance, job training and development, community education, and advocacy.

* * *

Notably, community economic development stands in sharp contrast to social services, insofar as development strategies attempt to build organizations with capacity for economic self-sufficiency and productivity rather than focusing on subsidized services to address the immediate needs of individuals. Therein lies a challenge for child care as a component of economic development--to build financially stable institutions as engines for entrepreneurship and creation of quality jobs. Despite the importance of child care as a social service, child care as an economic activity still remains marginal and its potential hardly tapped for building enterprise capacity in distressed communities.

In recent years, community development corporations have begun to increase the availability of child care services. In the 1970s and 1980s, many CDCs primarily focused on housing issues and saw their most substantial successes in housing development. But given a lasting slump in the housing market and, more importantly, the growing need for child care, an increasing number of CDCs have sponsored child care programs as an explicit component of their development strategies.

* * *

Child care development is well suited to the broad social and economic goals of community development corporations. Particularly in low- and moderate-income communities, which are the geographic focus of many CDCs, affordable child care is a sine qua non for parental employment. Sponsoring child care services supports labor force participation, one basic goal of community development. If the community-based child care programs combine a quality educational curriculum with the custodial function, their investment in human capital--the children--is likely to strengthen the social and economic infrastructure of the community in the long term.

CDC emphasis on human capital mirrors the emphasis that community organizers place on leadership development. By building organization and opportunities for citizen participation, community organizers have crafted vehicles for the emergence of grass roots leaders. Similarly, CDC child care projects can provide motivation and a means for involvement by parents of young children. Parent participation would most likely begin with the child care project itself, as an interested parent or consumer, as a volunteer in the enterprise, or as part of a governing board, and, over time, would extend to the broader CDC agenda for community development.

Child care also presents CDCs with an opportunity for enterprise development. As in certain other service sector businesses, child care enterprises face growing local markets, are less vulnerable to global competition than the struggling manufacturing sector, and require little start-up capital relative to other industries and trade. Additionally, some government subsidies are available for child care providers that serve low- and moderate-income families. These subsidies, although inadequate to fully fund quality care, can provide start-up funds and a core income stream. With respect to job creation, child care ventures can create jobs at less cost than more capital intensive businesses that require investment in machinery, inventory, or other items not needed by a local service enterprise. Moreover, many of the jobs created are entry level, enabling CDCs to target employment to some of their constituents who have little formal education or work experience.

These very elements of enterprise opportunity, however, also reflect severe problems in child care enterprise as a development strategy. Easy market entry means the potential for significant local competition. Capital expenses may be low, but operating margins are quite narrow and thus increase the vulnerability of child care centers. A large portion of government support is in the form of demand-side subsidies, such as the Dependent Care Tax Credit or the AFDC income disregard, which only indirectly benefit the enterprise by partially subsidizing its clientele. Additionally, subsidies that directly benefit the enterprise may carry their own baggage, such as Title XX reimbursement rates set below the area market level or requiring costly bureaucratic paperwork and delay.

Most problematic about child care enterprise as a development strategy is that the primary subsidy for child care ordinarily is provided by the employees of the enterprise, in the form of low wages and limited employee benefits. Coupled with low prestige and little opportunity for advancement, this work environment yields high staff turnover and undermines the quality of care provided. It threatens basic tenets of community economic development--the quality of jobs created is as important as the quantity, and a central measure of success is the social impact of the enterprise.

Child care enterprise, nonetheless, retains the potential for a pivotal role in an affirmative development strategy if the strategy acknowledges and addresses the problems of child care work. . . . As a counterpoint to the dominant view that continues to undervalue child care work and workers, the community development efforts can demonstrate the combination of quality care and quality work. But they facc a hostile economic and social environment that perpetuates the view of child care cnterprise as marginal. In an industry whose work force is predominantly female, and in a society in which gender discrimination persists, the challenge facing community development efforts is even more formidable.

Notes and Questions

1. *Collaboration.* Peter Pitegoff noted the importance of collaborative efforts to the success of community economic development projects. What functions are served by collaboration? How would you build collaboration into a CED project?

2. *Human Capital.* Professor Pitegoff emphasizes the development of human capital in community economic development. What does he mean? How is this accomplished? What benefits flow from the sense of self-sufficiency created through CED?

3. *Expertise.* One of the reasons collaboration is required for succcssful CED projects is that communities need to import necessary expertise to guide their efforts. What are the trade-offs to importing expertise? Do lawyers with experience in representing poor clients possess the legal expertise needed for CED work? What type of training would lawyers need? Consider how the lawyers and students fared in the following example of a CED project.

Rebecca Arbogast, et al.

REVITALIZING PUBLIC INTEREST LAWYERING IN THE 1990S: THE STORY OF ONE EFFORT TO ADDRESS THE PROBLEM OF HOMELESSNESS

34 HOWARD LAW JOURNAL 91 (1991)

> You must find your own path to meet the great service obligation of our profession. All that is important is that you meet it. In the privileged world in which even the least prosperous of you will practice or work, the

> obligation of pro bono service must become a staple. In return for the privileged life your degree affords, public service is an obligation. It is the price of passage on the ship you have boarded today.[1]

Despite annual exhortations to graduating law students to accept the responsibilities as well as the benefits of entering the legal profession, the prognosis for public interest law in the 1990's is uncertain. There have been significant decreases in federal and private funding of public interest organizations, sweeping changes in the composition of the federal judiciary, and a decline in the matriculation of public interest lawyers due to the increasing salary gap between the private and public sector. Together these factors raise serious questions about the future effectiveness of the traditional model of the full-time public interest litigator and call for the development of alternative models of public interest lawyering suited to the financial, judicial, and personnel constraints of current practice.

We were four students at the Yale Law School who were involved in an innovative clinical program that has sought to revitalize public interest lawyering through an approach which we term "community institution building." Community institution building is a model of social activism which seeks to build coalitions--of individuals, skills, and funds--and to translate these coalitions into permanent community institutions designed to address a targeted community problem. We applied this approach to address the problem of homelessness in New Haven, Connecticut; although its clearest application is in those areas of public interest law that deal with poverty, it might also be successfully applied to other areas of public interest law.

* * *

Lawyers using the community institution building approach work on behalf of themselves or clients to build coalitions, which in turn create institutions to address a targeted community problem. These coalitions bring together public and nonprofit organizations with private individuals, techniques, and resources.

---

[1]Address by Eleanor Holmes Norton, Yale Law School Commencement (May, 1988).

* * *

The creation of Housing Operations Management Enterprises, Inc. ("HOME") is the story of bringing together diverse individuals and groups into a coalition that succeeded in building a community institution to address the problem of homelessness in New Haven. HOME was created with the assistance of the Yale Shelter Project, an innovative law school clinical program. Since the success of HOME, the Shelter Project has helped to establish other community institutions. However, HOME, the first creation of its type, provides a detailed illustration of what we propose as an alternative approach to public interest law.

While New Haven, historically, has been the focus of anti-poverty programs at both the local and national level, the large urban renewal projects of the 1960's and 1970's actually eliminated more units of affordable housing than they replaced. In addition, the New Haven Housing Authority, which managed the majority of the public housing built to replace what was lost in urban redevelopment, has a history of poor management. Consequently, many of the units quickly deteriorated and became unusable. Today, ten percent of the approximately 3,750 public housing units in New Haven are vacant because of disrepair. The speculative real estate boom between 1984 and 1989 led to the demolition of affordable housing to make way for middle-income and luxury condominiums or office space. As a result, currently over three thousand people in New Haven have no place to live.

In analyzing the shortage of affordable low-income housing in New Haven, the Yale Shelter Project identified the lack of adequate management as one of the prime causes. Incentives to encourage the private sector to create low-income housing have been limited mostly to mortgage subsidies and tax deductions and credits; these up-front subsidies essentially guarantee that developers and investors will receive the bulk of their profit within fifteen years or less, and therefore they do little to encourage capital expenditures and successful subsequent management. In addition, the low revenue generated by a low-income housing project provides a strong incentive to keep operating expenses and management fees to a minimum in order to make a project economically feasible. Poor management leads to disrepair and abandonment.

Taking a close look at the homeless population of New Haven helped us to understand that management of low-income housing is key on the demand side of housing as well. Good management requires not only attending to the physical health of the building, but also addressing the problems faced by the poor through the provision of services such as day-care and job counseling. In addition to addressing these effects of poverty, effective management must also be sensitive to the problems of mental illness and substance abuse. Therefore, the problem is not only a need for physical shelter but also a need for counseling and care. Addressing these challenges is difficult, particularly when the funds to support management and development are no longer available from traditional sources.

The Yale Shelter Project grew out of a more traditional clinical program where students represent individual clients in a variety of legal matters including landlord/tenant disputes, prisoner parole hearings, and entitlements advocacy. While students working in the clinical program had engaged in successful impact litigation which gained new rights for homeless people in Connecticut, any long-term solution to the problems of homelessness had to provide for the development of new low-income units sufficient to offer physical shelter for those who could not afford the rent of existing units. Additionally, a new type of shelter was needed that could better integrate low-income people into the larger community by offering social services as an integral part of the housing package. These were solutions that litigation could not provide.

Recognizing that the problem of homelessness cuts across traditional disciplinary lines, a group of students and faculty formed the Yale Shelter Project as a new clinical program to bring together resources from many different disciplines.

* * *

The need for a multidisciplinary approach in creating the Shelter Project paralleled the need for a similar approach in the community to address the problem of homelessness.

* * *

Accordingly, members of the New Haven professional, business, and political community were brought together with the poor, their advocates, and the providers of services to the poor communities. This group was institutionalized in the Board of Directors of HOME. The initial HOME Board included private lawyers, private developers, a private management consultant, a city official, a program supervisor for the State Office of Human Resources, a building contractor, a director of a social services agency working with African-American families, a former bank president, a legal aid attorney, a child care consultant, the executive director of a tenant services organization, and a former homeless mother.

Incorporating members of groups that traditionally differ in their support and approach to low-income housing into the HOME structure has resulted in institutional permanence for three reasons. First, HOME became a forum through which traditional adversaries could work out mutually acceptable solutions to a problem that affected each in a different, yet related manner. Second, HOME has been able to preempt potential opposition by including representatives of such sectors (i.e., developers and landowners) as part of its Board. Third, the broad representation of voices and groups within HOME makes it more likely that its decisions will be viewed by the public as the consensus of a broad coalition rather than simply the will of any one particular group. The potentially thorny issue of situating low-income housing can be mitigated more by the participation of a broad-based community coalition than if the government or a social services group acting alone attempts to force its acceptance.

* * *

With regard to funding issues, HOME was quickly faced with the problem of financing the development and management of affordable low-income housing at a time of diminishing government resources. In order to obtain such financing, we needed to tap private sector techniques and create a complex funding package.

* * *

The Yale Shelter Project obtained initial equity on behalf of HOME by applying for federal low-income housing tax credits available under the 1986 Tax Reform Act, which we in turn sold to for-profit partners. To provide enough income to cover operating and management expenses, we increased the value of the rent rolls by obtaining federal and state rental subsidies for many of the tenants who were eligible. In addition to these public sources of funding, HOME sought out private sector money from a variety of sources. As part of a $50 million investment pledge to the community of New Haven, Yale University loaned HOME $1 million for the development and management of low-income housing in New Haven. Under the Community Reinvestment Act, banks must make a certain percentage of loans to low-income communities; the Shelter Project has been using the Community Reinvestment Act to encourage banks to increase the amount of affordable credit available to community nonprofits such as HOME.

These coalitions of individuals and groups, of skills and resources, and of public and private funding sources, have set the stage for effectively addressing the twin problems of shelter and services. HOME currently owns 32 units of housing and is in the process of building four additional units. HOME is refining innovative management techniques that provide social services to the tenants of those units and over 200 units that it manages under contract with others. HOME has also created a track record that will enable it to tap these same coalitions of funding again in the future to acquire different properties. Through grants from the New Haven Foundation and the City of New Haven, HOME has been able to hire an executive director and has sufficient funds to provide for its continued operating expenses.

* * *

First, by accumulating technical expertise and developing relationships with different political groups and funding sources, we in some sense began to act as more than lawyers and strategists. As the Shelter Project itself became institutionalized, we became a player in the local political arena. We embraced an expanded notion of lawyering, acting more in the role of principal than agent.

The most blatant example of our acting as a principal came when we helped to create our own client. In theory, it is the client that dictates policy, and the attorney who advises and facilitates. Although in practice this division often becomes blurred in a traditional attorney-client relationship, the demarcation was shattered with our role in the creation of HOME. We were intimately involved with the initial policy discussions defining HOME's goals, as well as how HOME should be structured and staffed. We acted in a dual role as counsel and staff for over a year until the hiring of an Executive Director.

* * *

A second tension that became apparent may be peculiar to the dynamics of New Haven. We realized that most of our clients were predominantly white organizations that had grown out of the dominant political and economic center of New Haven. We had yet to undertake a project with any of the predominantly African-American neighborhood groups.

At the inception of the Shelter Project, we made a preliminary decision not to get involved in the neighborhoods in part because of neighborhood reactions to the siting of homeless shelters in these neighborhoods, and in part because we were not sufficiently knowledgeable about local political conditions to understand the dynamics of what was happening. . . .

Tensions in the client selection process were not limited to race and class issues. We also accepted and rejected clients so as to match our vision of what the Shelter Project should be. We declined to take on a client that was housing low-income teens because of its anti-abortion stance, which did not mesh with the broader social goals of a majority of the members of the Shelter Project. We rejected another client who, on her own and with limited means, was managing to provide housing for homeless individuals. She was using methods that violated certain zoning laws. If we took her on as a client, we could not assist her and allow her to continue these practices, but nor did we wish to stop her from accomplishing her good works. As we become more experienced with the community institution building approach, our awareness of some of the tensions this model presents has helped us mange them more effectively.

* * *

With community institution building, the role of the lawyer has changed. The lawyer acts as a facilitator, planner, and sometimes initiator. However, "legal" advice is not all that is necessary; business consulting and political activity are part of the job. Most importantly, the model depends upon building coalitions: bringing together people, resources, and skills from the private, public, and nonprofit sectors.

* * *

The distinctive feature of the community institution building model--its broad base--may be both its greatest strength and a source of weakness. When a group of diverse individuals with varied backgrounds and disparate agendas chooses to come together to focus on a single problem or project, the absence of a core ideological perspective may give rise to divisiveness which would not exist in a more homogeneous group. At its worst, this tension can be either diluting or diverting. At its best, it can be dynamic and invigorating. It casts the net wider, bringing in law students and professionals who would not otherwise have participated in public interest work. Corporate lawyers, in particular, now have available to them a vehicle to do public interest work that is more engaging than the traditional provision of discrete and limited services such as incorporating a string of nonprofit organizations. By bringing together diverse talented individuals and forging links among community groups, the broad base that community institution building develops can make a greater range of expertise available to tackle a problem. But perhaps even more importantly, it can rejuvenate public interest lawyering.

* * *

Notes and Questions

1. *Limitations of Litigation.* Why did the faculty and students at Yale's legal clinic choose community institution building as their strategy to address the problem of homelessness in New Haven, rather than litigation?

2. *Role of Lawyers.* The authors describe their experience as being more of the principal and less of the agent. Is this an appropriate role for lawyers? Did the duality involved in placing students in roles as both counsel and as client create a conflict of interest? Are law students trained to act as organizers, financiers, lobbyists and coalition-builders? Is there any reason why lawyers can't fulfill these other functions?

3. *Who Benefits?* Where are homeless people and their interests in this account? Did they benefit from the creation of HOME? Did they request and control this project? Must the intended beneficiaries of lawyers' strategies serve the traditional client function of directing the lawyers' efforts?

4. *Ideas from Urban Policy.* The literature regarding urban policy is one helpful source for ideas for low income advocates. *See, e.g.,* Michael A. Stegman, *National Urban Policy Revisited,* 71 NORTH CAROLINA LAW REVIEW 1737 (1993); E. Douglass Williams and Richard H. Sander, *The Prospects for "Putting America to Work" in the Inner City,* 81 GEORGETOWN LAW JOURNAL 2003 (1993).

5. *Other Legal Tools.* Advocates should be mindful of other legal tools available to help residents of low-income communities, such as the Community Reinvestment Act and enterprise zones. *See,*

e.g., Richard D. Marsico, *Fighting Poverty Through Community Empowerment and Economic Development: The Role Of The Community Reinvestment And Home Mortgage Disclosure Acts*, 12 NEW YORK LAW SCHOOL JOURNAL OF HUMAN RIGHTS 281 (1995); Mildred Wigfall Robinson, *Empowerment Zones and Enterprise Communities Under the Omnibus Budget and Reconciliation Act of 1993: A Promising Concept with Some Modifications*, 11 JOURNAL OF LAW & POLITICS 345 (1995).

6. *Housing and Environmental Community Based Initiatives.* Some of the most positive developments in recent times have been the collaboration between law students, lawyers, and communities. In addition to his work on child care initiatives, Peter Pitegoff described a variety of law school clinics which assist communities on issues related to housing. *See* Peter Pitegoff, *Law School Initiatives in Housing and Community Development*, 4 BOSTON UNIVERSITY PUBLIC INTEREST LAW JOURNAL 275 (1995). The Virginia Environmental Law Journal devoted its 14th volume in 1995 to describing community-based environmental law clinics. *See also*, Hope Babcock, *Environmental Justice Clinics: Visible Models of Justice*, 14 STANFORD ENVIRONMENTAL LAW JOURNAL 3 (1995); Luke W. Cole, *Empowerment as the Key to Environmental Protection: The Need for Environmental Poverty Law*, 19 ECOLOGY LAW QUARTERLY 619 (1992).

INDEX

References are to Pages